ART FOR THE NATION

SUPPLEMENT TO

Art for the Nation

Entries for eleven gifts received after the publication deadline
and corrected pages 246, 256, and 257

ASHER BROWN DURAND
1796–1886

Pastoral Landscape, 1861
Oil on canvas
39 x 60 (99.1 x 152.4)

Gift (Partial and Promised)
of The Manoogian Foundation

Asher Durand, whose first career was as an engraver, turned to painting landscapes after an 1837 sketching trip with his friend Thomas Cole. Following two years of study and travel in Europe in 1841–1842, Durand established a routine of sketching in the Catskill, Adirondack, and White mountains in the summers and painting finished works in his New York studio during the winters. By the mid–1840s he was considered one of the most prominent landscape painters in the country and in 1845 he was elected president of the National Academy of Design in New York, a position he would hold for almost twenty-five years. With the death of Thomas Cole in 1848 Durand assumed leadership of the Hudson River School.

During the 1850s Durand developed two types of landscapes that became fundamental to the Hudson River School. One was the vertical format canvas of quiet forest recesses, such as *In the Woods* (1855, The Metropolitan Museum of Art, New York), which celebrated the pristine beauty of untouched American wilderness. The second was the panoramic view of a great expanse of rural scenery. *Pastoral Landscape*, painted when Durand was at the height of his powers, is one of the most majestic and accomplished examples of his panoramic landscape style.

The view in the painting moves from a detailed foreground of precisely painted rocks and underbrush across a placid body of water and into a vast distance softened by a radiantly glowing atmosphere. Large, painstakingly individualized trees frame the left side of the composition, providing a shadowy contrast to the more brightly lit fields and hills of the distance. Various buildings, including an Italianate villa just glimpsed among the trees, a gabled house by the water, and several churches in the distance, establish man's presence but do not intrude upon the peaceful serenity of nature.

Pastoral Landscape is the largest and most important painting known by Durand from 1861, and may be the work known as *Hillsdale*, which has been unlocated since the nineteenth century. Durand sketched in and around Hillsdale, in Columbia County, New York, in the summer of 1861 and created a major landscape based on his experiences that fall. *Hillsdale* was sold to a Baltimore collector for $1,200, a sum that indicates it was a large and important work.

Whether or not *Pastoral Landscape* may be identified with *Hillsdale*, it is a summary example of Durand's mature art and a quintessential Hudson River School painting. It presents America as a pastoral paradise where devout and industrious citizens live in harmony with nature. Ironically, it was painted at the very moment when just such reassuring visions were about to be undermined by the turmoil and tragedy of the Civil War. Durand was too old to serve in the war, but he, like other Hudson River School artists, was profoundly affected by it. Although he continued to paint in the later 1860s and in the 1870s and 1880s, the optimistic and celebratory vision of American nature and civilization that makes *Pastoral Landscape* so appealing disappeared from his art.

Although the Gallery's collection includes two landscapes by Durand (as well as two portraits), both are smaller and less important than *Pastoral Landscape*. A full-scale example of the artist's best work, this painting will be a worthy counterpart to major paintings by other Hudson River School artists such as Thomas Cole, Frederic Church, and Jasper Cropsey already in the collection. But unlike paintings such as Cole's *Sunrise in the Catskills* (also included in this exhibition), which celebrate the drama of untamed wilderness, *Pastoral Landscape* gives us the quiet harmony of the settled American landscape.

Franklin Kelly

JEAN DUBUFFET
1901–1985

Site à l'homme assis, 1969/1984
Painted polyester resin
120 (304.8); base 3 ½ x 144 x 102
(8.9 x 365.76 x 259.08)

Gift of Robert M. & Anne T. Bass
and Arnold & Mildred Glimcher

Arguably the most important artist to emerge in postwar France, Jean Dubuffet is known as a painter, sculptor, theorist, and collector of what he termed "l'art brut": the art of the insane and the dispossessed, those at the margins of culture and society. His earliest sculptures, the *Petits statues de la vie précaire* of 1954, were figurative constructions composed of cast-off or fugitive materials. They were made of lava and clinker, newspapers, twine, and sponge. In the late 1960s Dubuffet's career as a sculptor entered a new phase as he pioneered the use of polyester resin and began to produce public and environmental sculpture.

Site à l'homme assis is exemplary of this later phase of Dubuffet's career. Both witty and grand, the sculpture represents a figure seated in a landscape of rocks and trees. Thick black lines energetically curve and twist across the sculpture's intricate surface, keeping the viewer's eyes moving while giving to this three-dimensional work a powerful graphic punch. In fact, Dubuffet described works such as *Site à l'homme assis* as "peintures monumentées"...paintings turned into monuments.[1] Their formal vocabulary was translated into sculpture from the meandering script of the Hourloupe series of paintings that Dubuffet began in 1962.

The transition from painting into sculpture was first accomplished in 1966. Wielding an electrically heated wire, Dubuffet was able to work Styropor, a polystyrene, as easily as he painted and drew.[2] The same looping gestures of the hand evidenced in the Hourloupe paintings, then, could be employed for the creation of sculpture. Once cut out of the relatively fragile Styropor, Dubuffet's sculptures could be cast in a durable polyester resin, "pointed up," and recast in polyester resin at a larger scale. The original polyurethane maquette for *Site à l'homme assis* measured 23 ½ x 25 x 14 ⅞ inches (60 x 64 x 38 cm).[3] The final cast of the sculpture is composed of six separate elements.

Dubuffet had conceived of his Hourloupe series as "the figuration of a world other than our own or, if you prefer, parallel to ours."[4] By turning to sculpture he was able to concretize that separate world, eliding the difference between it and our own lived world. In addition to discrete sculptures, Dubuffet created grand monuments and ensembles, Hourloupe rooms, and outdoor environments.

Compared to Dubuffet's largest sculptural creation, the nearly two-thousand-square-yard *Closerie Fabala* at the Fondation Jean Dubuffet in Périgny-sur-Yerres, *Site à l'homme assis* may seem relatively modest. Yet *Site à l'homme assis* embodies Dubuffet's ambitions as well as any of the artist's larger Hourloupe sculptures. Dubuffet noted that "the works that belong to the *Hourloupe* cycle are linked one to the other, each of them an element destined to become part of the whole."[5] The landscape of *Site à l'homme assis*, with its writhing forms and odd protrusions, seems at once complete and contained, yet suggests a world of the imagination magically made real and present and capable of infinite extension.

Since before the opening of the East Building of the National Gallery in 1978, the Gallery has sought a major sculpture by Dubuffet. The acquisition of *Site à l'homme assis* makes for a spectacular realization of that ambition. *Site à l'homme assis* joins an important early Dubuffet painting in the collection, *La dame au pompon*, 1946, as well as a group of 106 lithographs.

Jeremy Strick

PROVENANCE
The Pace Gallery, New York.

NOTES
1. Andreas Franzke, *Dubuffet*, trans. Robert Erich Wolf (New York, 1981), 183.
2. Franzke 1981, 183.
3. Max Loreau, *Catalogue des travaux de Jean Dubuffet*, fasc. 25 (Lausanne, 1974), 54.
4. Jean Dubuffet, "Remarks on the Unveiling of the Group of Four Trees," in *Jean Dubuffet: A Retrospective* [exh. cat. The Solomon R. Guggenheim Foundation] (New York, 1973), 35.
5. Dubuffet in New York 1973, 35.

GEORGE RICKEY
Born 1907

Divided Square Oblique II, 1981
Stainless steel
138 x 82 x approx. 12
(350.52 x 208.28 x 30)

Gift of Mr. and Mrs. William A. Nitze

Divided Square Oblique II is an outdoor wind-powered work highly characteristic of Rickey's mature oeuvre. Symmetrical and abstract, the sculpture consists of an eleven-foot-tall center post and four identical three-sided hollow spars that are each six feet long. These slightly tapering spars or blades are attached to the center post with ball bearings. Each has the capacity to rotate 360 degrees in a plane, to describe a circle perpendicular to the ground. The blades are internally weighted so that when the air is completely still (an unusual circumstance) and the blades are thus at a position of rest—which in the case of this work are positions at a 45-degree angle from the upright center post—the four blades together form the "square" of the title. "Oblique" is the term Rickey uses to describe moving sculptural parts that at rest have a slanting position, neither parallel nor perpendicular to the ground.

The artist's neat geometry is constantly broken by air currents that send the blades into motion. In this respect the work, like much of Rickey's sculpture since the early 1960s, fascinates because it embodies both order (his vocabulary of parts) and randomness (the unpredictability of the wind). This contrast of order and randomness is characteristic of the appearance of Rickey's sculptural parts as well: the almost rigid geometry of the components is countered by the appearance of their stainless-steel surfaces. These Rickey has treated with free-form strokes of a carborundum disk, creating marks that catch light fleetingly as the parts move.

A descendant of Yankees who emigrated to America from England in the seventeenth century, Rickey was born in South Bend, Indiana, and raised near Glasgow, Scotland, where his father, a mechanical engineer, managed the Singer sewing machine company's British branch. Rickey read modern history at Balliol College, Oxford, where he also took art classes at the Ruskin School. Later he studied cubism in Paris at André Lhote's academy and in the late 1940s attended the Institute of Design, the Chicago outpost of Bauhaus pedagogy. Intrigued by both the history of constructivist art (on which he wrote a pioneering book in the 1960s) and by the example of Calder's mobiles, and encouraged by his friend David Smith's advice to be lavish with materials, in the course of the 1950s and early 1960s Rickey developed systems of motion for his sculpture that were acutely responsive to the slightest variation in currents of air. During the past twenty-five years he has developed sculpture with parts made of lines, planes, rotors, volumes, and space churns, moving in paths that describe planes or volumes in a variety of ways, from simple oscillation to conical gyrations, according to his engineering and the flow of air and, in certain cases, the pressure of water. Many works since the early 1960s have been large-scale public commissions for sites in the United States, Europe, and Japan. Recently Rickey has divided his time between his home in East Chatham, New York, and studios in Berlin and Santa Barbara, California.

Divided Square Oblique II, number one in an edition of three, is the first work by Rickey to enter the collection of the National Gallery. It complements a related group of much earlier works, also with blades or lines, in the collection of the Hirshhorn Museum and Sculpture Garden. Between 1981 and 1983 Rickey made a number of objects nearly identical in design to the Nitze sculpture but in different sizes (with three-foot, four-foot, eight-foot, four-foot-five-inch, and seven-foot blades), as well as two much smaller indoor examples that also form an oblique square. The Nitzes' gift is the first sculpture of the "divided square oblique" type to enter any public collection.

Nan Rosenthal

WILLEM DE KOONING
Born 1904

Woman with a Hat, 1966
Oil on paper, 50 x 21 (127 x 53.34)

Gift (Partial and Promised) of
General Dillman Atkinson Rash
in Memory of
Nancy Phillips Batson Rash

The great American abstract expressionist Willem de Kooning moved from New York City to eastern Long Island in 1963. But in leaving the city he took with him one of his most profound subjects, the Women series. This theme, running as a vital thread through his work from the late 1930s to his critically acclaimed and controversial Women of the early 1950s, changed at that time, however. Most of his previous Women were depicted either seated formally in a studio or standing in a cool gray light, cut apart by sharp fractures of paint.[1] The new Women, the so-called Women in the Country,[2] were standing, floating, glowing in bright outdoor sunlight. They had lush curvilinear bodies, more like tribal fertility idols than their tense, splintered predecessors. The artist indulged in the oily, fluid qualities of paint.

Today this nude is acclaimed for its expressive beauty. However, when *Woman with a Hat* was presented to the public for the first time, Thomas Hess recorded the contemporary view that the figure was frightening. He wrote: "De Kooning's radical departure was toward a controlled Expressionism which holds the image to the surface, but reveals the drama of the destructive forces and anxieties that went into its conception...."[3] "The full-scale Women of 1964–66 face you directly. Visage, torso, and waist are arranged on a vertical axis.... The arrangement is a bit like a totem pole, or a ceremonial spear. Face, breasts, and sex are pulled apart; the eyes twist away from the nose, the mouth is forced open in a gape, revealing dangerous teeth.... It is a gesture of ferocious display.... The anatomy is cut apart and reassembled, and sections are visualized from different points of view.... Some of the Women wear big, lumpy hats, like cushions or loaves of bread, which block off the top of the picture. The anatomy generally fills the whole narrow format, like a closet packed to bursting. There is no background, only a brief indication of exterior space which writhes with an energy even more muscular than that of the figure itself."[4]

Woman with a Hat is a critically important member of this distinguished series of tall vertical paintings. Two larger versions are *Woman Sag Harbor*, 1964, in the Hirshhorn Museum and Sculpture Garden and *Woman Acabonic*, 1966, in the Whitney Museum of American Art. In all three, de Kooning imposed broad, abstract, expressive gestures upon the figure, leaving just enough of this image to allow identification, and perhaps even sympathy, for the model. The work is filled with juicy, bloody red and fleshy pink paints merged with vivid yellows, bright greens, and blues from outdoors. The glowing pigment is slathered on in strokes that keep their spontaneous look even as we know the artist carefully considered every mark.

Beginning in the early 1960s de Kooning began painting more works on paper. *Woman with a Hat* is one of these, where the artist pushed or slid the paint around, rubbing and scraping off areas, exploiting the paper's slickness. This gives a "fatted," greasy look to the surface, one quite in keeping with the visceral nature of the subject. At the same time de Kooning invented a new canon of expressive beauty in these ample Rubensian blonds. Simultaneously frightening and brilliant, the subject in *Woman with a Hat* seems deformed, obese, but nonetheless arresting, compelling. The iconic figure, perhaps with raised arms helping to make the "hat" shape, is penned in by the tight picture frame. The caricatured face, distended breasts and belly, and flattened, hanging legs and feet challenge the viewer in 1991 perhaps as much as they did in 1966.

The National Gallery owns an early de Kooning series of four painted mural panels dated 1940, twenty-one prints, and three drawings. The gift of this remarkable painting from General Dillman Rash provides the Gallery with its first major de Kooning painting and our first work from the artist's long and celebrated Women series.

Jack Cowart

PROVENANCE
The artist; Knoedler Gallery (1967).

NOTES
1. Not all the early Women were painted in the studio, but their preponderant attitude was visibly different from the bright and lush works of the 1960s. For further discussion of the evolution, their more obvious relations to cubism, and the settings for the 1950s series of Women see E. A. Carmean, "Willem de Kooning: The Women," in *American Art at Mid-Century: The Subjects of the Artist* [exh. cat. National Gallery of Art] (Washington, 1978), 154-182.
2. Jörn Merkert, "The Painting of Willem de Kooning," in *Willem de Kooning* [exh. cat. Whitney Museum of American Art] (New York, 1983), 128.
3. Thomas Hess, *de Kooning: Recent Paintings* [exh. cat. M. Knoedler & Co.] (New York, 1967), 14.
4. New York. 1967, 21.

CLAES OLDENBURG
Born 1929

Glass Case with Pies
(Assorted Pies in a Case), 1962
Burlap soaked in plaster, tins, paint,
glass and metal case
18¾ x 12¼ x 10⅞
(47.63 x 31.12 x 27.62)

Gift of Leo Castelli

The elder of two sons of a Swedish diplomat, Oldenburg was born in Stockholm and grew up in Chicago. He attended Yale where he majored in English and in art. In the early 1950s he worked as a police reporter and at odd jobs while studying art. He also traveled in northern California, and in 1953 became naturalized as a U.S. citizen. In 1956, increasingly experienced as a draftsman, he moved from Chicago to New York, settled in the gritty environment of the Lower East Side of Manhattan, and pursued his career as an artist who rejected abstract painting while absorbing lessons of abstraction expressionism.

From childhood Oldenburg kept detailed written and illustrated notebooks, at first about his imaginary utopia of "Neubern," an island in the south Atlantic whose language was half English and half Swedish and whose universe Oldenburg imagined and inventoried in concrete detail. As Barbara Rose observed, the precise parodies of reality in Oldenburg's Neubern anticipate his adult art.[1] While, as Rose also proposed, Oldenburg rejected in his work the idealist aesthetics of European art, he was at the same time a sensitive intellectual whose artistic clowning (a kind of costume or disguise) criticized consumerist values of American society of the late 1950s and early 1960s while nonetheless acknowledging its popular attractions.

Oldenburg's first important work to be shown in New York, in 1960, was two versions of an environment called *The Street*. These consisted of many related two-dimensional cut-out figures, objects, and signs, painted brown and black, that either were attached to the wall or hung or stood in space. Made of burlap, newspaper, other found materials, wire, and cheap paint, the figures were childlike, ragged-edged creations that appeared to reflect the poverty and palette of New York slums and, to a degree, the style of Jean Dubuffet. *The Street* marked one of the first appearances of Oldenburg's seriocomic alter ego, Ray Gun, an object with human attributes such as phallic potency.

The Ray Gun Manufacturing Corporation, with C. Oldenburg as president, in 1961 began to produce "commodities" for Oldenburg's second important environment, *The Store*. *The Store* contained brightly painted burlap and plaster reliefs and three-dimensional objects chiefly representing processed or cooked foods and manufactured clothing. There were two main versions of *The Store*: the first at Oldenburg's Lower East Side studio (itself a former store) at 107 East Second Street in December 1961–January 1962, where the artist-proprietor sold the goods; the second at the Green Gallery on 57th Street, where in addition to plaster pieces approximately the size of their real-world counterparts, Oldenburg showed his first giant soft sculptures, of food such as a ten-foot-long ice cream cone and a bed-size hamburger.

Leo Castelli's generous fiftieth-anniversary gift, a classic icon of Pop art, was made at Oldenburg's Second Street studio in summer 1962 and first shown at the Green Gallery version of *The Store* in September–October 1962, when Castelli purchased it. The unique sculpture consists of six "pies" formed from burlap and plaster in real pie tins, placed in a vertical glass and metal display case that the artist purchased from a restaurant supplier. Several "flavors" appear identifiable (lemon meringue, pumpkin, chocolate cream), while others appear more generic. According to the artist his main concern at the time, when he was using six or seven hues of an inexpensive commercial oil enamel, was never to mix or blend the colors but to use them on his objects just as they came from the can.[2] The flat or slightly mounded pies are themselves a kind of low relief, with the glass and metal case constituting a kind of frame provided by the artist.

Glass Case with Pies is the earliest of three works by Oldenburg to enter the Gallery's collection on the occasion of the fiftieth anniversary. It relates closely to two other important works of the early 1960s that are also anniversary gifts: Roy Lichtenstein's *Look, Mickey*, 1961 and Wayne Thiebaud's *Cakes*, 1963. In Oldenburg's oeuvre *Glass Case with Pies* was preceded by two smaller works of 1961 consisting of slices of pie in glass and metal cases. Two larger, horizontal pastry cases with foodstuffs also date from 1962 and another dates from 1965. Oldenburg also made four works with French vitrines and "tartines" for an exhibition in Paris in 1964.

Nan Rosenthal

PROVENANCE
Green Gallery, New York; Leo Castelli.

NOTES
1. Barbara Rose, *Claes Oldenburg* [exh. cat. The Museum of Modern Art] (New York, 1970), 19.
2. Conversation with the artist, 10 January 1991.

FREDERIC-AUGUSTE BARTHOLDI
1834–1904

Allegory of Africa, cast c. 1863/1865
Bronze, 12½ x 20 x 6¾
(31.8 x 52 x 17.2)

Gift of the 50th Anniversary Gift Committee

Few sculptors are more familiar to the American public, even if not by name, than Bartholdi.[1] He created the colossal statue of *Liberty Enlightening the World*, installed in New York Harbor in 1886. Patriotic monuments had long been his specialization by that time. This impressive bronze *Allegory of Africa* had been conceived earlier for one of his first such monuments, a fountain commemorating a hero of his native city of Colmar in the Alsace region of France.[2]

Shortly after the sudden death from cholera of Admiral A. J. Bruat (1796–1855), the city of Colmar proposed a monument to him. The young Bartholdi, who had recently completed his first such local monument (to General Rapp), was approached for a design. In March 1856 he submitted a project for a fountain. After delays and revisions occasioned by financial problems and debate over a site, Bartholdi produced a bronze maquette that was exhibited in the Salon of 1863 in Paris.[3] The monument, completed and inaugurated in 1864, featured a bronze statue of Bruat standing above a basin of pink Vosges sandstone. From the same stone were carved reclining figures symbolizing the four parts of the world in which the admiral had triumphed, Europe (or "Oceania") and Asia represented by women, America and Africa by men.

This bronze, the only known example of an apparent reduction of *Africa* from the finished monument,[4] symbolizes the continent through the majestic figure of a black man reclining on a lion skin. His pose, powerful physique, and brooding expression recall not only ancient sculptures of river gods, but even more Michelangelo's *Times of Day* on the Medici tombs in the new sacristy of San Lorenzo in Florence. Cast at an as-yet-unidentified foundry, the bronze shows highly refined execution, with a rich dark brown lacquer selectively applied to enhance the modeling.

The bronze suggests the intense impact the full-scale stone figure must have exercised. Striking testimony to this comes from the reminiscences of Albert Schweitzer, the great theologian and mission doctor in equatorial Africa:

"It was the Colmar sculptor Bartholdi... who directed my youthful thoughts toward distant lands. On his monument to Admiral Bruat... he carved a Negro in stone, which is certainly the most impressive thing to come from his mallet: a Herculean statue, with a profound and sorrowful expression.... The sight of it spoke to me at length about the misery of these black brothers. Whenever I'm in Colmar, I still go to see it."[5]

The figure that inspired Schweitzer was destroyed, along with the rest of the Bruat monument, during the German occupation in 1940. The present bronze gives an idea of the expressive quality Schweitzer found so moving. Other than reductions of the *Liberty Enlightening the World*, Bartholdi bronzes are rare in American collections.[6] In the National Gallery this one will reveal to the American public another aspect of the talents of an artist best known for a great national icon.

Alison Luchs

NOTES
1. On Bartholdi see Stanislas Lami, *Dictionnaire des sculpteurs de l'école française au dix-neuvième siècle*, 4 vols. (Paris, 1914–1921), 1 (1914): 63-69; Jacques Betz, *Bartholdi* (Paris, 1954); Marie Busco in Peter Fusco and H. W. Janson, eds., *The Romantics to Rodin* [exh. cat. Los Angeles County Museum of Art] (Los Angeles, 1980), 121; and *Liberty: the French-American Statue in Art and History* [exh. cat. New York Public Library] (New York, 1986).
2. On the Bruat monument see Betz 1954, especially 45–50; 57, 60, 68; and Société d'histoire et d'archéologie de Colmar, *Bartholdi. Annuaire 1979* (Colmar, 1979), 11, 151–154. Thanks are due to William Agnew for additional information.
3. For the bronze maquette see Lami 1914–1921, 1:65; on a plaster cast that appeared in the Salon of 1864 see Betz 1954, 57. A photograph, possibly of that cast, showing the complete monument is reproduced in Betz 1954, 50.
4. Bronze reductions of two other parts of the world from the Bruat monument, as yet unidentified, are reportedly in private collections in London. The terra cotta sketch model for *Africa*, differing in detail, is in the Musée Bartholdi in Colmar, along with the bronze and plaster maquettes.
5. Schweitzer is quoted in Betz 1954, 60; translation author.
6. An iron fountain by Bartholdi, however, may be seen not far from the National Gallery of Art at First Street and Independence Avenue, SW. See James Goode, *The Outdoor Sculpture of Washington, D.C.* (Washington, 1974), 250–251 and 546.

PIERRE-JEAN DAVID D'ANGERS
1788–1856

François-Pascal-Simon,
Baron Gérard, 1838
Plaster, 24 (61)

Gift of the Christian Humann
Foundation

Pierre-Jean David, who styled himself "d'Angers" after his birthplace and to distinguish himself from the famous painter Jacques-Louis David (1748–1825), enjoyed a reputation during his lifetime as the greatest sculptor of his time.[1] He left Angers in 1808 to study in Paris with the sculptor Philippe-Laurent Roland (1746–1816).

David is best known for his portraits, usually of famous or worthy contemporaries. He felt that sculpture had the moral obligation to proclaim the importance of great persons.[2] His choice of subjects often reflects his staunch Republican sympathies. His first portrait was a medallion of the composer Louis Joseph Ferdinand Herold, in 1814. He made more than five hundred portrait medallions during his career, depicting such luminaries as Lord Byron, Baron Gros, Chateaubriand, Harriet Beecher Stowe, and Paganini. He also made numerous large-scale monuments including the *Thomas Jefferson* in the rotunda of the U.S. Capitol and the *Ambroise Paré* in Lavel. Both of these are represented in the National Gallery by small bronze reductions.[3] The present bust is the first full-scale portrait by this important master to enter the collection.

The subject, the painter Baron Gérard (1770–1837), was a student of Jacques-Louis David and was one of Napoleon's favorite portraitists. David d'Angers inscribed the bust to Gérard on the front, with his signature and the date 1838, the year following the sitter's death. It bears a second inscription to the sitter's

widow: "à Madame Gerard, David." Gérard may have sat for the portrayal before his death, as well as for David's medallion of him from 1837. This plaster bust was apparently cast after a marble version made for the vestibule of the Institut de France. Two other plasters are known, both in the Musée David in Angers; one of these was apparently the model for the marble, while the other is a twin to the present plaster.[4] An engraving of the marble illustrates a collection of Gérard's correspondence.[5]

The portrait bust gives a quiet, thoughtful dignity to Gérard, who was a fellow instructor with David d'Angers at the Ecole des Beaux-Arts. He appears in contemporary dress, coiffed to allow the artist to emphasize the high, noble forehead. David was very interested in Gall's and Lavater's studies of phrenology and physiology, and his emphasis here on the physical shape of Gérard's head, unobscured by strands of hair, may have been purposeful.[6] David does not spare his sitter, but depicts clearly the bags and wrinkles below the eyes, the large ears and strong nose, and the determined set of the mouth. These qualities, together with Gérard's concentrated gaze to the right, give a picture of vitality even in advanced age. The hatched texture of Gérard's collar and coat emphasizes the soft pliancy of the face above them.

The bust makes an instructive comparison with another given for the National Gallery's fiftieth anniversary, the terracotta bust *A Lady* by Joseph Chinard (1755–1813). That work, a generation earlier, depicts a woman in antique drapery that contrasts with the Parisian overcoat worn by Gérard. The later bust, though retaining a truncation following an ancient Greco-Roman type and a certain ageless, classical air, is more explicitly rooted in time and place and probes the subject's features more intensely than does Chinard's relatively idealized depiction.

Donald Myers

PROVENANCE
Madame Gérard; Private collection; André Lemaire, Paris.

NOTES
1. James Holderbaum, *The Romantics to Rodin* [exh. cat. Los Angeles County Museum of Art] (Los Angeles, 1980), Peter Fusco and H. W. Janson, eds., 212.
2. Los Angeles 1980, 211.
3. Accession numbers 1975.11.1 and 1977.27.1, respectively.
4. For the marble, see Stanislas Lami, *Dictionnaire des Sculpteurs de l'École Française au dix-neuvième siècle*, vol. 2 (Paris, 1916), 91. Thanks to Jacques de Caso for his assistance regarding the two plasters in Angers.
5. Henri Gérard, ed., *Correspondance de François Gérard Peintre d'Histoire avec les Artistes et les Personnages Célèbres de son Temps* (Paris, 1867), between pages 208 and 209.
6. This observation was made by Suzanne Glover Lindsay.

HUGH DOUGLAS HAMILTON
c. 1739–1808

*Frederick North, Later Fifth Earl
of Guilford, in Rome*, late 1780s
Pastel, 37⅜ x 26¾ (95 x 68)

Gift of the 50th Anniversary
Gift Committee

This magnificent pastel by the Irish-born portraitist Hugh Douglas Hamilton is one of his masterpieces. It presents an elegant Englishman, presumed to be the young Frederick North (1766–1827),[1] against the grand ruins of Rome. The figure itself is exceptionally fine in both the handling of the face, enlivened by deft accents of unblended pastel, and the smooth and rich rendering of the clothes. Particularly compelling is the execution of the crumpled glove, a marvelous contrast to the smoother textures of the breeches and coat. Equally brilliant are the bold red band inside the hat, the only bright spot of color in the composition, and the gleaming metal buttons of the coat. The setting, too, is wonderfully rich in texture and detail, providing a suitably grand backdrop for this impeccable portrait.

Frederick North, later fifth earl of Guilford, was the third son of Lord North, second earl of Guilford, well known to Americans as the prime minister of England during the American Revolution. Frederick, who succeeded his two brothers to the earldom in 1817, spent most of his adult life abroad. He served as governor of Ceylon from 1798 to 1805 but otherwise preferred scholarship to politics. Greece and the Greek language were his particular passion and he is known to have had an impressive library of books and manuscripts. When the Ionian Islands came under British protection in 1815, he helped to found the University of the Ionian Islands on Corfu and served as its first chancellor. It is thought that his portrait came to the Sheffield family, in whose possession it remained until 1909, through his sister, Anne, who married the first earl of Sheffield in 1798.

The works of Hugh Douglas Hamilton are now generally known only to specialists, but in his day he was an artist of considerable stature. Born in Dublin the son of a wig maker, Hamilton trained there in the drawing school of Robert West (?–1779), where he won several prizes. As an independent artist he first specialized in portrait miniatures, working mainly in chalks and pastels. His rapid success in Dublin encouraged him to move to London in about 1764, where he soon established himself as a fashionable society portraitist. Moving to Italy in 1778, he continued to make portraits for English travelers but also experimented with history subjects during his twelve-year stay. In the late 1780s Hamilton was convinced by his countryman and fellow artist John Flaxman (1755–1826) to devote himself more to oil painting and accordingly made very few pastels thereafter. He finally settled permanently in Dublin in 1791 and continued to enjoy considerable success as an artist until poor health forced him to give up painting in about 1804.[2]

Within Hamilton's oeuvre the most impressive and inventive works are without question the full-length portraits. Those in his very best manner, such as this great pastel of Frederick North, have all the presence and power of oil paintings and can rival the best work of Hamilton's older contemporary, the great Italian portraitist and history painter Pompeo Batoni (1708–1787).

During the past decade the acquisition of British drawings has been a high priority for the National Gallery. The purchase of this impressive piece is thus most opportune, adding to those holdings both an exceptionally glorious portrait drawing and the first eighteenth-century British pastel.

Margaret Morgan Grasselli

PROVENANCE
The sitter; his sister, Anne North Sheffield?; by descent to Henry North Holroyd, 3rd earl of Sheffield (sale, London, Christie's, 11 December 1909, no. 3); Gooden and Fox, London, 1909; Hazlitt, Gooden & Fox, London, 1990

NOTES
1. See *English Drawings* [exh. cat. Hazlitt, Gooden & Fox] (London, 1990), no. 38, where the identification of the sitter as representing John Baker Holroyd, first earl of Sheffield (1735–1821), who would have been fifty or more when the portrait was made. A lithographic portrait of Frederick North by the great French artist Jean-Auguste-Dominique Ingres (1780–1867), made in Rome in 1815—nearly thirty years later—shows marked similarities with the Hamilton portrait in the full lower lip and the high-bridged aristocratic nose. The Gallery owns two impressions of Ingres' print.
2. The most complete article on Hamilton and his work was published nearly eighty years ago. See Walter G. Strickland, "Hugh Douglas Hamilton, Portrait-Painter," *The Walpole Society* 2 (1912–1913), 99–110. Hamilton' years in Italy are the subject of a more recent article by Finten Cullen, "Hugh Douglas Hamilton in Rome 1779–92," *Apollo* (Feb. 1982), 86–91.

JEAN-BAPTISTE GREUZE
1725–1805

The Ungrateful Son, c. 1777
Red chalk
16 ½ x 12 ¾ (41.9 x 32.4)

Gift in Memory of
Douglas Huntly Gordon

This stunning drawing is an exceptionally powerful and moving example of the *tétes d'expression* or expressive heads that were one of Greuze's greatest achievements as a draftsman. Remarkable for their monumental scale and vigorous execution as well as the broad cross-hatching that is such a distinctive feature of Greuze's drawing style, these heads were intended to stand on their own as portraits of specific psychological states such as grief, joy, and anger. Rarely, though, did these emotionally charged images attain the eloquence, intensity, and sheer physical beauty of the exceptional sheet presented here.

As is generally the case with Greuze's expressive heads, this elaborate drawing was not made in preparation for a painting, but rather was derived from one, in this case his work in 1765 and 1777 on *The Father's Curse: The Ungrateful Son*.[1] The drawing is based on the head of the son who, in choosing to leave his family to enlist in the army, is cursed by his father. The shock, pain, and sadness elicited by the unexpected malediction is simply conveyed in the sharp twist of the head, the puckered brow, the intense gaze, and the parted lips. Greuze based such expressions on the formalized representations of emotions established a century earlier by Charles Le Brun (1609–1690), but injected them with new vigor and immediacy.[2] His very best efforts in this genre, including the head presented here, are brought to life by both the force and speed of his chalk strokes and the naturalness of the pose. These imposing head studies were widely praised and collected by Greuze's contemporaries; many served as models for aspiring artists. The existence of several copies of this work gives a clear indication of the admiration it must have elicited in Greuze's time.[3]

This magnificent drawing joins two other fine red chalk heads by Greuze in the National Gallery, both of female subjects and both very different in execution. The addition of this one sheet elevates the Gallery's representation of Greuze's work in this genre to the very highest level and puts the artist in his rightful place on a par with some of the greatest draftsmen of the eighteenth century in France.

Margaret Morgan Grasselli

PROVENANCE
Charles Fairfax-Murray, London; Prince W. Argoutinsky-Dolgoronkoff, Paris (Lugt 2602d; sale, London, 4 July 1923, no. 41); Tancred Borenius; Mrs. W. H. Hill, Boston; Mrs. Smith, New York; Douglas H. Gordon, 1942.

NOTES
1. Greuze made a compositional drawing of the subject, now in the Musée des Beaux-Arts, Lille, in 1765; he then made an important painting in 1777, in which he reversed the composition (Musée du Louvre, Paris). Both are reproduced and discussed by Edgar Munhall in *Jean-Baptiste Greuze 1725-1805* [exh. cat. Wadsworth Atheneum] (Hartford, 1976), nos. 48, 84. This red chalk expressive head seems to have stemmed from an intermediate stage of Greuze's work on the subject, since it is in the same direction as the drawing but is closer to the expression of the son in the final painting.
2. The present head was based on Le Brun's rendition of physical pain, which in turn was based on the head of one of the sons in the famous antique sculpture of *Laocoön*, now in the Vatican. See Hartford 1976, 15, fig. 7.
3. Munhall (in Hartford 1976, 174, no. 85) mentioned four copies of this head (in the Pierpont Morgan Library, New York; the Musée du Louvre, Paris; the Musée des Beaux-Arts, Lyon; and a private collection in Paris) and a counterproof in the Musée Greuze, Tournus.

SIMBOLO APOSTOLICO
CREDO
IN SEGNO CON IL QVALE SI
CONOSCESCESSERO LI FEDELI, E PER
TENERLO PER VN SOMMARIO BREVE
E COMPENDIOSO DI QVELLO CHE ESSI
DOVEVANO PREDICARE, E CREDERE

GIOVANNI DOMENICO TIEPOLO
1727–1804

The Apostles' Creed, c. 1771 or after
Pen, brown ink, and wash over
graphite, 18⅝ x 14⅛ (46.5 x 35.6)

Gift of Stephen Mazoh and
Company, Inc.

This is a very handsome and typical sheet from Domenico's so-called Large Biblical Series, a corpus of more than two hundred fifty drawings that the artist executed over a period of time following his return from Spain to Venice in 1770. As James Byam Shaw has pointed out, the series consists of "album drawings," that is, sheets made as independent works of art rather than as preparatory studies for paintings or prints.[1]

This particular drawing is one of many devoted to the apostles of Christ. The apostles here occupy a clearly defined room with one figure, probably Peter, enthroned in the center below a wall tablet inscribed with Domenico's rather cryptic designation of the subject. The prayer referred to in the drawing, not found in the Bible and likely dating from the second or third century in its first form, might here be interpreted as the apostles professing their belief in Christ and dedication to the preaching of Christianity.[2]

As the prime apostle grandly and rhetorically gestures toward the left, the others respond to his gesture by glancing upward, some with their hands raised in prayer. The figures appear to be infused with religious fervor, and their almost ecstatic states are greatly enhanced by Domenico's characteristically nervous pen line and brilliant use of the white of the paper; the light seems to fall erratically, illuminating parts of bodies and clothing.

During his own lifetime, Domenico Tiepolo labored under the shadow of his famous and revered father, Giovanni Battista, who died in 1770. Domenico was accused of a lack of imagination and invention, traits deemed essential for the best eighteenth-century artists. Supposedly stung by such criticism, he demonstrated his originality in several large series of drawings and one of etchings. The Large Biblical Series sheets, as here, may be seen as part of this endeavor. Modern scholars have readily recognized his own unique talent and vision as a draftsman, painter, and etcher.[3]

This is the seventh drawing by the artist to enter the Gallery's collection and the second from the Large Biblical Series.

H. Diane Russell

PROVENANCE
Jean F. Gigoux, Paris, sale, Hôtel Drouot, 1882 (Lugt 1164); Eugène Feral, Paris, sale, Hôtel Drouot, 1901; private collection, Paris; Stephen Spector, New York; Peter Josten, New York.

NOTES
1. See J. Byam Shaw, *The Drawings of Domenico Tiepolo* (Boston, 1962), 36–37.
2. Further research may clarify the subject matter.
3. For other comments on this sheet, see Eric Van Schaack, *Master Drawings in Private Collections* (New York, 1962), 86–87, cat. 64.

LUCA SIGNORELLI
c. 1450–1523

Bust of a Youth Looking Upward
c. 1500
Black chalk on tan paper,
partially indented with a stylus
8⅞ x 6¹⁵⁄₁₆ (22.5 x 17.7)

Gift of the Woodner Family
Collection

This compelling drawing, the first by Signorelli in the National Gallery, shows with remarkable clarity why the artist has been characterized as the first great Italian master of black chalk, the medium in which nearly all his extant drawings were executed.[1] Very much an artist of his time in the facial types and expressions he gave his figures, Signorelli stood apart from his contemporaries in the bold forms and powerful physiques that he presented with uncompromising directness. Both his deep understanding of the human form and his brilliant execution are revealed in exemplary fashion in the Woodner drawing, not only by the arresting figure on the recto, but also by the two excellent nude studies on the verso, discovered only in 1987.

Figures gazing upward with their heads tilted back to reveal the underside of the chin are found throughout Signorelli's oeuvre, though the precise figure for which the Woodner drawing was made has not yet been identified. Since 1928, scholars have suggested connections with several different figures in the great frescoes in Orvieto cathedral,[2] but the strange, pointed, earlike forms that jut from the sides of the head of the drawn figure seem to indicate that this study was made for some other project altogether.[3] None of the figures in the Orvieto frescoes have such ears, which seem to resemble the long, pointed ones usually associated with Pan and his followers.

Nor do any of the Orvieto figures have quite the same pose, with the chest thrust forward and the arms pulled back in a way that suggests the youth may be bound. (His pose is in fact very close to that of Amor in *The Triumph of Chastity*, now in the National Gallery, London, but in reverse.)[4] Since the study on the recto was incised for transfer, Signorelli presumably used the figure in one of his paintings, though not apparently in one that has survived to this day.

As a prime example of Signorelli's draftsmanship and the earliest black chalk Italian drawing to enter the National Gallery, this exceptionally fine sheet assumes immediate importance within the Gallery's small but treasured group of Italian Renaissance drawings. To make it even more precious, it comes to the Gallery from the collection of a very close friend and donor, the late Ian Woodner, whose special love for drawings of the Italian Renaissance is thus movingly honored.

Margaret Morgan Grasselli

PROVENANCE
De Clementi; A. G. B. Russell (sale, London, Sotheby's, 22 May 1928, no. 89); Durlacher; John Nicholas Brown, Providence; David Tunick, New York, 1986.

NOTES
1. Bernard Berenson, *The Drawings of the Florentine Painters* (Chicago, 1938), 1:30.
2. Tancred Borenius was the first to propose the connection to the Orvieto frescoes, specifically to the *Crowning of the Elect* (in the catalogue for the sale held in London at Sotheby's on 22 May 1928, introduction and no. 89). Berenson later suggested a direct relationship with a "youth forming a group with a woman embracing another man, just under r. foot of trumpeting angel l. in the fresco of Resurrection" (*Drawings of the Florentine Painters*, 1938, 2:334, no. 2509F). More recently, Nicholas Turner has suggested that the drawing was made in connection with the fresco of *The Damned*.

See *Master Drawings, The Woodner Collection* [exh. cat. Royal Academy of Arts] (London, 1987), no. 4. For reproductions of all the Orvieto frescos, see M. G. de la Coste-Messelière, *Luca Signorelli* (Paris, 1975), 47–150.
3. The ears were first pointed out by Nicholas Turner (London, 1987, no. 4), who posited a relationship between the drawing and the Orvieto fresco of *The Damned*, which features a number of horned and winged demons. Those demons' horns, however, grow out of the forehead and have a very different shape from the forms in the Woodner drawing.
4. Reproduced by La Coste-Messelière 1975, xxix.

ISRAHEL VAN MECKENEM
c. 1445–1503

Saint George and the Dragon
c. 1465-1470
Engraving, diameter 6¾ (17.1)

Gift of the 50th Anniversary Gift
Committee

This fine impression of Israhel van
Meckenem's roundel print illustrating
Saint George slaying the dragon is one
of about thirty known impressions of
this version and is the first to enter a
public collection in North America.[1]

Meckenem, who was trained also as a
goldsmith, executed his first engravings
around 1465, soon becoming one of
the most prolific artists in this medium
in the fifteenth century. It has been
noted that about one-fifth of all German engravings executed before Dürer
are attributable to Meckenem.[2] Though
a large portion of his oeuvre consists of
copies after prints by other early printmakers, including Master E.S., the
Housebook Master, Martin Schon-
gauer, and the young Albrecht Dürer,
Meckenem did possess a strong degree
of originality and inventiveness, which
he displayed even in his earliest prints
such as this present engraving.

The style and technique of *Saint
George and the Dragon* suggest an early
date of c. 1465–1470. As Alan Shestack
has noted, Meckenem's early prints
combine hard, rigid outlines with soft,
delicate modeling.[3] They are also reminiscent of the engravings by Master
E.S., especially in the sculptural quality
of the drapery and in the stacking-up of
landscape forms. In this print Meckenem filled the space with decorative
and flowing lines, creating rich surface
patterning that is harmonious with the
artist's concurrent work as a goldsmith.
Equally ornamental is the fluid Gothic
script of the artist's prominently placed
signature.

The story of Saint George slaying the
dragon was a favorite subject among
Renaissance artists. According to the
Golden Legend, Saint George was a Roman soldier of steadfast Christian faith.
He was traveling through the countryside of Silene at a time when the
people were being terrorized by a dragon. To appease the beast, human sa-
crifices, chosen by lot, were offered.
The next victim was to be Princess
Cleodolinda, daughter of the king.
George arrived at this perilous moment.
Protecting himself from harm by making the sign of the cross, he slew the
dragon with his spear, thereby saving
the princess and liberating the frightened people. According to the story, many
who had witnessed the power of Saint
George's faith were converted to Christianity. As a devotional image, Saint
George slaying the dragon is an allusion
to the triumph of good over evil.

The Gallery's collection of 105 Israhel
van Meckenem prints, all given by
Lessing J. Rosenwald, is considered the
finest in the United States. The collection contains several rare prints, including three unique sheets.[4] The present
impression strengthens the small group
of early prints by the artist in the collection, of which this is clearly the most
accomplished. Meckenem's *Saint George
and the Dragon* also joins the Gallery's
other depictions of the story: the paintings by Raphael and Rogier van der
Weyden and a pen and ink drawing
attributed to Hugo van der Goes.

Gregory Jecmen

PROVENANCE
William Esdaile (Lugt 2617), London;
Christie's, London, 1839–1840; Brisard,
Bibliothèque Royale de Belgique, stamp
(Lugt 257); Ducs d'Arenberg, stamp (Lugt
567), Brussels and Nordkirchen, 1849;
William H. Schab, New York; Dr. Albert W.
Blum, Short Hills, N.J., 1952; Sotheby's,
New York, 27 February 1988, no. 1027;
Private collection; Frederick Mulder,
London.

NOTES
1. Max Lehrs, *Geschichte und kritischer
Katalog des deutschen, niederländischen und
französischen Kupferstichs im XV. Jahrhundert* (Vienna, 1934), 9:281–282, no. 344,
state ii of ii.
2. Fritz Koreny, preface to vol. 24 of Holl-
stein's *German Engravings, Etchings, and
Woodcuts, 1400–1700* (Blaricarum, 1986), vi.
3. Alan Shestack, *Fifteenth-Century Engravings of Northern Europe* [exh. cat. National
Gallery of Art] (Washington, 1967), in
biography preceding cat. 54.
4. See Washington 1967, cats. 155, 156,
162.

Art for the Nation

Gifts in Honor of the 50th Anniversary of the National Gallery of Art

NATIONAL GALLERY OF ART · WASHINGTON

The exhibition is supported by a
grant from GTE Corporation

Art for the Nation was organized by the
National Gallery of Art

Exhibition Dates
17 March–16 June 1991

Library of Congress
Cataloging-in-Publication Data

National Gallery of Art (U.S.)
    Art for the nation: gifts in honor of the 50th
anniversary of the National Gallery of Art.
    p. cm.
    Catalog of an exhibition held Mar. 17–June
16, 1991 at the National Gallery of Art.
    Includes indexes.
    ISBN 0-89468-158-3
    1. Art—Exhibitions. 2. National Gallery of
Art (U.S.)—Exhibitions.
    I. Title.
N5963.W18N38   1991
708.153—dc20   91-6918
                                          CIP

Cover: Vincent van Gogh, *Roses*, 1890, oil on
canvas. Gift (Partial and Promised) of W. Averell
Harriman and Pamela C. Harriman

Back Cover: Edgar Degas, *Little Dancer Fourteen
Years Old*, 1878–1881, wax and other materials.
Promised Gift of Mr. and Mrs. Paul Mellon

Produced by the Editors Office, National Gallery
of Art
Editor-in-Chief, Frances P. Smyth
Edited by Jane Sweeney
Designed by Cynthia Hotvedt
Editorial Assistance by Abigail Walker
Production Assistance by
Meg Alexander

Typeset in Galliard by VIP Systems, Inc.,
Alexandria, Virginia
Color Separations by PhotoColor, Inc., Newark,
Delaware
Printed on Karma by Garamond/Pridemark Press,
Baltimore, Maryland

PHOTO CREDITS

Credit is due the Photographic Services of the National Gallery of Art for photographing most of the
works of art in this exhibition. Other copyrights as
follows: p. 157, © 1982 Malcolm Varon, N. Y. C.;
p. 283, © 1980 Aperture Foundation, Inc.; p. 295,
© 1989 Aperture Foundation, Inc.; p. 296 (left and
right), © Aperture Foundation, Inc.; p. 297, © 1971
Aperture Foundation, Inc.; p. 299, © 1950 Aperture Foundation, Inc.; p. 329, © August Sander
Archive; pp. 340-341, © Lisette Model Foundation; p. 359, © 1990 Trustees of the Ansel Adams
Publishing Rights Trust; p. 398, © Malcolm Varon,
N. Y. C.; p. 419, Disney characters © The Walt
Disney Co.; p. 430, Geoffrey Clemens, New York,
and Sidney Janis Gallery, New York.

NOTE TO THE READER

Dimensions are given in height in inches, followed by width and depth (and by centimeters in
parentheses). In books and portfolios, page size is
given.

CONTENTS

FOREWORD

Art for the Nation celebrates the fiftieth anniversary of the opening of the National Gallery of Art on March 17, 1941. That event was the culmination of many years' effort by Andrew W. Mellon to establish an art museum of the highest possible quality in the nation's capital, to show that America stood not only for the successes of industry and business but also for the highest standards in culture. The gift of his superlative collection of paintings and sculptures, as well as the original Gallery building and endowments, remains the greatest single private donation to any government.

Andrew Mellon's vision and generosity were quickly followed by major donations from other collectors, most notably Joseph E. Widener, Lessing J. Rosenwald, Samuel Henry Kress and Rush Harrison Kress, Chester Dale, Ailsa Mellon Bruce, and Paul Mellon. These Founding Benefactors continued Andrew Mellon's vision that America's national gallery should collect and show the best of European and American art from the late Middle Ages forward. Their donations and the extraordinary gifts of art from many other private citizens have built the heart of the National Gallery of Art—its permanent collection—into a remarkably comprehensive and fine collection in an extraordinarily short time.

Since those early years the Gallery has grown into a multifaceted institution involved in numerous projects. Our exhibitions, loans to other museums, publications, research, concerts, filmmaking, extension services, center for scholars, programs in public schools, lecture series, internships, and numerous additional activities have brought the Gallery into the lives of people throughout this country and the world. These activities are very important to our mission. But we remain, above all, a museum with a dedication to the quality and display of its collection, and in that sense the vision of the Gallery's founders continues.

We celebrate the Gallery's fiftieth anniversary this year with numerous activities in all our areas of interest, but our focus is above all on the permanent collection. Under the leadership of our deputy director, Roger Mandle, we are reinstalling many of the galleries of the original building to take into account the latest changes in the collection and scholarship on it; we have emphasized the use of period frames as integral components of the major paintings. The Gallery's conservation department has accelerated the treatment of a number of important works, resulting in discoveries such as those celebrated in our recent exhibition on the artistic complexities of one of the greatest paintings in the collection, Giovanni Bellini's *Feast of the Gods*. Our new systematic catalogue on the main fields of painting, sculpture, and decorative arts is a scholarly work incorporating the latest art-historical and conservation research that will eventually grow to twenty-six volumes.

The most appropriate way to celebrate the foundation of the National Gallery of Art and the extraordinary contribution of its original benefactors is, of course, to further their work. Thus the theme of this exhibition is the new donations of works of art to enhance the permanent collection. *Art for the Nation*, which opens to the public fifty years to the day from the Gallery's original opening, matches the range of the Gallery's main collections: European and American paintings, drawings, sculpture, prints, illustrated books, and photographs from the late Middle Ages to the present. The primary intent has been to make major additions to the collection, building on its strengths but especially filling its gaps. It is remarkable to see how, even in areas of the Gallery's greatest strength, such as Italian Renaissance painting and sculpture or French impressionist painting, major new works play crucial artistic and historical roles.

Some of our visitors may not realize that the collection is far larger than what is seen on the walls on any given day. The various objects on paper, for example—prints, drawings, photographs, rare books—cannot be exposed to light for long periods and therefore are exhibited in rotating groups, otherwise being fully available for study and enjoyment in our print study rooms. The Gallery is a latecomer in these fields compared to many great centers, particularly European ones, and therefore seeks to augment the depth and breadth of its holdings in the graphic arts. Even in the areas of paintings and sculpture, the Gallery needs greater resources than can be shown at one time in order to satisfy the demands of loans to exhibitions elsewhere, photography, conservation, and research.

Beyond that, as it is a national gallery, the Trustees have emphasized our duty to lend original works of art to sister institutions across the land, as well as to other official public spaces. Our vision for the Gallery in its next fifty years—and beyond—is to provide a rich asset sustaining the Gallery's public trust and national mission as well as justifying its sources of support.

More than one hundred fifty benefactors, including many old friends and very many new ones from throughout America and from Europe, are represented in this exhibition by more than three hundred works of art. These donors are remarkable in their magnanimity and personal sacrifice in that they have agreed to share the works of art they love and prize with the wider audience of visitors to the Gallery. Our gratitude to them is boundless. Each donor represented in the exhibition will have made a significant present gift to the Gallery in honor of its anniversary. Most objects are given fully; some, in part; all objects in the exhibition not given outright in their entirety are committed to the Gallery. Many more gifts of art have been received than could be included here, and even as this is being written further donations are being made, all of which will be acknowledged in a second volume to be published at the end of this anniversary year.

Art for the Nation has been a project involving the Trustees of the Gallery, under the leadership of Franklin D. Murphy, chairman, and John R. Stevenson, president, the Trustees' Council, the executive officers, and most of the Gallery's staff. A 50th Anniversary Gift Committee of more than seventy donors, organized, chaired, and inspired by Gallery trustee Robert H. Smith, has contributed funds, and with the help of the Gallery's development office under Joseph Krakora and Laura Smith Fisher, assisted by Catherine Conger, the committee collected more than five million dollars to enable the acquisition of major additions in each of the principal fields in which we collect, and most notably one of our most crucial desiderata, *The Martyrdom of Saint Bartholomew* by Jusepe de Ribera.

The Gallery's other support groups—the Collectors Committee, chaired by Ruth Carter Stevenson and Edwin L. Cox, and the Circle, chaired by Robert H. Smith and Katharine Graham—are represented, together with the 50th Anniversary Gift Committee, in the acquisition of Wayne Thiebaud's celebratory *Cakes*. Trustees and staff alike, the deputy director, the senior curators, curators, and assistant curators were involved in visiting collectors to discuss the fiftieth anniversary and ask their help. The entire curatorial staff did research and wrote entries on gifts offered, as seen in their signed contributions to the catalogue. The catalogue was edited and designed with grace under utmost pressure by Jane Sweeney and Cynthia Hotvedt of the editors office, under the supervision of Frances P. Smyth. The registrarial coordination of hundreds of works from the large number of donors was ably handled by Mary Suzor, Ann Halpern, and Judi Cline; D. Dodge Thompson, Ann B. Robertson, and Debbi Miller of the department of exhibitions were of great help as well. The installation was beautifully designed by the Gallery's team under Gaillard Ravenel, Mark Leithauser, and Gordon Anson. The opening festivities have been elegantly supervised by Genevra Higginson.

If there was one person principally in charge of the entire project, however, it was senior curator Andrew Robison. His organization of the curatorial research, his optimism about the response of our friends as well as the necessity for high standards, his unflagging energy for each new possibility, and his enthusiasm for building the Gallery's collection propelled the campaign, as many of our donors will remember. And with the talented help of Barbara Ward he has supervised the final contacts, the selection, the organization of the exhibition, and the catalogue through every stage to the Gallery walls.

Joining with us in support of this exhibition is the GTE Corporation, an outstanding corporate patron under its chairman, James L. Johnson, and its president, Charles R. Lee, to whom we are most grateful once again.

To all the above, our deepest thanks, and also the thanks of millions of future visitors from throughout the world who will appreciate and enjoy these many outstanding gifts honoring the National Gallery's past and continuing to build its future.

J. Carter Brown
Director

DONORS OF WORKS OF ART

AS OF 7 FEBRUARY 1991

Maida and George Abrams
The Harry N. Abrams Family
Virginia Adams
Walter H. and Leonore Annenberg
Anonymous Donors
Aperture Foundation
Jeffrey Atlas
Martin and Liane Atlas
Sally Michel Avery
Dr. and Mrs. George Baer
Robert M. & Anne T. Bass
Patricia Bauman and
　John L. Bryant, Jr.
Mr. and Mrs. Daniel Bell
Katrin Bellinger
Dr. Ruth B. Benedict
Mr. and Mrs. Donald M. Blinken
C. G. Boerner
Warren and Grace Brandt
Mr. and Mrs. Harry Brooks
J. Carter Brown
Yvonne tan Bunzl
Iris and B. Gerald Cantor
Edward William Carter and
　Hannah Locke Carter
Leo Castelli
The Circle of the National Gallery of Art
Collectors Committee
Catherine Gamble Curran
Lois and Georges de Menil
Mr. and Mrs. Richard Diebenkorn
Louisa C. Duemling
Mr. and Mrs. James T. Dyke
Mercedes Eichholz
David, James, Miles, Richard, and
　Sarah Carianne Epstein
Sarah G. Epstein
Mr. and Mrs. Thomas M. Evans
Kathleen Ewing
Frank R. and Jeannette H. Eyerly
50th Anniversary Gift Committee
Mr. and Mrs. Donald G. Fisher
Aaron I. Fleischman
Mrs. Daniel Fraad

Robert Frank
Helen Frankenthaler
Mr. and Mrs. John R. Gaines
Galerie Arnoldi-Livie
Galerie Cailleux
Jo Ann and Julian Ganz, Jr.
Kate Ganz
Isabel and Fernando Garzoni
Mr. and Mrs. Anthony Geber
Gemini G.E.L.
The Howard Gilman Foundation
Arnold & Mildred Glimcher
The Horace W. Goldsmith Foundation
Graphicstudio, U.S.F.
The Clive Gray Family
The Grinstein Family
Guest Services, Inc.
Helena Gunnarsson
Mr. and Mrs. Nathan L. Halpern
Mr. and Mrs. Gordon Hanes
Pamela C. Harriman
Mrs. Robert A. Hauslohner
Mrs. Rudolf J. Heinemann
Mr. and Mrs. H. John Heinz III
George F. Hemphill and
　Lenore A. Winters
John D. Herring and
　Mr. and Mrs. Paul L. Herring
Margaret Mellon Hitchcock
Mr. and Mrs. Jem Hom
Mr. and Mrs. Raymond J. Horowitz
The Christian Humann Foundation
Dora Donner Ide
Jean Jacques
Jasper Johns
Peter Josten
Ruth and Jacob Kainen
Mr. and Mrs. Stephen M. Kellen
Ellsworth Kelly
Mr. and Mrs. Gilbert H. Kinney
Richard A. and Lee G. Kirstein
Robert P. and Arlene R. Kogod
Mrs. Rush Kress
Mr. and Mrs. Leonard A. Lauder

50TH ANNIVERSARY GIFT COMMITTEE

Robert H. Smith
Chairman

ART FOR THE NATION

JACOPO BELLINI
c. 1400–c. 1470

Saint Anthony Abbot and
Saint Bernardino of Siena, 1459 or 1460
Tempera on wood
43¼ x 22½ (110 x 57)

Gift (Partial and Promised) of
an Anonymous Donor

Jacopo Bellini was a pivotal figure in the history of Venetian Renaissance art. In two remarkable sketchbooks, one in the Louvre, Paris, and the other in the British Museum, London, dating from about the mid-fifteenth century, he experimented in a highly personal way with the new invention of linear perspective and with the classical subject matter that was then coming into vogue.[1] But Jacopo's few surviving paintings, mostly half-length Madonnas in various European and American museums, remain faithful to his origin in the late or International Gothic style of his teacher Gentile da Fabriano. Major credit for instilling Renaissance values in Venetian painting has, accordingly, been given to Jacopo's son Giovanni (c. 1430–1516). We must revise this theory now that a major painting by the elder Bellini has unexpectedly come to light — an arched panel that depicts a noble pair of saints, Anthony Abbot and Bernardino of Siena, standing in a landscape. This newly discovered masterpiece by Jacopo almost certainly belonged to an altarpiece which, according to early sources, he completed, together with Giovanni and his other son Gentile (1429–1507), in 1459 (or 1460) for the funeral chapel of the famous *condottiere* Gattamelata in the basilica of Sant'Antonio (the Santo) in Padua.[2] Dismantled in the seventeenth century, the Gattamelata altarpiece has been hypothetically reconstructed, with the present panel, its figures facing right, forming the left wing of the complex.[3] Donatello worked in the city for more than a decade sculpting the high altar of the Santo and the equestrian monument commemorating Gattamelata outside the church. The structure of Jacopo's altarpiece, with the figures placed before a landscape instead of a gold ground, seems to have responded to the Florentine's example.[4] Though clearly designed by Jacopo, the fragments that formed the predella, or base, of the altarpiece appear to have been painted by Giovanni Bellini.[5] Likewise, the master may well have been assisted by Gentile in executing the *Saints Anthony and Bernardino.* Tall upright figures

and stratified rocks like those in the present panel abound in Jacopo's sketchbooks.[6] And the sinuous curls of Anthony's beard are a hallmark of the International Style in which he was trained. But the more austere treatment of the saint's recently canonized companion, holding the Name-of-Jesus monogram, finds closer analogies in the work of Gentile Bellini, who massed such figures together to create the large-scale narrative scenes in which he excelled.[7] Designed by Jacopo and probably executed in collaboration with Gentile, the rediscovered panel from the Gattamelata altarpiece ushered in a new age in Venetian painting.

David Alan Brown

PROVENANCE
Private collection, the Netherlands; Private collection, New York.

NOTES
1. For the albums and all other aspects of Jacopo's work see the definitive monograph by Colin Eisler, *The Genius of Jacopo Bellini* (New York, 1989).

2. Sold with an incorrect attribution to Crivelli by Sotheby's, London (8 April, 1981, lot 124), the panel was attributed wholly to Jacopo by Miklós Boskovits ("Per Jacopo Bellini pittore [Postilla ad un Colloquio]," *Paragone* 36, nos. 419–421–423 [Jan.–May 1985], 113–123) and in part by Colin Eisler ("'Saints Anthony Abbot and Bernardino of Siena' Designed by Jacopo and Painted by Gentile Bellini," *Arte Veneta* 39 [1985], 32–40). See also Boskovits, "Giovanni Bellini. Quelques suggestions sur ses débuts," *La revue du Louvre* 36, no. 6 (1986), 386–393; and Keith Christiansen, "Venetian Painting of the Early Quattrocento," *Apollo* 125 (March 1987), 174–176.

3. Eisler reconstructs the altarpiece as a triptych (1985, 39, fig. 7; and 1989, 62, fig. 47).

4. Peter Humfrey in *Gothic to Renaissance. European Painting 1300–1600* [exh. cat. Colnaghi] (London and New York, 1988), 15–26.

5. For the problem of the predella see in addition to the writers previously cited, Rona Goffen, *Giovanni Bellini* (New Haven and London, 1989), 8–9, figs. 3 and 4.

6. Compare, for example, Eisler 1989, plates 220 and 239.

7. In his monograph of 1989, Eisler credits the authorship of the picture to "Gentile Bellini, after Jacopo's design" (pp. 60, 63, and 517). About Gentile see Jürg Meyer zur Capellen, *Gentile Bellini* (Stuttgart, 1985).

3

ANONYMOUS GERMAN

Christ on the Cross, 1485
Woodcut with gouache and
gold leaf on vellum
12⅝ x 7¹³⁄₁₆ (32.0 x 19.8)

Ruth and Jacob Kainen Collection

This magnificent German fifteenth-century hand-colored woodcut comes from a missal printed in 1485 by Johann Sensenschmidt in Bamberg.[1] The tradition of illustrating missals, which contained the prayers and rites of the mass, with Christ on the Cross was firmly established in the printed book by the end of the 1470s. The image, almost always a woodcut, was inserted at the beginning of the Canon of the Mass. As in the case of this present woodcut the illustration was often printed on vellum even in an otherwise paper book.[2] The devotional image follows the standard iconography of the Crucifixion with Christ on the Cross flanked by the Virgin Mary at the left and Saint John at the right. The skull at the foot of the cross not only symbolizes the Mount of Golgotha where Christ was crucified; along with the nearby scattered bones it also refers to the remains of Adam whose original sin was atoned for by Christ's sacrifice.[3]

Early woodcuts such as this were frequently the combined effort of several people. The artist would have provided the design while possibly another person transferred the design to the block. The woodcutter did the actual cutting of the block. Others were then responsible for the printing and finally the coloring of the woodcut.

The bold, expressive printed lines of the figures in this woodcut are counterbalanced by the delicate and jewellike hand-coloring. Also exceptional is the extensive use of gold in the background and in Christ's halo. The gold background has been incised and stamped to create a decorative diamond and floral pattern. The extraordinary and individual attention to the hand-coloring of the print makes it comparable to a page from an illuminated manuscript. The fine condition of this print is unusual, given the fact that missals were in daily use and for the most part are worn out or have been destroyed.[4]

This rare woodcut further strengthens the National Gallery's outstanding collection of fifteenth-century woodcuts, metalcuts, and engravings formed and then given by Lessing J. Rosenwald beginning in 1943. The woodcut joins other similar missal illustrations in the collection, these dating from the same time but coming from Basel, Speyer, and Strassburg. The Kainen *Christ on the Cross* attests to the couple's love for the woodcut, from the beginnings of the medium in the fifteenth century to those done by the twentieth-century German expressionists. The latter is superbly represented by another Kainen Fiftieth Anniversary gift, Ernst Ludwig Kirchner's *Blond Painter Stirner*.

Gregory Jecmen

PROVENANCE
Purchased Kennedy Galleries, New York, 1965.

NOTES
1. Wilhelm Schreiber, *Handbuch der Holz-und Metallschnitte des XV. Jahrhundert* (Leipzig, 1926), 1:122, no. 375.

2. Richard S. Field, *Fifteenth-Century Woodcuts and Metalcuts* [exh. cat. National Gallery of Art] (Washington, 1965), cat. 52.

3. Louis Réau, *Iconographie de l'art chrétien* (Paris, 1957), 2:488–489.

4. Arthur M. Hind, *An Introduction to a History of Woodcut* (Boston and New York, 1935), 2:283, n. 1.

Et famulum tuū epm nr̄m cū oīb' sibi cōmissis: ab oīi
aduersitate custodi. et pacē ecclie nr̄is ꝛcede tpibus.

HARTMANN SCHEDEL
1440–1514

Liber Chronicarum (Nuremberg Chronicle)
Koberger, Nuremberg, 1493
Bound volume with 1,809 hand-colored woodcuts
18½ x 12½ (46.9 x 31.6)

Gift of Paul Mellon

Hartmann Schedel's *Liber Chronicarum*, commonly known as the *Nuremberg Chronicle*, is the first truly monumental printed illustrated book of the fifteenth century.[1] Published in 1493 by Anton Koberger in Nuremberg, the book is a world history from the Creation to the year of its publication. The book's structure follows popular late medieval chronicles and is divided according to the six ages of mankind: the Creation to Noah; Noah's ark to the destruction of Sodom and Gommorrah; Abraham to Saul; David to the destruction of Jerusalem; the Babylonian captivity of the Jews to the death of John the Baptist; and the birth of Christ to the present.

The *Chronicle* was written for the scholar as well as for the general audience and was published in both a Latin and a German edition. The Mellon Latin edition is one of the finest extant copies of the *Chronicle*. The woodcut illustrations are exquisitely hand-colored and the volume was handsomely bound specially for Raimund Fugger (1489–1535), a member of the eminent Augsberg mercantile-banking family.

The *Chronicle* was commissioned by Sebald Schreyer and Sebastian Kammermeister, two leading Nuremberg citizens, who contracted the artists Michael Wolgemut and Wilhelm Pleydenwurff to illustrate Schedel's text. They also engaged the publisher, Anton Koberger. The artists first produced an "exemplar," or layout model, which set out in manuscript and sketch form the placement of text and image.[2] The workshops of Wolgemut and Pleydenwurff produced the 645 different woodblocks, many of which were then used more than once, particularly for some of the historical figures. The young Albrecht Dürer, the godson of Koberger and apprentice to Wolgemut in 1488, was probably a member of this workshop.

One of the most interesting parts of the *Chronicle* is the description and depiction of various cities. These woodcut illustrations, oftentimes spreading across two facing pages, include both authentic city views of European cities, such as Strassburg (illustrated here), Rome, Venice, Basel, and, of course, Nuremberg, and imaginary views of ancient cities, such as Babylon, Carthage, and Troy.[3] The volume also contains two early printed maps. The first, a world map, follows the tradition of Ptolemy, showing only the three continents of Europe, Africa, and Asia. The second map is one of middle Europe and comes from the cosmographer Hieronymus Münzer. It is the first map of middle Europe to be included in a printed book.[4]

In the late fifteenth century Hartmann Schedel became the leading figure of Nuremberg's humanist circle, which also included Schreyer and Koberger. Trained as a physician, Schedel also studied Greek and law. He collected the works of ancient writers along with contemporary texts on medicine, geography, and mathematics. Schedel's own major literary work, the *Liber Chronicarum*, reveals his careful scholarship and critical approach to earlier sources. The *Nuremberg Chronicle* initiated the collaboration between the city's humanist scholars, artists, and publishers, which was to continue into the following century.

The high quality of the woodcuts in the *Nuremberg Chronicle* paved the way for Albrecht Dürer's own handling of the medium in his series of The Life of the Virgin, The Large Passion, and The Apocalypse, dating from the late 1490s and early 1500s. All three series were published together in 1511 and appeared with Latin texts written by Benedictus Cheldonius. This publication is a high mark of book production in early sixteenth-century Nuremberg and the Gallery is fortunate to possess a single bound copy of all three series, bequeathed by Lessing J. Rosenwald. The Mellon *Nuremberg Chronicle* is the first illustrated German book printed before 1500 to enter the Gallery's collection, and is an exceptional complement to the extensive holdings of early German single-sheet woodcuts.

Gregory Jecmen

PROVENANCE
Raimund Fugger, Augsberg; purchased Hôtel Drouot, Paris, November 21, 1960.

NOTES
1. Wilhelm Schreiber, *Manuel de l'amateur de la gravure sur bois et sur metal au XVe siècle* (Leipzig, 1911), 5: cat. 5203.

2. Adrian Wilson, *The Making of the Nuremberg Chronicle* (Amsterdam, 1976), and by the same author, "The Early Drawings for the Nuremberg Chronicle," *Master Drawings* 13 (1975), 115–130.

3. Elisabeth Rücker, *Die Schedelsche Weltchronik—Das grösste Buchunternehmen der Dürer-Zeit* (Munich, 1973), 85–135.

4. Rücker 1973, 77–81.

ANONYMOUS GERMAN

Christ on the Cross, c. 1500–1525
Hand-colored woodcut with gold leaf
12⅝ x 8¹³⁄₁₆ (32 x 22.3)

Gift of C. G. Boerner

This exquisitely designed and executed woodcut of Christ on the cross between Mary and Saint John originally formed the canon page of a missal. The sensitive hand coloring and incised gold leaf of the figures' halos gives this print a sumptuous character usually associated with manuscript illustrations. Though it is not yet possible to attribute this work to a specific artist, the print displays some affinities with the woodcuts produced in Strassburg during the first quarter of the sixteenth century. The intricate monogram to the left of Mary, composed of the letters *HKA* (or *M*) *T*, is probably that of either the printer or the cutter of the block.

The woodcut displays an overall sophistication in the drawing and cutting of the block. A subtle delineation of form is particularly evident in Mary's elegant face and her splendidly elongated fingers, in the curly hair of Saint John, and in the agitated folds of Christ's garment. This refined style together with the long parallel hatching, seen notably in Mary's robe and in the foliage of the trees, suggests a similarity with certain prints executed in the workshop of Johann Grüninger, a printer and publisher active in Strassburg between c. 1483 and 1530.[1] Another striking feature of this woodcut is the realistic landscape in the background. The artist not only created a convincing recession of space but also implied a sense of a particular place in the small village or monastery just beyond the main figural group. Similarly composed and executed landscapes can be found in the illustrations from Grüninger's *Virgil* published in 1502.[2] A landscape comparable to that in the present print appears in another woodcut of Christ on the cross included in a later edition of Martin Luther's *September Testament* published by Johann Schott in Strassburg in 1523.[3] While the Boerner print follows an established iconography in the placement of figures and the inclusion of the skull and bones of Adam near the base of the cross, the depiction of an isolated clump of flowers in the lower right corner is unusual. This plant, while lacking enough details for a specific identification, is perhaps a symbolic reference to the suffering and passion of Christ.

This woodcut is a welcome addition to the National Gallery's collection of early sixteenth-century German woodcuts, which includes works by Albrecht Dürer, Albrecht Altdorfer, Lucas Cranach the Elder, Hans Baldung Grien, and Hans Burgkmair.

Gregory Jecmen

NOTES
1. For Grüninger's work see Albert Schramm, *Der Bilderschmuck der Frühdrucke* (Leipzig, 1937), 20:3–9, and Arthur M. Hind, *An Introduction to a History of Woodcut* (Boston and New York, 1935), 2:339–344.

2. The illustration for the First Eclogue from Grüninger's *Virgil* is reproduced in Hind 1935, 2: fig. 154.

3. See Heimo Reinitzer, *Biblia deutsch. Luthers Bibelübersetzung und ihre Tradition* [exh. cat. Herzog August Bibliothek] (Wolfenbüttel, 1983), cat. 127 and ill. 134.

TITIAN
c. 1490–1576

Study of an Eagle, c. 1515
Pen and brown ink
3⅝ x 3⅝ (9.3 x 9.2)

Gift of J. Carter Brown

This vibrant pen and ink study of an eagle, which once belonged to the English painter and critic Sir Joshua Reynolds, was believed to be by Leonardo da Vinci until Konrad Oberhuber recognized Titian as its true author.[1] The former attribution was based on the superb quality of the drawing and on Leonardo's well-known interest in animals rather than on any consideration of style. The rapid "staccato" pen strokes, suggesting the eagle's feathers, are characteristic of the Venetian master, especially of his early landscape studies, in which foliage is treated in the same luminous manner. In its fluid handling of the pen and its painterly texture, the Washington drawing most closely resembles the sketch of a *Landscape with an Eagle* in the Uffizi Gallery, Florence, which Oberhuber also convincingly identified as Titian's.[2] The eagle in the Uffizi drawing is shown entire, and so are the others represented by Titian in the woodcut of the *Triumph of Christ* of c. 1511; the woodcut of a *Landscape with a Milkmaid* of c. 1525; and the painting of the *Vision of Saint John the Evangelist* (fig. 1) of the mid-1540s in the National Gallery's collection.[3] These birds all have a heraldic air typical of coats of arms (after he was knighted, Titian added a double eagle to his family escutcheon), while their forms are straightforwardly naturalistic. Though limited to the bird's head and outspread wing, the Washington study is both more expressive and more fantastic. With its ruffled crest, piercing eye, sharply hooked beak, and long curling tongue, Titian's eagle shares much of the ferocity of the winged dragon in his later drawing of *Roger and Angelica* in the Musée Bonnat at Bayonne.[4] In the Washington drawing Titian has well captured the eagle's fighting spirit. Few of his studies have survived, so it is not surprising that although the Gallery can boast the finest group of Titian paintings in America, the *Study of an Eagle* is the first drawing by the master to enter the collection.

David Alan Brown

NOTES
1. Konrad Oberhuber in *Recent Acquisitions and Promised Gifts. Sculpture, Drawings, Prints* (National Gallery of Art, Washington, 1974), 119, cat. 74.

2. Harold E. Wethey, *Titian and His Drawings* (Princeton, 1987), 157, cat. 33 and fig. 76.

3. About the two woodcuts see David Rosand and Michelangelo Muraro, *Titian and the Venetian Woodcut* [exh. cat. National Gallery of Art] (Washington, 1976), 37–44, cat. 1 and ill. 47; and 140–145, cat. 21 and ill. 141; and about the painting see Robert Echols in *Titian, Prince of Painters* [exh. cat. National Gallery of Art] (Washington, 1990), 272, cat. 42.

4. Wethey 1987, 158–159, cat. 42, fig. 102, and frontispiece.

Fig. 1. Titian, *Saint John the Evangelist on Patmos*, 1544, oil on canvas, 93½ x 103½ (237.6 x 263). National Gallery of Art, Washington, Samuel H. Kress Collection

POLIDORO CALDARA, called POLIDORO DA CARAVAGGIO
c. 1499–1543?

A Deathbed Scene (recto)
Woman Seated with a Piece of Cloth (verso), c. 1521–1522
Chalk
8½ x 11½ (21 x 29)

Gift (Partial and Promised) of David E. Rust

Although Lombard by birth, Polidoro received his training in the entourage of Raphael. He worked in Raphael's Logge at the Vatican, where he painted grisaille panels and biblical scenes alongside Perino del Vaga, Giovanni da Udine, and others.[1] Following the Sack of Rome in 1527, Polidoro fled to Naples, working there and in Messina until his death, probably in 1543.[2] In the 1520s Polidoro became famous for his monochromatic facade frescoes of Roman subjects on some of the most notable palaces of the city. Destroyed or faded today, these frescoes were copied by most painters coming to Rome and became a kind of school for young artists. Consequently, they are preserved in numerous drawings.[3] Polidoro is also important for introducing a new conception of landscape painting, which portrayed classical ruins and nature in a new fantastic or emotionally charged manner.[4]

The present drawing,[5] is a study for a fresco in the Palazzo Baldassini, Rome.[6] The commission for the *palazzo* was given to Perino del Vaga, whose hand is evident in the contiguous main *salone*. This sheet is proof, however, that Polidoro painted some of the histories in the palace, as Vasari contended.[7] The preparatory study varies little from the fresco, although more figures appear in the final painting and their positions have been refined. The verso must be a study of an additional woman to have been seated to the left of the bed, perhaps ministering to the dying figure. Who this figure is has not been determined, but it is possible that he was a classical sage who wears a scholar's hat. Frescoes in the palace already identified indicate that the patron Melchiorre Baldassini, a distinguished lawyer, had devised a program relating to erudite ancient jurists.[8]

The Palazzo Baldassini and its frescoes were completed by 1522; stylistically Polidoro's drawing should be dated then, before the artist's brief trip to Naples (1523–1524).

The composition derives from Perino and Raphael, and the sketchily indicated figures do not yet exhibit the elongation of form and emotional anxiety of the drawings produced in the mid-1520s.

The *Deathbed Scene* is the first drawing by Polidoro da Caravaggio to enter the Gallery's collection and one of the last of this quality still in private hands. As one of Polidoro's major graphic works, it will be an important addition to our collection of drawings by artists working in Rome in the 1520s.

Diane De Grazia

NOTES
1. Nicole Dacos, *Le Logge di Raffaello* (Rome, 1986).

2. Pierluigi Leone de Castris, ed., *Polidoro da Caravaggio fra Napoli e Messina* [exh. cat. Museo e Gallerie Nazionali di Capodimonte] (Naples, 1988–1989), 1.

3. Lanfranco Ravelli, *Polidoro Caldara da Caravaggio* (Bergamo, 1978).

4. See his frescoes in San Silvestro al Quirinale, repr. Alessandro Marabottini, *Polidoro da Caravaggio* (Rome, 1969), 2: pl. xxx; and drawings in Ravelli 1978, 102–103.

5. Marabottini 1969, 1:310–311, cats. 51–52; Ravelli 1978, 121, cats. 52–53; Leone de Castris 1988–1989, 7 and fig. 6; Elena Parma Armani, *Perin del Vaga, L'anello mancante* (Genoa, 1986), 39, fig. 36; John Gere, *Drawings by Raphael and His Circle* [exh. cat. Pierpont Morgan Library] (New York, 1987), cat. 82.

6. Parma Armani 1986, 39, fig. 35.

7. Giorgio Vasari, *Le vite de'piu eccellenti pittori, scultori, ed architettori*, ed. Gaetano Milanesi (Florence, 1906), 5:146. On Perino in the Palazzo Baldassini see Parma Armani 1986, 36–40 and 254–257. Konrad Oberhuber first connected Polidoro's drawing with the Palazzo Baldassini fresco. Marabottini suggested that Polidoro's drawing was a copy of Perino's fresco. Scholars now agree that both drawing and painting can be attributed to Polidoro.

8. Linda Wolk, "Studies in Perino del Vaga's Early Career," Ph.D. diss., University of Michigan, 1987, 191–195, identified the figures in the *salone* as ancient doctors of the law. She also identified (225, n. 117) some of the scenes in this room, which she suggested may have been Baldassini's *studiolo*, as historical subjects based on Livy's *History of Rome*.

13

Attributed to
PIETER CORNELISZ. KUNST
1489/1490–1560/1561

Landscape with the Baptism of Christ
c. 1530
Pen and ink
7⁷⁄₁₆ x 9¹⁵⁄₁₆ (19 x 25.2)

Gift of Maida and George Abrams

The ostensible subject of this spirited drawing, the baptism of Christ in the lower left foreground, serves merely as a pretext for the depiction of an expansive, fanciful landscape. The composition has been carefully composed. Note, for example, how the massive rock outcroppings and mountains at the left are balanced by the deep space at the right, and how this spatial recession, on the diagonal, is accentuated and counterbalanced by the framing device of the foreground tree. The rocks, windswept trees, and ruined buildings are created out of a varied mixture of cross-hatchings, parallel and curved lines, and looping rounded lines in the foliage, all marked by skillful and vigorous pen work.

Landscape with the Baptism of Christ is most likely by the same hand as a *River Landscape with Classical Buildings* (Foundation Custodia, coll. F. Lugt, Paris) and several other drawings.[1] They show an affinity with a group of drawings that traditionally have been attributed to Pieter Cornelisz. Kunst. One of the three sons of the artist Cornelis Engebrechtsz., Pieter Cornelisz. Kunst was trained in Leiden by his father and was active in that city as a painter and designer of stained glass windows. His name is associated with drawings for stained glass dated between 1517 and 1537, several of which are monogrammed *PC*.

Not all critics are agreed that the *Landscape with the Baptism of Christ* and its companion in Paris are by the same hand as the group attributed to Pieter Cornelisz. Kunst. Even if anonymous, the *Landscape with the Baptism of Christ* can be localized in Leiden on the basis of stylistic similarities to drawings by other artists active in that area, such as Aertgen van Leyden. Moreover, the ruined classical buildings and obelisks at the upper left recall similar structures found in the background of drawings by and attributed to Jan van Scorel. Scorel acquired a first-hand knowledge of contemporary and antique art in Rome in 1522/1523; he was back in Utrecht by 1524 and worked in Haarlem in 1527/1530, and thus motifs from his work could have been available in the northern Netherlands from the late 1520s onward.

The creation of landscape as an independent genre was one of the major achievements of northern Renaissance artists in the course of the sixteenth century. *Landscape with the Baptism of Christ* is the earliest Netherlandish landscape drawing in the National Gallery of Art and thus is the first step on a path that leads to Matthijs Cock's *Landscape with Castle above a Harbor* (1978.19.2), to the panorama of Pieter Bruegel the Elder's *Landscape with Saint Jerome* (1972.47.1) of 1553, and on to another fiftieth-anniversary gift, Hans Bol's *Winter Landscape with Skaters*, c. 1584/1586.

John Oliver Hand

PROVENANCE
Lord Milford; Sir John Philipps; C. R. Rudolf.

NOTE
1. Discussed by Karel Boon in *L'Epoque de Lucas de Leyde et Pierre Bruegel. Dessins des anciens PaysBas. Collection Frits Lugt. Institut Néerlandais, Paris* [exh. cat. Istituto Universitario Olandese di Storia dell'Arte, Florence; Institut Néerlandais, Paris] (1980–1981), 143–144, no. 101, and J. Richard Judson in John Oliver Hand et al., *The Age of Bruegel: Netherlandish Drawings of the Sixteenth Century* [exh. cat. National Gallery of Art] (Washington, 1986), 125–126, no. 41.

15

ANTONIO DA TRENTO
c. 1508–after 1550

The Martyrdom of Two Saints, c. 1530
after Parmigianino
Chiaroscuro woodcut printed from
three blocks in three tones of blue
11⅛ x 18½ (28.3 x 46) (sheet size)

Gift of Andrew Robison

Antonio da Trento was one of the most accomplished Italian woodcutters of the second quarter of the sixteenth century. His body of chiaroscuro woodcuts was done after the designs of the artist Francesco Mazzola, called Parmigianino.[1] Antonio worked under Parmigianino in Bologna between 1527, the year Parmigianino left Rome, and 1531. Nothing is known about Antonio after 1531, nor do any prints by him exist after this date. Giorgio Vasari, in his *Lives of the Most Eminent Painters, Sculptors, and Architects*, informed his readers that Antonio da Trento suddenly left the city one day after stealing his master's drawings and copper plates, adding that "he must have gone off to the Devil, for all the news that was ever heard of him."[2]

The first Italian chiraroscuro woodcuts were produced by Ugo da Carpi who, in 1516, asked for and was granted a patent for the "invention" of the technique. Actually, the very first chiaroscuro woodcuts originated in Germany some ten years before. Though the process was initially conceived to reproduce pen and wash drawings, the resulting prints were soon praised for their own unique visual impact.

Traditionally the subject of the present woodcut has been identified as the martyrdom of Saints Peter and Paul. However, Saint Peter met death by crucifixion whereas in the print both saints appear about to be beheaded. While alternative saints have been suggested, a satisfactory identification is still lacking and thus the present title has now been generally accepted.[3]

This present print is undoubtedly one of the most successful early impressions of *The Martyrdom of Two Saints*.[4] The image is strong and clear, with even tone and crisp line. It has none of the imperfections in later impressions caused by the breaking down or cracking of the wood block. The choice of the three distinct tones of blue is visually successful, giving an outstanding coordination of tonalities that is lacking in other impressions printed in different colors. This coherence gives great depth to the image itself. The tones of blue are close to those found in contemporary chiaroscuro drawings that these early chiaroscuro prints imitate. These images needed to be bold and clear in order to provide an immediate visual impact upon the viewer, since they were often meant to be hung.

Though the National Gallery started off with just a few early Italian chiaroscuro woodcuts, the past twenty years have seen an accumulation of a small but important collection with outstanding individual examples. Andrew Robison's gift complements seven others by Antonio da Trento after Parmigianino in the Gallery's collection. These include two other early impressions of *The Martyrdom of Two Saints*. One, a recent purchase, is printed with a dark green line block and gray-green and light gray-brown tone blocks, on the verso of which is a very rare proof printed from the darker of the two tone blocks.[5] The present impression also joins six fine chiaroscuro woodcuts by Ugo da Carpi, the so-called inventor of the chiaroscuro woodcut in Italy, and three chiaroscuro woodcuts by Gian Nicolo Vicentino also after Parmigianino.

Gregory Jecmen

PROVENANCE
Harry Salomon, Milan.

NOTES
1. Parmigianino's early compositional designs as well as several figure studies related to the present chiaroscuro woodcut are today in the collections of the British Museum and the Louvre. See Arthur E. Popham, *Drawings of Parmigianino* (New Haven and London, 1971), 1: cats. 191, 192, 379, 380, 417.

2. Giorgio Vasari, *Lives of the Most Eminent Painters, Sculptors, and Architects*, trans. Philip Lee Warner (London, 1913), 5:249–250.

3. Jan Johnson, "States and Versions of a Chiaroscuro Woodcut," *Print Quarterly* 4 (June 1987), 154.

4. Adam Bartsch, *Le peintre graveur* 12:79, no. 28 i/ii; Johnson 1987, 158, version B.

5. Colnaghi and Co., *Chiaroscuro Woodcuts, Sixteenth to Eighteenth Century*, New York (10/12–11/5/88), no. 21.

ITALIAN MASTER

Presentation in the Temple, c. 1540
Chiaroscuro woodcut
16⅛ x 11⅝ (41 x 29.5)

Gift (Partial and Promised) of
Daryl R. Rubenstein and
Lee G. Rubenstein

Because chiaroscuro woodcuts, printed from two or more blocks, convey the qualities of a wash drawing, Renaissance painters were quick to perceive their aptness for reproducing compositional ideas. The design of the *Presentation in the Temple* was credited to Giuseppe Salviati in an inscription on the second state of the print. Most writers, beginning with Adam Bartsch in his vast print corpus, have preferred, nevertheless, to associate the woodcut with Francesco Mazzola, called Parmigianino (1503–1540).[1] Parmigianino is known to have employed the woodcutters Antonio da Trento and Ugo da Carpi to record his designs, and Niccolò Vicentino continued the process after the painter's death.[2] The exceedingly elegant figure style of the *Presentation* and the secular interpretation of the theme unquestionably derive from Parmigianino. Except for the altar, the infant's gesture and radiance, and the motifs of the sacrificial knife and doves, we might mistake the sacred drama for a festive occasion. The protagonists—the Virgin and Child, the High Priest, and Joseph—are nearly lost in a crowd of supernumeraries, much as in a painting of the *Circumcision* in the Detroit Institute of Arts, which is now accepted as by Parmigianino himself.[3] This picture and a group of related drawings by the artist are not sufficiently close to the woodcut, however, to state for certain that Parmigianino was himself responsible for the design and supervised its execution.[4] The present work, made from four blocks in black and reddish-brown tones (rather than the gray-green found in most other examples), is the first of two states. Its technique bears comparison with that of Ugo da Carpi, to whom it is sometimes tentatively attributed.[5] Exhibited in Washington in 1984, the chiaroscuro woodcut of the *Presentation* well demonstrates the appeal for artists and collectors of Parmigianino's drawings, six of which are in the National Gallery's collection.[6]

David Alan Brown

NOTES

1. Adam Bartsch, *Le Peintre Graveur Illustré. I. Italian Chiaroscuro Woodcuts* (Bartsch vol. XII), ed. Caroline Karpinski (University Park, Pennsylvania, and London, 1971), no. 31.6 I; and *The Illustrated Bartsch. 48. Formally Volume 12. Italian Chiaroscuro Woodcuts*, ed. Caroline Karpinski (New York, 1983), 31. For the attribution to Parmigianino see Konrad Oberhuber, *Parmigianino und sein Kreis* [exh. cat. Graphische Sammlung Albertina] (Vienna, 1963), 42, cat. 97.

2. A. E. Popham ("Observations on Parmigianino's Designs for Chiaroscuro Woodcuts," in *Miscellanea. I. Q. van Regteren Altena* [Amsterdam, 1969], 48–51) attempted to distinguish between those prints Parmigianino designed and those that merely reproduce his ideas.

3. Sydney J. Freedberg, "Parmigianino's *Circumcision*," in *Bulletin of the Detroit Institute of Arts* 55, no. 3 (1977), 129–132.

4. William H. Trotter, "Chiaroscuro Woodcuts of the Circles of Raphael and Parmigianino: A Study in Reproductive Graphics" (Ph. D. diss., University of North Carolina, Chapel Hill, 1974), 296–299, plate 99.

5. Luigi Servolini, *Ugo da Carpi. I chiaroscuri e le altre opere* (Florence, 1977), cat. 27, plate XXXVIII.

6. *Master Prints from Washington Private Collections* [exh. cat. National Gallery of Art] (Washington, 1984), cat. 14.

HEINRICH ALDEGREVER
1502–1556/1561

Portrait of a Bearded Man with a Beret
c. 1540
Colored chalks
11¹¹⁄₁₆ x 8 (29.7 x 20.3)

Gift of
Mr. and Mrs. Stephen M. Kellen

It is common to speak of the spread of the Italian portrait to a wide range of persons and classes during the fifteenth and sixteenth centuries as an embodiment of the Renaissance evaluation of individual human worth, power, and dignity, even with the still-pervasive awareness of the transitory nature of the human form and the invisibility of the human spirit. The same is true of the Renaissance in the north. Especially after 1500, portrait paintings proliferated. And, even more distinctive of German than Italian art, so did portrait drawings. Throughout the major German territories, portraits play an important role in the oeuvre of artists from whom we have a substantial body of surviving work. However, very few of them have found their way to American collections; outside of a half-dozen Dürers and a few Holbeins, fewer than twenty sixteenth-century German portrait drawings are recorded in this country. With what we like to think of as the finest collection of early German drawings in America, the National Gallery has only five: Dürer's portrait of his brother Hans, an unidentified man by Leonard Beck, a pair by Peter Gertner of an unidentified man and wife, and Joseph Heintz's portrait of Giovanni da Bologna.

Heinrich Aldegrever, who lived most of his mature life in the Westfalian city of Soest, was a painter and artist in several media. However, he is now known primarily from his three hundred prints, including a few etchings and woodcuts but primarily engravings. Mostly in small format, they include biblical, mythological, allegorical, and genre subjects as well as ornament prints, each typically a miniature but brilliant world unto itself, filled with telling details, a traditional delight in the bravura portrayal of textures. His eight engraved portraits continue many of these features but are on the whole larger both in conception and in size, with particularly fine portrayal of the human personality conveyed through facial expression and through bright "living" eyes.

When it was in the famous Prag collection of Adalbert von Lanna, this portrait of a blond bearded man was thought to be by Hans Holbein the Younger, undoubtedly because of its subject and format, its quality, and its use of colored chalks, all so characteristic of Holbein. In fact in the von Lanna sale in 1910 this drawing was highlighted as one of the few works to be reproduced, the better of the two Holbeins, called "a major drawing of the highest rank." However, with the wider knowledge of the individual stylistic characteristics of early German drawings now available, it is evident that this portrait is clearly not by Holbein, not even from Augsburg or Basel, but closest to the north-German works by Heinrich Aldegrever.[1]

For the attribution to Aldegrever we can compare his engraved portraits as well as the securely attributed chalk drawings in London and Berlin.[2] Although such features are found in work by a number of artists of this period, the general format of this drawing: the three-quarter view, the costume, flat cap, and high, tightly ruffled collar are special favorites of Aldegrever. In distinction from many other artists, and particularly close to Aldegrever, are the strongly individualized treatment of the nose, thinly pursed lips, finely delineated ear, and strong outlines at the edges of the nose and profile. It is true that, as a personal characteristic, Aldegrever frequently emphasized the tear duct area of the eye, in strongly rounded form, more than here. Further, his Berlin and London drawings show less fine detail and hatching than is here, for example, on the cap, eyelashes, and nose; though as such detail is evident in Aldegrever's engravings, it would not be untoward for it also to be seen in a drawing. In conclusion, it seems most likely this fine drawing should be added to the oeuvre of Heinrich Aldegrever, and dateable from the costume to c. 1540.[3]

Andrew Robison

PROVENANCE

Baron Adalbert von Lanna, Prag; his sale H.G. Gutekunst, Stuttgart, 6–11 May 1910, item 299, plate XXI; Mr. and Mrs. Paul von Schwabach, Berlin; Mr. and Mrs. Hans Arnhold, Berlin and Paris; Anna-Maria Arnhold Kellen, New York.

NOTES

1. Such reattribution from the relatively fewer famous names of the past is, of course, common with old master drawings. It is especially difficult with finished portrait drawings. For other contemporary examples of the problems in the specific realm of early German portraits, see Giselsa Hopp's entries in Werner Hoffmann, ed., *Köpfe der Lutherzeit* (Hamburg, 1983), especially nos. 102 and 124–130.

2. Reproduced, for example, in John Rowlands, *The Age of Dürer and Holbein* (Cambridge, 1988), no. 138, color plate XX; Fedja Anzelewski, *Dürer and His Time* (Washington, 1965), no. 93. Compare the Louvre portrait of a man, which also may be regarded as a secure Aldegrever, and with a number of analogies to our present work; Colin T. Eisler, *German Drawings* (Boston, 1963), color plate 55.

3. This judgment, with various degrees of qualification, is supported by Hans Mielke (personal conversation in Berlin, based on a photograph and transparency, 1984) and Fritz Koreny (conversation based on the original in Washington, 1988).

FRENCH MASTER
Active 1561

Portrait of a Member of the
Quaratesi Family
Oil on wood
39¾ x 33½ (101 x 85.2)

Gift (Partial and Promised) of
Mrs. Rush Kress in Memory of
Her Husband, Rush Kress

This elegant likeness of a thirty-four-year-old gentleman was formerly believed to be the work of Antonis Mor (c. 1516/1520–c. 1575/1576), painter to King Philip II of Spain and other members of the Hapsburg court.[1] Mor (known in Spain as Antonio Moro) created a type of coolly aristocratic portraiture that was influential not only on his contemporaries but also on such later artists as Van Dyck.[2] Comparison of the newly acquired portrait with authentic examples by Mor, including the National Gallery's own *Portrait of a Gentleman* (fig. 1) reveals, nevertheless, a distinctly different approach to the portrayal of high-born subjects.[3] The sitters are similarly shown standing at knee length and in three-quarter view, with one arm held akimbo and the other at rest. But Mor's portrait is more realistic in the spatial projection of the sitter, the careful depiction of his costume, and the aloof glance he directs at the viewer. The Gallery's new acquisition, by contrast, depends for its effect on the way the sharply angled forms of the sitter's dark costume are silhouetted against the olive background. This decorative planar quality and restrained use of color have suggested to Colin Eisler that the portrait is French, not Flemish, in origin.[4] The sitter's mannered hands resemble those in the great *Portrait of François Iᵉʳ*, traditionally ascribed to Jean Clouet, in the Louvre, while the abstract character of the picture finds a parallel in the *Portrait of Pierre Quthe* by François Clouet, dated 1562, also in the Louvre.[5] The author of the Washington portrait remains unknown, but the date 1561, inscribed together with the sitter's age in the upper left corner, indicates when he was active. The subject has been identified from the (partly repainted) coat of arms in the upper right as a member of a distinguished Florentine family, the Quaratesi.[6] He might be one of the many Florentines who accompanied Catherine de' Medici to France. The initials *AM* placed on his handkerchief and alongside the coat of arms should provide a clue to his individual identity.

David Alan Brown

PROVENANCE
A. Contini Bonacossi, Florence.

NOTES
1. William Suida, *Twenty-Five Paintings from the Collection of the Samuel H. Kress Foundation* [exh. cat. University of Arizona] (Tucson, 1951), cat. 13. So-called manuscript opinions by G. Fiocco, Roberto Longhi, Adolfo Venturi, and Raimond van Marle, written on the backs of photographs in the Kress files at the National Gallery, give the painting to Mor.

2. Lorne Campbell, *Renaissance Portraits. European Portrait-Painting in the 14th, 15th and 16th Centuries* (New Haven and London, 1990), 236–246.

3. Martha Wolff in John Oliver Hand and Martha Wolff, *Early Netherlandish Painting* (Washington, 1986), 202–205.

4. Colin Eisler, *Paintings from the Samuel H. Kress Collection. European Schools Excluding Italian* (Oxford, 1977), 252–253.

5. Hélène Adhémar, *Portraits français XIVᵉ, XVᵉ, XVIᵉ siècles* (Paris, 1950), nos. 22 and 11.

6. Eisler 1977, 252–253.

Fig. 1. Antonis Mor, *Portrait of a Gentleman*, 1569. National Gallery of Art, Washington, Andrew W. Mellon Collection

ANNO ÆTATIS SVE 34
ET·DE ANNO·1561

MAERTEN VAN HEEMSKERCK
1498–1574

The Triumph of Job, 1559
Pen and ink, traces of chalk
7⅛ x 10⅜ (18.2 x 26.2)

Gift of
Walter H. and Leonore Annenberg

This handsome drawing was made in preparation for an engraving in a series entitled Patientiae Triumphus (the triumph of patience) that was engraved by Dirck Volckertz. Coornhert (1522–1590) and published in 1559. The drawing is signed and dated by Heemskerck in the lower right corner.[1] Although Heemskerck included the word "Inventor" in the inscription, it is likely that he was strongly influenced by the ideas of Coornhert, who at times worked as an engraver but was also a noted humanist and religious philosopher. The *Triumph of Job* (fig. 1) was fifth in the series of eight. It was preceded by the triumphs of Patience, Isaac, Joseph, and David and was followed by Tobias and Saint Stephen, culminating with the triumph of Christ.

Here the Old Testament figure of Job is shown sitting on a tortoise, clad only in a rough woven cloth. As explained in the Latin inscription accompanying the engraving, Job steadfastly endured his trials and torments, "and he remained as strong as a tortoise, whose shell no one can break." Pulled along behind him are his three false friends at the far left, his wife, and Satan. On the banner held by Job are objects that Veldman[2] has interpreted iconographically: the winged heart symbolizes hope; the balanced scales indicate an equitable temperament; and above the world orb surmounted by a cross a flaming sword signifies the power of Christ to sever man's heart from the things of this world. In the background at the right are events from the biblical narrative in which Job's faith is tested: the destruction of his eldest son's house and all of Job's children; the death of his cattle; Job sitting on a dung heap berated by his wife; and the visit of the three friends who argue with Job that if he is being punished by God he must therefore be guilty. From the Middle Ages onward Job was the exemplar of patience and an Old Testament prefiguration of the suffering and resurrection of Christ. Job's troubles were especially pertinent for a series that ends with Christ Triumphant.

The son of a farmer, Maerten took his last name from the north-Netherlandish town of his birth, Heemskerck. Between 1527 and 1530 he worked in Haarlem with Jan van Scorel and emulated Scorel's Italianate style. A decisive influence in Heemskerck's life was his stay in Italy, which began in 1532 and lasted until 1536/1537. In Rome Heemskerck filled his sketchbooks with drawings of antique sculpture and architecture as well as studies after the paintings of Raphael and Michelangelo. These studies served as the inspiration for his art for the remainder of his long and successful career as a painter and draftsman in Haarlem. The popularity of his mannered "Romanist" style is attested to by his numerous drawings for prints, which, as the biographer Karel van Mander observed, "filled the entire world with inventions."

Since the National Gallery owns the series of engravings of the Triumph of Patience,

the *Triumph of Job*, which is in superb condition, is an especially welcome addition to its already distinguished collection of sixteenth-century Netherlandish drawings.

John Oliver Hand

PROVENANCE
Freiherr Richard von Kuehlmann; Curtis O. Baer, New Rochelle, New York; Dr. George Baer, Atlanta.

NOTES
1. Other drawings for the series are to be found in private collections and museums in Europe and the United States. See Eric M. Zafran, *Master Drawings from Titian to Picasso. The Curtis O. Baer Collection* [exh. cat. High Museum of Art] (Atlanta, 1985), 60–61, no. 27.

2. Ilja M. Veldman, *Maarten van Heemskerck and Dutch Humanism in the Sixteenth Century* (Maarssen, 1977), 66; the series is discussed 62–70.

Fig. 1. Dirck Volckertz. Coornhert, *The Triumph of Job*, engraving. National Gallery of Art, Washington, Ailsa Mellon Bruce Fund

GIORGIO VASARI
1511–1574

Vita de' gran Michelagnolo Buonarroti
Giunti, Florence, 1568
Bound volume with woodcut
illustrations
8¼ x 6 (21.8 x 15.1)

VIRGIL SOLIS

David and Bathsheba, 1540–1550
Pen and ink and wash
3¹³/₁₆ x 3¹³/₁₆ (9.7 x 9.7)

Gift of Elmar W. Seibel

Vasari's biography is one of the crucial early works on Michelangelo. It is notable not only for what it says, but also for the manner in which it was published. The first edition of Vasari's *Le vite de' più eccellenti architetti, pittori, et scultori* . . . was published in Florence in 1550, and in it was included a biography of Michelangelo, the only living artist to be so honored. Until Michelangelo's death in 1564, the only other account of his life was Ascanio Condivi's *Vita di Michelagnolo Buonarroti* published in Rome in 1553. Vasari issued this 1568 edition to correct what he felt were errors in Condivi's account[1] and also to incorporate new information found in Benedetto Varchi's *Orazione funerale*[2] (Florence, 1564), which describes the ceremonies at Michelangelo's funeral.

It was clear to Vasari that this revision was necessary. He explained in the dedication to Alessandro de' Medici that he had long felt the need to write a new biography of Michelangelo and would have done so but for the pressures of other work. By 1566 the text had been written and prepared for editing[3] but was not printed until 1568, when it appeared in both the new edition of the *Vite*, which contained for the first time the woodcut portraits designed by Vasari, and in this separate biography with new title page, new dedication, and new colophon. It was Vasari's decision to print the Michelangelo text by itself as well as to in-

clude it in the larger work. In the dedication to the present work he stated that many would want the life of Buonarroti separate from the other lives; "I have published some copies of Buonarroti alone for those who do not want or cannot have the whole book."

Copies of this offprint are exceedingly rare and are found in only a few libraries in this country. There may have been only a very limited number of copies printed, or some other reason may explain its scarcity today. This homage to Michelangelo is a bibliographic rarity as the first offprint ever published.[4] Its content qualifies it also to be called one of the finest offprints in history. With this gift, the National Gallery now has six of the seven earliest biographical sources for Michelangelo: the 1550 and 1568 editions of Vasari's lives; the Condivi biography; and two of the three versions of the Michelangelo funeral ceremonies, those of Varchi and Tarsia (Florence, 1564).

To this outstanding illustrated book Elmar Seibel has added a second fiftieth-anniversary gift to represent his other primary interest, old master drawings. Virgil

Solis' *David and Bathsheba* is a charming example of the artist's refined style in designing ornamental engravings and book illustrations. Solis was the most important graphic artist in Nuremberg in the sixth decade of the sixteenth century. He continued the old German tradition in his love for textures and complex draperies. But he also showed the new winds of mannerism in his delicacy of posture and line, as in the sprightly fountain in the center of this drawing, which might be a forecast for a sculpture by Giambologna or Adrian de Vries.

Neal Turtell
Andrew Robison

NOTES

1. Paola Barocchi, *Giorgio Vasari, La Vita di Michelangelo* (Milan, 1962), 1:xxxi–xxxii.

2. Zygmunt Wazbinski, *L'Accademia medicea del disegno a Firenze nel cinquecento; idea e istituzione* (Florence, 1987), 101.

3. Barocchi 1962, xxxviii–xxxix.

4. B. H. Breslauer, "The Origin of Offprints," in *Book Collector* 6, no. 4 (1957), 403.

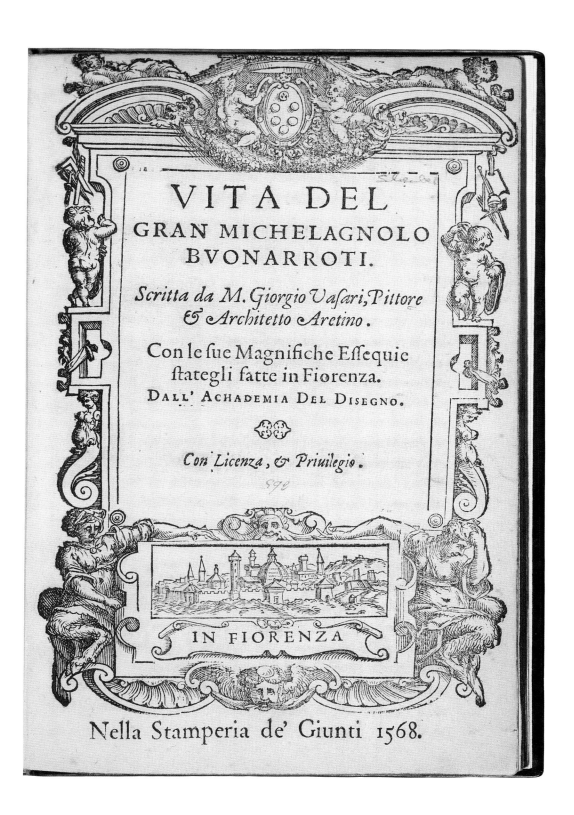

VITA DEL
GRAN MICHELAGNOLO BVONARROTI.

Scritta da M. Giorgio Vasari, Pittore
& Architetto Aretino.

Con le sue Magnifiche Essequie
stategli fatte in Fiorenza.
DALL' ACHADEMIA DEL DISEGNO.

Con Licenza, & Priuilegio.

IN FIORENZA

Nella Stamperia de' Giunti 1568.

LATTANZIO GAMBARA
c. 1530–1574

Study for a Prophet, 1567–1573
Chalk with white heightening,
squared in chalk
14¼ x 9¾ (36.5 x 25)

Gift of Yvonne tan Bunzl

The Brescian artist Lattanzio Gambara was well known for his grand fresco cycles, especially those with complicated compositions of figures seen from below (*di sotto in su*). Besides his native city he worked also in Cremona and Parma. He was influenced by Pordenone and Giulio Romano as well as the Campi family, with whom he worked.[1] In Parma between 1567 and 1573 Gambara painted the extensive cycle of the scenes of the life of Christ in the nave of the duomo. Below these horizontal narrative compositions he frescoed prophets on clouds in the pendentives of the arches.[2] The present drawing of a figure seen from below is possibly a preliminary study for one of these prophets, though this particular figure does not appear there. The immediacy of the muscular figure suggests it could be based on a live model; however, it probably was inspired by Michelangelo's *ignudi* on the Sistine Chapel ceiling in the Vatican, known through the many copies circulating in Italy. The muscle and bone structure of the nude is rather generalized, further supporting the contention that Gambara was drawing from memory instead of from a studio model. Like some of Gambara's other drawings for the prophets,[3] the artist employed the edge of a piece of black chalk for broad strokes in order to render an atmospheric ambience for the figure. The squaring indicates an intention to transfer the composition to another sheet or a cartoon.

Yvonne Tan Bunzl's gift is a welcome addition to the National Gallery's graphic arts collection, as this vigorous study will be the Gallery's first drawing by any of the sixteenth-century artists from Brescia and Cremona.

Diane De Grazia

NOTES

1. On Gambara's paintings see Pier Virgilio Begni Redona and Giovanni Vezzoli, *Lattanzio Gambara, Pittore* (Brescia, 1978).

2. See Begni Redona and Vezzoli 1978, 181–199, for reproductions of the narrative scenes and the pendentives below.

3. See, for example, the drawing in the collection of David Rust, repr. Diane De Grazia, *Correggio and His Legacy* [exh. cat. National Gallery of Art] (Washington, 1984), 280–281, cat. 93.

FEDERICO BAROCCI
c. 1535–1612

Head of a Woman, 1582–1586
Colored chalks with some stumping
on blue paper
15⅜ x 10⅝ (38.8 x 27.0)

Gift of Peter Josten in Memory of
Stephen Spector

The naturalness of the handmaiden's pose as she is caught in midturn was based on studies directly from life: Barocci drew continually from persons on the street and from his own models as they walked around the studio. It is this natural quality of this artist's figures and the immediacy and believability of his subjects that made him popular with church authorities intent on conveying religious concepts in a direct manner understandable to a large audience; it is his color and vibrantly dramatic compositions that made him influential with seventeenth-century artists and writers. Barocci's beautiful and direct chalk studies of heads such as this one were imitated immediately, and the type was developed throughout the seventeenth century in Italy, culminating in the elaborate pastel portraits fashionable in eighteenth-century France.

Federico Barocci worked in Rome briefly at the beginning of his career (in the 1550s and again in the early 1560s), returning for the rest of his life to his native Urbino because of poor health caused, it was said, by poison from jealous Roman artists. In spite of his residence in far-off Umbria, his paintings were highly prized in the papal city. It often took years for a commission by Barocci to be completed, yet Roman confraternities and cardinals waited patiently for his dramatic and emotionally charged religious subjects representative of the current Counter-Reformation taste.

In 1582, after negotiations with the duke of Urbino, the Oratorian Fathers successfully obtained Barocci's consent to paint a *Visitation* for the Chapel of the Visitation in their church, Santa Maria in Vallicella (the "Chiesa Nuova"). In 1586, when the painting was installed, it was admired by both artistic and religious visitors to the church and helped secure the artist's fame in Rome. (Barocci's biographer, Giovanni Pietro Bellori, writing in 1672, said that the Oratorians' founder, Saint Filippo Neri, was so impressed by Barocci's painting that he

came to this chapel to perform his private devotions.)[1] Barocci's slowness in finishing this and other paintings was caused not just by the illness that often kept him idle but by the elaborate care and preparation in his working procedure, attested by his immense graphic output. After setting the basic elements of a painting in compositional sketches, Barocci made numerous chalk studies of individual figures and combinations of figures, including separate studies for heads and limbs and drapery. After this came full compositional chalk and oil sketches (*modelli*), the full-scale cartoon, and other oil sketches of single figures and heads to correct color and pose. At all stages of this elaborate process the artist would modify the design as he saw fit.

Our drawing, a study of the head of Mary's attendant at the right of the *Visitation,* belongs to this second phase of individual chalk study. Here Barocci worked with colored chalks on blue paper, the drawing type for which he is celebrated and which he helped develop into a painterly medium. By combining colored and black chalk in this head, Barocci sought to test the play of light on the woman's face with the colored chalks and to reevaluate her pose with the black chalk outlines. The pentimenti to the nose and eyes indicate he was not yet satisfied with the angle of her head. Indeed, in further studies her profile was altered subtly to its final position in the painting, where her head is tilted slightly more at an angle and her features are somewhat more visible to the viewer as she looks up toward the Virgin she is serving.

This drawing is the fifth by Barocci to enter the National Gallery. Three of these are studies of figures in which the artist was contemplating poses for paintings[2]; the other is an oil sketch of the head of Saint John the Evangelist.[3] The *Head of a Woman* is a wonderful complement to this nucleus of a great draftsman's oeuvre and the first of its type, the pastel head study, in the collection.

Diane De Grazia

PROVENANCE
Peter Lely (Lugt 2092); Jonathan Richardson, Sr. (Lugt 2184).

NOTES
1. Most of the information we have on Barocci comes from Bellori's biography. Giovanni Pietro Bellori, *Le vite de' pittori scultori et architetti moderni* (Rome, 1672), 165–196. It is translated into English and published in its entirety in Edmund P. Pillsbury and Louise S. Richards, *The Graphic Art of Federico Barocci* [exh. cat. The Cleveland Museum of Art, Yale University Art Gallery] (New Haven, 1978), 11–24. The present drawing is discussed by Pillsbury and Richards on pages 76–77, cat. no. 53.

2. Chalk studies for *The Crucifixion* of 1565–1567 (1983.17.1); a sheet of pen studies from the early 1590s (1983.74.2); and chalk studies for the *Last Supper,* 1591–1592 (1981.33.1).

3. For the *Entombment* in Senigallia, 1579–1582 (1979.11.1).

HANS BOL
1534–1593

Winter Landscape with Skaters
c. 1584/1586
Pen and brown ink, brown wash
7⁹⁄₁₆ x 10⅛ (19.2 x 25.8)

Gift of Robert H. and Clarice Smith

Hans Bol's spirited drawing depicts several of the delights of winter in the Netherlands. The populace has turned out to skate or simply to enjoy a stroll on the frozen waterway that runs through their town. Elegantly posed even when they are falling down, the groups of skaters form gentle curves that carry the viewer's gaze into the distance. The leafless trees on either side of the canal also define the space of the landscape. Working only in brown ink and wash, Bol deftly captured the cold, pale light of winter.

One of the most productive and talented Netherlandish artists of the sixteenth century, Hans Bol was born on 16 December 1534 in Mechelen (Malines) and trained there as a painter. Following a trip to Germany, including two years in Heidelberg, Bol returned to Mechelen and in 1560 joined the painters' guild. The Spanish occupation forced him in 1572 to leave Mechelen for Antwerp, where he entered the guild in 1574. Because of the spreading political and religious conflict Bol left Antwerp in 1584 and went northward. He settled in Amsterdam in 1591 and died there in 1593. Although Bol was a skilled painter and miniaturist, he is best known for his drawings, which num-

ber in the hundreds, and for many prints both by and after him.

Bol's drawings were often made for prints, but William W. Robinson has shown that *Winter Landscape with Skaters* is related to a miniature (Residenzmuseum, Munich) depicting winter, part of a series of the Four Seasons.[1] Although the drawing is not directly preparatory to the more elaborate miniature there is a clear relationship between the two. The miniature is dated 1586 and thus suggests a date of c. 1584/1586 for the drawing, which is in accord with our understanding of Bol's late style.

While the National Gallery of Art owns several prints based on his designs, *Winter Landscape with Skaters* is the first drawing by Hans Bol to enter the collection. A work of outstanding quality, it significantly enriches the Gallery's holdings and joins a number of other extremely fine Netherlandish drawings, including David Vinckboon's *Venetian Party in a Château Garden* (1986.76.1), which have been generously given over many years by Robert H. and Clarice Smith.

John Oliver Hand

PROVENANCE
Heinrich Wilhelm Campe (Lugt 1391); Dr. Carlos Gaa (his sale, Boerner, Leipzig, 9–10 May 1930, no. 56); Koutuzow collection; (Schaeffer Galleries, New York); J. Theodor Cremer, New York (his sale, Sotheby Mak van Waay, Amsterdam, 17 November 1980, no. 96).

NOTE
1. In John Oliver Hand and others, *The Age of Bruegel: Netherlandish Drawings of the Sixteenth Century* [exh. cat. National Gallery of Art] (Washington, 1986), 73–74, no. 15. The miniature in Munich is reproduced 74, fig. 2.

Hans. Bol.

HENDRIK GOLTZIUS
1558–1617

Ignis, 1586 or before
Pen and brown ink, gray wash, and
white heightening
8⁹⁄₁₆ x 6½ (21.7 x 16.4)

Promised Gift of
Ruth and Jacob Kainen

Unquestionably one of the greatest graphic artists of the Renaissance, Hendrik Goltzius was born in Mühlbracht (now Bracht) on the Lower Rhine and in 1574, while still in Germany, he apprenticed with the Netherlandish engraver Dirck Volkertsz. Coornhert. Soon after 1576 Goltzius followed his teacher to Haarlem and it was there in 1583 that he met the artist, theoretician, and biographer Karel van Mander. Van Mander introduced Goltzius to the mannerist style of Bartholomeus Spranger and from 1585 on Goltzius made engravings after Spranger's drawings.

Goltzius' drawing, here shown for the first time, was made in preparation for an engraving of *Ignis* (fire) dated 1586, which is one of a series depicting the Four Elements—air, earth, fire, and water—and is the work of an anonymous engraver who was probably a member of Goltzius' workshop. *Ignis* is personified as a young male, nude except for a billowing cloak, who holds aloft a bolt of lightning with one hand and in the other a sphere or cannonball out of which burst

flames. Next to his right foot is the artist's monogram, *HG* in ligature. At the lower left is a dragonlike creature who is appropriately surrounded by flames and smoke. At the right background a group of figures are gathered near a burnt offering on an altar, a possible reference to the sacrificial use of fire in the Old Testament.

Ignis is an excellent example of the free and somewhat sketchy preliminary drawings that Goltzius often made for engravings and demonstrates his assured spontaneity in rendering the human figure and his virtuoso handling of line, wash, and heightening. The influence of Spranger's mannered style can be seen in the elegant pose and attenuated proportions of *Ignis.*

By virtue of its comparatively early date, freshness, and finesse of execution, *Ignis* is a vitally important addition to the collection. With five drawings already in its possession the National Gallery is a major repository of Goltzius drawings in the United States.

John Oliver Hand

PROVENANCE
Anne Verriest Badgley.

GIAMBOLOGNA
(Jean Boulogne, Giovanni Bologna)
1529–1608

Christ Crucified, before 1588 (?)
Bronze
14⅛ x 10¹/₁₆ (36 x 25)

Gift of Mr. and Mrs. John R. Gaines
in Memory of Clarence F. and
Amelia R. Gaines, and Gloria Gaines

Giambologna, born in Flanders but active for most of his career in Florence, in his lifetime achieved fame as a sculptor second only to that of his older contemporary Michelangelo. With superlative command of anatomy and graceful twisting movement, he brought unsurpassed mastery of bronze and marble technique to his creation of a population of elegantly idealized human types, finished with exquisite refinement. Because Giambologna worked in the portable medium of the small bronze as well as large marbles, his sculpture reached and influenced a wide international audience. His principal patrons, the Medici grand dukes of Florence, collected his works and commissioned them as diplomatic gifts to other rulers so that they became treasures of the courts of Europe.[1]

Giambologna conceived a fragile, spiritualized human ideal in this crucified Christ. The ethereally slender figure appears to float almost weightlessly against the cross. Only the head, drooping heavily on the chest, and the bulging, closed eyes give a sense of suffering. The elegantly curling hair and beard and the subtle spiral torsion of the pose are characteristic of the artist. A dark red lacquer with golden highlights that once covered the surface is abraded, perhaps from extensive handling in devotion or a connoisseur's appreciation. Clinging to indentations, the remaining lacquer accentuates the sensitive modeling of ribs and musculature.

This bronze figure is one of many crucified Christs Giambologna modeled, in different sizes and attitudes, for churches and for private clients. It seems to be a smaller variant or conceivably a forerunner of those at the convents of San Marco and Santa Maria degli Angiolini in Florence, which have been dated before 1588.[2] A bronze like this would have been cast in Giambologna's workshop by his expert assistants, using molds taken from the master's wax model. Besides this one, five other known casts evidently derive from the same model.[3]

The exact date and relationship of each example to the original model continue to be studied and debated. In the present bronze, the sharp, fine detail of the hair and facial features may indicate a cast from the artist's lifetime, skillfully capturing the delicate nuances of the model.[4] Since the version of Giambologna's celebrated *Mercury* in the National Gallery of Art's rotunda is now regarded as a late eighteenth-century cast, this fine Renaissance bronze is an especially significant addition to the collection, bringing us all the closer to the genius of a great master of western sculpture.

The ebonized cross set with semiprecious stones on a base with scrolled forms corresponds to late sixteenth-century Florentine taste. It is nevertheless uncertain how long the cross and corpus have been together. The lacquer on the beautifully modeled back of the bronze figure is as worn as that on the front, suggesting the bronze Christ long lacked the protection of a cross behind it.

Alison Luchs

PROVENANCE
European art market; Michael Hall Fine Arts, before 1971; Mr. and Mrs. John R. Gaines, c. 1983.

NOTES
1. On Giambologna see Elisabeth Dhanens, *Jean Boulogne Giovanni Bologna Fiammingo* (Brussels, 1956); James Holderbaum, *The Sculptor Giovanni Bologna* (New York, 1983; Ph. D. diss., Harvard University, 1959); Charles Avery and Anthony Radcliffe, eds., *Giambologna 1529–1608: Sculptor to the Medici* [exh. cat. The Arts Council of Great Britain] (London, 1978), and Charles Avery, *Giambologna* (Mount Kisco, N. Y., 1987).

2. The Florentine Christs cited are 45.8 and 46.8 cm high, respectively. On Giambologna's crucifixes see Katharine J. Watson in London 1978, 45–47, 140–146 (present example illustrated on 146, cat. 110); Avery 1987, 202.

3. Douai, Musée municipal de la Chartreuse, reportedly from the collection of Giambologna's devoted patron Bernardo Vecchietti; Pitti Palace, Florence; Liebieghaus Museum alter Plastik, Frankfurt; and the J. B. Speed Art Museum, Louisville, Kentucky. The example in the Royal Ontario Museum, Toronto, may have been cast from a later, slightly modified version of the model. For these versions see Adolfo Venturi, *Storia dell'Arte Italiana* 10. *La Scultura del cinquecento*, part 3 (Milan, 1937), 782, fig. 650; Anton Legner, "Neuerwerbungen der Frankfurter Museen 1945–1966," *Städel-Jahrbuch* 1 (1967), 254–256, 269; Watson and Avery in London 1978, 145–146, cats. 108–111, and K. Corey Keeble, *European Bronzes in the Royal Ontario Museum* (Toronto, 1982), 51–53, cat. 22 and literature cited there.

4. On bronze production in Giambologna's workshop see Avery in London 1978, 42–44; Watson there, 33–41, 45–47; and Keeble 1982, 51–53.

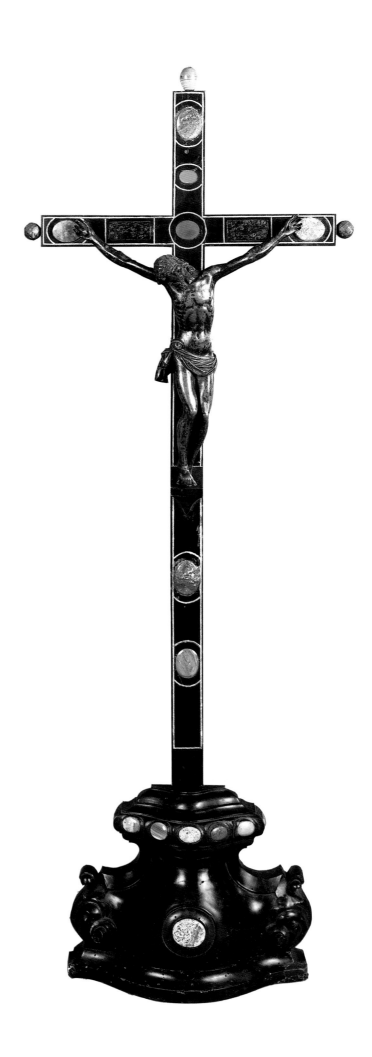

HENDRIK GOLTZIUS
1558–1617

Hercules and Cacus, 1588
Chiaroscuro woodcut, printed in
olive and pale ocher
15⅞ x 13 (40.7 x 33.4)

Gift of Dr. Ruth B. Benedict in Honor
of Andrew Robison

Hercules and Cacus is the largest, most impressive, and perhaps earliest of Hendrik Goltzius' chiaroscuro woodcuts and is the only one to be dated in the block.[1] The woodcut was made in three blocks, one line and two tone blocks in olive and ocher, a striking visual combination. In this beautiful and clean impression the crisp lines and the contrasting olive green and pale ocher tones make the entire image bright and bathe the scene in a warm, glowing light. The woodcut is full of the contrasts of light and shade for which the chiaroscuro technique was invented.

While the number of Goltzius' engravings is large, his known woodcut oeuvre is small, between eighteen and twenty-four prints, but it comprises some of his best-known work.[2] During the mid-1580s, when Goltzius came under the influence of the Antwerp artist Bartholomeus Spranger, Goltzius' first woodcuts were made. The bravura and freedom of line, energy, and treatment of light and dark in this early woodcut reflect Spranger's mannerist style,[4] while at the same time creating an image that is distinctly Goltzius' own.

Hercules and Cacus depicts the ancient Roman legend as told by Ovid and Virgil of the fire-breathing, half-human son of Vulcan. Cacus stole some of the cattle of Geryon, shown on the right, which were being driven home to Greece by Hercules. Following the sound of the lowing cattle, Hercules entered the cave of Cacus in the Aventine Hills, and after a battle killed the giant.

This extremely fine print further strengthens the Gallery's excellent woodcut holdings by this key printmaker, which include the *Arcadian Landscape* on blue paper, *Cliffs of a Seashore,* also on blue paper but with white highlights done by hand, and the complete chiaroscuro woodcut series of the four landscapes and the Gods and Goddesses. The Gallery has a later impression of Goltzius' *Hercules and Cacus* in shades of brown. The much earlier printing and rarer olive and ocher tones of Dr. Benedict's gift, together with its unusually fine impression and condition, make it a crucial addition and a highlight for the Gallery's graphic collection of Goltzius' woodcuts.

Gretchen A. Hirschauer

PROVENANCE
Acquired in 1977 from Zeitlin & Ver Brugge, Los Angeles.

NOTES
1. The signature, *HGoltzius Inue* [invenit], leaves out the usual *fecit,* suggesting that Goltzius did not actually cut the block himself as was the case in some of his later blocks, but instead entrusted that task to a master cutter. Walter L. Strauss, ed., *Hendrik Goltzius 1558–1617: The Complete Engravings and Woodcuts,* 2 vols. (New York, 1977), 2:696.

2. Walter L. Strauss (in "The Chronology of Hendrik Goltzius' Chiaroscuro Prints," *Nouvelles de l'estampe* [Sept./Oct. 1972], 9–13) accepts twenty-four autograph prints, while Nancy Ann Bialler (in *Hendrick Goltzius and the Netherlandish Chiaroscuro Woodcut,* Ph.D. diss., Yale University, 1983 [Ann Arbor, Mich., University Microfilms, 1986], 82) recognizes only eighteen.

3. Goltzius learned of Spranger's work through drawings provided by his friend and biographer Karel van Mander. Clifford S. Ackley, *Printmaking in the Age of Rembrandt* [Exh. cat. Museum of Fine Arts] (Boston, 1981), 2.

4. Bialler 1986, 105–106.

HENDRIK GOLTZIUS
1558–1617

Pietà, 1596
Engraving
6⅞ x 4⅞ (17.5 x 12.6)

Promised Gift of
Ruth and Jacob Kainen

The *Pietà*, dated 1596, is an extraordinary example of Goltzius' skill with the engraver's burin. The pose of the Virgin lamenting and holding the dead Christ recalls Michelangelo's *Pietà*, which Goltzius saw in Rome during his Italian sojourn of 1590/1591. The overwhelming influence on this print, however, is that of the great German artist Albrecht Dürer (1471–1528). The technique of precisely controlled stipplings and hatchings, the richly textured night sky, the small size, and even the way the monogram in the foreground is presented are thoroughly in Dürer's style. In the *Schilder-boek* of 1604, Karel van Mander characterized his friend as a "phenomenal Proteus." Here Goltzius has not copied or paraphrased Dürer, but rather achieved a Protean transformation that enabled him to create new images imbued with Dürer's spirit. Van Mander reported that, when their monograms were erased, certain of Goltzius' prints were hailed as long-lost originals by Albrecht Dürer and Lucas van Leyden. The virtuosity of hand and mind required to convincingly assimilate another artist's style is at once a mannerist conceit and an act of homage. In a larger context, the *Pietà* is part of the "Dürer Renaissance" that took place in northern and central Europe at the end of the sixteenth century.

Until now the National Gallery's large and representative collection of prints by Hendrik Goltzius has included two impressions of the *Pietà*. Both, however, are eclipsed by the brilliance, richness, and outstanding state of preservation of this impression so generously offered by Ruth and Jacob Kainen.

John Oliver Hand

PROVENANCE
R. Esmerion.

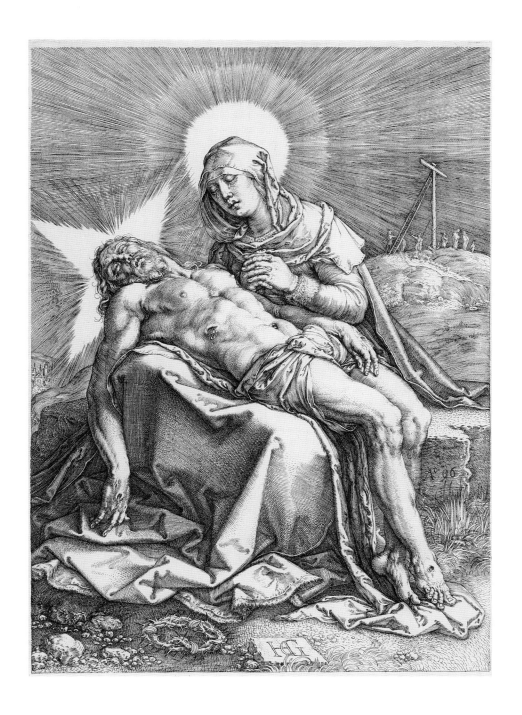

SOUTH GERMAN (Augsburg?)

Pietà, 1580s, after El Greco
Gilded bronze relief plaquette
7¹³⁄₃₂ x 5¹⁄₁₆ (18.6 x 12.9)

Gift of Mr. and Mrs. Anthony Geber
in Memory of Dr. Antal and
Klarissza Geber

As Ulrich Middeldorf remarked about another cast of this design, "this *Pietà* was perhaps the most famous sacred image in Europe around 1600."[1] Its figural composition was developed by an unknown plaquette maker, probably in Rome, from the closely related design of a small oil sketch by El Greco, which in turn was based on Michelangelo's marble *Pietà* of c. 1547–1553.[2] El Greco's sketch of the early 1570s[3] (fig. 1) apparently also inspired a marble altar relief, *The Dead Christ Supported by Two Angels*, in San Giuliano, Venice, signed by Girolamo Campagna in 1577/1578.[4] The plaquette replicates the figural composition of the Greco sketch except that it substitutes a position of Christ's legs common to Campagna's relief and to a 1571 painting by Bronzino in Santissima Annunziata, Florence. In reducing Greco's four-figure group to two, the plaquette artist substituted his seated Virgin's lap for Greco's right-hand figure; but his retention of Christ's right arm as extended only over a void, rather than a left-hand figure, demonstrates not only that the Greco sketch was certainly his prototype, but that he did not trust his own ability to make fundamental revisions to its design.

The composition's group of Christ and the Virgin is reproduced or closely reflected in pictures by Otto van Veen (1556–1629), Leandro Bassano (1557–1622), and Lodovico Cigoli (1559–1613) as well as Anthony van Dyck (1599–1641). Although none of their pictures happens to be dated, two large-scale sculptural derivations of the figure group (from as far afield as central Germany) are dated by inscriptions to 1589, proving the design to have been in existence by that date. Casts of the plaquette were even imported by Christian missionaries into Japan, presumably before a severe phase of religious intolerance swept that country in 1614.[5] Those "exports," however, like the version exhibited here, represent the second form in which early examples of the plaquette are widely found. In the rarer original (Roman?) type, the group of the Virgin with the Dead Christ is silhouetted on a blank background; such plaquettes, of which seven specimens are known, measure about 19 x 14 cm on average. In this immediately subsequent variant type, whose eleven specimens average about 18 x 12.5 cm, a characteristically south German background is inserted.

The National Gallery's example of this handsome relief is the largest specimen of its type and also one of the finest. The Gallery's outstanding collection of Renaissance plaquettes is principally focused on Italian designs, and what northern European examples are included are mostly of the earlier sixteenth or later seventeenth centuries. The nearest parallel to the date and origin of this important object is an Augsburg silvered plaquette of c. 1600, the *Adoration of the Shepherds*, itself a recent gift to the Gallery's collections; together they make particularly strong additions to an area still underrepresented in our holdings.

Douglas Lewis

Fig. 1. *El Greco, Pietà*, c. 1570/1572. Philadelphia Museum of Art, John G. Johnson Collection

PROVENANCE
Dr. Antal Geber (1879–1962), Budapest, Hungary (by 1924); by gift in 1946 to Mr. and Mrs. Anthony Geber.

NOTES
1. Ulrich Middeldorf, *Medals and Plaquettes from the Sigmund Morgenroth Collection* (Chicago, 1944), 28, no. 186, pl. 14.

2. Charles de Tolnay, *Michelangelo: The Final Period*, 6 vols. (Princeton, 1971), 5:86–88, 149–152, pls. 77, 159, 340–373.

3. Harold Wethey, *El Greco and his School*, 2 vols. (Princeton, 1962, and Madrid, 1967), 1: pl. 16; 2:80–81, no. 101.

4. Wladimir Timofiewitsch, *Girolamo Campagna: Studien zur venezianischen Plastik um das Jahr 1600* (Munich, 1972), 235–236, no. 2, pls. 2–3.

5. Anthony Geber, "Name Inscriptions: Solution or Problem?" in *Italian Plaquettes*, Studies in the History of Art 22 (Washington, 1989), 254–259, fig. 12.

43

SOUTH GERMAN (Nuremberg?)

Striding Stag, c. 1590s
Bronze (technically "red brass")
11¹⁄₁₆ x 11³⁄₈ x 2¹¹⁄₁₆
(28.1 x 29 x 6.8)

Gift of Asbjorn R. Lunde

This vivid characterization exemplifies a genre of small sculptures whose production brought fame to the Renaissance cities of south Germany, especially Nuremberg and Augsburg. Indeed Nuremberg was regarded as the birthplace of the metal now called brass,[1] a copper alloy whose second principal ingredient (instead of tin, which produces bronze) is zinc, of which this cast is typical in containing some fifteen percent.[2] The relatively easier casting and attractive golden color of this alloy made it a favorite for fine metalworking, a craft in which Nuremberg artisans were particularly distinguished during the late Renaissance.

This delicately poised *Stag* closely reproduces a type developed in the 1580s as hollow drinking vessels, usually in gilded silver, that were produced by master goldsmiths for their princely patrons in the south German courts. An early example in the same pose as the National Gallery bronze is the vessel made by Georg Hellthaler of Augsburg for Count Wolfgang von Hohenlohe-Neuenstein, who inaugurated it on 8 August 1581 at Hermersberg Castle.[3] For this project Hellthaler made a drawing that could well have been the model for successive versions of the object.[4] Another vessel of the same design was made in 1586/1589 by Abraham Altermann of Stuttgart for Prince Ludwig of Württemberg,[5] while a third—identical save for a reversal of the legs—was produced by Elias Zorer of Augsburg between 1586 and 1590.[6] These silver examples have collars encircling the stags' necks to mask the joint between cover and container; the removal of the stags' heads evidently prompted a subsidiary type, an antlered head designed as a wall ornament.[7]

Another bronze cast of the same model as the National Gallery's *Stag,* which has been published by Elisabeth Dhanens as a Nuremberg work of the end of the sixteenth century, is gilded.[8] Such a connection of surface as well as of form confirms the derivation of these anonymous bronze versions from the gilded silver examples by famous goldsmiths from other south German cen-

ters, especially Augsburg. The bronzes exhibit greater grace and suppleness in the musculature, silhouette, and implied motion of the animals as well as extraordinary refinement of texture. Such detailed surface treatment emphasizes a special advantage of their brassy alloys: much deeper and richer chasing than possible on a thin silver shell.

The surface characteristics of these bronzes of the 1590s are paralleled in a related bronze type of a *Leaping Stag Attacked by a Hound,*[9] which derives from a different series of goldsmiths' models of the 1590s through the 1620s[10]; a variant of this second bronze type has been tentatively ascribed to Francesco Fanelli.[11] The class of designs based on a leaping stag has been connected with a much-restored antique marble in the Vatican museums,[12] but in fact its silver cognates may have developed independently, in the same orbit of the south German goldsmiths who had previously produced the striding model reflected in the National Gallery bronze. Both types may reflect similar small bronzes from the ancient world,[13] while the leaping, multi-animal groups may recall the more movemented late sixteenth-century inventions of Giovanni Bologna in Florence.[14]

Douglas Lewis

PROVENANCE
Art market, London; acquired 24 January 1972.

NOTES
1. *Encyclopaedia Brittanica,* 11th ed., 29 vols. (Cambridge, England, 1911), 19:914 ("Nuremberg"); see also 4:433–434 ("Brass").

2. Surface composition of the alloy includes approximately 80% copper, 15% zinc, 3% tin, 2% lead, 0.3% iron, and 0.07% each of antimony and silver: preliminary analysis by energy dispersive x-ray fluorescence spectroscopy (XRF), on 11 December 1990 by Deborah Rendahl and Lisha Glinsman, of the National Gallery of Art Science Department.

3. Gilded silver, 47.0 cm high with base; private collection: *Die Renaissance im deutschen Südwesten,* 2 vols. [exh. cat. Heidelberg Castle] (Karlsruhe, 1986), 2:630–631, no. L 27, repr.

4. Lead point and sepia ink on unmarked paper, 54 x 38 cm, private collection; Karlsruhe 1986, 2:630–631, no. L 28, repr.

5. Gilded silver, 25.5 cm high with base, private collection, Switzerland; Karlsruhe 1986, 2:633, no. L 30, repr.

6. Gilded silver, 33 x 23 x 12 cm with base; Treasury of the Residenz, Munich: Helmut Seling, *Die Kunst der Augsburger Goldschmiede 1529–1868,* 3 vols. (Munich, 1980), 1:249, no. 149; 2: pl. 149.

7. Example in Museum für Kunstgewerbe, Berlin; gilded bronze, 16.5 cm high, Klaus Pechstein, *Bronzen und Plaketten* (Berlin, 1968), no. 13, repr.

8. Gilded bronze, 29.5 x 34.5 cm, private collection, Belgium; *Bronzes de la Renaissance* [exh. cat. Château de Larne] (Brussels, 1967), 156–157, no. 106, repr.

9. 10.5 x 12.7 cm, Michael Hall Fine Arts, New York; Penelope Hunter-Stiebel, *A Bronze Bestiary* [exh. cat. Rosenberg & Stiebel] (New York, 1985), 59, no. 41, repr.

10. *Welt in Umbruch: Augsburg zwischen Renaissance und Barock,* 2 vols. [exh. cat. Rathaus] (Augsburg, 1980), 2:417–418, no. 794; Seling 1980, 1:251–252, nos. 171–174, 2: pls. 171–174.

11. Bronzes, 19 cm high; two examples in private collections; Hans R. Weihrauch, *Europäische Bronzestatuetten* (Braunschweig, 1967), 237, fig. 288.

12. Walther Amelung, *Die Sculpturen [sic] des Vaticanischen Museums,* 2 vols. (Berlin, 1908), 1: pl. 33, 2: 340, no. 132.

13. Examples in Louvre, Paris; bronze, fourth century B.C., Greek, found at Sybaris in Italy: Marcel Brion, *Animals in Art* (London, 1959), 60, repr.; and in Museo Nazionale, Naples; bronze, 95.0 cm high, first century A.D., Roman, found at Herculaneum: Kenneth Clark, *Animals and Men* (London, 1977), 138, fig. 98, 232, no. 98.

14. For example *Hercules and the Arcadian Stag* in State Hermitage Museum, Leningrad, inv. 222; bronze, 38.0 cm high, c. 1581: Charles Avery and Anthony Radcliffe, *Giambologna, Sculptor to the Medici* [exh. cat. Royal Scottish Museum, Edinburgh] (London, 1978), 124–125, no. 77, repr.

ANNIBALE CARRACCI
1560–1609

Landscape with Figures by an Estuary with Sailing Boats c. 1590–1595
Pen and brown ink
4⁷⁄₁₆ x 7¼ (11.1 x 18.5)

Gift (Partial and Promised) of
Mr. and Mrs. David P. Tunick

In the many ways that Annibale Carracci changed the course of the history of art, perhaps the most lasting was his innovation in the portrayal of landscape. He was the first to represent views in a naturalistic manner, raising the genre to an independent status and freeing it from its role as adjunct to literary and religious themes. Very few of the artist's authentic independent landscape paintings survive, and the National Gallery is fortunate to possess one of the handful of his major paintings in this genre.[1] The *Landscape with Figures by an Estuary with Sailing Boats* is only the second drawing by Annibale and his first landscape drawing to enter the Gallery.[2] It will complement the two major landscape drawings by his brother Agostino already in the collection.[3]

This composition must have been an extremely popular image, for it was copied at least three times and etched once. The other versions differ little in content but greatly in quality.[4] Scholars agree that the present drawing is the prime version. Since the Chatsworth and Oxford drawings extend the composition at right and left, it is likely that our drawing was once somewhat wider at left: the tree at the edge may have been more complete. However, it is difficult to determine if the additions made at the right of the Chatsworth and Oxford drawings, which make less sense, were once evident in the National Gallery sheet. The extra windows on the building, the extension of the sloped roof, and the half-hearted completion of the tree suggest that Annibale's composition was either complete as it stands or already cut down when copied. These drawings also exhibit misunderstanding of the economical use of lines to indicate form found in Annibale's sheet. Jean Baptiste Corneille's etching, in reverse, also extends the composition on either side, embellishes the foreground with rocks and plants, and adds swirling smoke and clouds to the sky, showing failure to comprehend the simplicity of the original. Such embellishments make it impossible to know whether Corneille copied Annibale's drawing or one of the copies.[5]

With a minimum of strokes—outlines with little shading—the artist has evoked an atmosphere of calm tranquility on a clear day, much as Rembrandt was to do in drawings a generation later.[6] Although Annibale's landscapes are difficult to date, this economy of means and naturalism of setting indicate the drawing dates before Annibale's departure for Rome in 1595. In the Carracci academy artists often played graphic games, trying to suggest a subject with the minimum of strokes. The *Landscape* may belong to this category and consequently may date to Annibale's Bolognese years when he was still active in the teaching methods of the academy. In any case, this evocative sheet is one of the most copied of any of Annibale's landscape drawings, indicating its importance and that of its author.

Diane De Grazia

PROVENANCE
M. Jabach ?; Louis XV ?; Sir Frederick Wedmore; A. G. B. Russell (Lugt 2770a), his sale, London, Sotheby's, 22 May 1928, lot 46; John Nicholas Brown.

NOTES
1. *River Landscape*, NGA 1952.5.58. See Fern Rusk Shapley, *Catalogue of Italian Paintings*, 2 vols. (Washington, 1979), 1:20, 2: pl. 82.

2. *Satyr Holding a Roundel*, NGA 1978.44.1. Edmund P. Pillsbury and John Caldwell, *Sixteenth-Century Italian Drawings: Form and Function* [exh. cat. Yale University Art Gallery] (New Haven, 1974), 44.

3. *Landscape with Two Washerwomen*, NGA 1978.19.1 and *Woodland River with a Boat*, NGA 1978.70.1. See *Master Drawings* [exh. cat. National Gallery of Art] (Washington, 1978), 49–50.

4. (Formerly) Chatsworth 461, Chatsworth Settlement Sale, London, Christie's, see *Old Master Drawings from Chatsworth*, 3 July 1984, under lot 3; Oxford, Christ Church 1017, see James Byam Shaw, *Drawings by Old Masters at Christ Church Oxford* (Oxford, 1976), 1:249–250 (under cat. 944); and Edinburgh, National Gallery of Scotland, D852, see Keith Andrews, *National Gallery of Scotland: Catalogue of Italian Drawings* (Cambridge, 1971), 1:33 (under cat. 37). The etching by Jean Baptiste Corneille is found in *Recueil de 283 Estampes . . . d'après les Dessins des grands Maîtres que possedoit autrefois M. Jabach et qui depuis ont passé au Cabinet du Roy* (Paris, 1754), 47.A.

5. This places the provenance of the National Gallery sheet into question since Corneille published his etching in a book after drawings in Jabach's collection.

6. Rembrandt knew and owned Annibale's drawings. It has been suggested in the Christie's sale catalogue that the Chatsworth sheet may be a copy by Rembrandt of the National Gallery drawing.

17

JAN BRUEGHEL THE ELDER
1568–1625

*A Basket of Mixed Flowers and a
Vase of Flowers,* 1615
Panel
21⅝ x 35⅜ (55 x 90)

Promised Gift of Mrs. Paul Mellon

This beautifully preserved panel painting will be the earliest Flemish still life in the National Gallery's collection, and the first painting there by this extremely important master.

Referring to one of his own paintings in a letter of 1606 to Cardinal Federico Borromeo, Jan Brueghel the Elder queried "whether these flowers do not surpass gold and jewels."[1] Certainly the artist's prosperity and his nickname "Flower" Brueghel suggest that he was not alone in holding his work in high regard. In the early years of the seventeenth century, Brueghel had turned increasing attention to flowers, probably in response to a growing demand for still-life and flower paintings. His vibrant colors, delicate yet painterly application of paint, and innovative arrangements were greatly admired.

The son of Pieter Brueghel the Elder, Jan Brueghel was trained in Antwerp by the painter and art dealer Pieter Goetkindt and probably by Gillis van Coninxloo. In the early 1590s he traveled extensively and visited, among other centers, Cologne, Rome, Naples, and Milan. In Milan he met his lifelong patron Cardinal Federico Borromeo. Over the years the cardinal would correspond with this Flemish artist whose works he considered "the lightness of nature itself."[2] Brueghel returned to Antwerp in 1595; there he married twice, raised a large family, and established an atelier. He served as dean of the Guild of Saint Luke, owned some five houses by the age of fifty, and received numerous privileges and honors in his role as a court painter to Archduke Ferdinand and Archduchess Isabella. These ranged from a remission from taxes to the right to study rare plants and animals in the royal gardens. Throughout his Antwerp years Brueghel collaborated with numerous artists, most

notably his friend Peter Paul Rubens. When he died of cholera in 1625 Rubens wrote his epitaph.

This work is a fascinating example of Brueghel's flower paintings, for it juxtaposes the natural splendor of a random arrangement of cut flowers in a basket with an arrangement of tulips, buttercups, and other delicate flowers in a Venetian glass. This combination of motifs provided Brueghel with a wonderful vehicle for emphasizing the freshness of the flowers, for it seems that the floral arrangement has been created from blossoms that have just been brought from the garden. Brueghel's manipulation of paint, which ranges from thick impastos to thin glazes, conveys the delicacy of thin forms with such naturalness that his contemporaries could even imagine their fragrant odors. Brueghel's basket of flowers, however, could never have existed in reality. The blossoms represented did not all grow at the same season of the year. Late-winter snowdrops mix freely with spring narcissus and summer roses while stems of wild buttercups tangle with those of cultivated carnations.

The unusual combination of a basket containing a profusion of blossoms and an informal arrangement of flowers in a small glass vase must have been admired, for Brueghel repeated the composition two years later.[3] Contemporary appreciation of Brueghel's flower arrangements, however, embraced far more than recognition of their beauty and the artist's skill: Brueghel's patron Cardinal Borromeo saw in such paintings a means for contemplating God's grandeur. This remarkable painting still invites the viewer to delight in a glorious profusion of flowers that reflects the deeply abiding faith in God's munificence that Brueghel shared with his contemporaries.

Arthur K. Wheelock, Jr.

PROVENANCE
Sold, Galerie Paul Brandt, Amsterdam, 10 October 1967.

NOTES
1. Jan Brueghel the Elder to Cardinal Federico Borromeo, letter of 1606, in Guhl-Rosenberg, *Künstlerbriefe*, 2d ed. (Berlin, 1880), cited in Gertraude Winckelmann-Rhein, *The Paintings and Drawings of Jan "Flower" Brueghel* (New York, [1969]), 22.

2. Cited in Winckelmann-Rhein [1969], 28.

3. *A Basket of Mixed Flowers and a Vase of Flowers* [exh. cat. De Boer] (Amsterdam, 1934), no. 272.

JAN TENGNAGEL
1584–1635

Abraham Entertaining the Angels
1610–1620
Black chalk, pen, brown ink,
and washes, with touches of graphite
13⅝₁₆ x 9⅜ (33.6 x 23.7)

Gift of Mrs. Alice Steiner

In one of the most delightful episodes of the Old Testament (Gen. 18.1–10), the hundred-year-old Abraham is visited by three angels. The anxious host rushes to greet his guests, offering them water with which to wash, shade in which to rest, and fresh milk, bread, and a dressed calf with which to refresh themselves. Unknown to the patriarch, they have come to foretell the birth of the son of whom he had abandoned all hope.

Typological readings of this scene abound. The visitation of the angels and the breaking of the bread have been read as Old Testament prefigurations of the Annunciation and the Last Supper. Saint Augustine stressed the trinitarian aspect of the visitors, while during the Counter-Reformation a new emphasis was placed on Abraham's gracious behavior: his example of providing hospitality to strangers was associated with one of the acts of mercy.[1]

The subject was particularly popular in the Netherlands in the seventeenth century. It was treated by a number of Dutch artists who traveled to Rome early in the century and were influenced by the work of German expatriate Adam Elsheimer. Tengnagel, who was in Rome in 1608, and his brother-in-law, Pieter Lastman, were members of this group, which has come to be known as the "Pre-Rembrandtists." Rembrandt and members of his school also treated this scene.

Tengnagel's drawing, although neither signed nor dated, is characteristic of his style in the 1610s, when he had returned from Rome and had come under Lastman's influence. Characteristic is the emphasis on gesture and expression to clarify the dramatic moment of the story. Here Abraham is clearly responding to the announcement that he will father a son. Sarah peers out from behind the door of the house while a figure in the lower right reaches into a basket for food for the guests. The entire scene is animated by quick rhythms of pen strokes and bold accents in wash.

Finished drawings such as this are extremely rare in Tengnagel's oeuvre. The Gallery has no other work by this master and no work by any of the other Pre-Rembrandtists. This drawing thus is of particular importance to our collection.

Arthur K. Wheelock, Jr.

PROVENANCE
Colnagy; Herbert Feist Gallery, New York (1973), no. 35 as by "Lambert Jacobsz"; collection of Alice Steiner, Larchmont, New York, by 1977.

NOTE
1. Louis Réau, *Iconographie de L'Art Chrétien* (Paris, 1955–1959), 2: part 1, 131–132.

JACOPO PALMA IL GIOVANE
c. 1548–1628

Lamentation, c. 1620
Oil on canvas
52½ x 42¾ (134 x 108.5)

Given in Memory of William E. Suida
by Bertina Suida Manning
and Robert L. Manning

By the end of the sixteenth century the four artists who had created the golden age of Venetian painting—Titian, Jacopo Bassano, Tintoretto, and Veronese—had all passed into history. The younger generation, which looked back nostalgically to their predecessors, was headed by Jacopo Palma, known as "il Giovane" to distinguish him from his great-uncle Palma Vecchio.[1] After returning to Venice from a Roman sojourn about 1570, Palma assisted Titian, completing the *Pietà* meant for Titian's tomb (Accademia, Venice) and leaving an eyewitness account of his aged master's unorthodox working methods. In his production from this period Palma was an eclectic, combining elements from all of the major sixteenth-century Venetian masters. But increasingly it was Tintoretto who emerged as Palma's chief source of inspiration. Tintoretto's manner, like the late Titian's, was highly personal. Palma transformed their styles into a more straightforward visual idiom, one well suited to his vast output (more than six hundred paintings survive). Palma's style also effectively conveyed the ideals of the Catholic Counter-Reformation, which called for a more direct and moving presentation of religious themes.

The *Lamentation* is a late work (c. 1620), which epitomizes Palma's approach as an artist: though the elongated proportions and poses of the figures and the dramatic lighting recall Tintoretto, Palma has arranged his figures in a simple arc surrounding Christ's body, which tilts forward, casting the head in shadow.[2] The Savior's pale form, emerging from the darkness into the light, is the fulcrum of the composition. To heighten the emotional impact of the painting, Palma spotlighted the sorrowful gestures and expressions of the mourners, who include the Virgin shown on the right, opposite the Magdalen, as she displays Christ's wounded hand. Above are a third Mary, the bearded Nicodemus, and Saint John, dressed in tones of blue, red, green, and gold, which set off the ghostly white of Christ's body and shroud. This small altarpiece by Palma is the first work by the artist to join the Gallery's superb holdings of Venetian Renaissance paintings.

David Alan Brown

NOTES

1. About the artist see Nicola Ivanoff and Pietro Zampetti, *Palma il Giovane* (Bergamo, 1975); and Stefania Mason Rinaldi, *Palma il Giovane. L'opera completa* (Milan, 1984).

2. Bertina Suida Manning and Robert L. Manning, "Palma Giovane and Matteo Ponzone in New York private collections," in *Dedicato a Pietro Zampetti nei suoi settanta anni*, ed. Ileana Chiappini and Giuseppe Cucco (*Notizie da Palazzo Albani*, Rivista semestrale di Storia dell'Arte, Università degli Studi di Urbino, vol. 12, nos. 1–2, 1983) (Urbino, 1983), 173–174 and fig. 4 (170–175).

53

HENDRICK TER BRUGGHEN
1588–1629

The Mocking of Christ, c. 1625
Oil on canvas
37⅛ x 49 (95.2 x 125.7)

Promised Gift of David E. Rust

Ter Brugghen is rightly considered the first and most important of the Dutch Caravaggists, the designation of a number of artists from Utrecht who traveled to Italy in the first decades of the seventeenth century and returned to the Netherlands under the influence of Caravaggio. The dramatically conceived history paintings and genre scenes of the Caravaggists had tremendous impact in the north, and their influence can be seen in the works of artists as diverse as Frans Hals, Rembrandt van Rijn, and Johannes Vermeer.

New biographical information about Hendrick ter Brugghen has recently been discovered that has changed our understanding of the origin of this fascinating Dutch artist. Ter Brugghen was neither born in the province of Overijssel as has always been thought, nor was he the son of a Catholic family.[1] His father originally came from Utrecht, but had moved to The Hague as a process-server ("deurwaarder") for the court of Holland ("Hof van Holland") prior to Hendrick's birth in 1588. It is not known when the family returned to Utrecht, but Hendrick certainly studied with the important Utrecht painter Abraham Bloemaert before he set off to Italy around 1604.

Little is known about the ten years he is reputed to have stayed there other than he traveled to Rome, Naples, and Milan. Without doubt, however, he was struck by the revolutionary work of Caravaggio. Shortly after Ter Brugghen returned to Utrecht in 1614 he joined the Guild of Saint Luke and executed his first known painting, *The Supper at Emmaus,* 1616 (The Toledo Museum of Art), a work that is clearly based on Caravaggio's depiction of the same subject (National Gallery, London).

It is possible that he returned to Rome for a short stay around 1620, but this proposed second trip to Italy remains a controversial idea.[2] Such a renewed contact with the Italian followers of Caravaggio, in particular Orazio Gentileschi, may account for the transformations in Ter Brugghen's style that occur around 1621. On the other hand, returning to Utrecht at just this time were the other two important Utrecht Caravaggisti, Gerrit van Honthorst and Dirck van Baburen, and their influence may have encouraged Ter Brugghen's stylistic transformation, which consisted of more focused compositions, a lighter palette, and broader brushwork than seen in his earlier work. Ter Brugghen enjoyed considerable success during the 1620s and seems to have developed a workshop in which replicas and versions of a number of his compositions were created. No specific information about the nature of this workshop, however, is known.[3]

The designation "Utrecht Caravaggisti," however appropriate for Ter Brugghen and his contemporaries, obscures the complex character of Ter Brugghen's art, for his work, as is clear from this fascinating painting of *The Mocking of Christ,* is also imbued with the spirit of early sixteenth-century northern traditions. In this striking work Ter Brugghen has intensified Christ's humiliation by tightly cropping the composition and bringing the confrontation to the immediate foreground. In this respect and in the broadly executed forms and the light tonality of the colors, Ter Brugghen's style relates to the work of Caravaggio. Thematically, however, Ter Brugghen has taken his subject from the graphic work of Lucas van Leyden and Albrecht Dürer. The stark contrast between Christ's serenity and the intense degradation inflicted by the mocking youth and the brute force exerted by the figure pressing the crown of thorns on the Savior's head are elements found in both Dürer's and Lucas van Leyden's work. The fusion of these two traditions gives Ter Brugghen's work an extraordinary intensity that is unlike that of any of his contemporaries.

Dating this painting, as is often the case with Ter Brugghen's oeuvre, is quite complicated. Nicolson placed it about 1620, at the moment that Ter Brugghen executed his large *Mocking of Christ* in Copenhagen.[4] This painting also contains many references to prints by Lucas van Leyden and Dürer.[5] Such an early date, however, seems unlikely given the broad execution of the painting, which is more compatible with Ter Brugghen's style from the mid-1620s.[6] At that time Ter Brugghen seems to have had renewed interest in a consciously archaizing style similar to that evident in this work.[7]

A number of pentimenti exist, particularly in the robes of Christ, that are consistent with those found in other of Ter Brugghen's authentic works. Nevertheless, the execution in the background is quite stiff and falls below the standard generally associated with the artist. Nicolson already had suggested that the painting may have been executed with the help of studio assistants.[8] However, the problems are more likely the result of overpainting. X-radiographs reveal a pattern of vertical lines that indicate that the canvas was once rolled. Restoration, especially in the background, is quite extensive.

This work, which is the first painting by Ter Brugghen or any of the Utrecht Caravaggisti to enter the Gallery, is an extremely important addition to our collection. It represents both an artist and a type of painting that had tremendous influence in Dutch art in the seventeenth century.

Arthur K. Wheelock, Jr.

NOTES

1. The fact that Ter Brugghen married in 1616 in the Reformed Church in Utrecht and had his children baptized in the Reformed Church indicates as well that he was a Protestant and not a Catholic. The most recent biographical information comes largely from the result of discoveries by Marten Jan Bok and is contained in *Nieuw Licht op de Gouden Eeuw: Hendrick ter Brugghen en tijdgenoten* [exh. cat. Centraal Museum] (Utrecht, 1987), 65–75. This account modifies an earlier publication of many of the new documents: M. J. Bok and Y. Kobayashi, "New data on Hendrick ter Brugghen," *Hoogsteder-Naumann Mercury* 1 (1985), 7–34.

2. C. Schuckman, "Did Hendrick ter Brugghen Revisit Italy? Notes from an Unknown Manuscript by Cornelis de Bie," *Hoogsteder–Naumann Mercury* 4 (1986), 7–22. See also Utrecht 1987, 66.

3. Leonard Slatkes in Utrecht 1987, 109, speculated that Ter Brugghen shared a workshop with Dirck van Baburen after the latter's return to Utrecht in 1621 and until his death in 1624.

4. Benedict Nicolson, "Terbrugghen Since 1960," in *Album Amicorum J. G. van Gelder* (The Hague, 1973), 239.

5. See Paul van Kooij, "Ter Brugghen, Dürer and Lucas van Leyden," *Hoogsteder-Naumann Mercury* 5 (1987), 11–19.

6. This date was first suggested to me by Leonard Slatkes, whose observations about this painting have been most helpful.

7. See, for example, his *Crucifixion with Mary and Saint John,* c. 1624–1626, The Metropolitan Museum of Art, New York.

8. Nicolson 1973, 239.

ROELANDT SAVERY
1576–1639

Landscape with Animals and Figures, 1624
Oil on panel
21½ x 36 (54.6 x 91.4)

Gift of Robert H. and Clarice Smith

In a dense mountainous forest several groups of cattle, sheep, and goats have been brought to drink from a trough fed by a fountain, while the herdsmen rest or talk with one another. In addition to the domestic animals there are numerous wild creatures: birds fill the air and in the shadowy woods at the left are deer, mountain goats, and two storks. Prominently displayed in the center is a round tower, which is in ruins and in the process of being overgrown with vegetation. One wonders whether this landscape might be imbued with an allegorical or moralizing meaning and, in particular, whether the tower and accompanying ruins might allude to the triumph of nature and time over man's creations or perhaps be a nostalgic reference to a "Golden Age" now fallen into decay.

A figure of considerable importance for the history of northern European art, Roelandt Savery was born at Kortrijk (Courtrai) in Flanders in 1576, but he and his family fled during the religious upheavals of the 1580s. It is likely that he went northward to Antwerp, Dordrecht, and Haarlem, and probably was in Amsterdam in 1591 where his older brother and teacher, Jacques Savery (c. 1565–1603) had acquired citizenship. The most decisive phase of Roelandt's career began in 1603 when he traveled to Prague. There he entered the employ of Rudolf II and in 1606/1607 was sent by the emperor into the Tyrolean Alps to record "their marvels of nature." Following Rudolf's death in 1612 Savery worked briefly for his successor, the Emperor Matthias, but returned to the Netherlands by 1613 or 1614. He was intermittently in Amsterdam until 1619, when he moved to Utrecht and joined the painters' guild. He remained in Utrecht until his death in 1639. Roelandt Savery played a key role in transmitting the Netherlandish landscape and genre tradition of Pieter Bruegel the Elder to early seventeenth-century Holland.

Landscape with Animals and Figures, signed and dated 1624 at the lower left, is a splendid example of the mannerist style that Savery continued to practice during his years in Utrecht. Typical of the mannerist landscapes created by Savery and his contemporaries are the strong contrasts and striking patterns of sunlight and shadow and the abrupt shifts in depth, such as the juxtaposition of foreground to distant trees and hills at the right. The robustness and vitality of the scene are testimony to the impression made on Savery by his earlier travels in the woods and mountains of Bohemia and the Tyrol. The same motifs of herdsmen watering their stock in front of a ruined tower appear in earlier landscape paintings formerly in a private collection in France (dated 1616) and the Museum voor Schone Kunsten, Kortrijk.[1]

It is only relatively recently that northern mannerism has been appreciated and collected in the United States, and the National Gallery of Art possesses very few paintings in this area. Therefore *Landscape with Animals and Figures,* which evidently has never been exhibited, is an addition of singular importance.

John Oliver Hand

PROVENANCE
Sale, Sotheby's, New York, 14 January 1988, no. 86.

NOTE
1. Kurt J. Müllenmeister, *Roelant Savery. Kortrijk 1576-1639 Utrecht. Hofmaler Kaiser Rudolf II. in Prag. die Gemälde mit kritischem Oeuvrekatalog* (Freren, 1988), 272, no. 168, 278, no. 169. The Gallery's painting is published here for the first time, 272, no. 168A.

FRANS SNYDERS
1579–1657

Still Life with Fruit and Game
c. 1615–1620
Oil on canvas
37¼ x 55¼ (94.5 x 143)

Gift (Partial and Promised) of
Herman and Lila Shickman

Frans Snyders was the foremost seventeenth-century Flemish painter of still lifes and game pieces. Trained under Pieter Brueghel the Younger and probably Hendrik van Balen, Snyders was admitted to the Antwerp Guild of Saint Luke as a master in 1602. He traveled to Italy in 1608, carrying with him an introduction to Cardinal Borromeo's secretary from Jan Brueghel the Elder who recommended him as "one of the best painters in Antwerp." By 1609 he was back in Antwerp and in 1611 married to Marguerite, sister of Cornelis and Paul de Vos. By 1617 Snyders' renown was such that Toby Matthew, English agent in the southern Netherlands, described Snyders as "that other famous Painter."[1] Snyders painted extensively throughout his life, owned a significant art collection, and died a wealthy man.

Drawing on the game piece and still-life traditions established in the sixteenth century by Pieter Aertsen and Joachim Beuckelaer, Snyders brought a new richness to this genre through his compositional sensitivity, with bold brushwork and rich colors. Moreover, he could effectively convey textures as varied as the soft fur of a deer, the feathers

of a bird, and the translucent sheen of a grape. He influenced a number of other Flemish artists, particularly Adriaen van Utrecht and Jan Fyt, and also had an impact on Dutch artists in their representations of game pieces after 1650. Aside from his independent creations Snyders also collaborated with Peter Paul Rubens and other members of Rubens' circle.

Still Life with Fruit and Game, the first work by Snyders to enter the National Gallery of Art, is a particularly rich example of the artist's large tabletop compositions. This pyramidal composition of fruits, vegetables, and dead game centers on a basket of pears, apples, a melon, and grapes on top of which an eager squirrel gazes toward fruit slightly beyond his reach. Around the basket are displayed the bounties of nature: assorted dead birds, a pear, a deer, an artichoke, a patterned porcelain dish of berries, and several bundles of asparagus. The entire arrangement is positioned on a red-draped tabletop thrust close to the picture plane; the backdrop is in earthen browns.

The image conveys the richness and bounty of the Flemish countryside that was so ad-

mired in Snyders' day. Painted in a bold and free manner, *Still Life with Fruit and Game* contains the vibrant reds and greens that made Snyders one of the outstanding colorists of his time. Although undated, by style and composition it appears closest to Snyders' works of c. 1615–1620. This painting is the first work by this artist to enter the National Gallery's collection.

Arthur K. Wheelock, Jr.

PROVENANCE
Collection of Herman and Lila Shickman.

NOTE
1. Toby Matthew to Sir Dudley Carleton, 25 February 1617, in Noel Sainsbury, *Original Unpublished Papers Illustrative of the Life of Sir Peter Paul Rubens* (London, 1859), 18.

GIOVANNI FRANCESCO BARBIERI, called GUERCINO
1591–1666

Landscape with the Taming of a Horse, 1620s
Pen and ink and wash
7³⁄₈ x 10⁵⁄₁₆ (18.8 x 26.2)

Gift (Partial and Promised) of
Mr. and Mrs. Harry Brooks

Guercino was born in the provincial town of Cento, near Bologna.[1] His self-taught genius was recognized early by local patrons and by the archbishop of Bologna, Cardinal Alessandro Ludovisi. When Ludovisi became Pope Gregory XV in 1621, Guercino's career was launched. The artist's few years in Rome (1621–1623) began a slow but steady change in his style, which tempered the exuberance and drama of his early period. Guercino's works gradually began to reflect a more subdued, idealistic manner. *Landscape with the Taming of a Horse* probably dates from the 1620s and reflects the style of these transitional years. Guercino's early pen and ink drawings are rapidly drawn with circular pen lines that by their movement alone suggest continual action. This virtuoso draftsmanship, although apparent here, is balanced by the strong stable verticals at left and by the planar disposition of the composition.

The National Gallery possesses eight other drawings by Guercino, which range in date throughout the artist's career, cover subjects both religious and profane, and vary in technique. However, we have no drawing of the type exemplified by this one: a large figural composition of everyday life set in a landscape. In fact, there are few comparable drawings by the artist. One such composition with two fighting horsemen is found in the collection of the earl of Leicester, but it dates somewhat earlier and is unconnected except for the rearing horse closely placed near the picture plane.[2] Horses and riders or horses with standing figures appear as *staffage* in several of Guercino's drawings but never dominate the landscape as here. The subject matter too appears to be unique. The untamed horse has just thrown off a rider as the trainer attempts to calm him. The singularity of the genre theme and the virtuosity of the technique, so characteristic of this artist's multifaceted talent, make the *Landscape with the Taming of a Horse* an important testament to Guercino's interest in quotidian life. As such this sheet is an important addition to our varied group of great drawings by this master.

Diane De Grazia

NOTES

1. The old inscription at lower right, "di Gio: franco Barbieri da/ Cento," acknowledges the artist's place of birth.

2. Repr. Thos. Agnew and Sons Ltd., *Old Master Drawings from Holkham* (London, 1977), cat. 49. This drawing was pointed out to the author by David Stone.

61

GERARD SEGHERS
1591–1651

Repentant Magdalene, c. 1625–1630
Oil on canvas
47¼ x 68¼ (121 x 175)

Gift (Partial and Promised) of
Patricia Bauman and John L. Bryant, Jr.

Lying before the grotto to which she had retreated after Christ's death, Mary Magdalene gazes with sad longing at the crucifix in her hand. With long golden tresses covering her shoulders and flowing over her back as well as underneath her body, the still-voluptuous repentant has surrounded herself with reminders of the suffering and death of Christ, including the blood-stained scourge that had inflicted pain on his body. The evocative fusion of sensual beauty and remorse, which makes this image of the Magdalene so poignant, was intended to reinforce the importance of the sacrament of penance for the Counter-Reformation viewers who beheld this devotional work.

Gerard Seghers is a fascinating Flemish artist from the early years of the seventeenth century whose career has never been fully explored.[1] He was inscribed as a master in the Guild of Saint Luke in Antwerp in 1608 and apparently remained in that city until 1611, at which time he visited Rome and Naples. It is also possible that he traveled to Spain. By 1620 he had returned to Antwerp. His work during the 1620s reflects his Italian experiences, particularly his responses to Caravaggio perhaps as made known to him by Italian followers of the master, including Bartolomeo Manfredi and Orazio Gentileschi. It has been suggested that Seghers traveled to Utrecht during the 1620s to visit Gerrit van Honthorst, whom he may have met in Rome, but no documentary evidence of such a trip exists.[2] In any event, by 1630 Seghers seems to have been firmly installed in Antwerp, where he worked for Jesuit patrons and for the Archduchess Isabella. In 1637 he was named court painter at the Flemish court by the Cardinal-Infante Ferdinand. In his later works Seghers abandoned his Caravaggesque style and created images that are more closely related, stylistically and thematically, to paintings by Peter Paul Rubens.

The attribution of this painting, which has only recently been discovered, is con-firmed by an engraving after a similar image of the *Repentant Magdalene* by Lucas Vorsterman in which Seghers in named as the inventor of the composition.[3] A comparable painting by Seghers is the *Saint Jerome at Prayer* in the Musée des Beaux-Arts, Lille. Saint Jerome, who had also removed himself to the wilderness in penitence, is shown by Seghers at his grotto praying fervently before a crucifix while books, a skull, and a whip lie on the ground. In both works the flesh tones and facial features are carefully rendered with smooth brushwork and luminous paint. In each instance as well, the distant landscape is rendered more softly than the foreground, in a style reminiscent of the landscape painter Jan Wildens (1586–1653). Since Wildens often collaborated with other artists in this manner, it is very likely that he worked with Seghers in the *Repentant Magdalene* as well.[4]

Seghers' *Magdalene* draws on Italian traditions of the late sixteenth and early seventeenth centuries.[5] One of the first images of a Magdalene reclining in a landscape was a work by Correggio that was well known through copies by Cristofano Allori (1577–1621).[6] The subject was also depicted a number of times by Orazio Gentileschi, an artist whose gentle brand of Caravaggism must have had great appeal for Seghers.[7] However, neither Correggio's nor Gentileschi's interpretations of the subject depict Mary Magdalene gazing at the crucifix. This emphasis on her psychological state of mind is consistent with northern traditions and is found in contemporary religious images by Rubens and by Anthony van Dyck.

We are particularly pleased to have this beautifully preserved painting as the first work by this artist in the National Gallery's collection. Not only does it broaden our representation of Flemish painting, which is dominated with works by Rubens and Van Dyck, but it also introduces a Counter-Reformation theme that was central to the artistic concerns of the day.

Arthur K. Wheelock, Jr.

NOTES

1. The basic study on the artist is D. Roggen and H. Pauwels, "Het Caravaggistisch Oeuvre van Gerard Zegers," *Gentse bijdragen tot de Kunstgeschiedenis* 16 (1955–1956), 255–301.

2. Roggen and Pauwels 1955–1956, 268, make this suggestion on the basis of Joachim von Sandrart's statement that he met Seghers in Amsterdam when visiting that city in 1645 (see Joachim von Sandrart, *Academie der Bau-Bild-und Mahlereikünste von 1675,* ed. A. R. Peltzer [Munich, 1925], 171). They reason that Sandrart may have met with Seghers at that time was because they had met in Utrecht in the mid-1620s when Sandrart was staying with Honthorst.

3. An impression of this print is in the Albertina, Vienna.

4. The suggestion that the landscape might have been executed by Wildens in the Lille painting was first made by Herve Oursel in *Trésors des musées du Nord de la France, III, La Peinture Flamande au Temps de Rubens* [exh. cat. Musée des Beaux-Arts] (Lille, 1977), 120–121, no. 56.

5. For traditions of the representation of Mary Magdalene see Marilena Mosco, *La Maddalena tra Sacro e Profano* [exh. cat. Palazzo Pitti] (Florence, 1986).

6. See Cecil Gould, *The Paintings of Correggio* (London, 1976), 279–280.

7. R. Ward Bissell, *Orazio Gentileschi and the Poetic Tradition in Caravaggesque Painting* (University Park and London, 1981), 173–174, suggests that Gentileschi could have depicted the first of his representations of *Saint Mary Magdalene in Penitence* in Rome before he left the city in 1621.

JUSEPE DE RIBERA
1591–1652

The Martyrdom of Saint Bartholomew
1634
Oil on canvas
41 x 44½ (104 x 113)

Gift of the 50th Anniversary Gift
Committee

Jusepe de Ribera can be considered both Spanish and Italian. Little is known for sure of his early years or training in Spain; after a probable study trip to northern Italy he was documented in Rome in 1615,[1] listed there as a follower of Caravaggio.[2] Ribera settled in Naples in 1616 where he enjoyed a long and prosperous career, with abundant commissions from King Philip IV of Spain, his viceroys in Naples, the Neapolitan and Spanish aristocracy, and the numerous religious establishments in the city. His emotional renderings of saints in ecstasy captured in a tenebrist atmosphere influenced all subsequent Neapolitan painters (particularly Luca Giordano, whose work appears in this exhibition).

The charge of the Counter-Reformation Church to encourage the faithful to participate in the suffering of the martyred saints was keenly felt in Spain and Naples. The Spaniard saint Ignatius Loyola, founder of the Jesuits, recommended the participation of the individual in the mystical passion of Christ and his saints. Ribera, more than any other artist of his time, evoked the spirit of Saint Ignatius by combining the physical reality of his subjects with the underlying mysticism of their religious experience.

One of the seventeenth century's and Ribera's favorite subjects was the martyrdom of Saint Bartholomew.[3] Legend relates that during a festival Ribera hung a painting of this subject across from the Palazzo Reale, attracting the attention of the viceroy (the duke of Osuna) and launching his Neapolitan career.[4] Ribera's other paintings of the subject situate in a landscape a full-length figure bound to a tree, often with several executioners and onlookers; only in this powerful depiction did the artist focus on Bartholomew's mystical experience before death rather than his physical suffering. The figures are placed against the forward picture plane, the saint almost falling into the observer's space. By this concentration on large half-length figures and on the frozen moment between Bartholomew and his executioner, the spectator feels an intensity of devotion and truly participates in the religious experience. Ribera here employed his usual *X*-shaped composition to heighten the drama: after being made party to Bartholomew's vision the viewer focuses on the sharpening of the blade, which curiously resembles a cross. Thus the executioner inadvertently reminds the saint and the viewer, as mystical participant, of Christ's own suffering.

When Ribera signed and dated this painting in 1634,[5] his style had evolved away from deep chiaroscuro contrasts to softer gradations of light and shade, bringing out the rich color tones in the half light such as that of the executioner's cape. The lush and thick impasto of his long brushstrokes, characteristic of Ribera, give the scene a tactile reality. This virtuoso handling of paint and mystical fervor set Ribera apart from Caravaggio and make his paintings singularly important. Ribera scholars Craig Felton and William Jordan have noted that the *Martyrdom of Saint Bartholomew* is among the artist's masterpieces of his full maturity.

The Martyrdom of Saint Bartholomew is all the more significant for its remarkable state of preservation: the delicate glazes and layers of impasto have remained intact, giving the surface a lustrous, vibrating quality. This exceptional painting is the first by this artist to enter the National Gallery. It will have a notable effect on our holdings of both Spanish and Italian paintings and should act as a catalyst to further collecting in this important area of baroque art.

Diane De Grazia

PROVENANCE
Bought for George Cranstoun, Lord Corehouse, by his nephew-in-law Lord Ashburton in Italy c. 1810; by descent to Colonel Cranstoun of that Ilk; his sale London, Sotheby's 6 July 1983, lot 39; Private collection, London; London, Sotheby's 4 July 1990, lot 83.

NOTES
1. Jeanne Chenault, "Ribera in Roman Archives," *Burlington Magazine* 111 (Sept. 1969), 561–562.

2. Giulio Mancini (*Considerazione sulla pittura*, c. 1620, ed. Adriana Marucchi and Luigi Salerno [Rome, 1956], 149–150) noted Ribera as among the followers of Caravaggio.

3. Examples exist in New York, Rome, Florence, Princeton, Stockholm, Barcelona, Grenoble, and Osuna. An etching of the subject is dated 1624. For reproductions see Nicola Spinosa, *L'opera completa di Ribera* (Milan, 1978).

4. Bernardo De' Dominici, *Vite de'pittori, scultori ed architetti napoletani* (Naples, 1742), 3:4.

5. Signed lower right "Jusepe de Ribera español F." and dated "1634." A copy of the painting exists in the Alte Pinakothek, Munich (Spinosa 1978, cat. 260, but repr. as 259, a confusion with the present painting).

REMBRANDT VAN RIJN
1606–1669

The Return of the Prodigal Son, 1636
Etching
6⅛ x 5⅜ (15.6 x 13.7)

Gift of Ruth B. Benedict
in Memory of William S. Benedict

Rembrandt van Rijn ranks among the outstanding interpreters of the Bible in the history of art. He especially was fascinated by biblical stories that emphasize human compassion, love, and forgiveness. One of his favorite tales was the return of the prodigal son (Luke 15.11–32). He illustrated the parable at many points during his long career, beginning with this signed and dated 1636 etching.[1] He took up the theme again in six drawings dated between c. 1642 and 1659. His last depiction occurs in a painting done the year before his death.[2]

In his etching Rembrandt illustrates the moment when the repentant son returns home, falling into the forgiving arms of his father. As was often the case with Rembrandt, he embellished the text by including in the doorway at the right the elder brother and mother who are not mentioned in Luke as being present at the reconciliation. The scene is also witnessed by a young woman, probably a servant, who leans out of an upper window. Rembrandt masterfully conveyed the emotional and psychological intensity of the scene through the individual expressions of the characters as they react to the event. These range from the anguish of the prodigal to the love and compassion of his father, the embarrassed glances of the elder son and mother, and finally the direct curiosity of the servant girl.

A maturing of Rembrandt's graphic art can be detected in 1636 and the *Return of the Prodigal Son* marks this transition, both in the artist's technique and in his sense of composition.[3] Rembrandt began then to abandon the quick, broken strokes of his earlier etchings, though this technique is still present in the far-off landscape, in favor of a more regular system of hatching and cross-hatching. This hatching, most effectively rendered in the father's tunic, defines form and suggests tone and becomes an increasingly important element in Rembrandt's mature prints. However, Rembrandt's etched line, always retaining its fluidity and spontaneity, never becomes fully systematized. The composition is simpler and more monumental than that of the early prints. The interlocking figures of the father and son form a pyramidal shape placed horizontal to the picture plane. This classical design is reinforced by the parallel lines of the steps and architecture. Just three or four decades later Bartolomé Esteban Murillo used this composition as a prime basis for his painting of the same subject, which is in the collection of the National Gallery of Art.

As with all of her many gifts to the National Gallery, this print reveals Ruth Benedict's keen eye and refined connoisseurship. It also appropriately strengthens for this anniversary the Gallery's superb collection of Rembrandt prints, the earliest of which were given in the founding year of 1941 by the eminent Boston curator and collector Philip Hofer. The collection of Rembrandt prints quickly grew with major gifts by Lessing J. Rosenwald and R. Horace Gallatin, making it today one of the strongest in the country. Though the collection already has two impressions of this print, this is a much finer and earlier impression, with strong line and contrast, and as such is far superior to the other two. This *Prodigal Son* is an especially appropriate addition to the permanent collection as it provides our first outstanding impression of the etching on which a major painting in our collection was based.

Gregory Jecmen

PROVENANCE
Richard Gutekunst (Lugt 2213a).

NOTES
1. Christopher White and Karl G. Boon, *Rembrandt's Etchings: An Illustrated Critical Catalogue* (Amsterdam, 1969), no. B. 91.

2. For the drawings see Otto Benesch, *The Drawings of Rembrandt* (London, 1973), 3: cats. 519, 562; 5: cats. 983, 1011, 1017, 1037. For the painting see A. Bredius, *Rembrandt: The Complete Edition of Paintings*, rev. H. Gerson (London, 1971), cat. 598.

3. Christopher White, *Rembrandt as an Etcher: A Study of the Artist at Work* (University Park, Pa., 1969), 40–41.

CLAUDE LORRAIN
1600–1682

The Departure for the Fields, c. 1637
Etching
5⅛ x 7⅛ (13 x 18.2)

Promised Gift of
Ruth and Jacob Kainen

This is the kind of bucolic image for which the French landscape artist is best known. Two shepherds, a shepherdess, and a flock of goats and cows are shown leaving for a day in the fields. With its large trees in the middle ground and mountains, lake, and small town in the distance, the countryside is characterized as an idyllic environment for people and animals.

The print is an exceptionally fine impression, being very rich and fresh in its inky black lines. It is undoubtedly an earlier impression than another now in the National Gallery's collection. It might be a first state (and is certainly a second), for no scholars of Claude's prints have yet found any impression without the number "12," as here, in the left margin.[1]

The image is related to a painting by Claude of about the same time, now in the North Carolina Museum of Art, Raleigh, but the print is most likely an independent work, for it does not reproduce the painting. Indeed it speaks above all for Claude's remarkable and seemingly infinite ability to vary the compositions and moods of his many hundreds of pastoral scenes, whatever the medium.

The print joins two paintings and a number of the artist's drawings and prints in the National Gallery, and it delightfully strengthens the representation of this august and highly influential master.

H. Diane Russell

NOTE
1. For a discussion and illustrations of the purported states of the print, see Lino Mannacci, *The Etchings of Claude Lorrain* (New Haven and London, 1988), 204–209, cat. 34.

ADRIAEN VAN OSTADE
1610–1685
CORNELIS DUSART
1660–1707

Peasants Fighting in a Tavern, c. 1640
Pen and ink over graphite with wash
5¼ x 10⅛ (14.9 x 25.9)

Gift of Edward William Carter and
Hannah Locke Carter

Disputes in taverns are not usually resolved with diplomacy, but Adriaen van Ostade's raucous scene captures an innkeeper's nightmare. The two adversaries brandish jug and knife while others rush to restrain them. In the meantime the table and a bench have been overturned, throwing spoons and a dish onto the floor. Adding to the commotion is a yelping dog and other figures who try to leap into the fray. The source of the dispute is not explicitly revealed, but it almost certainly was the outgrowth of gaming and drink. The makeshift table is similar to those in other scenes in which it serves as a support for such pastimes as backgammon, while the contents of the upraised jug have undoubtedly been consumed by its bellicose owner. Ostade's drawing thus falls within a broad tradition of Dutch drawings, prints, and paintings that condemn and ridicule the effects of intemperance.

Ostade undoubtedly derived this subject from the example of Adriaen Brouwer, when Brouwer was in Haarlem during the 1620s as a student of Frans Hals. Since Ostade was a pupil of Hals' around 1627, Ostade and Brouwer probably met at that time. Ostade, who joined the Haarlem Guild of Saint Luke by 1634, was a prolific painter, draftsman, and graphic artist. In his early works Ostade concentrated on vigorous depictions of peasant life within the dark interiors of their homes and taverns. Frequently he delved into the same subject types as did Brouwer, including peasants drinking, singing, smoking, or fighting. Ostade, however, focused more on the physical activities of the protagonists than did the Flemish artist, who emphasized the figures' facial features for expressive effect.

In this boldly executed drawing Ostade first indicated the figures with rapid strokes of graphite before he worked out the composition in pen. In the process he made a large number of changes, eliminating certain figures and adding others to give greater emphasis to the confrontation between the two main protagonists. Behind the seated man with the knife, for example, can be seen the first idea in graphite for another figure holding a jug aloft, which Ostade decided not to include in his final design.

The definition of the interior space in the lighter brown ink was added by Ostade's trusted pupil and follower Cornelis Dusart.[1] Dusart, who worked in Ostade's workshop in the late 1670s before his admission to the Haarlem Guild of Saint Luke in 1679, inherited the contents of Ostade's workshop after the master's death in 1685. Dusart then worked up a number of Ostade's drawings in this manner, presumably to make them more salable. In the late seventeenth century collectors admired drawings with a more finished appearance than those produced in the first half of the century, and Dusart was clearly responding to that market.

This drawing, thus, is both a major example of Ostade's draftsmanship from about 1640 and a fascinating document of studio practices and changes in taste in the Netherlands during the seventeenth century.[2] While the National Gallery has an excellent painting by Adriaen van Ostade and a fine group of his etchings, this work is the first drawing by Ostade to be acquired by the Gallery and the first large-scale Dutch genre scene in the drawings collection.

Arthur K. Wheelock, Jr.

PROVENANCE
Sybrand Feitama, sale Amsterdam, 16 October 1758, no. 14; John McGouan, sale London, 26 January 1804, no. 422 or 424; Sale, Amsterdam, Christie's, 1 December 1986, no. 13; C. G. Boerner, cat. 1987, no. 18.

NOTES
1. The monogram "AVo" and the borderline are even later additions by another hand.

2. The quality of the drawing has been praised by Bernhard Schnackenburg, the author of the standard monograph on Ostade's drawings, in a letter dated 16 June 1986 (curatorial files).

ISACK VAN OSTADE
1621–1649

Workmen before an Inn, 1645
Oil on panel
26 x 23 (66 x 58.4)

Partial Gift of
Richard A. and Lee G. Kirstein

The artistic milieu of the Dutch city of Haarlem flourished during the seventeenth century. Here were found many proponents of the vibrant naturalism so characteristic of Dutch painting of this period, among them Frans Hals, Philip Wouwermans, Adriaen van Ostade, and Jacob van Ruisdael. Another artist of this circle whose untimely death at the age of twenty-eight cut short a promising career was Isack van Ostade.

Born in 1621, Isack van Ostade was trained by his elder brother, the genre painter Adriaen van Ostade. Documentation for Isack's career is scarce although guild records tell us that he entered the Haarlem painters' guild in 1643. In that year Ostade began to free himself from his brother's style and subject matter (such as barn interiors) and to develop his own direction. He broadened his range of subject matter to include genre scenes set before an inn. His style acquired a sense of light and atmosphere more characteristic of Bamboccianti painters, particularly Pieter van Laer, who had returned to Haarlem from Italy in 1639. Also influential for Ostade were the Haarlem landscapists Pieter de Molijn and Salomon van Ruysdael.[1]

Isack van Ostade's *Workmen before an Inn* of 1645 is a magnificent signed example of his oeuvre.[2] A horse-drawn sledge has paused before the mottled, brown stone facade of a rustic village inn. One laborer bends to unload a keg from the sledge while another turns in the doorway. Yet a third more youthful figure, jug in hand, pauses in a cellar entry. Farther down the village lane a cripple hobbles along on his cane and stick; a woman, her back to us, busily sells her goods under a canopy; while in the far left background a quack peddles his wares. Ostade added to the charm of the scene by including a plethora of animals. Hens and roosters scratch and peck; two dogs, nose to nose, snarl at each other while a third, anxious to be part of the quarrel, demands the full-time attention of the very young child who holds him; and a stork gazes down from a chimney top. Ostade's organization of the scene along the diagonal provides a sense of depth and continuity to its otherwise episodic subject matter. Sunlight, breaking through thick painterly clouds, bathes the scene in warm browns and golds.

While Ostade frequently represented travelers halting before an inn, as in the National Gallery's fine example from the Widener Collection, such a focus on the activities of workmen restocking an inn is exceptional. The juxtaposition of these two fine paintings will significantly enrich our appreciation of this painter and his portrayals of the seventeenth-century Dutch world.

Arthur K. Wheelock, Jr.

PROVENANCE
Sale (Van Tol) in Souterwoude, 15 June 1779, no. 13 (1,300 florins, Wubbels); J. E. Fiseau in Amsterdam, 30 August 1797, no. 165 (1,000 florins, J. de Bos); in the collection of Baron van Brienen van de Grootelindt, Amsterdam, in 1842 (Smith valued it at £200); sale (Van Brienen van de Grootelindt), Paris, 8 May 1865, no. 23 (25,200 francs); Marq. H. de V. . . , London, 1871 (£157, 10s); Comte Greffulhe of Paris, Sotheby's, London, 22 July 1937, no. 74; in the collection of the late Adolf Mayer, The Hague, in 1948; in Brod Gallery, London, as a "recent acquisition," 13 October–30 November 1977.

NOTE
1. Schnackenburg speculated that Van Ostade may well have studied briefly under the latter, although he also allowed for Van Laer's direct influence. Bernhard Schnackenburg, *Adriaen van Ostade, Isack van Ostade: Zeichnungen und Aquarelle,* 2 vols. (Hamburg, 1981), 34–36.

2. I would like to thank Lea Eckerling Kaufman, who is writing her Ph.D. dissertation on the paintings of Isack van Ostade, for her helpful comments about this work.

NICOLAES BERCHEM
1620–1683

View of an Italian Port, c. 1660s
Oil on canvas
18⅞ x 23⅜ (48 x 59.5)

Partial Gift of
Robert H. and Clarice Smith

Nicolaes Berchem was one of the most popular and successful of the Dutch seventeenth-century Italianate landscape painters. Aside from views of Italy, his extensive oeuvre consists of hunt scenes, biblical and mythological paintings, drawings, and etchings.[1] Born in Haarlem in 1620, Berchem's early training was under his father, the still-life painter Pieter Claesz. Berchem.[2] He entered the Guild of Saint Luke in 1642 and married in Haarlem in 1646, but spent much of his later career in Amsterdam. Berchem traveled through northwest Germany with Jacob van Ruisdael in 1650 and was clearly influenced by this great Haarlem master early in his career. After 1655, however, presumably as a result of a trip to Italy, he developed into one of the most sensitive interpreters of both the pastoral and the exotic character of that distant land. His luminous vistas are painted with a facile sensitivity to the effects of light and color.

View of an Italian Port, a work signed by the artist, contains many of the qualities that made Berchem so popular. An elegant couple on horseback has paused along the riverbank to speak with a staff-bearing attendant. As in many of Berchem's works, a figure on horseback wearing a splash of red drapery provides a central focus to the more incidental nature of the rest of the painting. The shoreline is populated with men and animals engaged in day-to-day activities. For instance, two figures in the right middle ground wrestle a recalcitrant sheep onto a cattle boat while a crouching figure in the left foreground idly fondles a dog's ears. An

anchored ship lists nearby while another ship, with sails unfurled, edges around the distant, cliff-lined shore. Atop these cliffs and in the distance are Italianate buildings. Brilliant Mediterranean sunlight breaks through a clouded sky; the resultant blues, greens, and browns lend a rich earthiness to the image. The restless movements of the horses, outstretched wings of the falcon, and conversational gestures of the figures not only instill a sense of vitality but also temper the exotic atmosphere of the landscape with the immediacy of the moment.

While the National Gallery has a particularly strong representation of views of the Dutch landscape by, among others, Meindert Hobbema and Aelbert Cuyp, only one very early painting by Adam Pynacker contains Italianate motifs in the midst of a wooded landscape. *View of an Italian Port* is the first Italianate landscape in the collection to fully suggest the luminosity and marvelous rhythms that so inspired Dutch artists in that distant land. It is particularly fitting that this be a work by Berchem who was not only one of the most prolific Dutch painters but also one central to the evolution of the Italianate landscape style. His style and choice of subject matter reflect the work of his immediate predecessors Pieter van Laer, Jan Both, and Jan Asselijn and influenced innumerable followers. His work was particularly admired in the eighteenth century. In splendid condition, *View of an Italian Port* contributes significantly toward broadening the spectrum of Dutch paintings offered by the Gallery's collection.

Arthur K. Wheelock, Jr.

PROVENANCE
Collection J. van Lanschot, Leiden, in 1753; Sale Van Leyden, Paris, 10 September 1804, no. 8 (price 4,800 F according to Laroche); Sale J. Parke, London, 8 September 1812 (price 400 guineas); House J. Smith, London, to John Webb, Esq. (price 300 guineas); Sale Chevalier Erard, Paris, Château de la Muette, 7 August 1832 (Mr. Henry), no. 62 (price 6,600 F according to Perignon); Chez George, Paris, 1853 (price 5,600 F); Sale by Steengracht van Duiveenvorde of The Hague, Paris, Galerie Georges Petit, 9 June 1913 (M. Lair-Dubreuil and Baudoin), no. 4 (price 7,900 F per M. Boyer), acquired by the grandfather of the 9 April 1990 seller; Sale Adar Picard Tajan, Paris, 9 April 1990, no. 82, to Robert Smith.

NOTES
1. C. Hofstede de Groot, *Beschreibendes und kritisches Verzeichnis der Werke der hervorragendsten holländischen Maler des XVII. Jahrhunderts* (Esslingen, 1926), 9:53–292, catalogues more than eight hundred paintings by the master.

2. Arnold Houbraken, *De Groote Schouburgh der Nederlantsche Konstschilders en Schilderessen* (The Hague, 1753), 3:111, however, enumerated other teachers including Jan van Goyen, Claes Moeyaert, Pieter de Grebber, Jan Wils, and—somewhat improbably—Berchem's cousin Jan Baptist Weenix.

LUCA GIORDANO
1634–1705

Diana and Endymion, c. 1675–1680
Oil on canvas
58¾ x 64¼ (149.5 x 163.5)

Gift of Joseph F. McCrindle in Memory
of Mr. and Mrs. J. Fuller Feder

Luca Giordano, known as "Luca fa presto" (for his quickly executed paintings, unceasing activity, and prolific output), was one of the most famous Italian painters of the second half of the seventeenth century. He traveled throughout Italy, executing influential frescoes in Florence, Rome, and his native Naples.[1] He also spent ten years in Spain (1692–1702), working at the Escorial and the Buon Retiro. Private patrons enjoyed his virtuoso oil paintings of religious and mythological themes, which he repeated with variations. The size and intimate theme indicate that the *Diana and Endymion,* a work signed by the artist,[2] must have been executed for such a patron.

The subject of Diana and Endymion was popular in seventeenth-century Italy, possibly for the opportunity it gave artists to portray the beauty of the human body both at rest and in action. In Giordano's painting, Diana, flying on a cloud, caresses the shepherd Endymion, whom she has put to sleep solely in order to kiss him "at her pleasure"[3] as his dogs look on in silence. As was usual with the artist he took up the theme several times, changing only slightly the positions of the protagonists and surroundings. Two other autograph versions of this subject, in Verona and Philadelphia, vary in the number of animals and putti present, the depth of slumber of Endymion, as well as the energetic speed of the goddess' flight.[4] All three paintings have been dated by Oreste Ferrari

to c. 1675–1680,[5] a period in which the influence of Pietro da Cortona was especially evident. The luminous colors, soft contours, graceful movement, and hair styles of the figures in the three works reflect a Cortonesque inspiration.

Unlike the Verona and Philadelphia paintings, which add cupids and animals, the McCrindle painting reduces the subject to its essentials. The two figures fill the picture space as Diana, the goddess of the moon, emerges from the dark of night surrounded by shadows to embrace the resting Endymion. The turbulence of her draperies and the churning sky contrast with the tenderness of her caress. More immediate than the other versions, *Diana and Endymion* suggests Giordano's Neapolitan origins in the school of Ribera, whose dramatic lighting and candidly direct forms are echoed here. The face of Diana, half hidden in shadow, and the use of the dark ground to intensify the contrasts of light and dark reflect what Giordano absorbed from Ribera, suggesting that the present painting may date slightly earlier than the other two.

Diana and Endymion is the first painting by Luca Giordano and the first Neapolitan baroque painting to enter the National Gallery collections. The Gallery is especially grateful to Mr. McCrindle for his gift of this fine painting, which is from one of the most important schools of the seventeenth century.

Diane De Grazia

PROVENANCE
Sotheby & Co., London, 10 May 1967, lot 147.

NOTES
1. For Luca Giordano's life see Bernardo De'Dominici, *Vite de'pittori, scultori ed architetti napoletani* (Naples, 1742), 3:394–456. For his paintings see Oreste Ferrari and Giuseppe Scavizzi, *Luca Giordano* (Naples, 1966), 3 vols. See also Clovis Whitfield and Jane Martineau, *Painting in Naples 1606–1705 from Caravaggio to Giordano* [exh. cat. National Gallery of Art] (Washington, 1983), 168–180.

2. Signed "Jordanus/F" on the rock at lower right.

3. The myth is repeated in various forms by many ancient authors, but Giordano seems to refer to the one told by Vincenzo Cartari in *Le Imagini de i Dei de gli antichi* (Venice, 1571), 125: "Questo dice, perche le favole finsero, che la Luna s'innamorasse di Endimione pastore, e l'addormentasse sopra certo monte solo per basciarlo à suo piacere."

4. Verona, Museo di Castelvecchio, repr. Ferrari and Scavizzi 1966, 3: no. 137; Philadelphia, Collection Carlo Croce, repr. Christie's, New York, 5 June 1985, lot 119. De'Dominici 1742, 3:415, mentioned another version, now lost, for the queen of Spain, made before her death in 1689 but sold to another patron. The sizes of the surviving paintings for the queen's series to which this belonged have different measurements from the three known paintings of the subject and have more figures and extensive landscape backgrounds.

5. Verbal communication 10/24/90.

SAMUEL VAN HOOGSTRATEN
1627–1678

*Inleyding tot de Hooge Schoole
der Schilderkonst*
Fransois van Hoogstraten, Rotterdam,
1678
Bound volume with
20 etchings and engravings
8 x 6¼ (20.4 x 15.7)

Gift of Arthur and Charlotte Vershbow

Samuel van Hoogstraten's *Inleyding tot de Hooge Schoole der Schilderkonst* (Introduction to the Noble School of Painting) is superbly illustrated with Hoogstraten's own etchings and engravings, which will be the first prints by the artist to enter the National Gallery's collection. The volume also forms a valuable source for the theory and practice of art in the time of Rembrandt, standing with only a handful of other seventeenth-century Dutch texts devoted to art theory. This paucity of contemporary literature on the subject contrasts curiously with the enormous number of paintings being produced at this time in the Netherlands.[1] Hoogstraten intended his work to be a handbook for the professional artist and dilettante alike. He divided his text, written in both prose and verse, into nine "instructional workshops," each dedicated to one of the nine muses.

The prints in the *Inleyding* include a self portrait; a frontispiece in which the artist is crowned with laurel by the surrounding muses; figurative title plates to the nine individual books that depict the muses in allegorical settings; and nine plates and half-page illustrations displaying the proportions of the human body and demonstrating various theories of perspective and the representation of light and dark. Among the title plates, for example, the one for the sixth section of the book, which discusses color, depicts Terpsichore, the muse of choral song, as the guiding parent and teacher of young artists. In the section about light and shadow there is an arresting and bizarre scene in which small mythological figures cast eery shadows across a curtain enclosing a stage. Tiny observers emerge from around the right half of the curtain, gazing upon this mysterious shadow box.

Hoogstraten was one of the most versatile and well-traveled artists of his day. After first studying with his father, the painter and engraver Dirck Hoogstraten, Samuel left his native town of Dordrecht in 1640 for Amsterdam where he then was apprenticed to Rembrandt, probably until 1648.[2] In 1651

in Vienna Hoogstraten was awarded a gold chain and medallion by the Holy Roman Emperor Ferdinand III, who particularly liked one of the artist's still lifes. Hoogstraten proudly wears this prize, the most coveted award given to an artist at this time, in his self-portrait for the *Inleyding*. Hoogstraten's great interest in the problems of perspective, which found written and visual expression in the *Inleyding*, culminated in his trompe l'oeil paintings and in his remarkable perspective peep boxes.

The Vershbows have generously given many important illustrated books to the National Gallery over the years. These gifts demonstrate their wide range of interests and devotion to the highest quality in book collecting. They include outstanding copies of *Imprese Nobili* published in 1583 with illustrations by Giovanni Battista Pittoni; the 1619 French edition of *Les Metamorphoses d'Ovide*; Ferdinando Galli Bibiena's *L'Architettura Civile* of 1711; and the large paper 1827 edition of John Milton's *Paradise Lost* with mezzotint illustrations by John Martin.

Gregory Jecmen

PROVENANCE
Purchased Emil Offenbacher, New York, 1978.

NOTES
1. See Beatrijs Brenninkmeyer-de Rooij's chapter in Bob Haak, *The Golden Age: Dutch Painters of the Seventeenth Century* (New York, 1984), 60–70; Jaap Bolten, *Method and Practice: Dutch and Flemish Drawings Books, 1600–1750* (Landau, 1985), 212–214.

2. Rembrandt's name frequently appears in the *Inleyding*. Hoogstraten, a loyal former pupil, nevertheless criticized some aspects of the master's art. See Seymour Slive, *Rembrandt and His Critics, 1630–1730* (The Hague, 1953), 94–100.

TERPSICHORE.
de Poeterse.
6.

S.v.H.

ANTHONY VAN DYCK
1599–1641

Le Cabinet des Plus Beaux Portraits . . .
H. & C. Verdussen, Antwerp [1700]
Bound volume with 124 plates,
including etchings by Van Dyck
and engravings after his designs
14¾ x 9¾ (37.4 x 24.8)

Gift of Arthur and Charlotte Vershbow

One of the most fascinating if least under-stood enterprises undertaken by Anthony van Dyck is the *Iconography*, a series of prints that portrays political and military leaders, scholars, artists, and amateurs, most of whom were contemporaries and even friends of this great Flemish master. Just when Van Dyck, who was above all a painter and not a graphic artist, came upon the idea to create this series, how he chose whom he would repre-sent in it, how he worked with other en-gravers and with his publisher to produce the prints, and the exact form he intended the *Iconography* to take are only a few of the questions for which no satisfactory answers can be given. However Van Dyck came upon the idea for this series and whatever the process through which he created it, the extraordinary popularity of the *Iconography* throughout history has played no small role in extending Van Dyck's fame and his in-fluence on portrait conventions of later generations.

The *Iconography* was never published as a corpus during Van Dyck's lifetime.[1] The first eighty prints of the series, engraved by other printmakers after Van Dyck's designs, were apparently issued during the mid-1630s by Martin van den Enden. Since no title page exists it does not appear that these portraits were ever contained in a bound volume. The next edition of the *Iconography*, which num-bered one hundred prints, was published in 1645 by Gillis Hendricx in Antwerp. Hen-dricx compiled his prints from the plates that had been used by Van den Enden, eighteen plates that had been executed by Van Dyck himself (some of which he had engravers bring to a greater state of completion), and newly executed engravings that were based on Van Dyck's designs.[2]

The remarkable volume here exhibited, which was published in Antwerp about 1700, is one of the most visible manifestations of the importance placed upon Van Dyck's en-terprise by later generations. The publishers, H. & C. Verdussen, wishing to make this volume as complete as possible, brought to-gether 124 prints and added a new title page. Included are all of the prints originally printed by Van den Enden and Hendricx as well as other engravings that were executed later in the seventeenth century on the basis of Van Dyck's paintings. This edition is beautifully preserved and is particularly noteworthy in that it is complete. With the addition of this handsome volume, the Gallery now pos-sesses a full range of Van Dyck's *Iconography*. This work complements the existing collec-tion of prints from this series, which in-cludes excellent impressions executed by the artist himself and a large number of images engraved by artists after his designs.

The complex history of the *Iconography* makes it difficult to assess just how Van Dyck envisioned the final appearance of this project, although it does seem that the orig-inal scheme called for three main divisions among the portraits: princes and military commanders, statesmen and philosophers, and artists and art lovers. Significantly, the largest group is the last. The dispropor-tionately large size of this group may not have been intentional, perhaps the conse-quence of a project never brought to com-pletion by the artist, but it does signify Van Dyck's interest in placing these individuals in the company of esteemed political, mil-itary, and scholarly figures. Indeed, in these half-length images, for example, the splen-did image etched by Van Dyck of Joos de Momper, artists are presented with as much dignity, intelligence, and graceful bearing as are aristocrats and men of learning. The *Iconography*, thus, is a fascinating document about the efforts that were still being made to elevate the role of the artist within his society. It also is of great sociological in-terest in that it celebrates, for the first time, art lovers and collectors.

Arthur K. Wheelock, Jr.

PROVENANCE
Frances Molesworth (inscribed 1777, and again as a gift to [illegible] 1780); Juliana Woodforde (inscribed "Oct. 14, 1832").

NOTES
1. The basis source on the *Iconography* is Marie Mauquoy-Hendricx, *L'Iconographie d'Antoine van Dyck, Catalogue Raisonné*, 2 vols. (Brussels, 1956).

2. Interestingly, none of Van Dyck's original etchings were printed by Van den Enden. The number of these plates added by Gillis Hendricx is given as fifteen by Arthur M. Hind, *Van Dyck: His Original Etchings and His Iconography* (Bos-ton, 1925), 23. The more recent assessment by E. Haverkamp-Begemann and Stephanie S. Dickey, "The Iconography," in *Anthony van Dyck* [exh. cat. Art Life] (Tokyo, 1990), 28, lists eigh-teen plates.

Judocus de Momper Pictor.
montium Antuerpiæ.

Ant. van Dyck fecit aqua forti.

ANTOINE COYPEL
1661–1722

Seated Faun, c. 1705
Red and black chalks heightened
with white on blue paper
15¾ x 10¾ (40.2 x 27.4)

Gift of Lois and Georges de Menil

This enchanting drawing belongs to a small group of studies by Coypel of fauns supporting floral garlands, all seen from below and all brilliantly executed in *trois-crayons*. These once formed part of an album. Because most of the other drawings in the album were by Coypel's contemporary Louis de Boullogne the Younger (1654–1733), who had signed and dated a number of the sheets, all of the faun studies were thought until very recently to be by Boullogne.[1] Boullogne, however, worked almost exclusively in red or black chalk combined with white, or in red chalk alone, but never seems to have used the three chalks together.[2] Coypel, on the other hand, was a master of *trois-crayons*.

Although the faun drawings are not related to any of Coypel's known decorative projects, most of which were destroyed in the eighteenth century, both the bold combination of the chalks and the vibrant, monumental forms link them to the hundreds of figure drawings he made in preparation for his paintings. Closest in execution and spirit are his numerous studies for the decoration of the Gallery of Aeneas in the Palais-Royal, Paris, painted between 1702 and 1706.[3] Perhaps Coypel had considered using fauns such as these in place of the caryatids and male nudes with which he finally decided to surround the central ceiling design.

Coypel's masterful use of the *trois-crayons* technique here as in so many other drawings by him bears striking witness to his leading role in the *Rubéniste* faction of the French Academy, which championed Rubensian color, rather than Poussinist line and design, as the essential element of good painting. He was in fact one of the most admired artists of his day and was rewarded toward the end of his life with two of the highest honors of his profession: the directorship of the French Academy in 1714 and the post of first painter to the king in 1715. It was at about that time that Antoine Watteau (1684–1721), who soon became the unri-valed master of the *trois-crayons* technique, made his first three-chalk drawings. One cannot help wondering if his decision to experiment with that medium was due in part to Coypel's marvelous example.

This magnificent drawing fills two important gaps in the Gallery's collections in a most impressive way: it is the first work of any kind by Antoine Coypel to enter the museum and it is the first drawing by anyone of his generation to join the collection. This monumental piece not only represents Coypel in his most exquisite manner, but also adds considerable power to the Gallery's holdings of French drawings from the first quarter of the eighteenth century.

Margaret Morgan Grasselli

PROVENANCE
From an eighteenth-century album of French drawings that was dismantled in the early 1950s; P. & D. Colnaghi & Co., London, 1953; Hardy Amies, London (sale, London, Sotheby-Parke Bernet, 8 December 1972, no. 7, as Louis de Boullogne the Younger; to Bailey); Sale, London, Sotheby's, 6 July 1987, no. 57, as Boullogne; W. M. Brady & Co., New York.

NOTES
1. Antoine Schnapper first proposed the attribution to Coypel in a notation he made on the mount of a faun drawing that is now in the Ashmolean Museum, Oxford; Eunice Williams, working independently, suggested the same attribution for the present drawing, another now in the National Gallery of Canada, Ottawa, and two others that were sold by Sotheby's in London on 17 March 1975, nos. 33, 34.

2. See Antoine Schnapper and H. Guicharnaud, *Louis de Boullogne. Cahiers du dessin français, no. 2* (Paris, 1987).

3. See Nicole Garnier, *Antoine Coypel (1661–1722)* (Paris, 1989), figs. 185–282, and especially figs. 195–198.

ANTOINE WATTEAU
1684–1721

The March of Silenus, c. 1715–1716
Red, black, and white chalks on brown
paper; verso, two shades of red chalk
6¹⁄₁₆ x 8¼ (15.4 x 21)

Gift of Mr. and Mrs. Paul Shepard
Morgan in Honor of Margaret Morgan
Grasselli

This extraordinarily boisterous drawing
represents a startling departure for Watteau,
whose great fame as a draftsman rests primarily on his exquisite drawings of graceful
ladies and gentlemen. The raucous subject
and correspondingly wild execution make
this drawing unique in his oeuvre, but his
authorship is indisputable, for the application of the chalks, even in this exuberant
idiom, matches exactly that of many of Watteau's more typical efforts in his favorite *trois-
crayons.*[1] Further, the rapidly sketched nudes
in the compositional jottings on the verso
are nearly identical in both form and execution to other such figures by Watteau,
including those in the National Gallery's own
drawing, *The Bower.*[2]

The key to this drawing's position in Watteau's work lies in the date of its execution,
c. 1715–1716. By that time Watteau had
mastered the *trois-crayons* technique and was
almost routinely turning out bravura studies
of great beauty. At the same time he was
experimenting with a number of history
subjects in both his paintings and his drawings, perhaps in search of a suitable idea for
his reception piece, the painting that would
earn him full membership in the French
Academy.[3] Normally the subject of his reception piece would have been assigned by
the director of the academy at the time of
his provisional admission in 1712. In a most
unusual departure from tradition, however,
the choice of subject had been left up to
Watteau himself. Silenus' drunken progress
may have been one of the ideas he considered and rejected.

In Greek mythology Silenus was a fat,
balding drunkard endowed with nearly en-
cyclopedic knowledge of both the past and
the future. He is said to have educated the
young Dionysus, god of wine, and is often
found in depictions of the god's retinue. He
is generally shown swaying drunkenly on an
ass or, as is the case in the present drawing,
supported by a band of carousing nymphs
and satyrs.

Watteau's composition was probably inspired by a painting that is now in the National Gallery, London, *The Triumph of
Silenus* by Peter Paul Rubens (1577–1640).[4]
Like his older contemporaries Antoine Coypel (1661–1722) and Charles de La Fosse
(1636–1716), Watteau greatly admired
Rubens' paintings and drawings, even to the
extent of making copies after many of them.
It was partly from studying Rubens' drawings, in fact, that Watteau learned the subtleties of combining red, black, and white
chalks in his own studies. The example of
La Fosse and Coypel, both skilled in the
trois-crayons technique, may also have influenced him to experiment with it. Indeed,
the figure at far left in Watteau's *Silenus* is
unusually close to La Fosse's style of drawing, especially in the way the flowing, multiple contours are used to search out the
form and establish the pose.

This exceptional drawing is a significant
addition to the National Gallery's collection
of French drawings not only because of
Watteau's established importance as one of
the great draftsmen of all time, but also because of this sheet's unique place within his
oeuvre. With its mythological subject, fu-
rious execution, and delightful verso sketches,
not to mention its allusions to the art of
both Rubens and La Fosse, this one highly
complex drawing expands the Gallery's representation of Watteau's art in several important new directions.

Margaret Morgan Grasselli

PROVENANCE
De Wailly collection (sale, Paris, 17–18 February
1853, no. 159); Baron Louis Auguste de Schwiter
(sale, Paris, 20–21 April 1883, no. 174); Henri
Michel-Lévy (sale, Paris, 12 May 1919, no. 135);
Mme. Piez, Paris; P. & D. Colnaghi, London,
1959; Private collection, England (sale, Monte
Carlo, Sotheby's, 12 February 1979, no. 51).

NOTES
1. One example is the *Couple Seated on a Bank*
from The Armand Hammer Collection, now on
deposit at the National Gallery. See *Watteau,
1684–1721* [exh. cat. National Gallery of Art]
(Washington, 1984), 151, where it is reproduced
in color. Comparison of the two drawings shows,
for example, that the black accents in the faces
and the thick, greasy quality of many of the red
chalk accents are closely identical, as are the character and quality of the white highlights.

2. The head study on the verso, which is executed in a red chalk of different hue and quality
from that used for the figure sketches, does not
appear to have been drawn by Watteau. *The Bower*
is reproduced in color in Washington 1984, 138.

3. History painting, which included mythological, biblical, allegorical, and historical subjects,
was the most highly regarded and prestigious of
all the genres of painting in France. Watteau finally decided against a history subject and was
admitted to the French Academy in 1717 as a
painter of *fêtes galantes*, a category that was invented especially for him.

4. Reproduced in Washington 1984, 211,
fig. 1.

JEAN-BAPTISTE OUDRY
1686–1755

Misse and Luttine, 1729
Oil on canvas
38⅜ x 57½ (97.5 x 146.1)

Promised Gift of
Mr. and Mrs. Eugene Victor Thaw

In 1729, when Jean-Baptiste Oudry signed and dated *Misse and Luttine*,[1] he was already one of the most sought after animal painters in France, having received his first commission from the king five years earlier. Before he settled into his niche as an artist of hunt scenes and animal fights he had painted an array of subjects. He had been apprenticed to the famed portraitist Nicolas Largillière (c. 1705/1707–1710/1712), but his forte did not seem to be in this genre.[2] Today he is still best known and appreciated as a draftsman and painter of animal subjects (the National Gallery has several important animal and bird drawings)[3] and a designer of royal hunt tapestries for both the Gobelins and the Beauvais tapestry factories, each of which he oversaw for some time.[4] His competitors in painting animals were François Desportes (1661–1743), today less known than Oudry to the American public, and Jean-Baptiste Chardin (1699–1779), who, interestingly, turned to this genre only late in Oudry's lifetime, perhaps to avoid a rivalry.

Although portraits of animals were known from at least the fifteenth century, Desportes and Oudry raised the genre to a level welcomed in the French Academy. *Misse and Luttine* are related to a group of portraits of dogs belonging to King Louis XV and destined as overdoors for the king's chambers and cabinet rooms at the royal chateau of Compiègne.[5] The hunting dogs were portrayed singly or in pairs against a landscape similar to that surrounding Compiègne. Each was identified in bold gilt letters. According to contemporary accounts, Oudry painted these on the orders of the king, who was so pleased that he had Oudry paint at least one portrait, that of *Misse and Turlo*, in his presence; twenty-five others were shown at court in 1726. More portraits followed, all destined for Compiègne where they were documented in 1732.

Misse and Luttine does not appear in the chateau's inventories, but it is certainly related to the Compiègne series. Misse, an English greyhound, is portrayed running to our left, in the opposite direction from the earlier portrait. The markings that continue around her flank show that she is the same dog in both pictures. Alongside Misse stands the black Gordon setter Luttine, another of the royal hunting dogs. As in the earlier painting the dogs are placed against an architectural and landscape background.

Typical of this period of the artist's career and unlike Desportes' realistic and dramatic portrayals, Oudry's dogs are perceived as decorative forms in a stagelike setting. In later years Oudry rejected this type of portrayal for simpler, more naturalistic forms approaching the sentimentality of Chardin. In fact *Misse and Luttine*, the National Gallery's first painting by Oudry, will be a fine counterpoint to our rich collection of Chardin genre paintings and will broaden our representation of this important current in eighteenth-century French painting.

Diane De Grazia

PROVENANCE
Peter Coats, London.

NOTES
1. The inscription on the socle reads "J.-B. Oudry / 1729."

2. On Oudry's life see Hal N. Opperman, *Jean-Baptiste Oudry*, 2 vols. (New York and London, 1977), with the appropriate bibliography; Hal Opperman, *J.-B. Oudry* [exh. cat. Kimbell Art Museum] (Fort Worth, 1983). On his close relationship with Largillière see Hal N. Opperman, "Largillière and His Pupil Jean-Baptiste Oudry," in Myra Nan Rosenfeld, *Largillière and the Eighteenth-Century Portrait* [exh. cat. The Montreal Museum of Fine Arts] (Montreal, 1981), 310–339. On our painting see Georges de Lastic, "Desportes et Oudry Peintres des chasses royales," *Connoisseur* 196:790 (December 1977), 293–294.

3. There are presently ten Oudry drawings in the collection from La Fontaine's *Fables* and Scarron's *Romain comique*.

4. On these activities see Opperman 1983, 54–62. Oudry followed the royal hunt to capture the immediacy of the events.

5. For complete information on the commission, provenance, and location of these paintings see Opperman 1983, 126–127.

MISSE   LVTTINE

GIOVANNI BATTISTA PIAZZETTA
1682–1754

Saint Stephen, 1738–1742
Black and white chalk on faded
blue paper
15⅞ x 13⅞ (40.4 x 35.4)

Promised Gift of
Mrs. Rudolf J. Heinemann

This outstanding and moving drawing is a highly characteristic work by the important eighteenth-century Venetian painter and draftsman Piazzetta. The artist made many such bust-length studies of men, women, and children, usually in black and white chalk as here. There are sheets of single figures, but also sometimes two or more figures are grouped. A number of these drawings were made for presentation to patrons, associates, or friends. Others were detailed studies for paintings, and still others were reproduced as engravings or mezzotints by various printmakers.

Saint Stephen is very similar to drawings used by Marco Pitteri for a series of engravings, *The Twelve Apostles,* although, in fact, it was never engraved.[1] It is, in any case, one of the most beautiful of all his works. Piazzetta has used the chalk in a softly painterly way to model the forms and to create brilliant white highlights, as on the figure's upturned eyes and the tip of his nose. Piazzetta often drew such figures from life, using ordinary people as models. Certainly *Saint Stephen* thoroughly convinces the viewer of his physical reality.

Stephen has traditionally been considered the first martyr for Christ, and he holds the martyr's palm and his attribute, a stone. He was chosen by the Apostles as a disciple after Christ's resurrection, and he was ultimately stoned to death for his preaching and faith (Acts 6–7). His somber and pleading expression conveys his supplication to God to forgive his executioners (Acts 7.60).

This is one of five bust-length figure studies being given to the National Gallery by Mrs. Heinemann. These join four drawings by the artist already in the collection, only one of which, *Boy with a Lute,* is comparable in type. Hence Piazzetta's representation is more than doubled and greatly strengthened by these splendid sheets.

H. Diane Russell

PROVENANCE
Rudolf J. Heinemann.

NOTE
1. See George Knox, *Piazzetta: A Tercentenary Exhibition of Drawings, Prints, and Books* [exh. cat. National Gallery of Art] (Washington, 1983), cat. 58.

GIOVANNI BATTISTA PIAZZETTA
1682–1754

Saint James Major, 1738–1742
Chalk on buff paper
15¾ x 13 (40.1 x 33.1)

Promised Gift of
Mrs. Rudolf J. Heinemann

This is another of the five outstanding drawings by Piazzetta being given to the Gallery by Mrs. Heinemann. As George Knox has pointed out, it is "one of the most notable" of the drawings of heads of apostles that were subsequently engraved by Marco Pitteri.[1] It is thought that the drawing was made as an independent work, however, rather than as preparatory to the engraving. Another version of the head, in a private collection, is closer in its details to the print.[2]

In the present drawing, James' visage is presented with great strength and intensity, his eyebrow, nose, mouth, and chin jutting out to the left. His forceful facial features contrast with the summary treatment of his hair, the hat he wears against his back, and his hand and the standard it holds. The vigor of the black chalk strokes, however, adds further to the effect of his fierce determination.

James, together with Peter and John, was favored by Christ to witness his transfiguration and agony in the garden of Gethsemane. He was also the first apostle to be martyred. The pilgrim's hat alludes to the story that James traveled to Spain to preach the gospel. During the Middle Ages, it was believed that his bodily relics were entombed at Santiago del Compostela, and the shrine became an enormously popular destination for Christian pilgrims.

H. Diane Russell

PROVENANCE
Rudolf J. Heinemann.

NOTES
1. See George Knox, *Piazzetta: A Tercentenary Exhibition of Drawings, Prints and Books* [exh. cat. National Gallery of Art] (Washington, 1983), cat. 57.

2. See *Drawings from the Collection of Lore and Rudolf Heinemann* [exh. cat. The Pierpont Morgan Library] (New York, 1973), cat. 33.

GIOVANNI BATTISTA TIEPOLO
1696–1770

Bacchus and Ariadne, c. 1744
Pen and brown ink, traces
of black chalk
8¹⁄₁₆ x 6¹⁵⁄₁₆ (20.5 x 17.5)

Gift of Mrs. Rudolf J. Heinemann

This is the ninth drawing by the Venetian master to enter the National Gallery's collection, but it is the first drawing by him that is a preparatory study for a painting. Hence, in addition to its pronounced beauty, it is a sheet of particular importance for the Gallery as it is the only example of this type by Tiepolo. George Knox has connected it with a ceiling fresco in one of the subsidiary rooms of the Palazzo Labia, Venice.[1]

Bacchus (or Dionysus), the Greek god of wine, discovered the mortal Ariadne, daughter of King Minos of Crete, on the island of Naxos, where she had been abandoned by her lover, Theseus. Most versions of the myth relate that Bacchus and Ariadne married and had four sons. The story was frequently depicted by Italian artists of the sixteenth through eighteenth centuries.

Between this drawing and the fresco, a number of changes are observable.[2] First, the drawing is vertical and the fresco is horizontally oriented within a curvilinear shape. Second, in the fresco Ariadne's head has been turned to the right, and her glance directed toward Bacchus. The putti, moreover, have been moved to the right, separated from the main figures; they seem to dance on a long leafy branch, one holding a bunch of grapes and the other a bowl. Bacchus' pose, by contrast, has been changed only slightly; his right leg has been turned to the right. The objects he holds in the drawing have been made clear: a crown of stars over Ariadne's head and a flagon of wine.

As in the Palazzo Labia's frescoes, this drawing demonstrates Giambattista's consummate artistic skill. With both freedom and dazzling virtuosity he has defined the human forms and clouds as well as their spatial relationships to each other and to the viewer, who seems to see the image from below. His deft use of washes, moreover, creates the effect of a celestial scene touched by bright sunlight, a worthy realm for Bacchus and for Ariadne, who was to become the constellation Corona Borealis.

H. Diane Russell

PROVENANCE
Sale, Paris, 11 December 1919; Birtschansky Collection, Paris; Probé Collection, Basel; Galerie Cailleux, Paris.

NOTES
1. Knox has further noted that the present drawing is especially close in its composition as well as its vertical format to a drawing for the same fresco in a New York private collection. See George Knox, *Tiepolo. A Bicentenary Exhibition, 1770–1790* [exh. cat. Fogg Art Museum, Harvard University] (Cambridge, 1970), cat. 36. He connected three other drawings with this project.

2. For the fresco, see Antonio Morassi, *A Complete Catalogue of the Paintings of G. B. Tiepolo* (London, 1962), 59 and fig. 265.

93

JOSEPH SEBASTIAN KLAUBER
c. 1700–1768
JOHANN BAPTIST KLAUBER
1712–1787

Historiae Biblicae Veteris et Novi Testamenti
Klauber, Augsburg, 1748
Bound volume with 100 etched illustrations
8½ x 13 (21.5 x 33)

Gift of Andrew Robison

During the eighteenth century Augsburg maintained the position it had achieved during the previous hundred years as a great center of print and book publishing, bringing forth some of the greatest graphic works of the German rococo.[1] It was primarily for religious art that the printmakers of Augsburg were known: sacred images printed on single sheets, in series, and as book illustrations. In Augsburg, as in the rest of central Europe at this time, there was a great passion for abundant ornament: a taste for extravagance that is as evident in printed art as it is in architectural decoration. An additional predilection for landscape and genre among Augsberg's extensive middle-class community led to the frequent inclusion of this type of motif within the context of sacred and decorative art.

One of Augsburg's important publishing houses was owned and operated by the brothers Joseph Sebastian and Johann Baptist Klauber.[2] One or both of them had been associated with the publisher Gottfried Bernhard Goetz before they established their own business around 1740. Typical of Augsburg printmakers and publishers, they produced a great number of ornamental sheets as well as illustrated series, such as the four seasons, elements, winds, and temperaments. They specialized, however, in religious subjects and were known as the Fratres Klauber Catholici. The work of the two brothers is so similar that it is difficult or impossible to identify which of them was responsible for any particular print; they both signed their works as "Klauber Catholici."

Among the many fine religious and devotional works that the Klaubers produced, their *Historiae Biblicae* is outstanding and considered one of the finest examples of eighteenth-century German book illustration. The volume consists of one hundred etched plates with Latin inscriptions, preceded by a title page printed in both Latin

and German that clearly announces its didactic purpose.[3] The work visually recounts the events of sacred history from the Creation to the advent of the heavenly city. The main scene represented on each page is set within a complex framework replete with details that amplify the central event like the marginalia of a medieval manuscript. This ancillary imagery includes further episodes from the narrative as well as related genre motifs. Each frame is designed specifically for its particular scene and no two are alike, proof of the wonderful fertility of the Klaubers' creative imagination.

For example, the representation of Samson destroying the temple of the Philistines is cleverly enframed by the building's collapsing ruins that form a proscenium in midair. Other events from the Book of Judges appear in the two lower corners. Toward the end of the volume the Klaubers created one of their most remarkable images to represent episodes in the life of Saint Peter. A view of Rome showing some of its greatest architectural monuments spreads across the page and is penetrated by a fantastic frame. This frame contains scenes of the imprisonment and martyrdom of Saint Peter, and it defines a stage-set interior space for Peter to occupy as he composes his epistles. The relationship of this interior space to the scene of Rome is ambiguous and somewhat disorienting. The frame wittily mimes the room with a make-believe dome on whimsical columns, but the continuity of space between the inner and outer realms is steadfastly maintained: are we witnessing a supernatural vision, as we might see in a rococo frescoed dome?

The National Gallery is steadily developing its fine though not yet comprehensive holdings of illustrated books as part of the graphic arts collection. This volume nicely complements others in the area of eighteenth-century German books. For exam-

ple, a recent acquisition is Johann Jacob-Scheuchzer's four-volume *Kupfer-Bibel*, another important monument of German biblical illustration published in Augsburg and Ulm between 1731 and 1735. Like the Klaubers' work this series presents its illustrations in elaborate frames filled with decorative motifs related to the central illustration; these framing devices do not, however, possess the highly inventive and playful spirit of those in the *Historiae Biblicae*. For this we must seek analogues in architectural decoration.

Virginia Tuttle Clayton

PROVENANCE
Grande Bibliothèque Ecole Libre, Nôtre Dame de Mont-Roland.

NOTES
1. On eighteenth-century book illustration in Augsburg, see Maria Lanckoronska and Richard Oehler, *Die Buchillustration des XVIII Jahrhunderts in Deutschland, Österreich und der Schweiz* (Frankfurt, 1932), 1:19–40.

2. Lanckoronska and Oehler 1932, 22–23.

3. It states that it is a picture book of Old and New Testament history that is intended to encourage easy instruction for children, revived memory in older people, swift recollection for preachers of the divine word, and useful and holy inquisitiveness in all.

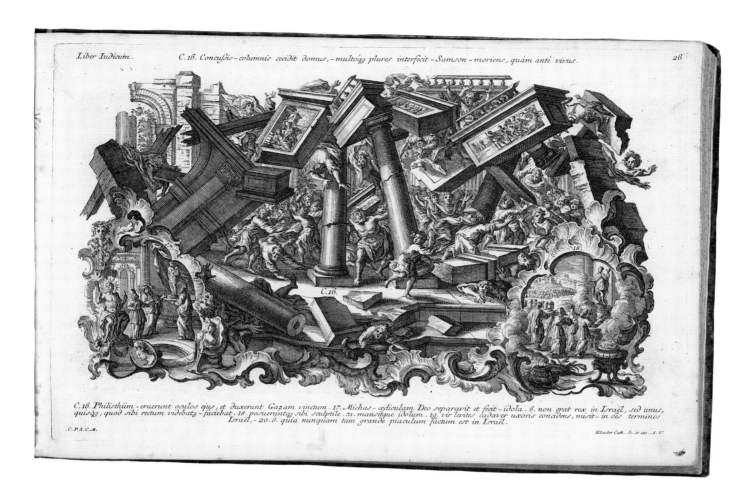

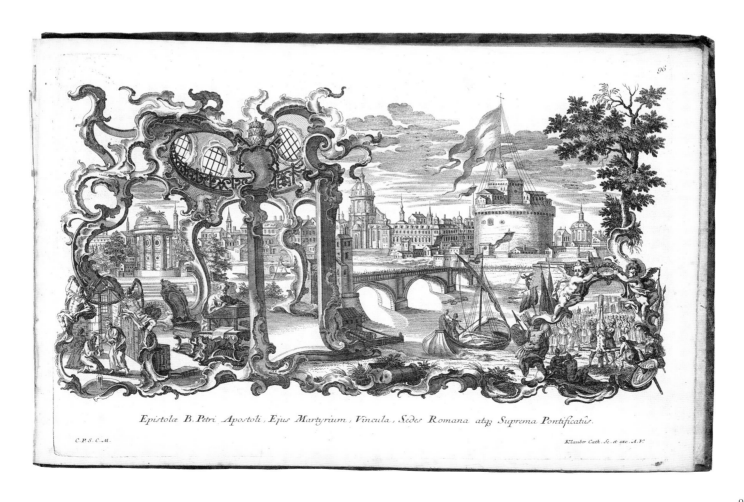

C.16. *Philisthüm - eruerunt oculos ejus, et duxerunt Gazam vinctum. 17. Michas - ædiculam Deo separavit et fecit - idola. 6. non erat rex in Israël, sed unus,*
quisq̃, quod sibi rectum videbatq̃ - faciebat. 18. posueruntq̃ sibi sculptile. 31. mansitque idolum. 19. vir levites cadaver uxoris concidens, misit - in oes terminos
Israël, - 20. 6. quia nunquam tam grande piaculum factum est in Israël.

C.P.S.C.M.   Klauber Cath. Sc. et exc. A.V.

Epistolæ B. Petri Apostoli, Ejus Martyrium, Vincula, Sedes Romana atq̃ Suprema Pontificatûs.

C.P.S.C.M.   Klauber Cath. Sc. et exc. A.V.

CANALETTO
1697–1768

Courtyard of the Palazzo Pisani
c. 1760
Pen, brown ink, and gray wash
18⅛ x 13⁷⁄₁₆ (45.9 x 34.1)

Gift of Robert H. and Clarice Smith

The Venetian painter, printmaker, and draftsman Canaletto is famous for his many views of Venice and the surrounding mainland. His style in all three media is marked by a devotion to brilliant effects of light and dark through which he evoked Venice's richly colorful environment.

Canaletto used a horizontal format for many of his works in order to render panoramic and sometimes spatially deep vistas. In the present drawing he chose a vertical format for an unusually intimate view, that of the inner courtyard of a palazzo. Such details as adults and children engaged in conversation, laundry baskets, a small dog, curtains flapping gently in the breeze, and a birdcage in the upper left window contribute to this casual intimacy. This is Venice and Venetians in a private everyday mode.

The principal building in the drawing has been known as the Palazzo Pisani, but it may be instead the east courtyard of the Procuratie Nuove or simply a *capriccio*, that is, a fanciful scene.[1] While the artist frequently recorded sites with great topographical accuracy, he also enjoyed creating imaginary places. He sometimes would combine parts of actual locales in inventive ways.

Canaletto's use of brown ink and gray wash is very characteristic of his finished drawings. With a deft use of the pen he has discreetly defined the forms suggested by the washes.

The National Gallery owns several fine paintings by the artist, as well as excellent impressions of his etched series, *Views of Venice*. This drawing, however, is only the second by Canaletto to enter the collection. The other sheet depicts Ascension Day festivities on the Grand Canal. Hence the present drawing forms a marvelous complement and contrast to that work, both in its setting and the mood it conveys.

H. Diane Russell

PROVENANCE
W. Mayor, London; J. P. Heseltine; Henry Oppenheimer; Duc de Tallyrand.

NOTE
1. See W. G. Constable, *Canaletto. Giovanni Antonio Canal, 1697–1768*, second ed., rev. by J. G. Links (Oxford, 1976), 2: no. 623.

HUBERT ROBERT
1733–1808

*The Oval Fountain in the Gardens of
the Villa d'Este, Tivoli,* 1760
Red chalk over graphite
12⅞ x 17¾ (32.7 x 45.1)

Gift (Partial and Promised) of
Mr. and Mrs. Neil Phillips and
Mr. and Mrs. Ivan Phillips

During the eleven years he spent in Italy from 1754–1765, nine of them as a special student at the French Academy in Rome, Hubert Robert devoted himself completely and passionately to studying and drawing the Italian countryside and the ruins and monuments of ancient Rome. With an unerring eye for picturesque juxtapositions of man-made and natural forms and an impeccable talent for seamlessly merging fantasy and reality, he created brilliant images of an idyllic world in which past and present coexist in perfect harmony.

The magnificent drawing presented by the Phillips brothers depicts with some artistic license (in the ornamental sculptures and the overall scale) the Oval Fountain in the private gardens of the Villa d'Este at Tivoli, about twenty miles east of Rome.[1] Tradition has it that Robert made this drawing during the summer of 1760 when his friend and fellow student Jean-Honoré Fragonard (1732–1806) and the wealthy *amateur* Jean-Claude-Richard, abbé de Saint-Non (1727–1791), with whom Robert had earlier traveled to Naples, spent several weeks at the villa. Although no written document attests to Robert's presence there that summer,[2] this drawing suggests that he did at least visit: the youthful vigor and delicate control of the chalk strokes, the brilliant patterning of light and shade, and the bold monumentality of the composition place the drawing squarely in 1760, the year Robert reached the height of his powers as a draftsman.

Indeed this superb drawing is one of Robert's greatest Italian landscape drawings, a nearly miraculous combination of virtuoso chalk work, dazzling light effects, and grandiose conception. Especially commanding is Robert's organization of the light, flooding in brightly from both sides and gently filtering through the tree boughs in the center. Equally admirable are the lively, infinitely varied chalk strokes, ranging from the vigorous, jagged lines that texture the cascading foliage to the delicate hatchings that evoke distant shadows suffused with light. Seemingly oblivious to their grand surroundings are the two washerwomen going about their business. Favorite motifs in many of Robert's landscapes, they here offer a witty contrast to the grandly formal figures of the sculptured women who seem to watch over them.

Robert rarely equaled and never surpassed the magnificence of the Phillips drawing, which thus becomes for the National Gallery both the greatest single example of his draftsmanship and one of the major masterpieces in the collection of French drawings.

Margaret Morgan Grasselli

PROVENANCE
Private collection, England; Wildenstein Gallery, New York, 1965.

NOTES
1. For photographs of the Oval Fountain as it looks today, see David R. Coffin, *The Villa d'Este at Tivoli* (Princeton, 1960), figs. 30, 31.

2. The information that Fragonard and Saint-Non were staying in Tivoli comes from Charles Natoire, director of the French Academy in Rome, in a letter of 27 August 1760 to the Marquis de Marigny: "M. the abbé de Saint-Non has been at Tivoli for the last month and a half with the *pensionnaire* Fragonard, painter." Robert is mentioned in the next paragraph as "also still doing very well" but in a way that suggests no link to the pair at Tivoli. See Anatole de Montaiglon and Jules Guiffrey, eds., *Corréspondance des Directeurs de L'Académie de France à Rome avec les Surintendants des Bâtiments*, vol. 11 (Paris, 1901), 354.

FRANCESCO ZUCCARELLI
1702–1788

Mountain Landscape with
Washerwomen and Fisherman, c. 1760s
Gouache
16 x 25 (40.7 x 63.5)

Gift of John Morton Morris

Zuccarelli, a prolific painter and draftsman, was born in Tuscany and trained in Florence and Rome. He was in Venice by about 1730, and he is usually associated with the Venetian landscape artists of the eighteenth century, owing to his specialization in pastoral scenes. These are especially close in style to those of Marco Ricci (1676–1729).[1] Zuccarelli later spent some fifteen years in England, where he was a founding member of the Royal Academy.

This large, handsome drawing is the first landscape by Zuccarelli to enter the collection. It is an exceptionally fine example of his Arcadian landscapes in which he stressed the simple and peaceful tasks and pleasures of country life.

Like most of his drawings this sheet is a work of art in its own right, not a preparatory study for a painting. Indeed, he has here employed the medium of gouache so as to stress the highly finished appearance of the scene. The fresh condition of the object suggests that it may have been kept in an album, although drawings of this type were sometimes framed and glazed in the eighteenth century.

Zuccarelli's landscape drawing, like many of his works, may be seen as a culminating point in the tradition of Italian pastoral scenes that originated in sixteenth-century Venetian art. As such it provides a fitting terminus to the National Gallery's increasingly significant holdings of Italian landscapes. These include such stellar sheets as Domenico Campagnola's *Landscape with Boy Fishing* (c. 1520), Annibale Carracci's *Landscape with Figures by an Estuary with Sailing Boats* (c. 1590–1595), another fiftieth anniversary gift, Guercino's *Landscape with a Waterfall*, and Marco Ricci's gouache *Stormy Landscape* (c. 1725).

At the same time, Zuccarelli's sojourn in England and the high regard in which his work has been held by British collectors and connoisseurs make this drawing a meaningful art historical link to our growing collection of eighteenth and nineteenth-century British landscape drawings.

H. Diane Russell

PROVENANCE
English private collection.

NOTE
1. See, for example, the remarks by Marco Chiarini, *Mostra di disegni Italiani di paessaggio del seicento e del settecento* [exh. cat. Gabinetto disegni e stampe degli Uffizi, XXXVIII] (Florence, 1973), cats. 94–95.

ROBERT ADAM
1728–1792

*A Design for Illuminations to Celebrate
the Birthday of King George III,* 1763
Watercolor over pencil
heightened with white
16½ x 22¾ (42 x 57.5)

Anonymous Gift

George III became king of England in 1760 and was married the following year. Seeking more room than was available in crowded St. James's Palace, in 1761 he acquired Buckingham House. Two years later his wife commissioned Robert Adam, who had recently been appointed one of the Architects of the King's Works, to design a fanciful temporary structure in the garden behind Buckingham House in honor of the king's twenty-fifth birthday.[1] The framework, which was rapidly completed with the aid of stage carpenters, was placed just outside the house's windows and was designed to be illuminated at night. Painted transparencies lit from behind were placed in three arches. The king was kept diverted at the palace from Saturday, 4 June, his birthday, until the following Monday. When he was taken to Buckingham House that night, he was completely surprised by the apparition that greeted him as the shutters were thrown open. According to one source, he was "much affected by this tribute of wifely and loyal devotion."[2]

This watercolor, long attributed to the French architect and draftsman Charles-Louis Clérisseau (based on an inscription by a later hand on the verso), is now believed to be by Adam himself.[3] The design apparently represents Adam's full intentions for the project and closely follows a meticulous elevation drawing still in the royal collection.[4] Apparently a much reduced version was actually executed, perhaps because of the constraints of time. Only the three arched pa-vilions with the illuminated transparencies were built, and they were joined not by elaborate arcades but by the standing sculptures first designed as roof ornaments.[5] However, when Adam and his brother James prepared the illustrations for the first volume of their ambitious publication, *Works in Architecture,* they chose to portray the complete design, no doubt proud of the wonderful architectural fantasy as originally conceived.[6]

Robert Adam, one of Britain's greatest and most influential architects, was born in Edinburgh, Scotland, in 1728.[7] After several years of successful architectural practice in Edinburgh, he went to Italy in 1754, where he remained for three years. While there Adam came under the spell of the two men he considered his greatest mentors, Clérisseau and the Venetian artist Giovanni Battista Piranesi. When Adam returned to London in January 1858 he quickly established himself as an architect of note. He and his brother were the dominant forces in British architecture for much of the next thirty years.

The Gallery's collection includes only one other work by Adam, a watercolor entitled *River Landscape with a Castle.* The present example, with its wealth of architectural detail and its charming evocation of a particularly interesting and unusual incident in Adam's career, is an especially welcome addition. It also comes with a distinguished provenance, having been owned by the great collector of British watercolors, J. Leslie Wright.[8]

Franklin Kelly

PROVENANCE
J. Leslie Wright, acquired 1936; by descent to Mrs. Cecil Keith; sold Sotheby's, London, 27 April 1988, no. 416; John Davidson.

NOTES
1. Details of the commission are given in Arthur T. Bolton, *The Architecture of Robert and James Adam* (London, 1922), 1:48–49, and A. P. Oppé, *English Drawings; Stuart and Georgian Periods; in the Collection of His Majesty the King at Windsor Castle* (London, 1950), 22.

2. Bolton 1922, 49.

3. See Oppé 1950, 22; the figures were ascribed to Antonio Zucchi. The watercolor was sold at Sotheby's, London (*English Drawings and Victorian Watercolours; Architectural Drawings and Watercolours,* 27 April 1988, no. 417) as by Robert Adam.

4. Oppé 1950, no. 18, plate 25.

5. Sotheby's 1988, no. 416. The captions and texts for nos. 416 and 417 are reversed in the catalogue.

6. See the engraving by D. Cunego in *The Works in Architecture of Robert and James Adam,* vol. 1, pt. 5 (London, 1778; reprint ed. London, 1931), plate 5, which has the following inscription: "Original Design of an Illumination and Transparency part of which was executed by Command of the Queen in June 1762 [sic], In Honor of His Majesty's Birthday."

7. Alistair Rowan, *Robert Adam* (London, 1988), 11–22.

8. See *Masters of British Water-Colour (17th–19th Centuries): Exhibition of the J. Leslie Wright Collection* [exh. cat. Royal Academy of Arts] (London, 1949).

GIOVANNI BATTISTA PIRANESI
1720–1778

Prospettiva della Scala . . . , 1764
Etching and engraving
$16\frac{1}{16}$ x $11\frac{11}{16}$ (40.8 x 29.6)

Promised Gift of
Arthur and Charlotte Vershbow

In his published prints and books Piranesi spared no costs. He created luxuriously scaled works on the very best paper, appropriate homage to what he saw as the magnificence of Roman architecture. But when it came to artistic work not for public display, his private frugality took over.

Sufficient examples survive for us to surmise that Piranesi made large preparatory drawings for most if not all his large *vedute*, both those in his most famous series, *Vedute di Roma*, and those included in his archaeological books of the 1750s and 1760s. However, extremely few survive. Further, like any good printmaker, Piranesi printed proofs as he was completing a plate to decide whether to make further artistic changes, or to consider it finished and engrave his signature and caption. Likewise, few survive of these fascinating proofs before the letters, which show his artistic progress and decisions. In general, preparatory drawings and artists' proofs were intently prized and avidly collected by his contemporaries, especially the French; but Piranesi must have considered his to be simply unfinished and private works, so he cut them up to use the blank backs as scrap paper. We find such fragments of proofs and drawings as well as spoiled prints on the versos of many of his smaller drawings, especially his studies for his *Camini* series and his figure drawings, as with the fine example given by Kate Ganz in honor of the fiftieth anniversary and also in this volume.

Of all Piranesi's 135 etchings in the *Vedute di Roma*, his largest and most popular series, of which proof impressions would be most likely to be preserved, it appears that only thirteen proofs before the letters survive intact. And of the hundreds of different prints in his archaeological books, including many large *vedute*, the present gift from the Vershbows appears to be one of only two proofs still intact.[1] Undoubtedly this proof survives only because it was itself printed on the verso of a proof page from an archaeological text, so there was no gain in cutting it up for scrap paper.

This etching became plate XIV in Piranesi's book on the *Antichità d'Albano e di Castel Gandolfo* (Rome, 1764). The series was dedicated to Pope Clement XIII, who maintained his summer residence at Castel Gandolfo and had become interested in Piranesi's research and publications on the outlet and the grottoes of Lake Albano. The book considers and magnificently portrays various types of Roman antiquities in the vicinity. The present plate is a perspective view of the staircase leading down into a large underground cistern, which was used in antiquity to supply a neighboring barracks for Roman soldiers. Comparison between this artist's proof and a regular impression shows that Piranesi added not only the caption, signature, plate number, and a dozen reference letters scattered throughout the image, but also reworked the plate at the top with patterns of heavy engraved parallel hatching to darken the foreground, emphasize the curvature of the vault, and further variegate the patterns of light and shade.

This etching illustrates how for Piranesi, even in his technical publications, there was no such thing as a perfunctory explanatory plate. When he designed formal plans they were elegantly laid out in collages of trompe-l'oeil scrolls. When he wanted to give a sense of the appearance of a structure, a classical *prospettiva* to explain a complicated corner of his ground plan, then he could not neglect the variety of materials and textures, or the grandeur of ancient Roman construction, but produced this view rakishly composed to reveal the magnificence of the ancients' work, bathed in the light of Italian sun as it penetrates the haze of the underground ruins picturesquely corroded by humidity and vegetation.

Andrew Robison

PROVENANCE
Inscribed as from Karl & Faber, Munich, 13 May 1955, item 324; Private Collection; P. & D. Colnaghi, London; Arthur and Charlotte Vershbow, Boston.

NOTE
1. The other is a proof of plate V of the series on the Aqua Giulia, preserved on the verso of a large drawing in Berlin. See Sabine Jacob, *Italienische Zeichnungen der Kunstbibliothek Berlin* (Berlin, 1975), no. 872.

GIOVANNI BATTISTA PIRANESI
1720–1778

Young Man With a Staff, c. 1765
Pen and brown ink with brown wash
6¼ x 4⅛ (15.9 x 10.5)

Gift of Kate Ganz

This *Young Man* shows the fire and dash of Piranesi's figure drawings, which have long been admired by connoisseurs. Piranesi's figures represent his lifelong fascination with capturing the stance and movement and gestures of human beings. He virtually never used these drawings—as other Italian artists did—as direct models or studies for inclusion in larger compositions, or for sale or presentation. Instead, they were for more private purposes, perhaps a kind of continued training so he could spontaneously create different but convincing figures in his compositions, or perhaps a straightforward personal reaction to the people he saw and a desire to record them.

Piranesi drew very few nudes, and his work shows virtually no evidence of his having used professional artists' models. His figures are tortured, twisting, ragged, gesticulating, hunchbacked. Their subjects include a wide catalogue of street types, which Piranesi would naturally have seen in Rome, but extremely few of the more refined and elegant types of acquaintances that we know he did have. After the 1750s Piranesi's figures also included numerous studies of dressed young men standing or working at counters. These have frequently and plausibly been thought to be helpers in his own printing and publishing establishment, set up in 1761.

The present *Young Man* is dressed in working-class garments, carrying a pouch or large wallet at his belt and holding a long staff. It is striking how much this particular figure recalls the classical pose of a professional studio model—one foot raised and body steadied by holding a model's pole or a suspended rope. However, given the overwhelming consistency of Piranesi's other figures, this is most likely a notable accident. This is surely a young man of the streets beginning to ascend a staircase, turning back to see something that has drawn his attention. Barely visible at the bottom right is an earlier drawing, one of Piranesi's unusual nude studies, here of a man's thigh, knee,

and shin, which the artist erased before beginning the present work.

This standing figure shows distinctive stylistic characteristics in its multiple bands of zig-zag hatching of irregularly differing widths and lengths and directions, created with a fairly thin nib, combined with much thicker strokes that accentuate crucial outlines or forms. In addition to the morphology of the figure, these characteristics of pen work closely associate this drawing with a standing man in the Gemeentemuseum, Amsterdam[1]; a kneeling (praying?) man currently at Artemis, London[2]; and a sheet of three figures in the Ecole des Beaux-Arts, Paris.[3] The fragments of a drawing and of a print on the verso of two of these can both be dated to 1764, suggesting the rectos date soon afterward. The present figure drawing is also on the back of a fragment of a print, specifically a section from the bottom right of Piranesi's *Antichità Romane*, vol. 3, plate XLIX. However, comparison with impressions in two different copies of the *Antichità Romane* in the National Gallery, one datable c. 1757 and one c. 1770, shows the impression in this fragment closer to the latter. A dating of these four drawings in the mid-1760s is confirmed by the similar stylistic characteristics of pen work in Piranesi's signed and precisely dated architectural fantasy (31 December 1765) now in the National Gallery of Art (1986.32.1), as well as in many of the preparatory drawings and drawings directly related to his *Camini* etchings,[4] which we know were at least partially finished and printed by 1767.[5]

A most unusual characteristic of this *Young Man* is its touches of golden brown wash. Though Piranesi did use wash in his multi-figured compositions drawn in the 1740s, subsequently he used only pure chalk or pure pen for figure drawings. The capturing of light and modeling of form with touches of wash does occur rather similarly on the standing figures included in one of Piranesi's large preparatory drawings for the architec-

tural fantasies of his *Parere* dating c. 1766.[6] However, the present *Young Man* is the only case I know of this extra care by the artist in a single figure study. Its brio and its distinctive features thus make this drawing a particularly welcome addition to the works by an artist the National Gallery has made a special attempt to collect in depth.

Andrew Robison

NOTES

1. Ben Koevoets, *Oude Tekeningen in het Bezit van de Gemeentemusea van Amsterdam . . .* (Amsterdam, 1976), no. 34a.

2. Pen and brown ink; 15.2 x 12.7; ex coll. JPH.

3. Hylton Thomas, *The Drawings of Giovanni Battista Piranesi* (London, 1954), no. 74.

4. See for instance Sabine Jacob, *Italienische Zeichnungen der Kunstbibliothek Berlin* (Berlin, 1975), nos. 871–898; and Felice Stampfle, *Giovanni Battista Piranesi: Drawings in the Pierpont Morgan Library* (New York, 1978), nos. 59–100, and especially nos. 66–68 and 61 (which also has touches of wash).

5. Robert O. Parks, *Piranesi* (Northampton, Mass., 1961), 36.

6. Now at David Tunick, Inc., New York; formerly Christie's, *Old Master Drawings* (London, 1989), no. 104.

FRANZ EDMUND WEIROTTER
1733–1771

Weathered Boulders, c. 1769
Red chalk
12⁵⁄₁₆ x 11¹¹⁄₁₆ (31.5 x 29.5)

Gift (Partial and Promised) of
Andrew Robison

Known principally for his numerous land-scape prints and drawings, Weirotter's most common subjects are charming country scenes and broad panoramic views, usually executed in ink and wash. Toward the end of his short life, however, he made more personal drawings from nature, monumental chalk studies of isolated rocks and vegetation. These remarkable drawings, including the great pile of boulders presented here, rank among his most memorable works.

Having trained as a landscape painter in his native Austria, Weirotter settled in Paris in 1759. There he came under the influence of Johann Georg Wille (1715–1808), a German engraver and draftsman who introduced Weirotter to drawing from nature and occasionally took him on sketching expeditions with other young artists into the French countryside.[1] A trip to Italy in 1763–1764 confirmed Weirotter's devotion to drawing in the open air. He continued the practice as professor of landscape drawing at the Kupferstecherakademie in Vienna from 1767 until his death in 1771, frequently accompanying his students into the Austrian countryside.

This grand drawing, together with several similar sheets in the Akademie der Bilden-den Künste, Vienna,[2] and a study of a waterfall in the British Museum,[3] attests in the most remarkable way to Weirotter's intense study of isolated corners of nature. As *Weathered Boulders* shows, he sought to cap-ture not only the picturesque qualities of his subject, but also the rocks' massive weight and scarred surfaces.

Weirotter's choice of red chalk for this and other nature studies certainly stemmed from his years in France and reflects especially his knowledge of the drawings of Hubert Robert (1733–1808) and Jean-Honoré Fragonard (1732–1806). But the strokes that Weirotter used to carve out the huge, weather-beaten rocks are very different from the Frenchmen's more refined hatchings and calligraphy. While Weirotter comes closest to the French in the patterns of his occasional grasses and plants, the substance of his drawing is the more irregular, forceful, and repeated strokes that capture the rough edges and crevices of the boulders. He shares the widespread eighteenth-century love for brilliant and broken light, but is distinctive in focusing on the strength and power of the natural forms. Weirotter's drawing, moreover, shows no clear human presence but presents its subject in splendid isolation.

During the last decade, the National Gallery's collection of eighteenth-century German and central European drawings has grown steadily and is now one of the strongest in the United States. This splendid Weirotter, his first to enter the collection, becomes the best landscape drawing in this category while adding impressive weight and dimension to that important group.

Margaret Morgan Grasselli

PROVENANCE
Kurt Meissner, Zurich.

NOTES
1. Wille described two sketching expeditions with Weirotter and other young artists in his diary, 14–22 September 1761 and 8 September 1765. Georges Duplessis, ed., *Mémoires et Journal de J.-G. Wille, Graveur du Roi*, vol. 1 (Paris, 1857), 178–179, 300.

2. Thomas DaCosta Kaufmann has noted similarities with inv. nos. 4769, 9929, 9931, and 15711. See *Central European Drawings 1680–1800, A Selection from American Collections* [exh. cat. The Art Museum] (Princeton, 1989), 246, n. 2.

3. Black and white chalk on gray-blue paper; inscribed *Wasserfall in den Steyermärkischen Gebürgen/nach der Natur gezeichet (sic) von Weirotter. 1769*. Inv. no. 0.0.4.1; Gernsheim 29153.

GEORGE STUBBS
1724–1806

White Poodle in a Punt, c. 1780
Oil on canvas
50 x 40 (127 x 101.5)

Promised Gift of Paul Mellon

Known in his lifetime primarily as a horse painter, George Stubbs is now considered one of England's great masters. Essentially self-taught, at an early age Stubbs showed an ability for and an interest in depicting anatomy, which culminated in his ten-year study and publication in 1766 of *The Anatomy of a Horse.* However, Stubbs considered himself an artist, not a scientist, signing the title page of his *Anatomy* "George Stubbs, Painter."[1] He developed a reputation in the 1760s for painting horses, but he also turned his keen powers of observation upon men and women, wild and domestic animals, conversational groups, and scenes of hunting, racing, and shooting.

Long an essential element of English country life, dogs had frequently been painted by Stubbs as part of larger scenes, often being used as clever design links in compositions, as in *Lord Torrington's Hunt Servants Setting out from Southill, Bedfordshire,* c. 1765–1768, and *John and Sophia Musters Riding at Colwick Hall,* 1777.[2] Stubbs portrayed dogs, horses, and human beings with equal sympathy and equal distinction. His individual dog portraits reveal the same attention to detail, understanding of the subject, and even intellectual curiosity as do his great portraits of horses.

Now considered companion dogs, poodles were originally bred as water dogs, outstanding retrievers of game. *White Poodle in a Punt* has been characterized as not a dog at work, but perhaps a dog going to work.[3] The poodle is balanced in a punt, confident in his task, and ready to jump in the water at any moment. Stubbs captured the woolly texture of the dog's coat and the wet feel of his soft, pinkish nose. He has also sensitively depicted the psychology of the moment, where, gazing out at the spectator instead of in a more neutral profile view,[4] the dog

is mindful of his unsteady position on a floating object. The *Poodle* has been dated in the past from the 1760s to around 1800. Scholars now date it to around 1780 because of its close similarity to *Water Spaniel,* dated 1778, also in the collection of Paul Mellon, and because the artist often used the weeping willow tree as background in paintings of that date.[5]

White Poodle in a Punt is only the second Stubbs painting in the Gallery's British collection, joining *Captain Pocklington with His Wife Pleasance (?) and His Sister Frances,* 1769. The Mellon gift exemplifies Stubbs' great achievement, which lay in his sympathetic portrayal of the inner nature of animals combined with an anatomist's attention to their exact physical appearance.

Gretchen A. Hirschauer

PROVENANCE
Mrs. Esme Smyth, Ashton Hall, near Bristol, Somerset; Lord de Mauley, sold Christie's 8 July 1949, lot 131, bought F. T. Sabin; 21st Earl of Shrewsbury and Waterford, Ingestre Hall, Staffordshire, 1951, sold Sotheby's 23 March 1960 (lot 63), bought Colnaghi for Paul Mellon.

NOTES
1. Judy Egerton, *George Stubbs 1724–1806* [exh. cat. Tate Gallery] (London, 1984), 31.

2. Both paintings are in private collections. See London 1984, cats. 46 and 116.

3. Venetia Morrison, *The Art of George Stubbs* (Seacaucus, N.J., 1989), 154.

4. Robert Rosenblum, *The Dog in Art from Rococo to Post-Modernism* (New York, 1988), 24.

5. London 1984, cat. 97; and for a discussion of the dating of the *Brown and White Norfolk or Water Spaniel,* see cat. 101.

JOHN HOPPNER
1758–1810

Portrait of Miss Frances Beresford
c. 1784–1785
Chalks on tinted paper
Oval, 9⅝ x 7⅝ (24.5 x 19.4)

Gift of the Leger Galleries, London

John Hoppner was one of the most successful English portrait painters of the late eighteenth century and one of the last to work in the grand tradition established by Sir Joshua Reynolds. His mother was a German attendant at the court of George II and it was widely rumored in Hoppner's lifetime that George III, who came to the throne in 1760, was his father. Although this was apparently not the case, the artist did little to dispel the belief and was, in fact, greatly liked by the king during his youth. Supported by a royal annuity Hoppner began formal study of art at the Royal Academy in 1775. In 1780 two of his works were accepted for the academy's annual exhibition, and by the time he was in his mid-twenties he was steadily attracting commissions.[1]

In 1781 Hoppner married Phoebe Wright, daughter of the well-know American artist Patience Wright. The elder Wright had left America during the Revolution, bringing her family to London, where her wax figures and busts of famous individuals became much admired. Unfortunately, Hoppner's marriage led to a fall from the king's favor. It is traditionally said that the king objected because his consent had not been asked, but more likely he disapproved of the bride's mother, who had spied for the Americans during the war. In any event, Hoppner quickly recovered from the blow. He and his wife moved to a grand home on St. James's Square, fitted it with an elegant gallery and studio, and were soon well-established members of London's artistic community.

Hoppner was not inclined toward stylistic innovation, preferring instead to assimilate the most successful elements of the works of other artists such as Reynolds, Thomas Gainsborough, and George Romney. In 1793 he was appointed Portrait Painter to the Prince of Wales, which caused great demand for his work among members of the fashionable circles around the prince.

Hoppner's chief competitor was the younger Sir Thomas Lawrence, with whom he carried on a long and highly public rivalry. Lawrence's appointment in 1791 as Portrait Painter to George III was a source of great personal frustration for Hoppner, who never succeeded in regaining the king's favor.

Hoppner created many of his finest works in the 1780s, and he was at his best in painting women and children.[2] Around 1784 he received a commission to paint portraits of the four daughters of Francis Beresford of Ashbourne, Derbyshire. In addition to the resulting oil paintings, Hoppner executed this lovely chalk drawing of Frances (1763–1831).[3] The second eldest daughter, she would have been about twenty-one when she sat for the artist. In the oil portrait she is shown in similar costume, but seated in a landscape and turned at an angle to the picture plane.[4] The painting is a conventional example of Hoppner's portrait style, but has a slight sense of stiffness and formality and some incongruity between the figure and the landscape setting. The drawing gives quite a different impression. Although fully worked and clearly conceived as a finished portrait in its own right, it has an appealing air of informality. Frances seems more relaxed as she sits on a red chair in front of a red drape with her hands crossed in her lap, her head slightly tilted. Her eyes gaze out at us with just a hint of wistfulness.[5] There is a sense of the momentary and the fleeting, both in the informality of the pose and in Hoppner's lively and quick strokes of chalk that animate the surface of the sheet.

There are several major oils by Hoppner and a number of reproductive prints after his work in the Gallery's collection, but the only other drawing is a more formal and more tightly worked male portrait. *Portrait of Miss Frances Beresford* is thus an especially welcome addition to the collection, representing a less familiar but engaging side of Hoppner's accomplishments.

Franklin Kelly

PROVENANCE
Selina Beresford (younger sister of the sitter); Her husband, Reverend Samuel Martin; Their son, Major William Martin; Their daughter, Miss Martin; Her brother, Marcus Trevelyan Martin, 1905; Leger Galleries, London.

NOTES
1. The best source of information on Hoppner's life and art remains William McKay and W. Roberts, *John Hoppner, R.A.* (London, 1909), which also includes a catalogue raisonné.

2. Ellis Waterhouse, *Painting in Britain, 1530 to 1790* (Baltimore, 1953), 226.

3. For these paintings see McKay and Roberts 1909, 21–22, 165.

4. The painting is reproduced in McKay and Roberts 1909, facing page 24.

5. In McKay and Roberts 1909, 21, it is stated that the drawing was done "for" the painting, but, given their completely different formats, that was clearly not the case.

HENRI ROLAND LANCELOT TURPIN DE CRISSÉ
1754–before 1800

*A View through a High Arch
in Tivoli,* c. 1775–1780
Black chalk
16¹³⁄₁₆ x 11⁷⁄₁₆ (42.8 x 29)

Gift of the Galerie Cailleux, Paris

The author of this striking view through a foreground arch was the talented young marquis de Turpin, a career soldier whose skill as an artist earned him an honorary membership in the French Academy in 1785. This handsome drawing, like so many of Turpin's views,[1] is dominated by tall architectural forms whose monumental scale is dramatically enhanced by both the artist's low viewpoint and the diminutive size of the charming figures that populate the scene.

Other than such momentous events as his election to the French Academy in 1785 and his participation in the Salon of 1787, the details of Turpin's activities as an amateur artist remain obscure. Some information about his training and development can be deduced from his drawings, however. For example, as the present drawing shows, Turpin must have been intimately familiar with the art of Hubert Robert (1733–1808), to the extent that he may even have studied with Robert in Paris. The intensely focused sunlight, the vigorously hatched shadows, the wiry sprigs of foliage, and especially the tiny figures with round heads all evoke Robert's work. Further, Turpin's many views in and around Rome, some bearing abbreviated inscriptions noting the location, indicate that he made at least one trip to Italy,[2] though the specific dates are unknown. Presumably he traveled there when he was still quite young, before he joined the military. In that case most of his Italian views, including the sheet presented here, would have been made in the mid-1770s.

One of the two paintings Turpin exhibited in the Salon of 1787, the only known public exhibition of his work, was a vertical composition representing *Les Portiques d'une rue de Tivoli,* a title that seems to correspond exactly to the scene in the Cailleux drawing. Since Turpin also exhibited "several drawings made from nature in Rome and its environs," it is tempting to speculate that this grand drawing was not only a study for the exhibited painting, but was also itself included in the Salon. It would then have been one of the remarkable group of works by Turpin that were briefly mistaken for the work of Robert by more that one connoisseur.[3]

As an excellent example of Turpin de Crissé's art and one of the very few outside France, this impressive drawing is a most welcome addition to the National Gallery's collection. The fact that Turpin fled France during the revolution and ended his days here in the fledgling United States adds to its importance for the Gallery and makes it even more appropriate for the collection.

Margaret Morgan Grasselli

PROVENANCE
Paul Prouté, Paris, 1981; Private collection.

NOTES
1. More than 150 of Turpin's drawings are conserved in the Musée Turpin de Crissé, Angers, many bearing the same red stamp as this sheet, *M.T.O.* in a triangle. Although the stamp's origin and meaning remain unknown, it was presumably applied by a family member since the Angers drawings came directly from Turpin's son, Count Lancelot Théodore Turpin de Crissé (1782–1859). All of the drawings were mistakenly attributed for many years to the son, who was also an artist; two were included under the son's name in *The Finest Drawings from the Museums of Angers* [exh. cat. Heim Gallery] (London, 1977), nos. 93, 94.

2. The partially trimmed initials *L. T.* at the bottom of the Cailleux drawing may originally have been followed by an *R,* the top of which is still visible. That shorthand notation is sometimes found on the drawings Turpin made in and around Rome.

3. Baron F. M. de Grimm noted in reference to Turpin's two exhibited paintings that "some practiced eyes were tempted to think them by Robert." See M. Tourneux, ed., *Corréspondance littéraire, philosophique* (Paris, 1881), 15:148. One of those who was fooled was Count Stanislas Potocki, who wrote a critique of the Salon. See M. E. Zoltowska, "Stanislas Kostka Potocki, David, Denon et le Salon de 1787, ou la première critique d'art écrite par un polonais," *Antemurale* 24 (1980), 9–65.

PIERRE-FRANÇOIS BASAN
1723–1797

Dictionnaire des graveurs anciens et modernes
Basan, Paris, 1789
Two volumes with etchings and engravings by various artists
7½ x 4⅝ (19.1 x 11.8)

Promised Gift of Andrew Robison

The eighteenth century witnessed a great rise in print collecting and writing about prints, particularly in France. This taste was initiated at the beginning of the century by the Parisian dealer and publisher Jean Pierre Mariette (1634–1716) who had formed an impressive private collection of graphic arts. By mid-century there were many collectors in Paris eager to learn about and purchase prints. With the proliferation of these collectors and dealers grew an increasing number of manuals, treatises, histories, and catalogues exclusively devoted to printmaking and printmakers.[1] To this body of literature belongs Pierre-François Basan's *Dictionnaire des graveurs anciens et modernes*. Printed in two volumes, the dictionary of printmakers was first published unillustrated in 1767, with a second, illustrated edition appearing in 1789. A third edition was published in 1809.

Basan began his career as a reproductive engraver. In about 1776 he turned to print collecting and dealing, later professing in his own biography in the *Dictionnaire* that he had "too lively a character for engraving." As a dealer Basan had one of the largest businesses in Paris. However, his most lasting contribution to the field of prints is his *Dictionnaire*. Andrew Robison's superb copy is from the illustrated edition of 1789, which contains additions and corrections to the first publication. More important, however, it is illustrated with actual impressions from the original plates Basan had gathered from many sources with the intention of providing prints to exemplify the work of artists he discussed in his text. Among the prints are examples by seventeenth-century artists whose work found particular favor in eighteenth-century France, including etchings by the Dutch artists Rembrandt van Rijn, Jan Lievens, Joris van Vliet, Adriaen van Os-

tade, Cornelis Bega, Pieter van Laer, and Anthonie Waterloo; by the Italian artists Giovanni Benedetto Castiglione and Stefano Della Bella; and by the French printmaker Pierre Brebiette. Basan's dictionary is also noted for its inclusion of prints by eighteenth-century etchers and engravers, especially the French, such as Augustin de St. Aubin, Charles Eisen, Charles-Nicolas Cochin *fils*, and Noel Le Mire as well as the Viennese Franz Edmund Weirotter (see Weirotter's fine red chalk drawing *Weathered Boulders* in this volume).

The present copy of the *Dictionnaire* is unique. It was owned by a contemporary amateur printmaker, Jules-Armand-Guillaume Bouchier,[2] who had the volumes bound with interleaves on which he meticulously added manuscript notes on additional prints and printmakers. His annotations, which range in date from the 1790s to 1824, attest to a wide knowledge of printmaking as they include contemporary artists outside France, such as the British Paul Sandby and the German Raphael Morghen. Quite amusing is Bouchier's penned remark *hic* (or "here") near his own entry in which he also corrected one of the initials of his name.

Basan's *Dictionnaire*, a product of the French Enlightenment in general and the *encyclopédique* tradition in particular, remains an important reference tool for the twentieth-century scholar. The library of the

National Gallery has a copy of the 1767 edition; this is the first illustrated edition to enter the Gallery. The Basan *Dictionnaire* joins its nineteenth-century British counterpart, a unique set of seven specially bound volumes of Michael Bryan's *A Biographical and Critical Dictionary of Painters and Engravers* (originally published in London in 1858 with supplements by Henry Ottley appearing in 1866). Bequeathed to the Gallery by Lessing J. Rosenwald in 1980, that set contains over 1,400 original prints, hand-tipped into each volume, as illustrations for selected artists.

Gregory Jecmen

PROVENANCE
J.A.G. Bouchier; F. de Nobele, Paris.

NOTES
1. See Jean Adhémar, *Graphic Art of the 18th Century* (New York, 1964), 230–234; George Levitine, "French Eighteenth-Century Printmaking in Search of Cultural Assertion," in *Regency to Empire: French Printmaking, 1715–1814* [exh. cat. The Baltimore Museum of Art and The Minneapolis Institute of Arts] (Minneapolis, 1984), 10–21.

2. For additional biographies of Bouchier see: Ulrich Thieme and Felix Becker, *Allgemeines Lexikon der bildenden Künstler* (Leipzig, 1910), 4:433; and Frits Lugt, *Les marques de collections de dessins et d'estampes* (Amsterdam, 1921), under no. 284.

DES GRAVEURS. 91
BOUCHIER, (J. A. 9.) amateur né en Provence, a gravé pour fon amufement, en 1786, plufieurs petites têtes & payfages, d'après *Rubens* &c.

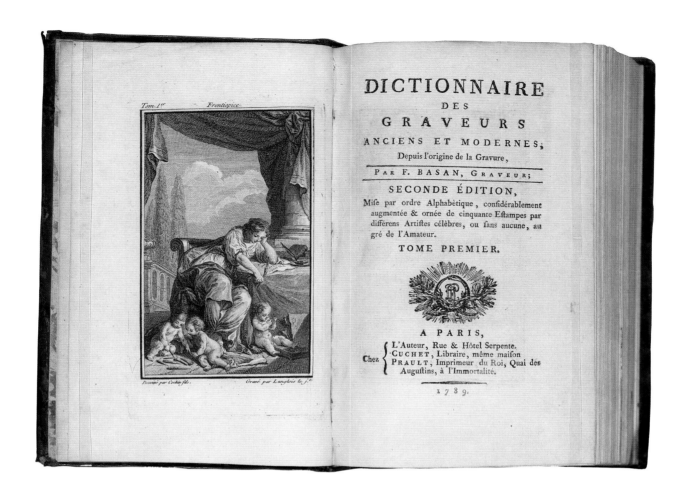

Tom. 1er.   Frontispice.

DICTIONNAIRE
DES GRAVEURS
ANCIENS ET MODERNES,

Depuis l'origine de la Gravure,

Par F. BASAN, GRAVEUR;

SECONDE ÉDITION,

Mise par ordre Alphabétique, considérablement augmentée & ornée de cinquante Estampes par différens Artistes célèbres, ou sans aucune, au gré de l'Amateur.

TOME PREMIER.

A PARIS,

Chez {
L'Auteur, Rue & Hôtel Serpente.
CUCHET, Libraire, même maison
PRAULT, Imprimeur du Roi, Quai des Augustins, à l'Immortalité.

1789.

Dessiné par Cochin fils.   Gravé par Langlois le j.e

Tom. II.   Page 261.

né à Anvers, vers l'an 1642, fut élève de Pierre de Bailliu, & a gravé entr'autres morceaux,

Une Descente de Croix. g. p. en h. d'après *Rubens.*

L'Assomption de la Vierge. p. p. en h. *id.*

Divers Sujets de Vierges, d'après *Van Dyck.*

Mars & Vénus. m. p. en h. d'après le même.

Les Portraits d'Antoine de Funiga, de Marie-Claire de Croi, de Frédéric-Henri, Prince d'Orange. *idem.*

WAUTERS, (Jean-Louis) né à Gand en 1731, a gravé plusieurs jolis paysages.

WEIROTTER, (François-Edmond) peintre Allemand, né en 1730, mort à Vienne en Autriche. Il vint à Paris où il séjourna plusieurs années pendant lesquelles il a gravé à l'eau-forte un très-grand nombre de p. paysages d'après nature, ou de son invention, dans lesquels on trouve une pointe fine & légère, & de très-jolies fabriques. Il a fait le voyage d'Italie, est revenu à Paris, & en est reparti en 1767, pour aller à Vienne y fixer son séjour. Il y fut nommé professeur de l'académie de dessin, et y mourut en 1773.

WEIS, (Jean-Marie) peintre né en Alsace en 1720, a gravé à l'eau-forte un des morceaux qui fait partie du vol. des fêtes données à la convalescence de Louis XV, à Strasbourg.

R iij

F. E. Weirotter fecit.   14.

GIUSEPPE BERNARDINO BISON
1762–1844

Coriolanus before the Women of Rome
late 1780s
Pen and ink and wash over chalk
7³⁄₈ x 12⁷⁄₁₆ (18.8 x 31.6)

Gift of Katrin Bellinger

Giuseppe Bernardino Bison was an artist from the region of Friuli whose art was formed in Venice. As a specialist in ornamental painting he frescoed many palaces in the Veneto, Trieste, and Milan. It is not surprising that the present drawing was once attributed to Canova,[1] whose neoclassical style Bison approached. The scene represented here, related by both Livy and Plutarch,[2] tells the story of Coriolanus, a Roman general who was banished from the city in 491 B.C. Later, as head of the army of nearby Volsci, he attacked Rome with his forces. There he was met by his wife and his mother who begged him to resist advancing on his native city. Swayed by their pleas Coriolanus returned to Volsci, where he was condemned to death as a traitor. Bison here depicted the powerful moment when the women kneel before Coriolanus in supplication. Behind them the artist sketchily indicated the ancient city. Further evoking the classical origin of the story, Bison placed the figures parallel to each other and close to the picture plane, reminiscent of a Roman frieze. The upright figures in strict profile and frontal views also suggest the formality of sculptural relief. In choosing this theme Bison followed a long tradition in Italian art. *Coriolanus before the Women* was often painted on Italian marriage chests and elsewhere to encourage loyalty to the family and its values. The National Gallery of Art, in fact, owns a series of Renaissance plaquettes illustrating the story of Coriolanus.[3] The lighthearted and ornamental quality of the sheet, however, may suggest a less serious purpose. By the late eighteenth century, scenes from Roman history were often employed for mere decoration. A similar drawing by Bison in the Metropolitan Museum of Art has been connected with Bison's trompe l'oeil reliefs in the Palazzo Manzoni in Padua of 1787–1790.[4] Our drawing may well have had the same destination.

Italian neoclassical drawings have become extremely popular in the last twenty years. Bison's combination of informal linear execution with weighty subject matter and formal compositional arrangements has made his drawings especially appreciated. The Gallery possesses very few of these drawings and none by Bison, which makes the addition of this sheet to the collection especially welcome.

Diane De Grazia

NOTES

1. The drawing is inscribed "Canova" on the verso.

2. Livy, *History of Rome*, 2:40 (*Ab Urbe condita libr.*) and Plutarch, *Life of Coriolanus*, 40.

3. See John Pope-Hennessy, *Renaissance Bronzes from the Samuel H. Kress Collection* (London, 1965), cats. 85–88.

4. For the drawing in the Metropolitan of an antique sacrifice see Jacob Bean and William Griswold, *18th Century Italian Drawings in the Metropolitan Museum of Art* [exh. cat. The Metropolitan Museum of Art] (New York, 1990), 32–33, cat. 11. For the frescoes see Franca Zava Boccazzi, "Gli affreschi di Bison," *Arte Veneta* 22 (1968), 142–166.

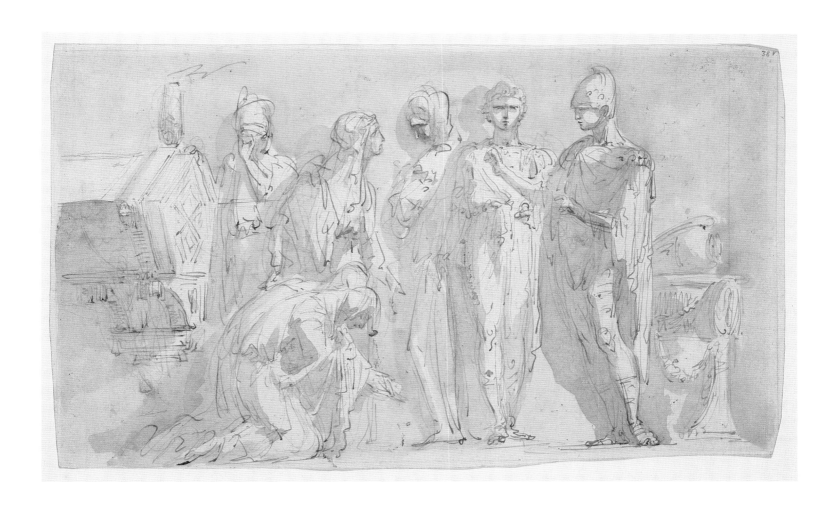

JACQUES-LOUIS DAVID
1748–1825

Portrait of Thirius de Pautrizel, c. 1795
Pen and ink, brush and wash, graphite,
white gouache
7⅝ in diameter (19.3)

Gift of
Walter H. and Leonore Annenberg

Rarely were David's considerable talents as both portraitist and draftsman as brilliantly combined as they are here in this portrait of Jean-Baptiste-Louis Thirius de Pautrizel (1754–?). Presenting his subject against a simple gray ground and in a rather austere profile pose reminiscent of ancient coins and medals, David created not only an arresting image but also a wonderfully eloquent likeness. The jutting profile, the deeply set, heavy-lidded eye, the luminous flesh, and the coarsely waving hair are all defined and shaped with consummate skill. A few quick strokes of the pen add expression to the eye and mouth; rapid flicks of the brush animate the figure as a whole.

David undoubtedly knew Thirius de Pautrizel between 1792 and 1795 when they were both members of the revolutionary Convention, Thirius as a deputy for Guadeloupe, where he owned property, David as a deputy for Paris.[1] Like so many others, David included, Thirius was eventually denounced before the Convention (in his case for a "seditious attitude") and imprisoned in 1795, at about the time this portrait was made. The same medallion format was in fact used by David during his own incarceration in 1795 for at least two portrait drawings he made of his fellow prisoners.[2] An inscription on one of those indicates that the drawing was made as a gift from the artist to the sitter.[3] The portrait of Thirius may well have been made for the same purpose, for the sense of human warmth and sympathy with which it is imbued suggests that the sitter was a close friend of the artist.

This exquisite drawing provides the impressive finale that has long been missing from the National Gallery's strong collection of eighteenth-century French drawings. Not only does it represent David's draftsmanship in a most striking way and at a level commensurate with his stature as the greatest French artist of his age, but also it establishes the highest standard for future collecting in this area. By happy chance it also complements in a particularly meaningful way the two David paintings in the collection, both of which are portraits from later in the artist's career and thus very different in presentation.

Margaret Morgan Grasselli

PROVENANCE
Gairac collection, Paris; Wildenstein and Company, New York; Curtis O. Baer, New Rochelle; his son, Dr. George Baer, Atlanta.

NOTES
1. The inscription on the drawing's mount, *THIRUS DE PAUTRIZEL, Capitaine de Cavallerie en 1785, Représentant de la NATION FRANÇAISE en 1794 et 1795,* indicates that Thirius was a representative only from 1794 to 1795, but records show that he was actually appointed in October 1792. See Adolphe Robert and Edgar Bourloton, *Dictionnaire des Parlementaires Français* (Paris, 1891), 2:562.

2. A portrait of Jeanbon Saint-André (1748–1813) in The Art Institute of Chicago is inscribed as having been made in prison on the 20th of Messidor (8 July) in the third year of the republic (1795). See Martha Tedeschi, *Great Drawings from The Art Institute of Chicago, The Harold Joachim Years 1958–1983* (Chicago and New York, 1985), 108–109, no. 46. One representing André Bernard des Jeuzines (1751–1818) was made just sixteen days later, on the 6th of Thermidor (24 July). See *Nineteenth-Century French Drawings* [exh. cat. Hazlitt, Gooden & Fox] (London, 1990), no. 1.

3. The drawing in Chicago is inscribed *Donum amicitiae. amoris solatium* (gift of friendship, solace of affection).

PHILIPPE-LAURENT ROLAND
1746–1816

Bacchante with a Goat, model 1796,
cast 1798
Bronze group, 16⁵⁄₁₆ (41.4) high;
base, 10½ x 6 (26.7 x 5.2)

Gift of Mr. and Mrs. John R. Gaines

Lithe and long-limbed, a smiling young woman balances on the back of a rearing goat, an ancient symbol of lusty animal high spirits. The ivy leaves crowning her hair and the thyrsus — a staff topped with a pine cone — she uses to goad the animal mark her as a devotee of Bacchus, the classical god of wine. In the wild ride her hair flies out behind her and her drapery clings to her body, often in ridged folds whose swirling patterns accentuate the rounded forms beneath. Elegant contours wind their way down from her outstretched neck through her curving back and bent legs. The contrasting textures of wavy fur, smooth flesh, cloth, and leaves, reflecting careful study of nature, are shown to advantage in the modeling and in the final cleaning and chasing of the fine bronze details. Louis-François Jeannest, who did the superb finishing work, was allowed to add his name to that of his teacher Roland in the inscription on the base.

Roland's successful career, which included royal commissions for Louis XVI and Marie Antoinette, spanned the Bourbon monarchy, the French Revolution, and the Napoleonic period.[1] A favorite pupil of the prominent sculptor Augustin Pajou, he produced architectural decoration, portrait busts, and figures for public monuments as well as small sculpture. This bronze, of a size and refinement suited to domestic enjoyment, was made under the Directoire, the government of the transition from the revolution to the empire of Napoleon. The great nineteenth-century sculptor David d'Angers, Roland's most successful pupil, wrote of the *Bacchante with a Goat*: "The vivacity of this sculpture, the grace of its pose, and the purity of its form place it among the most beautiful works he ever executed."[2]

Such subjects from ancient Greek and Roman mythology, representing ideally beautiful and lightly clothed human figures in action, had been favored by European artists and patrons since the Renaissance. The sculpture's light-hearted theme and mild eroticism look back to the art of the earlier eighteenth century. But Roland's mutually balancing movements, clear, sharp contours, carefully articulated structure, and linear drapery style would have suited the neoclassical taste that predominated later in the century. So would the composition, offering alluring views from many angles yet most complete and effective from direct front and back views, like a relief or a painting. In fact, the twisting pinwheel pose Roland gave his *Bacchante* suggests an interest in the energetic seated figures of Renaissance painting, such as those of Michelangelo and Raphael in Italy, where Roland studied for five years, or in the sixteenth-century French art influenced by the Italian Renaissance. Related poses appear, for instance, in the enamel decoration by Léonard Limousin, c. 1560, on a dish representing the *Wedding Feast of Cupid and Psyche* in the National Gallery, (1942.9. 293).

A terra-cotta model for this sculpture is in the Metropolitan Museum of Art, signed and dated 1796. The bronze shows important differences from this model. The changes were probably introduced in a wax version that was cast from the clay model and then reworked before itself being cast in bronze. This bronze example may be the one that Roland showed in the officially sponsored Salon exhibition of 1798 in Paris.

In a collection with great strength in the eighteenth-century rococo terracottas of Clodion, the style of the Roland *Bacchante* subtly broaches the turn toward neo-classical taste. It introduces to the collection a type of supremely refined bronze that embodies, in its approach to classical antiquity, both the transition and the continuity between the arts of the *ancien régime* and those of the early nineteenth century.

Alison Luchs

PROVENANCE
Location unknown before 1981 (possibly shown at the Salon exhibition, Paris, 1798); Nouveau Drouot sale, "Tableaux anciens et modernes . . ." (Paris, 10 June 1981, lot 79, illustrated); Brooks Beaulieu, Northampton, Massachusetts, 1981–1983; Mr. and Mrs. John R. Gaines, 1983–1989.

NOTES
1. On Roland see D. Genoux, "Philippe-Laurent Roland Décorateur. Ses Travaux au Palais de Fontainebleau en 1786," *Bulletin de la Société de l'Histoire de l'Art français* 1964 (1965), 119–125; articles by the same author in the same journal 1965 (1966), 191–200; 1966 (1967), 189–198, and references cited in O. Raggio, *The Fire and the Talent: A Presentation of French Terracottas* [exh. cat. The Metropolitan Museum of Art] (New York, 1976), no. 8.

2. P. J. David d'Angers, *Roland et ses ouvrages* (Paris, 1847), 25, translated by Raggio in New York 1976, no. 8.

WILLIAM BLAKE
1757–1827

The Death of Saint Joseph, 1803
Watercolor on paper
14¼ x 14 (36.20 x 35.56)

Gift (Partial and Promised) of
Louisa C. Duemling

Throughout his career William Blake struggled to find an artistic language capable of expressing the purity and intensity of his visionary subjects. To many of his contemporaries he was an enigma, a man distracted by a fanciful imagination and naive in his understanding of art and artistic practice. For others his extraordinary genius made him one of the most sophisticated and innovative artists of the era.[1]

Blake was trained in reproductive engraving, which would provide income throughout much of his life. His true ambitions, however, lay in poetry and painting and in 1779 he entered the Royal Academy, only to drop out during his first year. Drawings and watercolors from the late 1770s and early 1780s indicate that Blake quickly mastered the current styles of history painting and could produce accomplished work in the academic tradition. But he soon found such work restrictive, believing he had a God-given mission to convey higher truths to his fellow man through the means of art. Gradually, Blake evolved a personal style; by the late 1790s his art had taken on an intensely expressive and visionary character markedly different from the works of any of his contemporaries.

As early as 1785 Blake had begun executing biblical subjects in watercolor, finding the Bible more entertaining and instructive than any other book because of its appeal to the imagination and spiritual sensation.[2] In 1793 Blake announced his intention to undertake a series from the Bible, but not until 1799, when Thomas Butts commissioned fifty temperas, did he actually commence this project.[3] Butts, a military clerk, was not a wealthy man, but he managed to amass the largest contemporary collection of the artist's works. His first commission was quickly followed by a second order for watercolors; Blake would eventually paint more than eighty for him.

The first years of the new century were filled with deep personal frustration and anguish for the painter. In January of 1802 Blake wrote to Butts that he was struggling with his art: "I have recollected all my scatter'd thoughts on Art and resumed my primitive and original ways of Execution in both painting and engraving. . . . I am not ashamed, afraid, or averse to tell you . . . I am under the direction of Messengers from Heaven, Daily and Nightly. . . ."[4] Blake then developed a powerful new style employing bold colors and dramatic light effects, as is evident in the watercolors he painted for Butts in 1803, including *The Death of Saint Joseph.*

Like its companion watercolor *The Death of the Virgin* (1803, Tate Gallery, London), *The Death of Saint Joseph* shows figures in an otherworldly, undefined space surmounted by a vivid rainbow of angels' heads and wings. Like the archivolts of a medieval tympanum, this angel-rainbow circumscribes and defines a separate spiritual realm. There is no natural source of illumination; instead light emanates from the figures of Joseph, Mary, and Christ, filling the scene with supernatural radiance. That Blake chose to depict the very moment of transition from earthly to heavenly life was made clear by the inscription originally found at the bottom of the sheet: "Into Thine hand I commend my spirit: Thou hast redeemed me, O Lord God of Truth."[5]

The Death of Saint Joseph, with its superbly delineated figures, evocative colors, and profound spirituality, is a significant addition to the Gallery's extensive Blake holdings. Joining three other watercolors from the Butts commission, including the well-known *Great Red Dragon and the Woman Clothed with the Sun* of c. 1805, it helps represent the finest achievements of a crucial phase in Blake's art.

Franklin Kelly

NOTES
1. David Bindman, *William Blake: His Art and His Times* [exh. cat. Yale Center for British Art] (New Haven and London, 1982), 10.

2. Gregory Keynes, *Blake's Illustrations to the Bible* (Clairvaux, 1957), ix.

3. Keynes 1957, ix. David Bindman, *Blake as an Artist* (Oxford and New York, 1977), 117. One of these temperas, *The Last Supper* (1799), is in the National Gallery's collection.

4. Quoted in Bindman 1977, 135–136.

5. This inscription, based partly on Jesus' dying words in Luke 23.46, was long ago cut from the sheet; it is recorded in William Michael Rossetti's "Annotated Catalogue of Blake's Paintings and Drawings," in Alexander Gilchrist, *Life of William Blake,* 2 vols. (London, 1880), 2:213. See also Martin Butlin, *The Paintings and Drawings of William Blake,* 2 vols. (New Haven and London, 1981), 1:365–366. The death of Saint Joseph, of course, is not a biblical subject in the strict sense, for the only accounts of it are found in apocryphal sources.

LOUIS LEOPOLD BOILLY
1761–1845

The Vaccine, 1806
Pen and ink and wash
17⁷⁄₁₆ x 23³⁄₈ (44.3 x 59.4)

Gift of Dora Donner Ide in Honor of
William Henry Donner

The surprising subject of this superb drawing is the now-ordinary act of inoculating a child against smallpox. Presented as an emotionally charged domestic scene that is one of the principal hallmarks of Boilly's art, the drawing bears witness not only to the artist's special brilliance as a chronicler of contemporary life but also to the considerable trepidation with which the still-new vaccination process was regarded in his time.

As is always the case in Boilly's work, attention is focused entirely on the figures, whose every nuance of expression and gesture is precisely orchestrated to convey as complete an emotional tale as possible. The execution, with its strong contours, crisp pen lines, exquisitely controlled washes, warm light, and smoothly sculpted forms, is also vintage Boilly. Especially fine is the group of two young women comforting a child at the left, skillfully defined by a few patches of light coupled with some beautifully modulated veils of translucent wash.

Smallpox is still a highly feared disease, not inevitably fatal but often hideously disfiguring for survivors. It was not until the end of the eighteenth century that a safe method of inoculation against the disease was discovered by the British physician Edward Jenner (1749–1823). His procedure involved introducing under the skin of his patients the vaccinia virus (hence the term vaccine), commonly known as cowpox, a

disease related to smallpox that affects only cattle. Those who were exposed to the cowpox virus in this manner were effectively immunized against smallpox without risking an outbreak of the disease itself.

In spite of the safety of Jenner's well-publicized inoculation technique, public fears and misconceptions were slow to fade. A significant advance was made in 1805, however, when Napoléon ordered that all his troops be vaccinated. The very next year, perhaps to help allay public mistrust, Boilly began detailed preparations for a painting on the subject of vaccination — tellingly subtitled *Le préjugé vaincu* (prejudice vanquished) — for which this extraordinary drawing is the largest and most complete study.[1]

As the first drawing by Boilly to enter the collection, joining only a small handful of French works dating from around 1800, this magnificent sheet is of critical importance for the National Gallery. Not only does it represent Boilly's draftsmanship in particularly memorable and moving fashion, but also it adds a notable masterpiece and considerable power to the collection of early nineteenth-century drawings. This gift is made even more special for the Gallery by the work's personal meaning for the donor, who was originally attracted to it because of her father's abiding interest in the history of medicine.

Margaret Morgan Grasselli

PROVENANCE
Probably Julien Boilly, Paris (sale, Paris, 4 May 1868, no. 94); Madame Variot, 1930; Jacques Seligmann, Paris; Mrs. Russell Pope, New York (sale, New York, Parke-Bernet, 25 May 1946, no. 775); Lock and Baer, New York; Baron Cassell Van Doorn, from 1946; private collection; M. R. Schweitzer and Didier Aaron, Inc., New York.

NOTE
1. The painting of 1807, almost identical in size to this drawing but differing in many details of pose, was exhibited in London in 1986. See *From Claude to Géricault, The Arts in France 1630–1830* [exh. cat. Thos. Agnew & Sons, Ltd.] (London, 1986), no. 4. A number of other preparatory drawings are known for this composition: a wash drawing of the central group (private collection, Paris), which probably preceded the composition presented here; a black chalk study of the figures at left (sale, London, Sotheby's, 28 May 1935, no. 271); a black chalk study of the maid and two children at right (Robert F. Johnson and Joseph R. Goldyne, *Master Drawings from the Achenbach Foundation for Graphic Arts, The Fine Arts Museums of San Francisco* [Geneva, n.d.], no. 51); a black chalk study of the woman holding a child at center and the girl standing behind (sale, Paris, Galerie Petit, 16–19 June 1919, no. 217); and a black chalk study for the doctor (Henry Harrisse, *L.-L. Boilly, peintre, dessinateur et lithographe, sa vie et son oeuvre 1761–1845* [Paris, 1898], no. 1189). The chalk drawings seem to have been made after the large-scale compositional drawing in order to modify and perfect the poses of individuals and specific groups. In 1824, Boilly made a lithograph of the painted composition (Harrisse 1898, no. 1202).

JOSEPH CHINARD
1756–1813

A Lady, 1810
Patinated terra cotta
26⅜ (67)

Gift of Daniel Wildenstein

The favorite portrait sculptor of Napoléon's family at the height of the Empire, Chinard depicted subjects including Napoléon himself and the Empress Josephine. The celebrated beauty Madame Recamier, a fellow citizen of his native Lyons, sat for some of the artist's most captivating busts and reliefs. Perhaps because he spent much of his career in Lyons rather than at the center of power in Paris, his portrait style kept a quality of "unforced freshness combined with a faintly pensive air."[1] This signed and dated bust of an unknown lady exemplifies this character, in the directly modeled feminine portraiture at which he excelled.

While his better-known sculptures often depict sitters with profuse details of coiffure and contemporary costume, this bust treats its subject with an austerity recalling certain ancient, imperial Roman portraits. Chinard must have known many such busts from his years of study in Rome, 1784–1787 and 1791–1793.[2]

In this late work the woman's gown, cut to emulate a classical chiton, falls from one shoulder to bare her chest. Covering one breast and just revealing the nipple of the other, the decolletage suggests less erotic flirtation than the antique use of nudity to represent the sitter as immortal. The treatment is monumental in its concentration on large, simple forms, yet intimate in the loose fall of the garment and naturalistic modeling of the face. In the latter respect Chinard "made no concessions, even to female sitters."[3] With honest yet sympathetic observation he showed a face in transition, its delicate contours yielding to the fullness and lines of age. While the pupils are left blank in the classical manner, indentations in the forehead and around the finely formed eyes and mouth betoken human imperfection and sorrow in this lady who regards us with a perplexed brow and gently sad smile. The level gaze and slightly projecting upper lip lend an air of persisting innocence. The mood, together with the stark simplicity of the costume and cubic base, may reflect an origin as a posthumous commemoration of the sitter.

Terra cotta (baked clay) could serve either for a finished sculpture or a preliminary model. While this bust could have been a study for a rendition in marble, the painted surface, through which the red color of the clay shows, implies a state of completion. Whatever the sculpture's purpose, the surfaces are vibrant with the touch of the artist's fingers, which he chose to leave visible rather than smooth away. Subtle movement animates the bust in this handling, in the lifted shoulder and turning head, and in the incised rivulets that flow through the tightly bound hair.

This bust is the first work of neoclassical portrait sculpture in the National Gallery of Art's collection. Yet it departs from neoclassical idealization in its concern for individuality, inner life, and impermanence. As one scholar has said of Chinard, "Face to face with another human being, he strove to understand his sitter, to pierce the mask and render the sitter's true personality in marble or clay. Thus he transcended time and fashion and took his place in the great tradition of the makers of the French portrait bust."[4]

Alison Luchs

PROVENANCE
Private collection, England; Wildenstein Collection, 1965–1990.

NOTES
1. Michael Levey in Wend Graf Kalnein and Michael Levey, *Art and Architecture of the Eighteenth Century in France* (Baltimore, 1972), 171. On Chinard see also Madeleine Rocher-Jauneau, *L'oeuvre de Joseph Chinard (1755–1813) au Musée des Beaux-arts de Lyon* [exh. cat.] (Lyons, 1978); *Skulptur aus der Louvre* [exh. cat. Wilhelm Lehmbruck Museum] (Duisburg, 1989), 198–199, 234–241, 251, 305, 310, 311, 313; Joseph Baillio, *The Winds of Revolution* [exh. cat. Wildenstein and Co.] (New York, 1989), 73–74, 104–106; a monograph on the artist by Rocher-Jauneau is in progress.

2. Chinard was expelled from Italy after imprisonment for the revolutionary sentiments expressed in his allegorical sculptures. Ironically, he then spent time in prison in Lyons (1793–1794) for his "moderation" in loyalty to the French Revolution. Thereafter he led an increasingly productive and honored artistic life there, with occasional visits to Paris and Italy.

3. Madeleine Rocher-Jauneau, "Chinard and the Empire Style," *Apollo* 80 (1964), 225. This bust is illustrated on p. 224 of that article.

4. Rocher-Jauneau 1964, 225.

THOMAS ROWLANDSON
c. 1757–1827

The English Dance of Death
Repository of Arts, London,
1815–1816
Two volumes with 74 hand-colored
etchings with aquatint after
Rowlandson, accompanied by verse
by William Combe
9½ x 6 (24.2 x 15.1)

The English Dance of Life
Repository of Arts, London, 1817
Bound volume with 26 hand-colored
etchings with aquatint after
Rowlandson, accompanied by verse
by William Combe
9½ x 6 (24.2 x 15.1)

The Vicar of Wakefield
by Oliver Goldsmith
Repository of Arts, London, 1823
Bound volume with 24 hand-colored
etchings with aquatint by Rowlandson
10 x 6⅛ (25.2 x 15.5)

Gift of Alexander Vershbow

Beginning around 1797, the British water-colorist and printmaker Thomas Rowlandson established a professional relationship with Rudolph Ackermann, a German-born publisher of prints and books. After commissioning several single-leaf prints from Rowlandson, Ackermann initiated a series of book-illustrating projects involving Rowlandson as artist and William Combe as author. The working relationship of artist and author was most unusual; the two never met. As Rowlandson completed the design for each illustration it was conveyed to Combe, who then composed verses to accompany it. The normal procedure for creating an illustrated book was thus reversed.

The outstanding product of this collaboration was the *The English Dance of Death*, a two-volume work that appeared in 1815 and 1816. It was followed by a sequel, *The English Dance of Life*, in 1817.[1] Here we see Rowlandson's finest illustrations, full of spirited inventiveness. Ackermann first published serialized portions of these books in his *Poetical Magazine* between 1814 and 1816. Rowlandson made watercolors for Ackermann's shop to render into etching and aquatint, hand colored according to Rowlandson's scheme. The *Dance of Death* gave Rowlandson the opportunity to dem-

onstrate his nearly inexhaustible imagination. He contrived to show Death interrupting mortal careers in all classes of society and all the ages of man.[2] In the second volume, for example, Rowlandson ridiculed an astronomer for his benighted manner of meeting Death. So intent is the astronomer on scouring the heavens that he is unable to recognize Death leering down his telescope at him.

In 1817 Ackermann employed Rowlandson to illustrate *The Vicar of Wakefield*.[3] As Rowlandson this time devised visual imagery to accompany an existing text, it was a more traditional project than that undertaken with Combe. Rowlandson himself made the hand-colored prints for this book, rather than Ackermann's shop. The tale of Doctor Primrose and his family recounts the misfortunes that the credulous and good must suffer in this world and their eventual rewards for virtue. Although the Primrose family was brought to grief by their petty sins of pride, both author and artist found them easy to forgive. Rowlandson never made them appear worse than just silly. In the episode of the *Family Picture*, only the artist is caricatured. The Primroses, in competition with their neighbors the Flamboroughs, who had recently had their portraits painted, commissioned a family portrait in historical costumes: "this would be cheaper, since one frame would serve for all, and it would be infinitely more genteel, for all families of any taste were now drawn in the same manner."[4] At the center of the composition Doctor Primrose solemnly presents his writings on the necessity of clerical mo-

nogamy to his wife, dressed as Venus. Their folly overcame them, however, as the painting was too big to fit into the house, and had to be left leaning against the kitchen wall "in a most mortifying manner . . . the jest of all our neighbors."[5]

Virginia Tuttle Clayton

PROVENANCE
Dance of Death and *Dance of Life*: bookplate of Joseph Ablett, Llandbedr Hall; Hofmann and Freeman, Cambridge, Mass., 1967; Mr. and Mrs. Arthur Vershbow. *The Vicar of Wakefield*: Dana's Old Corner Book Store, Providence, 1964; Mr. and Mrs. Arthur Vershbow.

NOTES
1. Joseph Grego, *Rowlandson the Caricaturist* (London, 1880), 2:317–355 and 359–361; Brenda D. Rix, *Our Old Friend Rolly* (Toronto, 1987), 84–85; Ronald Paulson, *Rowlandson: A New Interpretation* (New York, 1972), 93–116.

2. On the theme of the Dance of Death, see Robert R. Wark, *Rowlandson's Drawings for the English Dance of Death* (San Marino, California, 1966), 8–13.

3. Grego 1880, 2:356–359 and 375; Rix 1987, 85. The Vershbow copy is a second edition published by Ackermann in 1823.

4. Oliver Goldsmith, *The Vicar of Wakefield* (London, 1823), 96.

5. Goldsmith 1823, 97–98.

The Hounds the flying Stag pursue:
But Dian does the hunting rue.

Published Sept 2 1817 at R.Ackermann's, 101 Strand.

Plate 24.

THE FAMILY PICTURE.

London Pub. May 1817 ab R.Ackermann, Repository of Arts 101 Strand.

THOMAS ROWLANDSON
1757–1827

*The Travels of Doctor Syntax
in Search of the Picturesque*
Repository of Arts, London, 1812
Bound volume with 31 hand-colored
etchings with aquatint by Rowlandson
9 x 5½ (23 x 14)

*The Second Tour of Doctor Syntax,
in Search of Consolation*
Repository of Arts, London, 1820
Bound volume with 24 hand-colored
etchings with aquatint after Rowlandson
9 x 5½ (23 x 14)

*The Third Tour of Doctor Syntax,
in Search of a Wife*
Repository of Arts, London, 1821
Bound volume with 26 hand-colored
etchings with aquatint after Rowlandson
9 x 5½ (23 x 14)

The History of Johnny Quae Genus
Repository of Arts, London, 1822
Bound volume with 24 hand-colored
etchings with aquatint after Rowlandson
9½ x 6 (24 x 15.2)

Gift of Ann Vershbow

The earliest and most popular work that
Rowlandson and Combe accomplished for
Ackermann was *The Tour of Doctor Syntax
in Search of the Picturesque*. It first appeared
in 1809 as monthly serials in Ackermann's
Poetical Magazine. The success of the serialized version, titled *The Schoolmaster's Tour*,
far exceeded expectations, and in 1812 Ackermann published it as an independent volume. Rowlandson made a new set of plates
for the book, with the imagery mostly the
same as that used for the magazine issue.
The book was so enthusiastically received
that five editions were printed within one
year.[1] The British public was at that moment
enthralled with the "picturesque tour": a
journey through native countryside, especially the Lake District, in quest of scenery
that fulfilled the current aesthetic of the picturesque.[2] *The Tour* was a parody of the type
of illustrated travel account spawned by such
tours, particularly that of William Gilpin,
and as such presented a timely appeal to
popular humor. At the opening of the work

the long-suffering, impoverished Doctor
Syntax conceives the idea of making a picturesque tour and of turning a profit by
publishing, on his return, an illustrated journal recounting it:

> *I'll ride and write, and sketch and print,
> And thus create a real mint;
> I'll prose it here, I'll verse it there,
> and picturesque it ev'ry where. . . .
> At Doctor Pompous give a look;
> He made his fortune by a book:
> And if my volume does not beat it,
> When I return, I'll fry and eat it.*

Although his trip was ultimately a success
in the way that he had hoped, he was continually beset by comic misadventures along
the way. One of Rowlandson's illustrations
shows Syntax, at the end of his journey, in
a bookseller's shop. He is offering the bookseller his beloved journal for publication,
but the man, whose dinner has been inter-
rupted, rebuffs Syntax, and a heated quarrel
ensues.

So pleased was Ackermann with the public's warm reception of *The Tour* that he
decided to continue it as a series. The illustrations for these books were again made by
Ackermann's shop after watercolors by
Rowlandson. In 1820 a sequel was brought
forth after appearing in monthly install-
ments: *Doctor Syntax in Search of Consolation*.
In this book, Syntax embarks on a second
journey to distract himself from grief at his
wife's death. This time he is a much more
prosperous traveler, riding a better horse
and accompanied by his servant, Patrick, but
he becomes involved in the same type of
ridiculous situation that plagued him on his
previous trip. In 1821, Ackermann published *The Third Tour of Doctor Syntax — in
Search of a Wife*. Syntax gallantly sets forth,
with Patrick eager to join him. By the end
of the trip Syntax is not only successful in
finding a wife, but adopts a foundling child.
This character, Johnny Quae Genus, becomes the subject of the final book in this
series, *The History of Johnny Quae Genus*, in
which Johnny, orphaned and penniless after
the death of Syntax and his wife, sets out
to seek his fortune in the employ of a succession of eccentric characters.

The National Gallery was extremely fortunate in acquiring, from Lessing J. Rosenwald, an outstanding collection of Thomas
Rowlandson's separate prints, originally
mounted in a seven-volume nineteenth-century scrapbook containing 1,218 items.
During the past five years the Gallery has
also added a number of fine watercolors by
Rowlandson as purchases and as gifts from

DOCTOR SYNTAX SETTING OUT
in Search of a Wife.

Paul Mellon and William B. O'Neal. Now,
with these generous gifts from Ann and
Alexander Vershbow, the Gallery will be
able to count as part of its collection the
third major component of Rowlandson's art,
the eight volumes that represent his greatest
achievements as an illustrator of books.

Virginia Tuttle Clayton

PROVENANCE
The three Doctor Syntax volumes: stamped
N. J. Bartlett and Company, Boston; inscribed
in graphite "ex coll J. T. Spaulding" [John Taylor
Spaulding]; Goodspeed's Bookshop, Boston,
1964; Mr. and Mrs. Arthur Vershbow. *Johnny
Quae Genus*: Norman Hall, Boston, 1960; Mr.
and Mrs. Arthur Vershbow.

NOTES
1. Joseph Grego, *Rowlandson the Caricaturist*
(London, 1880), 1:38–39, and 2:247; Brenda
D. Rix, *Our Old Friend Rolly* (Toronto, 1987),
82–83.

2. On the picturesque, see Christopher Hussey,
The Picturesque: Studies in a Point of View (London, 1927), 83–127; Ronald Paulson, *Rowlandson: A New Interpretation* (New York, 1972), 38–
45; John Dixon Hunt and Peter Willis, eds., *The
Genius of the Place: The English Landscape Garden,
1620–1820* (London, 1975), 337–341; J. H.
Plumb, *The Pursuit of Happiness: A View of Life
in Georgian England*, with entries by Edward J.
Nygren and Nancy L. Pressly [exh. cat. Yale Center for British Art] (New Haven, 1977), 5–11.

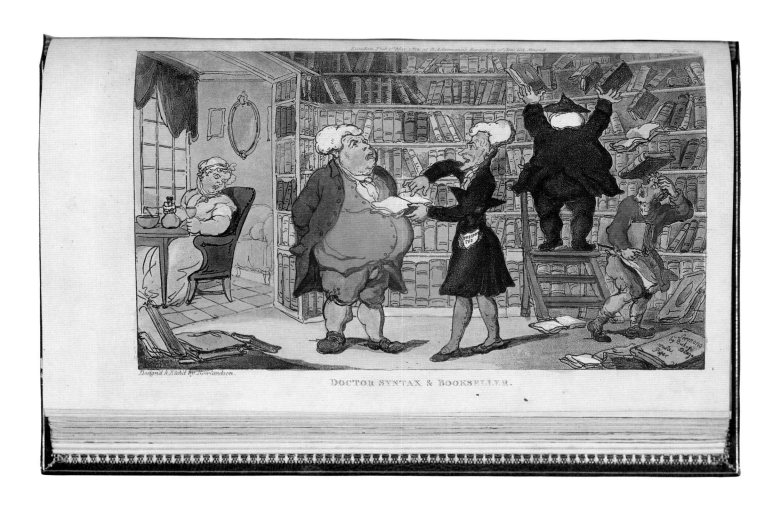

DOCTOR SYNTAX & BOOKSELLER.

QUÆ GENUS WITH A PORTRAIT PAINTER.

WILLIAM BLAKE
1757–1827

Evening, c. 1820–1825
Aqueous medium and chalk on
pine panel
36⁷⁄₁₆ x 11¾ (91.8 x 29.7)

Gift of Mr. and Mrs. Gordon Hanes

Evening is one of a group of nine paintings Blake executed in the 1820s, several of which are on wood panels.[1] For these late paintings Blake worked in a manner that is close in effect to the transparency of his watercolors and distinctly different from the heavily worked temperas he painted during various periods of his life.

Evening and a companion panel *Winter*, now in the Tate Gallery, London, are among the last of these late, thinly worked paintings to be completed. Both are thought to have been painted for installation at the sides of a fireplace (along with *Frieze: Olney Bridge*, now lost) for the Yaxham Rectory in Norfolk, which the Reverend John Johnson had rebuilt in 1820–1821.[2]

Both *Evening* and its companion in the Tate illustrate lines by Johnson's cousin, William Cowper, in *The Task*, Book IV, in the case of *Evening*, lines 243–260:

Come, Ev'ning, once again, season of peace;
Return, sweet Ev'ning, and continue long!
Methinks I see thee in the streaky west,
With matron-step slow-moving, while the
*   night*
Treads on thy sweeping train; one hand
*   employ'd*
In letting fall the curtain of repose
On bird and beast, the other charg'd for
*   man*
With sweet oblivion of the cares of day:
Not sumptuously adorn'd, nor needing aid
Like homely featur'd night, of clust'ring
*   gems;*
A star or two, just twinkling on thy brow,
Suffices thee; save that the moon is thine
No less than her's, not worn indeed on high
With ostentatious pageantry, but set
With modest grandeur in thy purple zone,
Resplendent less, but of an ampler round.
Come then, and thou shalt find thy vot'ry
*   calm,*
Or make me so. Composure is thy gift.[3]

Evening, like many of Blake's transparent watercolors, has changed over the years and is now less intense in hue; however, it reveals much about the artist's masterful draftsmanship. The extraordinary grace of his line is best seen, perhaps, in the clarity of the hands and in the swirls of the drapery enfolding the figure. In addition, the touches of color—a warm flesh tone in the feet, hands, cheeks, and robe of the elongated figure, as well as blue in the background—serve to enhance the assuredness of Blake's flowing line. The artist's great sympathy with his subject is clearly evident in the gentle serenity of her expressive face.

As much a drawing as a painting, *Evening* is an important addition to the Gallery's collection of Blake's art, given earlier by Lessing J. Rosenwald, W. C. Russell Allen, and William B. O'Neal.[4] In addition to other Blake watercolors, the Gallery's holdings also include individual plates from several of Blake's illuminated books, numerous drawings in a variety of media, prints made by many different processes, and several of Blake's original etching plates, one of which is a fragment of copper that is the only known example of Blake's distinctive relief etching. Of his paintings, we have two temperas on canvas: *The Last Supper*, c. 1799, and *Job and His Daughters*, 1823–1825 (fig. 1). Both of these are quite different in technique and sense of finish from *Evening*, which adds a distinctively new dimension to the Gallery's representation of Blake's art.

Ruth E. Fine

PROVENANCE

Rev. John Johnson; Canon Cowper Johnson; Bertram Vaughan-Johnson; his widow; the Rev. B. Talbot Vaughan Johnson; the Vaughan Johnson Trust; Sotheby's 18 July 1979 (59, repr.) to Agnews for Mr. and Mrs. Hanes.

NOTES

1. Martin Butlin, *The Drawings and Paintings of William Blake*, 2 vols. (New Haven and London, 1981), 549–553, nos. 803–811.

2. Butlin 1981, 552, no. 809.

3. H.S. Milford, ed., *Cowper Poetical Works*, 4th edition with corrections and additions by Norma Russell (London, 1971), 188.

4. On Lessing J. Rosenwald's donations, See Ruth Fine Lehrer, "Blake Material in the Lessing J. Rosenwald Collection," *Blake Newsletter* 35 (winter 1975–1976), including the Blake collections Rosenwald donated to the National Gallery of Art and the Library of Congress.

Fig. 1. William Blake, *Job and His Daughters*, c. 1799/1800. National Gallery of Art, Washington, Rosenwald Collection

JOHN CONSTABLE
1776–1837

Yarmouth Jetty, 1822
Oil on canvas
12½ x 20 (31.7 x 50.8)

Promised Gift of
Ruth Carter Stevenson

John Constable, unlike his well-traveled contemporary J. M. W. Turner, spent much of his artistic life close to home. Born in the small town of East Bergholt, Suffolk, Constable early on developed a deep affection for the bucolic scenery of East Anglia. There he found the subjects for many of his best-known paintings, including the famous *Hay Wain* of 1821 (National Gallery, London).[1] So strongly was he identified with the region that in his own lifetime part of it, the Stour Valley, came to be known as "Constable's Country."[2]

Yarmouth Jetty is one of the finest of a small group of seascapes, most of modest scale, that Constable executed in the 1820s; they were, according to the artist, "much liked."[3] Great Yarmouth, in Norfolk at the mouth of the river Yare, was the most important town and port on the East Anglian coast, a notable tourist destination and active fishing center.[4] Only one visit by Constable to Norfolk is recorded, in the 1790s long before this painting was executed.[5] No drawings or oil sketches related to the painting are known, so it is impossible to say whether it was based on his recollections or on a more recent unrecorded trip.

Whatever the case, the carefully delineated pier and building suggest that the artist worked from a drawing or sketch made on the spot. The sky, however, was based on one Constable had used in 1820 for several small paintings of Harwich Lighthouse.[6] The painting fairly sparkles with light and atmosphere and has an almost palpable sense of swiftly moving clouds and sea breezes playing across the tops of the waves. In these years Constable constantly painted oil studies of the sky that are marvels of careful observation, and it was from these that he often derived the effects in his finished pictures. He attached great importance to the role of skies in his paintings, for as he said in a now-famous statement: "It will be difficult to name a class of landscape, in which the sky is not the '*key note,*' the *standard of 'Scale,'* and the chief '*Organ of sentiment.*' "[7] The potency of Constable's vision was evident to his contemporaries: according to the artist, one owner of a Yarmouth painting often ate his breakfast with the picture beside him on the sofa so that he might imagine himself "on the seashore enjoying its breezes."[8]

Yarmouth Jetty will join three other works by Constable already in the collection of the National Gallery: *Wivenhoe Park, Essex* of 1816, the full-scale sketch for *The White Horse* of 1819, and *A View of Salisbury Cathedral* of c. 1825. More spontaneously handled and more intimately conceived than these works, *Yarmouth Jetty* will help give a fuller view of Constable's achievement and will also provide a link to the works of other artists in the Gallery's collection such as Richard Parkes Bonington, Eugène Boudin, and Eugène Delacroix, who were in various ways profoundly influenced by him.

Franklin Kelly

PROVENANCE
John Gibbons (d. 1851); the Reverend B. Gibbons, Corbyns Hall, Staffordshire; sale, Christie's 26 May 1894, no. 6; purchased by Agnew for Sir Charles Tennant; by descent in the family until 1975; Agnew's, London, 1975; Ruth Carter Stevenson, 1975.

NOTES
1. For a discussion of this and other paintings from Constable's maturity, see Graham Reynolds, *The Later Paintings and Drawings of John Constable,* 2 vols. (New Haven and London, 1984).

2. Michael Rosenthal, *Constable: The Painter and His Landscape* (New Haven and London, 1983), 5.

3. "Half an hour ago I received a letter from Woodburne to purchase . . . one of my sea-pieces—but I am without one—they are much liked. . . . " Letter of 18 August 1823, quoted in R. B. Beckett, *John Constable's Correspondence,* 6 vols. (Ipswich, 1962–1968), 6:128. Most of his other seascapes depicted scenes of Brighton, in East Sussex, and Harwich, in Essex. At least three versions of *Yarmouth Jetty* survive: the present example, another in a private collection, and a third in the collection of the Tate Gallery. This version is considered the original and the finest because of its full signature and date and its comparatively high degree of finish, and is most likely the "Yarmouth Jetty" that Constable exhibited at the British Institution in London in January 1823. For a discussion of the various versions see Leslie Parris, *The Tate Gallery Constable Collection* (London, 1981), 106, and Reynolds 1984, 108–109.

4. Karl Baedeker, *Great Britain: A Handbook for Travellers* (Leipzig and New York, 1890), 448–449.

5. Parris 1981, 106. According to Parris, an anonymous manuscript account of Constable's life mentions a sketching trip to Norfolk.

6. See Reynolds 1984, 46–47, and Parris 1981, 85–88.

7. Letter of 23 October 1822, quoted in Beckett 1962–1968, 6:76–77.

8. Undated letter (probably July 1831), quoted in Beckett 1962–1968, 5:89.

JAMES PEALE
1749–1831

Fruit Still Life with Chinese Export Basket, 1824
Oil on panel
14⅞ x 17⅝ (37.8 x 44.8)

Gift of Mr. and Mrs. Thomas M. Evans

Fruit Still Life with Chinese Export Basket, the first painting by James Peale to enter the collection of the National Gallery, is an elegant distillation in both subject and technique of the qualities that distinguish the work of one of the founders of the American school of still-life painting. An important addition to the Gallery's holdings of works by the Peale family,[1] James Peale's masterwork serves as the ideal opening note for the museum's small but select collection of American still-life paintings that includes works by Peale's artistic successors William Michael Harnett (*My Gems*, 1888) and John Frederick Peto (*The Old Violin*, c. 1890). Peale's painting also bears an intriguing relationship to *Peaches—Still Life* (fig. 1), a theorem, or stencil painting, given to the Gallery in 1953 by Edgar William and Bernice Chrysler Garbisch. As an example of a popular technique that allowed amateurs to work from stenciled designs, *Peaches—Still Life* testifies to the widespread appeal of the still-life paintings produced by several members of the Peale family.

James Peale, a younger brother of Charles Willson Peale (1741–1827), spent much of his career as a painter of portrait miniatures in Philadelphia. When the strain of producing images on such a small scale threatened his health he turned to large-scale portraits, landscapes, and still lifes. His interest in still life may have been sparked by his nephew Raphaelle Peale (1774–1825), who had begun exhibiting still-life paintings as early as 1795.[2] A gifted artist with a taste for visual trickery, Raphaelle Peale produced trompe l'oeil "deceptions" as well as a series of masterfully composed still lifes.[3] Like his nephew, James Peale constructed his still-life paintings with a mathematician's eye for geometric form. In *Fruit Still Life with Chinese Export Basket* James skillfully balanced the circular forms of apples, grapes, and the ceramic dish with the sharp linear edge of the supporting table and the diag-

onal thrust of broken grape stems. Though asymmetrical in structure, the composition exhibits an equilibrium of classical purity. Equally skilled at rendering subtle variations in surface texture, Peale successfully juxtaposed translucent grapes, pitted apples, and serrated leaves. The golden apples at the center of the composition, spotted with signs of decay, suggest that Peale was aware of the European tradition of still-life painting. In placing blemished fruit at the center of his composition, Peale allied himself with generations of European artists whose carefully composed still lifes addressed the ephemeral and transitory.

Despite its *memento mori* overtones, Peale's painting is a glorious celebration of nature's color. The apples that rest on the rim of the porcelain basket attest to the artist's ability to individualize each piece of fruit through subtle variations of color and tone. Thus the clear red of one apple serves as the foil for the pale yellow of another and the green grapes that crown the bowl complement the purple cluster at the far left. The same colors are echoed in the spray of leaves that forms the backdrop for the highlighted fruit. The stark white basket at the center, man-made and flawless, serves as both a pedestal for Peale's richly colored fruit and by contrast a powerful reminder of the imperfect and fragile character of the natural world.

At once solemn and celebratory, *Fruit Still Life with Chinese Export Basket* also contains a note of whimsy, for the grape tendril that twists toward the upper edge of the picture forms the artist's initials.

Nancy K. Anderson

PROVENANCE
Private collection, New Jersey; Frank S. Schwarz & Son, Philadelphia, 1987; Jeanne Rowe Mathison Trust, 1987.

NOTES
1. The permanent collection includes three works by Charles Willson Peale: *John Philip de Haas*, *Benjamin and Eleanor Ridgely Laming*, *John Beale Bordley*; and six by or attributed to Rembrandt Peale: *Richardson Stuart*, *Thomas Sully*, *George Washington*, *Rubens Peale with a Geranium*, *George Washington*, and *Timothy Matlock*.

2. Raphaelle Peale exhibited seven still lifes and a "deception" at the Exhibition of the Columbianum in Philadelphia in 1795. For Raphaelle Peale see Nicolai Cikovsky, Jr., *Raphaelle Peale Still Lifes* [exh. cat. National Gallery of Art] (Washington, 1988).

3. *Venus Rising from the Sea—A Deception* (The Nelson-Atkins Museum of Art, Kansas City), also known as *After the Bath*, is perhaps the best known of Raphaelle Peale's trompe l'oeil "deceptions."

Fig. 1. American School, *Peaches—Still Life*, c. 1840, theorem velvet, glazed, 16½ x 24½ (41.9 x 62.2). National Gallery of Art, Washington, Gift of Edgar William and Bernice Chrysler Garbisch

THOMAS COLE
1801–1848

Sunrise in the Catskills, 1826
Oil on canvas
25½ x 35½ (64.8 x 90.1)

Gift of Mrs. John D. Rockefeller 3rd

The story of Thomas Cole's dramatic rise to fame and the founding of the Hudson River school is among the most familiar in the history of American art. In October 1825, when he was twenty-four years old, three of his landscapes were sold to three prominent figures in the young nation's art community, John Trumbull, William Dunlap, and Asher B. Durand. Recognizing that Cole's Hudson River Valley scenes captured the character of the American wilderness with a freshness and vigor that was stunningly new and original, they immediately spread word of his achievement. One of the first to hear was Robert Gilmor, a highly knowledgeable and sophisticated Baltimore collector. Cole met the collector in New York in the spring of 1826, and Gilmor commissioned a view of the Catskill Mountain House. In July Cole informed Gilmor that the subject was causing him difficulty and proposed choosing a new subject to "ensure a better picture."[1] That "better picture" would be *Sunrise in the Catskills*.

Gilmor readily agreed, but also offered copious advice as to what style Cole should use and what details should be included.[2] For Cole, corresponding with this astute though highly opinionated connoisseur proved of great importance. He was still forming his artistic beliefs, and expressing his intentions to Gilmor on paper during the very time he was painting the picture for him forced Cole to clarify his ideas both in his own mind and on canvas. The letters they exchanged provide fascinating evidence of a lively, often argumentative interplay between artist and patron and are among the most celebrated documents in the history of American art.[3]

Sunrise in the Catskills was delivered to Gilmor on Christmas Day 1826.[4] Its subject, according to the artist, was a view from Vly Mountain near the headwaters of the Delaware River.[5] Using a daringly elevated point of view, Cole presented a vista toward several other mountains and across valleys filled with mists rising in the morning light. In the foreground are tangled bits of underbrush, contorted and fallen trees, and rough outcroppings of rock. Clearly, this is not a tamed and cultivated portion of the American landscape, but a remote, wild place. A primeval scene of "desolate wildness," as Gilmor described it, it confronts the viewer with something fundamental about the American landscape, American landscape painting, and the formation of an American national identity during the first half of the nineteenth century. As a writer for the art magazine *The Crayon* would observe: "Our country *is* wild, and must be looked at by itself, and be painted as it is. . . . untamed nature everywhere asserts her claim upon us, and the recognition of this claim represents an essential part of our Art."[6] It was Thomas Cole, with works such as *Sunrise in the Catskills*, who first asserted that claim pictorially.

Sunrise in the Catskills, as a key early work in Cole's development, is an especially meaningful addition to the National Gallery's collection. In company with a splendid work from Cole's maturity, *The Notch of the White Mountains (Crawford Notch)* of 1839, and his famous four-part allegorical series, *The Voyage of Life* of 1842, it allows a superb overview of the artist's entire career. And in the broader context of nineteenth-century American landscape painting, represented in the collection by works by Asher Durand, John Kensett, Frederic Church, Jasper Cropsey, and other members of the Hudson River school, *Sunrise in the Catskills* provides a compelling beginning for one of the most glorious episodes in the history of our national art.

Franklin Kelly

PROVENANCE
Robert Gilmor, Jr., Baltimore, 1826–1848; Private collection, New Haven, 1967; Kennedy Galleries, New York, 1968; Mr. and Mrs. John D. Rockefeller 3rd, 1968.

NOTES
1. 28 July 1826, quoted in Howard S. Merritt, ed., "Correspondence between Thomas Cole and Robert Gilmor, Jr.," in *Studies on Thomas Cole, and American Romanticist* (Baltimore, 1967), 43.

2. See Merritt 1967, 43–44.

3. Ten letters (see Merritt 1967) dating from 1826–1828 between Cole and Gilmor have survived, and several others are known to have existed.

4. In a now-unlocated letter of 4 December 1826 Cole announced the completion of the picture and described it to Gilmor. Something of the content of this important letter can be deduced from Gilmor's response of 13 December (Merritt 1967, 44–45): Cole's painting depicted "the desolate wildness of American nature," did not include figures, and represented a scene "near the headwaters of the Delaware."

5. On Cole's list of pictures painted in New York in 1825–1826 (see Ellwood C. Parry III, *The Art of Thomas Cole: Ambition and Imagination* [Newark, Del., London, and Toronto, 1988], 22), Gilmor's picture is recorded as "Sunrise from the Fly [sic] Mountain." However, the first letter of "Fly" has been written over by a later hand. The word must have originally read "Vly," which is the name of a mountain in the Catskills about eight miles from the east branch of the Delaware.

6. "Sketchings; Exhibition of the National Academy of Design, No. III," *The Crayon* 1 (11 April 1855), 234.

JEAN-BAPTISTE-CAMILLE COROT
1796–1875

Clump of Trees at Cività Castellana
1826
Graphite, pen, and ink
heightened with white
10⁷⁄₁₆ x 13⁷⁄₈ (26.5 x 35.2)

Gift of
Walter H. and Leonore Annenberg

The inscription on this drawing, *Civita Castellana / 1826*, identifies it with a significant time and place in Corot's development.[1] One of the most prolific artists of the nineteenth century, Corot began his career at the comparatively advanced age of twenty-six. After nearly four years of academic training in Paris, Corot, like many aspiring French artists, traveled to Italy to continue his studies. As was customary, Corot left Rome when hot weather arrived to make sketching tours of the surrounding Roman campagna. He arrived in Cività Castellana toward the end of May 1826, remained there most of June, and returned again in September and October of 1827, approximately three months of the two and a half years Corot was in Italy. Yet the paintings and drawings that originated in Cività Castellana in that comparatively brief time form nearly one-fourth of Corot's output from that period.[2]

During his first stay in Italy, from the end of 1825 until the end of summer in 1828, Corot attained artistic maturity and decided on the course of his life. In a letter to a friend in Paris written shortly after Corot made this drawing, he noted first that he was sitting in a dense wood with the noise of a waterfall in the background. He continued with the assertion that he had "only one goal in life that [he] wished to pursue with constancy: to make landscapes."[3]

It is in carefully worked drawings like *Clump of Trees at Cività Castellana*, done on the scene in several concentrated hours, that we see Corot's artistic personality emerge. Corot first established the principal lines of the composition in graphite, then articulated individual components of the scene in crisp notations in both graphite and ink. Ink

was placed over the preliminary graphite line both to strengthen the paler graphite and to create space and atmosphere in the composition by emphasizing prominent features of the foreground in contrast to the distant hillsides. The effectiveness of that approach and Corot's mastery of these materials are evident, for instance, in two adjacent areas of hatching near the center: the darker lines indicate foliage extending out from the trees at right, while paler, delicate hatchings summarily describe the overgrown cliffs beyond. Corot followed this method of composition throughout his career, an approach that he recommended to pupils and followers including the impressionists Camille Pissarro, Berthe Morisot, and Auguste Renoir.

It is not uniqueness that distinguishes *Clump of Trees at Cività Castellana* from contemporary works. Corot's chosen subject and technique do not differ substantially from the norm. Rather, Corot's individual and particularly responsive handling of these traditional forms and the acuity and conscientious freshness of his observation set him apart from his coevals. On one convivial evening in a Roman café, teasing by some of Corot's artist friends was stopped abruptly when Caruelle d'Aligny, another French landscape painter, declared, "My friends, Corot is our master."[4] Edgar Degas echoed those words some sixty years later, saying "I believe that Corot drew a tree better than any of us."[5]

Clump of Trees at Cività Castellana is especially welcome at the National Gallery as the only drawing by Corot in a collection rich in his paintings.

Florence E. Coman

PROVENANCE
A. Stroelin, Lausanne; Sale, Gutekunst and Klipstein, Bern, 22 November 1956, no. 66; Curtis O. Baer, New Rochelle; his son, Dr. George Baer, Atlanta.

NOTES
1. The most complete discussion of Corot and Cività Castellana is in André and Renée Jullien, "Les Campagnes de Corot au nord de Rome (1826–1827)," *Gazette des Beaux-Arts* s. 6, 99 (May–June 1982), 179–202.

2. Jullien 1982, 189.

3. "Je n'ai qu'un but dans la vie, que je veux poursuivre avec constance: c'est de faire des paysages." Jean-Baptiste-Camille Corot, letter from Papigno dated 8 August 1826 to Abel Osmond, Paris, in *Corot raconté par lui-même et par ses amis* (Paris, 1946), 1:179–180.

4. Etienne Moreau-Nélaton, "L'Histoire de Corot et de ses oeuvres," in Alfred Robaut, *L'Oeuvre de Corot: Catalogue raisonné et illustré* (Paris, 1905), 1:33–34.

5. "Je crois que Corot dessine un arbre mieux qu'aucun de nous." Degas reportedly made this statement to Frémiet in Gérôme's studio on 20 June 1887. Jean Diéterle in *Exposition Corot 1796–1875* [exh. cat. Galerie Schmit] (Paris, 1971), 15.

SAMUEL PALMER
1805–1881

A Cascade in Shadow, 1835 or 1836
Watercolor, gouache, and pen
and brown ink over graphite
18⅝ x 14¾ (46.4 x 37.5)

Promised Gift of Malcolm Wiener

Samuel Palmer made sketching tours of northern Wales in 1835 and 1836, accompanied by the artists Edward Calvert and Henry Walter.[1] He returned to London with dramatic sketches of the Cambrian Mountains, romantic views of castles, and finely wrought studies of waterfalls such as this cascade near the junction of the Machno and Conway rivers.[2] Charged with poetic feeling, this watercolor not only exemplifies the love of the picturesque typical of the romantic period, but also Palmer's distinctive sensitivity to nature. Palmer's son wrote that his entire soul was in these Welsh works,[3] and indeed it seems that not a single nuance escaped his attention, from the radiance of golden light on distant leaves to the lustrous and mirrorlike surface of the mountain stream.

Palmer's childhood was in many respects exceptional. His mother encouraged him to make copies after prints and drawings, and his father, a bookseller, introduced him to literature. The elder Palmer was a brilliant but erratic man whose nature Samuel inherited. As Samuel matured he became a habitual soul searcher, prone to radical shifts of temperament.

At age seventeen Palmer met the artist John Linnell. Linnell was thirteen years his senior, forceful, engaging, and marked for success. Linnell exerted a tremendous influence on Palmer's life—introducing him to the poet and painter William Blake and to his daughter Hannah whom Palmer married—and provided lifelong artistic and financial support. This support was not without its cost, however, for Palmer suffered under the domineering influence of his father-in-law.

Without question Blake's visionary art had a profound influence on Palmer and inspired his early Shoreham period, so named after the Kent village where Palmer lived from 1827 to 1832. These imaginative works, remarkable for their high degree of spirituality, were followed by a shift in the mid-1830s toward greater naturalism. In the Welsh subjects of 1835 and 1836, which include at least six studies of waterfalls,[4] Palmer was able to balance his Shoreham stylization with natural observation. The sweeping pen lines that shape the framework of *Cascade in Shadow* are richly inventive and form a counterpoint to Palmer's fidelity to texture and color. The play of light and shadow in pure earth tones not only enlivens the scene but also imbues it with radiant warmth.

Although the National Gallery has a choice group of Palmer etchings primarily from the Rosenwald Collection and a bound copy of Palmer's Milton illustrations donated by William B. O'Neal, until now the Gallery had only one drawing by Palmer, an 1830 Shoreham work from the Paul Mellon Collection. *A Cascade in Shadow* embodies ideal beauty balanced with inventiveness and is a superb example of the picturesque.

Judith Brodie

PROVENANCE
(Probably) Leonard Rowe Valpy; Sir Robert Young CBE, sold Sotheby's 17 March 1954, lot 45; The Fine Art Society; Lord Clwyd; Private collection, sold 1988; Leger Galleries Ltd., sold 1989.

NOTES
1. Calvert and Walter, along with Palmer, were members of an artistic brotherhood called "The Ancients." For a catalogue on The Ancients see Raymond Lister, *Samuel Palmer and "The Ancients"* [exh. cat. Fitzwilliam Museum] (Cambridge, England, 1984).

2. Raymond Lister, *Catalogue Raisonné of the Works of Samuel Palmer* (Cambridge, England, 1988), no. 241.

3. "His soul was in this work; he rejoiced in the rugged beauty of wild impetuous currents, no less than in the still translucent depths; and held that a landscape, however lovely, was never perfect without at least a glint of water." A. H. Palmer, *Samuel Palmer: A Memoir* (London, 1882), 9.

4. Lister 1988, nos. 221, 222, 226–228, and 241.

No. 7

Samuel Palmer

JOHN MARTIN
1789–1854

View on the River Wye, Looking towards Chepstow, 1844
Watercolor, gouache, oil (?) over graphite, scraped, heightened with varnish and/or gum arabic
12³⁄₁₆ x 25⅛ (31 x 64)

Gift of The Circle of the
National Gallery of Art

John Martin, generally recognized as a painter of apocalyptic visions,[1] was also a painter of visionary landscapes, mostly in watercolor. Martin's preference for dramatic river landscapes seems to have been shaped by his formative years spent in the Tyne River Valley in Northumberland. Although he moved to London in 1806 and acquired an urban outlook, he never confined himself solely to the city. The surrounding countryside was a frequent haven for Martin, as was Wales where so many of the British watercolorists had found inspiration. During the last decade of his life he traveled to southeast Wales and turned his attention to the beauty of the Wye River Valley, in particular the area near Chepstow. This astonishing watercolor, which is a view of the river with Chepstow Castle barely discernible in the distance, is one of a series of Wye views that the artist painted in 1844.[2]

Martin eventually exhibited four of the Wye watercolors at the Royal Academy.[3] Yet it was this sheet that he chose to exhibit first and singly.[4] Another in Ottawa from the series[5] provides a similar spatial sweep from a heightened aerial perspective, but without the overwhelming vertiginous and awe-evoking aspect. In the National Gallery watercolor the immense mountain range curves dramatically inward and threatens to engulf the tiny and almost transparent figures moving upstream in their boats. The imminence of the view actually provokes a sense of fear, an idea central to Edmund Burke's thoughts on the sublime and one favored by artists of Martin's generation.[6] No less remarkable is the immensity and strength of the effect achieved with the utmost delicacy of brushwork.

Although the National Gallery has only one other watercolor by John Martin, a small pastoral scene, the collection of British drawings has been notably strengthened over the past decade. Among outstanding recent acquisitions were two superb watercolors, one by Thomas Girtin and the other by Paul Sandby, both donated by The Circle of the National Gallery of Art.[7] Through The Circle's continued generosity our British collection has been further strengthened by the addition of this magnificent work by Martin. The *View on the River Wye, Looking towards Chepstow* is one of Martin's finest watercolors, spectacular in scope, and is an impressive example of what has been termed the natural sublime.[8] It will unquestionably form a keystone in the Gallery's collection of British romantic works.

Judith Brodie

PROVENANCE
Mrs. R. Frank, the sale of the beneficiaries of her estate, Christie's, London, 1 March 1977, lot 176; Robert Tear, London; Michael Simpson Ltd., London.

NOTES
1. Most notably the *Fall of Babylon*, 1819, *Belshazzar's Feast*, 1820, *Adam and Eve Entertaining the Angel Raphael*, 1823, *The Deluge*, 1826, and the Last Judgment trilogy, 1852–1853. Repr. William Feaver, *The Art of John Martin* (Oxford, 1975), pls. 26, III, 38, IV (1834 version), 147, VII, and 155.

2. Aside from the present drawing, three can positively be identified: *View on the River Wye, near Chepstow*, National Gallery of Canada, repr. *Master Drawings from the National Gallery of Canada* [exh. cat. National Gallery of Art] (Washington, 1988), no. 84; *The Wye Valley*, Whitworth Art Gallery, repr. Washington 1988, 265; and *View on the River Wye, Looking towards Chepstow Castle*, present whereabouts unknown, repr. Sotheby's *Eighteenth- and Nineteenth-Century British Drawings and Watercolors* (London, 14 July 1988), lot 131.

3. See entries 707 (1845), 977 (1847), 954 (1850), and 976 (1850) in Algernon Graves, *The Royal Academy of Arts: A Complete Dictionary of Contributors . . .* , 8 vols. (London, 1905–1906), 5:205.

4. Among other evidence, the present sheet is inscribed by an unknown hand on the verso: ". . . Exhibited at the Royal Academy, London, 1845 No 707. Inspected and authenticated by D. Kighley Baxandall of the Cardiff Art Gallery. . . ."

5. Repr. Washington 1988, no. 84.

6. For a discussion of Burke's philosophy, see Morton D. Paley, *The Apocalyptic Sublime* (New Haven and London, 1986), 1.

7. Thomas Girtin (1775–1802), *Village along a River Estuary in Devon*, 1797/1798, watercolor over graphite and Paul Sandby (1725–1809), *The Tide Rising at Briton Ferry*, 1773, watercolor over graphite.

8. Paley pointed out that "the natural sublime represented scenes of great heights and depths which in nature produced the effect Burke termed 'astonishment.'" See Paley 1986, 3.

ALBERT BIERSTADT
1830–1902

Lake Lucerne, 1858
Oil on canvas
72 x 120 (182.9 x 304.8)

Gift of Richard M. Scaife and
Margaret R. Battle

In the spring of 1990 Albert Bierstadt's most important early painting, *Lake Lucerne*, a work long thought to be lost, came to light under dramatic circumstances. Unaccounted for since the nineteenth century, the painting was discovered in the home of the late Pearl J. Rose, who had lived in seclusion near Exeter, Rhode Island, for many years. The first of Bierstadt's large panoramic landscapes, *Lake Lucerne* had long been sought as the missing link between the artist's early European paintings and the heroic western landscapes of the 1860s and 1870s.

Albert Bierstadt was born in Solingen, Germany, in 1830, the son of a Prussian soldier and his wife. Two years later he came to America when his parents immigrated to New Bedford, Massachusetts. In 1850 he moved to Boston and began advertising his services as a drawing instructor. Self-taught and reportedly lacking in natural gifts, Bierstadt struggled to raise enough money to travel and study abroad, for despite family opposition he had determined early on that he wished to become an artist.

In the fall of 1853 he set sail for Düsseldorf where he hoped to obtain the sponsorship of Johann Peter Hasenclever (1810–1853), a distant relative and a prominent member of the Düsseldorf circle of artists. Hasenclever died shortly before his arrival, however, and Bierstadt turned to Emanuel Leutze (1816–1868) and Worthington Whittredge (1820–1910), two American artists working in Düsseldorf, for assistance. It was Whittredge who later recalled that Bierstadt arrived in the German art capital with a group of presentation drawings that were "absolutely bad."[1] Despite his inauspicious beginning, Bierstadt studied, observed, experimented, and within an astonishingly short period of time transformed himself into a technically accomplished painter.

In the summer of 1856, after more than two years in Düsseldorf, Bierstadt joined Whittredge and several other companions on an extended sketching tour up the Rhine and on into Switzerland and Italy. In the fall of 1857 he returned to New Bedford after nearly four years of European travel and study. Almost immediately he set to work on *Lake Lucerne*, the painting with which he would make his exhibition debut at the National Academy of Design in New York the following spring.

On a canvas larger than any he had attempted before (six by ten feet), Bierstadt composed his landscape from numerous plein-air sketches completed in Switzerland the previous year. Though based on a specific geographic site, *Lake Lucerne* is a masterful combination of fact and fiction. Beneath alpine peaks identified in a contemporary review as Ematten, Oberbauen, Uri Rothstok, and Saint Gotthard are crystalline Lake Lucerne, the river Muotta, and the village of Brunnen.[2] In the foreground, however, Bierstadt allowed his imagination free rein. The elevated knoll, rutted road, and framing trees that direct viewer attention to the middle and far distance are pure invention, as is the camp of nooning gypsies gathered near a blazing fire at the left. Just a few years later Bierstadt would utilize the same compositional technique to produce the first of his panoramic views of Yosemite Valley.

Lake Lucerne was a stunning achievement for an unknown twenty-eight-year-old painter from New Bedford. When placed on view at the National Academy of Design in April 1858, the picture drew astonished praise from critics. Within six weeks Bierstadt had been elected an honorary member of the academy and by the end of the year he had sold *Lake Lucerne* to Alvin Adams, founder of the Adams Express Company, for $925.[3] In 1882, following Adams' death, *Lake Lucerne* was sold at auction to Hezekiah Conant, a private collector from Pawtucket, Rhode Island.[4] The painting has not been seen publicly since the Adams sale.

On the occasion of its fiftieth anniversary, the National Gallery is pleased to accept, as a gift to the nation, its first painting by Bierstadt. *Lake Lucerne* is the most important of Bierstadt's "lost" works and the pivotal painting of his early career.

Nancy K. Anderson

PROVENANCE
Purchased from the artist in 1858 by Alvin Adams, Watertown, Mass.; purchased by Hezekiah Conant, Pawtucket, R. I., at the sale of the Alvin Adams collection, 1882, lot 109; reported to have entered the collection of William L. Sunderland, Exeter, R. I., first husband of Pearl J. Rose, by 1920; listed in the estate inventory of Pearl J. Rose, Exeter, R. I., May 1990.

NOTES
1. Worthington Whittredge, *The Autobiography of Worthington Whittredge*, John I. H. Baur, ed., *Brooklyn Museum Journal* (1942), 26.

2. *Home Journal* (3 April 1858), 2.

3. Bierstadt's election to membership in the academy was reported in the *Crayon* (June 1858), 180. The *New Bedford Daily Mercury* noted the sale of *Lake Lucerne* on 14 December 1858.

4. On 18 March 1882 the *Boston Globe* reported that Mr. Conant had purchased *Lake Lucerne* for $3,375 at the sale of the Alvin Adams collection the previous afternoon.

FITZ HUGH LANE
1804–1865

Becalmed off Halfway Rock, 1860
Oil on canvas
29 x 48½ (73.7 x 1.23)

Promised Gift of
Mr. and Mrs. Paul Mellon

During the last decade of his life Fitz Hugh Lane created his most memorable paintings, which are characterized by refined, elegant compositions and a crystalline depiction of light and atmosphere. His subject matter had not changed—the beaches, harbors, ships, boats, and watermen of maritime New England remained the principal focus—but now a more meditative mood of stillness and quiet came to predominate. These qualities are clearly evident in *Becalmed off Halfway Rock,* a splendid example from this culminating phase of Lane's career.

Halfway Rock, named for its location between Cape Ann and Boston, would have been well known to Lane, for he lived in nearby Gloucester.[1] Rising some forty feet above the sea, the rock is three miles offshore of the harbors of Salem, Beverly, and Marblehead.[2] Halfway Rock was and is frequently used as a marker in sailing races, and in Lane's day outbound fishermen often tossed pennies on it to buy good luck and safe return.[3] In Lane's painting the rock serves as the focal point of the composition, with the becalmed vessels lying seaward to either side. Although the arrangement of the ships and boats convincingly suggests they have merely chanced to drift together on the tide, Lane carefully positioned each to give the painting perfect equilibrium. Stillness and quiet pervade the scene, and other than the motion of a small lobster dory being rowed, all is calm.

Modern eyes are most impressed by the masterful compositions and remarkable clarity of Lane's paintings, but to the artist's contemporaries it was his accuracy in depicting watercraft that ensured his success. He knew, according to one source, "the name and place of every rope on a vessel," and his

paintings "delighted sailors by their perfect truth."[4] Recent research has indeed shown that Lane had a remarkable understanding of ship construction and handling, and that he was sensitive to subtle details of hull design and rigging.[5] *Becalmed off Halfway Rock* testifies to Lane's knowledge of his subject, for it presents a veritable panoply of precisely identifiable craft.[6] The vessel seen broadside at the left is a topsail schooner laden with a cargo of lumber, presumably en route from Maine to Boston. On the right a large merchant brig lies in the middle distance and in the foreground are a "pinky" (a double-ended schooner) and a small fishing sloop. The latter, to judge from the demeanor of its occupants, is being sailed simply for pleasure, but the pinky, carrying fish barrels and towing net-setting dories, is clearly fitted for fishing. Lane thus not only presents the viewer with several different types of vessels, but also surveys the variety of functions and purposes, ranging from the commercial to the pleasurable, for which they can be used.

The National Gallery owns one other work by Lane, *Lumber Schooners at Evening on Penobscot Bay,* also from 1860. That painting, with its two lone schooners, spare composition, and pink twilight sky, strikes a note of wistful revery that evocatively complements the mood of *Becalmed off Halfway Rock.* Both works remind us that Lane lived in rapidly changing times; while he faithfully chronicled the great age of sail in his paintings, he was also a witness to its passing. The majestic sailing ships he so lovingly portrayed were, even in his day, fast being outmoded by steam-powered vessels that moved with or without the wind.[7]

Franklin Kelly

PROVENANCE
Private collection, Boston; Mr. and Mrs. Harrison G. Reynolds, Beverly Farms, Mass., c. 1940s; Mr. and Mrs. Kennedy B. Middendorf, Oyster Bay, New York; Middendorf Gallery, Washington, 1985; Mr. and Mrs. Paul Mellon, 1988.

NOTES
1. On Lane's life and art, see John Wilmerding, *Fitz Hugh Lane* (New York, 1971) and his *Paintings by Fitz Hugh Lane* [exh. cat. National Gallery of Art] (Washington, 1988).

2. Information provided by the Cape Ann Historical Association.

3. *Massachusetts: A Guide to Its Places and People* (Boston, 1937), 274. Young boys were known to row out to the rock and harvest the pennies, but if caught they faced stiff fines.

4. Quoted in William H. Gerdts, "'The Sea Is His Home': Clarence Cook Visits Fitz Hugh Lane," *American Art Journal* 17 (Summer 1985), 49.

5. See Erik A. Ronnberg, Jr., "Imagery and Types of Vessels," in Washington 1988, 61–104.

6. See Ronnberg in Washington 1988, 85, 89–93.

7. Although Lane often included steam-powered vessels in his works of the 1850s, they rarely appear in his paintings after 1860.

EDOUARD MANET
1832–1883

The Balloon, 1862
Lithograph
16 x 20⅛ (40.7 x 51.l)

Promised Gift of
Mr. and Mrs. Paul Mellon

The Balloon, Manet's second lithograph, was far more ambitious and precocious in style and subject than his first, the *Caricature of Emile Ollivier* of 1860. He chose the subject when the print dealer-publisher Cadart invited him to participate in a project for a portfolio of prints by five artists that the dealer hoped would lead to a renewed interest in lithography. Because the results were regarded with contempt by Cadart's printer, the project collapsed with only a few trial proofs produced of each image. Five examples of *The Balloon* are known, including the particularly rich impression from the Mellon collection.[1] This exceedingly rare image is a superb complement to the Gallery's collection of thirty-four prints by Manet.

The exact subject of *The Balloon* eluded scholars until 1983 when Druick and Zegers identified it as a balloon launch that took place 15 August 1862.[2] The launch was arranged in connection with the Fête de l'Empereur, a national holiday celebrated every 15 August since 1852. The date had been chosen by Emperor Louis-Napoléon to encourage the impression of a direct connection between his reign and that of his uncle, Napoléon I, who had also declared 15 August a holiday. It was Napoléon I's birthday; the birthday of the fictitious Saint Napoléon; the Feast of the Assumption; the date established by Napoléon I to celebrate his reauthorization of religion in France; and the date of the Vow of Louis XIII.[3] In short, the date enhanced the illusion of legitimacy of his reign, but in reality Louis-Napoléon had obtained dictatorial powers through a coup d'état in December 1851.

The fête, which always took place on the Esplanade des Invalides, included displays of imperial generosity such as support for the needy, amnesties, pardons, free entertainment, distributions of inexpensive gifts,

and a lavish fireworks display.[4] The festival was, in effect, an enormous propaganda event. The balloon launch fascinated and entertained the public, but it also served as a display of modern technological accomplishment and a symbol of the ascendancy of the empire.

To the left and the right of the balloon are two slippery, soaped poles known as *mâts de cocagne*, which agile individuals climbed in order to retrieve prizes at the top. Behind are three so-called "Venetian masts" bearing imperial ensigns. In the left and right background are stages for pantomimes glorifying imperial military achievements. The crowd is a cross-section of the Parisian populace "whose diverse social components emerge clearly, but whose individual portraits are sacrificed to a vigorous handling that conveys Baudelaire's image of the crowd as 'an immense reservoir of electrical energy'."[5]

In front of the crowd is a crippled figure on a wheeled platform just above the ground. He is the antithesis of the accomplishments represented actually and symbolically by the balloon. How he became crippled is not known, but Manet portrayed him as isolated within a society that ignores him. He anchors the composition and literally brings us down to earth. Ironically, he is the only true invalid visible at an occasion that took place on the Esplanade des Invalides not far from the Hôtel des Invalides, which is faintly visible in the background. Moreover, the alignment of the cripple and the balloon is by no means accidental.[6] On 15 August 1862 the balloon launch actually took place at the other end of the esplanade.[7] Clearly Manet organized the composition in order to draw attention to the failed social contract of the Second Empire.

Charles S. Moffett

PROVENANCE
André Bloch, Paris; D. David-Weill; sale, D. David-Weill, 25–26 May 1971, Hôtel Drouot, Paris; R. M. Light & Co., Inc., as agent for Paul Mellon.

NOTES
1. Marcel Guérin, *L'Oeuvre Gravé de Manet* (Paris, 1944), 17 and no. 68; Anne Coffin Hanson, *Edouard Manet 1832–1883* (Philadelphia, 1966), 63; Jean C. Harris, *Edouard Manet: Graphic Works* (New York, 1970), 82; Frances Carey and Antony Griffiths, *From Manet to Toulouse-Lautrec: French Lithographs 1860–1900* [exh. cat. British Museum] (London, 1978), 12–14, 32 (no. 14); Douglas Druick and Peter Zegers, *La Pierre Parle: Lithography in France 1848–1900* [exh. cat. National Gallery of Canada] (Ottawa, 1981), 5–6; Douglas Druick and Peter Zegers, "Manet's 'Balloon': French Diversion, The Fête de l'Empereur," *The Print Collector's Newsletter* 14/2 (May–June 1983), 38.

2. Druick and Zegers 1983, 38.

3. Druick and Zegers 1983, 40.

4. Druick and Zegers 1983, 41.

5. Druick and Zegers 1983, 39.

6. Theodore Reff, *Manet and Modern Paris* [exh. cat. National Gallery of Art] (Washington, 1982), 260; George Mauner, *Manet: Peintre-Philosophe* (University Park and London, 1975), 175; Druick and Zegers 1983, 40; Kathleen Adler, *Manet* (Oxford, 1986), 44.

7. Druick and Zegers 1983, 40.

CLAUDE MONET
1840–1926

Sainte-Adresse, 1867
Oil on canvas
22⅝ x 31¾ (57 x 80)

Gift (Partial and Promised) of
Catherine Gamble Curran and Family

As the first landscape of the 1860s by Claude Monet to enter the National Gallery of Art, *Sainte-Adresse* is a superb complement to two other Monets of the 1860s already in the collection: *Camille and Bazille,* 1865–1866 (1970.70.41) and *Interior, after Dinner,* 1868–1869 (1983.1.26). In addition it joins an important canvas by the artist's close friend Frédéric Bazille, *The Ramparts at Aigues Mortes* (1985.64.1), also painted in 1867, as well as an outstanding landscape painted the following year by Camille Pissarro and also a gift in honor of the fiftieth anniversary, *Landscape near Pontoise* (Gift [Partial and Promised] of Mr. and Mrs. David Rockefeller).

Monet spent the summer of 1867 in Sainte-Adresse, a village on the coast of Normandy near Le Havre. He was there because he was virtually penniless and therefore had to accede to arrangements made by his father to live with his father's sister, Madame Lecadre. His father made the offer to ask Madame Lecadre to take in her nephew with the understanding that Monet would end his relationship with his pregnant mistress, Camille Doncieux (she would give birth to their son, Jean, in July). They married in the summer of 1870.[1]

Reluctantly, Monet left Camille with a friend in Paris and went to Sainte-Adresse in June. In a letter of 25 June to Bazille he reported that he was at work on a group of pictures that most certainly included *Sainte-Adresse*: "I am slaving away; I have about twenty canvases coming along nicely, some stunning marines as well as figures and gardens. . . . Among the marines, I am doing the regattas of Le Havre with lots of people on the beach and the roadstead covered with small sails."[2] The group of paintings cited in the letter included, in addition to *Sainte-Adresse,* several other important early works, such as *Terrace at Sainte-Adresse* (The Metropolitan Museum of Art, New York), *The Beach [Races] at Sainte-Adresse* (The Met-

ropolitan Museum of Art, New York), and *The Beach at Sainte-Adresse* (The Art Institute of Chicago). In short, *Sainte-Adresse* takes its place among a group of exceptional paintings that are of critical significance to the artist's early development and to the rise of the impressionist movement.

Of the beach scenes Monet painted in the summer of 1867, *Sainte-Adresse* is the only view toward the west. However, consonant with the others, it records specific climatic conditions characterized by particular effects of color and light. The overcast sky, the gray-green water, the clarity of the air, and the quality of the light indicate that the artist hoped to convey an actual experience, in marked contrast to the idealized, formulaic approach of painters trained at the Ecole des Beaux-Arts. Of course truth to the experience of color and light would become a hallmark of the impressionist movement, but the beach scenes of 1867 reflect Monet's still-close ties to the realist-naturalist ideas that dominated much of the best French landscape painting in the fifties and sixties.

However, in *Sainte-Adresse* it is apparent that Monet kept descriptive detail to a minimum, and his growing preoccupation with the arrangement of touches of color on the picture plane is easily recognized. Furthermore, in details such as the rich orchestration of the grays of the vigorously painted sky and the blacks and grays in the hulls of the boats on the beach, one finds the willingness to experiment and improvise that is so important to his technique. As William Seitz has noted in connection with *The Beach at Sainte-Adresse,* "Monet was unfettered by traditional formulas, and relied instead on an innate optic sensibility. . . . Were his images not enriched by vigorous brushwork, selective placing of mobile elements, and an intangible quality of artistry, one would say that he perceived objects as a camera does — in colored patterns rather than solid masses."[3]

Indeed, *Sainte-Adresse* and the beachscapes of 1867 reveal Monet as a central figure in the emerging impressionist movement. These accomplished and beautiful images are early but unequivocal evidence of the talent and prowess of the young artist long since recognized as a driving force of nineteenth-century French modernism.

Charles S. Moffett

PROVENANCE
Probably Jean-Baptiste Faure, Paris; Sale, A. Tavernier, Galerie Georges Petit, Paris, 6 March 1900 (no. 58); Sale, Th. Revillon, Paris, Galerie Georges Petit, 1 March 1924, no. 25, to V. Revillon; Sale, Galliera, Paris, 23 November 1965, no. 198; Fritz and Peter Nathan, Zurich, c. 1967; Catherine G. Curran, New York.

NOTES
1. Gaston Poulain, *Bazille et ses amis* (Paris, 1932), 74–77.

2. Daniel Wildenstein, *Claude Monet, Biographie et catalogue raisonné,* vol. 1 (Paris and Lausanne, 1974), 423–424, letter 33, inscribed and dated "Ste. Adresse ce 25 juin [1867]."

3. William C. Seitz, *Claude Monet* (New York, 1960), 74.

CAMILLE PISSARRO
1830–1903

Landscape at Les Pâtis, Pontoise, 1868
Signed and dated, lower right,
C. Pissarro 68.
Oil on canvas, 32 x 39½ (81 x 100)

Gift (Partial and Promised) of
Mr. and Mrs. David Rockefeller

Between October 1866 and January 1869, Pissarro lived in Pontoise, a town about fifteen miles northwest of Paris on the banks of the Oise. The lanes, farm buildings, hillsides, and plowed fields of Pontoise and the surrounding area provided the subject matter for a group of landscapes that are among the artist's most important works.

Les Pâtis is situated in the Viosne valley between the château of Marcouville and Osney. Brettell has noted that the Rockefeller picture "was painted from the hillside near the village of Cernay overlooking the Viosne valley with its hamlet, Les Pâtis. Yet it is clear that topographical accuracy was not Pissarro's concern. The floor of the Viosne valley with its distinctive mills, old farms, quarries, and small forests, all of which would have fascinated a topographical tourist illustrator, play a minor role in Pissarro's landscape. The rich human and architectural character of the site is eschewed."[1]

Landscape at Les Pâtis, Pontoise is one of at least seventeen views of Pontoise and its environs that Pissarro painted in the late sixties.[2] Its dimensions identify it with a group of large, ambitious works that were apparently painted for exhibition, such as *Jallais Hill, Pontoise,* 1867 (The Metropolitan Museum of Art, New York) and *Hillsides of l'Hermitage,* 1867 (Solomon R. Guggenheim Museum, New York), which were apparently shown in the Salon of 1868.[3] Interestingly, the Rockefeller picture was neither sold nor exhibited during the artist's lifetime, suggesting that Pissarro deliberately reserved it for his own collection. As Margaret Potter has observed, Pissarro was in the habit of keeping some of his best work for himself and his family "in spite of [the] material hardship" that plagued him for much of his career.[4]

The orderly, structured character of the composition very likely reflects the influence of the early work of Corot, whom Pissarro had long admired and to whom he occasionally turned for advice.[5] In addition, the present work suggests that Pissarro had looked carefully at the work of a wide range of nineteenth-century landscapists including Valenciennes, Daubigny, Chintreuil, Courbet, and Pissarro's younger friend Monet. Nevertheless, possible sources and influences not withstanding, this painting and the other large landscapes of 1867–1868 have a particular character and strength of their own. The combination of relatively broad paint handling,[6] the emphasis on rectilinear forms, the rich orchestration of greens, and the panoramic view of a grand but patently agrarian landscape is unmistakably the work of Pissarro. Moreover, the depiction of the productive and harmonious relationship between peasants and the land addresses overarching political and philosophical beliefs that were an increasingly important aspect of Pissarro's imagery. As Emile Zola wrote of *Jallais Hill, Pontoise* after seeing it in the Salon of 1868: "There is the modern countryside. One feels that man has passed, turning and cutting the earth. . . . And this valley, this hillside embody a simplicity and heroic freedom. Nothing could be so banal were it not so great. From ordinary reality the painter's temperament has produced a rare poem of life and strength."[7]

Landscape at Les Pâtis, Pontoise, the first painting of the 1860s by Pissarro to enter the Gallery's permanent collection, joins twelve other canvases by the artist. Unquestionably an outstanding early work and one of Pissarro's greatest paintings, it is a major addition to the National Gallery's collection of impressionist paintings.

Charles S. Moffett

PROVENANCE
Mme Alexandre Bonin (Jeanne Pissarro, the artist's second daughter), Paris; Emile Lernoud, Buenos Aires; Dr. Carlos Zubizarreta, Buenos Aires; Wildenstein and Company, New York; acquired by Mr. and Mrs. David Rockefeller, New York, February 1955.

NOTES
1. Richard Brettell, *Pissarro and Pontoise: The Painter in a Landscape* (New Haven and London, 1990), 147.

2. Brettell 1990, 145.

3. Vivian Endicott Barnett, *The Guggenheim Museum: Justin K. Thannhauser Collection* (New York, 1978), 182.

4. Margaret Potter, private communication, 1990.

5. John Rewald, *The History of Impressionism,* 4th rev. ed. (New York, 1973), 16, 17, 33, 48, 49, 75, 76, 101; Brettell 1990, 145, 147.

6. Richard Brettell, "Camille Pissarro, A Revision," *Pissarro* [exh. cat. Hayward Gallery, London and Museum of Fine Arts, Boston] (London and Boston, 1980), 16: "Pissarro chose to enlarge what had been appropriate forms for *plein-air* oil-sketches to the scale of a Salon landscape. His realism was therefore hardly new in itself, but the context in which it was presented was certainly new."

7. As quoted in Charles S. Moffett, *Impressionist and Post-Impressionist Paintings in the Metropolitan Museum of Art* (New York, 1985), 85.

ALPHONSE LEMERRE

Sonnets et eaux-fortes
Lemerre, Paris, 1869
Bound volume
13¹⁵⁄₁₆ x 10¼ (35.8 x 26)

Edouard Manet, 1832–1883
Fleur Exotique
Etching and aquatint

Victor Hugo, 1802–1885
L'Eclair
Etching and drypoint

Jean François Millet, 1814–1875
Sur une composition de F. Millet
Etching and drypoint

Gift of Richard A. Simms

Sonnets et eaux-fortes is one of the most important illustrated books published in France during the third quarter of the nineteenth century. Its illustrations were created by some of the leading artists of this time, many of them better known as painters than printmakers. Its illustrations were treated with equal importance as the text, and it has been described as a precursor to the *livres de peintres* that flourished around the turn of the century.[1] So outstanding are its illustrations that few copies of the book remain intact, most having been disbound and their pictures sold individually. The National Gallery's graphics collection already includes a large and fine assortment of eighteenth-century French illustrated books from the Widener Collection and one of the great French books of the early nineteenth century, Goethe's *Faust* illustrated by Eugène Delacroix. Until now however, it has included only one other volume with illustrations by an impressionist artist: Jules Champfleury's *Les Châts*, with an etching and aquatint by Manet. The addition of *Sonnets et eaux-fortes* will help make the Gallery's holdings of illustrated books more representative of this important period in the history of art.

Lemerre, the editor of *Sonnets et eaux-fortes*, enlisted Philippe Burty to commission prints as illustrations for the poems. This was an eminently wise choice because Burty, a critic for the *Gazette des Beaux-Arts*, was closely involved with the etching revival and able to interest in the project such notable artists as Gustave Doré, Jean Léon Gérôme, Seymour Haden, Camille Corot, Félix Braquemond, Jules Jacquemart, Johan

Jongkind, and Charles-François Daubigny. The etching revival in France began in 1862 when Alfred Cadart organized the Société des Aquafortistes and began publishing albums of prints to demonstrate the tremendous potential of etching as an artistic medium.[2] Etching had fallen into disuse since the early nineteenth century, but Cadart's efforts served to return it to favor. *Sonnets et eaux-fortes* was one of the few illustrated books that resulted from the creative forces of this renaissance of etching.

Manet was among the artists whose prints were published by Cadart. His experimentation with re-creating images from his own paintings — as well as from works by such artists as Velázquez and Goya — helped convey the graphic media to an increasingly elevated plateau; rather than merely reproducing existing images, he would alter them in ways appropriate to the graphic processes, a declaration of the autonomy of the print.[3] Manet's *Fleur Exotique*, which faces the text of the poem by Armand Renaud, is one of the most striking in the volume. It attests to the fascination with Spain and earlier Spanish artists that held sway over Manet's imagination at this time. The National Gallery's painting collection includes such important Manets from this period as *The Dead Toreador*. The image he created for *Sonnets et eauxfortes* is based upon a plate in Goya's *Caprichos* and embodies the mysterious and sometimes sinister enchantment of that work.[4]

The diversity of styles that was fostered within the etching revival is manifest in a comparison of Manet's work with that of

Jean François Millet and Victor Hugo, which also appear in *Sonnets et eaux-fortes*. Millet's etching, like his paintings, addresses the guileless simplicity of the peasant figure with a direct and unassuming approach; Hugo's *L'Eclair* is filled with romantic power, a visualization of the forces that inspired his writings.

Virginia Tuttle Clayton

PROVENANCE
Victoria Keilus Dailey, 1977.

NOTES
1. Philip Hofer, *The Artist and the Book: 1860–1960* [exh. cat. Museum of Fine Arts] (Boston, 1961), no. 64; Gordon Ray, *The Art of the French Illustrated Book: 1700–1914* (New York, 1982), 2:359–362. On the *livres de peintres*, see the entry in this catalogue for Pierre Bonnard's *Parallèlement*.

2. See Gabriel P. Weisberg, *The Etching Renaissance in France: 1850–1880* [exh. cat., Utah Museum of Fine Arts, University of Utah] (Salt Lake City, 1971); Janine Bailly-Herzberg, *L'Eauforte de peintre au dix-neuvieme siecle: La Société des aquafortistes 1862–1867* (Paris, 1972).

3. Manet's work had an important impact on the collecting public's perception of printmaking as art: "it would find . . . in Manet's output, especially in the artist's proofs, the premises for this reappraisal, this promotion of the print as an alternative art form, not subordinate to painting" (Michel Melot, "Manet and the Print," in Françoise Cachin and Charles S. Moffett, *Manet: 1823–1883* [exh. cat. The Metropolitan Museum of Art] (New York, 1983), 37.

4. Manet's illustration is an interpretation of the image in plate 15 of the *Caprichos*.

SIR EDWARD COLEY BURNE-JONES
1833–1898

Saint Barbara, c. 1866–1870
Egg tempera with oil glazes (?)
and shell gold, charcoal, graphite
37½ x 16¼ (95.3 x 4.13)

Gift of Professor William B. O'Neal

The *Saint Barbara* is an impressive example of Burne-Jones' mature style. Its confident brushwork shows him at the height of his development. Broad strokes of thickly applied pigment lend texture and density and give the impression of oil paint, a technique favored at the time.[1] Although the Gallery has acquired Pre-Raphaelite drawings in recent years,[2] this is the first work that bridges the gap between drawing and painting. It is the National Gallery's most technically complex and ambitious Pre-Raphaelite work, an exhibition piece of the highest quality.

Edward Burne-Jones did not set out to be a painter. In 1853 he enrolled at Exeter College, Oxford, to take holy orders. There he met William Morris who introduced him to the Pre-Raphaelite movement and the work of its leader, Dante Gabriel Rossetti. Both Morris and Burne-Jones were passionate admirers of the medieval, and it was the romantic medievalism of Rossetti's work that inspired them. Burne-Jones left Oxford in 1856 to study with Rossetti, and in time became the most acclaimed of the second-generation Pre-Raphaelite painters.

Although the Pre-Raphaelite Brotherhood, a semi-secret society founded in 1848, decreed an interest in realism and nature, Burne-Jones was always more concerned with art than with nature.[3] For inspiration he looked to the painters of the quattrocento such as Mantegna and Botticelli, as well as to those of the High Renaissance. Matters of design and decoration were of utmost importance to him. And myth held sway over contemporary reality. The subject of the present work is the legendary Saint Barbara,[4] posed gracefully with a peacock's feather, symbol of her birthplace, and the tower of her imprisonment to her left.

It was that ability to translate myth into gracefully composed designs that William Morris surely recognized. For thirty-five years Burne-Jones provided the firm of Morris, Marshall, Faulkner & Co.[5] with some of its most successful designs for tapestries, painted tiles, and stained-glass windows. Evidence suggests that in its original form the *Saint Barbara* was a design for a stained-glass panel. Its underdrawing (seen with infrared reflectography) is exquisitely rendered in charcoal and graphite and relates to a series of designs completed in 1866 for the east window of All Saints Church in Cambridge, England.[6]

Probably Burne-Jones later retrieved the design and reworked it to its fully realized and lushly colored state.[7] We know that he presented it as a wedding gift in 1870 to Alfred and Louisa Baldwin, brother-in-law and sister of the artist's wife. The industrious Mr. Baldwin was dismayed with the artist's lack of efficiency (the gift arrived four years and four months after the nuptials),[8] but the work was treasured and remained in the Baldwin family for almost a century, passing into the collection of Earl Stanley Baldwin, prime minister of England, before it was acquired by Professor O'Neal.

Judith Brodie

PROVENANCE
Mrs. Alfred Baldwin, née Louisa Macdonald, England; Earl Stanley Baldwin, England; Durlacher, New York, sold 1964.

NOTES
1. Marjorie B. Cohn, *Wash and Gouache* [exh. cat. Fogg Art Museum] (Cambridge, Mass., 1977), 13, 56.

2. Most notably Dante Gabriel Rossetti's *Jane Morris Reclining on a Sofa*, 1870, Ailsa Mellon Bruce Fund and an earlier work by Burne-Jones, *Ariadne*, 1863–1864, The Armand Hammer Collection.

3. Quentin Bell, "The Pre-Raphaelites and Their Critics," *Pre-Raphaelite Papers*, ed. Leslie Parris (London, 1984), 18.

4. Barbara was the daughter of a heathen nobleman who wished to shield her from suitors. For her protection, he confined her to a tower with only two windows for light. Barbara turned to Christianity for salvation and as a testament to her new faith had a third window added to the tower, symbolizing the spiritual light of the Holy Trinity. Her father was so enraged by her new beliefs that he beheaded her.

5. Founded in 1861, changed to Morris & Company in 1875.

6. Burne-Jones' account book of 1866 lists eight designs for stained-glass panels, including the *Saint Barbara*. See A. Charles Sewter, *The Stained Glass of William Morris and His Circle—A Catalogue*, 2 vols. (New Haven and London, 1975), 2:42. See also Sewter 1975, 1:41 and 2: pl. 263 for catalogue entry and illustration of the east window at All Saints.

7. Burne-Jones preferred using a water-based medium for color, usually assumed to be gouache. In this instance we know the water-based medium was egg tempera made from egg white and not yolk. See Susana Halpine, National Gallery of Art Analytical Report, 16 March 1990.

8. Ina Taylor, *Victorian Sisters* (Bethesda, Md., 1987), 106.

MARTIN GENSLER
1811–1881

The Ruins of Saint Nicolai
Church in Hamburg, 1871
Watercolor over brown ink
22³⁄₁₆ x 16 (56.4 x 40.7)

Gift of Galerie Arnoldi-Livie

This highly finished watercolor of *The Ruins of Saint Nicolai Church in Hamburg* records the aftermath of the disastrous fire that swept through the city on 7 May 1842. During that calamity many of the monuments of the historic old town were destroyed, including the famous thirteenth-century church of Saint Nicolai. With virtuosic control of this difficult artistic medium, Gensler shows the interior in ruins, open to the sky, with streams of sunlight articulating the massive piers and shadowy vaults and flickering off the last vestiges of architectural decoration. Nearly lost in the cavernous and disorienting space, workers remove a green-draped sarcophagus from a vault under the pavement. The inscription in the lower right "Vormalige S. Nicolaikirche zu Hamburg 1842, im Sommer," identifies the church and tells us that the picture represents events of the summer following the great fire.

Martin Gensler was the youngest of three brothers, all prominent Hamburg artists. Günther (1803–1884), the eldest, was primarily a portrait painter. The middle brother Jakob (1808–1845) specialized in landscapes and studies after nature; one of his most famous and ambitious paintings depicts *Hamburg after the Fire of 1842* (Hamburg, Kunsthalle). Martin Gensler is known best for his watercolors of the architecture of medieval German towns and of his native Hamburg, although he also painted genre scenes.[1]

In the wake of the fire of 1842, Martin Gensler's drawings in many instances were the city's only records of the important old buildings and churches that were destroyed.[2] Given his interest in these subjects, the Senate appointed him to the commission for the preservation of Hamburg landmarks. The ruins of Saint Nicolai were one of Gensler's most frequent subjects. In fact, his name came to be inextricably linked with the building in local legend. He nearly lost his life while executing one of these pictures when the scaffolding on which he was sitting collapsed, sending him fleeing into an adjoining house.[3]

The crumbling Gothic vaults with mysterious, dangling pieces of twisted metal and the macabre nature of the laborers' excavations place *The Ruins of Saint Nicolai Church* directly in the tradition of German romantic art. One thinks immediately of the Gothic ruins in deserted landscapes represented by Caspar David Friedrich and his followers. These nineteenth-century German works also are related to an even more pervasive and equally romantic eighteenth-century tradition of depictions of Roman ruins, most notably by Piranesi and Hubert Robert. Although the present work is dated 1871, it is very similar to the views Gensler executed in 1842, at the time of the fire.[4]

The Ruins of Saint Nicolai Church is the National Gallery's first fully finished German romantic watercolor, setting a precedent for the Gallery's small but growing collection of nineteenth-century German graphic works.

Elizabeth Pendleton Streicher

PROVENANCE
Busch Collection, Dortmund; Arnoldi-Livie, Munich.

NOTES
1. For information on the Gensler brothers, see Fritz Bürger, *Die Gensler: Drei Hamburger Malerbrüder des 19. Jahrhunderts* (Strassburg, 1916); for Martin Gensler, see especially 29–49, 89–174. See Alfred Lichtwark, *Hermann Kauffmann und die Kunst in Hamburg von 1800–1850* (Munich, 1893), 60–67; for Martin Gensler, see especially 63–67. See also *Katalog der Meister des 19. Jahrhunderts in der Hamburger Kunsthalle*, ed. Eva Maria Krafft and Carl Wolfgang Schumann (Hamburg, 1969), 80–93, especially 89–93.

2. Bürger 1916, 43–44.

3. Bürger 1916, 43–44, 129.

4. See especially *Katalog der Meister des 19. Jahrhunderts*, 91, no. 2003; also Bürger 1916, 129, nos. 294, 295, 296, 297.

WILLIAM STANLEY HASELTINE
1835–1900

Natural Arch at Capri, 1871
Oil on canvas
34 x 55 (86.4 x 139.7)

Gift of Guest Services, Inc.

In 1953 William Stanley Haseltine's daughter, Helen Haseltine Plowden, gave the National Gallery of Art *Marina Piccola, Capri* (c. 1856/1858), a remarkably fresh painting her father had completed following his first visit to the island in the 1850s. On the occasion of its fiftieth anniversary, the National Gallery welcomes the gift of a second painting by Haseltine, *Natural Arch at Capri*, completed fifteen years later in 1871. As complementary works, the two paintings testify to the artist's continued fascination with the rugged terrain and historical resonance of the island held by some to be the home of the mythical sirens.

William Stanley Haseltine was born in Philadelphia, the son of John Haseltine, a successful businessman, and his wife Elizabeth, an amateur landscape painter.[1] While still a teenager he began studying painting with Paul Weber, a German landscape and portrait painter who had settled in Philadelphia. Haseltine graduated from Harvard University in 1854 and returned to Philadelphia where he resumed his studies with Weber. In 1855, having determined that he wished to become a professional artist, Haseltine journeyed to Düsseldorf where became a student of Andreas Achenbach. The following year he joined Worthington Whittredge and a group of fellow students on an extended sketching trip up the Rhine, into Switzerland, and on to Italy. Haseltine remained in Italy for two years traveling and sketching. It was during this period that he visited Capri and completed *Marina Piccola, Capri*. In 1858 Haseltine returned to Philadelphia. The following year he moved to New York, took a studio in the Tenth Street Studio Building, and set to work composing paintings from sketches completed abroad. Personal tragedy struck in 1862 when his wife died in childbirth. Four years later Haseltine remarried and shortly thereafter departed for Europe. By 1869 he had settled in Rome where he remained for more than twenty years. *Natural Arch at Capri* was completed in Rome in 1871.

Although based on plein air sketches like *Nature's Arch* (fig. 1), *Natural Arch at Capri* offers both a close-up view of the island's distinctive limestone cliffs and a more distant view of the Italian coast. In the immediate foreground is the Arco Naturale, the celebrated rock formation located on the southeastern side of the island. In the distance is the peninsula of Sorrento, the southern arm of the Bay of Naples. To the right sheer rocky crags rise abruptly from the sea. At the far left, atop the most distant cliff, are the ruins of the Villa Jovis, built by the Roman emperor Tiberius. Although Augustus Caesar was the first of the Roman emperors to discover the beauties of Capri, it was Tiberius, his successor, who left a lasting mark on the island by building twelve villas.[2]

By the mid-1850s, when Haseltine made his first visit to the island, Capri had become a tourist mecca. Drawn by ancient ruins, spectacular views, the famous Blue Grotto, and a warm sunny climate, visitors arrived year-round. In June 1857 two of Haseltine's compatriots from Düsseldorf, Albert Bierstadt (1830–1902) and Sanford Gifford (1823–1880), spent nearly two weeks on the island sketching.

Haseltine's own sketches of Capri's distinctive rock formations and splendid views suggest that he was as intrigued by the play of light on the rough surface of the island's limestone crags and the shimmering waters of the Mediterranean as he was by the arch itself. Thus the chief protagonist in *Natural Arch at Capri* is the sunlight that defines the serrated edge of the arch and casts the foreground in deep shadow. In the distance the same light bathes land, sea, and clouds in soft pastel hues.[3]

As painted by Haseltine, Capri exhibits all the charms of the mythical island where the melodious songs of sirens lured sailors to their deaths on rocky shores.

Nancy K. Anderson

PROVENANCE
Ader, Picard, Tajan sale, Nouveau Drouot, Paris, 27 April 1987, lot 145; Jody Klotz, New York, 1987; Berry-Hill Galleries, Inc., 1987–1989.

NOTES
1. Helen Haseltine Plowden's biography of her father (*William Stanley Haseltine* [London: 1947]) remains the standard source for biographical information about the artist. Andrea Henderson, who is currently working on Haseltine for an upcoming exhibition, kindly supplied additional information.

2. Augustus Caesar landed on Capri in 29 B.C. while returning to Rome from a campaign in the East. He later turned the island into a private estate. At his death in 14 A.D. Tiberius inherited the empire and Capri. Attracted by its impregnability and isolation as well as its beauty, Tiberius spent the last decade of his life (27–37 A.D.) on the island.

3. In 1876 Haseltine contributed two paintings to the Centennial Exhibition in Philadelphia: *Ruins of a Roman Theatre in Sicily* and *Natural Arch in Capri*. At present it is not clear which of the several pictures Haseltine completed of the Natural Arch was exhibited at the Centennial.

Fig. 1. William Stanley Haseltine, *Nature's Arch*, watercolor and pencil on paper, 14¾ x 21½ (37.47 x 54.61). The Georgia Museum of Art, The University of Georgia, Gift of Mrs. Helen Plowden, Courtesy of National Academy of Design, New York

CLAUDE MONET
1840–1926

The Artist's Garden in Argenteuil
(A Corner of the Garden
with Dahlias), 1873
Signed, lower left, *Claude Monet.73.*
Oil on canvas
24⅛ x 32½ (61 x 82.5)

Partial Gift of
Janice H. Levin

Between 1871 and 1878 Monet lived in Argenteuil. "Located just down the Seine from Saint-Denis," Paul Tucker has written, "where the river loops for a second time on its course north from Paris to the Channel, Argenteuil was a picturesque, historic, and progressive suburban town. It was twenty-seven kilometers by water from the capital but only eleven kilometers by railroad, a fifteen-minute trip. . . . Well known in the nineteenth century as an *agréable petite ville* . . . it was a place, as one contemporary journalist noted, that had 'flowers, large trees, green grass, and a breeze; isn't that enough to make us forget everything?'"[1]

From 1871 until 1874 Monet rented a house at 2 rue Pierre Guienne before moving around the corner to another house on the boulevard Saint-Denis.[2] The present work depicts the garden behind the first house, but Auguste Renoir's *Monet Painting in His Garden at Argenteuil*, 1873 (Wadsworth Atheneum, Hartford), which must have been painted at approximately the same time as *The Artist's Garden in Argenteuil*, indicates that Monet considerably altered the scene for his composition. For example, the flower bed has been enlarged and apparently moved from his neighbor's property to his own; the house in the background of Monet's painting has been moved from a position to the left; several houses visible in the background of the Renoir have been eliminated altogether; and trees have been moved and/or given different shapes. The suburban realities depicted by Renoir seem not to have appealed to Monet; instead, he created an image that he must have found visually, aesthetically, and personally more satisfying.[3] Moreover, as Tucker has observed, "The en-

ergy of [this] view seems to derive from the conflict between myth and reality, between what Monet wanted the site to be and what it was."[4]

Of course the result contradicts Monet's reputation for recording visual truths that he actually experienced. Indeed, Monet cultivated his image as a painter who always worked in the open air and directly from the subject,[5] but careful examination of many paintings reveals that he often made changes for compositional and aesthetic reasons. As his career progressed, studio work and manipulation of compositional elements became an increasingly important characteristic of his work. The question of topographical accuracy notwithstanding, the present painting is an excellent example of the "high" or "classic" phase of impressionism in the early and mid-1870s. The emphasis on color and light, the palette, the attention to atmospheric and meteorological effects, the subject, and the prominence of the open brushwork are hallmarks of the style that established the reputations of the young avant-garde artists who held their first group show the following year and were immediately dubbed "impressionists."

This composition is also important as one of the many views of gardens that first appeared in Monet's work in 1866 and continued to the end of his career. Indeed, the imagined changes in *The Artist's Garden in Argenteuil* foreshadow the constant changes, alterations, and modifications that he made to his garden and water garden in Giverny. Interestingly, there his garden became both a changing work of art in its own right and the ongoing subject of his art.

The Artist's Garden in Argenteuil adds

meaningfully to the Gallery's twenty-one paintings by Monet. Moreover, it joins another of his celebrated garden paintings, *The Artist's Garden at Vétheuil*, 1880 (1970.17.45), and is an excellent complement for the two other Argenteuil pictures in the collection, *The Bridge at Argenteuil*, 1874 (1983.1.24), and *Bridge at Argenteuil on a Gray Day*, c. 1876 (1970.17.44).

Charles S. Moffett

PROVENANCE
Purchased from Monet by Durand-Ruel, December 1873; Baroux Collection; Durand-Ruel, 1896; Gallery Thannhauser, Berlin, c. 1928; Sam Salz, New York; Mr. and Mrs. David O. Selznick, New York; Sam Salz, New York, 1965; Mr. and Mrs. Konrad H. Matthaei, c. 1966; Mr. and Mrs. Philip J. Levin, New York, 1971.

NOTES
1. Paul Hayes Tucker, *Monet at Argenteuil* (New Haven and London, 1982), 9.

2. For a thorough discussion of Monet's life and work in Argenteuil, see Tucker 1982. Also see Daniel Wildenstein, *Claude Monet, Biographie et catalogue raisonné*, vol. 1 (Paris and Lausanne, 1974), 58–62, 75–78; and 236, no. 286.

3. Tucker 1982, 143 and 145, made many of the same observations and offered an extended discussion and analysis of the differences between the two paintings.

4. Tucker 1982, 43.

5. Duc de Trévise, "Pilgrimage to Giverny," *La Revue de l'Art Ancien et Moderne* (Jan. 1927, Feb. 1927) as reprinted in Charles F. Stuckey, ed., *Monet: A Retrospective* (New York, 1985), 334.

WINSLOW HOMER
1836–1910

Dad's Coming, 1873
Oil on panel
9 x 13¾ (22.86 x 34.93)

Promised Gift of
Mr. and Mrs. Paul Mellon

Among the many idylls of childhood that Winslow Homer made in the late 1860s and early 1870s in the aftermath of the Civil War, none are more beautiful and charming than the ones he painted in watercolor and oil at Gloucester, Massachusetts, in the summer of 1873. And among those, the most compelling is *Dad's Coming.*[1]

The image exists in three versions, all nearly identical in size: the Mellon oil; a watercolor at Mills College that depicts the boy seated on the beached dory, which probably preceded the oil; and a wood engraving published in *Harper's Weekly* in November 1873 that, like the oil, includes the standing figure of the woman and child at the right, and was probably made after it.

When it was first exhibited, and also when it was published in 1873, it was titled affirmatively *Dad's Coming.* In the poem of the same title that accompanied its illustration in *Harper's Weekly* that affirmative interpretation was reinforced by an exclamation point and by verses that made it clear that the father's boat has been sighted and all was well. About the middle of this century, however, an alternative title came into use, *Waiting for Dad.* While incorrect, it interestingly reflects a modern inclination to interpret the subject less affirmatively and more ambiguously. For in *Dad's Coming,* as in a number of Homer's oils and watercolors of the period, it does indeed seem that child-

hood innocence is infiltrated by tension, anxiety, and even incipient tragedy, which, in a modern understanding of the subject, makes them so much better, so much truer and more perceptive, than the usual Victorian depictions of childhood. Added to that, the stately cadenced compositional order and simple geometries that endow *Dad's Coming* with an almost classical clarity of form and, despite its actual smallness, a monumental largeness of effect give to the reading of its meaning a profundity and timeless universality.

Dad's Coming is a major addition to the National Gallery's rapidly growing collection of the works of Winslow Homer, one that includes definitive holdings of his watercolors, wood engravings, and oils ranging from his last great painting, *Right and Left,* to this singularly beautiful and equally moving example of his first maturity.

Nicolai Cikovsky, Jr.

PROVENANCE
Wildenstein & Co., 1954; Mr. and Mrs. Paul Mellon.

NOTE
1. The painting has been most closely studied by John Wilmerding, "Winslow Homer's Dad's Coming," *Essays in Honor of Paul Mellon, Collector and Benefactor* (Washington, 1986), 389–401.

EDOUARD MANET
1832–1883

Polichinelle, 1874
Gouache, watercolor over lithograph
18⅞ x 12¾ (48 x 32.3)
Inscribed by Manet with a couplet by
Théodore de Banville

Gift (Partial and Promised) of
Malcolm Wiener

Marcel Guérin recorded only "three or four" copies of the exceedingly rare first state of Manet's lithograph *Polichinelle*.[1] One impression in black is in an American private collection; a second in black was used for the "pierre de report"; and a third, the present unique and outstanding example, was reworked with watercolor and gouache, presumably to be used as a guide for the printer. However, the disposition of the colors in the final version of the lithograph is not exactly the same, and green appears in addition to the reds, yellows, blues, and whites that Manet added to this example. The most plausible explanation of the discrepancies has been offered by Juliet Bareau. She has observed that although Manet wanted to exhibit an impression of the finished color lithograph in the Salon of 1874, he could not show it because work on the lithographic stones had not been completed. Instead he reportedly exhibited a watercolor of *Polichinelle*, which is otherwise unrecorded. Bareau suggests that the image actually shown was probably the present work.[2]

Manet's wish to show the print at the Salon is easily understood, because the color lithograph would have been recognized immediately as a technical tour-de-force. However, since exhibiting the finished print was impossible, his insistence on including the hand-colored proof among the four works that he submitted to the Salon suggests that *Polichinelle* was also significant for another reason. Indeed, it seems very likely that the print incorporated political references that were not immediately apparent to the jury, which accepted only two of the four works Manet submitted.

Although Manet's friend, neighbor, and fellow artist Edmond André posed for *Pol-*

ichinelle, and although the image seems influenced by the painting of the same title that Meissonier exhibited in the Salon of 1860, evidently the figure depicted resembles Marshal MacMahon, president of France between 1873 and 1879.[3] To contemporary audiences the implied ridicule would have been clear: Polichinelle was an irascible, besotted buffoon who was a stock character in productions of the commedia dell'arte and the guignol theater as well as the carnival and the masked ball of the opera. The connection was considered sufficiently obvious for the authorities to force cancellation of the publication of the lithograph in an edition of the Republican newspaper *Le Temps* in June 1874.[4] Evidently the government was particularly sensitive to pointed criticism of MacMahon. He had commanded the French army at Sedan in 1870 that suffered one of the worst defeats of the Franco-Prussian War and later directed the brutal military response to the bloody civil disturbance known as the Commune.[5] Manet himself never offered any information about the meaning of *Polichinelle*, a subject that he also treated on other occasions.[6] However, the print is only one of several works in his oeuvre that comment either directly or indirectly on contemporary political and historical events.

This hand-colored impression of *Polichinelle* is an important addition to the Gallery's exceptional collection of works by Manet. It joins three watercolors; thirteen paintings; and thirty-four prints, including a superb, fully finished impression of the first printing of the third state of *Polichinelle* (1947.7.85) and a proof in brown of the second printing of the third state (1983.35.1).

Charles S. Moffett

PROVENANCE
Mme Charpentier, Paris, 1873 [?]; Mme Martinet, Paris, 1884; Etienne Moreau-Nélaton, Paris; Private collection, Paris; Paul J. Sachs, Cambridge, Mass.; Private collection; Malcolm Wiener, New York, 1988.

NOTES
1. Marcel Guérin, *L'Oeuvre Gravé de Manet* (Paris, 1944), no. 79.

2. Juliet Bareau Wilson, *Manet: Dessins, Aquarelles, Eaux-Fortes, Lithographies, Correspondence* [exh. cat. Galerie Huguette Berès] (Paris, 1978), no. 83.

3. Theodore Reff, *Manet and Modern Paris* [exh. cat. National Gallery of Art] (Washington, 1982), 124, no. 40.

4. Adolphe Tabarant, "Une Histoire Inconnue de 'Polichinelle'," *Bulletin de la Vie Artistique* (1 Sept. 1923), 368–369; Wilson 1978, no. 83; Washington 1982, 124; Marilyn R. Brown, "Manet, Nodier, and 'Polichinelle'," *Art Journal* 45 no. 1 (Spring 1985), 43.

5. Brown 1985, 43–44, has pointed out that de Banville's couplet, inscribed just below the figure, may also have been considered inflammatory because of its reference to drunkenness, an especially controversial issue at that time. The couplet reads: *Féroce & rose avec du feu dans sa prunelle / Effronté, saoul, divin c'est lui, Polichinelle!* ("Ferocious and flushed, with fire in his eyes, / Shameless, drunk, and divine, that's him, Polichinelle!").

6. Denis Rouart and Daniel Wildenstein, *Edouard Manet*, vol. 1, Paintings (Lausanne and Paris, 1975), 178, nos. 212, 213; the figure of Polichinelle also appears the extreme left of no. 216, *Ball at the Opera*, 1873 (National Gallery of Art, 1982.75.1).

Vivre et voir naître du feu dans sa prunelle,

Effront, saoul, divin, dit-lui, Polichinelle!

Th. de Banville.

WINSLOW HOMER
1836–1910

Blackboard, 1877
Watercolor
19⁷⁄₁₆ x 12³⁄₁₆ (49.4 x 32.6)

Gift (Partial and Promised) of
Jo Ann and Julian Ganz, Jr.

This magnificent sheet is one of the greatest works in any medium and from any period of Winslow Homer's career. It was painted just four years after he began making watercolors in earnest in the summer of 1873, following ten years of professional practice as a painter and illustrator.[1] At the end of his life Homer reigned unchallenged as America's greatest watercolor painter; this early work shows the stuff of his greatness. That consisted of an innately sympathetic feel for the medium, but it consisted also of a certain resistance to, or ignorance of, its conventions that gave his watercolors a range, reach, toughness, and daring that few others achieved. "Mr. Winslow Homer is fond of experiments," a critic said of the works (including *Blackboard*) the artist submitted to the 1877 exhibition of the American Society of Painters in Water Colors, sounding an often repeated note in the critical response to Homer's watercolors.[2]

Watercolors at their best are supposedly spontaneous and directly made, fluid and transparent in technique, immediate and intimate in effect. Homer, however, often painted watercolors like oils, thickly and opaquely, and he frequently reworked them as he did his oils. Sometimes, as *Blackboard* shows, he carried watercolors to the larger physical size of oil paintings and made them bear their more premeditated formative processes and meanings as well.

The nameless young woman in *Blackboard* appears repeatedly in Homer's art of this period. Her presence reflects a part of Homer's private life about which nothing is known otherwise, save that her sudden disappearance from his art about 1880, and therefore presumably from his life, was profoundly disturbing, producing the rebarbativeness and reclusiveness that marked his conduct for the rest of his life.[3]

Depicted as a teacher standing before a blackboard, she delivers a lesson in drawing. Homer's native state of Massachusetts was the first in the nation to require (in 1870) the teaching of drawing in public schools. The method developed by Walter Smith, the commonwealth's director of art education, stressed principles of design that could be taught by teachers without special gifts or training. In what might almost be a text for Homer's watercolor Smith described a beginning lesson in drawing: "In the very earliest lessons to the youngest children drawings on the blackboard by the teacher are the only examples used, the illustrations being vertical, horizontal, and oblique lines singly and in simple combinations, such as angles, squares, triangles. . . ."[4] With a wittiness he often indulged in his early work, the vertical, horizontal, and oblique lines by which Homer constructed his watercolor suggest that he was following a children's lesson in drawing taught by the teacher/model according to the very latest method. With further wit he signed the blackboard in the lower right-hand corner as if it were his creation.

Blackboard joins other watercolors that came to the Gallery through earlier gifts, bequests, and purchases to form a collection that embraces with conspicuous quality and remarkable range the body of Homer's work in watercolor, one of the most distinguished achievements in the history of American art.

Nicolai Cikovsky, Jr.

PROVENANCE
William Townsend, Boston; Estate of William Townsend, Boston; Rose Townsend, Boston; Thomas H. Townsend, Boston; Vose Galleries, Boston, 1977; Jo Ann and Julian Ganz, Jr., 1977.

NOTES
1. The definitive work on the subject is now Helen A. Cooper, *Winslow Homer Watercolors* [exh. cat. National Gallery of Art] (Washington, 1986).

2. "The Painters in Water Colors. Pictures by American Artists in the Exhibition," *New York Evening Post* (13 February 1877).

3. See Henry Adams, "The Identity of Homer's 'Mystery Woman,'" *Burlington Magazine* 132 (April 1990), 244–252, for recent speculation on the identity of Homer's sitter and on the nature of his sexuality.

4. Walter Smith, "Art Education and the Teaching of Drawing in the Public Schools," *Massachusetts Teacher* 24 (November 1871), 389.

JULES DALOU
1838–1902

Bust of a Young Boy, c. 1879
Marble
18¾ (47.6) including socle

Gift of the
Iris and B. Gerald Cantor Foundation

While he aspired successfully to be a sculptor of public monuments, Dalou often did his best work on more intimate sculptural types. This contemporary of Rodin, mentioned by critics of their time as of equal stature, excelled at portraits of children. They occur in his work, however, almost exclusively during the years 1871–1879, the period of his exile in England after involvement in the ill-fated Paris Commune of 1871. His English patrons, who came to include Queen Victoria, particularly appreciated his warm and accomplished images of contemporary mothers with children. Studies for the 1878 memorial to the grandchildren of the queen at Windsor, including a beautiful sketch model bust of a little boy,[1] suggest the gift for sympathy that he brought even to monumental commissions.

Recently discovered in an English private collection, this bust shows a small boy with his ringlets swept back as if to free his finely formed face. Conceived and carved with a sensitivity that captures the subtlest swellings and hollows, the delicate marble face looks soft to the touch. While the boy gazes out with a grave and innocent expression, the slight tilt of his head and the deliberately off-center tie falling in the opposite direction give a liveliness that breaks the potential formality. Above all the pupils of the eyes are carved with such crispness and depth that they dominate the composition, appearing to sparkle with light and shadow. A date in the late 1870s seems plausible, based on similarity to Dalou's terracotta bust of *Miss Helen Ionides*, 1879, in the Bethnal Green Museum, London; the pres-

ent marble is a near mirror image of that calm portrait.[2]

Like most sculptors of his day, including Rodin, Dalou employed *practiciens* (carving specialists) to assist with marble renditions of designs he created. His innate preference was for modeling in clay. Early in his career, however, he had developed the ability to perfect the carving of a roughed-out marble sculpture. By the mid-1880s he required a sitter to return several times so that he could personally carve the details.[3] In this bust the exquisitely sensitive handling of the face, compared with the relatively summary treatment of the curls, suggests the difference between the approaches of a technician and a master.

The former owner's grandfather was a partner in Bingham Brothers, marble masons of Fulham. This may one day prove a clue to the child's identity; Dalou was conceivably portraying the son of a colleague who provided him with marble for his sculpture.

The National Gallery owns a terra-cotta sketch of a *Mother and Child* by Dalou, as well as a bronze portrait of his artist friend and protector *Alfonse Legros*. Besides enhancing the holdings of this important artist, this bust takes its place among the fine portraits of children that are high points of the Gallery's sculpture collection. These include Desiderio da Settignano's solemn-faced *Little Boy,* c. 1460, and Houdon's *Alexandre Brongniart* and *Louise Brongniart* of 1777, with their sparkling eyes carved in a manner that Dalou may even have emulated.

Alison Luchs

PROVENANCE
Trevor Shaw Esq. of London by descent from his grandfather; Thos. Agnew & Sons Ltd., London, 1989.

NOTES
1. The sketch is illustrated in Maurice Dreyfous, *Dalou. Sa vie et son oeuvre* (Paris, 1903), 87. On Dalou's career see Dreyfous; Henriette Caillaux, *Aimé Jules Dalou 1838–1902* (Paris, 1935); John M. Hunisak, *The Sculptor Jules Dalou. Studies in His Style and Imagery* (New York, 1977), esp. 133–134, 137–138; and Hunisak in H. W. Janson and Peter Fusco, eds., *The Romantics to Rodin* [exh. cat. Los Angeles Country Museum of Art] (Los Angeles, 1980), 185–199.

2. For this connection, proposed by Hunisak, see *Master Drawings and Sculpture* [exh. cat. Thos. Agnew & Sons Ltd.] (London, 1989), with additional comparative works; for an illustration and discussion of *Miss Ionides* see Hunisak 1977, 133 and figs. 89a and b.

3. On Dalou and marble see Hunisak 1977, 93, and Dreyfous 1903, 48; both mention a carving accident early in his London career, but the 1885 account clearly indicates he continued to carve marble.

PAUL CEZANNE
1839–1906

Sketchbook, c. 1877–c. 1900
Pencil on paper
6 x 9⁵/₁₆ (15.2 x 23.7)

Promised Gift of
Mr. and Mrs. Paul Mellon

Cézanne used the Mellon sketchbook between c. 1877 and c. 1900.[1] It contains forty-six sheets, several of which are blank, and is of a slightly larger format than most of Cézanne's other sketchbooks. A hand other than the artist's has numbered the recto of each sheet a with a Roman numeral. Page XX was removed in 1923 by Cézanne's son and given to Georges Rivière (Kunstmuseum, Basel), and the Roman numeral XXXI was used twice. Seventy-three sides of pages have been used for drawings; the end papers, the recto of the first page, and half the verso of the final page have been used for notes, lists, and arithmetical figuring. There is a draft of a letter to the critic Octave Mirbeau on page II recto. Only one drawing, a landscape with houses, extends across two sides of sheets that face each other (III verso and IIII recto).

The Mellon sketchbook provides an excellent overview of Cézanne's interests from the beginning of his early maturity in the late 1870s to the late work of c. 1900. It includes portraits, a self-portrait, landscapes, figures, architectural and decorative details, vegetation, furniture, bathers, studies after antique sculpture, studies after works by Desiderio da Settignano, Puget, and Rubens, compositional studies, and drawings of ordinary objects such as a lamp, fireplace utensils, and a hat. Cézanne seems to have opened the sketchbook at random and used any page or part of a page without regard to sequence. As a result the location of drawings in the sketchbook is sometimes haphazard. For example, a sketch of c. 1887–1890 depicting a mill (XXVII verso) faces two studies of 1883–1886 for *The Judgment of Paris* (XXVIII recto).[2] Furthermore, work of different dates sometimes appears side by side on one page (VI verso), but a depiction of his son drawing (XVII verso) is several pages away from a directly related study (XXIII verso).

In addition to the many different subjects, there is a wide range in the finish and quality of individual drawings. There are drawings that are experimental and somewhat tentative, such as the page with two views of a woman's head (XIIII recto); but others, such as the self-portrait (X recto), are confident, direct, and well realized. Among the most impressive of the latter variety is a portrait of Madame Cézanne (VII recto) that is a study for *Madame Cézanne in the Conservatory,* 1891–1892 (The Metropolitan Museum of Art, New York).

The Mellon sketchbook as a whole permits a closer view of the artist who was the most reclusive of the impressionist and post-impressionist painters. We see a wide range of technique and sense Cézanne's unspoken delight with the medium. It offers an autobiographical glimpse of his fascination with Renaissance and baroque art, his delight in the shapes and rhythms of ordinary objects, his enduring interest in landscape, and his repeated contemplation and study of the two people closest to him, his wife and son. But most of all the Mellon sketchbook underscores an inexorable desire to search, investigate, probe, and realize imagery through drawing.

The Mellon sketchbook, one of the last Cézanne sketchbooks owned privately, is an outstanding addition to an exceptional group of works by the artist in the National Gallery's collection: twenty-one paintings, three drawings, two watercolors, and nine prints.

Charles S. Moffett

PROVENANCE
Paul Cézanne (the artist's son), Paris; Paul Guillaume, Paris; until 1967, Adrien Chappuis, Tresserve, Switzerland.

NOTES
1. Lionello Venturi, *Cézanne, son art—son oeuvre,* 2 vols. (Paris, 1936), 309–312, nos. 1301–1315 (troisieme carnet); Adrien Chappuis, *Album de Paul Cézanne* (Paris, 1967) facsimile edition; Adrien Chappuis, *The Drawings of Paul Cézanne, A Catalogue Raisonné* (Greenwich, Conn., 1973); John Rewald, *Paul Cézanne: The Watercolors, A Catalogue Raisonné* (Boston, 1983), 103, no. 69.

2. Venturi 1936, no. 537; Chappuis 1966, 60, 62.

Portrait of Madame Cézanne, 1890–1891

THE DEGAS WAXES

c. 1878–c. 1911

Promised Gift of
Mr. and Mrs. Paul Mellon

By Alison Luchs

INTRODUCTION

"It is the movement of people and things that distracts and even consoles . . . ," Edgar Degas (1834–1917) wrote in 1886. "If the leaves of the trees did not move, how sad the trees would be, and we too."[1] The sculpture he produced in the privacy of his studio throughout most of his artistic career testifies to the fascination and consolation he found in intensive study of the movement of living beings.

As in his paintings, pastels, and prints, Degas' principal subjects came from his immediate, late nineteenth-century Parisian world. They are race horses, jockeys, dancers, and nude women bathing or grooming. Yet only a few sculptures, notably the *Little Dancer Fourteen Years Old*, represent figures from contemporary Paris with the painstaking naturalism that was part of his jarring modernity. Even though Degas was a brilliant portraitist, relatively few of his sculptures are portraits.[2] In sculpture, with a few exceptions, he concerned himself less with the details that define the individual than with the form as a whole. He posed his figures in attitudes that achieve a rare synthesis between directly observed actions and motifs derived from the old masters. Thus his statuettes, immediate as their poses may look, frequently recall the ancient, Renaissance, and Far Eastern works that Degas admired and carefully studied. Above all he grappled with the problem of representing a figure in motion, explored from every angle, piercing space and penetrated by it in a configuration that implies imminent change. The spaces shaped by the limbs, changing as one moves around a figure, become as fascinating as the solid forms.

The process of sculpture excited Degas far more than the result. This is evident in these rough, willfully unfinished surfaces; almost all retain the abstract quality of sketches. He strove endlessly to perfect his orchestration of a movement, and often reworked a statuette until it fell to pieces. Experimenting freely just as he did with new methods for painting and printmaking, he devised his own mixtures of pigmented wax, plastilene (nondrying modeling clay), and other substances such as fats and starch. He applied these over armatures of flexible wire and rope, supported by a vertical shaft anchored in the wooden base and often external to the figure. Some limbs were stiffened with nails, brush handles, or matchsticks, and he frequently added corks to the wax for lightness and bulk. This method suited him because, even if the unstable materials easily crumbled or collapsed, they afforded the freedom he prized to revise again and again.[3]

From at least as early as 1870, Degas modeled in wax, devoting increasing attention to it in his last twenty years, as his vision deteriorated.[4] Beginning with horses, he claimed to have taken up modeling statuettes as an aid to working out poses and movements in his paintings.[5] But his sculpture quickly took on a life of its own. Even more self-critical in this pursuit than in his two-dimensional works, he exhibited only one sculpture during his lifetime, the *Little Dancer Fourteen Years Old*, in the sixth impressionist exhibition in April 1881. Critical reception ranged from profound admiration to fury and disgust. Probably less for this reason than because the process of bringing the *Little Dancer*'s highly naturalistic style to perfection took so long, Degas kept the rest of his sculpture private. Working at it for his own stimulation and exploration, not for an audience, he allowed only a few friends to see it. Nor would he permit it to be cast in a material other than plaster, and then in only four cases. He held out to the end against commitment to bronze, "that material for eternity."[6] But he carefully preserved his favorite waxes under glass vitrines and continued to model statuettes until 1912, when a forced move from his familiar studio in the rue Victor Massé precipitated his final decline.

The famous bronzes cast from Degas' waxes were produced after his death by the founder A.-A. Hébrard in an arrangement with the Degas heirs. Of about 150 sculptures that his dealer Durand-Ruel remembered finding, in widely varying condition, in Degas' studio in 1917, 74 were ultimately cast; many others must have fallen to pieces before and after his death. Before being cast the sculptures were repaired and the armatures and bases trimmed,

sometimes reinforced and sometimes replaced, probably with participation by Degas' sculptor friend Albert Bartholomé. Seventy-three chosen sculptures were then cast in bronze, beginning in 1919, in editions of at least 23 each, by the Italian expert Albino Palazzolo (the 74th, *The Schoolgirl*, was cast at an unknown date years later). The process Palazzolo used to make molds from the waxes left all but four of the fragile originals preserved. They were returned to Hébrard's cellar, not to emerge until after the Second World War. Restored further by Palozzolo, these 69 original sculptures were first exhibited as a group in 1955, at the Knoedler Gallery in New York. In 1956 they were all purchased by Paul Mellon.[7]

The bronzes today are widely known in public and private collections. Their brilliant compositions prompted even Degas' friend Mary Cassatt, who had initially opposed their casting, to write: "I believe [Degas] will live to be greater as a sculptor than as a painter."[8]

Yet Degas never saw the bronzes. The only sculptures he produced with his own hands are waxes like the ones in the present exhibition, and only these show the full extent of his sculptural genius. The improvised armatures, poking through the wax, reveal the "drawing in space" that underlies the figures. The direct work of the artist's hands appears with fresh immediacy, smoothing some areas to the look of polished wood, building up others with bits of wax slapped on in a rough, scaly texture that leaves the edges of each fragment visible. Vaguely suggested forms contrast with delicate hints of facial features or anatomical detail. Only the waxes reveal the softly organic substance, its unique response to light, and the varied colors and textures of Degas' revolutionary assemblage of objects and materials. Although the waxes were virtually unknown to most artists before 1955, this mixture of real and represented objects foreshadowed twentieth-century approaches to art.

Also evident only in the original wax sculptures is the essential role played by Degas' armatures and bases. He showed a lifelong preoccupation with the figure's relationship to the earth, its struggles against gravity for freedom and balance. In a few cases the armatures do not merely support a figure but seem to suspend it in the air, long before mobiles like those of Calder were conceived. These effects are lost in the bronze casts. Moreover each sculpture began with a wooden base that defined the ground above which the figure acts and also the spatial environment it charges with its movement. Some bases are multilayered constructions. Several have strips added at the ends to extend them, recalling the strips of paper Degas often added to expand the composition of a pastel. The dimensions of a base and a figure's orientation and movement in relation to it were evidently part of Degas' developing conception. It is true that changes in the bases and armatures, made after the artist's death, must be considered in each case. But the evidence of early photographs and of the waxes themselves take us far toward an understanding of the brilliant uses Degas made of these elements.[9]

A total of sixty-nine sculptures from Degas' hands survive.[10] Sixty-six are mostly of wax and plastilene, three of indefinable matter containing plaster. Today these original works can be seen in only three museums in the world: the Musée d'Orsay, Paris (four works), the Fitzwilliam Museum, Cambridge (three works), and the National Gallery of Art, Washington. In all cases these museum holdings result from the generosity of Mr. and Mrs. Paul Mellon, who donated seventeen waxes, five bronzes, and one plaster to the National Gallery in 1985. Their promised gift of thirty-one additional waxes—nearly half the surviving total—in honor of the Gallery's fiftieth anniversary will make possible the fullest public installation of Degas waxes anywhere since 1956. In addition, the *Little Dancer* appears here in an unprecedented grouping with three closely related works from the 1985 gift: the wax nude study, a bronze cast from that study, and a colored plaster produced in Hébrard's studio from the final 1881 version. These offer insight into the wax's production process, its subsequent history, and the important differences between Degas' original sculptures and the casts made from them.

PROVENANCE

Except for *The Schoolgirl*, all the waxes in this group have the same provenance. Found in Degas' studio in 1917, they passed to the artist's heirs and in 1919 to the founder A.-A. Hébrard. In 1955 they were placed on consignment with M. Knoedler and Co., New York. Paul Mellon purchased the entire group in 1956.

NOTES

The titles used for the waxes today, with the exception of *Little Dancer Fourteen Years Old*, were not devised by Degas. Their English form in most cases originates with John Rewald's *Degas, Works in Sculpture: A Complete Catalogue* (New York and London, 1944), translated with minor changes from the French titles used in the catalogue of the 1921 exhibition of the bronzes. Rewald's titles and Roman numeral catalogue numbers (retained in his *Degas: Sculpture* [New York, 1956]) have become standard.

The dates of the waxes are almost all conjectural. The *Little Dancer* is the best documented. Dates for others have been proposed based on relationships to other Degas works, clues in correspondence, and reminiscences of friends and models. It is usually uncertain whether Degas made a particular sculpture as a study for a related painting or pastel, or whether work on a two-dimensional image inspired him to continue exploring a movement in three dimensions. He repeated and varied certain poses, often over many years. Besides this he would sometimes put a sculpture aside and return to it later.

It is usually argued that his early sculptural style is smoother and more compact, closer to the precision of the *Little Dancer*, and that his treatment grew looser and more expressive in his late years. But certain cases raise the possibility that he worked in more than one manner at the same time. There is also evidence that his earliest sculpted figures are more tranquil and restrained; that they move with increasing freedom after c. 1885, and that in his final years they become heavier and more earthbound.[11]

The "Degas" inscriptions on the waxes are posthumous. Degas would scarcely have added a signature with its implications of completion and an expected audience. The inscriptions may have been added before casting in 1919 or in preparation for the 1955 exhibition.

Materials are described based on observations in Rewald 1956; in Charles W. Millard, *The*

Sculpture of Edgar Degas (Princeton, 1976); and by the author. Analysis of each piece to identify components more precisely remains to be undertaken. Heights given exclude the bases.

Warm thanks are due to Mr. and Mrs. Paul Mellon and to Beverly Carter for essential information and assistance in studying the waxes.

1. Letter of 1886, in Richard Kendall, ed., *Degas by Himself* (London, 1987), 209–210. See also Millard 1976, 86–87.

2. On Degas' portrait sculpture see Rewald 1956, 147–148; Millard 1976, 10–14, and Jean Sutherland Boggs, ed., *Degas* [exh. cat. Galeries Nationales du Grand Palais] (Paris, 1988), 455–456.

3. On his sculptural practices see Rewald 1956, 25–28; Millard 1976, 35–39; John McCarty, "A Sculptor's Thoughts on the Degas Waxes," *In Honor of Paul Mellon, Collector and Benefactor*, ed. John Wilmerding (Washington, 1986), 217–225, and *Sculptures en cire de l'ancienne Egypte à l'art abstrait* (Paris, 1987), 225–237.

4. On the impact of his lifelong visual problems on Degas' work see Richard Kendall, "Degas and the Contingency of Vision," *Burlington Magazine* 130 (1988), 180–197.

5. Degas implied this in an 1897 conversation recalled by François Thiébault-Sisson in 1921; translation in Jacqueline and Maurice Guillaud, eds., *Degas. Form and Space* [exh. cat. Centre Culturel du Marais] (Paris, 1984), 179.

6. On the plaster casts and Degas' reluctance to cast in bronze see Millard 1976, 30.

7. On the casting process and adjustments to the waxes see Jean Adhémar, "Before the Degas Bronzes," *Art News* 54 (November 1955), 34–35, 70; Rewald 1956; Millard 1976, 25–39, esp. 37 n. 54; Patricia Failing, "The Degas Bronzes Degas Never Knew," *Art News* 78 (April 1979), 38–41; Patricia Failing, "Cast in Bronze: the Degas Dilemma," *Art News* 87 (January 1988), 136–141; and Gary Tinterow in Paris 1988, 609–610. Archival photos of several waxes, taken before casting and showing the original forms of some armatures and bases, are published in Paul Gsell, "Edgar Degas, Statuaire," *La Renaissance de l'Art français et des Industries de Luxe* (December 1918), 373–378; Paul-André Lemoisne, "Les statuettes de Degas," *Art et Décoration* (Sept.–Oct. 1919), 109–117; Pierre Borel, *Les sculptures*

inédites de Degas—choix de cires originales (Geneva, 1949; some armatures deleted), and Rewald 1944.

8. Letter quoted by John Rewald in *The Complete Sculpture of Degas* [exh. cat. Lefevre Gallery] (London, 1976), 3.

9. See Boggs in Paris 1988, 23–26; on the armatures and bases: Millard 1976, 94, 104, McCarty in Mellon 1986, 219–223; on the problem of alterations, note 7, above, on expanded paper supports, Paris 1988, 202–203.

10. The census of his surviving sculptures usually includes a seventieth work, a *Torso* cast in plaster at his wish around 1900, of which the wax disappeared before 1919. This plaster is counted among the sixty-nine works in the 1955 Knoedler exhibition, which did not include *The Schoolgirl*.

11. On stylistic evolution of Degas' sculpture see Rewald 1956, 24–25, 140; Millard 1976, 20, 108–110; Boggs in Paris 1988, 484, 586. Failing 1988, 138–139, stressed the problems of any effort to date the sculptures.

Little Dancer Fourteen Years Old
(Petite danseuse de quatorze ans),
1878/1881
Wax, hair, ribbon, linen bodice,
satin shoes, muslin tutu, wood base
39 (99)
REWALD XX

The fame or notoriety of this statuette began even before Degas allowed it to go on view in the sixth impressionist exhibition in April 1881. He had delayed its installation twice over the preceding year, not yet satisfied that it was ready. The critics greeted it with excitement whether they praised or reviled it.[1] Degas had flouted conventions in choosing, as subject for an exhibition sculpture two-thirds life size, a coltish adolescent rather than an ideal beauty, and a denizen of contemporary Paris rather than a goddess or literary heroine. With her low forehead, thrusting jaw, and half-closed eyes, she stands defiantly self-absorbed in her wrinkled stockings. Several critics, based on common knowledge about the life of young dancers, read in her face a morally dubious future.[2] Guilt by association must have reinforced this prejudice, for Degas showed two drawings of *Criminal Physiognomy* in the same exhibition. Compounding the unease his dancer engendered, Degas presented her with what the admiring critic Huysmans termed a "terrible realism," suggesting an ethnographic display. He had modeled her in fleshlike tinted wax, dressed her in actual, miniature clothing rather than the illusion of it, and placed a wig of real blond hair on her head.[3] Thin coats of different colored wax, applied with a paintbrush over the hair, bodice, stockings, and shoes, unified the surface and subtly enhanced the polychromy. The *Little Dancer*, laboriously perfected over three years, became the only sculpture Degas ever exhibited publicly.

The model is generally agreed to be the dancer Marie van Goethem (or van Goethen), daughter of a Belgian tailor and a laundress, born in Paris on 17 February 1864.[4] Her name and address appear in Degas' notebook and on a drawn study; she presumably began to model for him in 1878. How he decided on her taut practice pose, a variation on the fourth position *ouverte*,[5] is uncertain. It went through several changes, but part of the inspiration may have come from a dancer seen from the back in a woodcut by the Japanese master Hokusai, whom Degas

greatly admired.[6] His sculptural interpretation, with arms and legs stretching away from the torso in opposing directions, gives an arresting effect of openness and tension.

The process of conceiving the statuette is documented in at least a dozen drawings of Marie, nude and clothed; and in the smaller (28½ in.) wax nude study in the National Gallery collection. This wax, the bronze cast from it (figs. 1,2), and the drawings record the most extensive preparation Degas ever devoted to a sculpture.

Degas set the nude figure on a plaster pedestal whose base shows the trace of a changed position of the right foot. The final clothed version restores the more strained position he had rejected in the nude study. A crack visible in the bronze nude's neck (repaired in the wax sometime after casting) reflects a crucial decision to tilt her head farther back, enhancing her look of absorbed concentration. The nude's shoulders are thrust back so that her arms hang freer of her body. In the final wax sculpture some of this pent-up energy is transferred to her sharply bent wrists. The difficulties Degas encountered in rendering the angular young figure, most visible where the right leg joins the pelvis, were resolved and turned to advantage by the addition of the costume.

The final, clothed wax has darkened with time; cracks that developed in the upper

arms, visible in the bronze and plaster casts[7] and early photographs, have been repaired. The figure received a new skirt, shorter and more curved than the original, around 1919.[8] It nevertheless retains the effects of freshness, delicacy, and vitality that the posthumous casts can only approximate. The original alone shows fully the fleshlike warmth of the wax, the precision and tenderness with which Degas outlined the girl's eyes, modeled her facial structure, and shaped her mouth, or the endearing details like the dangling end of a ribbon around the left ankle.

The critic Elie de Mont asked the artist in his review, "Could you really have met a model this horrible, this repellant? And admitting that you did meet her, why did you choose her?" Degas evidently chose her because she captivated him as an individual, a social type, and an image of promise. Her character and movements clearly belonged to his own time and place, and he portrayed her with an experimental method as true as possible to those. She embodies the determination of the street-urchin dancer Degas addressed in a sonnet, in which he savors the contrast between her common origins and the celebrated future he envisions for her. The artist wished that, even as the spirits of historical and mythical dancers endowed her with their gifts, she might "hold fast in the palace the race of her street."[9]

Fig. 1. Edgar Degas, *Study in the Nude for the Dressed Ballet Dancer*, c. 1878/1879, wax. National Gallery of Art, Washington, Collection of Mr. and Mrs. Paul Mellon

Fig. 2. Edgar Degas, *Study in the Nude for the Dressed Ballet Dancer*, model c. 1878/1879, cast 1919/1932, bronze. National Gallery of Art, Washington, Collection of Mr. and Mrs. Paul Mellon

NOTES

1. For the critical response see especially Millard 1976, 28–29 and (in French) 119–126; George Shackleford, *Degas. The Dancers* [exh. cat. National Gallery of Art] (Washington, 1984), 66–69; Charles W. Moffett and others, *The New Painting: Impressionism 1874–1886* [exh. cat. The Fine Arts Museums of San Francisco] (San Francisco, 1986), 336, 341–343, 362; Douglas W. Druick and Peter Zegers in Paris 1988, 343.

2. See above references; Washington 1984, 14, 31–38; Richard Thomson, *The Private Degas* [exh. cat. Whitworth Art Gallery, Manchester] (London, 1987), 64–67, and Anthea Callen, "Anatomy and Physiognomy: Degas' Little Dancer of Fourteen Years," in Richard Kendall, ed., *Degas Images of Women* [exh. cat. Tate Gallery, Liverpool] (London, 1989), 10–17.

3. Scholars disagree on whether the "réels crins" mentioned by the critic Huysmans are human hair or horsehair. That Degas probably obtained it from a maker of wigs for dolls, whose address he jotted down in his notebook, does not answer this question. See Rewald 1944, 8; Theodore Reff, "Degas Sculpture, 1880–1884," *Art Quarterly* 33 (1970), 288, and Millard 1976, 64, 124.

4. For these details see Millard 1976, 8, n. 26. On Marie and the history of the statuette see Reff 1970, 277–278; Theodore Reff, *Degas: The Artist's Mind* (New York, 1976; expanded version of Reff 1970), 239–248; Millard 1976, 8–9, 28–29, 60–65; Ronald Pickvance, *Degas 1879* [exh. cat. National Gallery of Scotland] (Edinburgh, 1979), 65–67; Washington 1984, 65–82; Paris 1988, 206–211 and 343–353.

5. Frederick Bohrer in *Joselyn Art Museum. Paintings & Sculpture from the European and American Collections* (Omaha, 1987), 102 and 104, n. 11.

6. Britta Martensen-Larsen, "Degas' *The Little Fourteen-Year-Old Dancer*: an Element of Japonisme," *Gazette des Beaux-Arts* 112 (September 1988), 107–114.

7. On the two surviving plasters see Bohrer in Omaha 1987, 101–104.

8. On the skirt see Lois Relin, "La Ballerina di quattordici anni, il suo tutù e la sua parrucca," in Ettore Camesasca and Giorgio Cortenova, eds., *Degas scultore* [exh. cat. Palazzo Strozzi, Florence] (Milan, 1986), 57–61; Paris 1988, 351 (letter 8 December 1919 from Mary Cassatt to Louisine Havemeyer). On the condition and repairs after 1900 see Paris 1988, 343, 350–351.

9. Trans. Shackleford in Washington 1984, 70.

The Schoolgirl (Woman Walking in the Street), c. 1880/1881
Red wax, 10½ (26.7)
REWALD LXXIV

This figure, as has often been noted, resembles *The Little Dancer Fourteen Years Old* in street clothes. The model might once again have been Marie van Goethem; but since her face is rounder and less clearly defined, she could just as well be one of Degas' young cousins, nieces, or the other girls who modeled for his sculpture around 1878/1882.[1] Many of his works of the early to mid-1880s also evince a fascination with the elegant, hourglass silhouette of a well-dressed contemporary woman walking, as in fig. 3.[2]

As with the *Little Dancer*, the artist's interest in portraying recognizable contemporary types shows in his attention to this figure's costume: her skirt, shorter than a grown woman's; her close-fitting jacket with a broad collar and buckled belt; and her hat with its upturned brim and ornament. The tilt of her head evokes the preoccupied, slightly insolent air of the *Little Dancer*. The girl clutches her book bag with a gangly right arm that stretches out of its sleeve while her left hand reaches back to grasp her pigtail nervously. Degas used a similar backward-reaching gesture in a portrait bust of *Hortense Valpinçon* in 1884 (destroyed).[3] He must have liked the tense projection it gives to the upper body and the way it silhouettes the torso, allowing light to penetrate through the bent arm in a play of angles and curves.

While sketchy in general treatment, *The Schoolgirl* is modeled with wonderful delicacy in many details. The broken edges of the collar suggest lace. Fine pinpricks define the nostrils and hint at teeth between parted lips. Degas formed the right eye with care, but only suggested the left. Definition of one eye but not the other often occurs in Degas sculptures, whether of humans or horses; one wonders if this may be related to the artist's own virtually monocular vision, with the right eye severely impaired.[4] The present supporting armature is not the one that existed in 1918, which rose from the base in front of the figure and curved to meet it near the belt buckle.[5]

Millard has seen in *The Schoolgirl*, with her broad-brimmed hat, crooked arm, and flexed left leg, a reminiscence of Donatello's bronze *David* in Florence.[6] Unlike the *David*,

however, the girl is moving forward; her skirt swishes out behind her to accentuate her progress. Thomson has raised the intriguing suggestion that Degas around 1880 planned a series of sculptures of Parisiennes, of which the *Little Dancer* was the only one to reach full realization.[7] *The Schoolgirl*, worked out in considerable detail, might by implication have been a study for one of these, conceived for a larger, clothed execution that never took place.

The close connection between this figure and a wood statuette exhibited by Gauguin in the 1881 impressionist exhibition, *Woman out for a Stroll*, is widely recognized. Given the mutual awareness and admiration of the two artists at that time, it is impossible to be certain which statuette was created first.[8]

This small figure has a history separate from the other waxes. It was not cast with them between 1919 and 1921. Yet it was probably in Degas' studio with the others, since it was photographed with them. The title *L'Ecolière (The Schoolgirl)* may have come from Durand-Ruel, Degas' dealer, as it is used in Borel's photo caption, presumably based on records kept with the photographs made for Durand-Ruel.[9] Only about five casts were made, for the artist's heirs, at an unknown date before 1955.[10] All this suggests the artist's heirs held back this solitary wax, the only independent dressed figure in Degas' sculpture besides *The Little Dancer*. This would support the claim that the model was a member of the family.

PROVENANCE
Degas studio; Degas heirs; A.-A. Hébrard; consigned or sold to Knoedler and Co., mid-1950s; Paul Mellon, 1956.

NOTES
1. See Reff 1976, 245–261; Millard 1976, 14–15; Paris 1988, 358–359 (on young models), and a useful summary on *The Schoolgirl* by Camesasca in Milan 1986, 213, no. 74. Failing 1979, 41, referred to a letter "issued early in 1955" by Hébrard's daughter Nell, asserting that *The Schoolgirl* is a portrait of a "sister or niece" of Degas, given to the Hébrards by Degas' niece at an unspecified date.

2. For the painting illustrated, see Tinterow in Paris 1988, cat. 267, 440–442. Works often cited in connection with *The Schoolgirl* include Degas' pastels *Project for Portraits in a Frieze* (dated 1879, exhibited 1881), Abs collection, Cologne, and *At the Louvre* (1879/1880), private collection; a print (1879/1880) of *The Actress Ellen Andrée*

(who has been suggested as the model for *The Schoolgirl*) and two other prints, *At the Louvre: Mary Cassatt in the Etruscan Gallery* and *At the Louvre: Mary Cassatt in the Picture Gallery*. Drawings for *The Schoolgirl*, from the front, back, and side, appear in a notebook datable c. 1881. See references in previous note; Edinburgh 1979, 67, no. 79, and Paris 1988, 318–324.

3. Reff 1976, 264–267; Millard 1976, 12–14.

4. See Kendall 1988, 180–181, 184.

5. For the early photo see Rewald 1944, 144, and Florence 1986, 213.

6. Millard 1976, 65; Degas had sketched Donatello's *David*, probably early in 1859.

7. Manchester 1987, 85–86.

8. See Florence 1986, 213, and Charles F. Stuckey in Richard Brettell and others, *The Art of Paul Gauguin* [exh. cat. National Gallery of Art] (Washington, 1988), 25–26, cat. 6.

9. Borel 1949. But Rewald 1944, 15, 28, who presumably had access to the same records, titled it *Woman Walking in the Street*.

10. Knoedler and Co., New York, having acquired the statuette in the mid-1950s, arranged for an edition of twenty bronzes to be cast by Hébrard in 1956; Rewald 1956, 158; Millard 32–33, n. 32.

Fig. 3. Edgar Degas, *Woman Viewed from Behind (The Visit to the Museum)*, c. 1885, oil on canvas. National Gallery of Art, Washington, Collection of Mr. and Mrs. Paul Mellon

HORSES

As a subject horses must have attracted Degas for the qualities they share with dancers. Alluring in the interplay with space of their highly trained bodies, both move with a natural yet disciplined grace. Their constant tension between transitory balance and movement holds the imagination. And both touch the heart as they escape the earth for brief instants of triumph in the hopeless struggle against gravity.

Also like dancers, horses performed for an audience in a particular modern setting and social context (the Longchamp racetrack in the Bois de Boulogne, Paris, where Degas went to observe and sketch, had opened only in 1857).[1] Degas took an interest not only in the "ritual movements" of performance, but perhaps even more in the accidental ones of horses breaking free from control, and dancers offstage.

Degas himself implied that his sculptural experiments had begun with horses, specifically inspired by his difficulties in painting *The Steeplechase* in 1866. Dissatisfied with his limited knowledge of "the mechanism that regulated a horse's movements," he found that sketches did not suffice; he had to try modeling. "The older I became, the more clearly I realized that to achieve exactitude so perfect in the representation of animals that a feeling of life is conveyed, one had to go into three dimensions."[2] Eighteen of Degas' surviving sculptures represent horses or, in two cases, jockeys. Eleven of these are on view here. Usually dated before 1890,[3] the horse sculptures must have been among the favorite works he preserved for decades under the glass vitrines visitors saw in his studio.

Degas had plenty of opportunity to study horses from life, not only at the racetrack but also in the streets of Paris and in the country. From the 1860s he often visited the estate of his friend Henri Valpinçon, near the horse-breeding center at Haras-le-Pin. He learned also and remembered much from his practice of drawing after the old masters. Study drawings survive of horses and riders from the Parthenon frieze, which he knew through casts; and Benozzo Gozzoli's *Adoration of the Magi* of c. 1459 in the Medici-Riccardi palace in Florence. His admiration for classical and Renaissance examples, such as the antique bronze horses at San Marco or Verrocchio's *Colleoni* of the 1480s in Venice, seems to be echoed in the calm gait of a wax like *Horse Walking*.[4]

More recent sources also offered Degas guidance in depicting the horse. These included English sporting prints and the works of the French painter-sculptor Théodore Géricault, whose wax anatomical study of a *Flayed Horse* (fig. 4) Degas drew, perhaps from a bronze or plaster cast. The *animalier* sculptor Antoine-Louis Barye, whose retrospective exhibition Degas must have seen in 1875, and his contemporary Ernest Meissonier must also have impressed Degas with their horse images. His grief over the death (1870) in the Franco-Prussian war of his friend Joseph Cuvelier, who had specialized in bronze equestrian statuettes, may have strengthened Degas' resolve to carry on with horse sculpture.[5]

The horses usually considered earliest, including *Horse Walking* and *Thoroughbred Horse Walking*, move slowly, primarily within a single plane, with the serene restraint of their most classical predecessors. Recent scientific and technological discoveries, always of interest to Degas in relation to his art, caught his attention as he experimented with increasingly movemented and spatially complex horses in the 1880s. Above all, photography instructed and stimulated him in this pursuit. By 1878 he was probably following, through illustrated reports in French journals, the experiments of the photographer Eadweard Muybridge, who was using stop-action photography to break animal movements visually into sequential phases. Degas may have known of Muybridge's illustrated lecture in the studio of Meissonier in Paris in November 1881, although records do not indicate he attended. He was evidently studying and even drawing from the photographs in Muybridge's major work, *Animal Locomotion*, within a year of its publication in 1887.[6]

Influence from Muybridge photographs has been proposed for at least six of Degas' horse sculptures, all of which are in the present exhibition: *Horse Galloping on Right Foot; Horse Balking; Horse Trotting, the Feet Not Touching the Ground; Rearing Horse; Horse Galloping on Right Foot, the Back Left Only Touching the Ground;* and *Horse Galloping, Turning the Head to the Right.* . . . Compare, for instance, *Horse Galloping on Right Foot* (Rewald VI) with fig. 5, or *Horse Balking* with fig. 6. The knowledge Degas gained from Muybridge certainly figured in the assurance with which he depicted increasingly complex equine movements. Yet the nature of the relationship is not beyond question in every case. *Horse Galloping, Turning the Head to the Right*, for instance, shows a striking resemblance to the horse ridden by a jockey on the right in the painting *The Races* (fig. 7), datable c. 1872.[7] One must consider whether this freely modeled wax could date earlier than 1887 (even if later than the painting), and whether, as Beaulieu has suggested, in some cases Muybridge simply confirmed what Degas had grasped with his own eyes.

In any case, Millard has cautioned that the evident importance of Muybridge for Degas should not be overstressed. The photographs provided him with valuable information on highly transient phases of movement and on the true relationships of the

Fig. 4. Théodore Gericault, *Flayed Horse I*, c. 1818/1824, wax. National Gallery of Art, Washington, Collection of Mr. and Mrs. Paul Mellon

Fig. 5. Eadweard Muybridge, *"Bouquet" Galloping, Saddled*, photograph from *Animal Locomotion* (Philadelphia, 1887), pl. 631. Courtesy of the Library of Congress, Washington

Fig. 6. Eadweard Muybridge, *"Daisy" Jumping a Hurdle, Saddled, Preparing for the Leap*, photograph from *Animal Locomotion* (Philadelphia, 1887), pl. 636. Courtesy of the Library of Congress, Washington

legs. But in sculpture Degas concerned himself not with a principal silhouette seen from a fixed position, but with movement fully realized in three dimensions. His horses are for the most part conceived to be looked at from many directions, not one main view in which all aspects fall into place. *Rearing Horse*, for instance, twists and tosses its head to the side as if frightened, inviting the eye to follow it. *Horse with Head Lowered* draws the gaze around and through the changing patterns of its swinging limbs. *Horse Balking* "combines forward, backward, rising and twisting motions in the closest approximation of a centripetal spiralling movement possible with a four-legged animal."[8] In his pursuit of balance in three-dimensional space and organic integration of his glimpses of living energy, Degas went beyond anything the camera could tell him. His own brilliant observation and control, strengthened by study of other images, brought forth some of the most persuasively alive sculptures of horses in the history of art.

Technical experiments of his own also figure in Degas' horse sculptures. Besides his usual mixture of modeling materials and his unorthodox armatures, including nails as well as wires, he devised a wax-coated cloth costume for one of his diminutive jockeys (Rewald XV), just as he had for the *Little Dancer*. Cloth also served as a saddle for at least two of the horses (both versions of *Horse Galloping on Right Foot*, in one of which only the imprint of the cloth remains). The jockeys, modeled independently, can change

mounts, and the artist may well have experimented with this himself.[9]

The armatures, with their main horizontal elements defining the long contour of a horse's back, work to splendid effect. This is evident, for instance, in *Thoroughbred Horse Walking*, where a gap in the neck leaves the wire exposed. McCarty has suggested plausibly[10] that the piece fell away during Degas' lifetime, and that the artist, recognizing the visual power of the charged void that remained, chose not to repair it. A wonderfully sinuous curve in three dimensions runs from the gently turning head through the spine to the tossing tail. In *Horse Balking* a wire projects from the end of the tail, and the wires shaping the structure of the head also emerge from the wax in many places. The vertical supports, two in this case, emphasize the precarious balance of this pose, also heightening its drama as the neck strains beyond the forked supporting piece in the chest as if against a barrier.[11]

Wit and imagination infuse the relationships between the horses and their bases. It is probably no coincidence that these bases all lie flat on the ground, as if surrogates for the earth. In contrast the bases for the statuettes of women, with a few exceptions, consist of a platform elevated by risers suggesting a stage, though in at least some cases the risers may be posthumous additions.[12] *Horse Walking* has its left hind foot teasing the base a fraction of an inch above the surface, with the wire armature visually completing its descent. The left hind foot of *Thoroughbred Horse Walking* extends over the rear edge as though the animal has just entered the base space from the world beyond. *Horse Galloping on Right Foot*, on the other hand, seems about to plunge forward off its high, multilayered base. This horse, like the fiery *Horse with Head Lowered*, has its base surface built up with cork as if the hooves were churning up the earth.

Fig. 7. Edgar Degas, *The Races* (detail), c. 1872, oil on canvas. National Gallery of Art, Washington, Widener Collection

Horse Trotting, the Feet Not Touching the Ground is the only one oriented along the diagonal axis of its base. This plays the silhouettes of its airborne legs with particular grace against the angled edges of the square, an effect missed in the bronze. The base beneath *Horse Galloping, Turning the Head to the Right* is smooth and narrow as a racetrack lane, while under *Horse Galloping on Right Foot, the Back Left Only Touching the Ground* the wax is worked up in mounds at front and rear, creating a low gully that horse and rider traverse.

The widely varying facture of the horses shows the range of Degas' modeling technique, from controlled precision to feverish freedom. *Horse Walking*, usually considered an early example, is relatively tight and compact in its modeling.[13] *Thoroughbred Horse Walking*, tiny as it is, evinces wonderfully delicate treatment in the head, eyes, and mouth, achieving a sensitive expression with different means than those used in the summary yet spirited head of *Horse Trotting*. In *Horse with Head Lowered*, a smooth back and hindquarters contrast with a lumpy mane and ruggedly expressive head. *Rearing Horse* has its back smoothed to a fine polish; its right eye, bulging in apparent terror, is well defined while the left remains a suggestive blob of wax.

Clear fingerprints are sometimes visible, for instance on the right side of the head of *Horse Galloping on Right Foot*; this figure also bears the pattern of a herringbone cloth that was once pressed into its back. Striations from a modeling tool, used to shape the forms in a faceted style, mark *Horse Trotting*. Vigorous, unblended applications of wax bits give a scaly surface to *Horse Balking*, fragmenting the light. Freest and most fantastic is *Horse Galloping on Right Foot, the Back Left Only Touching the Ground*, which looks to have been modeled with a swift excitement matching the animal's movement. The lower part of its outstretched neck, a roll of wax squeezed (over cork?) into a thin sheet, has wavy contours that enhance the spectral character of the gaunt steed.

NOTES

1. See especially Ronald Pickvance, *Degas' Racing World* [exh. cat. Wildenstein] (New York, 1968), n.p.; also Pickvance in Edinburgh 1979, 8–9.

2. Thiébault-Sisson in Paris 1984, 179; Henri Loyrette in Paris 1988, 137–139.

3. Rewald 1956, 140, catalogued the horses as a group c. 1865–1881, but recognized that some are probably later. Millard 1976, 20–23, argued that the calmer ones date from before 1881, the more active ones from c. 1881/1890, the period when the photographs of Muybridge had their greatest impact on Degas. Dates soon after the publication of Muybridge's *Animal Locomotion* in 1887 have been proposed for *Horse Balking* and *Rearing Horse* (Gary Tinterow in Paris 1988, 461–463).

4. Pickvance in New York 1968 and in Edinburgh 1979, 8–9; Millard 1976, 59; Thomson in Manchester 1987, 92–95.

5. Millard 1976, 4–5, 74.

6. For a summary on Muybridge's influence and the literature on this, see Tinterow in Paris 1988, 375, 459–462. See also Millard 1976, 20–23; Manchester 1987, 102. Degas copied two frames of plate 621 (*Annie G. in Canter*) in vol. 9 of *Animal Locomotion*. He also indicated interest in the studies of animal motion by the French professor of natural history Etienne Jules Marey. Millard 1976, 22, n. 82; Thiébault-Sisson in Paris 1984, 179.

7. Michèle Beaulieu, "Les sculptures de Degas: essai de chronologie," *Revue du Louvre* 19 (1969), 370, 374; she also notes similarities of this wax to two-dimensional works of 1877/1880; for the 1872 dating of the painting see Loyrette in Paris 1988, 160, fig. 87 (as *Before the Race*).

8. Millard 1976, 100–101, for this description and the limits of Muybridge's role.

9. See Rewald 1956, plates 12, 14, 20, 21.

10. McCarty in Mellon 1986, 223–224.

11. It was formerly known, perhaps more appropriately, as *Horse Clearing an Obstacle*; for the present title and proposed date see Tinterow in Paris 1988, 460–461, cat. 280.

12. The photo made before casting of *Woman Arranging Her Hair*, for instance, shows the base without the risers that are now present; Rewald 1944, 112. Failing 1988, 141, observed that the early photos show that the pre-casting condition of most of the horses corresponded fairly closely to their present state.

13. The finely pitted surface of this, presumably one of the earliest horses, may reflect age and wear rather than the modeling technique; Millard 1976, 97, n. 8.

Horse Walking, probably before 1881
Reddish wax, 8¼ (21)
REWALD X

Thoroughbred Horse Walking
probably before 1881
Yellow-brown wax, 5¼ (13.3)
REWALD V

Horse with Head Lowered, c. 1881/1890
Brown wax, cork, 7⅛ (18.1)
REWALD XII

Horse Galloping on Right Foot
c. 1881/1890
Brown wax, cork, 11⅞ (30.2)
REWALD VI

*Horse Trotting, the Feet Not
Touching the Ground,* c. 1881/1890
Dark red wax, 8⅝ (22)
REWALD XI

Horse Balking (previously called
Horse Clearing an Obstacle)
c. 1888/1890
Yellow wax, 11¼ (28.6)
REWALD IX

Rearing Horse, c. 1888/1890
Red wax, 12⅛ (30.5)
REWALD XIII

Horse with Jockey; Horse Galloping on Right Foot, the Back Left Only Touching the Ground, c. 1881/1890
Brown wax, cloth, 9⅜ (23.8)
REWALD XIV AND XV

Horse with Jockey; Horse Galloping, Turning the Head to the Right, the Feet Not Touching the Ground c. 1881/1890 (?)
Dark greenish- and reddish-brown wax 11¼ (28.6)
REWALD XVII and XVIII

WOMEN AT THEIR TOILETTE

Woman Washing Her Left Leg, c. 1890
Yellow, red, and olive-green wax;
small green ceramic pot
7⅞ (20)
REWALD LXVIII

"I have not yet made enough horses," Degas wrote in 1888 to the sculptor Bartholomé. "The women must wait in their tubs."[1] This remark and a description to Bartholomé in June 1889 of his work on a wax convincingly identified with his ingenious *The Tub* (fig. 8)[2] suggest it was around this time that figures of women bathing and grooming themselves entered his sculptural repertory. Some of his most innovative experiments in mixed media, as well as one of his most classical compositions, center on this theme.

The depiction of a woman bathing in a shallow tub or drying herself after a bath had occupied him at least since the late 1870s.[3] He focused on it with particular intensity in the mid-1880s, sending ten pastels he described as "a suite of female nudes bathing, washing, drying and toweling themselves, combing their hair or having it combed" to the eighth impressionist exhibition in 1886. Around 1890 he worked on a group of pastels of bathers stepping into tubs.[4] As usual with Degas these were not classical Aphrodites rising from the waves, even if their poses sometimes evoked ancient sculpture. They were anonymous women, often of less (or more) than ideal proportions, in settings clearly identified by the furnishings as modern. He presented them absorbed in their personal grooming, often bending to display the sensuous curves of their backs seen from above, from behind, or from oblique points of view. Although Degas carefully posed his models for these figures, they appear oblivious to any possible audience, as if the viewer "looked through a keyhole." These numerous images of bathers have inspired considerable debate about whether Degas' approach was perversely misogynistic or natural and sympathetic, as well as about the social station implied for the women by the settings, accessories, and actions.[5] In the sculpture, where the figure exists independent of a domestic setting, such questions are less insistent. Yet even here Degas felt the need to introduce accessories appropriate to a contemporary woman bathing. For this purpose he devised mixed-media creations that follow up on his experiments in the *Little Dancer* by incorporating objects from the real world. By such means he again attacked the barriers between illusion and reality in a way that anticipated the assemblage techniques of the cubists and futurists.[6]

The larger *Woman Washing Her Left Leg* has repeatedly been singled out as a masterpiece of the polychrome sculpture Degas first broached with the varied materials of the *Little Dancer*. Paul Gsell described this bather as "warmly tinted and translucent as honey, and the vase streaked with green and red harmonised perfectly with the golden amber of the wax."[7] These rich effects, perhaps a conscious parallel to the intense, anti-naturalistic color effects he introduced in his pastels of bathers in the late 1880s,[8] gain from his incorporation of the little ceramic vessel into which the woman prepares to step. The wide range of textures, playing her caramel-smooth, rounded back against the hard geometric forms of the tub and the ruggedly unformed masses of wax around her, is particularly intriguing. Degas built her a chair to lean on as she pokes an elbow into space, a gesture he used repeatedly to open up the mass of a figure and to heighten its tension.

In composing the sculpture Degas also played with differing heights. The woman and her chair stand on a small section of board set crosswise on top of the main base. She is poised to step down into the tub and her towel flows down over the chair toward it, connecting the different levels. The open form of the chair behind her balances the closed one of the tub in front to create an exceptionally complex and satisfying composition of solid forms, spaces, colors, and materials.

The smaller related wax assigned the same title presents questions. Here the base is a single board set on a pair of risers (possibly added after Degas' death). The woman supports herself not on a chair but on an armature rod bent like a cane, with her left elbow lifted higher than in the other wax. There is no tub, but she holds a piece of wax-coated fabric to dry her left foot. The front of her left foot is broken off; a nail protruding from the base below it may once have supported its precariously raised toes. Her right foot, in contrast, spreads over the base like a root system. This figure is highly sketchy and abstract, its squiggle of an arm across space recalling the wavy neck of the *Horse Galloping on Right Foot.* Should this

Woman Washing Her Left Leg
c. 1890/1900 (?)
Brown wax, cloth, 5¾ (14.6)
REWALD LXVII

Woman Arranging Her Hair
c. 1895/1910
Yellow wax, 18¼ (46.4)
REWALD L

Fig. 8. Edgar Degas, *The Tub*, c. 1889, wax, lead, plaster, cloth. National Gallery of Art, Washington, Collection of Mr. and Mrs. Paul Mellon

wax be understood as a first experiment at the composition that Degas later developed with the ceramic basin or a variation on the same theme, perhaps modeled years later in feverish haste?[9]

Woman Arranging Her Hair, which actually represents a woman drying her hair, must occupy a fairly late place in the artist's sculptural oeuvre. As often recognized, the composition relates to his plan announced in a letter of 6 July 1891 to Evariste de Valernes to begin two suites of lithographs: "a first series on nude women at their toilette" and a second on nude dancers.[10] The works associated with this project include recurring studies of a standing nude seen from the back, leaning to one side so that her torso curves and her hair falls heavily toward earth, and bending her elbows as she vigorously towels one hip (compare fig. 9).[11]

Later, in works around 1900, Degas modified the pose from a woman wiping her hip to one drying her long hair. Other closely related figures appear in the charcoal and pastel *Nude Woman Drying Herself*, c. 1900 (The Museum of Fine Arts, Houston) and the pastel *Woman at Her Toilette*, c. 1905 (Art Institute of Chicago), a bending nude with streaming hair seen from the back.[12]

The present statuette belongs to these explorations. The woman's large size and heavy proportions suggest the massiveness of his latest sculptured figures, several of which dry themselves while seated in armchairs.[13] The back view of this standing figure clearly appealed to Degas, as evident in the related lithographs and drawings. His attraction to this aspect of the sculpture shows in the attention he devoted to smooth modeling of the back and buttocks of the wax figure, leaving the front relatively rough.[14]

Paradoxically for a figure of such weight

and generally rugged treatment, the pose of a standing woman drying her hair has been recognized as one of the most "canonically classical" Degas ever chose. Its ancient prototype, of which many examples survive, is a standing Aphrodite wringing water from her tresses; a study drawing of one such sculpture exists in a Degas notebook.[15]

The original armature for this wax, presumably removed in the preparations for casting c. 1919, contributed significantly to the spatial composition.[16] The present external armature, piercing the left hip and seeming to confine the standing figure to a narrow space, was not present. To support her leaning torso and the horizontal extension of her hair Degas had run two strands of wire from inside the figure out through the hanging tress; these curved outward into space, then returned in their descent toward the board where they were fixed to the surface. Notches in the edge of the base below the hair still record the points where they made contact. This supposedly utilitarian support must have taken on a poetic character, suggesting the trajectory of falling drops of water or a visualization of the inexorable pull of gravity.

NOTES

1. Marcel Guérin, ed., *Lettres de Degas*, 2d rev. ed. (Paris, 1945), letter C, 127; cited in Millard 1976, 20. Internal evidence dates this letter to 1888, and the context suggests Degas was referring to sculpture.

2. Millard 1976, 9–10. Beaulieu 1969, 380, argued that the two versions of *Woman Washing Her Left Leg* and a third sculpture destroyed in casting, *Woman Leaving the Bath*, Rewald LXXII, are related to pastels dated 1883.

3. Paris 1988, 414–415, monotypes.

4. For the 1886 group see Martha Ward in San Francisco 1986, 430–434; Tinterow in Paris 1988, 443–450. For the bathers stepping into tubs, Tinterow in Paris 1988, 470–472. Rewald placed all the bather sculptures among Degas' last works, in his 1896–1911 group.

5. For useful summaries see Ward in San Francisco 1986, 430–434; Norma Broude, "Degas' 'Misogyny,'" *Art Bulletin* 59 (1977), 95–107; Eunice Lipton, *Looking Into Degas. Uneasy Images of Women and Modern Life* (Berkeley, 1986), 165–186; Kendall in Liverpool 1989, 56–57.

6. Reff 1976, 261, 291-292, 338; Millard 1976, 111–112. Millard and Reff also noted parallels with the approach of the Italian sculptor in wax and mixed media, Medardo Rosso, even before he and Degas were in contact.

7. Gsell 1918, 376; cited in Rewald 1956, 26; see also McCarty in Mellon 1986, 218.

8. See Tinterow in Paris 1988, 369.

9. The pose can be compared, for instance, to a pastel of c. 1886, *Bather Drying Her Legs* (Dayton Art Institute), but also to a pastel of *Woman Stepping into a Bath*, c. 1890 (The Metropolitan Museum of Art, New York), and to a series of drawings and pastels of bending bathers c. 1895–1905. Paris 1988, 599–602 and 518, figs. 294 and 471.

10. The connections have been noted by Thomson in Manchester 1987, 123, 127, 128, dating the sculpture c. 1890/1900 and observing the pose's derivation from a grieving woman in Delacroix's *Entry of the Crusaders into Constantinople*. Thomson, *Degas. The Nudes* (London, 1988), 197–199, dated the wax 1890/1895; Boggs in Paris 1988, 498, 598–599, dated it c. 1900/1910. Beaulieu 1969, 380, suggested a date c. 1903.

11. For the lithograph *Nude Woman Standing, Drying Herself* see Paris 1988, 499, cat. 294.

12. Manchester 1987, 119, 127–128; Paris 1988, 596, cat. 382.

13. For instance National Gallery of Art 1985.64.54, 58, 59 and 60, Collection of Mr. and Mrs. Paul Mellon; see Boggs in Paris 1988, 484 and 586, on proportions after 1900; Millard 1976, 108–110.

14. Boggs in Paris 1988, 598, cat. 384.

15. Millard 1976, 70 and fig. 108.

16. Early photo published by Rewald 1944, 112; the absence of risers under the base in this photo raises a question as to whether these were posthumous additions in some if not all cases.

Fig. 9. Edgar Degas, *Nude Woman Standing, Drying Herself*, c. 1891, lithograph. National Gallery of Art, Washington, Rosenwald Collection

ARABESQUES

Of all the movements of classical ballet, the arabesque seems to have held the greatest fascination for Degas as a sculptor. Eight of his surviving waxes[1] represent figures in phases of this movement, in which the dancer, balancing on one foot, extends the other leg backward and both arms out from the center. These figures range from a fragile child dancer only eight inches high, usually dated before 1880 (Rewald XXXVII, Fitzwilliam Museum, Cambridge) through firmly modeled mature and graceful women, the largest of the group (*Grande Arabesque, First Time* and *Grande Arabesque, Second Time*, in the present exhibition) to a sketchier figure, possibly of the mid–1890s, whose stocky proportions make the pose look all the more improbable (Rewald XXXIX, Musée d'Orsay).[2] The assured handling of movement in *Grande Arabesque First Time, Second Time,* and *Third Time* has suggested dates c. 1885/1890.[3] Their careful modeling, with lovingly smoothed backs and legs and even some attention to the hairstyle, may connect these three with the painstaking precision of the *Little Dancer*. Perhaps it was in pursuit of this smoothness that Degas experimented with plastilene as a principal material for these arabesque figures. *Arabesque over the Right Leg, Right Hand near the Ground, Left Arm Outstretched,* sketchier in modeling and more tentative in movement, is harder to date. Given Degas' known fondness for exploring an action over many years, Rewald's general dating of c. 1882/1895 still seems appropriate for the group.

Degas' fascination with the arabesque is understandable. In it the human figure often appears close to flight. The arabesque is a moment of balance in which the dancer reaches a peak of tension between submission to gravity and escape from it. Her body has one point of contact with the earth and endless directional possibilities for the other limbs that seem to strain for freedom. The essentials of the armature for a figure in an arabesque, a strong vertical element for the supporting leg with a pivotal point at the hip, allowed Degas to twist and bend the wires for the other limbs, constantly changing their relationship in a process that particularly delighted him. The surviving examples, whatever their chronological relationships, show various stages in the rise and descent of a dancer in an arabesque and

demonstrate the subtle variations of direction and muscle action possible even in the same pose (Rewald XL, XLI). One can only imagine how many more arabesque sculptures must have collapsed under Degas' impatient hands.[4]

The difficulty for a model to maintain the relevant poses must also have stimulated him to explore the arabesque in sculpture. The resulting waxes provided a three-dimensional aid for studying this human movement for the treatments that appear repeatedly in Degas' paintings and pastels from the 1870s through the 1890s.[5] The example and challenge of the old masters may have further attracted him to the arabesque. For *Grande Arabesque, First Time,* a figure poised at the inception of the movement, Millard has suggested ancestry in antique sculptures of a *Striding Diana* or a *Running Eros*.[6] Perhaps a work like Giambologna's Renaissance bronze *Mercury*[7] stirred Degas to attempt modern counterparts to the sculptural movements of the celebrated mythological figure. Or he may have been moved to surpass a recent feminine descendent of the *Mercury* in an arabesque-like pose, Jean-Alexandre-Joseph Falguière's *Hunting Nymph,* exhibited in plaster in the Salon of 1884.[8] His probable acquaintance with these works makes it all the more intriguing that Degas never chose to sculpt a dancer in an arabesque rising on her toes, as Giambologna's and Falguière's figures did, but always kept the supporting foot flat on the ground.

Experiments with suspension and flight produced sculptures like the remarkable *Arabesque over the Right Leg, Left Arm in Front*.[9] Wires secure the tiny figure to its metal frame, with its movement oriented along the narrow base. The result is an unusually pictorial composition in which the figure and wires form a pattern dividing up the open, rectangular field within the frame, at the same time allowing display of the taut belly and muscular legs that are the glories of its modeling. The interplay of two-dimensional and sculptural design fascinates as the wires simultaneously bind and liberate. A similar structure that once supported the even more tenuously balanced *Arabesque over the Right Leg, Right Hand near the Ground, Left Arm Outstretched* was apparently sacrificed in the preparations for casting. The role of the lost frame in the composition is still recorded by the narrow base (shortened and set on a new platform with risers), once probably close to the proportions of the base that survives for *Arabesque over the Right Leg, Left Arm in Front*. An early photograph suggests *Grande Arabesque, Third Time* also had a long narrow base, as well as suspension wires at the head and extended leg.[10]

Whether freestanding or suspended, the arabesque dancers as a group evoke the infinite potential stages in the movement. Individually each also implies rotation on an axis, with the sole of the extended foot (almost always the left) turned inward.[11] That Degas sought and savored this suggestion of a turning motion in arabesque figures is clear from an experiment he performed for Walter Sickert with the graceful, firmly modeled *Grande Arabesque, Second Time*.[12] Sickert recalled how the artist projected its shadow against a sheet by candlelight one evening, rotating the figure slowly to change the silhouettes and to create an effect of continuous movement. The dancer's height, augmented by a base heavily built up with wax over cork, must have enhanced the drama. This demonstration also suggests an element of fantasy and magic in Degas' conception of his small wax dancers. For a moment he was Pygmalion, wishing a figure into life by actualizing the movement latent in its pose.

The difficult and painful nature of the arabesque pose is as inescapable as its exhilarating grace. Even with their faces undefined, the dancers carry expressive implications in their twisting limbs, their reach for the unattainable, and their poignant, losing battle with gravity that call to mind Degas' description of sculpture as "a medium in which to express profound suffering."[13]

NOTES

1. Rewald XXXV, XXXVI, XXXVII, XXXVIII, XXXIX, XL, XLI, XLII.

2. On the arabesque in Degas' art see especially Millard 1976, 97–98, 102, 105–106; Linda D. Muehlig, *Degas and the Dance* [exh. cat. Smith College Museum of Art] (Northampton, 1979), 11–13; Richard R. Brettell and Suzanne Folds McCullagh, *Degas in the Art Institute of Chicago* [exh. cat.] (Chicago, 1984), 155–156; Tinterow in Paris 1988, 586, cats. 372–373. Tinterow, dating Rewald XXXIX in the mid–1890s, identified its position as *First Arabesque Penchée*. A similar title would therefore be appropriate for Rewald XL and XLI. I am grateful to Beth Noreen for advice on ballet terminology.

3. Millard 1976, 24, proposed dates around 1885/1890 for Rewald XXXV, XXXVI, XL and a date in the early 1880s for Rewald XXXVIII. Beaulieu 1969, 374, 380, dated the whole group c. 1877/1883.

On Degas' use of plastilene for several of these see Millard 1976, 37, n. 54.

4. For the kind of armature involved see the diagram and X-ray in *Sculptures en cire* 1987, 230–231. On Degas' delight in change to the point of destruction see Millard 1976, 36.

5. For a list of examples of the arabesque in his paintings and pastels from the 1870s through the 1890s see Tinterow in Paris 1988, 586, n. 1.

6. Millard 1976, 68 and figs. 49, 50, 88, 89.

7. See Charles Avery and Anthony Radcliffe, eds., *Giambologna, 1529–1608. Sculptor to the Medici* [exh. cat. Arts Council of Great Britain] (London, 1978), 84, cat. 33.

8. For the Falguière, recognized in its time as a descendant of the Giambologna, see Peter Fusco and H. W. Janson, eds., *The Romantics to Rodin* [exh. cat. Los Angeles County Museum of Art] (Los Angeles, 1980), 260, cat. 132.

9. Millard 1976, 102, 111, noted this was as close as Degas came to complete suspension of a figure. He saw it as a forerunner to the mobiles of Alexander Calder in the twentieth century.

10. On Rewald XLI see Failing 1988, 140–141. Rewald XLII (*Arabesque over the Right Leg, Left Arm in Line*) also had some sort of frame, no longer extant, to which it was attached by spiraling coils of wire. See photo in Rewald 1944, 97. For an early photo of *Grande Arabesque, Third Time*, see Gsell 1918, 376.

11. Millard 1976, 106.

12. Millard 1976, 105–106, citing Walter Sickert, "Degas," *Burlington Magazine* 31 (1917), 185; for identification of the specific sculpture Degas used see Walter Sickert, "The Sculptor of Movement" in *Works in Sculpture of Edgar Degas* [exh. cat. Leicester Galleries] (London, 1923), 180, reprinted in Oliver Brown, *Exhibition* (London, 1968), 179–181. See also Thomson in Manchester 1987, 130.

13. Millard 1976, 89–90.

Grande Arabesque, First Time
c. 1882/1895
Dark green wax, 19 (48.2)
REWALD XXXV

Grande Arabesque, Second Time
c. 1882/1895
Brown plastilene, wax, cork, 18½ (47)
REWALD XXXVI

Arabesque over the Right Leg,
Left Arm in Front, c. 1882/1895
Yellow-brown wax, metal frame
11⅜ (28.9)
REWALD XXXVIII

Grande Arabesque, Third Time
(First Arabesque Penchée), c. 1882/1895
Greenish-brown and black plastilene
15⅞ (40.4)
REWALD XL

Arabesque over the Right Leg,
Right Hand near the Ground,
Left Arm Outstretched
(First Arabesque Penchée), c. 1882/1895
Brown wax, 10¾ (27.3)
REWALD XLI

Dancer at Rest, Hands on Her Hips,
Left Leg Forward, late 1870s (?)
Brown wax
14¾ (37.5)
REWALD XXI

Could Degas have begun his sculpture of human subjects with the *Little Dancer Four-teen Years Old*? It is certainly difficult to imagine him reaching the level of accomplishment evident in that statuette or in the earlier nude study for it without prior experience. *Dancer at Rest* is the most convincing candidate for a work that preceded the *Little Dancer*.[1] As such it would be perhaps the earliest surviving Degas sculpture of a human figure.

The pose places the legs in a variation on the fourth position similar to that in the *Little Dancer*, but reverses them. This figure is relaxed and earthbound, with the weight planted firmly on the back leg. The stocky torso is none too clearly that of an adolescent model, with small breasts and only hints of anatomical details. The well-defined muscles at work in the arabesques or in the *Little Dancer* herself seem distant. The modeling, too, seems methodical rather than assured; the surface is covered with striations from a clawed tool, suggesting a sculptor finding his way in facture as well as in anatomy and movement.

Typically for Degas, the figure places her hands on her hips with her elbows pointing out and back. Besides opening out the mass of a figure, this gesture brings tightness and a challenging look to the exposed torso. The face, a bare suggestion, recalls the *Little Dancer* and *Schoolgirl* in the projecting chin and outlined eyes, only the right one defined. A casual stance evoking the impatient mood of practice, of waiting backstage, gives an effect of life and imminent change to the still figure.

Informal as the pose appears, it may, like so many Degas works, owe something to study of an ancient model. Millard has pointed to an antique bronze of a standing *Hercules*, which Degas could have known either directly or through a plaster cast be-

longing to his friend the painter-sculptor Gustave Moreau.[2] The restrained power and potential action in such a figure may have appealed to him.

McCarty has suggested[3] that the plaster block at the junction of the external armature shaft with the wood base, angled to prevent undercuts, may be a posthumous addition made to simplify the mold-making process when the statue was cast around 1919.

NOTES
1. Millard 1976, 23, 97, for a date in the mid 1870s, calling its pose a "preliminary stage" of that of the *Little Dancer*. Beaulieu 1969, 375, instead dated *Dancer at Rest* c. 1890, in connection with related poses in pastels of that year.

2. Millard 1976, 60, and figs. 21, 22.

3. McCarty in Mellon 1986, 225, n. 13.

Dancer at Rest, Hands Behind Her Back, Right Leg Forward, mid–1880s (?)
Dark greenish wax
17¼ (43.8)
REWALD XXII

Degas produced two other waxes of dancers in a pose similar to this, one nude (Rewald XXIII) and one dressed in a billowing tutu crammed with cork (Rewald LII, *Dressed Dancer at Rest . . .*). The dressed version, because of its rugged facture and resemblance to figures of dancers in Degas' late pastels, has recently been assigned a date c. 1895.[1] For the other example of the nude figure closely resembling this one, various dates within Rewald's general suggestion of 1882/1895 have been proposed.[2]

Although the pose of this figure superficially recalls that of *Dancer at Rest, Hands on Her Hips, Left Leg Forward* (Rewald XXI), it seems astonishing that they should have been assigned such similar titles. Muscular and dynamic, this dancer hardly seems "at rest." Even her orientation along the long axis of the base, compared with the static horizontal alignment of the base for *Dancer at Rest, Hands on Her Hips . . .* serves to charge her with movement (for unknown reasons, this is one of the few bases for a female nude that lacks risers). Chin thrust out, she lunges forward on her bent right leg; only her foot's sharp turn to the right seems to break an advance evoking the figurehead of a ship. Her tightly pulled back hair and her projecting cheekbones enhance the effect of a rush into a resisting element.

The forward surge of this figure with winglike elbows projecting behind her suggests nothing so much as a modern nude interpretation of the ancient Greek *Winged Victory* from Samothrace. Inspiration from that source is possible. The *Victory* had been erected in the Louvre in 1867. After the discovery of its pedestal in the form of a ship's prow in 1879, the statue received a dramatic new installation dominating the Escalier Daru in 1884,[3] which would have renewed its impact on its Parisian audience.

A date in the mid–1880s would seem to make sense for this *Dancer*, with her beautifully realized muscular torso, strongly constructed face, and modeling akin to *Grande*

Arabesque First Time, Second Time, and *Third Time.* Whenever it was made, the figure calls to mind Degas' reply to the question of why he so often portrayed scenes of dancers: "Because only there can I recapture the movements of the Greeks."[4]

NOTES

1. Boggs in Paris 1988, 515, cat. 309.

2. Millard dated Rewald XXIII to the early 1880s because of a pose somewhat similar to Rewald XXI, but handled with greater ability. Beaulieu 1969, 375, placed both nude versions c. 1890 because of their connection with the dressed version and the related pastels.

3. Francis Haskell and Nicholas Penny, *Taste and the Antique. The Lure of Classical Sculpture 1500–1900* (New Haven and London, 1981), 333–334, cat. 92.

4. René Gimpel, *Journal d'un collectionneur* (Paris, 1963), 186 (as cited in Paris 1988, 29). For full references on Degas' copies after antique sculpture see Millard 1976, 55.

*Dancer Fastening the String of
Her Tights,* c. 1885/1890 (?)
Yellow-brown plastilene
16¾ (42.6)
REWALD XXVIII

In the *Little Dancer Fourteen Years Old* Degas
was already engaged in "break[ing] down
the traditional hierarchy of views in favor
of a continous three-dimensional experience" of a sculpture.[1] He posed the young
girl with limbs so disposed that, although
she faces forward, no single point of view
dominates. The observer is urged around
her, each view leading on to another. *Dancer
Fastening the String of Her Tights* represents
a considerably more advanced stage in the
same process of experimentation. Bending
the forward leg and raising a shoulder, the
figure twists actively around and downward, her arms placed to accentuate the spiraling motion. The curves of her back and
hip, the crook of her right arm, and the
changing shape of the void between her legs
create endless appealing views as one turns
around the figure. The proposed date around
1885/1890 seems likely.[2]

Degas had the best of old master teachers
for a twisting pose of this kind. His principal
point of departure was evidently a figure in
Michelangelo's famous cartoon of 1504–
1505 for a mural planned for the Great
Council Hall in the Palazzo Vecchio in Florence, *The Battle of Cascina.* That influential
design, well known through Renaissance
copies and engravings, included a nude figure seen from behind, twisting to pull on
his stockings as he prepares for battle after
bathing. Degas had drawn this and other
figures from the *Battle of Cascina* in his notebook in the late 1850s.[3]

Such a figure, looking downward and
turning back on axis with bent arms and
knees, had a long life also in sixteenth-century
mannerist sculpture influenced by
Michelangelo. In particular it occurs in the
bronzes of Giambologna and his circle, such
as the *Apollo* or *Astronomy.*[4] Its respected
antecedents in ancient art may include a small
bronze dancing satyr noted by Millard or

the celebrated type of the *Venus Kallipygos,*
gazing down over one shoulder at her shapely
buttocks.[5]

Degas did not actually copy any of those
sculptures, and the *Dancer Fastening . . .* has
a pose closer to the Michelangelo drawing
than to any of the sculptures cited. But he
could easily have known them and sensed
the challenge of their deliberately difficult
poses, showing off the sculptor's mastery of
a figure performing a strenuous movement
in place. If so, he could hardly have resisted
tackling the problem in a modern context.
His main differences with the Renaissance
sculptural predecessors, besides the obvious
one of his willful lack of finish, involve the
degree of openness and conviction in the
pose. Degas' figure has both feet on the
ground rather than one raised. Her legs, like
the Michelangelo bather's, are widely separated, making the pose more stable and
dynamic and less affected, silhouetting the
legs and opening up an interesting changing
spatial shape between them. Degas brought
the conception into his own time by asso-
ciating the movement with preparation for
the dance and by giving the heavy-legged
figure individualized rather than ideal proportions. The work is modern also in its
abstract treatment of major features such as
the sketchy head and arms, scaly torso, or
left hand that seems to disappear into the
right hip.

The base beneath this statuette has no
risers. It was lengthened, possibly after Degas'
death, by the addition of a piece less than
an inch wide at the back end. The Durand-
Ruel photo made before the sculpture was
cast in bronze indicates that the lower legs
at that time were badly broken. Repairs evidently included addition of the missing left
foot in the present, impossibly double-jointed
position.[6]

NOTES

1. Millard 1976, 98.

2. Rewald placed it in his 1882/1895 group. Millard 1976, 24, dated it with other accomplished and controlled sculptures c. 1885/1890. Beaulieu 1969, 377, illustrated a closely related charcoal drawing as a much later "reprise," but did not date the statuette. On the material see Millard 1976, 37, no. 55.

3. Millard 1976, 68, fig. 86; Tinterow in Boggs 1988, 470–471.

4. Avery and Radcliffe, *Giambologna* (London, 1978), 68, cat. 12; 88–89, cat. 36–38.

5. For the satyr, Millard 1976, fig. 85; for the Venus, Avery and Radcliffe 1978, 65, cat. 7, and Haskell and Penny 1981, 316–318, cat. 83. Degas, who often visited his relatives in Naples, could have known the famous example there, as well as the marble copy now in the Louvre.

6. For the early photo see Borel 1949 (unnumbered) and Failing 1988, 138.

*Dancer Looking at the Sole of
Her Right Foot,* c. 1890/1900
Dark green wax, cork
18 (45.7)
REWALD XLV

Perfectionist that he was, Degas may have come unusually close to satisfaction with this statuette. The figure takes a pose to which he returned almost obsessively in at least six sculptured variants, presumably over several years.[1] The explorations carried out in these sculptures and a group of closely related pastels and drawings graphically realize his principle that "one must repeat the same subject ten times, a hundred times" in order to master it.[2] That he liked this particular sculpted version exceptionally well is evident from the fact that it is one of only three statuettes he allowed to be cast, in plaster, during his lifetime.[3]

The casting took place around 1900 as we know from Degas' remark to the model Pauline, who was taking the identical pose for him in December 1910. When she mentioned seeing a plaster cast "in the case downstairs" of a model in the same pose, he replied "Ah yes! I modelled it ten years ago! That's the last time the molder came here."[4]

Exactly why this particular version pleased him enough to cast it is not certain, especially without knowing for sure its place in the sequence.[5] Whatever he liked about it did not stop him from returning to the pose later, as Pauline's assignment shows. Compared with the others in this pose, it is apparently the most finished and the most serenely balanced. The smoothed thighs are relatively close together and the raised foot balletically pointed. Only in this version does the hair wind forward over one shoulder, deliciously echoing the curve of the shoulder blade as it enhances the spatial continuity. The angle of the bent right arm rhymes appealingly with those of the right knee and flexed torso as well as with the long, elbowed armature anchored far behind the figure on its long base.[6] With her full, rounded forms and supple torsion, this figure is perhaps the only one that makes the action look almost easy.

Degas himself shed some light on his attachment to this sculpture, or perhaps to its model, when he told Pauline, "The model who posed for it has started working in sculpture. . . . She left me, of course, just when she was doing exactly what I needed. . . ."[7]

The pose, in which her limbs assail and encircle space, belongs to a broader exploration in various media in Degas' late years, with two- and three-dimensional versions perhaps successively stimulating new forays in one or the other. The "athletic nudes" in his work after around 1885 include repeated variations on a bather seen from the back, reaching one arm downward and extending the other to steady herself as she steps over the edge of a deep tub (for instance *The Morning Bath,* c. 1887/1890, Art Institute of Chicago[8] or *After the Bath,* Phillips Collection, Washington, c. 1905/1910).[9] The waxes may well have assisted him in working out the related movement in some of the two-dimensional works.

Brettell mentioned one wax version—not identified—in which Degas broke, bent, and partially repaired the knee with hot wax as he rethought the pose. This may explain why one example fell apart during the casting process.[10] Thomson, who associated the climbing pose with a bather Degas drew in his youth after Michelangelo's *Battle of Cascina,* observes that the related works dwell on "an image which superbly coordinates balance and movement, and the venerable Degas was obsessed with balance."[11]

While the back view of this figure relates to the dynamic climbing bathers, the front and side views connect it strikingly with Degas' much admired "movements of the Greeks." The woman balancing on one foot, examining the other and extending the opposite arm to balance herself, took majestic form in the celebrated relief of a *Victory Loosening Her Sandal* from the parapet of the Temple of Athena Nike on the Acropolis at Athens. Degas' study drawings include one of a plaster cast of that figure.[12] The memory of such ancient grace may have inspired Degas to cast a modern woman in a related pose.[13]

NOTES

1. For the four versions of *Dancer Looking at the Sole of Her Right Foot* see besides this one Rewald IL, LX, and LXI; comparative illustrations in Rewald 1956, plates 58–61; Beaulieu 1969, 374–375 (dating them 1890/1895), and Boggs in Paris 1988, 527–529, cats. 321–323, with suggested dating c. 1895–1910 for the group. Rewald dated this version c. 1882/1895. For the type of armature see *Sculptures en cire* 1987, 235–236. The two versions of *Dancer Holding Her Right Foot in Her Right Hand* (Rewald LXII and LXV, National Gallery of Art 1985.64.53 and 1985.64.56) change the angle of the head and upper body in a similar balancing pose.

2. From Guérin 1945, 119, quoted in Shackleford 1984, 82.

3. The other two are *The Spanish Dance* (Rewald XLVII, this catalogue) and *Woman Rubbing Her Back with a Sponge, Torso* (Rewald LI), for which the wax has not survived. For photos of the plaster casts, two of which still belong to the Hébrard heirs (Millard 1976, 35), see Borel 1949 (unnumbered); Rewald 1944, 100, 104, and (for *Torso*) Millard 1976, pl. 110.

4. Rewald 1956, 149–150; quotation in Millard 1976, 30, 18–19, and Boggs in Paris 1988, 528 (on the pose). A casting date c. 1900 is confirmed by other sources; Millard 1976, 29–30.

5. Millard 1976, 18, n. 66, proposed an early date in the series, c. 1890.

6. McCarty in Mellon 1986, 220, 222, admired the way such an armature reinforces the dynamics of the figure by contrast and repetition. Its original pertinence to this wax remains to be confirmed (questioned in Failing 1988, 140), but its strong effect and spatial expansiveness, seemingly irrelevant to the more practical need for a support, argue that it is Degas' creation.

7. See Kendall 1987, 316.

8. Chicago 1984, 161, cat. 76.

9. Thomson 1988, 214, 221, 223, fig. 222 (the Phillips pastel and related works).

10. Chicago 1984, 161; Rewald 1956, 152, IL.

11. Thomson 1988, 214 and illustrations, 218–223.

12. Millard 1976, 55, figs. 78, 79, here mentioned only in connection with *Dancer Rubbing Her Knee*. He suggests a type of standing Aphrodite and a related ancient dancer as possible sources for *Dancer Looking at the Sole* . . . (69, figs. 100, 126).

13. Broude suggested the connection with the Acropolis figure in Broude 1977, 105–106, fig. 20.

Dancer Putting on Her Stocking
c. 1890/1895
Brown wax, 18¼ (46.4)
REWALD LVI

Degas made at least three sculptures of figures in this pose: the present wax and Rewald LVII and LVIII (assigned the same title). The last was reportedly destroyed in casting.[1] Rewald LXVII is in the National Gallery (1985.64.52), a gift of Mr. and Mrs. Paul Mellon. All three show the energetic modeling with rapid, unblended applications of wax associated with Degas' late style. The present version is evidently the most finished of the three in the firm contours of its torso, back, and legs and in the definition of the facial features. She also shows more spirit and grace than the other two versions, lifting her head and extending the raised leg. Even so this wax is rough in execution, with a gash in the belly and a cluster of nails or flat-sided wires poking from below the right thigh. This and the fairly heavy body with sagging breasts point to a late moment in Degas' sculpture. Yet it does not reach the rugged abstraction of the other two, especially the work that entered the National Gallery in 1985 with its lava-like clumping of wax, looking barely human, that was perhaps one of the last creations of the despairing artist. The sheer heaviness and failed balance of that wax may explain why Degas supported it with a vertical board against its left side.[2]

In the present pose Degas set himself a balance problem related to *Dancer Looking at the Sole of Her Right Foot*, but relinquished the free and aggressively multidirectional character of the movement. In bending and reaching toward her foot, *Dancer Putting on Her Stocking* seems to fold in upon herself, enclosing space as much as penetrating it. The struggle against gravity that draws down her arms and raised leg becomes gloomy rather than exhilarating. The everyday nature of her action also contrasts with the relatively artificial movement of *Dancer Looking at the Sole of Her Right Foot*. The stocking-puller's proposed ancestry in an ancient *Dancing Faun*, perhaps handed down to Degas through small eighteenth-century bronzes, seems remote.[3] Brettell, dating the destroyed version around 1900/1912, found its composition characteristic of the blend of realism and classicism that pervades Degas'

work. He noted that in sculptures like this one nothing specifically identifies the figure as a dancer. In spite of the title assigned to her for the 1921 exhibition, she is to all appearances an anonymous nude.[4] Yet Degas' stated intention in 1891 to produce a suite of lithographs of "nude dancers" may indicate he meant such sculptured nudes in balancing poses as dancers also.

The layered base is intriguing but problematic. The neat lower board and risers may be posthumous, which would presumably mean the same for the present round armature shaft and its anchoring block set on that board behind the figure. The upper board, on which the wax rests directly, shows additions at two corners that may be Degas'.

The wood addition wrapped around the rear corner has its outer edge trimmed to a curve as if reaffirming the figure's claim on space by tracing, on earth, the contours of her right hip and thigh.

NOTE
1. Rewald 1956, 154.

2. The armature was changed after his death, but a supporting vertical board is present in an early photo; see Borel 1949.

3. Millard 1976, 69 and fig. 105.

4. Todd Porterfield and Brettell in Chicago 1984, 182, cat. 87; for the same point with reference to *Dancer Fastening the String of Her Tights*, see Brettell in Chicago 198, 170.

DANCERS IN PERFORMANCE

*Fourth Position Front, on the
Left Leg*, c. 1883/1888
Brown wax, cork
22⅝ (57.5)
REWALD XLIII

Three of Degas' wax treatments of this classic ballet movement survive.[1] In them the artist moved far beyond the tentative steps of the *Little Dancer* to the accomplished balance and grace of an expert performer. Two of them, including this one, are among his largest wax dancers, suggesting this pose inspired a more monumental treatment than most. While a date of around 1883/1888 has recently been proposed for the trio, the Musée d'Orsay (Rewald LV) version could well be later. In that version sketchier execution is combined with a more perfect grasp of the position.[2]

Millard praised the present statuette as a peak of equilibrated balance and upward spiraling movement in Degas' work, with a position that seems "continually and effortlessly to rise and turn from the base upward to the curved arm that returns the motion on itself." The pose may also reflect Degas' admiration for a related dance movement in Indian sculpture.[3]

This version of *Fourth Position Front* is a little off balance, with the torso leaning backward slightly and the flexed right leg well above the horizontal. The equilibrium he eventually brought to his treatment of the pose was hard won. This is evident from the use of an external suspension armature in at least one version, recorded in an early photo of National Gallery of Art 1985.65.49, Rewald XLIV.[4] Not only was that figure suspended at the head from the overarching wire attached to a shaft behind her, but an additional *L*-shaped support also rose in front to bolster her extended foot. The armatures that produced that fascinating state of supported suspension were removed, probably in preparation for casting c. 1919.

The three waxes of *Fourth Position Front* illustrate the shifts in Degas' modeling technique between relative naturalism and greater abstraction. This example has a precisely defined body and face, navel, nipples, rounded forehead, and turned-up nose. The National Gallery of Art example (1985.65.49, Rewald XLIV) shows similar attention to anatomical details in the torso but rougher surfaces and a face less human, rendered in a shorthand of lines, lumps, and ridges. The

Musée d'Orsay wax, placed by Rewald in the 1896–1911 group, is the sketchiest. The torso is built up of wax scales, the head a blob pulled to a point at the back, yet the human forms reveal assurance and understanding even at their most abstract.

A crack in the right elbow of the example exhibited here, visible in the bronzes, was repaired after casting. The base beneath the wax is a virtual wedding cake, with four tiers of board and wax, so that the figure appears triumphantly poised on a summit. The lowest board with risers is perhaps a posthumous addition, but otherwise the substructure gives evidence of being Degas' work.

NOTES
1. The other two, with the same title, are Rewald XLIV (National Gallery of Art 1985.65.49), nearly identical in size to this one, and the smaller wax (Rewald LV), 16 inches high, in the Musée d'Orsay. See Rewald 1956, pls. 41–44, and Tinterow in Paris 1988, 473–474, cats. 290, 291.

2. Rewald placed this example in his 1882/1885 group. Beaulieu 1969, 380, dated all three c. 1877/1883, close to the presumed date of the arabesque figures. Millard 1976, 24, dated it 1885/1890, connecting it with the more finished and balanced of the arabesques. Tinterow, dating all three *Fourth Position* waxes c. 1883/1888, associated them with other works assigned to the mid-1880s, including *Spanish Dance* (Rewald XLVII) and *Dancer Moving Forward, Arms Raised* (Rewald XXIV).

3. Millard 1976, 106–107; for Indian dancing figures, of which Degas owned some casts, see Millard 1976, 67 and fig. 72.

4. Illustrated in Rewald 1944, 99.

Dancer Moving Forward, Arms Raised
c. 1885/1890
Greenish black wax,
metal armature, 13¾ (35)
REWALD XXIV

The movement and modeling in this wax are close to those in the more finished *Grande Arabesque, First Time*. Here the torso stretches tighter as both arms rise; the greater forward impetus and the angles of the feet make the balance less stable. The ongoing shift of the woman's weight suggests a stop-action photograph. In inviting us to imagine the movements immediately before and after what we see, this sculpture exemplifies Degas' passion for "the balance point between two movements."[1] The effect of grace and poise, comparable to *Fourth Position Front* and *Spanish Dance*, has prompted a dating for this wax in the mid-1880s. A second version of the pose, in worse condition (Rewald XXVI), perished during the casting process.[2]

To free the figure for an imminent forward rush, Degas suspended her from an armature anchored at the back of the base. Again, as in *Arabesque over the Right Leg, Left Arm in Front*, the suggestion of floating movement anticipates the concept of the mobile. The existing black metal armature sets a horizontal question mark, wrapped with wire and coated with wax, projecting from the shaft and arching to contact the top of her head. An early photo records that a flimsier wire armature, now removed, once played a similar role in the composition of another wax of about the same date, *Fourth Position Front* (Rewald XLIV).[3] The improvised form of that armature suggests that the present relatively neat and sturdy armature of *Dancer Moving Forward* may be a posthumous replacement. Thus the suspension armature was recognized, even by those who prepared the waxes for casting after Degas' death, as an element essential to preserve in the design of this sculpture. Perhaps it was kept only out of structural necessity, since it is omitted from the bronze.

Millard noted that the pose is prefigured in a famous ancient *Dancing Faun*, available to Degas in the original in Naples and also in a plaster reduction belonging to his friend Gustave Moreau.[4] That sculpture makes the dance relatively light-hearted and joyful. In Degas' interpretation the essential elements of the composition, the rising *U* of the arms against the vertical shaft behind them, sum up in simple terms the tragedy he seems to have sensed in a striving for the sky, perennially counteracted by the pull to earth.

NOTES

1. Julius Meier-Graefe, *Degas*, trans. J. Holroyd-Reese (London, 1923), 44; Millard 1976, 104.

2. Tinterow in Paris 1988, 473. Rewald placed this figure in his 1882/1895 group; Beaulieu 1969, 377, dated it 1898/1900. Rewald 1956, 146.

3. Illustration in Rewald 1944, 99.

4. Millard 1976, 69, figs. 97, 98.

Spanish Dance, c. 1883/1885
Dark green wax, 17 (43.2)
REWALD XLVII

This slender, tightly wound figure is one of the three sculptures with which Degas was sufficiently satisfied to permit casting in plaster around 1900.[1] He had evidently preserved it since the mid-1880s, a dating suggested not only by its careful modeling and command of movement but also by circumstances that might have inspired his study of this particular kind of dancer then. Spanish dancers were a frequent subject in the paintings of his friend and colleague Manet, who had died in 1883. Manet's *Spanish Dance* of 1862, showing several figures in related poses, was on view in 1884 in a memorial exhibition that Degas would surely have visited.[2]

A precedent for a Spanish dancer in sculpture existed in the popular statuette of 1837 by Jean-Auguste Barre that depicts the famous ballerina Fanny Elssler dancing a *cachucha*. Degas' friend Henri Rouart owned a plaster cast of that sculpture.[3] The Barre statuette concerns itself less with complex movement than with a faithful likeness and with the overwhelming richness of the Spanish costume. Degas' dancer, like almost all his others, is conceived as a nude. Her movements alone, in a taut, spiraling pose, define the nature of the dance. The dancer seems simultaneously to proffer and withdraw her body as she looks haughtily down over one shoulder at the observer. The model's face is barely sketched, with a slash of a mouth that recalls Renoir's comment on an early stage of Degas' *Little Dancer*: "a mouth, a mere hint, but what draughtsmanship!"[4]

The pose works brilliantly in three dimensions, with no single dominant view. Arching arms cut the air and intriguing contrasts appear everywhere—the slow curve of the stretching right side against the full one of the outthrust left hip, the sharp angles of knees, elbows, and right thigh against the pelvis. Degas chose an unusually slim model for this work, perhaps to emphasize the ardent and angular character of the movement. He heightened these effects by exaggerating the length of her right leg. A second *Spanish Dance* (Rewald LXVI), usually presumed to be later, is performed by a figure of similar slenderness. That rugged wax could represent an early sketch of the same fragile model, another model chosen later for her similar proportions, or a rough reprise based on the present statuette.

The effort Degas put into this design is documented in a measured drawing for legs in a similar pose.[5] The drawing reflects his concern with the proportional interrelationships of the parts of a figure. Showing the legs and pelvis only, it may also document his aspiration to design figures from the ground up.[6] The vertical inner armatures for his waxes must have facilitated such a process. Once the place of the weight-bearing leg was fixed, he could go on to articulate the figure "from the pelvis outward, thrusting and probing with volumes and axes until a balance is achieved."[7]

NOTES

1. See *Dancer Looking at the Sole of Her Right Foot*. For photos of the plaster cast, which belongs to the Hébrard heirs (Millard 1976, 35), see Rewald 1944, 104, and Millard 1976, fig. 73.

2. Todd Porterfield and Richard Brettell in Chicago 1984, 154. For a date in the mid 1880s see also Millard 1976, 24; Beaulieu 1969, 375, dated it 1882.

3. Los Angeles 1980, 112–114, cat. 4; Millard 1976, 74, 103, fig. 75; Chicago 1984, 153.

4. On the pose see Northampton 1979, 10–14, and Chicago 1984, 154. Renoir quotation in Rewald 1956, 17.

5. Millard 1976, 24, 61, fig. 74.

6. Millard 1976, 42.

7. William Tucker, *Early Modern Sculpture. Rodin, Degas, Matisse, Brancusi, Picasso, Gonzalez* (New York, 1974), 154.

Dancer in the Role of Harlequin
c. 1884/1885
Red-brown wax, 12¼ (31.2)
REWALD XLVIII

A recent interpretation gives this wax an exceptional place in Degas' sculptural oeuvre, one that challenges generalizations about the waxes as independent explorations of movement for its own sake. The statuette appears to represent a woman dancing a specific role at a specific time, and perhaps even an identifiable performer.

The evidence[1] lies in the similarity of the sculpture, the only one surviving in this pose, to a figure in one of a series of seven Degas pastels datable to 1884–1885. The pastels depict performers in *Les Jumeaux de Bergame*, the title of a comic opera and a ballet about the competing courtships of twin brothers.[2] Both twins are harlequins, the humorous stock characters in particolored costume from the eighteenth-century Italian Commedia dell'Arte. In the ballet version, women danced both parts.

In one pantomime scene in *Les Jumeaux*, Harlequin Senior, having leveled a rival with his stick, bends over the fallen figure with left hand on knee and the club-wielding right behind his back, about to recognize his brother Harlequin Junior in the adversary he has knocked to the ground. Degas represented this scene in a pastel dated 1885, now in the Art Institute of Chicago, which is the closest pastel to the sculpture. It shows a rear view of the bending Harlequin Senior, dated 1885.[3] There the figure holds a stick behind its back. Degas apparently reworked the back and right arm of the wax at some point so that it is now uncertain what the dancer holds. This may be one reason why the specific connection with Harlequin Senior has not been suggested earlier.

Degas made notes at a rehearsal that he attended on 23 July 1885 at the Paris Opera, in which Marie Sanlaville was dancing the role of Harlequin Senior. She went on to perform the part in 1886 in Paris. The few details of the wax figure's face support Tinterow's suggestion that Sanlaville may have served directly or from memory as the model. That she fascinated Degas is clear enough from a sonnet he dedicated to her. Praising her brilliance at pantomime and her "knowing grace," he spoke as a watcher "pierced by the mystery/ of the movements of a body eloquent and silent."[4]

One cannot be certain whether he made the sculpture to help realize a figure in the pastel or continued after the pastel was finished to explore the dramatic bending-stretching movement, with neck extended on the verge of discovery. His admiration for Sanlaville would make either a possibility. The likely connection with her performance in *Les Jumeaux de Bergame* makes one wonder if specific associations remain to be discovered for other Degas sculptures.

The proposed dating confirms Rewald's general suggestion of 1882/1895 and also lends support to the dates in the mid-1880s often proposed for similarly active and relatively smoothly finished figures among Degas' waxes. The dancer leans not along the axis of her base, but along a rectangular patch of wax set at an angle to it. This orientation, which accentuates the dynamism and attentive twist of her pose, was obliterated in the bronze. That and the absence of the club may help explain why this wax was taken for a figure at rest.

NOTES

1. For the arguments see Tinterow in Paris 1988, 431–435, esp. 433–435, cat. 262. Millard 1976, 24, already dated the wax c. 1885 based on a perceived connection with the Harlequin pastels.

2. The ballet was identified by Lillian Browse in *Degas Dancers* (London, 1949), 58. It was based on a 1782 play by Jean-Pierre Claris de Florian, which was adapted as a comic opera in 1875 and a ballet a few years later (Tinterow in Paris 1988, 432).

3. Tinterow in Paris 1988, 433, fig. 237; McCullagh in Chicago 1984, 157–159, cat. 75.

4. Tinterow in Paris 1988, 434.

Dancer Bowing (also called
The Curtain Call), c. 1880/1885
Yellow-brown wax, 8¾ (22.2)
REWALD XXXIII

Degas modeled a dancer bowing in at least two statuettes[1] in this diminutive scale. While the nearly identical sizes and poses would suggest they were produced around the same time, the figures seem to reflect the individual proportions of different models as well as some difference in facture and color. This one, about half an inch taller, is short-waisted and compact, with her face a complete abstraction. The other, of red wax, is more willowy and supple, with discernibly human facial features. Thus the two may testify to a continuing exploration.

The small size, restrained movement, and firmly defined surfaces of the present work have suggested an early date, probably in the early 1880s.[2] It was around then that Degas probably made several pastels of a dancer bowing, acknowledging the audience with her right hand brought toward her heart. Although less daring in her movements than his later sculptures, the figure is appealing in the graceful torsion of her turn to the right, with weight shifting forward onto her left leg as the right leg crosses behind it. This pose, implying that her body is about to bend, invites the observer's mind to complete the action. Degas also modeled a dancer actually sinking downward in a deep bow, with sharply bent knees (*The Bow*, National Gallery of Art 1985.64.50, Rewald LIII). Its larger size (13⅛ in.), rugged facture, and evident submission to gravity suggest that figure belongs to Degas' later sculptures. In the present wax the dancer remains free and light, with the lilting step of an ancient striding Diana or running Eros.[3] As Degas clearly preferred, it is her action and not her face that suggests the emotions of a completed performance as she moves forward and acknowledges an invisible shower of praise. This subtle little work fascinates in its evocation of the dancer's interaction with her audience, and in its implied place within a sequence of movements, foretelling a bend that is always about to come.

NOTES

1. The other is Rewald XXXII; see Millard 1976, 24, fig. 48, with a dating in the early 1880s.

2. Beaulieu 1969, 375 and 372, figs. 5–6, dated five related pastels. Browse 1949, 56, 389–391, cats. 160, 161, 165, placed several relevant pastels in the mid to late 1880s.

3. Millard 1976, 66, fig. 48 (Rewald XXXII) and figs. 49, 50.

FELIX BUHOT
1847–1898

Fan with Wildflowers and Butterflies against the Norman Coast, c. 1875
Tempera and gouache with gold highlights over graphite on silk
5⅞ x 20½ (14.9 x 52.1)

Gift of Agnes Mongan

As a struggling young painter in the early 1870s before he had found his niche as one of the great experimental etchers of the nineteenth century, Félix Buhot earned his living in a variety of ingenious ways, from decorating fans to designing covers for musical scores. For the fans his primary employer was a fashionable *éventailliste* by the name of Duvelleray, but Buhot also made them as New Year's gifts for patrons who had been especially kind to him. Although he disliked catering to the tastes and whims of contemporary society, Buhot seems to have taken fan painting seriously enough to have exhibited one in the Paris Salon of 1875.[1]

Few of Buhot's fans are known to have survived, either because of natural attrition in a genre that is inherently ephemeral or because unsigned pieces are now no longer recognized as his work. Indeed, were it not for the signature at left in the exquisite confection presented here, it, too, would have been lost to Buhot's oeuvre: the bold spray of flowers and lilting butterflies splashed before the sunlit Norman shore have little in common with the darkly mysterious etchings and lithographs that occupied him for most of his career. Only the solitary figure on the beach and the indistinct tower on the headland give a hint of the brooding spirit that permeates so many of his prints.

The addition of this remarkable fan to the Gallery's collection is particularly appropriate since the museum owns another rare example of Buhot's work as a fan painter, a watercolor and graphite study that is far less complete and very different in both subject and execution (fig. 1). Together these two pieces give a unique glimpse of this little-known aspect of Buhot's work and supplement in a most unusual way the Gallery's collection of his prints, including the impressive group that is also being given in honor of the fiftieth anniversary.

Margaret Morgan Grasselli

PROVENANCE
Purchased c. 1965 from a second-hand bookstore near the rue du Bac, Paris.

NOTE
1. See André Fontaine, *Félix Buhot, Peintre-Graveur, 1847–1898* (Paris, 1982), 40.

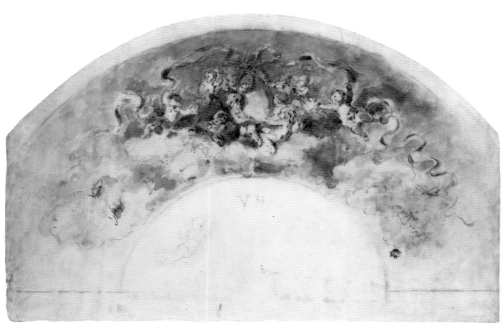

Fig. 1. Félix Buhot, *Design for a Fan,* watercolor over graphite, 11⅝ x 18⅛ (29.9 x 46.6). National Gallery of Art, Washington, Rosenwald Collection

213

CAMILLE PISSARRO
1830–1903

Crépuscule, 1879
Color etching and aquatint
4⅛ x 7⅛ (10.5 x 18)

Promised Gift of Jeffrey Atlas

Of all the impressionist artists, Pissarro was the most actively involved in printmaking. He produced approximately two hundred plates, compared to fewer than half that number created by Manet, Degas, or Renoir. This rare, superb impression of *Crépuscule* (twilight) is the tenth of approximately fifteen artist's proofs of the third and final state, and is one of the several versions printed by Degas. It is inscribed *No 10 Epreuve d'artiste,* and signed *C. Pissarro.* In addition it bears the special notation *imp. par E. Degas.*[1]

Pissarro's prints generally depict the same subjects as his paintings. The modest, rural theme of *Crépuscule* is typical of his art: under cloudy skies, two peasants walk along a curving road past a pair of haystacks. While we think of haystacks or grain stacks as staples of the impressionists' repertoire, Pissarro represented them only a few times: in this series of etchings and in several paintings. Monet may have been aware of Pissarro's etchings when he embarked nearly a decade later upon his series of haystacks seen at different times of day.

Crépuscule dates from the period of Pissarro's most active collaborations with Degas. The two artists met in 1878, and during the next few years Degas introduced Pissarro to new and complex printmaking techniques involving combinations of etching processes. In addition to the simple etched lines of his earlier works, he now employed softground, aquatint, and drypoint, and incorporated serendipitous acid accidents and printing imperfections into his designs. Because Pissarro did not yet have his own press, Degas printed some of his proofs for him. They also experimented with the expressive effects of different ink colors.[2]

Crépuscule is a virtuoso demonstration of the two artists' printmaking expertise. Barbara Shapiro described the three stages of the print's evolution:

Initially, a rhythm of forms including two small figures, a curved road, double haystacks, and a row of trees on the horizon were all established by means of liquid aquatint (grains of rosin mixed in ether or alcohol), that literally puddled into abstract shapes. Additional coarser aquatint grains then created different textures and deeper tones. In the third state fine etched and drypoint lines clarified forms, especially the imperfectly silhouetted trees. Touches of acid brushed directly onto the sky heighten the effect of skudding clouds.[3]

What is truly remarkable about this monochromatic print, however, is the way Pissarro has evoked the effects of color, light, and atmosphere that he and his fellow impressionists so successfully conveyed in their paintings. The print quite literally glows, with a luminosity achieved through an extraordinary range and depth of tone in the combination of different densities of aquatint and the highlighting effects of the touches of acid in the sky and haystacks. For just these reasons, *Crépuscule* is often described as the quintessential impressionist print. This impression in red-brown ink has at least one counterpart, in the National Gallery of Canada, Ottawa; other versions exist in black and white, Van Dyck brown, ultramarine, crimson lake, vermilion, and green.[4]

Pissarro made his etchings and lithographs for his own pleasure, with no real expectation of either exhibiting or selling them. He resisted turning his plates over to commercial publishers and printed most of the etchings himself, sometimes with the help of experienced friends such as Degas. Thus his prints were not issued as editions, but rather as a succession of evolving states, some of which he signed. After Pissarro's death, however, a number of posthumous editions were commissioned by his family. These much more numerous impressions are not nearly as fresh or subtle as those Pissarro printed himself. Thus early signed proofs such as this *Crépuscule* are especially important for understanding the subtlety and beauty of his art.

Elizabeth Pendleton Streicher

PROVENANCE
Galerie Kornfeld, Bern, Auktion 176, 1981, no. 678; David Tunick.

NOTES
1. On this proof, the notation "brun-rouge," identifying the brownish-red color of the ink, was not written by Pissarro. For essential catalogue information, see Loys Delteil, *Le Peintre-graveur illustré (XIX et XX siècles): Camille Pissarro, Alfred Sisley, Auguste Renoir,* 17 (Paris, 1923), no. 23, third state; and Jean Cailac, "The Prints of Camille Pissarro: A Supplement to the Catalogue by Loys Delteil," *Print Collector's Quarterly* 19 (1932), 79. See also Barbara Stern Shapiro, "Pissarro as Printmaker," in *Pissarro* [exh. cat. Museum of Fine Arts] (Boston, 1981), 205; see 48, 205–206, nos. 164–168. For a brief outline of Pissarro's career as a printmaker, see Barbara S. Shapiro, *Camille Pissarro: The Impressionist Printmaker* [exh. cat. Museum of Fine Arts, Boston] (Boston, 1973), "Introduction"; Jean Leymarie, catalogue by Michel Melot, *The Graphic Works of the Impressionists: Manet, Pissarro, Renoir, Cézanne, Sisley* (New York, 1972), 5–6, 19–25; Ludovic Rodo, "The Etched and Lithographed Work of Camille Pissarro," *Print Collector's Quarterly* 9 (1922), 275–301.

2. Shapiro 1972, "Introduction," 4.

3. Shapiro 1981, 205.

4. Shapiro 1981, 205.

no 10   Epreuve d'artiste   C. Pissarro
(Cuivre) Crépuscule   brun rouge
                                                       imp. par E. Degas

FELIX BUHOT
1847–1898

Un Débarquement en Angleterre, 1879
Third state: etching, drypoint, roulette,
and aquatint, with pencil additions
12⁹/₁₆ x 9⁷/₁₆ (31.9 x 24)

Une Jetée en Angleterre, 1879
First state: drypoint and roulette
11⁵/₈ x 7¾ (29.6 x 19.8)

Second state: etching, drypoint,
roulette, softground, and aquatint
11¾ x 7⅞ (29.9 x 20)

Seventh state: etching, drypoint,
roulette, and aquatint
11¾ x 7⁹/₁₆ (29.9 x 20.1)

Helena Gunnarsson Buhot Collection,
Partial and Promised Gift

These two images, which are the reverse of each other, are based on sketches that Buhot made during his second trip to England. Dated 9 September 1879, his visual notes record a landing at Ramsgate, north of Dover.[1] The rain-soaked, wind-swept pier was a subject ideally suited to Buhot, who was well known for his ability to capture the changing effects of weather. These English subjects, so characteristic of Buhot's painterly approach to printmaking, were exhibited in the Salon of 1880.

For these prints quick sketches were used as the basis not only of the primary images, but of the marginal scenes as well. Buhot's development of what he called *marges symphoniques* (symphonic margins) was a major contribution to the art of printmaking.[2] In one respect these subsidiary images resembled *remarques*, the small, witty devices that nineteenth-century etchers sometimes added just outside the main image. Buhot transformed these modest jottings into fully integral elements of his prints that provide a sort of commentary on the main action. His inspiration may have come from a boyhood aquaintance with illuminated manuscripts, or from vignette-encircled book illustrations or sheet-music covers.[3] *Un Débarquement en Angleterre* and *Une Jetée en Angleterre,* each with their heavily figured margins flanking one side of the main image, probably owe a special debt to Japanese woodcuts, some of which utilize this format. Certainly Buhot

and his contemporaries knew and admired the art of Japan.

Any one of Buhot's English subjects would have been an important addition to the National Gallery's holdings by this artist. The gift of these four related images is, however, especially fortuitous because it provides an opportunity to experience Buhot's virtuosity. The techniques and effects of these impressions of *Une Jetée en Angleterre,* representing three of eight known states, are startling and wide-ranging. Among them are the soft bleeding of rich black ink in the drypoint figures and dog; the illusion of light reflecting off wet pavement created by wiping the lower half of the plate almost clean after inking; the addition of seagulls in the stormy sky, drawn and burnished as highlights into the plate; and the remaking of the sky, once formed of billowing aquatint clouds, into a fine network of etched lines suggestive of descending wind and rain. Even in a period of unparalled creativity in the field of etching, Buhot's masterful manipulation of the medium was remarkable.

The six rare Buhots in this catalogue from Helena Gunnarsson exemplify her extraordinary collection of the artist's prints and drawings. The collection includes a wide range of Buhot's work but is most noteworthy for its remarkable quality, including beautiful impressions, rare states and working proofs, prints with hand additions, rare color proofs, and proofs with gold. In honor

of the fiftieth anniversary, the Helena Gunnarsson Buhot Collection has now been promised to the National Gallery. It will transform our collection of Buhot's work to represent the beautiful and moving art of this most subtle printmaker.

Deborah Chotner

PROVENANCE
Un Débarquement: C. & G. Goodfriend, New York; *Une Jetée* (three proofs): Helmut H. Rumbler, Frankfurt am Main.

NOTES
1. Jay McKean Fisher and Colles Baxter, *Félix Buhot: Peintre-Graveur. Prints, Drawings, and Paintings* [exh. cat. The Baltimore Museum of Art] (Baltimore, 1983), 42.

2. Gustave Bourcard, with additions and revisions by James Goodfriend, *Félix Buhot: Catalogue Descriptif de son Oeuvre Gravé* (New York, 1979). Buhot's symphonic margins are discussed in Goodfriend's unpaginated introduction.

3. Baltimore 1983, 53–54.

JOHN LA FARGE
1835–1910

Lesson Study on Jersey Coast, 1881
Watercolor and gouache
8 x 10⅝ (20.32 x 27.62)

Anonymous Gift

There was, as his contemporaries saw, something of the Renaissance, something almost Leonardesque, about the extraordinary versatility of the late nineteenth-century American artist John La Farge. "He was our sole 'Old Master,' our sole type of the kind of genius that went out with the Italian Renaissance," La Farge's biographer wrote in the year after his death.[1]

Born in New York to French parents, John La Farge was probably the most cultivated, learned, and literate artists of his age, numbering among his friends the philosopher William James and his brother Henry, the historian Henry Adams, and the geologist Clarence King. He was one of the first anywhere to be influenced by (and to write about) Japanese art, and one of the first to anticipate the impressionist study of light and color. He also touched, often as a pioneer, nearly every mode and medium of artistic expression—easel painting, mural painting, illustration, and stained glass; and nearly every subject—landscape, still life, and the human figure. La Farge's large-scale, ambitious public murals and decorative schemes are impressive and often very beautiful, but his smaller, more intimate works, ones more suited to the exquisite refinement of his sensibility, are consistently his most ingratiating. Among the loveliest of those are his watercolors.

La Farge did not begin painting watercolors in earnest until the later 1870s, although he had learned how many years earlier. He used watercolor for different purposes: for its own sake in still life, for decorative designs, and to record visual and emotional effects of nature. *Lesson Study on Jersey Coast,* as the title inscribed (with the date) on its backing suggests, is one of those nature studies (whether it was a lesson for La Farge himself or someone else is not clear). The process and purpose of such studies as this one may have been described by Henry Adams, who, ten years later, watched La Farge make a watercolor sketch in Hawaii by one day soaking on splashes of pigment and the next adding a few shaping touches: "Of course, it is not an exact rendering of actual things he paints, though often it is near enough to surprise me by its faithfulness; but whether exact or not," Adams added, "it always suggests the emotion of the moment."[2] La Farge himself wrote, "The painter of water-color exercises far more skill, must be far more resourceful, and, in the end, with his simple means, often suggests more than the oil painter is able to represent."[3]

In its richly textured surface and extreme, almost austere reductiveness of form and color, this sheet—poised between its nineteenth-century antecedents Turner, Courbet, and Whistler, and its successors in the twentieth, Rothko and Reinhardt—is a remarkable example of the almost infinite suggestiveness and profound emotion that, La Farge believed, the "simple means" of watercolor were capable of expressing.

Lesson Study on Jersey Coast is the first watercolor by La Farge to come to the National Gallery. It joins three drawings for La Farge's first great decorative project, the murals for H. H. Richardson's Trinity Church, Boston (1876), in the John Davis Hatch collection, and his largest and most important Tahitian painting, *After-Glow, Tautira River, Tahiti,* c. 1895.

Nicolai Cikovsky, Jr.

PROVENANCE
Private collection, Boston area, 1892–1977; Unidentified auction, Massachusetts, 1977; E. Guy Sawyer, Berlin, Mass., 1977; William Young and Co., Wellesley Hills, Mass., 1977–1978; Patricia Young Cerino (de George), Newport, 1978–1983; William Vareika Fine Arts, Newport, 1983–1986; Greg Shepherd, Newport and Providence, 1986–1988; David Nissensen, New York, 1988–1989; William Vareika Fine Arts, Newport, 1989–1990.

NOTES
1. Royal Cortissoz, *John La Farge, A Memoir and a Study* (Boston and New York, 1911), 261.

2. Quoted by James Yarnall, "Nature and Art in the Painting of John La Farge," in *John La Farge* (New York, 1987), 112–113.

3. Quoted in Kathleen A. Foster, "John La Farge and the American Watercolor Movement: Art for the 'Decorative Age'," in Yarnall 1987, 125.

JAMES McNEILL WHISTLER
1834–1903

Beach Scene, c. 1883–1885
Watercolor with body color
4¾ x 8⅛ (12.1 x 20.6)

Gift of Mr. and Mrs. Paul Mellon

Whistler left America for Europe in 1855 at the age of twenty-one. He remained abroad for the rest of his life, for the most part dividing his time between London and Paris and exerting a strong influence in important art circles in both cities. Nevertheless Whistler ranks among the central figures in nineteenth century American art.

Best known for his oils, notably the famous portrait of his mother (*Arrangement in Grey and Black: Portrait of the Painter's Mother*, Louvre, Paris) and for his prints, especially the etchings he executed in Venice in 1879–1880, Whistler also completed a body of approximately sixteen hundred drawings in a variety of media including watercolor and pastel.[1] Although he used watercolor occasionally throughout his career, he gave it particular focus during the 1880s.

In recent years this watercolor has been known as *Beach Scene*, and before that as *Beach in Brittany*, but Margaret MacDonald suggested that it is probably *Grey and Yellow—Sun and Sands, Trouville*, first exhibited at Dowdeswell and Dowdeswells in 1886.[2] It was included in the important Arts Council of Great Britain exhibition of Whistler's work held in England and New York in 1960, titled *Beach Scene* and dated to the 1890s.[3]

The main focus of activity in the upper right corner is unusual for Whistler who most frequently structured the compositions of his seascapes, and city scenes as well, with layered horizontal bands, as seen in *Return of the Fishing Boats*, c. 1888–1893, another fiftieth anniversary gift. In *Beach Scene*, vivid dabs and strokes of paint against the broad washes of neutral beach and pale blue sea and sky suggest the active gestures of distant figures clustering in small groups. The details of their colorful clothing, plaids and polka-dots, evoke a feeling of carefree festivity that is countered by the smoking vessel in the distance, a harbinger of the modern industrial world.

This is one of four watercolors by Whistler committed to the National Gallery of Art by Mr. and Mrs. Mellon in honor of the fiftieth anniversary.[4] All of the artist's important themes in this medium are represented by them: this beach scene, a seascape, a London street scene, and an elegant portrait. Although the Gallery's collection is quite rich in Whistler's other works, with nine oil paintings, several hundred etchings and lithographs, and sixteen drawings, these are our first watercolors. This gift, therefore, supplements our Whistler collection in an especially fine way.

Ruth E. Fine

PROVENANCE
Miss Rosalind Birnie Philip; P. & D. Colnaghi Co. Ltd.; Mrs. Frances L. Evans, Oxfordshire; Christie's, 19 May 1972, no. 37.

NOTES
1. Whistler's paintings are documented in Andrew McLaren Young, Margaret F. MacDonald, Robin Spencer, and Hamish Miles, *The Paintings of James McNeill Whistler* (New Haven and London, 1980), two volumes. His etchings are listed in Edward G. Kennedy, *The Etched Work of Whistler* (New York, 1910), reissued by Alan Wofsy Fine Arts, San Francisco, 1978; and his lithographs are listed in Mervyn Levy, *Whistler Lithographs, A Catalogue Raisonné* (London, 1975). A catalogue of his watercolors, pastels, and drawings by Margaret F. MacDonald is forthcoming.

2. I am grateful to Margaret MacDonald for sharing her entry on this work from her forthcoming catalogue of Whistler's drawings.

3. *James McNeill Whistler* [exh. cat. The Arts Council Gallery and The Knoedler Galleries] (London and New York, 1960), cat. 95. Introduction by Andrew McLaren Young. The watercolor has been redated since by Margaret F. MacDonald.

4. For an article on Whistler's watercolors in the collection of Paul Mellon at the time of its publication see Ruth E. Fine, "Notes and Notices: Whistler's Watercolors" in John Wilmerding, ed., *Essays in Honor of Paul Mellon: Collector and Benefactor* (Washington, 1986), 110–135.

JAMES McNEILL WHISTLER
1834–1903

Village Shop, Chelsea, c. 1884
Watercolor with body color
4¾ x 8⅜ (12.2 x 20.9)

Gift of Mr. and Mrs. Paul Mellon

Works of small size such as the four watercolors included in this exhibition are an important aspect of Whistler's art. Charles Lang Freer described them as "superficially, the size of your hand, but, artistically, the size of a continent."[1] *Village Shop, Chelsea* is a splendid example of the diminutive street scenes that punctuated Whistler's oils, watercolors, and etchings throughout the 1880s and into the 1890s.[2] Generally horizontal in format, Whistler established in them a counter-structure of verticals—doorways, window panes and shutters, and groupings of figures, usually engaged in conversation.

The barely discernible standing figure inside the building here—beyond the right doorway, about to be joined by a toddler on hands and knees—offers evidence of Whistler's proclivity to peer past the obvious, into windows and through doorways, to suggest the private life behind the street's activities.

Village Shop, Chelsea is marked by great formal subtlety, with color supplying an internal quality of light apparent, for example, in the delicate blue of the bricks between doorway and shutter at the far left; in the touches of red that move horizontally across the center of the composition, several spots in the window at left, in the wall between the windows, and ending with the relatively brilliant hue in the flowers at right. Equally subtle is the way in which dabs of green quite clearly suggest leaves at the upper right, and the way brief strokes of the brush, seemingly lacking in specificity, capture marvelous details of the children's clothing and gestures.

At the center of the composition is Whistler's distinctive butterfly signature, which is also visible in the three other watercolors by him included in this Fiftieth Anniversary gift. Evolved over a period of years from his initials *JMW*, the butterfly is a hallmark of Whistler's work. The details of its configuration are often useful in determining dates, if not of when a work was painted, then of when it was signed.

This watercolor has long been admired. Under the title *A Study (Houses)*, it was reproduced in *The Studio* magazine in November 1903, within months of Whistler's death. That title seems more apt than the one it has since taken on, as Whistler's shop scenes tend to give some evidence of the sort of shops they are. Much later the watercolor was included in an exhibition commemorating the 150th anniversary of the artist's birth, *Notes, Harmonies & Nocturnes: Small Works by James McNeill Whistler.*[3]

Ruth E. Fine

PROVENANCE
Brown & Phillips, London, 1903; John P. Elton, Waterbury, Connecticut; Lucy Cross (his granddaughter); Private collection, Los Angeles; acquired through Hope Davis Fine Art, 1988.

NOTES
1. Letter to H. H. Benedict, 26 November 1901, Freer letterbooks, 8:435. Freer Gallery of Art, Washington, quoted by Hope Davis in her preface to *Notes, Harmonies, Nocturnes: Small Works by James McNeill Whistler* [exh. cat. M. Knoedler & Co.] (New York, 1984), no. 9.

2. For a selection of London shop fronts, including a brief summary of Whistler's work in watercolor, see *Whistler: Themes and Variations* [exh. cat. Montgomery Art Gallery, Pomona College] (Stanford, 1978), 50–60.

3. New York 1984, 93.

JAMES McNEILL WHISTLER
1834–1903

*Study in Black and Gold
(Madge O'Donoghue)*, c. 1885
Watercolor with body color
9⁷/₁₆ x 6¾ (24 x 17.2)

Gift of Mr. and Mrs. Paul Mellon

This delicate watercolor is similar in several respects to some of Whistler's most important portraits in oil. Most notable is the manner in which the artist set off the figure: a dark, stark background, one that is lacking any qualities that would define it as a particular place. The dense blackness of the setting presents a dramatic contrast to the opaque mauve of the woman's dress, touched by rich blues in some of the shadows, and the browns and grays of the floor.

Broad watery washes are contrasted with delicate strokes that define the folds of the sitter's garment and details such as the tiny dabs of paint that suggest ruffles at the neck and wrists. On her lap, which is covered by a black shawl, she holds a wide-brimmed, feathered black hat. Both almost fuse with the surrounding darkness. Only the feathers spring free, carrying forward the gesture of her left hand into space.

Study in Black and Gold (Madge O'Donoghue) is one of several highly finished, elegant watercolors of women from the mid 1880s.[1] Whistler was proud enough of this one to include it in his 1884 exhibition at Dowdeswell and Dowdeswells as *Harmony in Violet and Yellow*. By 1905 it was on view in Paris under its present title, and it also appeared in the important exhibition of Whistler's work organized by the Arts Council of Great Britain in 1960.[2]

Study in Black and Gold (Madge O'Donoghue) was once owned by Alexander Arnold Hannay, a London solicitor who was friendly with Whistler in the late 1890s. Hannay was the owner of several of Whistler's oils as well. Whistler's portrait of him is among the paintings given to the National Gallery of Art by Lessing J. Rosenwald.[3]

Ruth E. Fine

PROVENANCE
E.J. Poole, London; Arnold A. Hannay, Esq. (from 1896 until at least 1905); with Scott and Fowles, New York, in 1926; Mr. and Mrs. Charles C. Henderson, New Orleans; M. Knoedler, Inc., New York, from whom acquired by Mr. and Mrs. Mellon in 1970.

NOTES
1. See Ruth E. Fine, "Notes and Notices: Whistler's Watercolors," in John Wilmerding, ed., *In Honor of Paul Mellon, Collector and Benefactor* (Washington, 1986), 119–120.

2. I am indebted to Margaret F. MacDonald's entry in her forthcoming catalogue raisonné of Whistler's drawings for much of my information on exhibition history and provenance.

3. See Andrew MacLaren Young, Margaret F. MacDonald, Robin Spencer, and Hamish Miles, *The Paintings of James McNeill Whistler*, 2 vols. (New Haven and London, 1980), no. 473.

PAUL ALBERT BESNARD
1849–1934

La Fin de Tout, 1883
Etching, 9½ x 8¼ (24.3 x 21)

Le Suicide, c. 1887
Etching, 12⁵⁄₁₆ x 9¹¹⁄₁₆ (31.2 x 24.5)

Gift of Mr. and Mrs. Daniel Bell

Morphinomanes, 1887
Etching, 9⅜ x 14½ (23.8 x 36.9)

Promised Gift of
Mr. and Mrs. Daniel Bell

These three etchings are from a large and extraordinary collection of prints and rare proofs by Besnard that has been gathered by Professor and Mrs. Bell. Most of these works were acquired in Paris and London from dealers who had in turn obtained them directly or indirectly from the Besnard family. In honor of the National Gallery's fiftieth anniversary the Bells are now donating fifty-two of these exceptional works and offering twenty-five more as promised gifts. This gift will greatly expand the National Gallery's small representation of this fascinating artist who, like other printmakers working at the end of the nineteenth century, became intrigued by the artistic possibilities of the various graphic processes. Besnard produced numerous working proofs for his prints, obsessively altering and adding to the image in successive states. The Bells' collection brings into focus this most important aspect of Besnard's graphic work by assembling sequential states of his prints.

After studying at the Ecole des Beaux Arts in the atelier of the great academic painter Alexandre Cabanel, and after a four-year sojourn in Rome following an award of the Prix de Rome in 1874, Besnard made a trip to London in 1879 that was to have an indelible influence on his career as a printmaker. Remaining in London for four years, he became closely acquainted with Alphonse Legros, James McNeill Whistler, and Félix Bracquemond, graphic artists well known for their original and innovative approaches to printmaking. As a result Besnard began to perceive the expressive power of the various printmaking techniques. *La Fin de Tout*, one of Besnard's first important prints, dates to the period he spent in London, and it presents a clear indication of both the technical acumen and sad eloquence that would

characterize his subsequent work. The striking light effects for which Besnard would become known are already apparent in this print. Acting on a suggestion made by Legros, he changed the print dramatically between the first and second states by cutting down the plate on all four sides, particularly the top and bottom.[1] This reduction of the image eliminated extraneous details of the setting and greatly intensified the work's psychological impact. The Bells' gift to the Gallery includes a copy of the fourth state as illustrated and a retouched proof of the very rare second state.

Back in Paris in 1883, Besnard continued to develop the distinctly coloristic, tonal qualities of his prints, creating evocative representations of light to convey a strong emotional content.[2] He explained that his attention to light resulted from his desire to "suggest the role of a thing by the way in which it concentrates in itself the light which comes from the objects around it."[3] From 1886 to 1887 Besnard executed a series of twelve prints titled *La Femme* in which he endeavored to "fix certain impressions of humanity" by charting the life of a woman — acting as humankind — through the terrible vicissitudes of fortune.[4] This desire to objectify and reveal mysterious, hidden truths with potent and personal motifs connects Besnard with the symbolist movement. This general approach as well as certain crucial images such as *La Fin de Tout* clearly shows his influence on Edvard Munch. *Le Suicide*, the next-to-last print in *La Femme*, embodies its subject in a suitably grim composition with a stark division of light and dark, of life and death. The rare second state of this print is illustrated; to the third state, also part of the Bells' gift, Besnard added aquatint to deepen the dark areas.

The *femme fatale* also occupied an important place in his creative imagination. *Morphinomanes* is another print that Besnard made around 1887, and it derives from this sinister perception of women.[5] This strange and disturbing work portrays two dissolute women seated at a table, one of whom gazes sullenly at us through a heavy-lidded torpor. The head of the figure behind the table seems to dissolve into the dark, vaporous atmosphere; swirls of smoke are nearly indistinguishable from her hair. Besnard made only one state of *Morphinomanes*, and this impression is particularly brilliant.

Virginia Tuttle Clayton

PROVENANCE
André Candillier, Paris, 1986.

NOTES
1. The plate was originally 17⅜ x 12 (44.4 x 30.5) (Louis Godefroy, *Albert Besnard*, in Loys Delteil, ed., *Le Peintre-Graveur Illustré*, [Paris, 1926], 30: no. 14).

2. His concern for depicting the varying qualities of light led to comparisons of his work with that of the impressionists; Degas responded sourly, "Besnard is flying with our wings." See John House and Mary Anne Stevens, eds., *Post-Impressionism: Cross-Currents in European Painting* [exh. cat. Royal Academy of Arts] (London, 1979), 45. A comparison of Besnard to the impressionists was also made by Claude Roger-Marx, *Graphic Art: The Nineteenth Century* (New York, 1962), 154–156.

3. Quoted in London 1979, 45.

4. Delteil nos. 47 to 58.

5. Delteil no. 65.

AUGUSTE RENOIR
1841–1919

Studies of Trees, 1886
Pencil, pen and ink, and watercolor
11¹³⁄₁₆ x 8⅞ (30 x 22.5)

Gift of Dr. and Mrs. George Baer

Study of Trees is one of a group of drawings using watercolor and pen and ink over graphite that Renoir created from about 1883 to about 1886, after which the artist abandoned this crisp method in favor of softer effects obtained with techniques such as charcoal, sanguine, pastel, and, toward the end of his career, pure watercolor.[1] The precise linear control evident in this sheet, particularly in the tree trunk at the top and the delineation of individual leaves in the two central images, are characteristics of Renoir's *manière aigre* (harsh manner). One of the founders of impressionism, during the early 1880s Renoir abandoned the style he had helped to create some fifteen years earlier. Dissatisfied by haphazard effects of light and color, Renoir wanted to create a more classical and monumental personal style. Renoir discussed this phase of his work in conversations with Ambroise Vollard initiated during the late 1890s. Vollard, writing in 1919, reported that Renoir spoke of "a sort of break that came in my work about 1883. I had wrung Impressionism dry and I finally came to the conclusion that I knew neither how to paint nor how to draw. In a word, Impressionism was a blind alley as far as I was concerned."[2]

According to Vollard, Renoir continued with an anecdote to explain his stylistic transformation: "I was painting in Brittany, in a grove of chestnut trees. It was autumn. Everything I put on the canvas, even the blacks and the blues, was magnificent. But it was the golden luminosity of the trees that was making the picture; once in the studio, with normal light, it was a mess."[3] *Studies of Trees* is closely related to that description. In the lower right section Renoir sketched the outline of a chestnut leaf in green, and the lobed leaves of the chestnut are clearly depicted in the principal study

on the sheet, a closer study of the foliage seen in the pair of trees immediately above it. The cascading leaves were first drawn with graphite, over which Renoir added ink to strengthen and define the shapes of the leaves. Then watercolor of varying density in golden yellow, red-orange, and yellow-green tones was laid onto the individual leaves.

Renoir was in Brittany in August and September of 1886,[4] staying in Saint-Briac, a village on the northern coast of Brittany. Writing to his dealer Paul Durand-Ruel in August, Renoir mentioned that he had "found a tranquil and pretty corner where he could work at ease."[5] Later in August he wrote again to inform the dealer that "I have here some pretty things to do until the end of September, but I make drawings and watercolors, in order not to be lacking in information [for paintings to be executed in the studio] this winter."[6] Like the majority of Renoir's drawings from this time, it is possible that this sheet was a preparatory study for a now-unknown or perhaps destroyed painting,[7] as suggested by Renoir's comment to Vollard.

This drawing reveals a distinctive aspect of Renoir's work not until now represented in the National Gallery. Our two pastels and two chalk drawings, all figurative works, differ from it in both medium and subject. The Gallery's extensive collection of paintings by Renoir includes only one from this important moment in the artist's development, the *Girl with a Hoop* (1963.10.58). There the landscape serves as a decorative backdrop for a commissioned portrait, whereas *Studies of Trees* reveals the full acuity of Renoir's vision and the finesse of his draftsmanship as he rejuvenated his style following the break with impressionism.

Florence E. Coman

PROVENANCE
Ambroise Vollard, Paris; Edouard Jonas; Curtis O. Baer, New Rochelle.

NOTES
1. This shift in graphic technique perhaps introduces the transition to Renoir's late style, a synthesis of the *manière aigre* and impressionism which did not appear in his oil paintings until about 1888.

2. Ambroise Vollard, *La Vie et l'oeuvre de Pierre-Auguste Renoir* (Paris, 1919), 127–128, as cited in *Renoir: A Retrospective*, ed. Nicholas Wadley (New York, 1987), 163.

3. Vollard 1919, 128, as cited in Renoir 1987, 163.

4. John House and others, *Renoir* [exh. cat. Hayward Gallery] (London, 1985), 303.

5. "J'ai trouvé un coin tranquille et joli où je pourrai travailler fort à mon aise." Auguste Renoir, letter to Paul Durand-Ruel, Paris, from Maison Perrette, La Chapelle-Saint-Briac, in Lionello Venturi, *Les Archives de l'impressionnisme* (Paris and New York, 1939), 1:135.

6. "J'ai ici de jolies choses à faire jusqu'à la fin de septembre, mais je fais des dessins et aquarelles, pour ne pas être à court de renseignements cet hiver." Auguste Renoir, letter to Paul Durand-Ruel, Paris, from Saint-Briac, in Venturi 1939, 1:136.

7. No Breton landscapes from this time in Renoir's career are presently known. Renoir wrote to Monet that he had "scraped everything" from his Breton canvases, a story that Monet repeated in a letter to Alice Hoschedé. See Barbara Ehrlich White, *Renoir: His Life, Art, and Letters* (New York, 1984), 166, 291 notes 65, 66. A few works executed or conceived in Brittany do survive, so landscapes may also exist. See François Daulte, *Auguste Renoir: Catalogue raisonné de l'oeuvre peint* (Lausanne, 1971), nos. 498–501, 504–505.

PETER HENRY EMERSON
1856–1936

T. F. GOODALL
1857–1944

Life and Landscape on the Norfolk Broads
Sampson Low, Marston, Searle, and
Rivington, London, 1886
Bound volume with text and 40
platinum photographs by Emerson and
Goodall
11¼ x 16⅛ (28.5 x 41)

Promised Gift of
Harvey S. Shipley Miller
and J. Randall Plummer

PETER HENRY EMERSON
1856–1936

Marsh Leaves
David Nutt, London, 1895
Bound volume with 16 photogravures
11¼ x 7⅛ (28.5 x 18)

Gift of Harvey S. Shipley Miller
and J. Randall Plummer

Peter Henry Emerson was an opinionated, feisty, and irascible man whose career was as intense and as brief as a meteor. He bought his first camera in 1882 and immediately started to photograph voraciously. By 1887 he had published *Life and Landscape on the Norfolk Broads*, which was hailed as "epoch-making . . . because such perfection of photography, such perfection of reproduction process and such perfection of artistic feeling have never before been brought together."[1] In 1889 in *Naturalistic Photography for Students of the Art*, described as a "bombshell dropped in a tea party," he insisted that photography in the hands of sensitive individuals could become an art. Yet only the following year, in 1890, he renounced this conviction. He published his last album of images, *Marsh Leaves*, in 1895, thus ending his brief and tumultuous career. *Life and Landscape on the Norfolk Broads* and *Marsh Leaves* are not only the end points of this remarkable work, but also the two publications that most effectively summarize his ideas, his contributions, and his influences.

Born in Cuba of American parents, Emerson spent most of his adult life in England. It was while he was studying for his medical degree in London that he discovered the Norfolk Broads. Entranced with the locale,

he began to work with the naturalist painter T. F. Goodall on a book about this region. Traveling by boat, they spent many days photographing and taking notes on the people as well as the natural vegetation.

The result was truly a joint effort: both Emerson and Goodall wrote the texts and collaborated on most but not all of the photographs. The rich platinum prints in *Life and Landscape*, such as *Rowing Home the Schoof-Stuff*, are quiet, sympathetic studies; the figures are solid and classical in their proportions, in tune with their environment and dignified in their posture. These photographs also reveal Emerson's strongly held and highly influential belief that photographers, in order to be truthful to nature, must not render all details with sharp outlines, but instead should use a differential focus. The eye, he believed, does not see all elements in a scene clearly at one time, and therefore the photographer must selectively render only the central elements in sharp focus, allowing peripheral information to become less distinct.

At heart, however, Emerson was both an artist and a scientist. And it is that duality that accounts for the schism in his work. As an artist he was intrigued with the simple, rugged beauty and the seeming purity of the people of the Norfolk Broads as well as their close communion with nature. But as a scientist he was also fascinated with the details of their lives and environment: their dress, their methods and habits of work, their patterns of speech, living conditions, and even their politics, as well as the flora and fauna of the area. His aesthetics would not allow him to clutter his imagery with such details, so he confined his discussion of these elements to the texts. It was also science — and to a lesser extent art — that caused him to abandon his claims for the artistic possibilities of photography: he had believed that tones could be made darker and lighter at will, but in 1890 the scientists Hurter and Driffield proved that tones always remained in the same relationship to each other. In addition, he wrote that conversations with "an artist," possibly Whistler, convinced him that the simple representation of nature was not art.[2]

Emerson made the photographs in *Marsh Leaves* most likely in 1890 and 1893, although the book was not published until 1895. Including many of his most minimal and abstract compositions, this work also contains images, such as *Marsh Weeds*, that clearly reveal the influence on his art of both Japanese prints, especially those of Hokusai, and Whistler. Using a long-focal-length lens

that compressed the space, Emerson created a spare composition with delicate banding of light and dark to construct a scene that is both formal in its structure yet evocative of the endurance of life within the depths of winter.

Emerson exerted a tremendous influence both on his own time and on subsequent generations. Alfred Stieglitz, whose work is represented so strongly in the National Gallery's collection, was a disciple of Emerson's in the late 1880s and 1890s, adopting his subject matter, style, and even his technique. However, until Harvey S. Shipley Miller and J. Randall Plummer graciously donated *Marsh Leaves* and promised to give *Life and Landscape on the Norfolk Broads*, Emerson's work was not represented in the collection.[3] Their donation is further enhanced by the inscription in *Marsh Leaves* from Emerson to "Mr. Dallmeyeren" (Thomas Ross Dallmeyer, who introduced the first telephoto lens in 1891, was Emerson's great friend and lens maker).

Sarah Greenough

PROVENANCE
Life and Landscape on the Norfolk Broads: Ken Jacobson; Harvey S. Shipley Miller and J. Randall Plummer, 1984. *Marsh Leaves*: Mr. Dallmeyeren, 1896; Christie's, London, 1985; Harvey S. Shipley Miller and J. Randall Plummer, 1985.

NOTES
1. As quoted by Nancy Newhall, *P. H. Emerson: The Fight for Photography as a Fine Art* (New York, 1975), 4. Although *Life and Landscape on the Norfolk Broads* was dated 1886, it was not released until the spring of 1887.

2. Newhall 1975, 90.

3. *Life and Landscape on the Norfolk Broads* is one of an edition of 175 copies. *Marsh Leaves* is one of a deluxe edition of 100 printed on Japanese vellum and bound in morocco and white linen.

VINCENT VAN GOGH
1853–1890

Harvest—The Plain of La Crau
31 July–4 August 1888
Pen and ink over pencil
9½ x 12⅝ (24.2 x 32.1)

Promised Gift of
Mr. and Mrs. Paul Mellon

The spring and summer of 1888 were one of the most productive periods in van Gogh's career. He had arrived in Arles from Paris in late February and immediately began to focus on subjects in the surrounding landscape. By the late spring, sowers, wheat fields, and harvest subjects had become his principal subjects. In June he executed an exceptional painting of the harvest in progress in the plain of La Crau near Arles.

The painting, which he titled *The Harvest* (Rijksmuseum Vincent van Gogh, Amsterdam), was done during an extraordinary ten-day period, 12–20 June, when he produced ten paintings and five drawings of harvest subjects.[1] He used a relatively large canvas (72 x 93 cm), only the third of that size that he had attempted since arriving from Paris. The authors of the catalogue of the recent retrospective exhibition of van Gogh's paintings have summarized: "He had first made two detailed drawings of the motif and, benefiting from the experience he had gained, completed the painting in a single, long session, adding the finishing touches to it in his studio a month later. . . . He later produced two drawings after it and contemplated making a copy after it in Saint-Rémy. Writing to [his brother] Theo from Arles, he explained his enthusiasm no fewer than three times: 'The [. . .] canvas absolutely diminishes all the rest.' "[2]

The Mellon drawing is one of the pair done after the painting; the other is in the collection of the Nationalgalerie der Staatliche Museen, Berlin.[3] Interestingly, both were done for other artists. The Berlin drawing was included in a group of fifteen that he did in July for Emile Bernard[4]; the Mellon example is one of twelve done between 31 July and 3 August that he sent to the Australian artist John Peter Russell, whom he had known in Paris.[5]

There are significant differences between the two drawings. Ronald Pickvance has observed, for example, that in the drawings sent to Bernard, van Gogh evidently accommodates his friend's dislike of neoimpressionism by using relatively few pointillist dots. However, in the group done for Russell, including the Mellon drawing, Pickvance noted a change of approach: "They are executed less hastily; as well as being more finished, they are more stylized. The major distinction lies in the prevalent use of the dot. Dots infest and overrun every sky."[6]

The two drawings differ in other important respects, too. In the Mellon version, the viewer is slightly nearer to the foreground, and the illusion of depth and distance is not as pronounced because the horizon line is lower. As a result, there is a stronger sense of engagement with the subject. In addition, the patently neoimpressionist style of the Mellon drawing offers a stronger expression of the energy of the landscape and the harvest. The sky shimmers and the landscape reverberates with rhythms and cadences, both natural and man-made. Clearly it is a more passionate and complete statement of van Gogh's interests than the cognate image made for Bernard.

Harvest—The Plain of La Crau, Arles is the second drawing by van Gogh to enter the National Gallery of Art; the first, known alternately as *Arles: View from the Wheatfields* and *The Harvest*, July 1888, also given by Mr. and Mrs. Mellon (1985.64.91), was among the batch of fifteen that van Gogh sent to Bernard in July. In addition to the drawing, *Harvest—The Plain of La Crau, Arles* joins three prints and seven paintings, one of which, *Farmhouse in Provence, Arles* (1970.17.34), was done in early June 1888, just before the painting of the harvest.

Charles S. Moffett

PROVENANCE
John Peter Russell, Belle-Isle-en-Mer, 1888; sale, Hôtel Drouot, Paris, 31 March 1920; Le Garrec Art Gallery, Paris; d'Audretsch Art Gallery, The Hague; Lutz Art Gallery, Berlin; George Hirschland, Werden on the Ruhr; Richard S. Hirschland, Englewood, New Jersey; Hector Brame, Paris, 1965; Mr. and Mrs. Paul Mellon, Upperville, Virginia.

NOTES
1. J.-B. de la Faille, *The Works of Vincent van Gogh: His Paintings and Drawings*, rev. ed. (Amsterdam and New York, 1970), 194, no. F 412, as *Harvest at La Crau, with Montmajour in the Background*. For the earliest thorough study of the relationship between the painting and four drawings of the composition, see Mark Roskill, "Van Gogh's 'Blue Cart' and His Creative Process," *Oud-Holland* 81/1 (1966), 3–18. The five works are again discussed in Evert van Uitert, Louis van Tilborgh, and Sjraar van Heutgen, *Vincent van Gogh: Paintings* [exh. cat. Rijksmuseum Vincent van Gogh] (Amsterdam, 1990), 122–123, and Johannes van der Wolk and Ronald Pickvance, *Vincent van Gogh: Drawings* [exh. cat. Rijksmuseum Kroller-Muller] (Otterlo, 1990), 231–232.

2. Van Uitert and others 1990, 122.

3. de la Faille 1970, 516 and 519, no. 1485 (Berlin) and 1486 (Mellon).

4. Van der Wolk and Pickvance 1990, 231–232.

5. Van der Wolk and Pickvance 1990, 232.

6. Van der Wolk and Pickvance 1990, 232.

FELIX BUHOT
1847–1898

Convoi Funèbre au Boulevard de Clichy
1887
Third state: photomechanical
reproduction, etching, aquatint,
roulette, drypoint, lift-ground, stop-out,
soft ground, and engraving
11¹³⁄₁₆ x 15⅝ (30.0 x 39.7)

La Falaise: Baie de Saint-Malo,
1886–1890
Fifth state of central image, second
state of margin
Photomechanical reproduction, etching,
drypoint, roulette, and aquatint
11¾ x 15⁹⁄₁₆ (29.9 x 39.6)

Helena Gunnarsson Buhot Collection,
Partial and Promised Gift

Buhot was a highly experimental print-maker, eagerly employing unusual treatments of his inks and papers as well as his plates. His open attitude even extended toward photo-reproductive processes, which he looked upon as a legitimate tool in the creation of original prints. He explained: "we will be happy tomorrow to have at hand a process of artistic enlargement that is still in its infancy, but which handled finally by true artists, men of resourcefulness, can in an instant or two, counting retouching, bring to life on copper those compositions that we are too lazy or too timid to recopy ourselves."[1]

Using such a reproduction as the basis for *Convoi Funèbre*, Buhot reworked the heliogravure plate into a much more ethereal and moody image. Flying cranes were added in the margins. Their graceful forms are a favorite theme in Japanese art, but their presence above this funeral scene acts also as a metaphor for the soul taking flight. The artist's application of colored inks in this, the most highly colored of all his prints, enhances its mysterious aura. In this impression the blue is bluer by contrast to the full moon and city skyline, a light area almost absent of ink. The japan paper on which the image is printed further adds to the luminous quality of the moonlit scene.

This impression of *Convoi Funèbre* provides an intriguing comparison to an earlier state of the same print in the National Gallery's collection.

Like *Convoi Funèbre*, the origin of *La Falaise* is a heliogravure reproduction. In this instance, the original image was a watercolor by the artist's father-in-law Henry Johnston,[2] which Buhot completely transformed. Dense, wiry vegetation has been added to the foreground and greater depth given to all other areas. A cross atop the cliff and the town across the bay were added as early as the second state.

Buhot is known to have used two different false margins (printed from a separate plate) for *La Falaise*.[3] One of the most remarkable aspects of this impression is the delicate little images that surround the main subject. Intricate figures, flora, and fauna that relate to life in the Breton countryside are printed in a black ink that contrasts with and frames the bister-colored landscape at center. Although he eventually lived in Paris, Buhot was born and raised in Valognes, Normandy, and had a strong affinity to the beauties of provincial France that is evident in this work.

La Falaise joins another version in the National Gallery collection, which lacks any printed margins.[4]

Deborah Chotner

PROVENANCE
Convoi Funèbre: Martin Gordon, New York; *La Falaise*: C. & G. Goodfriend, New York.

NOTES
1. Jay McKean Fisher and Colles Baxter, *Félix Buhot: Peintre-Graveur. Prints, Drawings, and Paintings* [exh. cat. The Baltimore Museum of Art] (Baltimore, 1983), 43.

2. This watercolor is illustrated in André Fontaine, *Félix Buhot. Peintre-Graveur. 1847–1898* (Paris, 1982), opp. 148.

3. Jay McKean Fisher and Colles Baxter, *Félix Buhot: Peintre-Graveur. Prints, Drawings, and Paintings* [exh. cat. The Baltimore Museum of Art] (Baltimore, 1983), 117.

4. Another Buhot print of Saint-Malo Bay, *Lever de Lune à Dinard*, may have been intended as a pendant to *La Falaise*, documenting the same location at a different time of the day. Baltimore 1983, 117.

Inquietant Flaneur, ennemi des Chloroses
Ce croquemort defunt trouvait plaisant de voir
Sur des ciels Parisiens aux tons bleus gris ou roses
Deux ou trois corbillards se detacher en noir
Felix Buhot 1887

PAUL CEZANNE
1839–1906

Boy in a Red Waistcoat, 1888–1890
Oil on canvas
35¼ x 28½ (89.15 x 72.4)

Promised Gift of
Mr. and Mrs. Paul Mellon

John Rewald has observed that following the death of Cézanne's father in 1886, the artist's inheritance permitted him to live relatively comfortably and made resources available that were previously beyond his means. In 1889–1890 he was able to hire the professional model who appears in *Boy in a Red Waistcoat*. We do not know precisely when or for how long Cézanne employed him, but the young man also appears in three other paintings and two watercolors.[1] Decorative elements in the interiors of at least two of the paintings in which he appears identify the setting as 15 quai d'Anjou on the Ile Saint-Louis, Paris, where Cézanne rented an apartment between 1888 and 1890.[2]

The use of a professional model represents a departure for Cézanne, who had long been in the habit of using relatives and friends as models. Little is known about the boy except his name and nationality. In the first catalogue raisonné of Cézanne's work published in 1936, Lionello Venturi stated that he was "a young Italian model dressed as a peasant from the Roman campagna," who, "according to tradition, was named Michelangelo di Rosa."[3]

Scholars and critics have long speculated about Cézanne's interest in di Rosa as a subject and about the possible meaning of the painting. Nearly all have found the figure melancholy or languid.[4] Schapiro noted "a mood of depressed revery,"[5] but Rewald, countering that interpretation, underscored the "considerable surface and vivid color" of the painting as well as the appeal of the model's "slenderness . . . youth, and, to a certain extent, the elegance of his bearing." He also asked "whether Cézanne really intended to convey a specific mood."[6] Indeed, the brilliant orchestration of reds in the waistcoat and the equally complex manipulation of broken blues, grays, mauves, and purples in, for example, di Rosa's sleeve and in the background, belie the subdued mood of the figure. Moreover, the composition as a whole is a carefully woven fabric of ex-

aggerations, distortions, seemingly arbitrary touches of color, and deliberate ambiguities that transcends the viewer's concern with the sitter's apparently wistful expression. The painting seems to exist principally not as a portrait but as a sophisticated, deliberate combination of formal elements that functions like a musical composition. Harmony, counterpoint, rhythm, theme and variation, and orchestration are far more important than illusionism, expressiveness, or the need to probe character. As Schapiro has noted, "Cézanne's art . . . lies between the old kind of picture, faithful to a striking or beautiful object, and the modern 'abstract' kind of painting, a moving harmony of color touches representing nothing."[7]

Rewald has also observed that di Rosa's posture in the Mellon picture resembles poses of those of models in academic life-drawing classes.[8] Schapiro, too, cited "the conventional classic pose of the academy nude" but also alluded to "that noble largeness of form we admire in the High Renaissance masters."[9] Indeed, *Boy in a Red Waistcoat* is reminiscent of a compositional type used by Agnolo Bronzino (1503–1572) and others. The three-quarter-length format, the pose with one hand on a hip, di Rosa's compositionally prominent long left arm, and the folds and rhythms of the draped fabric in the background appear at least indirectly related to portraits such as Bronzino's *Ludovico Capponi*, c. 1556–1559 (Frick Collection, New York), and *Gianettino Doria*, c. 1547 (Galleria Doria-Pamphilj, Rome). The undeniable modernity of *Boy in a Red Waistcoat* notwithstanding, the painting seems also to reflect Cézanne's admiration of sixteenth-century Italian art.

The importance of *Boy in a Red Waistcoat* to Cézanne's development and the history of modern art has long been recognized. Unquestionably one of his best paintings, *Boy in a Red Waistcoat* is an outstanding addition of the Gallery's already exceptional collection of twenty paintings by the artist.

Charles S. Moffett

PROVENANCE
Ambroise Vollard, Paris; Egisto Fabbri, Paris and Florence, until 1928–1929; Paul Rosenberg Gallery and Wildenstein Galleries, Paris; Jakob Goldschmidt, Berlin and New York, by 1939; estate of Jakob Goldschmidt, New York, sold at auction, 15 October 1958, Sotheby & Co., London, no. 6, purchased by Carstairs Gallery, as agent; Mr. and Mrs. Paul Mellon, Upperville, Virginia.

NOTES
1. Lionello Venturi, *Cézanne, son art—son oeuvre*, 2 vols. (Paris, 1936), nos. 680–683 (paintings); John Rewald, *Paul Cézanne, The Watercolors: A Catalogue Raisonné* (Boston, 1983), 174–175, nos. 375–376 (watercolors); John Rewald, "Paintings by Paul Cézanne in the Mellon Collection," in John Wilmerding, ed., *Essays in Honor of Paul Mellon* (Washington, 1986), 310.

2. Rewald 1986, 310.

3. Venturi 1936, 61, 211.

4. Jack Lindsay, *Cézanne, His Life and Art* (London and Greenwich, Conn., 1969), 239; Richard Murphy, *The World of Cézanne* (New York, 1968), 93; Bernard Dorival, *Cézanne* (Paris and New York, 1948), 57.

5. Meyer Schapiro, *Cézanne* (New York, 1952), 92.

6. Rewald 1986, 312.

7. Schapiro 1952, 9–10.

8. Rewald 1986, 311.

9. Schapiro 1952, 92.

VINCENT VAN GOGH
1853–1890

Roses, May 1890
Oil on canvas
28 x 35½ (71 x 90)

Gift (Partial and Promised) of
W. Averell Harriman and
Pamela C. Harriman

On Wednesday 8 May 1889, Vincent van Gogh left the Provençal town of Arles and traveled fifteen miles by train to the village of Saint-Rémy-de-Provence where he voluntarily committed himself to the asylum of Saint-Paul-de-Mausole for treatment of an illness characterized by epilepsy-like attacks, depression, and erratic behavior. About a year later, on the day of his release, his doctor, Théophile-Zacharie-Auguste Peyron, included the following passage in the remarks made for the hospital record: "Between his attacks the patient was perfectly quiet and devoted himself with ardor to his painting." Dr. Peyron also noted that van Gogh was "cured."[1]

The last three weeks that van Gogh spent in Saint-Rémy were a period of stability and calm but also a time of extraordinary artistic activity. As the artist reported in a letter to his brother, he "worked as in a frenzy. Great bunches of flowers, violet irises, big bouquets of roses. . . ."[2] Among the pictures he produced were two exceptional still lifes of roses, the painting in horizontal format titled *Roses* that has been committed to the National Gallery of Art by Pamela C. Harriman, and another in vertical format titled *Vase of Roses* in the collection of Walter H. and Lenore Annenberg.

In a letter of 11 or 12 May 1890, van Gogh mentioned that he was working on two still lifes of irises and "a canvas of roses with a light green background,"[3] referring to the Harriman picture. In a letter written on 13 May he cited a second still life of roses ("I have just finished another canvas of pink roses against a yellow-green background in a green vase"), the example in the Annenberg collection. A comparison of the two indicates that the flowers in *Roses* are slightly livelier and fresher; the rhythms of the petals

are crisper. There is also a greater sense of energy and vitality that includes the articulation of the background, which is richer and more complex in its rhythms and brushwork. The differences are noteworthy because of the artist's interest in the cycle of birth, death, and regeneration that is the underlying theme of nearly all of the work done in Arles and Saint-Rémy (February 1888–May 1890). *Roses* records the fullest and most impressive phase in the life of a rose; in contrast, *Vase of Roses* portrays the moment just beyond the peak, when petals begin to fall and the flowers begin to lose their vitality.

Although van Gogh assigned meanings to certain flowers in still lifes he painted, in his letters he never ascribed a specific significance to the roses depicted just before he left the asylum. Nevertheless, it is clear that he associated images of flowering and blossoming with a celebration of birth and renewal. *Blossoming Almond Tree* (Rijksmuseum Vincent van Gogh, Amsterdam), for example, was painted to celebrate the birth of his nephew in February 1890. It is very likely that he associated the flowering roses with his own renewal and his presumed "cure."

Roses is the first still life by van Gogh to enter the National Gallery of Art. It joins six other paintings, two drawings, and three prints by the artist already in the permanent collection. As one of his largest and most important still lifes, as a work that is simultaneously rooted in tradition and daringly modern, and as one of the most beautiful works in his entire oeuvre, *Roses* brings new distinction to the National Gallery's outstanding collection of post-impressionist paintings.

Charles S. Moffett

NOTES
1. Ronald Pickvance, *Van Gogh in Saint-Rémy and Auvers* (New York, 1986), 73; Joseph J. Rishel in Colin B. Bailey, Joseph J. Rishel, and Mark Rosenthal, *Masterpieces of Impressionism & Post-Impressionism: The Annenberg Collection* [exh. cat. Philadelphia Museum of Art] (Philadelphia, 1989), 109 and 196 (n. 2).

2. *The Complete Letters of Vincent van Gogh*, 2d ed. (trans. Johanna van Gogh Bonger and C. de Drood), vol. 3 (Greenwich, 1959), 469 (letter no. W 21).

3. Van Gogh letters 1959, vol. 3, 269 (letter no. 633).

JAMES McNEILL WHISTLER
1834–1903

Violet [Note?] . . . The Return of
the Fishing Boats, c. 1889–1893
Watercolor on board
8½ x 5 (21.6 x 12.8)

Gift of Mr. and Mrs. Paul Mellon

The wonderful contrast between sea and sky in *The Return of the Fishing Boats* suggests the great expressive range Whistler developed in his use of the watercolor medium. All of its fluidity was explored in his handling of the watery sea, as washes were applied over each other to surfaces already wet; alternatively, at the top of the sheet, using brushstrokes applied over paint that had dried, the artist suggested the weight of the clouds as they moved, swiftly, it appears, across the expanse of the sky.

A mood of serenity is evoked by the silvery tones of the piece that also suggest overcast weather that day, perhaps a chill in the air. The fuzzy quality of the boats' reflections on the water attest to the motion of the wind.

This seascape presents a stark contrast to *Beach Scene*, c. 1883–1884 by Whistler. There the beach itself is featured, with the distant sea and sky no more than a narrow band across the top of the composition. Figures, far away, are represented by dots of color, and while gestures are suggested, no true sense of the figures' solidity is offered. Here the sea itself is featured, with sailing vessels and their reflections accounting for much of the visual activity. The figures play an active role as well, not only visually but psychologically, looking as they are out to sea, awaiting the day's bounty on one level but perhaps also longing for distances unknown.

A vertical composition in contrast to the horizontal format of *Beach Scene* and *Village Shops, Chelsea, The Return of the Fishing Boats*, like them, is composed of layered horizontal bands. The latest of the watercolors by Whistler included in this exhibition, it is the only one worked fully in transparent washes without the use of opaque body color, a more forgiving medium that more readily allows for overpainting and correcting. By this late date Whistler's approach to watercolor had obviously become fully assured, although he still used body color occasionally.

Whistler's interest in the presentation of his work is legendary.[1] All four of his watercolors in this exhibition are framed in their original gilded oak frames in Whistler's distinctive reeding and panel design.[2]

Ruth E. Fine

PROVENANCE
Richard A. Canfield, Providence, Rhode Island; Knoedler Galleries, 1914; Charles S. Carstairs, 1915; Christie's, 19 December 1972, no. 58; acquired from Baskett & Day.

NOTE
1. For an essay on this subject see David Park Curry, "Total Control: Whistler at an Exhibition," in Ruth E. Fine, ed., *James McNeill Whistler: A Reexamination*, Studies in the History of Art 19 (Washington, 1987), 67–82.

2. I am grateful to Hugh Phibbs for discussing Whistler's frames with me.

THEODORE ROBINSON
1852–1896

*Drawbridge — Long Branch Rail Road,
Near Mianus,* 1894
Oil on canvas
12 x 17⅞ (30.5 x 45.4)

Gift (Partial and Promised) of
Mrs. Daniel Fraad in Memory of
Her Husband

Before 1893 Theodore Robinson's artistic life was spent largely in Europe, first as a student in Paris beginning in 1876 and later in a succession of visits to Italy and France. The most important of those visits were the summers he spent at Giverny from 1888 to 1892, where, more as a friend than a pupil, he worked with the greatest of the French impressionist painters, Claude Monet.

Among his American contemporaries Robinson was the only one to receive impressionism firsthand from one of its inventors. He was never Monet's imitator, however, even in the years when they were the closest. Nor did he, despite his many years abroad, succumb as several other American artists did to the temptation of expatriation. Indeed the chief concern of Robinson's full artistic maturity, which can be said to have properly begun in 1893 after his return to America and was cut prematurely short by his death in 1896, was American subject matter and style: "emancipation," he wrote in his diary in 1893, "from old formulae and ideas of what is interesting and beautiful, from the European standpoint, will work wonders."[1] He thought of American subjects, like "little square, box-shaped white houses," and, in a lost painting called *New Jersey Town*, "American figures and vehicles — perhaps a buggy."[2] And he rethought his style in more American terms, attracted to "severer design" and greater "frankness" and criticizing one of his own paintings that had "'sunlight' but little else" as "too floating, shimmery — and not firmly done."[3]

In the summer of 1894 Robinson visited Cos Cob, Connecticut, on the Mianus River. He first came to the region the previous summer in search of American subjects and to visit his friend John Twachtman who had settled in nearby Greenwich a few years earlier. The series of paintings of sailboats at anchor that he made that summer are some of Robinson's loveliest and most successful paintings, surely because he found in the pictorial architecture of the subject something of the frankness, firmness, and severity of design that were, as he was coming to see, elements of an American vision and language of style. In June, the day after he arrived at Cos Cob, Robinson, as he noted in his diary, "walked around by the R.R. bridge to Mianus and back," and found "some fine things — little white boats near the [Long Island] sound — anchored, also at Mianus, with the R.R. bridge in the distance."[4] A couple of weeks later he wrote, "Am getting well and strong [he suffered from debilitating asthma] and work with interest — especially from R.R. Bridge."[5] Most of his Cos Cob pictures, depicting boats at anchor in the yacht club harbor,[6] were probably painted from the Mianus railroad bridge, but in this case he expressed his growing concern for pictorial firmness and severity by painting the structure of the bridge itself. An 1894 sketchbook contains a drawing of the bridge and boat dated "14 Sept '94."

This painting from the Cos Cob series, intimate in scale, is the first Theodore Robinson to enter the Gallery's American collection, joining examples by his friends John Twachtman and J. Alden Weir and completing its representation of the major figures of American impressionism.

Nicolai Cikovsky, Jr.

PROVENANCE
Estate of the artist, 1896; Robinson estate sale, American Art Association, New York, 1896; J. B. Mabon, New York; Davis Galleries, New York, 1962; Rita and Daniel Fraad, 1962.

NOTES
1. Quoted in John I. H. Baur, *Theodore Robinson 1852–1896* (Brooklyn, 1946), 38.

2. Baur 1946, 37, 42.

3. Baur 1946, 40, 44–45, 51.

4. Collections of Mr. and Mrs. Raymond J. Horowitz, Mr. and Mrs. Richard Manoogian, Mr. and Mrs. Hugh Halff.

5. Baur 1946, 41.

6. Quoted in Sona Johnston, *Theodore Robinson, 1852–1896* [exh. cat. The Baltimore Museum of Art] (Baltimore, 1973), vii.

J. ALDEN WEIR
1852–1919

U.S. Thread Company Mills, Willimantic, Connecticut, c. 1893–1897
Oil on canvas
20 x 24 (50.8 x 60.9)

Gift (Partial and Promised) of
Mr. and Mrs. Raymond J. Horowitz

J. Alden Weir was one of the first of his generation of American artists to have a first-hand experience of French impressionism. In Paris in 1877, while a student of the academic artist Jean-Léon Gérôme, Weir attended the third impressionist group exhibition. "They do not observe drawing nor form but give you an impression of what they call nature," he wrote his parents of his reaction. "It was worse than the Chamber of Horrors. I was there about a quarter of an hour and left with a headache." His experience was all the worse for having to pay an entry fee of one franc.[1]

About fifteen years later, when he painted this thoroughly impressionist picture, Weir had clearly changed his mind about impressionism. By the 1880s impressionism had become more familiar, less disturbingly novel, and by the 1890s it had become virtually international in its acceptance and influence. More particularly, by that time several of Weir's close artist friends, such as John Twachtman and Theodore Robinson (who had befriended Claude Monet at Giverny in the later 1880s), had adopted their versions of an impressionist style.

The five or six paintings of the factories at Willimantic, Connecticut, near his wife's family home at Windham, are the high point of Weir's impressionist period. His impressionism was short-lived, lasting no longer than the decade of the 1890s, and on the whole timid and tentative. He seldom yielded to the relaxation of conventional form and drawing that he found objectionable in the impressionist paintings he first saw in 1877, nor did he often paint the subjects, such as modern industrial architecture, that figured in a number of those paintings.[2] He did both in *U.S. Thread Company Mills, Willimantic, Connecticut*, however, as if harking back to his first experience of impressionism and to pictures of the sort that he saw in the third impressionist exhibition and which, ironically, he had then found so horrible.

U.S. Thread Company Mills adds importantly to the Gallery's still small but very choice group of American impressionist pictures, broadening its range to include a major personality in the history of American impressionism not heretofore significantly represented in the collection and a type of subject of which Weir was, chiefly if briefly, the major exponent.

Nicolai Cikovsky, Jr.

PROVENANCE
Wickersham June; Robert Carlen, Philadelphia; Schoelkopf Gallery, New York, 1968; Mr. and Mrs. Raymond J. Horowitz, 1968.

NOTES
1. Dorothy Weir Young, *The Life & Letters of J. Alden Weir* (New Haven, 1960), 123.

2. For the 1877 exhibition, see *The New Painting: Impressionism 1874–1884* [exh. cat. The Fine Arts Museums of San Francisco] (San Francisco, 1986), 189–240.

245

PAUL GAUGUIN
1848–1903

Reclining Nude, 1894–1895
Charcoal, black chalk, and
pastel on paper
12¹⁄₁₆ x 24⁷⁄₁₆ (30.6 x 62.1)

Gift (Partial and Promised) of
Robert and Mercedes Eichholz

This stunning pastel is based on one of Gauguin's best-known paintings from the first Tahitian voyage, *Manao tupapau (The Spirit Watches over Her)*, 1892 (Albright-Knox Art Gallery, Buffalo, New York). In that work Gauguin's young Tahitian mistress Tehamana lies prone on a bed, terrified by the Tahitian night and the ancestral spirits it begets. Gauguin valued the painting highly, for he composed elaborate descriptions of it in his Tahitian manuscripts *Noa Noa* and *Cahier pour Aline* and derived from it a number of works on paper between 1893 and 1895 during his return to Paris from the South Seas.

This residence in France constituted one of Gauguin's most prolific periods of graphic experimentation. In addition to this pastel, the artist made a lithograph[1] based on the entire composition of *Manao tupapau* as well as a woodcut[2] that dramatically silhouettes Tehamana's head, shoulders, and hands. Of all of the graphic works generated from *Manao tupapau*, however, the present pastel relies least on the imagery of its predecessor. The threatening spirit and exotic trappings of the painting have disappeared. Instead, the tiny sleeping nude of the pastel inhabits an indeterminate locale, a peaceful world devoid of terror and superstition.

Judging from her slight figure the model was not Tehamana but Annah la Javanaise, a thirteen-year-old native of Ceylon who lived with Gauguin and was his principal model during the Paris years. This identification is confirmed by the presence on the verso of a sketch executed in pastel suspended in water, which is related to Gauguin's monumental painting of 1893-1894, *Aita tamari vahine Judith te parari (The Child-woman Judith Is Not Yet Breached)* (Private collection), which depicts Annah seated in a majestic blue armchair.[3] The color and composition of this preparatory study, mys-

teriously confined to half the sheet, differ significantly from the oil. Judging from the abrupt cropping of Annah's torso at the shoulder, Gauguin must have first made the sketch and later made the pastel on the recto, trimming the sheet to center the pastel figure.

Gauguin's transformation of the elaborate iconography of *Manao tupapau* into a straightforward depiction of his naked, sleeping mistress recalls the account he wrote of the painting in *Cahier pour Aline*. Following a long description of the "literary" aspects of the painting, that is its complex subject matter, Gauguin paradoxically added that, all subjects aside, "the picture is simply a study of a Polynesian nude."[4] When combined, the pastel and verso sketch constitute an intriguing pair of drawings linked to two of the artist's most important paintings of the 1890s. At the Gallery, the drawing will join twelve paintings by the artist, five of which date to the Polynesian years. In addition to a large number of Gauguin's prints, the Gallery owns a second drawing from 1894 that is also loosely based on a painting of Tehamana from 1892.[5]

Gauguin produced at least two counterproofs or transfer drawings from this pastel original, one of which is dated 1895, which were made using a process that Gauguin developed in the late 1880s.[6] He placed a dampened sheet of paper over the pastel and rubbed the surface to transfer some of the water-soluble pigment from the original drawing to the new sheet. The resulting transfer prints, like their pastel progenitor, are pale, diffuse images in a symbolist mode entirely consonant with their dreamy subject.

Marla Prather

PROVENANCE
Baron Gourgaud, Paris; Jacques Seligmann & Co. Inc., New York; purchased by Robert Eichholz in 1948.

NOTES
1. See Eberhard Kornfeld, Harold Joachim, and Elizabeth Morgan, *Paul Gauguin: Catalogue Raisonné of His Prints* (Bern, 1988), no. 23.

2. See Kornfeld 1988, no. 30.

3. On this painting as well as the drawing under discussion see Richard Brettell in *The Art of Paul Gauguin* [exh. cat. National Gallery of Art] (Washington, 1988), nos. 160 and 161 respectively.

4. Quoted from Gauguin's essay on the painting titled "Genèse d'un tableau," in *Cahier pour Aline*, c. 1892, Bibliothèque d'art et d'archéologie, Paris, Fondation Jacques Doucet, n.p.

5. *Te nave nave fenua*, 1894 (gouache and india ink; Rosenwald Collection) was derived from the painting of the same name (Ohara Museum of Art, Kurashiki, Japan).

6. Richard S. Field, *Paul Gauguin, Monotypes* [exh. cat. Philadelphia Museum of Art] (Philadelphia, 1973), nos. 11 and 12. The latter counterproof exists only as a fragment.

Verso

PAUL GAUGUIN
1848–1903

Reclining Nude, 1894–1895
Charcoal, black chalk, and
pastel on paper
12¹⁄₁₆ x 24⁷⁄₁₆ (30.6 x 62.1)

Gift (Partial and Promised) of
Robert and Mercedes Eichholz

This stunning pastel is based on one of Gauguin's best-known paintings from the first Tahitian voyage, *Manao tupapau (The Spirit Watches over Her)*, 1892 (Albright-Knox Art Gallery, Buffalo, New York). In that work Gauguin's young Tahitian mistress Tehamana lies prone on a bed, terrified by the Tahitian night and the ancestral spirits it begets. Gauguin valued the painting highly, for he composed elaborate descriptions of it in his Tahitian manuscripts *Noa Noa* and *Cahier pour Aline* and derived from it a number of works on paper between 1893 and 1895 during his return to Paris from the South Seas.

This residence in France constituted one of Gauguin's most prolific periods of graphic experimentation. In addition to this pastel, the artist made a lithograph[1] based on the entire composition of *Manao tupapau* as well as a woodcut[2] that dramatically silhouettes Tehamana's head, shoulders, and hands. Of all of the graphic works generated from *Manao tupapau*, however, the present pastel relies least on the imagery of its predecessor. The threatening spirit and exotic trappings of the painting have disappeared. Instead, the tiny sleeping nude of the pastel inhabits an indeterminate locale, a peaceful world devoid of terror and superstition.

Judging from her slight figure the model was not Tehamana but Annah la Javanaise, a thirteen-year-old native of Ceylon who lived with Gauguin and was his principal model during the Paris years. This identification is confirmed by the presence on the verso of a sketch executed in pastel suspended in water, which is related to Gauguin's monumental painting of 1893-1894, *Aita tamari vahine Judith te parari (The Child-woman Judith Is Not Yet Breached)* (Private collection), which depicts Annah seated in a majestic blue armchair.[3] The color and composition of this preparatory study, mysteriously confined to half the sheet, differ significantly from the oil. Judging from the abrupt cropping of Annah's torso at the shoulder, Gauguin must have first made the sketch and later made the pastel on the recto, trimming the sheet to center the pastel figure.

Gauguin's transformation of the elaborate iconography of *Manao tupapau* into a straightforward depiction of his naked, sleeping mistress recalls the account he wrote of the painting in *Cahier pour Aline*. Following a long description of the "literary" aspects of the painting, that is its complex subject matter, Gauguin paradoxically added that, all subjects aside, "the picture is simply a study of a Polynesian nude."[4] When combined, the pastel and verso sketch constitute an intriguing pair of drawings linked to two of the artist's most important paintings of the 1890s. At the Gallery, the drawing will join twelve paintings by the artist, five of which date to the Polynesian years. In addition to a large number of Gauguin's prints, the Gallery owns a second drawing from 1894 that is also loosely based on a painting of Tehamana from 1892.[5]

Gauguin produced at least two counterproofs or transfer drawings from this pastel original, one of which is dated 1895, which were made using a process that Gauguin developed in the late 1880s.[6] He placed a dampened sheet of paper over the pastel and rubbed the surface to transfer some of the water-soluble pigment from the original drawing to the new sheet. The resulting transfer prints, like their pastel progenitor, are pale, diffuse images in a symbolist mode entirely consonant with their dreamy subject.

Marla Prather

PROVENANCE
Baron Gourgaud, Paris; Jacques Seligmann & Co. Inc., New York; purchased by Robert Eichholz in 1948.

NOTES
1. See Eberhard Kornfeld, Harold Joachim, and Elizabeth Morgan, *Paul Gauguin: Catalogue Raisonné of His Prints* (Bern, 1988), no. 23.

2. See Kornfeld 1988, no. 30.

3. On this painting as well as the drawing under discussion see Richard Brettell in *The Art of Paul Gauguin* [exh. cat. National Gallery of Art] (Washington, 1988), nos. 160 and 161 respectively.

4. Quoted from Gauguin's essay on the painting titled "Genèse d'un tableau," in *Cahier pour Aline*, c. 1892, Bibliothèque d'art et d'archéologie, Paris, Fondation Jacques Doucet, n.p.

5. *Te nave nave fenua*, 1894 (gouache and india ink; Rosenwald Collection) was derived from the painting of the same name (Ohara Museum of Art, Kurashiki, Japan).

6. Richard S. Field, *Paul Gauguin, Monotypes* [exh. cat. Philadelphia Museum of Art] (Philadelphia, 1973), nos. 11 and 12. The latter counterproof exists only as a fragment.

Verso

CAMILLE PISSARRO
1830–1903

Baigneuses, gardeuses d'oies, c. 1895
Etching in four colors
3⅝ x 5⅞ (9.2 x 14.9)

Gift of Martin and Liane Atlas

Place du Havre à Paris, c. 1897
Lithograph
5½ x 8¼ (14 x 21)

Promised Gift of
Martin and Liane Atlas

Like *Crépuscule,* both *Baigneuses, gardeuses d'oies* and *Place du Havre à Paris* are inscribed or signed by the artist, confirming that they are among the small number of very fine prints produced by Pissarro during his lifetime. *Baigneuses, gardeuses d'oies* is one of only five color etchings created by Pissarro. This exceptional impression of the fourth state, inscribed *4ᵉ,* is printed with four different plates, in four colors: red, blue, yellow, and gray-brown.[1]

In the mid-1870s Pissarro turned from pure landscape subjects to the themes of rural peasant life that would preoccupy him for the remainder of his career. These bathers tending geese are a conflation of two frequent subjects in Pissarro's art: young girls tending farm animals and the bathers he introduced into his paintings and prints in the mid-1890s. This latter subject proved to be short-lived, however. In a letter to his son Lucien, Pissarro lamented his difficulties finding models in the rural town of Eragny who were willing to pose in the nude.[2] Nonetheless, he executed numerous paintings of bathers and more than a dozen prints,[3] at least three of which depict nude bathers watching over geese.[4]

Pissarro's treatment of this theme was consistent with his other peasant subjects. As Richard Brettell observed about the artist's late rural pictures, "For Pissarro one works in a paradise, and it is through work that one attains a state of harmony or grace. His peasants never toil. . . ."[5] Indeed, these two bathers exist in complete, arcadian harmony with their surroundings, and are neither monumentalized nor sentimentalized.

If prints in black and white may be said to defy one of the most fundamental tenets of impressionism—that of the importance of colors and their interactions—then Pissarro's color etchings occupy a very special place in the graphic oeuvre of these artists. Because it is nearly impossible to align four successive plates exactly the same way in printing an image such as this, each impression is unique. The three primary colors overlap, combine, and play off against each other. Jean Leymarie described their luminous effects: "The shades ranging from green to purple and brown, the broken reflections on the water, the mauve and purple nuances of the shadows, the light playing on the bodies, all reveal a typically impressionist feeling for color."[6]

In the last decade of his career Pissarro made a few trips to Paris, where he painted a famous series of views of the boulevards, *places,* and gardens of the city. In addition he produced two lithographs, one of them *Place du Havre.* This print from the second and final state is the third of twelve impressions.[7] Although Pissarro preferred to print his own etchings, the complexities of the lithographic printing process forced him to turn his stones over to the professional printer Tailliardat, whom he supervised very closely.[8]

The Place du Havre is located at the top of the rue Saint-Lazare, which is represented in Pissarro's other lithograph in this series, *Rue Saint-Lazare, Paris.*[9] Pissarro executed all of his urban views from indoors, from vantage points high above the street. In fact, *Place du Havre* is related to another work from exactly the same date in the collection of the National Gallery, Pissarro's painting *Boulevard des Italiens, Morning, Sunrise* (fig. 1). In *Place du Havre* the horizontal format and the absence of surrounding buildings further accentuate the sense of mystery and chaos that critics of the day ascribed to the new boulevards of Haussmann's Paris. Upon seeing Pissarro's paintings of Paris, the writer Gustave Geffroy praised their evocations of the "social conflict visible in the restless comings and goings in the streets . . . the senseless agitation of human beings living out their lives against their ever changing backgrounds."[10]

The three Pissarro prints in this exhibition represent a larger group of rare lifetime impressions of Pissarro's etchings, aquatints, and lithographs that have been collected by the Atlas family and which will eventually come to the National Gallery of Art. The Atlas' fine proofs will greatly expand the Gallery's collection of Pissarro's quintessentially impressionist prints. In particular they will add many of the most important images now missing from the Gallery's collection, in the early impressions that truly reflect Pissarro's sensitive art.

Elizabeth Pendleton Streicher

PROVENANCE
Baigneuses: Lucien Goldschmidt, Inc., cat. no. 46, 19, no. 113; *Place du Havre:* Private collection, England; Hom Gallery, Washington.

NOTES
1. Delteil knew of only one impression of this state. Loys Delteil, *Le Peintre-graveur illustré (XIX et XX siècles): Camille Pissarro, Alfred Sisley, Auguste Renoir,* vol. 17 (Paris, 1923), no. 119, fourth state; Jean Cailac, "The Prints of Camille Pissarro: A Supplement to the Catalogue by Loys Delteil," *Print Collector's Quarterly* 19 (1932), 83; Jean Leymarie, catalogue by Michel Melot, *The Graphic Works of the Impressionists: Manet, Pissarro, Renoir, Cézanne, Sisley* (New York, 1972), 24.

2. See Barbara Stern Shapiro, "Pissarro as Printmaker," in *Pissarro* [exh. cat. Museum of Fine Arts] (Boston, 1981), 221.

3. See Delteil 1923, nos. 114, 116–118, 142, 148–151, 159–160, 181.

4. See Delteil 1923, nos. 115, 161, 180.

5. Richard Brettell, "Camille Pissarro: A Revision," in Boston 1981, 36.

6. Leymarie 1972, 24.

7. Delteil 1923, no. 185, second state. See also Cailac 1932, 85; Boston 1981, 226, no. 197.

8. Barbara S. Shapiro, "Introduction," in *Camille Pissarro: The Impressionist Printmaker* [exh. cat. Museum of Fine Arts] (Boston, 1973), 6.

9. Delteil 1923, no. 184.

10. Quoted in Brettell, Boston 1981, 36–37.

Fig. 1. Camille Pissarro, *Boulevard des Italiens, Morning, Sunlight,* 1897. National Gallery of Art, Washington, Chester Dale Collection

4e État Baigneuses gardeuses d'oies

Ep def n° 3   C. Pissarro

PIERRE BONNARD
1867–1947

Woman with an Umbrella, 1895
Lithograph in two colors
12⅝ x 9⅞ (32.2 x 25.1)

Gift of Sidney and Jean Jacques

During the late nineteenth century the creative milieu in Paris was particularly diverse and stimulating as artists who had worked in the impressionist style were seeking a more complex and profound language of visual communication. Pierre Bonnard belonged to a group of artists who called themselves the Nabis—from the Hebrew word for "Prophets"—and who delighted in the use of strong colors and bold, linear effects. Bonnard was the first artist to experiment in achieving these effects with color lithography. His earliest poster, *France-Champagne,* was published in 1891, and drew broad acclaim and interest from fellow artists. It was, in part, Bonnard's success with lithography that led other artists, including Toulouse-Lautrec, to adopt it as the graphic medium most suitable to their new modes of expression.

Supporting this innovative approach to printmaking, a number of periodicals began to publish original prints by artists such as Bonnard. One of these was *La Revue blanche,* which began publishing in Paris in 1891 and for whom Bonnard made a promotional poster in 1894. Each month *La Revue blanche* featured one print by an artist from the ranks of the avant-garde, and in September 1894 Bonnard's *Woman with an Umbrella* appeared in issue thirty-five.[1] The same work was reprinted in an edition of fifty in 1895 for *L'Album de la Revue blanche,* whose cover Bonnard adorned with another lithograph. The print presented to the Gallery by Mr. and Mrs. Jacques is from this later printing, which was on a larger sheet of paper than had been used for the magazine.

Monet once remarked that Bonnard's most valuable asset as an artist was his ability to convey a sense of charm in his work; *Woman with an Umbrella* is a quintessential example of this. The attenuated figure of the young Parisienne dressed in black, her face glowing with a beguiling touch of peach—the only color on the sheet—is the very personification of elegance and dainty feminine charm. She has been identified as Marthe de Meligny, the "timid florist's assistant" whom Bonnard met in 1893 and with whom he would spend most of his life.[2]

The collection of the National Gallery includes a copy of Bonnard's 1894 poster for *La Revue blanche* and a lithograph from *Nib Carnavalesque,* a supplement to the journal; the lovely *Woman with an Umbrella* is a most welcome addition.

Virginia Tuttle Clayton

NOTES
1. Claude Roger-Marx, *Bonnard Lithographie* (Monte Carlo, 1952), no. 35; Colta Ives, Helen Giambruni, and Sasha Newman, *Pierre Bonnard: The Graphic Art* [exh. cat. The Metropolitan Museum of Art] (New York, 1989), cat. 31.

2. Colta Ives, "City Life," in New York 1989, 104–105.

HENRI DE TOULOUSE-LAUTREC
1864–1901

Marcelle Lender Dancing the Bolero in "Chilpéric," 1895–1896
Oil on canvas
57⅛ x 59 (145 x 149.8)

Gift (Partial and Promised) of
Betsey Cushing Whitney in Honor of
John Hay Whitney

In February 1895 a revival of the comic operetta *Chilpéric* by Hervé[1] opened in Paris at the Theatre de Variétés. Toulouse-Lautrec saw the production often, at least twenty times according to Romain Coolus who often accompanied him. However, the principal attraction for Toulouse-Lautrec was not the operetta, a story about the eighth-century French king Chilpéric, but rather the actress Marcelle Lender[2] who played Chilpéric's Spanish bride, Queen Galswintha.

After numerous performances Coolus asked Lautrec why he insisted on returning to *Chilpéric*. The artist answered unequivocally: "I come strictly in order to see Lender's back. Look carefully; you will seldom see anything as wonderful. Lender's back is sumptuous."[3] Her costume must have been as revealing in the back as the front, because Coolus reported: "The beautiful Marcelle Lender . . . was dressed, or rather undressed, in such a way that every muscle in her back was available for the scrutiny of opera glasses."[4]

Lautrec's fascination with Lender was shared by many, but her appeal was based on more than her physical traits. As John Rewald has observed, "Her back as well as her charm, her elegance, her vivacity, and the lithe grace of her body earned Marcelle Lender a prominent place in Lautrec's collection of inspiring models. She thus joined such picturesque figures as Yvette Guilbert, Jane Avril, May Belfort, and La Goulue. All these young women appealed to him not so much by their beauty (Yvette Guilbert was far from pretty and Marcelle Lender's finely drawn features were far more interesting than lovely) as by their personalities, their gestures, and their professional accomplishments, and the way in which they projected themselves in their performances."[5] Clearly Lender inspired him and served as both model and muse; between 1893 and 1896 Lautrec included her in no fewer than twenty-six works.[6]

Marcelle Lender Dancing the Bolero in "Chilpéric" is both Lautrec's most important depiction of the actress and one of his best paintings. In Fritz Novotny's estimation, "Of all Lautrec's works on the theme of the theatre this picture is the greatest in both size and in significance."[7] It chronicles the spirit, style, and spectacle of the nineties, and underscores Lautrec's fascination with the ambiguous boundaries between art and artifice and between "high" and "low" art. Lautrec combined elements of caricature, popular entertainment, and theatrical exaggeration to create an image that reflects the changing course of art. The open spaces and natural light of impressionism have been supplanted by a stage set, artificial light, and interests far removed from those of realism and naturalism. Indeed, Lautrec's very personal and expressive use of line and color look well beyond the nineteenth century. It is a picture that boldly and confidently signals the end of one era and the beginning of another.

The Whitney painting is surprisingly the first on canvas by Lautrec to enter the National Gallery of Art. It is an extraordinary addition to the Gallery's collection of post-impressionist art, especially to its extensive holdings of works by Toulouse-Lautrec on paper and *carton*. Moreover, it is an excellent complement for the five café and cabaret subjects of the nineties already in the permanent collection that depict other legendary figures of Marcelle Lender's generation including Jane Avril, La Goulue, Maxime de Thomas, and Alfred la Guigne.

Charles S. Moffett

PROVENANCE
Toulouse-Lautrec until at least 1897 (although reportedly offered by the artist to Paul Leclercq in 1895); estate of Toulouse-Lautrec, 1901[8]; Maurice Joyant; Madame M. G. Dortu; Mr. and Mrs. John Hay Whitney, 1950.

NOTES
1. Hervé's original name was Florimond Rouger (1825–1892).

2. Marcelle Lender's original name was Anne-Marie Bastien (1862–1926).

3. Romain Coolus, "Souvenirs sur Toulouse-Lautrec," *L'Amour de l'Art* 12, no. 4 (April 1931), 139.

4. Coolus 1931, 139.

5. John Rewald, *The John Hay Whitney Collection* [exh. cat. National Gallery of Art] (Washington, 1983), 74; see also John Rewald in *The John Hay Whitney Collection* [exh. cat. Tate Gallery] (London, 1961), no. 58.

6. Nora Desloge, *Toulouse-Lautrec, The Baldwin M. Baldwin Collection* [exh. cat. San Diego Museum of Art] (San Diego, 1988), 102, no. 30.

7. Fritz Novotny, *Toulouse-Lautrec* (London, 1969), 193, no. 92.

8. The painting bears the estate stamp (the monogram HTL in a circle, in red) at the lower left corner.

HENRI DE TOULOUSE-LAUTREC
1864–1901

Seated Clowness, 1896
Lithograph on wove paper
20½ x 15¾ (52.07 x 40)

Gift of
Mr. and Mrs. Robert L. Rosenwald

Seated Clowness is one of Toulouse-Lautrec's most famous lithographs. The subject, Cha-u-ka-o, performed as a clown, acrobat, and dancer at the Moulin Rouge and the Nouveau Cirque. Her name is an orientalized version of "chahut-chaos," a type of can-can dance.[1] Cha-u-ka-o, a known lesbian, sits with her elbows on spread legs, a decidedly masculine pose, while at the same time she is feminized by the jaunty yellow ribbon on her top knot and the yellow ruffle across her shoulders. Lautrec used Cha-u-ka-o as a model in a number of artworks between 1892 and 1897.

Seated Clowness is one of a suite of images entitled "Elles," which includes a cover, frontispiece, and ten lithographs. Cha-u-ka-o is the only model in the suite who is not a prostitute. As Jean Adhémar pointed out, the word *elles* was a general term for women, and by using this word as the title of a series about prostitutes and a woman of the dance halls, Lautrec implied that he considered them ordinary women who led ordinary lives.[2] There are several reasons why Lautrec may have chosen to produce a series on this subject. According to Thadée Natanson, a friend of many artists of the period, Lautrec's inspiration for the series came from a lesbian couple, and the binding theme is lesbianism, a subject that fascinated Lautrec.[3] Another possibility is that Gustave Pellet, the publisher of the series who was known to have an interest in erotica, may have suggested the idea to Lautrec. The Elles series was the first collaboration between Lautrec and Pellet. Whether due to poor sales or lack of erotic content of the series, the collaboration was short-lived.[4] The series was successful aesthetically, if not financially, garnering positive reviews from artists and critics. Sales were so bad that Pellet began selling the sheets separately.

Seated Clowness sold better than the others, undoubtedly because of the exotic subject, its brilliant use of color, and its striking composition. The vertical black wall section and the horizontal red step emphasize the contrast between Cha-u-ka-o's sly smile and her spider-like pose.[5]

As in so many of his lithographs, Lautrec used the spatter technique in *Seated Clowness.* In this technique, a short-bristled brush was dipped into ink and scraped with a knife, causing a fine mist of droplets to fall on the stone below. For large areas the inked brush was drawn over a metal grill held over the stone. Areas in which Lautrec did not want spatters were covered with a barrier of gum arabic.[6] In his approach to *Seated Clowness,* the lithographic crayon was used for outline and some shading. The yellow ruffle and hair ribbon and parts of the black leggings were printed separately as solid colors created by lithographic tusche or wash. The remaining series of steps involved the use of layers of ink spatters in multiple colors. *Seated Clowness* is one of the finest masterpieces by Lautrec in this technique, which he made distinctively his own. Especially surprising here is the way Lautrec manipulated the technique to give, with only three color printings, a remarkable variation of both density and hue throughout the entire image. The Rosenwalds' *Seated Clowness* is the "bon à tirer," the signed state approved by Lautrec to be published.

From Lessing J. Rosenwald, Robert Rosenwald's father, the National Gallery received in 1947 and 1964 the entire Elles series except for this, the most famous subject. Thus it is fitting that Mr. and Mrs. Robert Rosenwald's gift should complete the Gallery's set of these celebrated color lithographs.

Barbara Read Ward

NOTES
1. *Henri de Toulouse-Lautrec: Images of the 1890s* [exh. cat. The Museum of Modern Art] (New York, 1985), 186.

2. Jean Adhémar, *Toulouse-Lautrec: His Complete Lithographs and Drypoints* (New York, n.d.), xxviii. "Except for the first lithograph and the penultimate one, there is nothing to show that these are not ordinary women making an honest living." Adhémar also notes that Proust was surprised by the fact that prostitutes would offer him a cup of tea and engage him in conversation as if their lives were the most ordinary.

3. Charles F. Stuckey, *Toulouse-Lautrec: Paintings* [exh. cat. The Art Institute of Chicago] (Chicago, n.d.), 255–256.

4. Wolfgang Wittrock, *Toulouse-Lautrec: The Complete Prints* (London, 1985), 45. Pellet bought most of the monotypes of brothel scenes made by Degas.

5. Adhémar n.d., xxvii. Some sheets of the Elles suite were still owned by Pellet at the time of his death and were sold by his estate. See also Henri Perruchot, *La Vie de Toulouse-Lautrec* (Paris, 1958), 276.

6. Wittrock 1985, 38–41.

EDVARD MUNCH
1863–1944

Women on the Shore, 1898
Color woodcut with crayon
17⅞ x 20⅛ (45.4 x 51.1)

The Sarah G. Epstein and
Lionel C. Epstein Family Collection

One of Munch's most beautiful color woodcuts, this print is an important expansion of the small group of his outstanding color prints at the National Gallery, two of which were previously given by the Epstein family. Moreover, this gift joins five other impressions of *Women on the Shore* already at the Gallery, to complete a unique set of Munch's prints, one critical to the understanding of this artist. This group of six is the only case known where Munch chose a series of variant impressions of a single image, which had been printed at widely different times, and combined them to be hung and seen side by side.

Part of the power of Edvard Munch's art lies in his obsession with certain personal themes and "primal" images. Throughout his paintings and graphic work Munch repeatedly returned to these, altering their colors, their composition, their moods, their iconographic overtones to correspond with his new insights or intentions. The six impressions in this set were printed over the course of thirty years and show Munch's experimental, serial approach to color and mood.

The present gift conforms in coloring and carving with what might be called the "standard edition" of 1898: with blue sea-sky, green shore, black old woman, and ocher and white young girl. These basic color areas were achieved by Munch's distinctive method of carving the woodblock into several pieces, inking the pieces separately, and then fitting them together for a single pass through the press. Because of the tone and density of color this is clearly a very early impression, where the young girl appears the embodiment of innocence, standing erect on a bleak shore and facing an undifferentiated chasm, while an old woman in dark clothes stoops behind her. This fine early impression sets the stage for the other five variations already in the Gallery, all but one of them unique.

The printed part of the second impression (fig. 1), where the portion of the woodblock for the sea-sky has been omitted, is fairly early. However, Munch's watercolor additions of the yellow moon and reflection, the blue sea and forward edge of the shore, and the touches on the girl and the boulder were probably painted later. In the third impression (fig. 2) the subdued yellow shore and gray stripe projecting from the young woman's face across the sea-sky focus attention on her orange head and extend her gaze into an even bleaker environment of gray and dead white. Again without the woodblock sea-sky, the entire composition in the fourth impression (fig. 3) is overprinted in yellow and striations of purple with strong analogies to Munch's paintings of 1905 to 1907. The extraordinary purple color in the sky introduces a new note of luxuriance, which is enhanced by the denser yellow and blue and the increasingly redder key of the young woman's hair. They radically change the empty mood of the previous version so that now the girl seems balanced between a friendly shore and some extraordinary natural display she is watching.

The fifth impression (fig. 4) was printed after the shore block had been recarved. The coloring of the beach has now shifted to a higher key and corresponds to Munch's paintings of the twenties. The printing of the old woman has been deepened to a solid black, transforming her from an ambiguous attendant into a spectral figure of death. And the young girl's hair has moved from orange to blood red, evoking Munch's sense of violence in sexuality. The sixth impression (fig. 5) is distinguished from the previous one by the blue shore and the addition of the yellow sun-moon and reflection. This symbolic form so frequent in Munch's work, evocative not only of Nordic nature but also of male and female, was accomplished by a paper cutout inked separately and placed on the block. It reflects the completion of ideas tried by Munch in the hand coloring of the second impression.

These six impressions were selected by Munch for a close friend and kept together as a set until they came to the National Gallery in 1978. At that time the Epstein family generously helped in the acquisition of the group by buying this earliest impression as a promised gift. The promise is now fulfilled and the extraordinary set is happily reunited.

Andrew Robison

PROVENANCE
The artist; Christian Gierloff, Oslo; Sverre Munthekaas Munck, Bergen; his heirs; Kaare Berntsen, Olso; Sarah G. Epstein.

Fig. 1

Fig. 2

Fig. 3

Fig. 4

Fig. 5

EDVARD MUNCH
1863–1944

Girl with the Heart, 1899
Color woodcut
9¹³/₁₆ x 7⅜ (24.9 x 18.7)

The Sarah G. Epstein and
Lionel C. Epstein Family Collection,
Given by Their Children: David, James,
Richard, Miles, and Sarah Carianne

In 1894, when he made his first print, Edvard Munch inaugurated a lifetime involvement with graphic media, producing a vast number of etchings, lithographs, and woodcuts characterized by technical experimentation and pictorial invention. Considering that he only began making woodcuts in 1896, the innovative techniques he applied in this 1899 work are remarkable.

Beginning with his earliest woodcuts, Munch explored new methods of color printing. Because he cut his own blocks and pulled impressions on his own presses, he was well positioned to manipulate his materials, all the while stretching the potential of the medium. For example, Munch devised an ingenious method of printing in color that bypassed registration, a time-consuming task that involves inking areas of the block separately for each color and painstakingly aligning the sheet for every run through the press. Munch's solution consisted of sawing pieces into sections that could be individually inked. The sections were then pieced back together like a puzzle and pulled through the press simultaneously.

In *Girl with the Heart,* one can easily make out the individual color sections. The red heart is cut from one piece of the block; the blue-green face and shoulders from a second; the black hair and background from a third. Munch reserved the white of the paper to depict strands of hair, and the striations of wood grain, less pronounced here than in many of Munch's woodcuts, introduce an atmospheric quality. The interstices between blocks form undulating white lines that impart graceful rhythms and a bold clarity to the work. Munch's technique was well adapted to an imagery constructed of large planes of complementary colors. In its succinct, highly concentrated forms, *Girl with the Heart* brilliantly demonstrates how the artist could exploit a medium to maximize the psychological impact of his subject.

This beguiling image dramatically expresses the emotional complexity of Munch's view of women. It is an ostensibly innocent scene, a young woman kissing a heart in a gentle, almost reverent manner. However, it takes on sinister dimensions if we recognize the blood-red color and organic nature of the heart as no paper valentine but a mass of human tissue. Does she caress or does she consume it? Indeed, the image can be understood as a searing portrayal of the predatory female whose carnal appetites amount to a powerfully destructive force.

Munch had represented a similarly macabre subject in 1896 in both a sketch[1] and an etching.[2] In that image, the artist portrayed a nude girl seated on the ground who pulls a heart-shaped flower out of the ground. Blood trails from its roots, spilling over the girl's foot and collecting in a dark pool on the ground. *Girl with the Heart* forms a kind of sequel to this earlier treatment of one of Munch's most frequently depicted themes, the inevitable coupling of Eros and death.

The Epstein Family Collection, which is promised to the National Gallery of Art, will be a major expansion of the Gallery's holdings of the art of Edvard Munch, especially in the important area of his color prints. Two works from the Epstein collection have already been given by Sarah G. Epstein, in this exhibition joined by this, our third impression of *Two Women on the Shore.* The present gift is especially welcome as the first gift from the Epstein children, who are collectors in their own right, to the Gallery.

Marla Prather

PROVENANCE
Sold at auction 20–22 June 1979, Klipstein and Kornfeld, Berne, lot 917; Private Collection; Purchased by the Epsteins in 1984.

NOTES
1. For a reproduction of the sketch see Bente Torjusen, "The Mirror," *Edvard Munch: Symbols and Images* [exh. cat. National Gallery of Art] (Washington, 1978), 208, fig. 9.

2. Gustav Schiefler, *Verzeichnis des graphischen Werks Edvard Munchs bis 1906* (reprint, Oslo, 1974), no. 48.

Fig. 3

Fig. 4

Fig. 5

EDVARD MUNCH
1863–1944

Girl with the Heart, 1899
Color woodcut
9¹³⁄₁₆ x 7⅜ (24.9 x 18.7)

The Sarah G. Epstein and
Lionel C. Epstein Family Collection,
Given by Their Children: David, James,
Richard, Miles, and Sarah Carianne

In 1894, when he made his first print, Edvard Munch inaugurated a lifetime involvement with graphic media, producing a vast number of etchings, lithographs, and woodcuts characterized by technical experimentation and pictorial invention. Considering that he only began making woodcuts in 1896, the innovative techniques he applied in this 1899 work are remarkable.

Beginning with his earliest woodcuts, Munch explored new methods of color printing. Because he cut his own blocks and pulled impressions on his own presses, he was well positioned to manipulate his materials, all the while stretching the potential of the medium. For example, Munch devised an ingenious method of printing in color that bypassed registration, a time-consuming task that involves inking areas of the block separately for each color and painstakingly aligning the sheet for every run through the press. Munch's solution consisted of sawing pieces into sections that could be individually inked. The sections were then pieced back together like a puzzle and pulled through the press simultaneously.

In *Girl with the Heart,* one can easily make out the individual color sections. The red heart is cut from one piece of the block; the blue-green face and shoulders from a second; the black hair and background from a third. Munch reserved the white of the paper to depict strands of hair, and the striations of wood grain, less pronounced here than in many of Munch's woodcuts, introduce an atmospheric quality. The interstices between blocks form undulating white lines that impart graceful rhythms and a bold clarity to the work. Munch's technique was well adapted to an imagery constructed of large planes of complementary colors. In its succinct, highly concentrated forms, *Girl with the Heart* brilliantly demonstrates how the artist could exploit a medium to maximize the psychological impact of his subject.

This beguiling image dramatically expresses the emotional complexity of Munch's view of women. It is an ostensibly innocent scene, a young woman kissing a heart in a gentle, almost reverent manner. However, it takes on sinister dimensions if we recognize the blood-red color and organic nature of the heart as no paper valentine but a mass of human tissue. Does she caress or does she consume it? Indeed, the image can be understood as a searing portrayal of the predatory female whose carnal appetites amount to a powerfully destructive force.

Munch had represented a similarly macabre subject in 1896 in both a sketch[1] and an etching.[2] In that image, the artist portrayed a nude girl seated on the ground who pulls a heart-shaped flower out of the ground. Blood trails from its roots, spilling over the girl's foot and collecting in a dark pool on the ground. *Girl with the Heart* forms a kind of sequel to this earlier treatment of one of Munch's most frequently depicted themes, the inevitable coupling of Eros and death.

The Epstein Family Collection, which is promised to the National Gallery of Art, will be a major expansion of the Gallery's holdings of the art of Edvard Munch, especially in the important area of his color prints. Two works from the Epstein collection have already been given by Sarah G. Epstein, in this exhibition joined by this, our third impression of *Two Women on the Shore.* The present gift is especially welcome as the first gift from the Epstein children, who are collectors in their own right, to the Gallery.

Marla Prather

PROVENANCE
Sold at auction 20–22 June 1979, Klipstein and Kornfeld, Berne, lot 917; Private Collection; Purchased by the Epsteins in 1984.

NOTES
1. For a reproduction of the sketch see Bente Torjusen, "The Mirror," *Edvard Munch: Symbols and Images* [exh. cat. National Gallery of Art] (Washington, 1978), 208, fig. 9.

2. Gustav Schiefler, *Verzeichnis des graphischen Werks Edvard Munchs bis 1906* (reprint, Oslo, 1974), no. 48.

PAULA MODERSOHN-BECKER
1876–1907

Portrait of a Woman, 1898
Charcoal and graphite
13½ x 19¼ (34.4 x 49.1)

Gift of Mr. and Mrs. James T. Dyke

Paula Modersohn-Becker's superb portrait of a woman, incisively rendered with soft strokes of charcoal and graphite, is a tender yet powerful work that reveals her keen ability to reduce the figure to its most essential self. Modersohn-Becker's initial reputation stemmed from the popularity of her letters and journals.[1] Published ten years after her premature death,[2] they were an immediate classic and provide an insightful account of the life of an enlightened woman at the turn of the century. Ironically it was not until after the Second World War that Modersohn-Becker's reputation as a pioneering artist was widely recognized. She was the first painter in Germany to incorporate post-impressionist currents,[3] and her drawings exemplify her highly individual treatment of subject and form.

The brevity of Modersohn-Becker's career was counterbalanced at least by her precocious talent. As an adolescent in Bremen she took drawing lessons from a local painter and at sixteen attended a professional art school in London. When she was twenty she persuaded her parents to send her to Berlin where she attended classes at the Society of Berlin Women Artists. From that time forth her commitment to art was all-absorbing. While working in Berlin, and later at the artists' colony at Worpswede,[4] she was repeatedly drawn to the study of the human figure, especially women and children. Yet it was not merely realism or the anecdotal that motivated her. Her hallmark is a powerful disregard for conventional or idealized notions of beauty. She probed deeper in search of more essential truths.

This portrait of 1898 was executed at the very end of Modersohn-Becker's studies in Berlin. That spring she wrote to her father, "Today in class we had an old woman whose head and neck were wonderfully structured. I loved quietly following with my eyes the almost imperceptible flow of the lines. I don't think that I ever understood it quite so well before."[5] This work was a seminal one for the young artist. Her earlier drawings were more detailed and tied to realism. *Portrait of a Woman* signals a move toward simplicity of form. The shapes are distilled, and there is no line or mark that is superfluous. The model is depicted with dignity and a touching vulnerability. Perhaps it is the fold of her lips, or the oblique cast of her eyes. Certainly there is not a hint of sentimentality in this timeless portrait.

Although women are the subject of many late nineteenth-century works, their treatment is rarely impartial. Alternately portrayed as powerless figures or dangerous *femmes fatales,* they are seldom examined with the sort of unflinching objectivity that informs this portrait. The model's large-boned and sparely structured face is in no way idealized and suggests a rare autonomy of spirit. Indeed few portraits of women in the National Gallery's collection equal this one for its strength of characterization. Although the Gallery has an impressive body of works by modern German masters, prior to the fiftieth anniversary it had only one print by Modersohn-Becker. The addition of this superb drawing helps significantly to reconcile that imbalance.

Judith Brodie

PROVENANCE
Estate of the artist; Alice Adam Ltd., Chicago.

NOTES
1. For the first edition (rev. 1920) see Paula Modersohn-Becker, *Eine Kunstlerin, Paula Becker Modersohn, Briefe und Tagebuchblätter,* ed. S. D. Gallwitz (Hannover, 1917). For the most complete edition of the artist's letters and journals, see Paula Modersohn-Becker, *Paula Modersohn-Becker, The Letters and Journals,* ed. Günter Busch and Liselotte von Reinken, ed. and trans. Arthur S. Wensinger and Carole Clew Hoey (New York, 1983).

2. Modersohn-Becker died of a heart attack at the age of thirty-one.

3. Ann Sutherland Harris and Linda Nochlin, *Women Artists: 1550–1950* [exh. cat. Los Angeles County Museum of Art] (New York, 1976), 273.

4. Worpswede was an artists' colony located twenty miles north of Bremen. It was founded by Fritz Mackensen, Hans am Ende, and Otto Modersohn. Otto Modersohn and Paula Becker met at Worpswede in 1897 and were married four years later.

5. Modersohn-Becker 1983, 97.

PIERRE BONNARD
1867–1947

Parallèlement, by Paul Verlaine
Ambroise Vollard, Paris, 1900

Bound volume with 109 lithographs
and 2 inserted sheets with 4 drawings
in crayon, as well as 124 additional
lithographs and 12 woodcuts by
T. Beltrand after Bonnard
11⅝ x 9½ (29.5 x 24)

Album with 33 drawings in charcoal
and crayon on proofs of the text and
6 lithographs
11 x 9 (27.7 x 23)

Album with 64 drawings in charcoal on
proofs of the text and 8 lithographs
11 x 9 (27.7 x 23)

Promised Gift of
Mr. and Mrs. Paul Mellon

These three volumes chart the course of one
of the most significant developments in the
history of twentieth-century book illustration. This publication of Verlaine's *Parallèlement* was the first of the great *livres de
peintres* of this century, books illustrated in
innovative ways by the painters of the school
of Paris.[1] Departing from traditional modes
of pictorially accompanying a text, Bonnard
has interpreted Verlaine's verses with 109
images that sprawl freely across the pages
in response to sensations evoked by the
poems, images that are as suggestive and
compelling as their verbal prototypes. This
gift is especially exciting because the two
albums that contain Bonnard's preliminary
sketches made directly on early proofs of the
text pages show us how he developed his
ideas for the project.[2] This copy of the published volume is number 86, the copy that
once belonged to Ambroise Vollard himself,
and it is of extraordinary quality.[3]

The inspiration for this new approach to
book illustration can be attributed to Vollard, who as art dealer and publisher was
instrumental in bringing to press some of
the most important French graphic art of
the late nineteenth and early twentieth centuries. During the late 1890s Vollard published albums of prints by leading French
printmakers: in 1895, Bonnard's *Quelques
aspects de la vie de Paris,* followed by four
more albums in as many years by various
other artists. Undaunted by the lack of enthusiasm with which print collectors met

these enterprises, Vollard next embarked on
an even more adventurous undertaking, the
production of sumptuously illustrated *livres
de luxe.*

The first book he selected for this elegant
treatment was Verlaine's *Parallèlment.* This
series of poems, collected from different periods of the writer's career, gave rich expression to the erotic side of what Verlaine perceived as the dualism — parallelism — of
human experience, including both homo-
sexual and heterosexual love. Vollard convinced the Imprimerie Nationale to print
the letterpress for the book; apparently the
title caused them to mistake the work for a
geometry text! When it was published and
the error discovered, the Ministry of Justice
demanded that the book, which had previously been banned as immoral, be removed from circulation. Vollard effected a
compromise, however, agreeing to recall the
two hundred copies that had been printed
and to remove and change the cover and
title pages on which the mark of the Imprimerie Nationale appeared. The publication seems to have been too avant-garde for
contemporary book collectors also. Few
copies were purchased until many years later
when its importance in the history of book
illustration was finally recognized.

For the book, Auguste Clot printed Bonnard's sketches in a romantic rose-sanguine,
creating an association with the sensuously
appealing drawings of the French rococo.
The drawings and early proofs in the two
albums trace the evolution of these illustrations, which appear on nearly every page of
the book, from preliminary to final ideas.
Here we can see the first impulses of the
artist as he formulated pictorial equivalences
to the hedonistic language of Verlaine's
verses. Here we see Bonnard calling forth
profound visual recollections and impressions of sensuality, manifesting them with
searching strokes of charcoal and crayon.
These pages show the significant changes
that were made between Vollard's and Bonnard's preliminary ideas on how to lay out
the pages and their final revisions made in
response to the sketches Bonnard had de-

vised. All secondary decoration subsided in
the face of Bonnard's powerful and encompassing imagery. For example, in the text
proof the first letter of each title was left
blank to be filled in later with a historiated
initial; in the final version they are printed
the same as the other letters, not to distract
from the prevailing illustration.

Many interesting discoveries are made in
examining the three volumes together; for
example, the evolution of one of Bonnard's
most beautiful figures, a languorous, volup-
tuous nude for which his mistress, Marthe
de Meligny, probably served as model. The
drawing, originally made for the poem *Le
Sonnet de l'homme au sable,* was sufficiently
appealing for Bonnard to use more than
once. He maintained the double-page layout for the final version of *Le Sonnet de
l'homme au sable,* but modified the position
of the woman, drawing her legs together
and making her look more soundly asleep,
more "wooden," in conformity with the text
of the poem. He then used the original,
more sensual figure for another poem,
Seguidille.[4]

Virginia Tuttle Clayton

PROVENANCE
Published edition: Daniel Sickles; H. P. Kraus,
1962; First album: Daniel Sickles; H. P. Kraus,
1962; Second album: H. P. Kraus, 1962; Colin
and Charlotte Franklin, Fine and Rare Books,
Home Farm, Culham, Oxford, 1973; Sale, Kornfeld und Klipstein, Bern, 152, 12 June 1974, no.
18; private collection; acquired through John
Baskett, 1975.

NOTES
1. Claude Roger-Marx, *Bonnard Lithographie*
(Monte Carlo, 1952), no. 94; Gordon Ray, *The
Art of the French Illustrated Book: 1700–1914* (New
York, 1982), 2:496–521.

2. Ray 1982, 505–506.

3. Ray 1982, 504–505. See also Colta Ives, "An
Art for Everyday," in Colta Ives, Helen Giam-
bruni, and Sasha M. Newman, *Pierre Bonnard:
The Graphic Art* (New York, 1989), 27–30.

4. Sasha M. Newman, "Nudes and Landscapes,"
in Ives, Giambruni, and Newman 1989, 168–171.

E SONNET DE L'HOMME AU SABLE.

Aussi, la créature était par trop toujours la même
Qui donnait ses baisers comme un enfant donne des noix.
Indifférente à tout, hormis au prestige suprême
De la cire à moustache & de l'empois des faux-cols droits.

Et j'ai ri, car je tiens la solution du problème :
Ce pouf était dans l'air dès le principe, je le vois ;
Quand la chair & le sang, exaspérés d'un long carême,
Réclamèrent leur dû, — la créature était en bois.

C'est le conte d'Hoffmann avec de la bêtise en marge,
Amis qui m'écoutez faites votre entendement large,
Car c'est la vérité que ma morale, & la voici :

SÉGUIDILLE.

Brune encore non eue,
Je te veux presque nue
Sur un canapé noir
Dans un jaune boudoir,
Comme en mil huit cent trente.

Presque nue et non nue
A travers une nue
De dentelles montrant
Ta chair où va courant
Ma bouche délirante.

27

MAURICE PRENDERGAST
1858–1924

Docks, East Boston, c. 1900–1904
Watercolor and pencil on paper
14½ x 21¼ (36.8 x 54)

Promised Gift of
Mr. and Mrs. Paul Mellon

Maurice Prendergast, a pioneering American modernist, was born in St. John's, Newfoundland, but grew up in Boston. He aspired from his youth to be an artist and initially made his living lettering show cards. Unlike such famous contemporaries as John Singer Sargent who began studying in Europe at age fourteen, Prendergast was unable to afford formal training and foreign travel until he was in his thirties. By the time he enrolled in the Académie Julian and the Académie Colarossi in Paris in 1891 (he had visited England briefly in 1886), currents of dramatic artistic change were revolutionizing French painting. Prendergast was initially influenced most by the works of James A. M. Whistler and Edouard Manet, but soon a variety of sources inspired him, including Paul Cézanne (whose watercolors he particularly admired) and the Nabis, especially Edouard Vuillard and Pierre Bonnard. Like the Nabis and other post-impressionist painters, Prendergast found his subjects in the everyday life of Parisian cafes, parks, and streets and in the colorful scenes at nearby resorts.

Prendergast returned to Boston in 1895 and joined his brother Charles in his recently established framing business. He gradually began to make his reputation as a painter, concentrating at first on watercolors because the materials required were less expensive than those needed for oils. In Boston as in Paris he found his subjects in the parks and streets and nearby beaches. His watercolors of these years are remarkable for their loose handling, almost shorthand drawing style, and highly spontaneous feeling.[1] A pronounced emphasis on surface pattern, which would become a hallmark of his mature work, was evident in his work almost from the first.

After an eighteen-month stay in Europe in 1898–1899, spent mostly in Venice, Prendergast returned to Boston to a period of increasing artistic recognition. He continued painting watercolors of Boston scenes, but began making regular trips to New York where he also painted. Although most of his works of the early 1900s portrayed the leisurely activities of people in parks or on beaches, in several watercolors he explored the docks and waterfronts of both New York and Boston.[2] *Docks, East Boston*, with its myriad figures, is one of the most ambitious and highly animated of these works.[3]

The scene shows three large sailing vessels with furled sails berthed at parallel piers; behind them are a fourth sailing ship and a gray-hulled steamer. In the foreground a street bustles with activity as horse-drawn carts and pedestrians pass by. The whole scene is convincingly animated and energetic even though Prendergast's aim was clearly not a highly detailed realism. Some elements, such as the two brown horses in the foreground, are fully realized, but others are only sketched with thin washes. Pencil drawing, visible throughout the image, sometimes describes and contains forms, but often seems to exist independently. Throughout the sheet there are obvious traces of Prendergast's working method: he would first rough out the scene with quick pencil notations and then lay in washes of color, often overlapping them as he moved from one form to the next. No other American artist of the time was as unabashed in allowing the process of artistic creation to remain so evident in a finished work.

In works such as *Docks, East Boston* and other watercolors from around 1900 Prendergast had evolved a modernist aesthetic that was highly advanced for American art at the turn of the century. Although identifiable as images of external reality, these works also flirt with abstraction in the way shapes and colors cling to the picture plane, creating rhythms and patterns that seem to have a life of their own.

Franklin Kelly

PROVENANCE
Kraushaar Galleries, New York; Phillips Memorial Gallery, Washington, 1927; Kraushaar, 1928; Arthur F. Egner, by 1934; Kraushaar, 1935; Winthrop Taylor, 1935; Jeremy Taylor (his son); Peter H. Davidson, 1976; Mr. and Mrs. Paul Mellon, 1976.

NOTES
1. Milton W. Brown, "Maurice B. Prendergast," in Carol Clark, Nancy Mowll Mathews, and Gwendolyn Owens, *Maurice Brazil Prendergast and Charles Prendergast: A Catalogue Raisonné* (Munich, 1990), 19.

2. For example, *The East River* (1901, The Museum of Modern Art, New York) and *Dock Scene* (c. 1900–1905, Collection of the Montgomery Museum of Fine Arts, Blount Collection of American Art); see Clark, Mathews, and Owens 1990, 408, 417.

3. The work has also been known as *Docks, South Street, New York*, but is generally accepted to be a Boston scene; see Clark, Mathews, and Owens 1990, 417.

MAURICE PRENDERGAST
1858–1924

The Mall, Central Park, c. 1900–1903
Watercolor and pencil on paper
22 x 20 (55.9 x 50.8)

Promised Gift of
Mr. and Mrs. Paul Mellon

In September 1899 William MacBeth wrote to Maurice Prendergast, inviting him to join the group of artists represented by his new gallery in New York.[1] Prendergast agreed, and MacBeth honored him with a one-man show of watercolors and monotypes in March 1900. The artist began making regular trips to New York and started a new series of watercolors devoted to scenes in Central Park.[2] Although these works did not represent a departure from the style he had used in earlier park scenes in and around Boston, they are notable for their consistently high level of quality. Wonderfully fresh and spirited, the Central Park watercolors are among Prendergast's most satisfying works.[3]

The Mall, Central Park shows three young girls, gaily dressed and sporting sun bonnets and parasols, poised at the top of steps leading down into the park. Beyond are countless figures enjoying the pleasures of a summer day, some seated on benches, some strolling about. At the right in the middle distance is a fountain spraying water and at the far left the corner of a bandstand is just visible. As with *Docks, East Boston* the scene is lively and animated, but whereas that picture portrayed a world of work and commerce, *The Mall* celebrates one of leisure.[4]

With the addition of *Docks, East Boston* and *The Mall, Central Park*, Prendergast is especially well represented in the National Gallery's collection. The Gallery owns four other watercolors, *Parisian Omnibus, Revere Beach*, and *Figures on a Beach*, all given by Mr. and Mrs. Paul Mellon, as well as *Saint Mark's, Venice*. These six provide an excellent survey of his works in that medium. The collection also includes one of Prendergast's innovative monotypes, *Outdoor Café Scene*, and a splendid oil painting, *Salem Cove*.

Franklin Kelly

PROVENANCE
Kraushaar Galleries, New York; Margaret Sargent McKean (Mrs. Quincy Adams Shaw McKean), 1927; M. Knoedler and Company, New York, 1961; Mr. and Mrs. Edward Patterson (later Joan Roberts), 1961; Knoedler, 1966; Mr. and Mrs. Paul Mellon, 1966.

NOTES
1. Prendergast was in Europe at the time MacBeth wrote and was only able to reply early in 1900 after his return. It would be at MacBeth's gallery in 1908 that Prendergast joined Robert Henri, John Sloan, Arthur B. Davies, William Glackens, Everett Shinn, George Luks, and Ernest Lawson to exhibit as a group known as The Eight.

2. See Gwendolyn Owens, "Maurice Prendergast among His Patrons," in Carol Clark, Nancy Mowll Mathews, and Gwendolyn Owens, *Maurice Brazil Prendergast and Charles Prendergast: A Catalogue Raisonné* (Munich, 1990), 51. Owens suggested that Prendergast's choice of Central Park may have been in part inspired by a desire to find subject matter that would appeal to New York patrons.

3. Hedley Howell Rhys, *Maurice Prendergast, 1859–1924* [exh. cat. Museum of Fine Arts] (Boston, 1960), 40: "For many of his admirers his Central Park series rank with his first Venetian Series as a high point in his career. These Central Park pictures are a sustained demonstration of his artistic maturity, and of his control of his medium."

4. At least two other watercolors in the Central Park series show the same spot as *The Mall*, but both depict it from the opposite view. *Central Park* (Saint Louis Art Museum) portrays the view back up the stairs from just in front of them, and in *Fountain, Central Park* (collection of R. Philip Hanes, Jr.) the vantage point is from the other side of the fountain. See Clark, Mathews, and Owens 1990, 409.

KÄTHE KOLLWITZ
1867–1945

Woman with Dead Child, 1903
Engraving and soft-ground etching,
with chalk, graphite, and gold paint
16⅜ x 18⅝ (41.7 x 47.2)

Gift of Philip and Lynn Straus

Käthe Kollwitz produced some of her finest prints and drawings between the years 1900 and 1910. *Mother with Dead Child*,[1] a work of shattering power, is one of her most significant of the period. Over the engraved and etched proof impression Kollwitz added dense passages of black chalk and graphite, creating an effect that is exceptionally rich, a work that is as much a drawing as it is a print. Equally remarkable and rare is her addition of a subtle gold wash surrounding the figures.[2] Although Kollwitz used color infrequently, she did so with great subtlety of effect.[3] The thin veil of gold that washes up against the figures lends an ironic warmth to this otherwise brutal image.

In some respects this was a prophetic work for Kollwitz.[4] By 1903 she had long been interested in sculpture but had never actually worked in the medium. *Woman with Dead Child* speaks strongly of Kollwitz's preoccupation with three-dimensional form. The stark but eloquent figures are boldly modeled, representing volume and weight. One can almost envision the artist circling around the mass, chiseling out cavities and refining contours. A year after making this print she enrolled in a sculpture class at the Académie Julian in Paris and sought out Rodin whose works she had long admired. Although we think of Kollwitz primarily as a printmaker and draftsman, at the end of her long career it was her sculpture, less known today, that she valued most highly.

Historically Kollwitz cannot be placed within the context of a specific group or movement. Her early work was influenced by Max Klinger's realism, but unlike Klinger she was not strictly a symbolist. Her methods sometimes paralleled those of the expressionists, yet her aims were very different. Although she was not a disciple of Edvard Munch's, his influence is sometimes apparent, particularly in works such as *Woman with Dead Child*. Like Munch, Kollwitz was drawn to powerfully emotional subject matter, and a suggestion of Munch's vampirish figures is echoed in the depiction of the woman, whose face is pressed to the neck of the child.[5] Similarly one thinks of Goya's painting of *Saturn Devouring His Children*.[6]

Although Kollwitz provided the title *Woman with Dead Child*, the physical characteristics of the woman are strikingly androgynous, perhaps more characteristically male than female. In the absence of the artist's title it might be easy to surmise that the dead child is in the grasp of a male figure, perhaps even the figure of Death. Abundant associations exist, provoking layer after layer of meaning.

The National Gallery has a superb collection of prints and drawings by Käthe Kollwitz, thanks largely to the generosity of Lessing J. Rosenwald. Yet the Gallery has lacked any impression of *Woman with Dead Child*. Now, through the generosity of the Strauses, the National Gallery has one of the richest and rarest impressions known. Few Kollwitzes in the collection equal it for its power and beauty. Few lend greater distinction to an already singular collection.

Judith Brodie

NOTES

1. August Klipstein, *The Graphic Work of Käthe Kollwitz* (New York and Bern, 1955), no. 72 iv/x (trial proof).

2. Aside from the present work, there are only five known impressions with gold backgrounds: three bequeathed to the British Museum by Campbell Dodgson, see Frances Carey and Antony Griffiths, *The Print in Germany 1880–1933* (New York, 1984), cats. 29–31; one in the Städtischen Museum, Bielefeld; and one from the Schocken Collection now in private hands, see C. G. Boerner, *Neue Lagerliste 50* (Düsseldorf, 1968), no. 21.

3. See Tom Fecht, *Käthe Kollwitz: Works in Color*, trans. A. S. Wensinger and R. H. Wood (New York, 1988).

4. In one respect it was tragically prophetic. Kollwitz had used herself and her seven-year-old son as models for the woman and child. Eleven years later her son was killed in World War I.

5. See Munch's *Vampire* in Gustav Schiefler, *Verzeichnis des graphischen Werks Edvard Munchs bis 1906* (Berlin, 1907), no. 34.

6. Carey and Griffiths 1984, 66.

269

PABLO PICASSO
1881–1973

The Frugal Repast, 1904
Etching in blue-green ink
18³⁄₁₆ x 14¹⁵⁄₁₆ (46.3 x 37.7)

Promised Gift of Robert H. and
Clarice Smith

One of the greatest works of Picasso's Blue Period is found in this impression of his etching *The Frugal Repast*. Coming at the very end of this period, it is one of only two known impressions of the etching printed with blue-green ink, the other being in the Art Institute of Chicago.[1] The present print is a darker blue, a color extraordinarily important and appropriate for this work in this period.

As a young artist Picasso was influenced by Spanish art of the sixteenth to eighteenth centuries, with its mannerist elongation of limbs, and by the Modernistas, a Spanish group of symbolist artists.[2] The Modernistas were attracted to northern and medieval art and were interested in expressing mood rather than action; their figures were idealized, imprecise, and mystical.[3] El Greco was a hero of the symbolist artists and was studied and admired by Picasso. The influence of Gauguin is also seen during this period in the limited use of color and heavy outlining of the figures.[4]

The Blue Period evolved during Picasso's first trip to Paris in 1902 and lasted until 1904. His work from this early period, of lonely or sick people in a blue tonality, exudes an impression of despair; the people are sunk into themselves. The mouths of the figures are closed; their faces are gaunt. Picasso used the theme of people sitting at a table as he did many times in his career. In *The Frugal Repast*, the blind man puts his arm protectively around the shoulders of the woman as his face hesitantly turns over his right shoulder toward the darkness. Their thin faces and plain clothes as well as the scant food on the table may have been a reflection of the poverty of Picasso and his friends. Sketches of the man in the etching are found in one of Picasso's sketchbooks

from 1903. The woman is seen in a number of other works, including *Woman with Her Hair in a Topknot*, 1904, *Woman Ironing*, 1904, and *Seated Nude*, 1905.

Except for one failed earlier attempt in 1899, *The Frugal Repast* is Picasso's earliest etching and paradoxically one of his most successful. He was twenty-three in September 1904 when the painter Ricardo Canals taught him the craft in Paris. Picasso reused a zinc plate with incompletely erased traces of a landscape by Joan González; faintly visible tufts of grass and stones can be seen running up the right side of the image.[5]

With this etching Picasso began his lifelong experimentation with printmaking in all of its variants. Between 1919 and 1930 he etched the Vollard series and began to learn lithography. His lithographic work with Fernand Mourlot was started in 1945 when he also printed a series of large-format aquatints. When Picasso moved to the south of France practical problems precluded lithographic work and he began to print linoleum blocks until 1963, when a printing press was brought to Mougins. The presence of the press made his printmaking endeavors more practical and more spontaneous, giving him the freedom to experiment in all media.[6]

The National Gallery has two other examples of *The Frugal Repast*, both printed in black ink after the plate was faced with steel. However, the quality of this blue-green impression is far superior, the finest perhaps of all known from this plate. There are few examples of this etching before the steel facing, and, as there are only two in which blue-green ink was used, this rare print becomes a major addition to the National Gallery collection.

Barbara Read Ward

PROVENANCE
Sotheby's; David Tunick, 1978; Robert H. and Clarice Smith, 1979.

NOTES
1. Josep Palau i Fabre, *Picasso: Life and Work of the Early Years*, trans. Kenneth Lyons (Oxford, 1981), 383.

2. Marilyn McCully, *Pablo Picasso: The Artist Before Nature* [exh. cat. Auckland City Art Gallery] (Auckland, New Zealand, 1989), 10–11.

3. Ronald W. Johnson, "Picasso's *Old Guitarist* and the Symbolist Sensibility," *Artforum* 13/4 (Dec. 1974), 56.

4. Pierre Daix and Georges Boudaille, *Picasso: The Blue and Rose Periods* (Greenwich, Ct., 1967), 58, 62.

5. Palau i Fabre 1981, 383. The landscape is more visible in the impressions printed after the steel facing of the etching plate, when less ink was used, than in this version, which was printed before the plate was faced. See Bernhard Geiser, *Picasso Peintre-Graveur* (Bern, 1933).

6. Georges Bloch, *Picasso Catalogue of Graphic Work* [exh. cat. Musée des Beaux-Arts de Zurich] (Bern, 1968), 1:11–15.

r 3   Picasso

JACQUES VILLON
1875–1963

Another Time: 1830, 1904
Drypoint, color aquatint, and roulette
with hand coloring
17⁹⁄₁₆ x 13⅞ (44.6 x 35.2)

Gift of
Frank R. and
Jeannette H. Eyerly

Jacques Villon was in Paris in the 1890s when the vogue for color printmaking was escalating and many artists were investigating color lithography. The young artist made only a few color lithographs in his early career, and he never embraced the lithographic process with great enthusiasm. Instead he became intensely involved with making etchings. He created his first color aquatints in 1899, and his gifted understanding of the medium and its technical nuances is evident in many of the beautiful prints he produced over the course of the next seven years. *Another Time: 1830* is a superb example of what Villon could achieve.

Villon printed *Another Time: 1830* in addition to three color lithographs on the occasion of the Bal Henri Monnier.[1] This park setting with two seated models in 1830s dress against a background of equestrian figures and promenading gentry depicts the tranquil world of the Parisian middle class; Villon probably intended the print as the appropriate salute to the artist Monnier (1805–1877) and the romantic era in which he worked.

Another Time: 1830 is part of Villon's pre-cubist period when he followed closely the stylistic elegance of Henri de Toulouse-Lautrec's color prints and posters. It was also about this time that Villon found inspiration in the work of Paul Helleu, who was responsible for inspiring an aesthetic movement that popularized similar romantic scenes of fashionable Parisian ladies. *Another Time:*

1830 also gives evidence of the strong influence Japanese prints had on the development of color printmaking in the late nineteenth century. The juxtaposition of unmodeled patterns of color and the denial of linear perspective for a flat tilted space echo some of the compositional devices of the Japanese *ukiyo-e* woodcuts admired at this time.

Villon's graphic oeuvre is represented in the Gallery's collection by sixty-nine prints, the core of which are from his cubist period and the later subjects of the 1930s and 1940s. Among the early works in the collection there are now eleven examples of his color aquatints, many given in 1985 by Mr. and Mrs. Paul Mellon. The present gift from Mr. and Mrs. Eyerly is a striking compliment to the Gallery's small but choice group. Enhanced with touches of roulette and the marvelously rich burr of his drypoint line, *Another Time: 1830* offers an instructive look at the breadth and variety of Villon's intaglio skill, and thus holds an important place in the Gallery's collection.

Carlotta J. Owens

NOTE

1. Colette de Ginestet and Catherine Pouillon, *Jacques Villon, Les Estampes et Les Illustrations, Catalogue Raisonné* (Paris, 1979), G/P E. 116, 117, and 122.

THOMAS EAKINS
1844–1916

Rear Admiral George W. Melville, 1905
Oil on canvas
40 x 27 (101.6 x 68.58)

Gift (Partial and Promised) of
Mr. and Mrs. H. John Heinz III

When, two years before his death, Thomas Eakins said that American artists who "wish to assume a place in the history of the art of their country" should "remain in America, to peer deeper into the heart of American life [and] study their own country and portray its life and types,"[1] he was to a great extent describing his own artistic undertaking, the one he himself had pursued unremittingly for nearly fifty years.

Portraiture was the means Eakins chose to peer into America's heart and record its life and types. Virtually all of Eakins' paintings are portraits. Not conventional portraits, however, commissioned by people who wished and expected to be flattered. Only a few of his portraits had been commissioned — most often it was Eakins who asked people to pose for him, as he did Admiral Melville — and none were flattering. He depicted his subjects with such uningratiating honesty and unflinching objectivity, such profound psychological penetration, that some sitters refused to accept their portraits and some even destroyed them.

With the exception of four years' study in Europe from 1866–1870, Eakins spent his entire life in his native city of Philadelphia, painting his family, his friends, his students at the Pennsylvania Academy, and the professional people he admired — physicians, scientists, teachers, athletes, musicians, actresses, clerics, and fellow artists. His early portraits usually depict their subjects in some characteristic activity or environment — singing, playing instruments, rowing boats; in operating rooms or laboratories. But in the portraits he painted during roughly the last twenty years of his life, such as this one, he concentrated on his subjects alone, with little or no setting. Intensely observed, relentlessly probing, utterly candid, his late portraits are among the most profoundly moving examinations of human character ever painted.

Eakins painted two portraits of George W. Melville (1841–1912), of which this is the second version, done in 1905. When he first painted him in 1904 Melville had recently retired as engineer-in-chief of the U.S. Navy with the rank of rear admiral. His distinguished career was marked by numerous achievements as chief of the Bureau of Steam Engineering as well as acts of great heroism and resourcefulness in arctic exploration. His most notable exploit occurred on the *Jeanette* expedition of 1879–1882, in which the ship (of which he was chief engineer) was trapped in ice for almost two years and finally sank. Melville managed to bring the small boat he commanded and its survivors to safety in Siberia, and then returned to search for his dead shipmates. He was awarded a Congressional medal for his valor, and the Russian order of Saint Stanislaus that he wears in this portrait. In Eakins' first portrait (Philadelphia Museum of Art), Melville stands facing left, in full dress uniform. The second, slightly smaller version is simpler. More plainly dressed, the figure frontally posed and filling the picture space, attention now concentrated on the leonine head with piercing eyes and scarred and gnarled hands, it expresses with greater success than the first the full power of Melville's person and personality — his imposing size (he was more than six feet tall) and great physical strength, his sometimes gruff and irascible behavior, and his dauntless and indomitable spirit.[2] The second version, it seems, is the one Eakins himself preferred.[3]

The portrait of Admiral Melville is one of the finest of Eakins' late portraits and in every way a superb example of what he could achieve in them. It joins an important group of Eakins paintings and drawings in the Gallery's permanent collection, including such other late portraits as those of *Louis Husson* (1899), *Mrs. Louis Husson* (c. 1905), *Harriet Husson Carville* (1904), and *Archbishop Diomede Falconio* (1905).

Nicolai Cikovsky, Jr.

NOTES
1. *Philadelphia Press* (22 February 1914), quoted in Lloyd Goodrich, *Thomas Eakins* (Cambridge, Mass. and London, 1982), 2:268–269.

2. Charles O. Paullin, "Melville, George Wallace," *Dictionary of American Biography* 12 (New York, 1912), 522.

3. Goodrich 1982, 2:211.

THOMAS EAKINS
1844–1916

The Chaperone, c. 1908

Oil on canvas

18¼ x 14 (46.3 x 35.6)

Gift of John Wilmerding

Fig. 1. Thomas Eakins, *William Rush Carving His Allegorical Figure of the Schuylkill River*, 1908. The Brooklyn Museum, Dick S. Ramsay Fund

In 1877 Thomas Eakins painted a canvas showing the early Philadelphia ship carver and sculptor William Rush (1756–1853) working from a nude female model in sculpting a life-size allegorical figure.[1] The only other figure present in the painting is an elderly woman knitting. Eakins was generally known for his uncompromisingly realistic depictions of Philadelphia friends and associates engaged in various activities (such as *The Biglin Brothers Racing* c. 1873, National Gallery of Art), and only rarely took interest in subjects from the past. In his painting of Rush, Eakins altered historical fact to serve his own ends, for there is no evidence that the sculptor had worked from a nude model. Eakins believed that study from the nude was essential and he vigorously stressed this belief in his teaching at the Pennsylvania Academy of the Fine Arts. The painting of Rush was thus specifically intended to suggest that working from the nude was not unprecedented in Philadelphia and in fact had a venerable tradition. And by including the elderly woman chaperone, perhaps a relative of the model, Eakins legitimized the activity of posing nude, making it clear that this is a virtuous young woman, not a tramp or a prostitute.[2]

In 1886 Eakins was forced to resign his position at the Pennsylvania Academy, primarily because his unrelenting emphasis on working from the nude had become a controversial topic in staid Philadelphia. The dismissal affected him deeply and he increasingly withdrew from Philadelphia art circles to work independently. By the early 1900s he was already becoming forgotten; when the famous portrait painter John Singer Sargent visited Philadelphia in 1903 and asked to meet Eakins, his baffled hostess could only reply, "And who is Eakins?"[3]

In 1908 Eakins returned to the subject of William Rush in several paintings. In the most complete version (fig. 1), for which the present work is a study, the principal elements from the 1877 oil are retained but have been transformed to give the picture a different nuance. The figure of Rush is stockier and has come to resemble Eakins

himself, suggesting that the painter now identified with the sculptor. The chaperone is no longer a finely dressed elderly white woman sitting in an elegant Chippendale chair, but a black woman with a bandana on her head in a plain wooden chair. We do not know the identity of the woman who sat for this sketch, but Eakins gave her a quiet dignity that is markedly different from the less sympathetic images of African-Americans found in all too many works by his contemporaries.[4] Intent on her knitting and thus creating with her own hands, she makes an effective counterpart to the equally intent sculptor working with mallet and chisel.

The Chaperone will join three important images of blacks by Eakins already in the Gallery's collection: two oil studies for *Negro Boy Dancing* of c. 1878 and a watercolor, *The Poleman in the Ma'sh*, of c. 1881.

Franklin Kelly

PROVENANCE
Mrs. Thomas Eakins, Philadelphia; estate of Mrs. Thomas Eakins; Babcock Galleries, New York; Garelick Gallery, Detroit; Marshall M. Miller, Huntington Woods, Michigan; Hirschl and Adler Galleries, New York, 1981; John Wilmerding, 1982.

NOTES
1. This painting, *William Rush Carving His Allegorical Figure of the Schuylkill River* (Philadelphia Museum of Art) has been much discussed in the literature on Eakins; see Elizabeth Johns, *Thomas Eakins: The Heroism of Modern Life* (Princeton, 1983), 82–114.

2. Eakins often complained that his students could not learn to portray beautiful forms if they were only exposed to "coarse and flabby types" who came from brothels. He even asked the Pennsylvania Academy to advertise for respectable female models who could be "accompanied by their mothers or other female relatives"; see Kathleen A. Foster and Cheryl Leibold, *Writing About Eakins* (Philadelphia, 1989), 343. Eakins also believed that any student enrolled in a life class should be willing to pose nude if asked.

3. Lloyd Goodrich, *Thomas Eakins*, 2 vols. (Cambridge, Mass., 1982), 2:222.

4. For a discussion of Eakins' images of blacks see Guy C. McElroy, *Facing History: The Black Image in American Art, 1710–1940* [exh. cat. Corcoran Gallery of Art] (Washington, 1990), xix, 84–87.

ERNST LUDWIG KIRCHNER
1880–1938

Performer Bowing, 1909
Color lithograph
14⅞ x 12¼ (38.2 x 32.8)

Ruth and Jacob Kainen Collection

The first great flowering of twentieth-century printmaking was created by Die Brücke, a Dresden artists' association begun by four young architectural students in 1905. The Brücke artists, among whom Kirchner was the most creative and forceful, hoped to renew an artistic tradition, which they thought had grown stagnant and academic, through authenticity in both subject and style. The present work, an extremely rare color lithograph known in only three impressions,[1] is a true masterpiece of Brücke prints.

Performer Bowing is one of a number of Kirchner's cabaret, variety, and circus scenes, which in modern literature are variously dated from 1908, 1909, and 1910.[2] This performer wears the tights and suit appropriate for an acrobat or tightrope walker,[3] and is caught just at the moment of landing on her feet after leaping from a tightrope to take a bow. She epitomizes two crucial aspects of Kirchner's art: his love of motion and his love of drawing. Kirchner explained to Curt Valentin the year before he died that during his entire career he had attempted to show life—colorful, fleeting, full-blooded life in motion. Here the swift, short strokes of *Performer* remind one pointedly of Kirchner's own account of perhaps the only artistic influence he freely admitted. "But I had to find a technique with which I could capture everything in motion, and there Rembrandt's drawings in the Munich Print Room gave me the cue. Seizing something quickly with bold strokes, that is what I practiced, wherever I went or stood, everywhere."[4]

The *Performer* also crystallizes Kirchner's most advanced use of color and his distinctive use of texture. While still in some cases defining form in a general sense, color is also liberated to convey emotion and movement. Certainly the performer's tights and her suit are red, but there are also flashes of red below her nose, on the right side of the image, and in the lower left. They pick up the red of her body and spread it throughout the scene. Likewise, the mottled blue—on what seems to be a curtain hanging in the background and on what may be part of a stage set in the lower right—spreads color and texture throughout the image.

Texture and truth to materials were crucial to Kirchner and the other Brücke artists. While there are precedents for such themes in woodcut in the work of Munch, in lithographs like this Kirchner was totally original. Part of the Brücke artists' authenticity was to complete the entire process of preparation and printing themselves and to make evident the nature of the processes and materials from which their works of art were created. Thus the edges of the printmaking matrix were not disguised, as in earlier professional printmaking, but emphasized. Small hints of all three colors are left on the edges of the lithographic stone, to show just where the stone begins and ends, just what were its stony imperfections—the characteristic way it is chipped at the edge, and how each color is impressed on the paper, one on top of the other. But the most distinctive element of the *Performer* is the extraordinary mottled texture of the colors. This technique, apparently invented by Kirchner, involved the use of turpentine and unusually strong acid in some fashion still not entirely clear.[5] In any case, it was a technique that enabled him simultaneously to fulfill three ambitions. First, it expanded the range of lithography while emphasizing the sense of the stone—the irregular pools of color evoking the feeling of lichen-covered rock. Second, the turpentine etching created mottling in broad areas, which is a modern textured substitute for the traditional modeling of tone, at the same time giving a richness and variety both to the figures and to the background. Finally, in combination with his swift strokes of crayon, Kirchner's distinctive technique enhanced the sense of excitement from organic or almost randomly natural flashes of color throughout the image.

Andrew Robison

PROVENANCE
Kirchner Estate, stamp (Lugt 1570b) verso, with ink no. "L 81 II D"; Hauswedell & Nolte, Hamburg, 2 June 1978, no. 650; Ruth Cole Kainen, stamp (not in Lugt) verso.

NOTES
1. Annemarie and Wolf-Dieter Dube, *E. L. Kirchner: Das Graphische Werk* (Munich, 1967), lithograph no. 122, dated by the Dubes 1909; they list only the impression in the Stedelijk Museum, Amsterdam. Besides the Kainen impression, there is one in the Fogg Art Museum, Cambridge, Mass.

2. See Donald E. Gordon, *Ernst Ludwig Kirchner* (Cambridge, Mass., 1968), 272–282, where the dates of the relevant paintings are spread over three years. On the other hand, Lucius Grisebach and Annette Meyer zu Eissen, *Ernst Ludwig Kirchner: 1880–1938* (Berlin, Munich, Cologne, Zurich, 1979), 115–128, attempt to regroup virtually all the most closely related painted and graphic works into the single year 1909.

3. Compare the painting *Tightrope Dancers* (Gordon 114, dated by him 1910, but redated 1909 by Grisebach 1979, 126), as well as the woodcut *Ringturnerin* (Dube 167, dated by them 1910).

4. His letter quoted in Annemarie Dube-Heynig, *E. L. Kirchner: Graphik* (Munich, 1961), 19.

5. Compare Frances Carey and Antony Griffiths, *The Print in Germany 1880-1933* (London, 1984), 31–35, 37–38; and Jacob Kainen, "E. L. Kirchner as Printmaker," in Andrew Robison, *German Expressionist Prints from the Collection of Ruth and Jacob Kainen* (Washington, 1985), 40.

ERNST LUDWIG KIRCHNER
1880–1938

Green House in Dresden, 1909/1910
Oil on canvas
22 x 35½ (56 x 90)

Gift (Partial and Promised) of
Ruth and Jacob Kainen

Green House in Dresden is one of an innovative series of paintings, prints, and drawings Kirchner executed in 1909–1910 depicting the shores of the Elbe River and the buildings, gardens, and streets in and around the city.[1] Donald Gordon characterized the works of this period as "among the most successful formal compositions in twentieth-century German art . . . reveal[ing] a decorative unity of line and color so harmonious and so immediate that one could not wish to see a single stroke altered."[2] On the verso appears a later, less finished work by Kirchner, *Dancing Couple in the Snow* from 1928–1929.[3]

Kirchner and the other artists of the Brücke were committed to portraying the world around them—the human figure, nature, the city, and contemporary life—and to finding a style that could represent the inner or higher reality that lies beneath surface appearances. They were inspired by the spatial distortions, arbitrary colors, expressive brushwork, and psychological insights of van Gogh, Gauguin, and Munch, and by the pure colors and simplified compositions of French neoimpressionist artists, Matisse, and the fauves. The German artists knew the works of these painters well, from recent exhibitions in Munich, Dresden, and Berlin and from reproductions in books.[4]

In *Green House*, spatial recession is subtly exaggerated in a manner reminiscent of van Gogh or Munch. On the left, the lines of the building and road converge toward a vanishing point outside the picture. One's eye is arrested, however, by a cropped tree defining the edge of the canvas. This pull toward the left is partially offset by the lone figure pulling a wagon on the right.

These perspective effects are counterbalanced by patterns of color and line that emphasize the flatness of the surface. With no concern whatsoever for observed reality, Kirchner constructed the picture with bright patches of joyous, nonnaturalistic color surrounded by contrasting outlines. Glimpses of untouched, but heavily primed white canvas are visible throughout, especially in the road and around the windows in the green wall of the house. Overall, the paint layers are thin and dry, giving the canvas a chalky, matte surface. There are only a few touches of varnish, which may have been applied by Kirchner himself.[5]

During the first decade of his career, figural compositions, especially nudes, were Kirchner's preferred subjects. *Two Nudes* (fig. 1) from 1907–1908 epitomizes these early works in the natural poses of the models and the rich impasto of the brushwork. Around 1909–1910 Kirchner began portraying circus performers, cabaret artists, and other socially marginal types with whom he and his bohemian friends identified. His views of Dresden from this period mark a stylistic turning point in his oeuvre.

Green House and *The Visit*, which also is a gift of Ruth and Jacob Kainen, together will transform the National Gallery's small collection of modern German paintings. Heretofore our holdings of German painting have included only the earlier *Two Nudes* by Kirchner, three paintings by Lyonel Feininger, two canvases and a triptych by Max Beckmann, and one painting by Max Ernst.

Elizabeth Pendleton Streicher

PROVENANCE
Kirchner Estate; Galerie Roman Norbert Ketterer.

NOTES
1. Donald E. Gordon, *Ernst Ludwig Kirchner* (Cambridge, Mass.), 1968, 421, no. 923v; Galerie Roman Norbert Ketterer, *Ausstellung Ernst Ludwig Kirchner: Gemälde, Aquarelle, Zeichnungen, Graphik* (Campione d'Italia, 1971), 4–5, no. 2. See also Gordon 1968, nos. 98, 99, 100, 103, 104, 119, 128, 130, 132; and *Ernst Ludwig Kirchner 1880–1938* [exh. cat. Nationalgalerie Berlin, Staatliche Museen Preussischer Kulturbesitz] (Berlin, 1979), nos. 42–47, 86–92, and 121–124 (related works from 1911).

2. Gordon 1968, 65.

3. Gordon 1968, 400, no. 923.

4. Gordon 1968, 15, 20.

5. Conservation report prepared by Ann Hoenigswald, conservator, and Barbara Pralle, technician, paintings conservation department, National Gallery of Art.

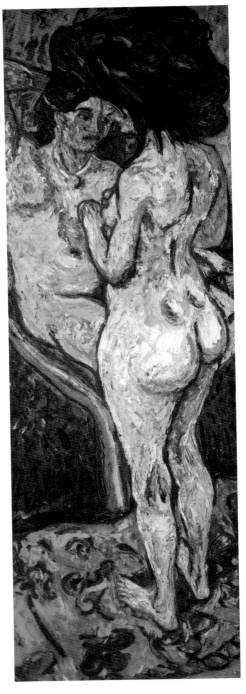

Fig. 1. Ernst Ludwig Kirchner, *Two Nudes*, 1907, oil on canvas, 77¼ x 25¾ (196.1 x 65.4). National Gallery of Art, Washington, Anonymous Gift

PAUL STRAND
1890–1976

Cambridge, England, 1911
Platinum photograph
10 x 11¼ (25.4 x 28.5)

Gift of the Aperture Foundation

Paul Strand has often been called the first modern photographer. In his early work he pioneered a style and subject matter that were radically different from existing conventions. At the youthful age of twenty-six his art was so certain and direct, so innovative and bold, that we have a tendency to assume it was always so sure, that, as if by magic, from the moment he picked up the camera he instinctively knew what he wanted to say and how to say it. But, of course, it was not that easy.

In 1907 when he was a high school student at the Ethical Culture School in New York City, Strand took a photography class with the now-famous documentary photographer, Lewis Hine. He later dismissed Hine's influence as minimal, and his earliest surviving work indicates that he was clearly intent on creating works of art rather than photographic records. Adopting the subject matter, printing techniques, and soft-focus style of the pictorialist photographers who were so popular at the turn of the century, Strand made some lovely but nevertheless conventional images in the first few years of his career. By the time he had adopted pictorialism, it was a well-worn path.

His earliest work, however, also reveals a tentative search for an alternate. After his graduation in 1909, he worked first in his family's enamelware business and then, very briefly, in an insurance company. In 1911 he decided to use his savings to travel to Europe, visiting more than twenty cities in a little more than fifty days. The photographs he made there use devices familiar to the pictorialists: for example, in some works water and reflection create a decorative pattern and heighten the sense of illusion, while in others, such as *The Garden of Dreams*, both the title and the subject—a temple at Versailles—evoke a sense of otherworldliness.

Certain photographs taken on this trip, such as *Cambridge, England*, are different. Although it depicts a bucolic subject that

was common among pictorial photographers, its point of view and strong formal complexity are strikingly at odds with the pictorialist vision. Strand later discounted the importance and complexity of several of these early images, noting that the lens he used "flattens and mushifies," allowing the beginning photographer to extract from reality essential elements and "pull things together."[1] Yet it is far more than just Strand's lens that accounts for the abrupt compression of space and formal strength of *Cambridge, England*. Like other modern European and American artists, Strand composed the picture right up to the edge of the frame, allowing bits of reality to push into the edge of the picture space. With the fence and haystack boldly and emphatically forcing their way into the picture, Strand constructed an image that is diametrically opposed to the quietly contained, closed, contemplative structures of the pictorialists. This image, while alluding to its heritage, dramatically breaks with the past: it is an open, fluid fragment, an abstract pattern cut from the larger whole.

Although Strand dismissed Hine's influence on his art, he did acknowledge that in 1907 his teacher introduced him to Alfred Stieglitz's experimental gallery, The Little Galleries of the Photo-Secession, later simply called 291 from its address on Fifth Avenue in New York. Strand subsequently recalled that he did not begin to frequent Stieglitz's gallery with regularity until 1913, yet he was well aware of its activities. It may have been the 1909 exhibitions at 291 of John Marin, Marsden Hartley, and Japanese prints or the 1910 shows of Arthur Dove, Max Weber, and Paul Cézanne that encouraged Strand's formal investigations. Or it may have been Hine's teaching that photographs function as "a symbol that brings one immediately into close touch with reality," telling a "story packed into the most condensed and vital form" that prompted Strand to make such an image.[2] Then too,

as is clearly evident in Strand's photographs made after 1915, he had a strong formal propensity, and *Cambridge, England* may simply be an early expression of what, for want of a better term, is usually called his strong eye.

Cambridge, England, donated by the Aperture Foundation, is the earliest Strand photograph in the National Gallery's collection. It is a superb addition to the sixty-one Strand photographs given and promised by the Southwestern Bell Corporation.

Sarah Greenough

PROVENANCE
Paul Strand Foundation, 1976; Aperture Foundation, Inc., 1984.

NOTES
1. Strand quoted in *Paul Strand: Sixty Years of Photographs* (Millerton, New York, 1976), 142.

2. Quoted by Alan Trachtenberg, "Ever—the Human Document," *America and Lewis Hine: Photographs 1904–1940* (New York, 1977), 121 and 133.

ODILON REDON
1840–1916

Large Vase with Flowers, c. 1912
Oil on canvas
28¾ x 21½ (73 x 54.6)

Gift (Partial and Promised) of
John C. Whitehead

In 1913 Redon called flowers "fragile perfumed beings, adorable prodigals of light."[1] *Large Vase with Flowers,* painted in about 1912, exemplifies his metaphoric description. Elusive and evanescent qualities of the graceful bouquet of real and imagined blossoms take precedence over concrete delineation. An indistinctly decorated blue-ground vase holding the brightly colored cluster of flowers, some bunched near the center and others floating on attenuated, arcing stems, is placed slightly off-center against an amorphous multicolored background. The use of frontal views or strict profile in the flowers, the absence of shadow, and Redon's technique, a combination of thinly applied, relatively dry pigments in imitation of the softened effects of pastel with occasional impasted areas that heighten separate components of the bouquet, give *Large Vase with Flowers* an eerie, unearthly quality.

Born in 1840, Redon was an exact contemporary of Claude Monet and Berthe Morisot and a year older than Auguste Renoir. His training and earliest works date from the same era as theirs, yet his work deliberately has little in common with that of his coevals. Reviewing the Salon of 1868 for a Bordeaux newspaper, Redon articulated the difference between his artistic goals and those of the realists and nascent impressionists. He wrote, "The weakness of M. Manet and of all those who, like him, want to limit themselves to the literal reproduction of reality, is to sacrifice man and his thought to good brushwork, to the brilliant handling of a detail. . . . It is on this point that true artists find themselves in decided opposition to paltry and restricted research. Although they recognize the necessity for a basis of seen reality, to them true art lies in a reality that is felt."[2] True art, for Redon, lay in a synthesis of the visual and the visionary, an attitude derived from the expressive force of paintings by Eugène Delacroix and the brooding intensity of the graphic works of Rodolphe Bresdin.

This preference for the evocative potential of a work of art characterizes Redon's entire oeuvre. Redon wrote, "I think I have made an expressive, suggestive, indeterminate art. Suggestive art is the irradiation of divine plastic elements, harmonized, combined in order to provoke reveries which it illuminates, which it inflames, by stimulating the thoughts."[3] From the late 1860s Redon was primarily a graphic artist whose macabre and mysterious charcoal drawings, etchings, and lithographs allied him with writers and artists of the symbolist movement. For no specific reason, although probably related to the artist's growing optimism at the birth of his sole surviving child, color became an important element in his work in about 1890. Floral motifs dominated Redon's work during the remainder of his career, in portraits and allegorical paintings and especially still lifes. As Berger wrote, "the flower pieces afford the best means of studying the development of the period of color which occupied his last years; they constitute the red thread running through his late art."[4]

Large Vase with Flowers will provide a striking complement to the National Gallery's *Flowers in a Vase* (1970.17.56), painted two years earlier in about 1910. The two are similar in content and composition but present poignantly different characterizations of the subject, illustrating the importance of the expressive and imaginary vein of Redon's art.

Florence E. Coman

PROVENANCE
Marcel Kapferer, Paris, bought from the artist; private collection, U.S.A.; Achim Moeller Limited, London.

NOTES
1. ". . . ces êtres fragiles de parfum, prodiges adorables de la lumière." Odilon Redon, *A Soi-Même* (Paris, 1922), 131.

2. Odilon Redon, "Salon de 1868, II—MM. Courbet, Manet, Pissarro, Jongkind, Monet," *La Gironde* (9 June 1868), as cited in John Rewald, *Odilon Redon / Gustave Moreau / Rodolphe Bresdin* [exh. cat. The Museum of Modern Art] (New York, 1962), 19–20.

3. ". . . je crois avoir fait un art expressif, suggestif, indéterminé. L'art suggestif est l'irradiation de devins éléments plastiques, rapprochés, combinés en vue de provoquer des rêveries qu'il illumine, qu'il exalte, en incitant à la pensée." Redon 1922, 111.

4. Klaus Berger, *Odilon Redon: Fantasy and Colour,* trans. Michael Bullock (New York, Toronto, and London, 1965), 88.

EGON SCHIELE
1890–1918

Dancer, 1913
Pencil, watercolor, and gouache
18½ x 12 (47 x 30.5)

Gift (Partial and Promised) of
Liselotte Millard

In the first decades of this century, Gustav Klimt, Egon Schiele, and Oskar Kokoschka were the leading avant garde artists in Vienna. Schiele is best known for his portraits and other figure compositions, although he also executed land- and cityscapes. Like their compatriot Sigmund Freud, these artists were preoccupied with probing the human psyche and the self and with questioning the assumptions and mores of modern life and society.

Dancer is one of Schiele's most elegant, serene, and discreet likenesses. It depicts the artist's model and mistress Valerie Neuzil, who was called "Wally." She is readily identifiable by her red hair, bangs, high cheekbones, and long nose.[1] Wally was introduced to the artist in 1911 by Klimt, for whom she had also posed, and she lived with Schiele until his marriage to Edith Harms in 1915.

Many of Schiele's portraits and self-portraits are nudes, often in agitated, provocative, or even overtly erotic poses. Although Schiele had a loyal clientele, his works were often controversial. In the spring of 1912, when he was living in the small town of Neulengbach near Vienna, Schiele was imprisoned for nearly a month on charges of immorality and the seduction of minors; at the end of his trial the judge symbolically burned one of his drawings. Schiele achieved a vindication of sorts in the spring of 1918, when his one-man exhibition at the Vienna Secession was a resounding artistic and financial success. Eight months later, he and

his pregnant wife died during an influenza epidemic. Schiele was only twenty-eight years old, but he had already produced approximately three hundred oil paintings and several thousand watercolors and drawings.[2]

Dancer is in many respects representative of Schiele's graphic art. The energized, jagged angularity of the drawing and the delicate passages of color — in the subject's reddish-brown hair and orange headband and the purplish-blue shading along the edges and folds of her garment — are closely related to Schiele's other watercolors of the period. Wally posed for many of Schiele's erotic drawings, and the position she adopts here, seated with her knees drawn up against her chest, often provided Schiele an opportunity to focus on the female genitalia. In this portrait, however, Wally is decorously dressed in a simple shift that envelops her from shoulders to feet. Her monumental, pyramidal form almost fills the entire sheet. The blank background concentrates our attention on her introspective expression and on her indolent gesture of raising — or lowering — her shoulder strap.

Dancer is a magnificent addition to the National Gallery's collection of modern German art. While the Gallery has eight of Schiele's prints and two of his black chalk portraits, Mrs. Mark Millard's gift is our first example of his extraordinary and much-coveted watercolors and joins the Mark J. Millard Architectural Collection of rare illustrated books and prints, which came to the Gallery during the 1980s.

Elizabeth Pendleton Streicher

PROVENANCE
Hans Ankwicz-Kleehoven; Rudolf Leopold; Serge Sabarsky; Sotheby Parke Bernet, New York, 16 May 1979, sale 4247, lot 72.

NOTES
1. See Jane Kallir, with an essay by Wolfgang G. Fischer; catalogue raisonné in collaboration with Hildegard Bachert and Wolfgang C. Fischer, *Egon Schiele: The Complete Works, Including a Biography and Catalogue Raisonné* (New York, 1990), 495, no. D1264; Rudolf Leopold, *Egon Schiele: Paintings, Watercolors, Drawings* (New York, 1972), 298, pl. 133; Serge Sabarsky, ed. Muni de Smecchia, *Egon Schiele: Erotische Zeichnungen* (Cologne, 1981), pl. 19. According to Leopold, the title *Dancer* originated with Otto Benesch, a champion of Schiele's art who may have gotten it from Schiele himself (Leopold 1972, 298).

2. For Schiele's relationship with Wally and his biography during these years, see Kallir 1990, 108–192; Comini 1974, 89–90, 92, 99–101, 105–107, 136–140, 144–145. See also Otto Kallir, *Egon Schiele: Oeuvre-Katalog der Gemälde* (Vienna, 1966), 19–35; Alessandra Comini, *Egon Schiele* (New York, 1976), 7–27; Christian M. Nebehay, *Egon Schiele 1890–1918: Leben, Briefe, Gedichte* (Vienna, 1979), 147–190, also 191–236, 437–496.

MAX WEBER
1881–1961

Interior of the Fourth Dimension, 1913
30 x 39½ (76.2 x 100.3)
Oil on canvas

Gift (Partial and Promised) of
Natalie Davis Spingarn in Memory of
Her Grandmother, Linda R. Miller

As the year that witnessed New York's Armory Show, 1913 marked a watershed in the development of American modernism and a critical moment in the career of one of its most sophisticated exponents. Max Weber painted *Interior of the Fourth Dimension* during this remarkably fertile year in which he forged a highly personalized cubist style.[1] Having returned to New York in 1909 from a formative sojourn in Paris, Weber easily kept apace with the most progressive international developments in painting. With *Interior of the Fourth Dimension* the artist gave form to the theories of an ideal geometry that he had begun to formulate during his three and a half years in Europe.[2]

By 1913 the concept of the fourth dimension was a fashionable topic of discussion among the New York intelligentsia and the subject of numerous articles in the popular press. Pseudoscientific in tone, these publications identified the fourth dimension with an unearthly sphere, one described in psychic and mystical terms. As early as 1910, however, Weber composed a short essay, "The Fourth Dimension from a Plastic Point of View," that was issued in Alfred Stieglitz' magazine *Camera Work.*[3] As the first publication that addressed the role of the fourth dimension in art, Weber's ideas would wield considerable influence in this country, particularly throughout the Stieglitz circle, as well as in France.[4] Although Weber's concept of the fourth dimension was fundamentally spiritual, he argued that its artistic expression must be firmly rooted in perceived reality, for the "greatest dream or vision is that which is *regiven* plastically through the observation of things in nature."[5]

When the painting was exhibited in Baltimore in 1915, Weber's description of it was quoted in a local newspaper: "The interior of the fourth dimension is the space around an art form which is stirred by the essence with which that form was vested by the artist."[6] It is this expressive, emotional potential of a higher dimension in art that Weber strove to achieve, and it could best be communicated through "a great and overwhelming sense of space magnitude in all directions at one time."[7]

As a pictorial analogue for this "dimension of infinity," *Interior of the Fourth Dimension* suggests an enormous, expansive space. Although the semiabstract nature of the composition lends itself to multiple readings, the forms suggest an immense architecture, one no doubt triggered by the spectacle of New York that Weber had begun to record in his paintings by 1912.[8] Cubist scaffolding evokes a myriad of towering edifices or the cavernous interior of an enormous Gothic cathedral, producing a dramatically modern image of sublimity. The somber palette, characteristic of much of Weber's work in 1913, and the black areas that border the composition suggest a nocturnally luminous city, anticipating *New York at Night* and other dynamic New York compositions of 1915. Weber's use of transparent planes and sequentially deployed forms suggests his familiarity with Marcel Duchamp's *Nude Descending a Staircase, No. 2,* 1912, that caused such a stir at the Armory Show. In 1915 Weber would paint his own interpretation of that work, *Rush Hour New York,* a work also in the National Gallery's collection.

Marla Prather

PROVENANCE
Purchased in 1915 by Nathan J. Miller from the artist for his wife Linda Miller, New York; passed to her daughter, Helen Miller Davis, in 1936; passed to Natalie Davis Spingarn around 1950.

NOTES
1. There is a preparatory study of the same title in gouache (18½ x 24 in.) for this painting in the Baltimore Museum of Art. It is incorrectly dated 1914.

2. On Weber and the fourth dimension in art see Linda Dalrymple Henderson, "A New Facet of Cubism: The Fourth Dimension and Non-Euclidean Geometry Reinterpreted," *The Art Quarterly* 25, no. 4 (Winter 1971), 410–433, and "Mabel Dodge, Gertrude Stein, and Max Weber: A Four-Dimensional Trio," *Arts Magazine* 57, no. 1 (September 1982), 106–111.

3. Max Weber, "The Fourth Dimension from a Plastic Point of View," *Camera Work* 31 (July 1910), 25.

4. The French poet Guillaume Apollinaire, whom Weber knew in Paris, actually used and partially copied Weber's essay for his own publication, *Les Peintres cubistes,* 1913. See Willard Bohn, "In Pursuit of the Fourth Dimension: Guillaume Apollinaire and Max Weber," *Arts Magazine* 54, no. 10 (June 1980), 166–169.

5. Weber 1910, 25.

6. Unidentified clipping from a Baltimore newspaper, March 1915, quoted in Henderson 1971, 176, n. 37.

7. Weber 1910, 25.

8. Weber scholar Percy North has described the painting as a boat pulling into New York harbor at night. *Max Weber: American Modern* [exh. cat. The Jewish Museum] (New York, 1983), 57.

289

MARC CHAGALL
1887–1985

Féla and Odilon, 1915
Gouache
16¾ x 13¼ (42.55 x 33.66)

Gift of Evelyn Nef in Memory of
John U. Nef

Féla and Odilon is a splendid gouache from Chagall's early period, with an especially free and playful technique. Chagall took the unusual step of using real lace to print the design in the shawl around the shoulders of the woman. The style is more natural than in most of Chagall's work from this period. There are no flying people, no dreamy visions.

Féla and Odilon is a much livelier and more colorful work, but is of the same size and is basically the same image as the painting *Maternity*, 1914. Several suggestions have been offered about their subjects, including that they portray Bella Rosenfeld, Chagall's future wife. If so, Chagall would have been projecting into the future in anticipation of their having a child of their own, for their first child, Ida, was not born until the spring of 1916.[1] However, Chagall seems to have painted no other works about the future. And if he were foretelling such an event, surely he would have inserted himself into the scene as the future father. Another suggestion is that the subject is Chagall's sister Lisa who had recently been married. However, she had not had a child at that point either.[2]

I would suggest a third possibility, that the two works are portraits of Féla Poznanska, the first wife of Chagall's close friend, the poet Blaise Cendrars.[3] Supporting the proposal that Féla is the mother in both the painting and the gouache are the facts that she was also the model for the painting, *Pregnant Woman*, 1913, and that she herself became a mother in the following year.[4] Féla's son, Odilon, named after Odilon Redon, was born in April 1914; Chagall dated the painting 1914 and this gouache 1915.

This proposal is confirmed by the resemblance of the mother in both the painting and the gouache to Féla. The woman in both works has straight hair that grows forward, falling toward her round face with its low forehead, just as Féla Cendrars appears in photographs.[5] Bella's forehead, on the other hand, was high and her hair, which looks very wavy both in photographs and paintings, seems to have grown away from her narrow face.[6]

Chagall knew the Cendrars well when he lived in Paris. As the couple spoke Russian, they undoubtedly helped to alleviate any homesickness that Chagall was feeling.[7] When Chagall was asked what the most important events in his life were, he answered, "My meeting with Blaise Cendrars and the Russian Revolution." Cendrars, in fact, provided titles for some of Chagall's paintings. Chagall inscribed the name Cendrars as one of four names surrounding a heart in his painting *Homage to Apollinaire*, 1911–1912. Unfortunately the friendship was fated to be a stormy one. Upon Chagall's return to Paris with Bella after the war, he discovered that paintings he had stored with the dealer Ambroise Vollard had been sold.[8] Chagall may have believed that Cendrars was partly to blame for this unwanted sale, since Cendrars had authenticated the paintings for Vollard. They rarely spoke again until they reconciled in 1961 when Cendrars was dying.[9]

This beautiful gouache is the National Gallery's first Chagall drawing. The Gallery owns a painting by Chagall, *Houses at Vitebsk*, 1917, given by the Nefs and the William Wood Princes.

Barbara Read Ward

PROVENANCE
Philippe Loeb; sold 1920s to John Nef.

NOTES
1. Sidney Alexander, *Marc Chagall: A Biography* (New York, 1978), 362.

2. Aleksandr Kamensky, *Chagall: The Russian Years 1907–1922* (New York, 1989), 81.

3. Jay Bochner, *Blaise Cendrars: Discovery and Recreation* (Toronto, 1978), 52–55.

4. Susan Compton, *Chagall* [exh. cat. Royal Academy of Arts] (London, 1985), 24–25.

5. Miriam Cendrars, *Blaise Cendrars* (Paris, 1984). See section of photographs.

6. Cendrars 1984, 275.

7. Cendrars 1984, 264–265 and Alexander 1978, Part 3. Chagall first lived in Paris in 1910–1914, returning to Russia via Germany in June 1914.

8. Alexander 1978, 261. Cendrars had written to Chagall to tell him that Vollard wanted him to return for a commission.

9. Bochner 1978, 52.

ERICH HECKEL
1883–1970

Young Woman, 1913
Woodcut on japan paper
10¾ x 6⅘ (26 x 17.3)

Gift (Partial and Promised) of
Daryl R. Rubenstein and
Lee G. Rubenstein

In the year the *Brücke* disbanded, Eric Heckel, one of the founding members of the group, had his first solo exhibition and also made *Young Woman*.

Born and raised in Saxony, Heckel studied architecture at the Dresden Technische Hochschule during 1904 and 1905. All the founding members of the Brücke were students at the Hochschule, and none of them originally trained to be professional artists. Heckel was the group's manager and practical organizer, and his strong concept of loyalty held the friends together for years.

During World War I Heckel voluntarily served as a Red Cross orderly in Flanders. After the war he returned to Berlin where he resided for most of each year until 1944, from then until his death making his home at Lake Constance. In 1937 his art was declared degenerate by the National Socialist government. More than seven hundred works were removed from German museums and confiscated. During a bombing raid in January 1944 his Berlin studio was destroyed; he lost numerous paintings as well as his wood blocks and etching plates. Between 1949 and 1955 he taught at the Fine Arts Academy in Karlsruhe.

Throughout his career graphics were a significant part of Heckel's artistic production. In 1903 he began with woodcut, and in 1906 he made his first etching; altogether some 460 woodcuts and nearly two hundred etchings are known. For Heckel and most of the Brücke artists, woodcut was the preferred graphic medium. The stark contrasts of black and white, the sharp linear definition, and the emphasis on surface over depth appealed to their search for new means of visual representation. Further, the resistance of the wood forced the carver to reduce forms to their simplest, most direct shapes.

The bold, stunning simplification of *Young Woman* equally derives from Heckel's personal preference for stylization over factual accuracy. This inclination emanates from two other influences. On the more immediate level, it comes from Heckel's exposure both to South Seas art in 1908 and to cubism in the years following his move to Berlin. On a more lasting level, it extends back to his architectural training and to his lifelong interest in discovering the basic structures that underlie natural phenomena.

The palpable feeling of ennui that pervades many of Heckel's works from this period, including *Young Woman*, strikes a discordant note within his oeuvre. It is at odds with the vital and dynamic images created during his years in Dresden and may well reflect the sense of crisis and impending doom that many German intellectuals so acutely perceived in the years immediately prior to World War I.

Several reworkings of *Young Woman* are known. In its final state, it was published in the periodical *Genius* in 1920. However, the proof presented to the National Gallery is unnumbered and was produced before the printing of the 1913 edition. The National Gallery has a small collection of Heckel's graphic art, including nine woodcuts but only three from the crucial year 1913. Thus, this fine proof on japan paper adds greatly to the collection with not only an intense and moving image but also an impression of high quality.

Christopher With

Eigendruck.   Erich Heckel 13

293

PAUL STRAND
1890–1976

The White Fence, 1916
Gelatin silver photograph, 1920s
9¹¹⁄₁₆ x 12¹³⁄₁₆ (24.6 x 32.5)

Workman, 1916
Satista photograph
9⅝ x 11⁷⁄₁₆ (24.5 x 29.2)

Toward the Sugar House, Vermont, 1944
Gelatin silver photograph
9½ x 7⅝ (24.2 x 19.3)

Gift of the
Southwestern Bell Corporation,
Paul Strand Collection

Like any artist with a career of more than sixty years, Paul Strand explored many different subjects and styles. Reflecting the influence on his thinking of several of the dominant artistic, social, and cultural ideas that gripped the twentieth century, his art includes such diverse subjects as softly focused, romantic landscapes and highly detailed studies of machines; precisionist celebrations of the urban environment and anthropomorphic photographs of nature; cubist-inspired abstractions and humanistic portraits. Despite this variety, his work is unified by his unwavering commitment to two principles, discovered just shortly before the First World War and defended until his death in 1976. Pledged to the belief that art must be intimately expressive of and responsive to the contemporary world of its maker, Strand was equally insistent that the artist must repeatedly reexamine his work, experimenting with new forms, subjects, styles, and even media to make this reality known. It was these beliefs that not only allowed him to respond to the changing world around him, but mandated that he do so.

It was also these tenets that propelled him to create a group of photographs in 1915, 1916, and 1917 that can only be described as prescient. Breaking from conventional style, he conducted a series of methodical yet inspired experiments, infusing his work with the most current issues of the art and culture of his time. Responding to the innovations of the cubists, he made a series of still lifes in the summer of 1916 in order to understand, as he wrote, "the underlying principles behind Picasso and the others in their organization of the picture's space, of their unity, of what that organization contained, and the problem of making a two-dimensional area have a three-dimensional character."[1] His aim, however, was not simply to create cubist-like abstractions, but to see what lessons he could apply to his studies of the real world. He used that knowledge in his photograph *The White Fence,* made in the fall of 1916. Unlike the abstractions, which were painstakingly constructed, this photograph is of a found object; it is an image discovered and extracted from the real world. And yet Strand's placement of the bold white fence in the foreground of the picture, coupled with the strong formal integration of light and dark tones throughout the photograph, creates a work that calls into question the same issues of space, dimensionality, and structure that the cubists addressed.

This was not the only experiment Strand made in 1916. At the same time he was also making a series of candid portraits, such as *Workman,* of people on the streets in New York City. Although such well-known photographers as Jacob Riis or Lewis Hine had documented the plight of the poor and the working class in the slums of New York, few had insisted, as Strand did, that the results were works of art. Like Picasso who incorporated newspaper and chair caning into his works, Strand wanted to inject the real world into his art. In addition, however, he also wanted to reveal distinctly American types that had often been overlooked by art and literature: for just as each of the pickets in *The White Fence* is slightly different from all the others and just as the fence, barn, and house are readily identifiable in their simplicity and solidity as American structures, so too is the workman, in his expression, stance, and clothing, a clearly recognizable American type.

Throughout the 1920s Strand continued

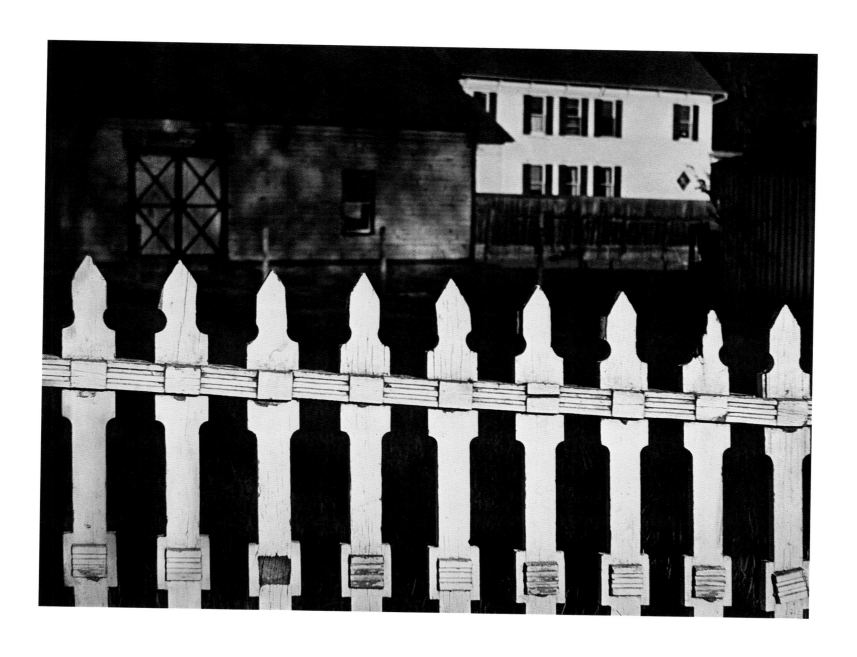

to be involved with these issues, using his photographs to scrutinize the American rural and urban landscape. His photographs from the early 1920s, such as *The Truckman's House*, 1922, reveal his continuing fascination with abstract art (fig. 1). In addition, like so many artists of his generation, Strand was preoccupied with defining the nature of the American experience. He wanted, as he wrote in a series of articles published between 1920 and 1924, to try "to come to grips with the difficult reality of America, to break through the crust of mere appearance" and create images that "shoved [us] into the core of our world," made us "experience something which is our own, as nothing which has grown in Europe can be our own." As in *Wild Iris, Maine* (fig. 2), Strand often brought his camera in extremely close to the objects he was photographing, making studies that are, as he insisted, "sharply particularized."[2]

During the Depression, Strand shifted his attention to filmmaking, believing that to be the most effective means to communicate the pressing social and political issues of the time. When he returned to still photography in the early 1940s, he again sought to define the nature of the American character and experience. Yet this time he decided to focus his attention on one region of the country, New England. As in his earlier works, in *Toward the Sugar House, Vermont* he again celebrated the straightforward functional grace of the simple wooden building. By framing the tree within the opening of the wooden structure, he also commented on the delicate balance between natural and man-made objects. In addition, however, Strand brought to this project his experience as a filmmaker and sought to create a more extended portrait that both visually and verbally addressed the underlying themes of social and cultural development of the region. Collaborating with Nancy Newhall, who selected texts by New England authors from the seventeenth to the twentieth century, Strand published *Time in New England* in 1950, a work that speaks of the spiritual and moral wholeness of New England,

Fig. 1. Paul Strand, *The Truckman's House,* 1922, gelatin silver photograph, 9½ x 7⅝ (24.1 x 19.4). National Gallery of Art, Southwestern Bell Corporation, Paul Strand Collection

Fig. 2. Paul Strand, *Wild Iris, Maine,* 1927, gelatin silver photograph, 9⁹/₁₆ x 7⁹/₁₆ (24.3 x 19.2). National Gallery of Art, Southwestern Bell Corporation, Paul Strand Collection

of its peoples' interaction with nature, their simplicity, and most of all their religious faith.

The Southwestern Bell Corporation has generously given six Strand photographs—these five plus *Rebecca, New Mexico, 1931*—to the National Gallery in honor of the fiftieth anniversary. Including the earliest known print of *The White Fence*, the only extant print of *Workman*, as well as excellent examples of other key works from his career, this gift is a significant addition to the Gallery's collection. In addition, Southwestern Bell has also promised to donate the remaining fifty-five works in their Paul Strand Collection. This will enable the Gallery to preserve the full range of Strand's art, from his earliest experiments in the 1910s to the last images in the 1970s. Southwestern Bell Foundation is also sponsoring the *Paul Strand* exhibition, which opened at the Gallery in December 1990 and will tour throughout the United States and Europe. With these two benefactions, Southwestern Bell has become the first corporation in the Gallery's history to fund an exhibition and at the same time give a major collection of works of art.

Sarah Greenough

PROVENANCE
Workman: Paul Strand Foundation, 1976; Aperture Foundation, 1984; Southwestern Bell Corporation, 1989. *The White Fence:* Hazel Kingsbury Strand; Michael E. Hoffman, 1980; Southwestern Bell Corporation, 1989. *Toward the Sugar House:* Paul Strand Foundation, 1976; Aperture Foundation, 1984; Southwestern Bell Corporation, 1989.

NOTES
1. Some of Strand's abstractions were also made after his release from the Army in the summer of 1919. Strand, quoted in an interview with William Inness Homer, *Alfred Stieglitz and the American Avant-Garde* (Boston, 1977), 246.

2. Paul Strand, "American Water Colors at the Brooklyn Museum," *The Arts* 2 (Dec. 1921), 149–152.

PAUL KLEE
1879–1940

Persische Nachtigallen, 1917
Gouache, watercolor, pen and ink,
graphite on paper, mounted on
cardboard
9 x 7⅛ (22.8 x 18.1)

Gift (Partial and Promised) of
Catherine Gamble Curran and Family

Although Paul Klee has generally been viewed outside the history of the avant-garde, his influence was widely felt and affirms his inclusion in it.[1] Having moved from Switzerland to Munich in his late twenties, he allied himself with the artists of the Blaue Reiter (Blue Rider).[2] Following the First World War his work was exhibited with the dadaists' in Zurich.[3] And from 1920 until 1931 he taught with the constructivists at the German Bauhaus. Even the surrealists working in Paris were keenly inspired by his art. They praised its miniature aspect and marveled at its poetic quality, particularly in works such as *Persische Nachtigallen* (Persian Nightingales).

In his teenage years Klee compiled three zoological notebooks, two devoted entirely to renderings and descriptions of birds. In years to come birds were a constant source of inspiration for Klee who must have envied their aerial view of the universe and freedom from earthly constraints.[4] Although he rarely designated an individual species, in 1917 in the midst of the Great War he devoted a series of works, including a poem,[5] to the nightingale. Probably it was the melodious song of this nocturnal bird that Klee, an ardent music lover, found so compelling.

Just as Klee integrated musical aspects into the plastic arts, so too did he experiment with the synthesis of language. In *Persische Nachtigallen* the Arabic letter *R* (balanced on the right by what appears to be an *N*) resides as an abstract sign and inhabits the same space and reality as the nonabstract elements: the nightingales, the stars, and the diversity of moons. These letters preside as symbols of language, as sounds that echo the nightingales' song, and as shapes within an abstract framework. Perhaps better than any artist of his generation, Klee understood the synthesis of parts and masterfully utilized its potential for poetic expression.

Hugo Ball, founder of the dada movement, wrote of Klee: "In an age of the colossus he falls in love with a green leaf, a star, a butterfly's wing, and since the heavens and all infinity are reflected in them, he paints those in too."[6] *Persische Nachtigallen* reflects in miniature this wondrous and microcosmic vision of the universe: the earth below, the heavens above, and God's creatures between. The nightingales teeter within a tensile space architectonic in its design. Individual shapes shift one against the other, each within the confines of Klee's wiry line, each flooded with thin washes of color. Although perfectly balanced for the moment, one senses that just a tiny slip of a line in one direction or another would set the whole structure tumbling.[7]

Prior to the occasion of the National Gallery's fiftieth anniversary, the Gallery had only three drawings by Paul Klee in its collection. Now three additional drawings of exceptional quality have been added. *Persische Nachtigallen,* the gift of Catherine Gamble Curran and her family, is especially welcome as the earliest work in the group and the National Gallery's only one from the nightingale series. It is perhaps one of the loveliest watercolors that Klee ever produced and sets the stage for his supremely inventive achievements that would follow.

Judith Brodie

PROVENANCE
Heinz Berggruen, Paris; Walter Feilchenfeldt, Zurich, 1973.

NOTES
1. For an insightful account of Klee's relationship to the avant-garde see Ann Temkin, "Klee and the Avant-Garde: 1912–1940" in *Paul Klee* [exh. cat. The Museum of Modern Art] (New York, 1987), 13–37.

2. In 1912 Klee participated in the group's second exhibition and had one work illustrated in their *Almanac.* See *The Blaue Reiter Almanac,* ed. Klaus Lankheit (New York, 1974), 197.

3. Hugo Ball included Klee's work in Galerie Dada's inaugural exhibitions, March and April 1917.

4. Richard Verdi, *Klee and Nature* (New York, 1984), 49.

5. "Because I came, blossoms opened, / Fullness is about, because I am. / My ear conjured for my heart / The nightingale's song. / I am father to all, / All on the stars, / And in the farthest places. / And / Because I went, evening came / And cloud garments / Robed the light. / Because I went, / Nothing threw its shadow / Over everything. / O / You thorn / In the silver swelling fruit!" Paul Klee, *The Diaries of Paul Klee, 1898–1918,* ed. Felix Klee (Berkeley and Los Angeles, 1964), 375.

6. Hugo Ball, *Flight Out of Time: A Dada Diary,* ed. John Elderfield, trans. Ann Raimes (New York, 1974), 103.

7. Klee may have been reflecting on the precariousness of life during World War I.

301

ALFRED STIEGLITZ
1864–1946

Georgia O'Keeffe: A Portrait—Hands
1918
Palladium photograph
9½ x 7¹¹⁄₁₆ (24.4 x 19.5)

Georgia O'Keeffe: A Portrait, 1918
Gelatin silver photograph
4⁵⁄₁₆ x 3³⁄₁₆ (11 x 8)

Gift of
The Georgia O'Keeffe Foundation
in Honor of Georgia O'Keeffe

Between 1917 and 1937 Alfred Stieglitz made more than 330 finished portraits of Georgia O'Keeffe. Entranced not just with her face, Stieglitz photographed all parts of O'Keeffe's body. However, from the very first time he photographed her in 1917 to his last images from the 1930s, he was also fascinated with her hands, making more than forty studies of them during this twenty-year period.

For Stieglitz, O'Keeffe's hands were as much an index of her personality as her face, and in many of these images they assume the same qualities and attributes he revealed in his other, more traditional portraits of her. For example, celebrating O'Keeffe as artist and creator, Stieglitz often recorded her hands encircling her own drawings; signaling her independence, he photographed her hands resting on the wheel of her car; or revealing her as nurturer and provider, he depicted her hands peeling apples and doing other chores. Yet surely one of the most expressive of these studies of hands is this work from 1918. Emerging from the black background, O'Keeffe's dexterous hands appear to dance before Stieglitz's camera. Her elegant, graceful fingers, glistening with the supple sheen of the skin, reverberate with energy, creating an image of great sensuality.

Stieglitz referred to his photographs of O'Keeffe as a composite portrait, noting that through a series of photographs made over an extended period of time he wanted to document O'Keeffe's "many selves." At the time, however, the term composite portrait had a well-defined meaning, one that adds a slightly different cast to Stieglitz's statement. A composite portrait was understood to be a single photograph that was made up of multiple images superimposed one on top of another in order to describe a generic type. It was presumed, for example, that if multiple portraits of several members of one race were superimposed one on top of another, the resulting image would reveal the characteristics of a racial type. The fact that Stieglitz used this term to describe his photographs of O'Keeffe indicates that, in addition to detailing O'Keeffe's persona, Stieglitz also wanted his composite portrait to address his understanding of woman in general.

In 1949 Georgia O'Keeffe gave the National Gallery what she later referred to as the key set of Stieglitz's work. She astutely realized that his major contribution to American art would be most thoroughly understood if there was one collection that represented all aspects of his art from the beginning of his career in the 1880s to his last works from 1937. The key set, which includes 1,269 photographs given in 1949, 329 portraits of O'Keeffe placed on deposit and subsequently given in 1980, and a specially bound set of the complete fifty issues of *Camera Work*, contains the finest example of each print that was in Stieglitz's possession at the time of his death. Because he rarely sold his work and only infrequently gave prints to friends, the key set is a very complete representation of his work. Moreover, if there were variant croppings or different kinds of prints of any one image—platinum, palladium, carbon, and gelatin silver prints, as well as photogravures—O'Keeffe put an example of each into the key set. The collection is, therefore, a testament not only to the artistry of the photographer, but also to the vision and commitment of the painter who preserved it.

When O'Keeffe donated the key set to the Gallery in 1949, *Georgia O'Keeffe: A Portrait—Hands*, 1918, and *Georgia O'Keeffe: A Portrait*, 1918 were noted on the list of objects to be given, but they were never transferred and were presumed missing. In the spring of 1990, after her death, they were discovered among O'Keeffe's possessions and, through the generosity of the O'Keeffe Foundation, have been added to the Gallery's collection, thus ensuring that the key set is the complete entity O'Keeffe originally envisioned.

Sarah Greenough

PROVENANCE
Georgia O'Keeffe; the Georgia O'Keeffe Estate, 1987; The Georgia O'Keeffe Foundation, 1990.

ERNST LUDWIG KIRCHNER
1880–1938

The Blond Painter Stirner, 1919
Color woodcut on oriental paper
24¹¹/₁₆ x 13⁵/₁₆ (62.7 x 33.8)

Ruth and Jacob Kainen Collection

In more than seventy large woodcuts from 1915 to 1919 Kirchner created the greatest series of portraits in twentieth-century printmaking. Primarily in black and white, these did include a small number in color. The latter culminated aesthetically in two works, the unique monotype version of Kirchner's 1917 *Self-Portrait* and this 1919 *Blond Painter Stirner,* itself recorded in only three impressions.

Kirchner painted, drew, and printed portraits throughout his life. However, during these five years the woodcut portraits are extraordinary in quality, scale, and number; they outnumber his portraits in any other single medium by three to one.

As a result of the disasters of his draft into the army in 1915 and again in 1916, his subsequent breakdowns and visits to sanatoria, and his auto accident in Berlin, Kirchner was physically and mentally debilitated. He clung to his life-giving art by force of will alone. This intensely inward period led to extreme sensitivity to the features and personalities of others and to a desire to capture a wide variety of acquaintances, intimate as well as casual, in portraits.

Karl Stirner (1882–1943) was a painter, illustrator, and author who concentrated on the Swabian landscape and people.[1] He visited Kirchner in the summer of 1919 for three weeks to study painting and woodcutting.[2] During that period Kirchner painted his portrait, seated at a table with a wine glass and a cat, with background elements that resemble landscape.[3] Like other cases where a monumental woodcut portrait succeeded a painting,[4] Kirchner has here greatly intensified the expressive and symbolic aspects.

As in the painted portrait, Kirchner's woodcut shows Stirner as a pensive, melancholy man. However, here the abstract background of deep purple heightens the inwardness of Stirner's look, a sense of solitude enhanced by the dark sickle moon that echoes and presses on the curve of his head. Stirner is no longer surrounded by his environment, which now, beyond the moon, consists of only three forms. Rather, he seems to be inwardly dreaming or mentally picturing it. The black cat, a frequent feature of Kirchner's years in Switzerland, no longer plays on a table in front of Stirner, but is reduced to a tiny image imprinted on his neck, inevitably reminiscent of Kirchner's interest in what he called "hieroglyphs." The figures on either side are much more ambiguous. Such subsidiary objects in Kirchner's woodcut portraits of this period are like comments on the sitter—sometimes open and straightforward, as in the peasants with their backgrounds of rural objects, sometimes more mysterious and evocative, as in the dark portrait of van de Velde with its abstract flurry of thrusting and pointed forms in the background. Here the figure on the left could be male or female, whereas the figure on the right is surely a nude woman with short hair. Her likeness to some of Kirchner's carved wooden statues leaves us wondering whether these may even be objects from the studio. Probably, however, like the provocatively similar face-à-face man and woman in the culminating image of Kirchner's 1918 series on Petrarch's Triumph of Love,[5] these are symbols of the eternal longing between man and woman, and may even represent Kirchner's perception of the ground for Stirner's melancholy. As he stands alone in the purple night under a dark moon and his intensely blue eyes rivet our gaze, is Stirner also what Kirchner called a "paraphrase," specifically a paraphrase of longing for lost or unattainable love?

This wonderful woodcut and Kirchner's 1909 *Performer Bowing* in this same exhibition mark a special and continuing contribution to the National Gallery. The Gallery had for some years a good collection of German expressionist prints, including a wide range of artists as well as extensive groups by Kollwitz, Müller, Barlach, Nolde, and Schmidt-Rottluff. However, the greatest printmaker of the period, Kirchner, was represented by only seven examples. Ruth and Jacob Kainen, in addition to their outstanding donations in other fields, have transformed the Gallery's collection of Kirchner's prints, beginning with their gift in 1985 of the great 1914 woodcut *Five Tarts* and continuing every year to add further masterpieces, so that the Gallery's collection is now three times as large in number and immeasurably stronger in the quality of works by this extraordinary artist.

Andrew Robison

NOTES
1. Thieme-Becker, *Allgemeines Lexikon der Bildenen Künstler,* vol. 32 (Leipzig, 1938), 66.

2. Kirchner's letter to Nele van de Velde of 14 October 1919, quoted in Lucius Grisebach and Annette Meyer zu Eissen, *Ernst Ludwig Kirchner: 1880–1938* (Berlin, 1979–1980), 258.

3. Donald E. Gordon, *Ernst Ludwig Kirchner* (Cambridge, Mass., 1968), 349. Kirchner also made a small etching of Stirner at work outdoors, also with the cat (Anne Marie and Wolfe-Dieter Dube, *E.L. Kirchner das Graphische Werk* (Munich, 1980), etching no. 281).

4. Compare Gordon's analysis of the 1917 portraits of Dr. Grisebach (Gordon 1968, 108).

5. Dube 1980, 342–350.

305

ERNST LUDWIG KIRCHNER
1880–1938

Umbra Vitae, 1924
Book by Georg Heym, designed and
illustrated with 50 woodcuts by Kirchner
Maquette 8⁹⁄₁₆ x 5¹¹⁄₁₆ (21.7 x 14.5)
Published version 9¼ x 6½ (23.5 x 16.5)

Promised Gift of
Ruth and Jacob Kainen

Frequently referred to as the finest German expressionist book and one of the finest illustrated books of the twentieth century, Kirchner's *Umbra Vitae* was entirely designed by him: typography, layout, binding, colors, endpapers, frontispiece, and illustrations. The Kainen maquette is Kirchner's own personal record of his trials and preparation for every aspect of the publication.

Kirchner was one of the best-read of modern artists, so it was quite natural for him to create series of woodcuts or book illustrations inspired by sympathetic literary texts. Walt Whitman was his favorite poet, his "leader and guide in perspective on life," and Kirchner saw Heym's poetry as a continuation of Whitman, "a Whitman translated into the German psyche, who prophetically saw and wrote of our times in the past decade."[1] Seen from the end of the second decade, Heym, who died at the age of twenty-four in a skating accident at the beginning of 1912, certainly did seem prophetic in his visions of the universal conflagration of war, the confusion in the individual's search for meaning in the face of death, and the strange ambiguities of environments both in nature and in the city.

Struck by Heym's provocative imagery and sympathetic themes, Kirchner began privately to prepare small woodcuts, which he printed by hand in his own copy of the 1912 first edition. Each of these powerful cuts was inspired by its own poem or stanza. The size of each was made to fit the varying blank spaces at the end of the poems in the 1912 edition; and in many cases Kirchner printed the cuts on top of his preliminary pencil sketches in those spaces. The strong differences in style and their relation to other works make it likely Kirchner prepared these woodcuts over four or five years, from the late teens through the early twenties.

The initiative to take this very personal document and turn it into a published presentation came from Hans Mardersteig,

Kirchner's neighbor in Davos who visited him occasionally and thus had seen his private copy. Mardersteig worked for the Munich publisher Kurt Wolff, who originally wanted to publish a new portfolio of Kirchner's prints. However, Wolff eventually took Mardersteig's advice in February 1922 to focus on *Umbra Vitae*.[2]

While his exact procedure can only be surmised from internal evidence in the maquette, it appears on stylistic grounds likely that after Kirchner agreed to the commission in 1922 he may have finished illustrations for three or four of the poems. Perhaps at this point he also added for the table of contents an impression from a much earlier woodblock of 1905, which he recut to bring it closer to his contemporary style. It was surely then that Kirchner decided to replace one of his smaller cuts (here apparently in a unique impression) with a full-page work incorporating his own cutting of Heym's text for the poem "Alle Landschaften Haben." Kirchner also prepared a two-color frontispiece as well as two different double-page cuts for endpapers and a wraparound two-color woodcut for the cover. As his sense for the total design of the book grew, Kirchner made impressions of all these additions, including a print of the cover woodcut on suede, and had his original edition taken apart and rebound with the appropriate insertions to give a true model of the finished work. This, the maquette copy, he then annotated with extensive instructions to the printer about type, arrangement of page, colors, method of printing—with some variation for individual cuts and a strong stress on the unity of picture and text throughout.

This fascinating maquette shows an extraordinarily sensitive printing and a personal quality in each woodcut, by comparison with its published version, as well as in the whole. The maquette's subsequent history can be traced through Kirchner's in-

scription, with understandable insistence, that the copy belonged to him and must be returned as soon as it was no longer needed by the printer. Kirchner completed its very personal meaning by inscribing and giving it to his wife Erna, in memory of her father who was a printer in Berlin.

Andrew Robison

PROVENANCE
Ernst Ludwig Kirchner; Erna Kirchner; Walter Kern, stamp (Lugt 1567a) and annotation "from Mrs. Kirchner, 20 June 1940"; Galerie Kornfeld, Bern, 21 June 1985, no. 104; Ruth Cole Kainen.

NOTES
1. Kirchner's letter to Curt Valentin, quoted by Annemarie Dübe-Heynig, *E. L. Kirchner: Graphik* (Munich, 1961), 94–96.

2. Eberhard W. Kornfeld, *Ernst Ludwig Kirchner: Nachzeichnung seines Lebens* (Bern, 1979), 216–217.

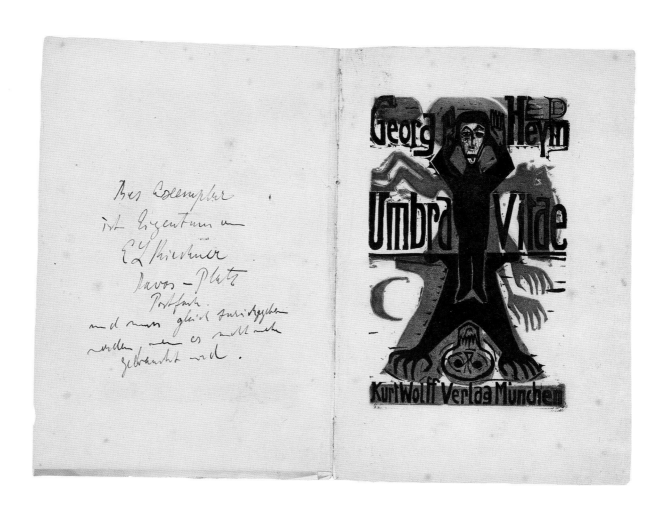

Dies Exemplar
ist Eigentum an
E L Kirchner
Davos — Platz
Postfach.
und muss gleich zurückgegeben
werden wenn es nicht mehr
gebraucht wird.

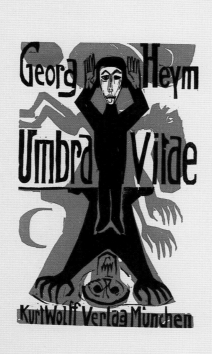

GEORG HEYM
UMBRA VITAE
NACHGELASSENE
GEDICHTE

MIT 47 ORIGINALHOLZSCHNITTEN
VON
ERNST LUDWIG KIRCHNER

KURT WOLFF VERLAG MÜNCHEN
1924

KURT SCHWITTERS
1887–1948

Mz 79. Herz-Klee, 1920
Collage
5⅞ x 4⅝ (15 x 11.8)

Merz 30, 7, 1927
Collage
6¼ x 4¾ (15.9 x 12.1)

Promised Gift of
Mr. and Mrs. Leonard A. Lauder

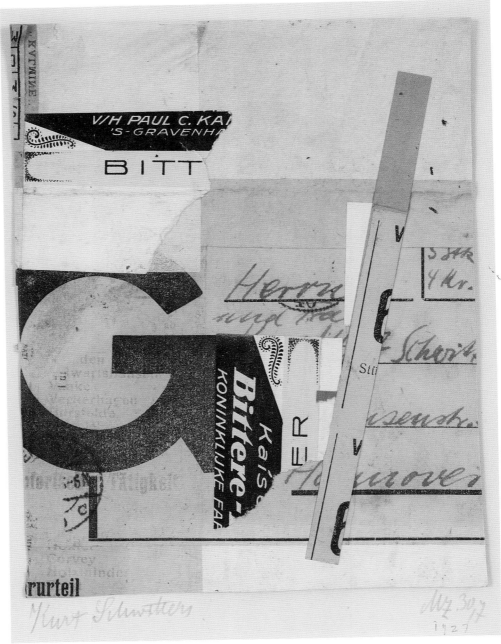

In the summer of 1919 Kurt Schwitters invented the concept of *Merz*, which amounted to a one-man art movement. *Merz* became the nomenclature by which Schwitters categorized his drawings, collages, and assemblages. These two collages are characterized as *Merzzeichnungen*, or "Merz drawings," abbreviated by the artist to *Mz*.

In 1920, Schwitters created a number of small, exquisite collages that are among the most satisfying works he ever made. A poet in his own right, he often gave humorous, wonderfully evocative titles to his works. *Herz-Klee* (Heart-Clover) delights both in German and English. Though the title refers to the hearts in the composition, the shapes of which are analogous to clover leaves, it is equally playful on a verbal level. "Merz" rhymes with "Herz," and the association between the two words evokes much of the charm of these works. Moreover, Paul Klee was among the artists Schwitters most admired, one who worked with similar materials on an equally minuscule scale. Thus "Herz Klee" becomes a humorous variation on "Herr Klee."

Like other collages produced around this time, *Herz-Klee* is composed of heterogeneous elements that, when assembled, produce a formally unified whole. Thin fragments of torn paper intersect and overlap, giving a dense textural quality, and painted passages of reddish-brown and black impart an overall softness and tonal warmth. Like nostalgic remnants from a past era, the papers seem darkened or stained with age, a mood underscored by glimpses of letters in a traditional Gothic typeface.

Schwitters worked intuitively and improvisationally, selecting his materials from the mounds of effluvia he collected and shifting them around a page until he achieved the desired composition. Although he wanted to disassociate them from any specific context, the contents of his collages have a timely, almost diaristic quality, like "miniature epistles of everyday experience."[1] The torn tram tickets or liquor labels constitute the ephemera of a life, here clearly an urban, specifically German one, and the charred effect produced by patches of black paint evoke the ravages of recent war.

Merz 30, 7 stands in strong contrast to the earlier work. Colors close in value make a spare, elegant work, light in both weight and tonality. In this more stringent composition, one informed by constructivist examples, Schwitters aligned the mostly scissor-cut forms with the edge. At the right, a letter addressed to Herrn and Frau Schwitters in Hannover constitutes the only handmade form, though in a writing not the artist's. On the same piece of paper a large *G* arrests the eye by its modern typeface and jarring disjunction of scale. It is no doubt a remnant from the magazine *G*, issued by Hans Richter and Werner Graeff in 1923–1924, to which Schwitters contributed.

Like the paper elements, words are cropped and elusive, deprived of their syntactic role but provocative nonetheless. "Bitt," for example, suggest a popular German beer named Bittburg. The label was probably taken from a Dutch cookie package, however, and is completed at the lower center where its other half is turned on its side.

These two collages are the first works by Schwitters to enter the National Gallery.

Marla Prather

NOTE
1. John Elderfield, *Kurt Schwitters* [exh. cat. The Museum of Modern Art] (New York, 1985), 71.

ANDRE DERAIN
1880–1954

Head of a Woman, 1920
Charcoal on paper
23⅞ x 18 (59.64 x 45.72)

MARSDEN HARTLEY
1877–1943

Plums and Pears, 1927
Pencil on paper
14½ x 11¾ (36.83 x 29.85)

Gift of Warren and Grace Brandt

As a soldier in the French army, André Derain wrote to his friend and fellow painter Maurice Vlaminck toward the end of the First World War: "I only want to paint portraits, real ones with hands, hair, life itself."[1] Following the demobilization in 1918, Derain made good that wish. For a time his prime subject became the figure, as he made numerous paintings and drawings of women.

Derain had long ago abandoned the fauve style upon which his fame still largely rests. Having fallen under the spell of Cézanne, he gradually developed an idiosyncratic, classicizing realism that emphasised clear outlines, strong modeling, and carefully balanced compositions. Above all, Derain drained his painting of that feature which had been central to fauvism: color. His post-fauve paintings are somber, thickly brushed in dark tones, browns, and black.

Although informed by the same principles as those paintings, Derain's later drawings make a quite different effect. Purity of line is emphasized and tonal transitions are subtle. In his many drawings of female heads and nudes from the 1920s, Derain seemed intent to reconcile the geometric simplifications of cubism with the tradition of French figure drawing stretching back to Ingres.

Head of a Woman is certainly among the strongest and most beautiful of Derain's drawings of female heads. Pulling thick charcoal against a roughly textured sheet of laid paper, Derain achieved a range of tonal gradations. Outlines of face and hair are firmly drawn, standing out against the white paper, while interior forms are delicately modeled. Smoothly curving lines that define chin and eyes betray an urge to generalize form while contrasting with the more specified treatment of nose and mouth and the lovely mass of freely drawn hair.

Derain's model for *Head of a Woman* ap-

pears in a number of his paintings and drawings of the early 1920s. The same woman takes a similar pose in Derain's painting *Woman in an Armchair*, 1920/1925, part of the Chester Dale bequest to the National Gallery. The Gallery's collection of Derains, which began with Dale's gift of eight paintings in 1963, now totals fifteen paintings, as well as a suite of engravings, a suite of woodcuts, a drypoint, a lithograph, and a color woodcut. *Head of a Woman* is the first Derain drawing to enter the collection.

Along with *Head of a Woman*, Warren and Grace Brandt have generously offered to the National Gallery for its fiftieth anniversary a pencil drawing by Marsden Hartley, *Plums and Pears*, 1927. Between 1926 and 1928 Hartley lived near Cézanne's home in Aix-en-Provence. There Hartley, a pioneer of American modernism who had produced strikingly original reinterpretations of the most advanced painting of the contemporary European avant-garde, devoted himself to the example of Cézanne. He painted and drew many of Cézanne's motifs in a style conspicuously indebted to that of the French master. A lovely example of those drawings, *Plums and Pears* is elegant and spare. Contours are more firmly drawn than in comparable works by Cézanne, and the flatness of forms rather than their volume is emphasised. An homage to his great predecessor, *Plums and Pears* is the work of an artist who understood and fully appreciated the use made of Cézanne's work by painters pursuing the ends of abstraction. Drawn in passages of parallel pencil strokes with graphite rubbed between passages making a delicate overall silver tone, *Plums and Pears* joins an earlier Marsden Hartley drawing, *Self-Portrait*, 1918, in the National Gallery collection, as well as two lithographs and three paintings.

Jeremy Strick

PROVENANCE
Dérain: Stoppenbach and Delestre, London; Hartley: Frances Mallek, New York.

NOTE
1. Denys Sutton, *André Derain* (New York, 1959), 36.

LOVIS CORINTH
1858–1925

Totentanz, 1922
Portfolio of 5 soft-ground etchings,
on japan paper, with title page
9⁷⁄₁₆ x 7 (23.9 x 17.78)

Gift in Memory of Sigbert H. Marcy

Lovis Corinth was born and raised in East Prussia. After studying in Königsberg and Munich, he spent three years in Paris where he trained with the academic painters Robert Fleury and William-Adolphe Bougereau. Back in Germany by 1887, Corinth eventually settled in Berlin in the summer of 1900, joining his friends and colleagues Max Liebermann and Walter Leistikow. Both of these artists were German impressionists who had broken away from the Berlin Academy and formed a splinter group known as the "Sezession" in 1898. Corinth actively participated in the Sezession and in its exhibitions, and was elected its president in 1915. During the first decade of the twentieth century, Corinth rapidly shed his academic background, and his palette grew lighter and his brushwork more bold and free. Together with Liebermann, Corinth quickly became one of the most important and fashionable painters in Berlin.

Although known primarily as a painter, the graphic arts were an intricate and significant part of Corinth's total output. His first etching was created in 1891 and, in 1894, he began lithography. By the early 1920s Corinth was producing more than a hundred prints yearly. At least nine hundred prints by Corinth have been documented.

Corinth treated the theme of the Dance of Death at various times in his career, in both painted and graphic versions. However, the *Totentanz* is his only extended commentary on the subject.

Recent scholarship suggests that the figures in *Totentanz* are either family members or close friends. The artist in *Death and the Artist* might be Corinth himself; the figures in the four other prints in the portfolio are probably his wife Charlotte, the etcher Hermann Struck and his wife, and his son

Thomas. The old man in the print *Death and the Old Man* is possibly Corinth's own father, Franz Heinrich Corinth.

The *Totentanz* portfolio was created during 1921 and published at the beginning of 1922 by Euphorion Verlag, Berlin. The image reproduced here, *Death and the Artist,* has its title etched into the plate directly above the head of the artist. The individual looks out at us with an intense yet doleful gaze. Holding either a pencil or engraving tool in his right hand, he attempts to copy the scene before him. Peering out from the background looms the skeletal figure of Death, who gently, yet noticeably, rests his hand upon the artist's arm. This gesture makes Death an active participant in the artist's struggle to commit his idea to paper.

In accordance with the traditional imagery of the *Totentanz,* Death is presented here as man's constant companion through life. However, Corinth added his own interpretation: that the making of visual images is an attempt to win immortality for their creator and thereby to cheat Death.

This perpetual dialogue with Death is reinforced by the style. The composition does not render the scene literally, but rather conveys Corinth's emotional response. This is especially evident in the treatment of light and dark and the handling of line. The finely nuanced varieties of highlights and shadows may derive from his knowledge of impressionism, but their total impact is less descriptive than evocative. Similarly, the linear patterns are both rationally calculated and willfully random in their placement across the page. This latter quality is especially striking in the delineation of the left side of the artist's face and shoulder. Taken together, these two aspects impart a calculated mix of control and arbitrariness, violence

and restraint, and reason and emotion. They express Corinth's often contradictory responses to Death, art, and life.

This portfolio, on japan paper, exemplifies the remarkable collection of Corinth prints formed by Sigbert Marcy. As a personal friend of Corinth, who even etched his portrait, Marcy had remarkable opportunities to obtain works of the best quality from the artist. His connoisseurship is reflected in the collection of more than 150 Corinths, all of which are stunning in their high quality and fine condition. The *Totentanz* in this exhibition represents the generous decision of the Marcy family to give the entire collection to the National Gallery. The Marcy Corinth Collection will transform the Gallery's holdings, making it an important center for the study of Lovis Corinth's prints.

Christopher With

ERNST LUDWIG KIRCHNER
1880–1938

The Visit, 1922
Oil on canvas
47¼ x 47¼ (120 x 120)

Gift (Partial and Promised) of
Ruth and Jacob Kainen

The Visit is a superb late expressionist masterpiece by Kirchner. It depicts the interior of the artist's Swiss mountain cabin *In den Lärchen* — named after the larch grove that surrounded it — where he moved in the autumn of 1918. The painting shows, on the left, Kirchner's companion and common-law wife Erna Schilling greeting the young Dutch artist Jan Wiegers as he comes up the stairs; and on the right, in the background, the artist himself lying on a sofa smoking a pipe. This painting once carried the subtitle *Couple and Guest*.[1]

Kirchner had gone to Switzerland to recover from his mental and physical collapse. At first he moved to a hut high on the Staffelalp, just south of Davos. Later, after a stay at a sanitorium on Lake Constance, he moved to the cabin at the foot of the mountain near Frauenkirch. The dramatic alpine scenery and simple peasant life proved restorative both artistically and personally. He decorated his abode, as he had his Dresden and Berlin studios, with textiles, sculptures and paintings. In *The Visit* we see a charming frieze of animals adorning the middle space.

During the postwar years, when he finally was free from the deleterious effects of the medicines he had been taking and began painting again, Kirchner enjoyed visits and letters from his friends and even dreamed of establishing a school of artists modeled on Gauguin's collaborations in Brittany and van Gogh's in Arles. During the twenties and thirties a number of young artists came to study with him, including Jan Wiegers who arrived in 1920.[2]

The Visit reflects the evolution of his art during the decade preceding its creation. Toward the end of his Dresden period, Kirchner became more concerned with expression, and turned for inspiration to the primitive art of Africa, New Guinea, and India among other places. In the years immediately before and during the First World War, he had created the Berlin street scenes populated with *demimondaines* for which he is best known, as well as views of the Baltic island Fehmarn. In these revolutionary canvases Kirchner communicated the anxieties of modern existence through spatial tensions and ambiguities, distorted forms, and arbitrary colors, often using jagged zigzag strokes.

Then in the early twenties, from his alpine retreat, Kirchner began once again to work in a more relaxed style and to represent the spectacular scenery and picturesquely costumed villagers of Frauenkirch as well as his own domestic world.[3] He came to favor large square canvases and his forms and spaces became equivalently monumental. While his earlier paintings contained few, if any, parallel lines, *The Visit* is a harmonious construction of right angles and perpendiculars. The dynamics of the composition are set up by the parallel horizontal lines in the foreground, which lead our eye into the picture and back into space on the right. Yet it is not at all certain what these lines represent: floorboards, a carpet with a geometric pattern, or even steps. The interior of the cabin remains provocatively ambiguous. Wiegers obviously ascends a staircase, but the positions of Erna Schilling and Kirchner are less clear. Is she standing on a landing or on another staircase? Does Kirchner occupy the same space or a loft-like area behind? The figures are blocky and geometrized, according to a canon that Donald Gordon characterized as "a rectangle with rounded corners."[4] Likewise the palette is simplified, consisting mainly of primary colors and their derivatives. These bright and cheerful colors imply a warm domesticity. They often are used non-naturalistically, however, especially in the figures' hair and in the modeling of their faces: Wiegers' hair is green streaked with light blue; Erna's hair is dark blue streaked with red; and the faces of all three figures are modeled with broad patches of blue paint. Throughout Kirchner created a surface pattern of long, constructive strokes of evenly applied pigment.

This late autobiographical painting by Kirchner is a welcome complement to the two early canvases by this artist, the *Two Nudes* already in the collection of the National Gallery, and *The Green House in Dresden*, also a fiftieth-anniversary gift from Ruth and Jacob Kainen.

Elizabeth Pendleton Streicher

PROVENANCE
Kirchner Estate; Galerie Wolfgang Ketterer.

NOTES
1. See Donald E. Gordon, *Ernst Ludwig Kirchner* (Cambridge, Mass.), 1968, 367, no. 693; Galerie Wolfgang Ketterer, *Ausstellung Ernst Ludwig Kirchner: Gemälde, Aquarelle, Zeichnungen, Graphik* (Munich, 1985), 26–27, no. 13.

2. See Gordon 1968, 27, 32, 107.

3. See Gordon 1968, 107, and nos. 662–755.

4. Gordon 1968, 107.

FERNAND LÉGER
1881–1955

Two Women, 1922
Oil on canvas
35¾ x 23 (90.8 x 58.4)

Gift (Partial and Promised) of
Richard S. Zeisler

Fernand Léger originated a distinct cubist style during the second decade of this century. In the early 1920s he both embraced and influenced the aesthetic of Purism as espoused by his friends Le Corbusier and Amedée Ozenfant. The clean, geometric forms of mechanized industry and mass production were prized as the harbingers of a renewed social and aesthetic order. Many of Léger's paintings took mechanical devices as their subject, and all of his paintings were informed by a style of cool precision and exacting workmanship.

Women occupied a traditional place within Léger's ideal new order. Counterpoints to the urban world of industry and work, Léger's many depictions of women embody a domestic realm of tranquility and leisure.[1] Nevertheless he treated his depictions of women no differently than the most austere mechanical form: edges are sharp, colors are distinct, and modeling follows a conspicuously stylized formula.

Léger often produced more than one version of his important compositions, and *Two Women*, 1922, is no exception. The first version (marked "1er ETAT" on its back), *Les deux femmes debout*, in the Musée National d'Art Moderne, Paris, is slightly smaller than *Two Women*.[2] The two paintings are close in almost every detail, differing principally in the landscape viewed from the window at upper left.

Two Women also relates in a more general fashion to a number of paintings by the artist of parallel subject. These include the monumental *La Mère et l'enfant* of 1922 and *Nus sur fond rouge*, 1923 (both in the Basel Kunstmuseum), and the *Deux femmes sur fond bleu* of 1927 (private collection, Solothurn), among others. All of these paintings show two women, one older, one younger, either in an interior or against a uniform background. In style and subject it relates as well to one of Léger's most famous series, that culminating in *Le Grand Déjeuner* of 1921 (The Museum of Modern Art, New York). Within this large group of paintings, *Two Women* is notable for its poignant combination of sharply delineated details of a domestic interior and precise human forms with the evident warmth and tenderness of the figures who clasp each other tightly.

The first major Léger to enter the National Gallery collection, *Two Women* makes an indispensable addition the Gallery's holdings. The collection already includes the quite fascinating Léger portrait *Maud Dale*, 1935, and *Woman with a Mirror*, 1929. *Two Women* is a particularly fine treatment of one of the artist's key subjects, painted at one of his most important and original moments.

Jeremy Strick

NOTES

1. Robert Herbert, "Léger's *Le Grand Déjeuner*," in *Léger's Le Grand Déjeuner* [exh. cat. The Minneapolis Institute of Arts] (Minneapolis, 1980), 26.

2. Claude Laugier and Michèle Richet, *Léger: Oeuvres de Fernand Léger* (Paris, 1980), 47.

PABLO PICASSO
1881–1973

Young Woman Seated in an Armchair
1921–1922
Brush and ink with white heightening
10⅝ x 9⅜ (27.11 x 23.71)

Promised Gift of Evelyn Stefansson Nef

Young Woman Seated in an Armchair is an idealized portrait of Olga Koklova, Picasso's first wife.[1] The idealized features of the woman in this gouache, her large body, and the classically inspired hairdo and clothing are typical for Picasso in this period.

Alfred Barr effectively located the origin and growth of Picasso's neoclassical style in the early 1920s as a part of the general movement in various arts in Paris toward classicism. This movement can be seen not only in the visual arts but also in music, dance, and theater, the latter of which were very important to Picasso at just this time. In 1917 Picasso had visited the antiquities in Pompeii, Naples, and Rome, which may have been a background foundation for his neoclassical style although it did not actually surface until three years later.[2]

Young Woman Seated in an Armchair is related to the huge female figures that Picasso made in 1920–1921. He has said that his interest in monumental proportions stemmed from his childhood experience of playing under the dining room table and seeing the thick ankles of his aunt, a solid and reassuring memory that he later transferred into his art.[3] However, his attraction was not only to the large size of such figures, but also to their serenity and balance. His portrayal of these classical female figures seated in armchairs began as early as 1920, but increased markedly in 1921 after the birth of his son, Paolo, when Picasso produced a series of paintings and drawings showing Olga, draped in a classical shift, holding their son and seated in this same clearly recognizable armchair. As usual with Picasso, his reworking of a vision transforms it, in this case leading from the heavier and heavier figures to a sudden break with this work and another where Olga is once more a relatively slim and youthful woman.

Drawn on a pale blue painted background, the woman's massive body fits comfortably into the sketchy upholstered chair. The chair is given just enough form to hold her rounded limbs and body. A few drawn lines behind the chair are all that is necessary to show that it occupies the corner of a room. Her long hair, caught with a bow and falling in curls down her back, makes this pensive woman seem less austere.

One of the fascinating aspects of Picasso's neoclassical works is his exploration through these massive figures of the artistic problem of scale. His images in this period appear monumental but may in fact be surprisingly small. That is undoubtedly the explanation for Zervos having mistakenly thought that this drawing was an oil painting on canvas.[4]

Young Woman Seated in an Armchair is a major addition to the National Gallery's small collection of drawings by Picasso. It is our earliest of his classical works, providing a background for the three paintings of 1922 and 1923 given by Chester Dale thirty years ago. Mrs. Nef has also made a gift of Marc Chagall's *Féla and Odilon* for the Gallery's fiftieth anniversary.

Barbara Read Ward

NOTES
1. See the side-by-side idealized and lifelike portraits of Olga in *Pablo Picasso: A Retrospective*, ed. William Rubin [exh. cat. The Museum of Modern Art] (New York, 1980), 242–243.

2. Alfred H. Barr, *Picasso: Fifty Years of his Art* (New York, 1946), 115.

3. Roland Penrose, "Beauty and the Monster," *Picasso 1881–1973*, ed. Roland Penrose and John Golding (London, 1973), 163.

4. Christian Zervos, *Pablo Picasso*, vol. 4 (Paris, 1951), cat. 360.

319

PAUL KLEE
1879–1940

Grüne Pflanzen Blutlaus, 1924
Watercolor, pen, and ink on gessoed
cloth, mounted on cardboard
8 x 12⁹⁄₁₆ (20.2 x 32)

Gift of Ruth Carter Stevenson

Paul Klee was a naturalist at heart.[1] As a young child he revealed a precocious interest in plants and animals, and in his adolescent years compiled meticulous renderings of mollusks, insects, and birds. His studio was filled with curious specimens, which he mounted to boards like collages. And in his teachings and writings he stressed repeatedly that the artist's dialogue with nature was a *conditio sine qua non.*[2] In this concise and deceptively simple composition of 1924, Klee tackles one of nature's most complex mysteries.

The literal English translation of *Grüne Pflanzen Blutlaus* is green plant-blood-louse. Lice were the artist's occasional subject in the 1920s, but by the thirties they appeared repeatedly.[3] Usually as predators, sometimes as male pursuers in a sexual relationship, their role was consistently insidious. And as Klee grew older and disease took hold of him[4] they became a harrowing symbol of his own inevitable end.

Klee classified his creations as scientists do nature. Using Roman numerals he indicated each work's respective rank. The National Gallery watercolor was originally inscribed on the mount with a Roman numeral II, which was later crossed out and replaced with the abbreviation for his highest ranking, *Sonderklasse* (special class). Certainly it is an acknowledgment of its highly inventive and complex nature. In nearly diagrammatic fashion and with remarkable economy of means, Klee explores nature's life cycle. And in so doing, he ingeniously suggests overlapping associations between plants and humans.

Three points of reference signal our attention. First is the tubular stem rising from an orifice in the plant's divided trunk. Not without sexual implications, it is crowned with an ovum-like mass symbolizing ger-

mination, growth, and reproduction. Second is the menacing blood louse, its stinger penetrating deep into the plant's flesh, literally sapping it of its vital juices. And last, wedged between the stem and the louse, is Klee's ubiquitous arrow aimed upward to the heavens. The arrow symbolizes both physical movement and man's yearning to free himself from earthly bonds.[5] With finite means Klee reveals an infinite vision of the universe, an ineluctable cycle of birth and death.

At the lower center of the sheet, almost unobserved, an eye and nose float free of gravity. Delicately rendered fragments of a face stare out at us, seemingly in acknowledgment of our presence, even signaling our inclusion. We are tellingly reminded that in this, one of life's greatest mysteries, we are both partners and silent witnesses.

Judith Brodie

PROVENANCE
Kornfeld und Klipstein, Bern, 25–26 May 1962, lot 530; L'Oeil Galerie, Paris, c. 1965.

NOTES
1. For a detailed account of Klee's responses to nature, see Richard Verdi, *Klee and Nature* (New York, 1984), 1–32.

2. Paul Klee, "Ways of Nature Study" (1923) in *The Thinking Eye: The Notebooks of Paul Klee,* ed. Jürg Spiller (New York and London, 1961), 1:63.

3. Verdi 1984, 67–69.

4. In 1935 Klee was diagnosed with scleroderma, a degenerative skin disease that severely impaired his manual dexterity.

5. For an account of the arrow as symbol, see Paul Klee, *Pedagogical Sketchbook,* intro. and trans. Sibyl Moholy-Nagy (London, 1984), section 4.

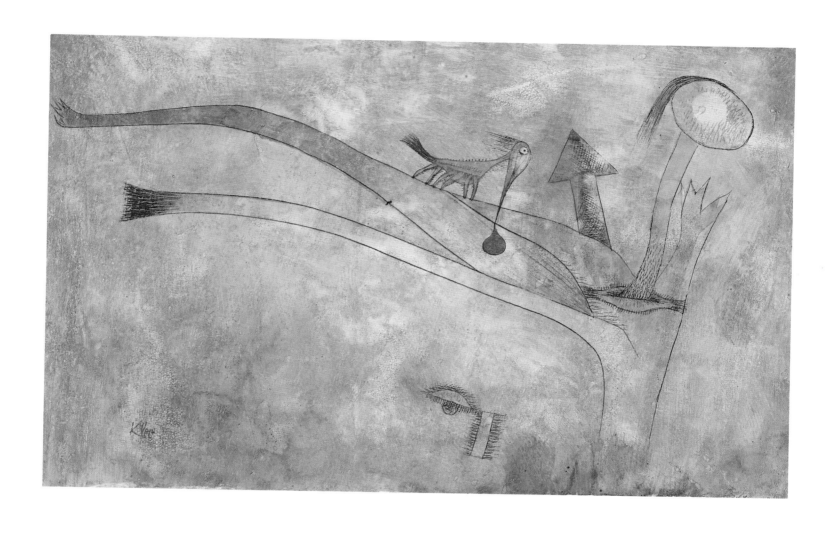

EGON SCHIELE
1890–1918

Self-Portrait, c. 1917,
cast c. 1925–1928
Bronze
10⅞ (27.6)

Gift of
Mr. and Mrs. Leonard A. Lauder

This bronze bust represents Schiele's only important sculptural work.[1] He probably made the original terra cotta, which is presumed lost or destroyed, around 1917. His friend and patron Arthur Roessler obtained the terra cotta from the artist's heirs and had one or two plasters cast from it. The first of these, which is today in the Historisches Museum der Stadt Wien, was reportedly used to make an edition of about two or three bronzes between 1925 and 1928.[2] The present bronze is from this earliest edition.[3]

The most obvious sculptural influence on Schiele is Auguste Rodin (1840–1917), who was much admired by Schiele and his Viennese compatriots and who was mentioned specifically by Schiele in a letter to Roessler in 1910.[4] It is instructive to compare Schiele's *Self-Portrait* with Rodin's portrait bust of *Gustav Mahler* in the National Gallery of Art.[5] Rodin employed a technique similar to that used only a few years later by Schiele, with an expressive face, rising out of a loosely defined neck, formed in an impressionistic manner. Both have a pathos that belongs entirely to the twentieth century, leaving the old world behind. Other Rodins can be considered stylistic kin to Schiele's bust, perhaps in particular the various figures rising out of the bronze voids of his *Gates of Hell*.

The *Self-Portrait*, which bears a beautiful dark- to golden-brown patina, depicts Schiele with his head turned upward, his lips slightly parted as if breathing, and his eyes wide open. The raised eyebrows and forehead and the blank eye sockets give the face a look different from Schiele's typical introspec-

tive, tortured, and knowing self-portraits on paper and canvas. The expression is similar to that in a photograph of Schiele from 1918[6] and in the large painting of *The Family* from the same year.[7] There the artist depicted himself with raised eyebrows, looking out at the viewer. In both the painting and the bust we are presented a wide-eyed figure who confronts the outside world directly, with relative equanimity. Both show Schiele less self-absorbed and brooding than in many of his earlier self-portraits.[8] Schiele looks out from himself with expectation and hopefulness, sadly cut short by his and his wife's premature death from influenza in 1918.

Schiele's *Self-Portrait* makes a significant addition to the National Gallery's holdings of early twentieth-century sculpture. It has an interesting parallel in the Gallery's wax *Flayed Horse* by Théodore Géricault (1791–1824)[9] as a sculptural essay by an artist who was primarily a painter and who died at a young age before having the opportunity to develop his sculptural talents.

Donald Myers

PROVENANCE
Arthur Roessler; Private collection; Sotheby's, London, sale of 26 June 1984 (lot 27).

NOTES
1. Jane Kallir, *Egon Schiele, The Complete Works: Including a Biography and a Catalogue Raisonné* (New York, 1990), 651; only three other sculp-

tural projects are known, all of little artistic significance.

2. Inv. no. 133.540; the second plaster, on loan to the Stanford University Art Gallery in California from a private collection, was probably cast from this plaster, though it may also have been cast from the terracotta. Although Roessler originally intended the bronze edition to be twelve to fifteen, he later maintained that it was limited to only two or three (Kallir 1990, 651).

3. This was verified by Jane Kallir, who was able to trace the provenance forward from Roessler to the present owner; see above. There were four later editions in bronze (1956, 1960, 1980, and 1987), and a 1965 edition in cast stone; the two most recent in date (which are also the most numerous in examples) were aftercasts, while the three earliest were from one or the other of the two plasters.

4. Quoted in Alessandra Comini, *Egon Schiele's Portraits* (Berkeley 1974), 38.

5. Accession number 1972.78.1, dating from 1909.

6. Reproduced in Erwin Mitsch, *The Art of Egon Schiele* (London, 1974), 13.

7. Österreichische Galerie, Vienna; see Mitsch 1974, 245, pl. 75.

8. Jane Kallir suggested that the fact that the number of self-portraits tapers off in the later years of Schiele's life indicates a more outward focus in his art. I thank Jane Kallir for all the assistance she generously provided.

9. Accession number 1980.44.7; the National Gallery also has two bronzes based on the *Flayed Horse*, accession numbers 1980.44.8 and 1980.44.9.

PAUL KLEE
1879–1940

Junger Wald, 1925
Pen and ink and watercolor,
mounted on cardboard
3⅞ x 12¹¹⁄₁₆ (9.8 x 32.2)

Gift (Partial and Promised) of
Lili-Charlotte Sarnoff

Paul Klee developed a pictorial language that was spare but richly inventive. Arrows form spindly trees, rows of saw-toothed lines arrange themselves into thickets, and swiftly penned dashes spell out clouds and sky. Set onto horizontal staff lines, these symbols resemble musical notation and underscore the melodious quality of this delicately patterned watercolor.

Much has been written about the role of music in Paul Klee's life and its relationship to his art.[1] His father was a professor of music in Bern. His wife was a piano instructor, and Klee himself was an accomplished violinist. As an adolescent he was torn between a career in painting and one in music and even wrote that he was apprehensive about his growing passion for the musical arts.[2] Ultimately he opted to study painting since he believed that music's glory was past and that painting's was still to come. Nonetheless Klee remained deeply involved with music and sought ways to integrate its theoretical aspects within the visual arts. Beginning around 1910 he experimented with musical-pictorial synthesis, and in the 1920s achieved a fully successful approach.

Works such as *Junger Wald* (Young Forest) have been referred to as "operatic,"[3] in the sense that the pen line is analogous to opera's libretto and the color analogous to its orchestration. The line develops the plot and the color enhances it. That is not to say that line is equal to libretto or color equal to orchestration. The emphasis is on theory: that autonomous components serve an integrated purpose.

Klee, who was blessed with an innate aptitude for drawing, recognized the expressive strength of his line and its intimate tie to narration. Although he customarily used line as a boundary for color, in works such as *Junger Wald* he sought to change line's restrictive role. Line and color would no longer define but enrich each other. Indeed Klee's ragged line seems adeptly suited to the hazy patches of underlying color. He allowed the ink to flow into the damp and absorbent paper, creating an effect not unlike early morning mist on trees. So too his line reflects the spindly and frail nature of the individual saplings. The color stains areas of the sheet in green and its uppermost edge in sky blue, but for the most part the color bears little reference to nature's actual tones. It represents a more general harmony that underscores the rhythmic sequence of the pen drawing.

Although Paul Klee was by no means the only twentieth-century artist who focused on the relationship between music and the visual arts, he did provide some of the most meaningful theories. Of the three watercolors by Klee donated on the occasion of the National Gallery's fiftieth anniversary, *Junger Wald* most ably demonstrates Klee's unique musical thinking. It succeeds an earlier operatic work donated by Lessing J. Rosenwald, *Alter Dampfer*, and looks ahead to Klee's further achievements in musical-pictorial synthesis, exemplified by the 1940 watercolor *Dampfer und Segelbote* given by Mr. and Mrs. Paul Mellon. *Junger Wald* pulses with melody and bears proof to the adage that "all art aspires to the condition of music."[4]

Judith Brodie

PROVENANCE
Robert von Hirsch, Basel, sold Sotheby's (*The Robert von Hirsch Collection*, vol. 5), June 1978, 115.

NOTES
1. For the most comprehensive studies of Klee's relationship to music, see Will Grohman, *Paul Klee* (New York, 1954); Richard Verdi, "Musical Influences on the Art of Paul Klee," *Museum Studies* 3 (Chicago, 1968), 81–107; Andrew Kagan, *Paul Klee/Art & Music* (Ithaca and London, 1983).

2. "As time passes I become more and more afraid of my growing love of music. I don't understand myself. I play solo sonatas by Bach: next to them, what is Böcklin? It makes me smile" (1897). See Paul Klee, *The Diaries of Paul Klee, 1898–1918*, ed. Felix Klee (Berkeley and Los Angeles, 1964), 14 (no. 52).

3. Andrew Kagan described operatic works as ones combining Klee's narrow-line drawing with absolute color composition. See Kagan 1983, 95–143.

4. Walter Pater, "The School of Giorgione" (1877), *The Renaissance* (London, 1961), 129.

1925 d. 8.

junger Wald

STUART DAVIS
1892–1964

Abstract Composition, 1927 [1921]
Watercolor and pencil
23¹⁵⁄₁₆ x 18¹⁄₁₆ (60.8 x 45.8)

Gift of
Mr. and Mrs. Frederick R. Mayer

Although *Abstract Composition* is signed and dated 1927, the painting was probably completed in 1921 during a period of rigorous experimentation that Davis undertook following the Armory Show in 1913.[1] The International Exhibition of Modern Art held in the Armory of the Sixty-Ninth Infantry in New York City in February 1913, more commonly called the Armory Show, was, according to Davis, the pivotal event of his early career: "I was enormously excited by the show . . . and I resolved that I would quite definitely have to become a 'modern' artist."[2] In coming to terms with what he had seen of European modernism at the Armory Show and subsequently in New York galleries and avant-garde journals, Davis spent more than a decade exploring the vocabulary of modernism and working through the styles of such European masters as Paul Gauguin, Vincent van Gogh, Henri Matisse, Fernand Léger, Georges Braque, and Pablo Picasso. By the early 1920s Davis had focused his attention on the pictorial issues raised by cubism. In such works as *Abstract Composition* he began to forge the personal style that would mark him as one of the most innovative abstract artists working in America during the early decades of the twentieth century.

Stuart Davis was born in Philadelphia in 1892, the son of Edward W. Davis, art editor of the *Philadelphia Press,* and Helen Stuart Foulke, a sculptor. In an autobiographical essay published in 1945, Davis acknowledged his good fortune by noting that, unlike many other artists, he had encountered no parental resistance when he declared that he wished to study art. On the contrary, Edward Davis, who employed John Sloan, George Luks, William Glackens, and Everett Shinn as illustrators, allowed his son to leave high school to enroll in Robert Henri's art school. Although Davis later

abandoned the urban realism championed by Henri, he repeatedly credited his teacher with providing the guidance and encouragement that later allowed him to create paintings that were not factual reports on the natural world but independent objects.

Abstract Composition, an important and rare work from what has been described as the artist's breakthrough period, is the first drawing by Davis to enter the National Gallery's collection.[3] An experimental work that foreshadows the spatially sophisticated compositions of the artist's maturity, *Abstract Composition* documents Davis' early engagement with the elements of cubism. The subdued colors and sharp linear quality of the picture reflect Davis' concern with planar and spatial relationships.

In a recent essay on the artist's early paintings, William Agee noted that between 1920 and 1922, the period during which *Abstract Composition* was completed, Davis "posed for himself the most fundamental questions about the art of painting, as if he was starting from the very beginning."[4] In 1920, for example, he proposed using only circles and squares to produce works whose simplicity would allow him to explore the purely formal character of art. The paintings that resulted from these experiments have been described as "in some ways radical works, unprecedented in American art."[5] Pictorially rooted in the 1913-1914 collages of Picasso and Braque, at least two paintings from the series seemed to echo "the suprematist and constructivist geometries of Malevitch, El Lissitzsky and Moholy-Nagy."[6]

The deceptively spare *Abstract Composition* reflects Davis' thorough investigation of the language of modernism. Though nonrepresentational in character, it already displays the same surface energy that quickly became the hallmark of the artist's mature style.

Nancy K. Anderson

PROVENANCE
Collection of the artist until his death; Roselle Springer Davis, the artist's widow, until 1979; private collection, New York, until 1986; Hirschl & Adler Galleries, Inc.

NOTES
1. Robert Hunter, co-author with William C. Agee of the Stuart Davis catalogue raisonné, believes this work was actually completed in 1921 and later exhibited at the Downtown Gallery, perhaps under the title "Coving" (no. 11) in *Stuart Davis Exhibition: Recent Paintings, Watercolors, Drawings, Tempera,* 26 Nov.–9 Dec. 1927. Hunter cited other works (private collections) similar in style and materials that are signed and dated 1921.

2. Stuart Davis, *Stuart Davis* (New York, 1945), n.p.

3. William C. Agee, *Stuart Davis: The Breakthrough Years, 1922–1924* (New York, 1987), n.p.

4. Agee 1987.

5. Agee 1987.

6. Agee 1987.

STUART DAVIS 1927

AUGUST SANDER
1876–1964

The Bricklayer, 1929
Gelatin silver photograph, 1950s
19⅞ x 14¾ (50.5 x 37.5)

Gift of Gerhard and Christine Sander

In many ways August Sander seems something of an anachronism. Although all of his important work was made in the twentieth century, his style, at least superficially, seems to have more to do with the nineteenth. Active during the years that witnessed the development and perfection of small, hand-held cameras, he nevertheless continued using a cumbersome, large-format view camera with a slow lens. While his contemporaries from Jacques-Henri Lartigue to Henri Cartier-Bresson celebrated their newfound ability to capture the beauty of the effervescent and transitory moment with fluid, often disjointed or fragmented compositions, Sander persisted in carefully composing and containing his images and in constructing frontal, symmetrical compositions. Like so many nineteenth-century portraits, Sander's bricklayers, farmers, bakers, or bankers, far from being caught unaware, were active participants in the process. His subjects stare directly into the camera with the same intensity and earnestness that their ancestors projected when they had daguerreotype portraits made.

Yet while the style may appear outdated, Sander's methodology and his intention were distinctly of the twentieth century. He wanted to establish a typology that would show the expressive possibilities of human physiognomy within his society; he wanted no less than to create a portrait of, what he called, "Man of the Twentieth Century." Beginning in 1910 he tried to accomplish this by photographing hundreds of different people whom he believed were archetypal subjects, reflective of universal human traits. He searched out individuals of all ages, from all levels of German society and all professions. Although he occasionally identified people by name, he was less concerned with their individual accomplishments and more interested in how they fit into the larger structure, the larger portrait, that he was organizing. Moreover, it was this larger portrait — as he wrote, of "the historical physiognomic

image of a whole generation" — that dictated the style, for it was only once Sander established a uniform method of presentation that the viewer could concentrate on physiognomic differences.[1]

Often Sander photographed people in their own environments — industrialists in their offices, the unemployed on the streets — but just as frequently people came to his studio where he photographed them against a white plane. Occasionally, however, he was forced to photograph outdoors against backgrounds that he found disruptive. In these cases, as in *The Bricklayer,* he retouched out the distracting elements, making the entire background black, with the result that our attention is riveted on the face and shoulders of the young man. While we may wonder how Sander has convinced this man with such a heavy burden to stop long enough to have his portrait taken, we are more immediately struck by the seeming ease with which he carries his load and the dignity with which he projects himself. Although he is a nameless brick carrier, he is nevertheless a person of great dignity.

Generously donated by the photographer's grandson Gerhard Sander and his wife Christine Sander, *The Bricklayer* is not only the first work by Sander to enter the National Gallery's collection, but also the first work by a European photographer, and thus indicates the Gallery's commitment to form a collection of photographs that represents artists of many different nationalities. *The Bricklayer* is one of four examples of this image known to have been printed by the photographer during his lifetime: one vintage eight- by ten-inch print exists in the J. Paul Getty Museum, as well as three prints from the 1950s. Of the three later prints, this is the only large example and one of the few enlargements made by Sander. Its size is an appropriate symbol of the monumentality of the project of which it was an integral part.

Sarah Greenough

PROVENANCE
Gunther Sander, 1964; Gerhard and Christine Sander, 1987.

NOTE
1. Sander, excerpt from "The Nature and Growth of Photography. Lecture Five: Photography as a Universal Language," translated by Anne Halley, printed in *The Massachusetts Review* 19 (Winter 1978), 678.

STANLEY WILLIAM HAYTER
1901–1988

Paysages Urbains, 1930
Portfolio of 6 prints incorporating
drypoint, engraving, and mezzotint
8⅛ x 10½ (20.7 x 26.8)

Gift of Mrs. Robert A. Hauslohner

In the late 1920s Stanley William Hayter made several prints based on urban themes, mostly Parisian street scenes. The culmination of that effort was the publication of *Paysages Urbains*[1] (Urban Landscapes), a portfolio that prefigures the surrealist thinking that characterized much of Hayter's work in the next decade. Each image in the set comprises two superimposed spaces: one a townscape, the other a landscape.[2] This unconventional mixture of settings creates some striking interactions and jarring ambiguities. Certain elements locate themselves fittingly in both settings. Others loom too large or seem oddly miscast. In either case there is an uneasy relationship between reality and invented space that sparks vigor in each print.

Hayter was born in London and studied chemistry and geology at Kings College, where he made his first experiments in printmaking. In 1926, after a brief career as a scientist, he moved to Paris and studied engraving with the Polish-born artist Joseph Hecht. One year later Hayter founded Atelier 17, the cooperative workshop that propelled printmaking to the forefront of modern artistic expression. The roster of artists who passed through Hayter's workshop is remarkably impressive. It includes Calder, Chagall, Ernst, Giacometti, Masson, Miró, Picasso, and—in New York where Hayter relocated during World War II—de Kooning, Motherwell, Pollock, Rothko, and David Smith.[3]

Hayter's association with the surrealists was an informal one based on personal friendships. He met André Masson in 1929 and was influenced by Masson's automatism: the acceptance of automatic impulses from the subliminal mind. That receptivity to the unconscious, without rational intervention, distinguishes even early works by Hayter. In the prints illustrated here the superimposition of landscapes and townscapes creates an eerie sense of isolation similar to surrealist works by Dalí. In *Rue d'Assas* the deeply recessive space is intersected by a barren landscape made up of a solitary moon and horizon line. A figure (in double outline) shadow-dances its way across a windowed facade that admits no hint of life. The landscape component in *Rue de Repos* is similarly barren and suggests a desert scene. A single cactus crosses the horizon, its form repeated in a tiny figure in the furthermost distance. In the foreground a pitcher, comparable in scale to the architecture and resting solidly on an oval shadow, bursts forth with finely scribbled designs and bits of graffiti.

The National Gallery has more than fifty prints by S. W. Hayter, most donated by Lessing J. Rosenwald who met the artist around 1944 and thereafter acquired prints from him directly.[4] In contrast to *Paysages Urbains,* the majority of these works represent Hayter's mid-career accomplishments. This exceptionally attractive group from 1930 is not only the first portfolio that Hayter made but also a striking example of his extreme openness to the process of discovery.

Judith Brodie

PROVENANCE
Purchased from Dolan/Maxwell Gallery, Philadelphia, 1987.

NOTES
1. To be included in Peter Black and Désirée Hayter's forthcoming catalogue raisonné. I thank Peter Black for providing titles for the individual prints.

2. The individual spaces can be identified by media. The townscapes are in drypoint and mezzotint, the landscapes are engraved.

3. From 1940 until 1949, Atelier 17 was associated with the New School for Social Research in New York. In 1950 it was transplanted once again to Paris where it functions to this day. The artists who have worked at Atelier 17 extend far beyond those listed.

4. Ruth E. Fine, *Lessing J. Rosenwald: Tribute to a Collector* [exh. cat. National Gallery of Art] (Washington, 1982), 213.

7/50 SWHayter

7/50 SWHayter

ALBERTO GIACOMETTI
1901–1966

No More Play, 1931–1932
Marble, wood, bronze
1⅝ x 22⅞ x 17¾ (4.1 x 58 x 45.2)

Gift (Partial and Promised) of
Raymond D. Nasher

In the early 1930s, Alberto Giacometti produced an extraordinary series of tabletop tableaux that may stand as his most remarkable sculptural achievement. Reversing the traditional relationship between sculpture and base, these objects, which have been compared to game boards, make the base the central focus of the sculptor's concern, radically redefining the relationship between viewer and object.[1] *No More Play*, a work of great mystery and evocative power, was the culmination of this series.

The title is provided by the words "On ne joue plus" that Giacometti inscribed in reverse script in one corner. The sculpture is a flat, rectangular marble base pitted with round, craterlike depressions that give an almost lunar appearance. In the center are three rectangular holes resembling tombs, each with a cover.

In addition to these marble elements, *No More Play* includes several wood and bronze figurines. Their correct placement is suggested by the earliest visual document of the sculpture, a photograph taken in 1932 by the American surrealist Man Ray.[2] There the top tomb is covered and the bottom two appear with lids ajar. In the bottom tomb lies a skeletonlike object and in the middle tomb a serpent. Two figures, one with upraised arms (probably male), one with only the barest suggestion of arms (probably female), stand in the largest circular cavities at upper right and lower left.

A number of sources have been suggested for *No More Play*, including African wooden game boards with craterlike depressions[3] and a Swiss wooden peasant table.[4] An especially suggestive and convincing source is an altarpiece of the *Last Judgment* by the Florentine master of the early Renaissance, Fra Angelico.[5] Commissioned in 1431 for the Florentine church of Santa Maria degli Angeli and now in the museum of San Marco, Florence, Fra Angelico's altarpiece depicts at center a double row of tombs, stone lids ajar, from which the elect have risen to heaven. The tombs recede in a straight line in sharp perspective, dividing the altarpiece into two halves, just as the area of tombs divides *No More Play* into two sides. At right in the altarpiece the damned are gathered in a series of pits and cauldrons that resemble the circular and oval depressions of *No More Play*. Giacometti may have remembered Fra Angelico's altarpiece from a trip to Florence in 1920, and he might also have seen it reproduced in a monograph on Fra Angelico published in Paris in 1929.[6]

No More Play was executed in a preliminary plaster (now in the Museum of Modern Art, New York). The marble version figured in Giacometti's first exhibition in America, held at the Julien Levy Gallery in December 1934. On that occasion the object was given by Giacometti to Levy, the gallery owner whose interest in surrealism was largely responsible for introducing the movement to this country.

The National Gallery collection now includes seven Giacometti bronzes, including another surrealist work, *The Invisible Object (Hands Holding the Void)*, 1935. *No More Play* will be the earliest Giacometti in the Gallery, and the only representation of his tabletop tableaux. This work, crucial to the history of twentieth-century art, makes a magnificent addition to the collection.

Jeremy Strick

NOTES
1. Rosalind Kraus, *Passages in Modern Sculpture* (New York, 1977), 118. This was subsequently discussed in Jeremy Strick, entry on *No More Play*, in *A Century of Modern Sculpture*, ed. Steven A. Nash [exh. cat. Dallas Museum of Art] (New York, 1987), 154–155.

2. *Cahiers d'Art 7*, nos. 8–10, 1932.

3. Rosalind Kraus, "Giacometti," in *"Primitivism" in 20th Century Art* [exh. cat. The Museum of Modern Art] (New York, 1984), 524.

4. Carola Giedion-Welcker, *Contemporary Sculpture: An Evolution in Volume and Space*, rev. ed. (New York, 1960), 98.

5. Nan Rosenthal, "Giacometti's *No More Play*, 1931–32," at Viewpoints and Visions, symposium on modern sculpture at Southern Methodist University, Dallas, 1987.

6. Paul Muratoff, *Fra Angelico* (Paris, 1929), LVII.

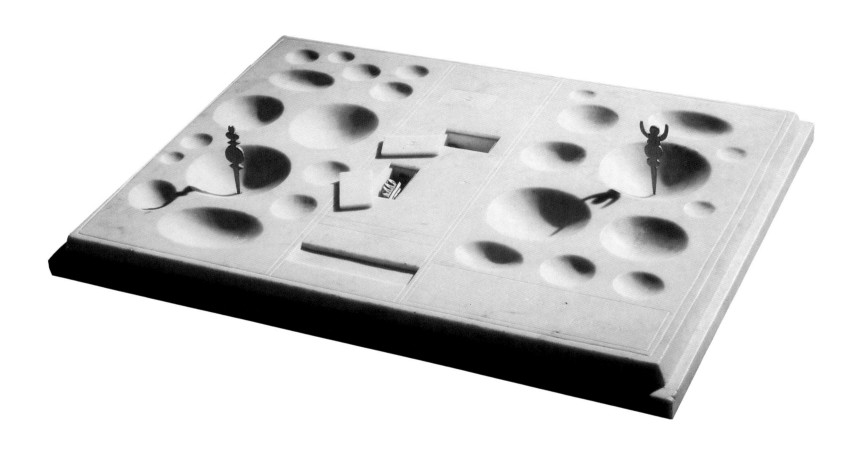

PABLO PICASSO
1881–1973

*Two Men Contemplating a Bust of a
Woman's Head,* 1931
Graphite
12¹³⁄₁₆ x 10¼ (32.9 x 26.1)

Six Circus Horses with Riders, 1905
Pen and ink
9¾ x 12⅞ (24.7 x 32.7)

Gift of
Walter H. and Leonore Annenberg

In the spring of 1931, in search of more
space than his Paris studio permitted, Picasso took possession of a seventeenth-
century chateau northwest of the city at
Boisgeloup, near Gisors. There he converted the stables into various studios, including one with an etching press and several others devoted to sculpture. In these
Picasso continued an activity he had begun
in the late 1920s, working on welded metal
constructions with the assistance of his old
friend and fellow Spaniard, the sculptor
Julio Gonzalez, who was a skilled smith
and welder. Picasso also returned in the
Boisgeloup studios to techniques he had used
years earlier for sculpture, modeling in plaster and clay. In the course of the early 1930s
he modeled a series of monumental female
heads inspired by the features of his mistress,
Marie-Thérèse Walter. These ranged in style
from nearly classical to deformations of
human form with enlarged rounded pro-
tuberances, such as noses seeming to grow
directly from foreheads, as they do in the
carved wooden figures of the African Baga
tribe, an example of which Picasso owned
and kept at Boisgeloup.

The serene yet introspective bust being
observed carefully by two men in the Annenberg pencil drawing, dated 27 November 1931, bears a close resemblance to the
most classical of the modeled heads of Marie-
Thérèse, *Head of a Woman,* 1931.[1] It is close
in subject to an ink drawing of 4 August
1931, in which two men in shorts observe
a sculpture of a female nude and to another
ink drawing of that date in which a bearded
figure in shorts is at work on a monumental
sculptural bust he derives from the features
of a model posing nearby.[2] In still other
drawings of the summer and autumn of 1931,
notably a pencil drawing (Phyllis Hattis Fine
Arts, New York) of the same size, date, and
medium as the Annenberg gift and an im-

portant painting, *The Sculptor,* completed 7
December 1931 (Musée Picasso, Paris), the
subject of the sculptor contemplating a bust
of Marie-Thérèse is further explored.[3] While
none of the male figures in these drawings
or the painting have features that resemble
Picasso's, the theme of the artist in his sculpture studio is an autobiographical one. It
seems reasonable to speculate that if one
of the male figures in the Annenberg gift
may be said to represent an idealized Picasso,
the other male figure may be his friend
Gonzalez, so frequently at Picasso's side at
Boisgeloup.

Both the Annenberg drawing and the
Hattis drawing of the same day, in which a
bearded male in shorts at left observes a
monumental bust in profile at right while a
model sits cross-legged on the floor in between, are drawn on glossy, parchmentlike
paper with a crisp, unhesitating line reminiscent of silverpoint.

The 1931 *Two Men* and one of the An-
nenbergs' other fiftieth-anniversary gifts, a
1905 ink drawing by Picasso, *Six Circus Horses
with Riders,* are two of three Picasso drawings given on this occasion, bringing to nine
the Gallery's total of Picasso drawings. The
1931 drawing is related to the Gallery's set
of a hundred etchings by Picasso, the Vollard Suite, 1930–1937, where the subject
of the sculptor in his studio with his model

and his work is richly explored in forty-five
prints. The *Six Circus Horses* relates closely
to the Gallery's great circus-period oil of
1905, *The Family of Saltimbanques* (Chester
Dale Collection), and especially to the drypoint *The Watering Place,* of which there is
a fine impression in the Gallery given by
Peter B. Josten.

Nan Rosenthal

PROVENANCE
Two Men Contemplating a Bust of a Woman's Head:
Curtis O. Baer Collection. *Six Circus Horses with
Riders*: Leo Stein; Henry Kleeman; Curt Val-
entin, New York; Curtis O. Baer Collection.

NOTES
1. In Werner Spies, *Sculpture by Picasso* (New
York, 1971), 304, the *Head* (no. 128) is dated
1932. However William Rubin, ed., *Pablo Picasso: A Retrospective* [exh. cat. The Museum of
Modern Art] (New York, 1980), 284, dated the
sculpture 1931, which seems confirmed by the
close resemblance of the drawn bust in the dated
Annenberg drawing to the sculpture.

2. Eric M. Zafran, *Master Drawings from Titian
to Picasso: the Curtis O. Baer Collection* [exh. cat.
High Museum of Art] (Atlanta, 1980), 154.

3. The Hattis drawing and a very similar work
(collection Marina Picasso) are reproduced in Ulrich Weisner, ed., *Picassos Klassizismus* [exh. cat.
Kunsthalle Bielefeld] (Bielefeld, 1988), 273, 335.

ARISTIDE MAILLOL
1861–1944

The Three Nymphs, 1930–1938
Lead
62 (157.5)

Gift (Partial and Promised) of
Lucille Ellis Simon

The ancient Mediterranean tradition of feminine beauty has received its most compelling twentieth-century sculptural interpretations in the work of Maillol. His nearly exclusive subject was a full-bodied, harmonious type of female figure, substantial, serene, and still. Carefully studied from nature, his statues transform their individual models according to the artist's ideal of purified forms and clear structure, recalling his comment, "I am seeking architecture and volumes. Sculpture is architecture, the balance of masses. . . ."[1]

The Three Nymphs represents one of his latest creations, developed over seven years from initial study of a single young model. His pupil Lucille Passavant posed in 1930 for a standing figure.[2] Over the next few years Maillol developed three variations on the resulting sculpture. The central figure, conceived first, raises both open hands to breast height in a gesture of greeting or offering. The other two statues, facing her, are almost mirror images of each other except for subtle differences in movement and gesture. Each stands with the weight on one sturdy leg, the arm above it bending to raise and extend a hand toward the central figure. The arm over the relaxed outer leg hangs serenely down, slightly away from the torso to leave its slowly curving contour visible. The sense of balance Maillol sought is achieved in these figures, individually and together.

The newly completed plaster group appeared as *Nymphs of the Meadow* in the exhibition *Les Maîtres de l'Art Indépendant* at the Petit Palais, Paris, in 1937. There the figures wore crowns of daisies, buttercups, and sweet marjoram. Their hands were united by a garland of unknown material, and the title *Meadow Flowers* was also considered for the group. Maillol rejected the inevitable suggestion that it be called "The Three Graces," claiming "they are too powerful to represent the Graces."[3] He nevertheless chose a timeless identification as beings from ancient myth and poetry, inhabitants of the fields and woods.

These majestic, entranced figures with their gentle smiles have particularly touched the imagination of Maillol's admirers. For Waldemar-George they evoke the goddesses of antiquity who "solicit the judgment of an unseen Paris."[4] Rewald, noting the aged sculptor's concentration on figures of "very young girls, radiant with youth and freshness, full of lyrical grace and a sensual poetic feeling," saw this as a work that sums up "all his knowledge and all his feeling."[5] For Cladel the nymphs embody "the most tender homage Maillol ever devoted to the springtime of woman."[6] The sculptor himself, around the time he finished this work, suggested what such images meant to him: "There is a limit to physical love, imposed by age, but the love of beauty does not grow old or change, and we artists have the consolation of translating it into forms."[7]

In the National Gallery *The Three Nymphs* will crown a series of individual Maillol figures, complete and partial, of standing women ranging in date from c. 1910–1933. This example, cast in lead, is the Gallery's first Maillol in that material frequently employed in the great tradition of French garden sculpture.[8]

Alison Luchs

NOTES

1. Judith Cladel, *Aristide Maillol. Sa vie — Son oeuvre — Ses idées* (Paris, 1937), 148.

2. Sotheby's, New York, *Important Modern Sculpture* (15 May 1984), 96, presumably based on information from the owner Dina Vierny, Maillol's last model, devoted friend, and the historian of his work.

3. Cladel 1937, 120–121.

4. Waldemar-George, *Aristide Maillol* (London, 1965), 58.

5. John Rewald, *Maillol* (London, 1939), 22.

6. Cladel 1937, 121.

7. Cladel 1937, 156.

8. Five other casts in lead, the material preferred by Maillol for this group, are recorded: at the Tate Gallery, London; the Musée National d'Art Moderne, Paris; the Kunsthalle, Bern; a U.S. private collection; and the Meadows Museum and Gallery, Dallas (formerly Wildenstein, New York). Bronzes, in addition to the one sold at Sotheby's in 1984 (see n. 2), are at the Minneapolis Institute of Arts and the Musée de Poitiers. See Ronald Alley, *Tate Gallery Catalogues. The Foreign Paintings, Drawings and Sculpture* (London, 1959), 130-132, with detailed bibliography. Ay-Whang Hsia of Wildenstein kindly updated the information.

WALKER EVANS
1903–1975

Berenice Abbott, 1929
Gelatin silver photograph
3½ x 3¹/₁₆ (8.9 x 7.8)

Gift of
Mr. and Mrs. Harry H. Lunn, Jr.
in Honor of Jacob Kainen

*Hudson Street Boarding House,
New York,* 1931
Gelatin silver photograph
6³/₁₆ x 8 (15.7 x 20.3)

Gift of the Clive Gray Family

Mount Pleasant, Pennsylvania, July 1935
Gelatin silver print
7³/₈ x 8⁷/₈ (18.7 x 22.5)

Gift of
Mr. and Mrs. Harry H. Lunn, Jr.

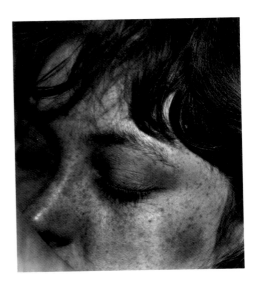

"I go to the street for the education of my eye and for the sustenance that the eye needs—the hungry eye, and my eye is hungry."[1]

Throughout his long career, Walker Evans was a voracious cataloguer of facts, accumulating vast archives of photographs of vernacular objects. He focused his camera on simple, everyday things—barber shops and billboards, Main Streets and back alleys—that had not yet through repeated use achieved the status of icon. Although he cultivated a style of presenting things simply as they are, and although his work overall takes on the quality of an inventory, he never confused his photographs for literal documents. When asked if photographs could be documentary as well as works of art, he responded, "Documentary? That's a very sophisticated and misleading word. . . . The term should be *documentary style.* An example of a literal document would be a police photograph of a murder scene. You see, a document has use, whereas art is really useless. Therefore art is never a document, though it certainly can adopt that style."[2] In another interview he amplified this statement, noting "the style of detachment and record is another matter. That, applied to

the world around us, is what I do with the camera."[3]

Evans, however, did not immediately discover this straightforward approach. His earliest work from the late 1920s is self-consciously artistic. For example, in his portrait of *Berenice Abbott,* he used extreme close-ups and unusual angles. And, more significantly, there is little psychological separation between the photographer and his subject, as his feelings for her are clearly expressed. Yet he quickly shed this more sentimental style and by the early 1930s, as in *Hudson Street Boarding House, New York,* adopted the cooler, more sharply-focused approach that characterized his work for the rest of his life. This photograph, as in *Mount Pleasant, Pennsylvania* and so many of his other works, is about emptiness. Empty bedrooms, empty living rooms, empty train stations, and empty streets are the subjects of many of his photographs. Devoid of people, they are, nevertheless, redolent of human life. The elegant, lucid details of the bed and bedroom, the street and its surroundings tell us more about their inhabitants than we could possibly garner if we saw them with our own eyes.

These two photographs are also indicative of the great influence on his art, not of the work of other visual artists, but of literature, and particularly Flaubert. Adopting the French author's naturalism and his objectivity of treatment, Evans emphatically stated that he believed "in staying out, the way Flaubert does in his writing."[4] A detached, non-existent observer, Evans did not project himself into either of these two photographs from the 1930s. Instead it is in the cumulation of details—the empty unpaved street, neatly trimmed hedges, and undulating shadows in the foreground of *Mount Pleasant, Pennsylvania,* for example—that impart meaning to the image.

These three works, along with the twenty-one other Evans photographs generously donated by Mr. and Mrs. Harry H. Lunn, Jr. and three more kindly given by the Clive Gray family, are significant additions to the Gallery's growing collection of this artist's work. Both the Lunn and Gray gifts include examples from throughout Evans' career, and they have particularly enhanced our representation of his work from the late 1920s to the late 1930s.

Sarah Greenough

PROVENANCE
Berenice Abbott and *Mount Pleasant, Pennsylvania*: George Rinhart, 1974; Lunn Gallery, 1975; Mr. and Mrs. Harry H. Lunn, Jr., 1982. *Hudson Street Boarding House, New York*: George Rinhart, 1974; Lunn Gallery, 1975; Clive Gray, 1982.

NOTES
1. "Walker Evans, Visiting Artist," quoted in Beaumont Newhall, *Essays and Images* (New York, 1980), 314.

2. Leslie Katz, "An Interview with Walker Evans," *Photography in Print,* ed. Vickie Goldberg (New York, 1981), 364.

3. Paul Cummings, "Walker Evans," *Artists in Their Own Words* (New York, 1979), 95.

4. "Walker Evans on Himself," ed. Lincoln Caplan, *The New Republic* 175 (13 November 1976), 25.

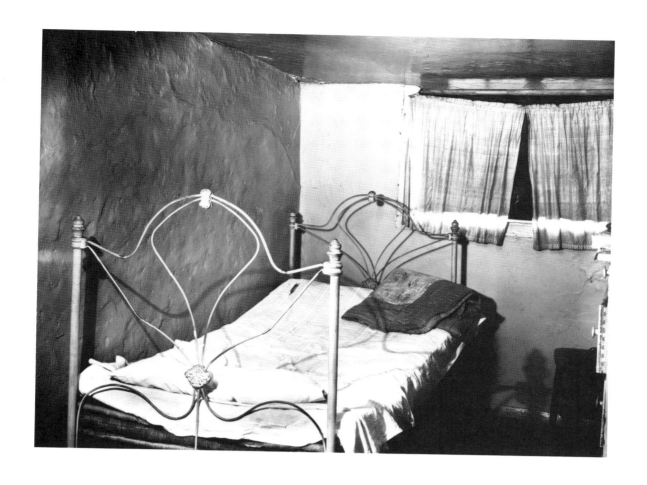

LISETTE MODEL
1906–1983

Promenade des Anglais, 1934
Gelatin silver photograph
13¾ x 10¹¹⁄₁₆ (35 x 27.2)

Man with Pamphlets, 1933–1938
Gelatin silver photograph
13¹³⁄₁₆ x 10¹³⁄₁₆ (35.1 x 27.5)

Gift of
Gerhard Sander and Kathleen Ewing

Often when a photographer presents us with a frozen slice of life we feel that if we were just quick enough in our reflexes, we too might be able to record such a scene. Yet we never have this sensation when looking at Lisette Model's photographs. The point of view in her works is so extreme that we are confident we would never see such a scene under normal circumstances. So highly charged and sharply described are her photographs that we feel she has somehow changed the real into the super real, the mundane into the extreme.

Model's famous statement, "Don't shoot 'till the subject hits you in the pit of your stomach," appears as if it could be applied both figuratively and literally to *Promenade des Anglais*. Made only a year after she began photographing, it was taken in Nice, France. One senses that she stalked this man sleeping in his chair, silently circling him like a lion moving in closer and closer, until she was so near that his toe could easily kick her camera lens, but her shot could not miss. Yet her prey is not caught totally off guard: although his left eye appears to be deep in sleep, rolling back into his head, his right eye is tracking her every action; his hands are not limp and relaxed with sleep but closed in careful circles, as if ready to move quickly. The woman in the background is also well aware of the intruder's presence and stares suspiciously at Model. And yet all is not quite as it seems: when we look at the full frame of the negative for this image it is apparent that much of its confrontational quality comes from Model's reconstruction of this image in the darkroom.[1] By cropping it from a square image to a vertical one, Model focused attention on the man and, more specifically, his shoe.

Much of Model's art is rooted in European painting in the 1930s. Her use of satire, as in the *Man with Pamphlets*, suggests the work of George Grosz of this same period. Making no attempt to remain an objective outsider, Model again brought her camera in very close. Although her photograph emphasizes his fatness and poor clothes, she did not make fun of him. Rather, one senses that she was as fascinated with him for his peculiarities as she was the man in Nice and wanted to learn more about both men by photographing them. In the 1950s she said, "When I want to discover something, when I want to get an answer in this world which I don't understand because nobody does, then I take the camera, and I find out what strikes me. And this thing that strikes me I photograph, and that is in one way or another the answer."[2]

Model claims an important place in the history of photography not only because of the strength of her images but also for her significant role as a teacher. She immigrated to the United States in 1938 and was an influential force on many younger American photographers, especially Diane Arbus. Until Gerhard Sander and Kathleen Ewing donated these two prints, plus *Reflections, Fifty-Seventh Street*, 1939–1940, the National Gallery had in its collection no examples of her bold, confrontational art, with its graphic predictions of so much post-World War II photography.

Sarah Greenough

PROVENANCE
Gerhard Sander, 1979; Gerhard Sander and Kathleen Ewing, 1990.

NOTES
1. Ann Thomas, *Lisette Model* (Ottawa, 1990), 48–49.

2. Ann Winters, transcript of a tape of Sid Grossman's class, 1950, quoted in Thomas 1990, 115.

EDWARD WESTON
1886–1958

Dunes, Oceano, 1936
Gelatin silver photograph
7⅝ x 9⁹⁄₁₆ (19.4 x 24.3)

Gift (Partial and Promised) of
Katherine L. Meier and
Edward J. Lenkin

In 1937 Edward Weston became the first photographer to be awarded a Guggenheim Fellowship. Freed from the necessity of running his portrait business, he packed up his car, married Charis Wilson, and together they traveled widely throughout the West. It has often been commented upon that, with this trip, Weston's work changed markedly: new subjects, new concerns, and a new style gradually begin to emerge in his art. Instead of focusing on the significant details of plants, rocks, or the human form, he quite literally pulled his camera back and addressed the object within its larger environment; instead of seeking reductive abstraction he sought complexity, photographing larger, more open and fluid scenes that frequently included many different and often competing elements.

In many ways, the photographs that he made in 1936 at the sand dunes in Oceano, California, are pivotal images. They both sum up his previous work and predict its future course. Entranced with peppers, rocks, and trees, Weston had made few nudes between 1928 and 1933. Yet beginning in late 1933, when he met Charis Wilson, his interest in this subject was rekindled, and in 1936, when Charis accompanied Weston to Oceano, he made many studies of her nude on the sand dunes. In addition, he also photographed the dunes alone. As with so many of his earlier works, the subject assumes the qualities of the female form. Using deep shadows contrasted with brilliant white sand, Weston created a series of photographs that are as sensual and sensuous as any of his studies of the human body. As in *Dunes, Oceano,* the forms undulate and twist with all the complexity, subtlety, grace, and bewitching charm of the human figure.

Yet in this work our eye is not contained entirely within the shallow and two-dimensional space of the foreground, but instead drifts up to the horizon, glimpsing the mountains and sky beyond this vista. In the years immediately prior to 1936, horizons had appeared very infrequently in Weston's work, for he preferred to focus his camera on a tightly contained and controlled detail. When they do appear one often suspects it is because there was no way to eliminate them. In *Dunes, Oceano* the horizon, mountains, and clouds serve to remind us, subtly but insistently, that this is not a surrogate human body, but a beautiful portion of nature that is part of a much larger, more complex, and potentially less controllable whole.

Katherine L. Meier and Edward J. Lenkin have graciously donated this superb photograph, the first Weston in the National Gallery's collection. As we build our holdings of strong representations of the art of major twentieth-century American photographers from Alfred Stieglitz to Robert Frank, Weston is and will be a crucial figure. *Dunes, Oceano* is further enhanced by Weston's inscription on the verso to Kurt Edward Fishback, the son of his friend Glen Fishback: "Dear Kurt Edward—This is from another Edward, a photographer, who made this photograph, perhaps for you; at least I hope you like it—your father does. By the way, you have been given one of my names, isn't that funny!" The young Fishback not only adopted Weston's first name, but also his profession as a photographer.

Sarah Greenough

PROVENANCE
Kurt Edward Fishback, 1942; sale (Sotheby's) to Katherine L. Meier and Edward J. Lenkin, 1987.

Edward Weston 1936

EMIL NOLDE
1867–1956

Red and Yellow Poppies and a
Blue Delphinium, c. 1930/1940
Watercolor
10⅞ x 17⅞ (27.5 x 45.5)

Gift of Alexander M. and
Judith W. Laughlin

Wherever Emil Nolde made a rural summer home for himself, he planted flowers—immense quantities of flowers that were said to have astonished his peasant neighbors who had never seen such dazzling displays.[1] Between 1906 and 1908 Nolde began painting flowers with the highly saturated, evocative colors that he preferred as he moved from his early impressionist phase into his mature expressionism. But it was in the 1930s and early 1940s that he produced his best and most renowned floral images. Nolde had by then established what was to be his final home on the Frisian coast at Seebüll, a few miles from the village in which he had been born. Here he made his most spectacular garden, which in turn provided inspiration and subject matter for some of his most cherished works.[2] He revealed his deep attachment to this site in his expressed wish that he and his wife, Ada, be buried there; he formed their initials with flower beds in the garden.[3] Many of the Seebüll flower pictures are watercolors, and, like the Laughlin's *Red and Yellow Poppies and a Blue Delphinium,* are signed but undated.

Red and Yellow Poppies and a Blue Delphinium is undoubtedly one of the watercolors that Nolde produced at Seebüll, and it is one of the most spectacular of this exalted group. The burning red-orange and gold of the poppies glow against the icy blue of the delphinium and limpid green of the foliage. It is a brilliant contrapuntal harmony, composed of the most intense chromatic themes. We can see that Nolde was intrigued by and that he encouraged the watercolor's tendency to spread freely from his brush across the damp paper, apparently of its own volition. He said that the running colors created forms "as if through themselves," forms that seemed to manifest powerful images from his subconscious. He felt as if he were working in partnership with strangely animated, profoundly expressive materials.[4]

This gift represents a significant addition to the National Gallery's present holdings of just two Nolde watercolors, and it complements works already in the collection by other German expressionists. The Gallery owns, for example, an exquisite watercolor of yellow iris by Karl Schmidt-Rottluff, painted at about the same time as *Red and Yellow Poppies and a Blue Delphinium.*[5] Nolde was briefly part of Die Brücke from 1906 to 1907, and the young artists in this group, including Schmidt-Rottluff, benefited greatly from their exposure to Nolde's work and ideas.[6] After leaving Die Brücke, Nolde remained friendly with its members. *Red and Yellow Poppies and a Blue Delphinium* is a quintessential expression of Nolde's profoundly felt spiritual link with the powerful forces of nature, a sensibility much admired and shared by the Brücke artists.

Virginia Tuttle Clayton

PROVENANCE
M. Knoedler and Co., Inc., New York, 1984;
Stiftung Seebüll Ada und Emil Nolde.

NOTES
1. Werner Haftmann, *Emil Nolde* (New York, 1959), no. 29.

2. Haftmann 1959, 36; Martin Urban, "Die Stiftung Seebüll Ada und Emil Nolde," in Walter Jens, *Emil Nolde* [exh. cat. Wurttembergischen Kunstvereins and Stiftung Seebüll Ada und Emil Nolde] (Stuttgart and Seebüll, 1988), 236–237.

3. Peter Selz, *Emil Nolde* [exh. cat. The Museum of Modern Art] (New York, 1963), 49.

4. Haftmann 1959, 34–35.

5. Karl Schmidt-Rottluff, *Yellow Iris,* c. 1935, National Gallery of Art, Rosenwald Collection, 1945.5.1324.

6. Haftmann 1959, 22–23; Manfred Reuther, "Die Graphik des Malers Emil Nolde," in Stuttgart and Seebüll 1988, 189–192.

EMIL NOLDE
1867–1956

*Sunflowers, Pink and White Dahlias,
and a Blue Delphinium,* c. 1930/1940
Watercolor
18½ x 14 (46.9 x 3.55)

Gift of Margaret Mellon Hitchcock

*Sunflowers, Pink and White Dahlias, and a
Blue Delphinium* is another significant addition to the National Gallery's group of
German expressionist watercolors. This resplendent work and *Red and Yellow Poppies
and a Blue Delphinium*[1] represent the first
of Nolde's magnificent flower pieces to enter our graphic arts collection. Here again
Nolde has crowded the foreground plane
with brilliant patches of color, conveying an
impassioned message with his "floral icons." [2]
He has focused closely on just the flowers
and a few of their leaves; looming toward
us and isolated from their setting, they become almost surreal in their intensity of
expression.

Sunflowers seem to have had a special
significance for Nolde.[3] An ardent admirer
of van Gogh and his sunflower paintings,
Nolde often portrayed sunflowers both in
watercolor and oil, sometimes showing them
as they pass their prime and bow their heads
toward the earth in preparation for drop-
ping their seeds. The sunflower at the lower
edge of this composition, just left of center,
is reaching that moment of somber acqui-
escence. While sunflowers and dahlias—frequently paired by Nolde—both blossom in
mid to late summer, delphiniums are an early
season flower. Such blues are scarce in the
garden as the summer wears on, however,
and Nolde's color harmony demanded this
hue. He must have felt compelled in this
instance to suspend the requirements of
horticultural veracity in the interest of
constructing a more perfect chromatic
composition.

Virginia Tuttle Clayton

PROVENANCE
Stuttgarter Kunstkabinett, 1962.

NOTES
1. Also a Fiftieth Anniversary Gift to the National Gallery of Art.

2. William S. Bradley, *Emil Nolde and German
Expressionism: A Prophet in His Own Land,* no.
52 in *Studies in the Fine Arts. The Avant-Garde*
(Ann Arbor, 1986), 106.

3. Peter Selz, *Emil Nolde* [exh. cat. The Museum
of Modern Art] (New York, 1963), 49.

GEORGES ROUAULT
1871–1958

Laquais, 1937
Sugarlift aquatint
17³⁄₁₆ x 13⁵⁄₁₆ (43.7 x 33.8)

Christ de face, 1938
Sugarlift aquatint
13¾ x 9¹³⁄₁₆ (34.9 x 24.8)

Gift of Dr. and Mrs. Frederick Mulder
in Memory of David Jonathan Mulder

These rare artist's proofs were made in preparation for a suite of thirty color aquatints that Rouault began in 1936. Though they were intended as illustrations for an edition of Charles Baudelaire's famous collection of poems, *Les Fleurs du Mal,* the twelve prints that Rouault actually completed were never published in book form. The artist had initially undertaken plans for the book in the late 1920s with his dealer Ambroise Vollard, but the publication never came to fruition. When Vollard died in 1939 in the midst of the *Fleurs du Mal* project, considerable conflict and litigation arose regarding the ownership of Rouault's works. This situation partially accounts for the termination of the venture.

Usually referred to as *Les Fleurs du Mal III,* this set of prints was Rouault's third in a series of projects related to Baudelaire's poetry. *Les Fleurs du Mal I* consisted of fourteen monochrome intaglios originally printed in 1926–1927. However, it was not until 1966 that Rouault's daughter Isabelle, who had acquired the plates, had them published in book form with thirteen of Baudelaire's poems. A second project, *Les Fleurs du Mal II,* consisted of several heliogravure studies, some of which were never completed, while others were modified and became part of the *Fleurs du Mal III* series. This set, along with a title page dated 1940, was issued by Roger Lacourière in an edition of 250. There were also a few maquettes of the 307-page book assembled by the Imprimerie Nationale.

Rouault conceived the project as a kind of posthumous collaboration between himself and Baudelaire, with whom he felt a deep, spiritual kinship. He did not create his prints as literal illustrations of the poems, but as pictorial evocations of the poet's highly metaphorical imagery. As the artist himself explained, "I shall count myself happy if it can be said of these engravings that I have entered a little into the atmosphere of the poem, not as an overscrupulous servant aim-

ing to make a commentary on the text, but as a modest and understanding brother."[1] In fact, the imagery of the prints is entirely in keeping with Rouault's work in other media from the same period. The face of Christ, particularly the closely cropped, elongated visage depicted here, is one of the most frequently repeated motifs of Rouault's oeuvre. The caricatured features of the *Laquais* (footman) relate to Rouault's countless images of clowns, judges, and grotesques.

Though an experienced printmaker by the 1930s, it was not until that decade that Rouault turned to the medium of aquatint. To make color prints in that medium, he used the sugarlift technique, which allowed him to draw directly on the copper plate with the freedom of a pen or brush. He achieved a rich, granular surface quality, made possible through the aquatint process, and lush, painterly layers of color. Characteristic of Rouault's style in the 1930s, the uncon-

ventional, almost dissonant color scheme is checked by the generous and emphatic use of black.

The National Gallery's extensive holdings of Rouault's graphic work include the twelve prints from *Les Fleurs du Mal III.* In comparing these proofs with the final edition one can detect many changes the artist made in the latter to clarify and tighten his composition, as well as to subdue the color. The proofs, so remarkable for their loose, vigorous handling, are even more dramatically expressionistic than the final product.

Marla Prather

PROVENANCE
Roger Lacourière; by gift to private collection; purchased by Frederick Mulder in 1988.

NOTE
1. Quoted in François Chapon and Isabelle Rouault, *Rouault: l'Oeuvre gravée* (Monte Carlo, 1978), 44.

WALKER EVANS
1903–1976

Untitled (Subway Portrait), 1938–1941
Gelatin silver photograph
4⅜ x 5⅜ (11.2 x 13.6)

Untitled (Subway Portrait), 1938–1941
Gelatin silver photograph
4⅞ x 7⁹⁄₁₆ (12.4 x 19.2)

Gift of Kent and Marcia Minichiello

According to section 1050.9 of the Metropolitan Transit Authority's rules for passengers, it is illegal to photograph in the New York subways.[1] But that is not what makes Walker Evans' subway series so arresting. Descending into the depths of the city, surrounded by deafening noise, blazing lights, cavernous shadows, grime, and pungent odors, Evans returned to the surface with a group of photographs that are striking not only for their subject matter but also for the conceptual framework that created them. With a 35mm camera concealed beneath his coat, its lens sticking out between two buttons, Evans imposed a rigid structure on this work that is remarkable for its lack of control. He consciously abdicated all the means that a photographer normally uses to make a picture: he did not look through the lens, he did not arrange his subjects or coach their expressions, he did not regulate his lighting or exposures, and he could not even determine what was in his frame. Evans further restricted himself to sitting on a bench—thus he could not change the angle of his shot—and, with one exception, he confined himself to photographing the people sitting across from him.[2] The only thing he did control was whether or when to press the shutter release in his sleeve.

At first glance these photographs seem radically at odds with Evans' previous work. When he began this project in 1938 he had just published *American Photographs*, which, although it contains some candid street photographs, is characterized by a cool, straightforward, documentary style. Emotionally detached, those photographs are, on the whole, carefully composed studies made with a large view camera of empty street scenes and quiet interiors in rural and suburban America. In his afterword, Lincoln Kirstein celebrated the cerebral, meticulous order of Evans' compositions and chastised the current craze of candid photography "with its great pretensions to accuracy, its promise of sensational truth."[3]

At precisely this same time Evans embarked on the subway series.[4] His aim was to invest portraiture with the same neutrality and seeming transparency of his other work. In order to do this not only did he have to become invisible so that his subjects did not become self-consciously aware of his purpose, but, in a very real sense, he also had to make them unaware of themselves. He found that the subway not only leveled society, but it also neutralized the individual. Within this environment Evans discovered that the masks people wore at all other times melted away. Lost in thought, these people are presented simply as they are, without artifice or sentimentality.

Striving for what he called "the ultimate purity" of the "record method," Evans equated this project to a "line-up" of average people and suggested that he would have liked to act like a photographic sponge, recording and displaying everybody who innocently sat across from him.[5] These two photographs are selected from fifteen generously given in 1990 by Kent and Marcia Minichiello in honor of the fiftieth anniversary of the National Gallery, fourteen of which were shown in the 1966 Museum of Modern Art exhibition of Evans' subway series. They graciously complement the Minichiellos' 1988 gift of fifty-seven subway photographs. Together they incisively comment on Evans' working methods and demonstrate that in the subway series he did not abandon all artistic control. This group contains numerous examples of different croppings of the same frame or variant shots of individuals or groups of riders, clearly demonstrating that Evans transferred artistic manipulation from the exposure of the film to the selective process in the darkroom.

Sarah Greenough

PROVENANCE
George Rinhart, 1974; Lunn Gallery, 1975; Kent and Marcia Minichiello, 1983.

NOTES
1. See "35-mm Crime: Shooting Photographs in the Subway," *New York Times* (20 October 1988), B1.

2. The exception is the last photograph published in *Many Are Called* (Boston, 1966), 177, a photograph—looking lengthwise down the center of the subway car—of a blind accordion player.

3. *American Photographs* (New York, 1938), 191.

4. These photographs are usually dated 1938–1941. However Jerry L. Thompson in *Walker Evans at Work* (New York, 1982), 15, noted that they were made in 1938 and 1941. Evans was not the only photographer at this time to photograph in the subways: among others, Lee Sievan and David Robbins, members of the Photo-League, also explored this subject.

5. In Thompson 1982, 160–161.

HENRI MATISSE
1869–1954

The Oriental, 1939
Charcoal on paper
24 x 16¹⁄₁₆ (60.96 x 40.96)

Gift of
Judith H. and Franklin D. Murphy

This large and fascinating work shows the great strengths of Matisse's mature charcoal drawing style and a quite unusual portrait subject. Though Matisse often sought interesting and exotic sitters, this drawing stands out as one of his most freely interpreted and stylistically extreme heads.

One of our century's greatest and most inventive draftsmen, Matisse believed the human body had connections to the vegetal world. In this sheet, originally titled *L'Asiatique,* he has given us a particularly organic and flowery shape. The face is portrayed as a large leaf or bulb, with treelike hair, trunklike neck, petal-shaped ears. The eyes are highly stylized and his signature "bow" mouth is doubled by another mouth outline to its left. The face and neck have been progressively tightened. As the artist compressed the forms he left the estompe erasures as shadows, ghosts of the previous drawing. The result is a vital, actively charged image.

A remarkable slightly smaller charcoal, *Portrait: Dancer (The Buddha),* also of 1939, presents another version of this same subject. Now in the Musée Matisse, Cimiez, that powerful drawing has even more exaggerated features and a tulip-shaped face. Recent research at the Archives Henri Matisse has confirmed that the subject of both these drawings was a dancer from the Ballets de Monte Carlo.[1] In 1937–1939 the artist was designing the costumes and stage sets for *Rouge et Noir,* a ballet "symphonically" choreographed by Léonid Massine to Shostakovich's First Symphony.[2] A number of smaller, more representational drawings of this model are documented in the Matisse Archives.[3]

Matisse's normal creative progression was to establish a "theme," where he sought to capture the identity of the directly observed subject in detail. Various drawings catalogued in the Matisse Archives perform this function. Next, Matisse would turn away from the sitter and work from memory, relating more the spirit of the elements he discovered in the first sittings. Their pure inventiveness is evidence that both the Cimiez and Washington drawings are these subsequent "variations."[4]

It is exciting to confirm that the exotic and sinuous curves of our drawing are related to the organic, flamelike forms found in Matisse's contemporary ballet designs. The Murphy drawing is thus connected to a critical moment when Matisse's lively theater designs were influencing so much of his work in other media, including his paper cut-outs, graphic oeuvre, and paintings.[5]

This is the first late Matisse drawing of this type or of this epoch in the National Gallery's collection. However, this drawing can be chronologically related to the Gallery's two 1940 Matisse paintings, gifts of Mr. and Mrs. Paul Mellon and of Rita Schreiber in memory of Taft Schreiber.

Jack Cowart

NOTES

1. I am indebted to Mme. Wanda de Guébriant of the Archives Henri Matisse, Paris, for her generous and timely reply to my questions on this matter.

2. Jack Cowart and others, *Henri Matisse Paper Cut-Outs* (New York, 1977), 92.

3. There are at least six of these figure in the Archives Henri Matisse.

4. See Louis Aragon, *Henri Matisse: Thèmes et variations* (Paris, 1943).

5. Cowart 1977, 91–96.

HENRY MOORE
1898–1986

Figures in an Underground Shelter, 1941
Wax crayon, watercolor, pen and brush
and ink, and colored chalks
13⅜ x 22⅛ (34.0 x 56.2)

Gift of Dr. Ruth B. Benedict

On the evening of 11 September 1940, Henry Moore and his wife were detained by air-raid wardens in the London Underground.[1] This was the first occasion on which Moore saw refugees taking shelter in subway stations far below ground in preference to the official air-raid shelters closer to the surface.[2] The experience was both cathartic and catalytic. Moore explained, "I found myself strangely excited . . . by the unbelievable scenes . . . of the Underground Shelters. . . . I went back again and again. . . . I began filling a notebook with drawings, ideas based on London's shelter life."[3]

The immediate products of this pivotal episode in Moore's career are 162 pages in two sketchbooks, which he drew from memory after two or three nights a week in the Underground.[4] Over the next year Moore developed from these prototypes some sixty-five to seventy-five large finished drawings, including this sheet.[5] Exhibitions of these probing yet sympathetic renditions of such a contemporary subject won Moore an enthusiastic public audience. The private sale of many of them made him independent enough to give up part-time teaching and devote himself full-time to his sculpture, on which especially the group compositions and drapery studies of the shelter drawings had an immediate and profound influence.

This superb sheet is a faithful enlargement of a detailed sketch in the second Shelter Sketchbook.[6] The prototype also prefigures its unusual technique. Moore had discovered that by laying down preliminary lines in white wax crayon and then washing over them with watercolor, the tone would "take" only outside these strokes; if they were then scraped free of wax and colored over again, more delicate tones could be made to adhere to their still-visible forms.[7] This is the technique used in the present sheet, where it is most apparent in the vertical texturing of the background, in the foreground highlights, and in the ghostly structures of the figures themselves.

The nature and meaning of the images in the shelter drawings have received much at-tention, beginning with Moore's own statement that he strove in them for "the creation of a unified human mood. The pervading theme of the shelter drawings was the group sense of communion in apprehension. . . . The only thing at all like those shelters that I could think of was the hold of a slave-ship on its way from Africa to America, full of hundreds and hundreds of people . . . quite powerless to resist."[8] His on-site notes written directly in the second Shelter Sketchbook bear out that sense of foreboding and anxiety: "Dramatic, dismal[ly] lit, masses of reclining figures fading to perspective point — Scribbles and scratches, chaotic foreground . . . (bundles of old clothes that are people)." Moore wrote above the preliminary sketch for this composition, "Two or three people under one blanket, uncomfortable positions, distorted twistings."[9]

All these formal and psychological tensions, however, are compassionately resolved by Moore's affecting rediscovery of humanity united and transfigured by suffering. "I was very conscious in the shelter drawings," he said, "that I was related to the people in the Underground. . . . Looking back, my Italian trip [of 1925] and the Mediterranean tradition came once more to the surface. There was no discarding of [my] other interests in archaic [and] primitive . . . art, but rather a clearer tension between this approach and the humanist emphasis . . . perhaps a temporary resolution of that conflict."[10] Such a resolution is achieved by Moore's opposing strengths, in the shelter drawings, of naturalistic accuracy on the one hand and originality of vision on the other. The gravely somber rhythms of his figure groupings suggest timeless images of endurance, monumentality, and grandeur. Moore's idiomatic invention of a generic new race populates these drawings with haunting echoes of Everyman.

The National Gallery owns thirteen prints by Moore and six sculptures. The present work is our first drawing by him and is one of the finest Moore drawings anywhere.

Douglas Lewis

PROVENANCE
Acquired from the artist by Sir Kenneth Clark (1941–after 1967); Marlborough Gallery, London (exhibitions in 1966 and 1967); William S. and Ruth B. Benedict (late 1960s).

NOTES
1. Alan G. Wilkinson, *The Drawings of Henry Moore* (New York, 1984), 300.

2. Alan G. Wilkinson, *The Drawings of Henry Moore* [exh. cat. Art Gallery of Ontario] (London, 1977), 29.

3. Letter of 11 January 1943, in James Johnson Sweeney, *Henry Moore* (New York, 1946), 67–68.

4. Sweeney 1946, 91, no. 78; Kenneth Clark, *Henry Moore Drawings* (London, 1974), 320, no. 139; Wilkinson 1977, 29–32, 152, n. 5; E. Petermann, *Die Shelterzeichnungen des Henry Moore* [exh. cat. Staatsgalerie] (Stuttgart, 1967), preface to catalogue section, n.p. See Donald Hall, *Henry Moore* (New York, 1966), 106–107.

5. Wilkinson 1977, 32 (estimating sixty-five finished drawings); Julian Andrews, *Henry Moore: Shelter and Coal Mining Drawings* [exh. cat. Nationalgalerie, Berlin] (London, 1984), 10 (estimating seventy-five drawings).

6. Petermann 1967, no. 21; John Russell, *Henry Moore* (New York, 1968), 83, fig. 85 top; Andrews 1984, 54, fig. 34 top.

7. Herbert Read, *Henry Moore* (New York and Washington, 1966), 149; Philip James, *Henry Moore on Sculpture* (London, 1966), 218; Hall 1966, 103.

8. James 1966, 103, 218.

9. Petermann 1967, nos. 6, 21, 25; Russell 1968, 83 (fig. 85), 85 (fig. 86); Robert Melville, *Henry Moore: Sculpture and Drawings 1921–1969* (London, 1970), 133, fig. 274.

10. James 1966, 216–218; Wilkinson 1977, 29. Moore had been particularly attracted to Masaccio while in Florence; later commentators have noticed parallels in his shelter drawings with Giotto, Michelangelo, Géricault, and Seurat as well.

HORACE PIPPIN
1888–1946

Interior, 1944
Oil on canvas
24⅛ x 29¾ (61.3 x 75.6)

Gift of
Mr. and Mrs. Meyer P. Potamkin

Horace Pippin's career as an artist began late in life, after years of working as a porter, furniture packer, iron molder, and soldier. Despite a World War I injury that crippled his right arm, the untrained Pippin developed his own method of image making, beginning around 1925 with a process of burning pictures into wood panels. After 1937, when his work was discovered by a critic in a West Chester, Pennsylvania, art show, his fortunes took a dramatic turn for the better. Examples of his work were featured in a 1938 exhibition at the Museum of Modern Art and Robert Carlen, a well-established Philadelphia dealer, became his enthusiastic representative.

Between 1940 and 1946, when he died, Pippin's paintings were included in numerous exhibitions and found a ready audience. Among his themes were his war experiences, the life of the abolitionist John Brown (whose hanging Pippin's grandmother had witnessed), a visionary series called Holy Mountain, and Pippin's recollections of his youth. The latter included both the overstuffed Victorian parlors that he may have encountered during his mother's days as a laundress and the simple homes of his and other black families.

The domestic scenes Pippin painted in the 1940s probably recalled his memories of Goshen, New York, where he lived from the age of three, in 1891, until 1912. Many of these paintings share common elements such as bare wood floors, cracked plaster walls, and chairs with broken back slats, all suggesting an austere existence. However, these images are tempered by notes that suggest poverty perhaps, but not misery. *Interior* depicts a woman and two children in a nearly cavernous room. At the center is a curtainless window partially covered by a shade, with darkness beyond. Although the windowpanes are layered with snow, there is a large stack of wood beside the iron stove and the kettle is steaming. Smoking her pipe, the woman relaxes as her child, on a quilt on the floor, plays with a doll and toy animal. A boy with his back to them leans over his work next to a candle on the table. He might be reading, or if he represents Pippin himself, perhaps drawing or painting.[1] There is no interaction among the inhabitants, yet the mood evoked is one of quiet anticipation, of the peaceful passing of time. The artist's enthusiastic recording of the textures and colors of the kitchen—the striped rag rugs, bright quilt, checkered tablecloth, and the woman's dotted kerchief—enlivens both the sparsely furnished interior and the canvas' design. Pippin excelled at utilizing surface patterns and interesting contours to vibrant effect.

With its strongly two-dimensional quality, unmodulated colors, and skewed perspective, Pippin's work is in some respects comparable to that of America's best-known twentieth century naive artist, Anna Mary Robertson ("Grandma") Moses (1860–1961). Moses' views of the pleasures of rural life, however, are laced with nostalgia whereas Pippin's embrace a grittier reality. At the same time Pippin confined his obvious messages to the John Brown paintings and a few other examples. In his everyday scenes he eschewed much of the direct social commentary of contemporaries such as Ben Shahn (1898–1968), Philip Evergood (1901–1973), and Jacob Lawrence (born 1917). The appeal of the best of Pippin's work is that it is absolutely straightforward, executed artfully but without artifice. Romare Bearden summarized the strength of Pippin's approach, recalling that upon meeting him Pippin was "positive that his paintings were completely realistic . . . to him these images were not distortions but perfectly literal translations of the actual world."[2] *Interior*, which was included in the important 1977 Pippin retrospective at The Phillips Collection, is such a work. It is the first painting by this artist to come to the National Gallery and joins a small but select group of works by African-American artists.

Deborah Chotner

PROVENANCE
Robert Carlen Galleries, Philadelphia; R. Sturgis Ingersoll, Esq.; Mr. and Mrs. Irving Vogel; Mrs. A. Lewis Spitzer; ACA Galleries; Mr. and Mrs. Meyer P. Potamkin, 1972.

NOTES
1. From a magazine contest Pippin at age ten won "a box of crayon pencils of six different colors. Also a box of cold water paint and two brushes. These I were delighted in and used often." Horace Pippin, "My Life's Story," as included in Selden Rodman, *Horace Pippin: A Negro Painter in America* (New York, 1947), 77.

2. Romare Bearden, "Horace Pippin," in *Horace Pippin* [exh. cat. The Phillips Collection] (Washington, 1976).

ANSEL ADAMS
1902–1984

*The Tetons and the Snake River, Grand
Teton National Park, Wyoming,* 1942
Gelatin silver photograph
39 x 59 (99.1 x 149.9)

Gift of Virginia Adams

During a war, when all physical and mental energy are focused on survival and victory, art can seem of secondary importance. The desire to be directly involved in and supportive of the struggle propels many to use their skills to document the disaster around them. During the Second World War the pressure, particularly for photographers, to create records of the war was intense. Many photographers saw their work as incontrovertible visual evidence, endowed not only with the authority of truth, but also with a moral order. It was a heroic stance, but not one that was possible or even acceptable to all.

Ansel Adams, born in 1902, was too old to serve actively in the Second World War, but he aided the war effort in many ways, doing what he called "bread-and-butter" work for the Department of the Interior, photographing Army convoys and teaching photography at Fort Ord.[1] His letters from the time, however, clearly indicate that he was both frustrated about not making a more direct contribution and deeply concerned about the kind of world that would emerge after the war. As a result, his images changed markedly during these years.[2] The quiet, more personal reflections on the beauty of mountains, trees, and water that had so characterized his work in the 1930s were replaced with grander, more emphatic, at times almost didactic images. Including such celebrated works as *Moonrise, Hernandez, New Mexico,* 1941, and *The Tetons and the Snake River,* the photographs made during the Second World War were clearly intended to be public statements: the scale, power, and purity of the massive vistas of the American West posited as antidotes to the forces that threatened civilization.

Like so many artists before him, Adams understood the American landscape in terms that closely approximate religion. As his letters demonstrate, during the late 1930s and 1940s he saw nature as a cleansing, redemptive power, yet as the war intensified he came to understand it also as a symbol of man's creative spirit. Shortly before the war openly erupted in Europe, he wrote that he wanted his photographs to show the "land and sky as settings for human activity," and to demonstrate "how men could be related to this magnificent setting," whereas in 1944 he wrote to Alfred Stieglitz that "as the war moves to a climax, the only enduring things seem to be the aspect of Nature—and its reciprocal, the creative spirit."[3] It is this sense both of endurance on a grand, heroic scale and of the equivalence between man's spirit and nature that is the subject of many of Adams' photographs made during the war and is most eloquently and emphatically affirmed in *The Tetons and the Snake River.* In his wartime work, Adams, as much as any other artist, constructed an art that not only embodied the ideals the nation was fighting to preserve, but also revealed the moral and spiritual order that he believed should be the foundation for the new postwar society.

As so many other artists had done in the 1930s, Adams experimented with scale and presentation. Beginning in 1935 and continuing for the next two decades, he occasionally made very large photographic prints. *The Tetons and the Snake River* was part of a group of mural photographs the Department of the Interior commissioned Adams to make in 1941 and 1942. Although he recognized that the large format could render some images trivial, revealing their weaknesses of subject, composition, and execution, it proved to be an extremely effective presentation of his images made during the war; their large physical size is a fitting reflection of the monumentality of their statement and intent. This rare mural print of *The Tetons and the Snake River,* so generously donated by Mrs. Adams, handsomely complements her previous gift of the Museum Set, a selection of seventy-five of Adams' finest photographs from throughout his long and productive career.

Sarah Greenough

PROVENANCE
Virginia Adams.

NOTES
1. Letter to Nancy Newhall, 1943, printed in *Ansel Adams: Letters and Images, 1916–1984,* ed. Mary Street Alinder and Andrea Gray Stillman (Boston, 1988), 143.

2. See Mary Alinder, *Ansel Adams: The Eightieth Birthday Retrospective* [exh. cat. The Monterey Peninsula Museum of Art] (Monterey, California, 1982), n.p.

3. Letters to David McAlpin, 4 November 1938, and Alfred Stieglitz, 25 December 1944, printed in Adams 1988, 110 and 154.

ARSHILE GORKY
1904–1948

Virginia Landscape, 1944
Pencil and wax crayon
22 x 30 (55.88 x 76.2)

Gift (Partial and Promised) of
Mrs. Walter Salant

In the summer of 1942, Arshile Gorky spent three weeks at the Connecticut farm of his friend Saul Schary. The close experience of the country occasioned a major change in Gorky's art. Rediscovering nature, he began an intense exploration of landscape and organic form.

The following summer Gorky and his family returned to the country, this time to the estate of his wife's parents, Crooked Run Farm in Hamilton, Virginia. The Virginia countryside captivated the artist, who found it reminiscent of his native Armenia. Gorky had recently begun to draw in a new medium, pencil and wax crayon, and he celebrated his renewed passion for nature in a series of large drawings. So involved was he with the spectacle of nature, and so pleased with the progress of his art, that he decided to pass a full nine months of the following year at Crooked Run Farm, drawing, painting, and observing the changes of the seasons.

Virginia Landscape dates from that second, extended stay at Crooked Run Farm in 1944. It is a wonderful and quite characteristic example of Gorky's landscape drawings of that year. Gorky, it has been noted, was more comfortable in both his drawing and painting with line than with color.[1] In his 1943 pencil and colored wax crayon drawings he attempted to fuse the two, melding the colors of his wax crayons, often smeared or rubbed across the paper sheet, to complex pencil contours.[2] In *Virginia Landscape* and other drawings of 1944, by contrast, line and color assert themselves as independent elements. He began with a scaffolding of strong, curving pencil lines, drawn in with a soft pencil. These are complemented by broad passages of color as well as several crayon lines that are drawn over or apart from the graphite. More subtle areas of silvery tone have been added by use of the stump and eraser.

Despite its title, *Virginia Landscape* derives more from a microscopic view than a macrocosmic vista. Gorky has been described sitting in the tall grass of the Virginia farm, dissecting "root, stem, insect, leaf and flower. . . . As he worked he sang the plaintive melodies of the East—and with the song came moods and deep-sprung impressions whose haunting beauty infused mere analysis with emotion."[3] His landscape drawings and paintings refer to nature seen close up; they are filled with strange forms that might be familiar were we to attend to the intimate details of the nature that surrounds us.

Although tied to that natural world, *Virginia Landscape* is quite evidently not a realist description. Gorky met and befriended the surrealist poet and theorist André Breton toward the end of 1944, but he was already familiar with the ideas of surrealism and practiced the surrealist procedure of automatic drawing. The lines and colors of *Virginia Landscape* occupy a middle ground between a transcription of the seen world and a brilliant improvisation based upon the nearly unconscious movement of the artist's hand.

The National Gallery is particularly fortunate in matters of Arshile Gorky. The collection already includes three of Gorky's most important paintings, *The Artist and His Mother*, c. 1926–1942, *Organization*, 1933–1936, and *One Year the Milkweed*, 1944, as well as six major drawings. *Virginia Landscape* is of considerable importance to this collection, for Gorky's landscape drawings of 1943–1944 are arguably his crucial achievement of those years. They form the basis for the style and provide many of the subjects for his paintings up until his death in 1948. *Virginia Landscape* complements its contemporary, *One Year the Milkweed*. Whereas the painting is subtle and atmospheric, a lovely demonstration of Gorky's subtle wash technique, *Virginia Landscape* is forthright and powerful, a compelling demonstration of the direct application of line, color, and imagination.

Jeremy Strick

PROVENANCE
World House Gallery, New York.

NOTES
1. Brooks Joyner, *The Drawings of Arshile Gorky* [exh. cat. University of Maryland Art Gallery] (College Park, Maryland, 1969), 2.

2. Joyner 1969, 14.

3. Ethel K. Schwabacher, *Arshile Gorky* (New York, 1957), 97.

ROBERT MOTHERWELL
Born 1915

Personnage, 1945
Oil on canvas board
23½ x 17½ (59.69 x 44.45)

Gift (Partial and Promised) of
Aaron I. Fleischman

A capsule history of abstract expressionist painting is familiar to many. The story goes that in the 1940s a young generation of American artists in New York turned away from the twin preoccupations of regionalism and social realism to embrace the tenets of advanced European art, especially cubism and surrealism. Influenced in part by the European modernists who came to this country in flight from the rise of fascism, these artists eventually came to forge in the 1950s a new abstract art founded upon gesture and immediacy and a grand, American sense of scale.

In recent years such capsule histories have been called into question. Not the least criticism is that in prizing the grand accomplishments of "classic" 1950s abstract expressionism, the early achievements of the New York school have been slighted. On the evidence of paintings like Robert Motherwell's *Personnage*, 1945, that criticism is just.

Personnage, one of several paintings of that title painted by Motherwell in the mid-1940s, no doubt reflects the artist's dialogue with Picasso, Matisse and, to a lesser degree, Mondrian. The picture can be read as an image of a painting, depicting a figure, set on an easel. The personage in the painting is described in an abbreviated, linear fashion—a version of the stick figures that Motherwell had first employed in his art in the seminal 1943 painting *Pancho Villa Dead and Alive* (The Museum of Modern Art, New York).[1] Motherwell's stick figures derive generally from Picasso's Studio paintings of 1927–1928, but that of *Personnage* relates most closely to Picasso's great *Wire Construction*, 1928.[2] The setting of the clearly outlined shapes of painting and easel against a lushly painted ground recalls Matisse, while the reduced, geometric organization of *Personnage* suggests the impact of Mondrian, whose studio Motherwell visited in 1944.[3]

If Motherwell has made no effort to hide his sources and influences, it is because he has transformed them into an intensely personal vocabulary.[4] Of his stick figures Motherwell stated, "The figure interests me when it fills the picture as in a full length portrait. It never occurs to me to have the figure do anything, its presence is sufficient; and I suppose it rarely occurs to me to do anything except feel my own presence."[5] *Personnage* might be read as a meditation upon the transcription of personal presence onto canvas. The artist draws his own identity into a painted figure, but it is the painting as a whole rather than the isolated image that reflects that identity–thus the relative stasis of the figure and the energetic, anthropomorphized quality of the outlined painting and easel.

For the past several years, the National Gallery has actively collected New York school paintings of the mid-1940s. That collection now includes a number of early Mark Rothkos given by the Mark Rothko Foundation, Arshile Gorky's *One Year the Milkweed*, 1944, William Baziotes' *Pierrot*, 1947, Ad Reinhardt's *Untitled*, 1947, as well as Barnett Newman's *Pagan Void*, 1946, one of several fiftieth-anniversary gifts of Annalee Newman. *Personnage* will make a distinguished addition to this company, while adding significantly to our representation of Robert Motherwell. Motherwell's mural *Reconciliation Elegy*, 1978 was commissioned for the opening of the East Building of the National Gallery, and the Gallery also owns one artist's book, one drawing, and twenty-two prints by the artist, none of these earlier in date than 1958. Among Motherwell's early paintings, *Personnage* is unusual for the degree to which it contains in germ so much of his later work. The brown, blue, and ocher of *Personnage* are colors typically associated with Motherwell, as is the compositional device of playing curving lines against straight verticals. *Personnage* will also make a provocative juxtaposition with another important image of a painting-within-a-painting in the collection of the NationalGallery, René Magritte's *The Human Condition*, 1933.

Jeremy Strick

PROVENANCE
Collection of G. David Thompson, Pittsburgh; Galerie Beyeler, Basel; James Goodman Gallery, New York; William Pall Gallery, New York; Waddington Galleries, London; Forum Gallery, New York; Collection of George Gilbert; André Emmerich Gallery, New York.

NOTES
1. Robert Saltonstall Mattison, *Robert Motherwell: The Formative Years* (Ann Arbor, 1987), 92.

2. Mattison 1987, 142.

3. Mattison 1987, 56.

4. Mattison 1987, 92–98.

5. Bryan Robertson, interview with Robert Motherwell, 1965, unpublished, cited in Mattison 1987, 93.

ISAMU NOGUCHI
1904–1988

Untitled, 1945
Painted wood
50 x 19 x 9¼ (127 x 48.26 x 23.50)

Gift (Partial and Promised) of
Robert P. and Arlene R. Kogod

Isamu Noguchi came into his own as a sculptor in the mid-1940s with a group of biomorphic assemblages made from thin sheets of wood, slate, and marble. Surrealist in inspiration, these sculptures had their most direct source in Picasso's "bone" figures of the early 1930s, and were close as well to the formal vocabulary of Yves Tanguy.[1]

Noguchi worked on these sculptures at the same time that he was engaged in producing set and costume designs for Martha Graham's dance company. He had first designed a set for Graham in 1935, for a production of *Frontier,* and had designed several other productions in the mid-1930s. The collaboration was renewed in 1943, when Graham invited Noguchi to work with her on the production of a trilogy of dances: *Imagined Wing, Appalachian Spring,* and *Herodiade,* which were performed for the first time in 1944. Noguchi's sets for these dances were spare and suggestive. That for *Herodiade* included three freestanding objects made of painted plywood. Representing a chair, a clothes rack, and a mirror, these combinations of rounded and elongated forms functioned at once as furniture, stage design, and full-fledged surrealist sculpture.[2]

Although the importance of Noguchi's set designs for the stylistic development of his sculpture is generally acknowledged, the artist's most common material in this period was the inexpensive marble slabs used to face buildings.[3] The black-painted wood *Untitled* is thus related to the three objects created for *Herodiade* in medium, and is also close to them in its furniturelike design. Indeed, one of Noguchi's earliest and most famous furniture designs, the table he produced for A. Conger Goodyear in 1939, also comprises a flat, horizontal "table" element supported by two legs.

Untitled was documented first in a photograph of Noguchi's studio taken in the mid-1940s by André Kertész.[4] There it appears unpainted, with a different "beak" shape where the tallest horned element is now. The sculpture is a complex union of curvilinear and geometric pieces, spiked projections, voids, and planes. Like many of Noguchi's sculptures of this period it evokes a standing figure, but it reads also as a family of figures, perhaps mother, father, and child.

Untitled joins three later Noguchis in the National Gallery collection: a monumental stone sculpture of 1974 and two galvanized steel edition sculptures of 1983 and 1983/1984. The first major early Noguchi to enter the collection, *Untitled* adds significantly to the Gallery's holdings of this major American artist, and adds as well to our representation of the surrealist movement.

Jeremy Strick

PROVENANCE
Family of the artist; Private collector, New York; Sold at Sotheby's, New York, 4 May 1984; Armand Bartos, Inc., New York.

NOTES
1. Sam Hunter, *Isamu Noguchi* (New York, 1978), 82.

2. Nancy Grove, *Isamu Noguchi: A Study of the Sculpture* (New York, 1985), 122–124.

3. Hunter 1978, 79.

4. Hunter 1978, 83.

BARNETT NEWMAN
1905–1970

Pagan Void, 1946
Oil on canvas
33 x 38 (83.8 x 96.5)

Gift of Annalee Newman

Annalee Newman's fiftieth anniversary gift of five paintings by her husband joins fifteen paintings by Newman already in the collection, the fourteen *Stations of the Cross—Lema Sabachthani*, 1958–1966, and the related oil, *Be II*, 1961–1964. The earliest of the five new gifts, *Pagan Void*, is one of Newman's most important works of the mid-1940s. A transitional painting with elements of both figuration and abstraction, it relates to other New York-school pictures of the mid-1940s in the permanent collection, among them works by Arshile Gorky and Mark Rothko.

One of the great figures of the abstract expressionist movement, Newman was a thinker who developed his ideas in painting, sculpture, and writing. In his insistence on the importance of the artist's intellect he often took issue with prevalent mythology about the art of his generation, writing, for example, in 1951 that an artist should be "approached . . . as an original thinker in his own medium," not "as an instinctive, intuitive executant who, largely unaware of what he is doing, breaks through the mystery by the magic of his performance."[1]

Born and raised in New York, Newman attended the Art Students League while in high school and while attending City College. There he majored in philosophy, graduating in 1927. In the course of the next fifteen years he operated his family's clothes manufacturing business, was a substitute teacher of art in New York high schools, and in 1933 ran as a candidate for mayor of the city on a platform advocating anti-pollution measures and civic programs for the arts. He also studied the writings of Henry David Thoreau and the anarchist Peter Kropotkin and became interested in botany, geology, ornithology, and tribal art. New-

man destroyed most paintings he made in the 1930s and early 1940s.

In the spring of 1945 Newman set down a number of his developing ideas about the proper goals of aspiring abstract painters in various drafts of an unpublished "monologue," "The Plasmic Image." There he asserted that, between the time of the impressionists and the 1940s, modernist painters had solved the technical problems of the language of painting (color, shape, atmosphere) and should go on to transcend such decorative aspects of art to project *concepts*. "Art," he wrote, "must become a metaphysical exercise."[2]

Around this time he embarked on a series of paintings and drawings with egglike circular forms, sometimes joined to strong vertical elements. Some had titles that proposed subjects relating to the beginning of creation, for example a 1945 oil and oil-crayon drawing, *Gea* (the goddess who in Greek mythology was the first being to emerge from chaos). Thomas Hess, who knew the artist well, has suggested that, like Newman's oil of 1947, *Death of Euclid*, *Pagan Void* has a combative title that refers to the lack of content of "Mohammedan" abstract art and by extension to all abstract art that is merely decorative geometric pattern and without subject matter.[3] In its intimations of naturalistic imagery, *Pagan Void* might also be read as a "genetic moment" (the words are the title of another Newman oil of 1947), that is, the moment when a sperm begins to penetrate an ovum. Newman's use in *Pagan Void* of rich green, blue, and red in thinly applied areas of paint anticipates the coloristic subtleties of his later abstractions and looks forward particularly to the palette of *Dionysius*, 1949.

Nan Rosenthal

NOTES

1. Barnett Newman, "Review of *Abstract Painting: Background and American Phase* by Thomas B. Hess," in *Barnett Newman: Selected Writings and Interviews*, ed. John P. O'Neill (New York, 1990), 121–122.

2. Newman, "The Plasmic Image," in Newman 1990, 145.

3. Thomas B. Hess, *Barnett Newman* [exh. cat. The Museum of Modern Art] (New York, 1970), 47, 52.

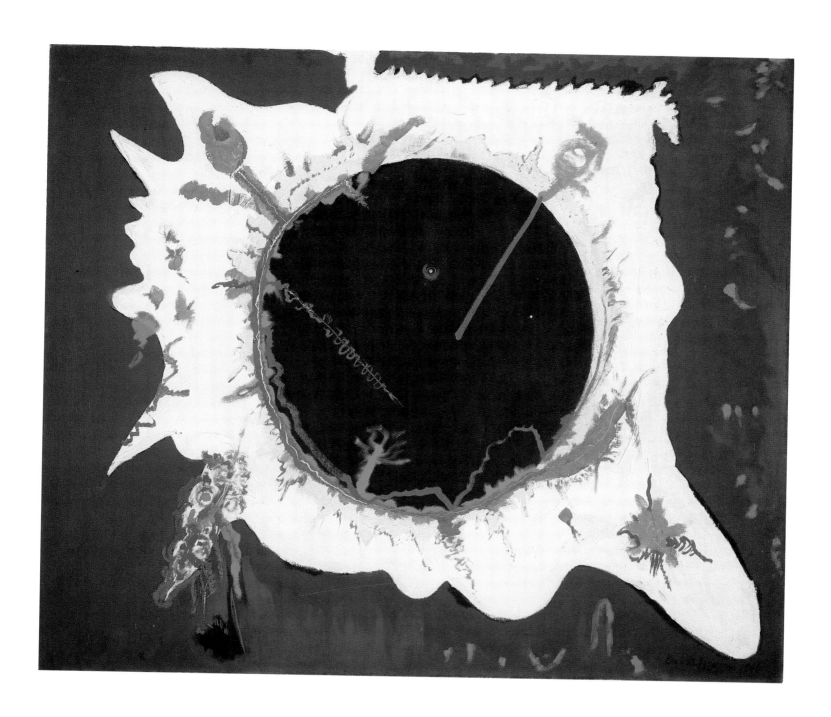

367

BALTHUS
Born 1908

Nude Girl Stretched Out on a Chair
1948
Graphite on brown paper;
black chalk on verso
12³/₁₆ x 16⁹/₁₆ (31 x 42)

Gift of Frank R. and Jeannette H. Eyerly

When the critic John Russell was preparing the catalogue for the Tate Gallery's 1968 Balthus retrospective, the artist instructed him to state, "Balthus is a painter of whom *nothing is known*."[1] This insistence on privacy, combined with fanciful interpretations of his background,[2] have made Balthus something of an enigma. Yet his artistic course has been markedly defined. Early on he determined the subject matter and style that would sustain him for a lifetime, and his devotion to that has been unfaltering.

Balthus' work is resolutely figurative, his subjects most often being pubescent girls. They recline in states of utter leisure, lost in daydreams or asleep. The National Gallery drawing is a study for one of the artist's most accomplished paintings, *Nude with a Cat* (1949),[3] a highly ordered and provocative work in the collection of the National Gallery of Victoria. The drawing also relates in a broad sense to a series of important works painted between 1949 and 1952.[4]

Balthus' paintings are carefully conceived works, formally constructed with an eye to the old masters. His drawings are strikingly different. They are spontaneous where the paintings are not. Their handling is varied and reveals a certain gentleness not admissible in the paintings. In the National Gallery drawing, fluid lines shift this way and that as the artist situates his model on the page. Her hand raised, she reaches up to the playful cat hovering above her. In the midst of unbroken movement, the model's composed face commands our attention, its contours accentuated with brisk cross-hatched shading. Her look is typically Balthusian: pensive, not truly focused on the cat, seemingly detached from her surroundings.

Four figure studies on the verso of this sheet probably relate to dance or theater projects. Balthus designed sets and costumes for five stage productions between 1948 and 1960.[5] In the very center of the sheet, a faintly drawn stage curtain is tied back with a pull. To the left of it are two figures, their bearing and physique suggestive of dancers. A figure to the right strongly resembles one of Cézanne's bathers and to the far right, barely discernible, is a crotchety-looking figure, seemingly in costume, pointing an accusing finger outward.

Works by Balthus are rare, exceedingly so in public collections. Although his reputation is legendary, admirers of his work seldom have the opportunity to see it in the original. Instead they must turn to photographic reproductions in books and catalogues. This beautifully rendered drawing, the first work by Balthus to enter the collection, will at long last offer visitors to the National Gallery an opportunity to study an original work by this twentieth-century master.

Judith Brodie

PROVENANCE
Albert Loeb & Krugier Gallery Inc., New York.

NOTES
1. John Russell, *Balthus: A Retrospective Exhibition* [exh. cat. Tate Gallery] (London, 1968), 7.

2. Following World War II, Balthus assumed the appellation Count Balthazar Klossowski de Rola. For an account see James Lord, "Balthus: The Curious Case of the Count de Rola," *The New Criterion* (December 1983), 9–25.

3. Repr. Sabine Rewald, *Balthus* [exh. cat. The Metropolitan Museum of Art] (New York, 1984), no. 31.

4. Most notably *The Week with Four Thursdays*, 1949, private collection, repr. Rewald 1984, no. 30 and *The Room*, 1952–1954, private collection, repr. Rewald 1984, no. 32.

5. Rewald 1984, 45–47.

MILTON AVERY
1893–1965

Laurels Number Four, 1948
Portfolio of 5 drypoints
16½ x 13 (42 x 33)

Gift of Mrs. Robert A. Hauslohner

Milton Avery's *Laurels Number Four* portfolio, published in 1948, brings together five drypoints. The copper plates for two of them, *Riders in the Park* and *Head of a Man*, had been worked in 1934 and 1935 respectively, but Avery had printed only a few proof impressions before setting them aside for what turned out to be more than a decade. The other three plates, *Reclining Nude*, *March at a Table*, and *By the Sea* were completed the year they were published.[1]

Avery's portfolio was the last of a series released by the Laurel Gallery in New York, owned by Chris Ritter who hoped thereby to raise some much-needed money. Issued for the sum of twenty-five dollars, the portfolio sold poorly even at that extraordinarily low price.[2] The drypoints were accompanied by a title page and an appreciation by the artist Joseph Solman. Both were hand set and printed by Douglass Howell on Howell Handmade Paper. His colorful sheets also served as wrappers for the prints and text and for the hand-printed labels on the gray paper-covered board portfolios.

These drypoints were printed by Stanley William Hayter at his New York Atelier 17 in warm black ink with rich tonal surface effects.[3] According to Grace Borgenicht, far fewer than the proposed edition of a hundred were printed.

The *Laurels Number Four* drypoint subjects are typical of Avery's work, including as they do portraits of friends and family (*Head of a Man* is a portrait of artist Louis Wiesenberg and *March at a Table* depicts Avery's daughter), the nude, the landscape, and the sea. The plates as a group present an intriguing compendium of drypoint markings, which the artist used to great advantage: for example, in building deep rich darks, as in the tree trunks in *Riders in the Park*; in developing a variety of middle tones, as in the necktie and background in *Head of a Man*; in suggesting delicately textured surfaces, as in *March at a Table*. As Solman said in his introduction, "this medium is ideal for Avery's concepts. Everything must be sacrificed to the barest notations. A few

abrupt strokes, several tender incisions, and the scene or personage is replete with life, warmth, and personality. . . . Avery's work reveals pure joy."

Avery is best known for his broadly composed, subtly colored paintings, as well as some two hundred monotypes executed toward the end of his life that take brilliant advantage of the painterly properties of the process. Throughout his career, however, he also completed a corpus of thirty drypoints, made intermittently between 1933 and 1950; eight lithographs, one completed in 1939, another, a color print, in 1963, and the rest published in editions of 2,000 in the souvenir catalogues for Artists Equity balls from 1950 to 1953; one linoleum cut and twenty-one woodcuts, many of them printed in variant impressions, all within the brief time between 1952 and 1955.[4]

Prior to this gift of *Laurels Number Four*, the National Gallery's collection included two prints by Avery, one early and one late: *Rothko with Pipe*, a 1936 drypoint portrait of the artist, purchased with funds donated by Ailsa Mellon Bruce; and the artist's only color lithograph, *Grey Sea*, the gift of Ruth B. Benedict. This splendid group of vigorously incised drypoints, therefore, represents a particularly significant addition to our representation of Avery's work.

Ruth E. Fine

PROVENANCE
Purchased from Dolan/Maxwell Gallery, Philadelphia, 1984.

NOTES
1. In *Milton Avery: Prints 1933–1955*, compiled and ed. by Harry H. Lunn, Jr. (Washington, 1973), these prints are nos. 6, 8, 26, 28, and 29. *Riders in the Park* was issued in 1973 in a restrike edition of one hundred unsigned impressions to accompany proof copies of the Lunn catalogue. *Reclining Nude* is also known as *Nude with Long Torso*; *March at a Table* also as *March on a Terrace*; *By the Sea* as *Umbrella by the Sea*.

2. I am grateful to Grace Borgenicht for supplying information about the Laurel Gallery portfolios, and to Harvey S. Shipley Miller for discussing this entry with Sally Avery and conveying to me that after Ritter closed his gallery several sets of these drypoints were assembled and issued without the portfolio and accompanying texts.

3. In "A Technical Note" in the Lunn catalogue, Alan Fern, citing Sally Avery as the source of his information, described Hayter's impressions as being in a brownish ink with surface tone and indicated they were less to Avery's liking than impressions printed in 1964 by Anderson and Lamb in black ink and wiped clean.

4. Alan Fern in the Lunn catalogue suggested more than two hundred monotypes. The others figures are based on this catalogue as well.

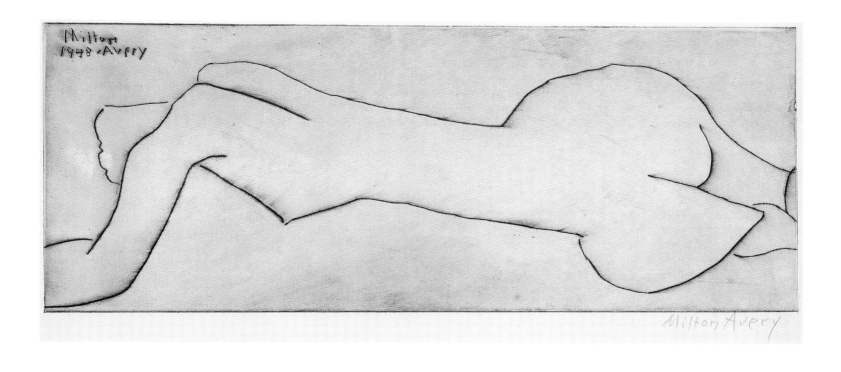

371

PABLO PICASSO
1881–1973

Young Woman in a Striped Blouse, 1949
Lithograph on paper
26 x 19⅝ (66 x 49.8)

Gift of Mr. and Mrs. Jem Hom

This arresting portrait belongs to a series of lithographic bust-length portraits that Picasso made beginning in January 1949.[1] One of only five printer's proofs of the first state, the work was dated by the artist 26 February of that year. Around the same time, Picasso was painting very similar portraits of this sitter in the same frontal pose and striped dress.[2]

Picasso made his first lithograph in 1919 and subsequently worked occasionally in that medium until 1930. After that it was not until 1945 that he seriously returned to lithography. Beginning in November, in the Parisian studio of the printmaker Fernand Mourlot, Picasso concentrated intensely on lithography, making more than two hundred prints in the next three and a half years. He was attracted to the medium by the seemingly infinite number of techniques it afforded, many of which are evident in this print. Printmaking appealed to him for the various permutations of an image that could be explored in successive stages of a print, such as the depiction of a bull that he increasingly abstracted in eleven states in 1945–1946.[3]

Picasso's first lithograph in 1945 was a portrait of Françoise Gilot, a young painter whom he met in Paris during the war in May of 1943. By the end of 1945 she gradually began to supplant Dora Maar's position in his life as well as his art. This portrait clearly depicts the dark, piercing features of Françoise, with whom Picasso was currently living in Paris. The artist's many images of Françoise during this period reflect the contentedness of their relationship. When Picasso drew this portrait, their son Claude was nearly two years old. Françoise was pregnant with a second child, Paloma, born April 19.

This emphatically frontal, nearly life-size image of Françoise offers a compendium of lithographic techniques. The striped bodice is wittily rendered with the side of a lithographic crayon, achieving a softly textured touch, while other areas such as the strands of hair or facial features have a painterly quality afforded by lithographic ink or tusche.

Having made the image, Picasso reworked the plate (here a zinc plate rather than a lithographic stone as in his earlier lithographs) on 4 March 1949, heavily retouching areas of the hair and face. This second state, like the first, was never published as an edition and exists only in five rare proofs. The same day he reworked another version of a very similar image that he had also originally composed on 26 February.[4] This series of lithographic portraits of Françoise, with their repetitious theme and variation, has a cumulative, incantatory effect, like obsessive investigations of both a beloved visage and the very process of image making.

The Gallery's graphics collection includes a large number of Picasso's prints, but this rare impression makes a significant contribution to our holdings in later prints by the artist.

Marla Prather

PROVENANCE
Private collection, London, acquired by the Homs in 1988.

NOTES
1. Fernand Mourlot, *Picasso Lithographe* (Paris, 1949), no. 157.

2. Christian Zervos, *Pablo Picasso* (Paris, 1965), vol. 15, nos. 136–141. In particular, no. 139 is dated 28 February 1949.

3. Mourlot 1949, no. 157.

4. Mourlot 1949, no. 158.

CHARLES SHEELER
1883–1965

Counterpoint, 1949
Conté crayon
20 x 28 (50.8 x 71.2)

Gift of Daniel J. Terra

Described as Sheeler's "last great conté crayon drawing," *Counterpoint* was completed in 1949 during a period of artistic rejuvenation sparked by an invitation three years earlier to spend several weeks as artist-in-residence at Phillips Academy in Andover, Massachusetts.[1] As was his practice, Sheeler spent much of his time in Andover gathering the photographic "notes" he would later use to produce paintings and drawings.[2] Although he took photographs of several campus buildings, the architectural structure that truly captured his imagination was not an academic building, but rather an abandoned mill at Ballardvale, near Andover. The dilapidated mill, much transformed, is the subject of *Counterpoint.*[3]

Sheeler began working with conté crayon very early in his career. Born in Philadelphia and educated at the School of Industrial Art and the Pennsylvania Academy of the Fine Arts, Sheeler later shared a Philadelphia studio and country house near Doylestown, in Bucks County, with fellow-artist Morton Schamberg. When it became clear that neither artist could support himself adequately on paintings alone, both Sheeler and Schamberg turned to commercial photography. Schamberg found work as a portrait photographer while Sheeler's subjects were more often art and architecture. About 1917, in a series of remarkable photographs and drawings of the Doylestown house and several Bucks County barns, Sheeler achieved artistic maturity.[4] Working his way through the vocabulary of modernism, he produced a number of drawings based on the barn images that allowed him to explore one of the central issues of cubism: spatial ambiguity. Although based on identifiable subjects, the drawings are often so spare that they verge on abstraction.

During the 1920s and 1930s Sheeler continued to produce conté drawings, often in conjunction with works in other media. In 1929, for example, he traveled to France where he took a series of photographs of Chartres Cathedral. As he had with the Bucks County barns, Sheeler explored the formal issues raised by his photographs in drawings. The only other work by Sheeler presently in the collection of the National Gallery is a drawing of Chartres Cathedral dated 1929.

Between 1930 and 1937 Sheeler produced at least sixteen of these drawings before he abandoned the difficult medium for more than a decade. It was, in fact, an invitation from Bartlett Hayes, director of the Addison Gallery of American Art at Phillips Academy, that initiated Sheeler's return to the medium. Hayes wished to inaugurate a new acquisition program whereby contemporary artists would be invited to spend a period of time on campus and the gallery would then purchase the "creative results of this term of residence."[5] Sheeler, the first artist invited to participate in the program, spent about six weeks in Andover in the fall of 1946. Intrigued by the old mill he discovered in Ballardvale, Sheeler took many photographs and subsequently produced an oil titled *Ballardvale* that was acquired by the Addison Gallery. Three years later Sheeler completed *Counterpoint,* a large-scale drawing that displays all the tonal richness of the earlier drawings, but also a new compositional complexity drawn from his more recent work in oil. As others have noted, *Counterpoint* is "at once entirely legible and intriguingly abstract."[6] The image was initially conceived as a composite of superimposed photographs. Though it is not clear exactly how many negatives were used, at least one shows the mill in reverse. The result is a multifaceted composition that reprises in a far more sophisticated manner Sheeler's earlier investigation of cubist space.

In 1946 Sheeler wrote that he undertook conté crayon drawing "to see how much exactitude I could attain."[7] *Counterpoint,* perhaps the finest of the artist's late drawings, demonstrates that he was capable of extraordinary conceptual and technical "exactitude."

Nancy K. Anderson

PROVENANCE
Downtown Gallery, New York; Bernard Heineman, Jr., New York; Berry-Hill Galleries, Inc., New York; Daniel J. Terra, 1985.

NOTES
1. Carol Troyen and Erica E. Hirshler, *Charles Sheeler: Paintings and Drawings* (New York, 1987), 192.

2. Troyen and Hirshler 1987, 35.

3. A photograph of Ballardvale mill by Sheeler is reproduced in Troyen and Hirshler 1987, 192.

4. Theodore E. Stebbins, Jr., and Norman Keyes, Jr., *Charles Sheeler: The Photographs* (New York, 1987), 8–14.

5. Troyen and Hirshler 1987, 35.

6. Troyen and Hirshler 1987, 192.

7. "Sheeler," *Art News* 45 (March 1946), 30.

BARNETT NEWMAN
1905–1970

Dionysius, 1949
Oil on canvas
67 x 49 (170.2 x 124.5)

Gift of Annalee Newman

Dionysius is one of four oils dating from 1949 in which Newman explored turning his characteristic bands or zips ninety degrees to cross the canvas from side to side rather than top to bottom. There are no drawings in this format, and Newman returned to it only once later, in 1951, with *Day before One* (Oeffentliche Kunstsammlung, Basel), a strongly vertical oil with narrow lateral bands at the top and bottom edges.

In the four 1949 oils with horizontal zips, the bands do not edge the canvas but cut across the fields, dividing them into sections. *Untitled (No. 3)*, 24 x 28 (Collection Annalee Newman), is the smallest and most likely the earliest of the four. Newman positioned two light blue bands in a dark red field. The upper band changes midway to a darker blue, and there are other contrasting streaks of paint applied laterally part of the way across the field, creating a faint suggestion of atmosphere, as if the painting were an abstract landscape with the upper band functioning as a horizon line.

Two other 1949 paintings with horizontal zips, *Argos* (Collection Annalee Newman) and *Horizon Light* (University of Nebraska-Lincoln Art Galleries, Gift of Mr. and Mrs. Thomas Sills) are emphatically horizontal in format and nearly the same size (30½ x 72 and 33 x 72 inches respectively).

Dionysius, probably the last of the four, is vertical in format. The rich blue-green field, with some yellow underpainting, is crossed above by a wide orange band and below by a narrow yellow band. In the orange zip Newman's brushwork is conspicuous and travels in patches onto the green field; the yellow zip has rigid edges apparently formed by using tape. The coexistence of the contrary kinds of paint handling creates tension in the work and calls attention to the way the field is divided: into bottom and middle sections of the same height and a top section half the height of each of the other two. The painting is signed on the front at the lower

right, and its stretcher bars are covered along the sides with black tape.

It was not unusual for Newman to title his abstract paintings with words referring to members of his family, aspects of Greek culture, the Old Testament, or places in American literature. These references were not meant as depictive allusions but rather, as Newman said, as metaphors describing his feelings when he did the paintings. "It's not literal but a cue," he told an interviewer.[1]

Given Newman's great interest in light as a metaphor of creation and revelation as well as his interest in Gothic architecture (there are paintings called *Cathedra* and *Chartres*), it seems possible that his title for this painting was prompted by Dionysius' the Pseudo-Areopagite, a fifth-century theologian from Syria whose writings, a synthesis of Neoplatonism and Christian mysticism, were highly venerated in medieval France at the time of the invention of Gothic architecture. The theology of Dionysius was the chief source of a metaphysics of light that stimulated the planners of the first Gothic cathedrals.[2] Newman may have discussed Dionysius' light metaphysics with the art historian Meyer Shapiro, a close friend whose special field is the medieval period.

Nan Rosenthal

NOTES
1. Barnett Newman, "From *Barnett Newman: The Stations of the Cross, Lema Sabachthani*," in *Barnett Newman: Selected Writings and Interviews*, ed. John P. O'Neill (New York, 1990), 187.

2. Otto von Simson, *The Gothic Cathedral* (New York, 1956), 103–107. In his monograph on Newman, Thomas Hess wrote that *Dionysius* refers to the Greek god of fertility, "the creator . . . of special interest to Newman as the god of tragic art." The name of that god, however, is spelled "Dionysus" or "Dionysos," an error Newman is unlikely to have made. Thomas B. Hess, *Barnett Newman* [exh. cat. The Museum of Modern Art] (New York, 1970), 82.

BARNETT NEWMAN
1905–1970

Yellow Painting, 1949
Oil on canvas
67½ x 52⅜ (171 x 133)

Gift of Annalee Newman

On 29 January 1948, his forty-third birthday, Newman made a small painting, *Onement I*, whose innovative characteristics provided strategies for much of his subsequent art. He first covered the entire surface of the vertical rectangle with cadmium red dark, brushing on the red-brown earth color with up-and-down strokes that were evenly applied yet faintly visible nonetheless. Thus his artist's touch was manifest in a straightforward, dignified manner that appeared to eschew qualities typical of art contemporary to it, on the one hand the straight-edged rigidities of much geometric abstraction and on the other the rhetorical flourishes of more painterly abstract pictures. In contrast to Newman's abstract surrealism and abstractions of the previous several years, the evenly applied paint eliminated any suggestion of shading from light to dark and therefore of atmosphere or depth. On top of the unshaded red-brown, Newman placed a strip of masking tape vertically down the center of the canvas and painted over this tape with cadmium red light, a red-orange he applied so that his brushwork showed somewhat at the ragged edges of the strip of color. It was a test smear that Newman studied for months before concluding that his painting was indeed finished and a revelation.

The forthright symmetry of the composition of *Onement I*, established by the vertical Newman would call a "zip," was unusual for the time. While his symmetrical composition was perhaps not unlike that of some of the northwest coast Indian art he admired, it differed from the studied, balanced asymmetry common to postmedieval western painting. Whether a landscape by Claude Lorrain, in which a narrow tall tree at the left is matched by a shorter yet fuller tree at the right, or an abstraction of around 1921 by Mondrian, in which rectangles of different size, color, and orientation counterweigh one another, much western painting has involved balancing acts or what the artist Frank Stella has termed "relational painting."

Newman's method with *Onement I* involved using the surprising impact of symmetry—something so simple that it risked appearing obvious or dull—together with contrasting manners of paint application (flat and thinly applied versus moderately brushy strokes over tape). In addition he made use of the impact of rich color that shifted very little in hue but a good deal in chromatic intensity. To viewers attempting to calculate the reasons for the force of such a seemingly simple picture, it became clear when the nuances were taken into account that a mind was at work and further that the intellect was intended to show.

Between the fall of 1948 when Newman decided that *Onement I* was, in fact, finished, and the end of 1949, Newman was immensely prolific, completing twenty paintings including *Yellow Painting*. Newman had earlier used saturated yellow dramatically with black in a work of 1946–1947, *Euclidian Abyss*. *Yellow Painting*, a particular favorite of Mrs. Newman's because of its color, was, like each of her fiftieth anniversary gifts, a present to her from the artist.

The work partakes of the discoveries made in *Onement I*. It is a symmetrical composition with a green-yellow ground. Near the left edge and the right edge there are white stripes or "zips"; both are fairly straight-edged yet clearly made by hand. In the middle of the canvas, establishing the symmetry echoed by the side bands, is a zip of yellow, slightly darker in value and more orange in hue than the yellow ground. It is nearly impossible to discern at a glance which of the three colors has been put on first. This of course contributes to the absence of depth the picture maintains. The painting is much larger than the breakthrough *Onement I*, and its expanses of color, in the absence of spatial cues, caused the critic Clement Greenberg to define such works by Newman as not easel paintings but rather "fields," thus giving rise to the term "color-field painting."

Nan Rosenthal

378

BARNETT NEWMAN
1905–1970

The Name II, 1950
Oil and Magna on canvas
108 x 96 (274.32 x 243.84)

Gift of Annalee Newman

Several months after Newman's first one-man exhibition, which took place at the Betty Parsons Gallery in New York in January–February 1950, he moved from his studio on East Nineteenth Street in Manhattan to a considerably larger space on Wall Street. One result of the move was that he could execute pictures much larger than previously possible, such as the eighteen-foot-long canvases *Vir Heroicus Sublimis* and *Cathedra*. One of the first paintings executed in 1951 in the Wall Street studio was *The Voice* (The Museum of Modern Art, New York, Sidney and Harriet Janis Collection). An eight- by nine-foot canvas, *The Voice* has two contrasting whites: a field of fairly evenly applied egg tempera and, five-sixths of the way toward the right, a vertical zip in glossier enamel or oil paint.

The Name II, Newman's second white-with-white painting of 1950, is virtually identical in stretcher size to *The Voice* but vertical in format, nine by eight feet. It contains four zips: two vertical bands at either side and two in the middle that divide the canvas into three more or less equal sections. The zips are in oil. The field areas, in Magna, probably mark Newman's first use of the new acrylic resin paint, sent to him by his friend Leonard Bocour, the paint manufacturer. While these white-with-white paintings have an obvious precedent in Kasimir Malevich's suprematist white-on-white canvases of 1918, such as the Museum of

Modern Art's square work with a white square on a white ground, the Newmans are inventive in their expansive scale, which relates them to the human body. They also anticipate many subsequent works, such as Robert Rauschenberg's entirely monochrome white paintings of 1951.

It has been proposed that the words of the title refer to the ancient Hebrew Tetragrammaton of four consonants, YHVH or the acronym Yahweh, used in place of the unutterable holy name for the creator. Newman earlier titled an oil of 1949 *The Name*. A four- by five-foot gray canvas, the 1949 *Name* is divided into four identical sections and one smaller one to the right by four vertical red zips. There is also a drawing of 1949 in the collection of the National Gallery of Art (fig. 1), on which the words "the name" appear toward the top of the verso.

The compositions of the National Gallery drawing and the 1949 painting *The Name* bear no apparent relationship to *The Name II* of 1950, which was first exhibited at Newman's second one-man show in April 1951 at Betty Parsons Gallery. The importance of the white-with-white pair of paintings (*The Voice*, *The Name II*) to Newman's thinking at the time is suggested by the announcement of the Parsons exhibition, which Newman designed and had printed in white ink on white cardboard.

Nan Rosenthal

Fig. 1. Barnett Newman, *The Name*, 1949. National Gallery of Art, Washington, Gift of the Woodward Foundation

ALBERTO GIACOMETTI
1901–1966

The Table before the Dormer Window, 1950
Graphite
20⅛ x 14 (51.2 x 35.7)

Gift of John D. Herring and
Mr. and Mrs. Paul L. Herring
in Memory of
Mr. and Mrs. H. Lawrence Herring

"What I believe," Giacometti said, "is that whether it be a question of sculpture or of painting, it is in fact only drawing that counts. One must cling solely, exclusively to drawing. If one could master drawing, all the rest would be possible."[1] Giacometti came as close to achieving that goal as any artist of his generation, especially in his mature works after 1945. Without pause he moved flawlessly from one medium to another, his sculpture fortifying his drawings and his drawings informing his paintings. Giacometti's unfaltering eye absorbed all that surrounded him: his friends and family, the landscape of his native Switzerland, and the familiar objects that filled his home and studio. Yet it was not the appearance of his subjects that interested him but the physical act of seeing. Vision after all is not a fixed sense; it shifts continuously, and Giacometti was able to capture that quality in brilliant drawings such as this one, whose swiftly coursing lines suggest a reality that is momentary rather than constant.

As a child Giacometti was an enthusiastic draftsman, constantly drawing the people and everyday objects that surrounded him, including reproductions that he found in art books. From all accounts he possessed a keen intelligence and insatiable curiosity.[2] He would return again and again to the same subject, always attuned to its possibilities. Although he began his studies in Geneva, he concluded them in Paris where he settled in a Montparnasse studio in 1927. During the late twenties and early thirties he explored the avant-garde styles in vogue at the time: primitivism, cubism, and surrealism. But by the end of World War II Giacometti had sifted through these numerous influences and arrived at the signature style that defined his work thereafter. It is that style that marks the present drawing, the first by Giacometti to enter the National Gallery's collection.

Giacometti made annual visits to his family home in Stampa, a Swiss village in the Italian-speaking Bregaglia Valley. There he devoted his energies to painting and especially to drawing. He drew incessantly, recording the home's intimate interiors: its vaulted ceilings, the mullioned dormer windows, the rustic tables and sideboards, and the various beloved objects that graced their surfaces. This scene is of the kitchen table at Stampa with a basket and a pitcher of flowers, set against a dormer window with a bottle of Chianti on its sill.[3] In attempting to capture the transitory experience of seeing, Giacometti relied solely on his lines: those thinly defined marks that speed from point to point, propelled by a hand that seems never to lose touch with the sheet. Tangled and rapidly executed, they describe objects in an atmosphere that seems palpable. Their contours are gapped and in places erased so that air and light pass through. For Giacometti there was no such thing as empty space. It was part of his encompassing vision and was as tangible to him as the flowers that fill the pitcher or the bottle that rests on the sill.

James Lord's numerous essays on Giacometti are some of the most insightful writings on the artist. Lord knew him well and was keenly attentive to his demeanor.[4] In writing about Giacometti's passion for drawing, he recounted that "even when his fingers were not engaged, his eye was. And often when he was seated somewhere without a pen or pencil in hand, his fingers would move round and round with the insistent gesture of drawing—on the table of a café, or on his knee as he rode along in a taxi—as if the mere motion of drawing might induce some new fragment of reality."[5] For Giacometti drawing was an essential means of clarifying his vision and of committing to line the transient nature of his surroundings.

Judith Brodie

PROVENANCE
Mr. and Mrs. H. Lawrence Herring, acquired c. 1952.

NOTES
1. As quoted in James Lord, *Alberto Giacometti Drawings* (Greenwich, Conn., 1971), 26.

2. Sylvio Berthoud, "Some Personal Memories," in Valerie J. Fletcher, *Alberto Giacometti 1901–1966* [exh. cat. Hirshhorn Museum and Sculpture Garden] (Washington, 1988), 16.

3. For related drawings and other interior views at Stampa, see Lord 1971, nos. 88–90, 95, 96, 98, 102, 104, 114.

4. Giacometti made several portraits of James Lord, as illustrated in Bernard Lamarche-Vadel, *Alberto Giacometti* (Paris, 1984), 98.

5. Lord 1971, 26.

JACKSON POLLOCK
1912–1956

Untitled, c. 1951
Black ink on mulberry paper
25 x 38¾ (63.5 x 98.4)

Promised Gift of
Robert P. and Arlene R. Kogod

Around 1947 Jackson Pollock put aside the traditional tools and concepts of making art. Instead of brushing paint onto canvas or applying pencil or crayon to paper, he poured or flung paint onto surfaces. Instead of illustrating feelings, he attempted to express them. And in spite of the fact that these works seem uninhibited, they are in essence highly controlled. The sheer effusion and velocity of lines in this strikingly bold drawing belie its ingeniously ordered invention.

Pollock grew up mainly in Arizona and California, the youngest of five sons. Although his family's resources were limited, his mother was a determined believer who fostered artistic potential in each of her children. In 1926 Jackson's oldest brother enrolled at the Art Students League in New York City where Jackson joined him four years later. Both brothers studied with Thomas Hart Benton, the titan of American scene painting and a staunch opponent of European modernism. Although Jackson revered Benton he eventually sought new directions. Years later Pollock wrote with some irony and a good deal of affection that his work with "Benton was important as something against which to react . . . it was better to have worked with [Benton] than with a less resistant personality who would have provided a much less strong opposition."[1]

Pollock absorbed influences from divergent directions. He admired the work of the Mexican muralists, asserted that Albert Pinkham Ryder was the only American master who interested him,[2] found inspiration in the work of Picasso and Miró, assimilated the surrealist's thoughts on the unconscious, and was affected by Jungian symbolism. Somehow Pollock took account of all these influences and forged an approach to art-making that was entirely unique. That approach was dubbed action painting[3] or abstract expressionism and was largely responsible for the ascendency of American art after World War II.

Pollock's work was basically linear with little distinction made between drawing and painting. As one commentator remarked, Pollock had the "impulse to draw with paint."[4] The present drawing is from a series of works done in ink and sometimes watercolor on absorbent Japanese papers. The artist began by making an ink drawing on the top sheet of a stack of Japanese papers. Because oriental paper is very absorbent, the primary image would bleed through to the sheets beneath. These were later separated and frequently reworked with either ink or watercolor. The present drawing, a vigorously worked and enormously powerful image, was the primary work in a sequence; its immediate undersheet is in a private collection; and the remaining two undersheets were acquired by the National Gallery in 1985.[5] It is very rare indeed to have three directly associated works from a Pollock series. Rarer still is a primary work of such exceptional impact and brilliance, now promised by the Kogods to join the sheets already in the Gallery.

While many of Pollock's so-called poured works are centrifugally structured, the present drawing is essentially episodic. Two wildly energetic vortexes mirror each other on alternate sides of the sheet. One is underlaid by a burst of gridlike lines (to the left), the other by a more tightly compacted grid (to the right). Toward the center four dynamic spatters of ink punctuate the whole and slow the frenzied motion. A line spills onto the page at top and decisively parts and isolates the activity. Barely compressed into the lower corner is a diminutive vortex, acting like a brilliant coda. It is an exquisite orchestration that calls to mind the poet Frank O'Hara's statement about Pollock's draftsmanship: "that amazing ability to quicken a line by thinning it, to slow it by flooding, to elaborate that simplest of elements, the line— to change, to reinvigorate, to extend, to build up an embarrassment of riches in the mass of drawing alone."[6]

Judith Brodie

PROVENANCE
The artist to Lee Krasner Pollock, acquired 1986 from the Lee Krasner Pollock estate.

NOTES
1. Jackson Pollock, *Arts and Architecture* 61 (Feb. 1944), 14.

2. Pollock 1944, 14.

3. The critic Harold Rosenberg coined the name "action painting." He wrote that at "a certain moment the canvas began to appear to one American painter after another as an arena in which to act—rather than as a space in which to reproduce, re-design, analyze or 'express' an object, actual or imagined. What was to go on the canvas was not a picture but an event." See his "The American Action Painters," *Artnews* 51 (Dec. 1952), 22.

4. Bernice Rose, *Jackson Pollock: Drawing into Painting* [exh. cat. The Museum of Modern Art] (New York, 1980), 16.

5. For the present drawing and its associated sheets see Francis Valentine O'Connor and Eugene Victor Thaw, *Jackson Pollock: A Catalogue Raisonné of Paintings, Drawings, and Other Works,* 4 vols. (New Haven and London, 1978), 3: nos. 821 and 822 and 4:165.

6. Frank O'Hara, *Jackson Pollock* (New York, 1959), 26.

DAVID SMITH
1906–1965

Untitled (Virgin Islands), 1933
Ink and graphite
17⅛ x 27⅛ (43.5 x 69)

Untitled (Oct 4 1951), 1951
Ink and gouache
26⅛ x 19¹⁵⁄₁₆ (66.4 x 50.6)

Untitled (11–22–58), 1958
Ink and egg yolk
17⅝ x 26¹⁄₁₆ (44.8 x 66.1)

Untitled 5 (Sept 13–58), 1958
Graphite, ink with egg yolk, and
gouache
26¾ x 39¹⁵⁄₁₆ (68 x 101.5)

Untitled (9/3/59), 1959
Ink
26¹¹⁄₁₆ x 39⅝ (67.8 x 101.3)

Untitled, 1962
Enamel spray paint
11⁹⁄₁₆ x 17⅝ (29.4 x 44.7)

Untitled, 1963
Enamel spray paint
17⁹⁄₁₆ x 11⅝ (44.6 x 29.5)

Gift of Candida and Rebecca Smith

Although David Smith is best known as a sculptor, he was a painter first; and he continued to work in painting and drawing throughout his career.[1] He "drew every day. He kept a note-pad by the bed, to capture those images so vivid in sleep. Another waited on the table in the workshop beside the telephone, in addition to notebooks which were rather larger. Sometimes he'd sketch a detail of an object seen in a museum, Assyrian or Egyptian art, or something as intricate as a lock. He had to draw."[2]

These seven drawings and an eighth work in enamel paint on canvas, also part of this gift, present important aspects of the artist's work in two dimensions. Smith himself made no distinctions between his drawings and his paintings; and in fact, many of the drawings are quite painterly whereas some of the paintings emphasize draftsmanship.

Some of Smith's drawings relate directly to sculpture, either as working ideas or as portraits after the fact; others relate more tenuously. All of them share with the sculpture Smith's unflagging sense of authority as expressed in his statement "From the artist there is no conscious effort to find universal truth or beauty, no effort to analyze other men's minds in order to speak for them. His act in art is an act of personal conviction and identity. If there is truth in art, it is his own truth. If beauty is involved it is only the metaphor of imagination."[3]

The earliest work in this group, *Untitled (Virgin Islands)*, dates from 1933, the moment Smith began working in sculpture. It is part of a group associated with the Virgin Islands, either because they were made there or because they stemmed from drawings made during a sojourn in Saint Thomas from fall 1932 through June 1933.[4] Like others

in the group this drawing features broad sweeping strokes of varying widths juxtaposed with delicate, meandering lines that suggest an interest in automatism. Some of the lines map out shapes with no obvious references to the visible world whereas others evoke images of shells or trees. The drawings call to mind the work of Stuart Davis and of Arshile Gorky, as if Smith instinctively was tracking a wide field on which to base his understanding of ideas about abstract art.

Particularly dramatic in this sheet are the broad areas of black that function between forms, as hollows or shadows, while also establishing dramatic compositional elements across the surface. The components of the drawing relate closely to those in Smith's sculptures of the period that incorporated wire, wood, shells, and other found materials. Smith's own comments about cubism seem apt in reference to his scheme: "The overlay of line shapes, being a cubist invention permits each form its own identity and when seen through each other highly multiplies the complex of associations into new unities."[5]

The next of this group of drawings, *Untitled, (Oct 4 1951)*, in ink and tempera, is the most painterly and also the most sculptural of them. Its rich palette of oranges, blues, black, and white is somewhat unusual for Smith, although the daring use of color in two dimensions is not. Aggressive shifts in space, strongly defined forms, and agitated draftsmanship combine to impart a distinctive sense of strength. The drawing presses to the edges of the sheet, yet remains contained. A layering of materials suggests an additive approach similar to that in Smith's sculpture.

There is a sense of grandeur about the drawing, which summarizes many of the formal themes Smith had been using, while also posing new ideas. Specific recognizable forms, either tied to Smith's sculpture or to elements in nature, are included in the drawings of this period: bones, for example, like the one horizontally displayed here across the left center of the sheet.[6] A heroic work, it was made during the period of the artist's Guggenheim Foundation Fellowship, which enabled him the financial freedom to work ambitiously with greater ease.

Three drawings provide a window into the richness of Smith's calligraphy, showing that the variety and range of his work even within this one realm is extraordinary. Some sheets feel quite close to the abstractness of the Oriental calligraphy that served as part of Smith's inspiration.[7] The individuated strokes maintain a life of their own, as in *Untitled (11–22–58)*, 1958, painted with a broad brush and the distinctive mixture of egg yolk and black Chinese ink that Smith began to use in the early 1950s.

The sensuous overlapping of strokes plays a crucial role in developing the energy of the sheet. Its dancing hieroglyphs vary in density. Also of importance is the beautiful yellow paper, an example of Smith's keen interest in beautiful sheets, their textures, colors, weights, and the effect of these qualities on the drawings themselves. "David took pride in good paper. . . . In part, quality was a solace for the fact that he couldn't buy steel large enough to make the sculpture he dreamed of."[8]

Many of Smith's calligraphic drawings of the late 1950s suggest mountain landscapes, a clear response to the surroundings of Bolton Landing, New York, his full-time home

Untitled (Oct 4 1951), 1951

from 1944.[9] In *Untitled*, 1959, which reveals no clear descriptive characteristics at all, the energetic speed of Smith's strokes and their shifts in scale suggest distant hills and close, dense foliage, perhaps a cloud in the sky, and a definite sense of the grandeur of the Appalachian Mountain landscape that surrounded the artist's studio.

Less characteristic of Smith's calligraphy is *Untitled 5 (Sept 13–58)*, in which there is both a suggestion of an underdrawing and of overpainting with white tempera to modify the black ink line.[10] While retaining the flowing overall qualities characteristic of the calligraphic drawings, spontaneity is not a salient characteristic here.

The two latest of these seven are from a group called the spray drawings, which Smith made starting about 1958. His process involved placing found objects—scraps of metal, paper, and other materials—on the sheet as a mask and then spraying automobile enamel around them. The mask established the image; the spray paint established the color world, which tended to be both layered and speckled, with a rich interaction of several hues as seen in both examples here. Smith often used metallic paints, and sometimes added strokes with white tempera to reinforce shapes and gestures.

The "sprays" are of two types, those that relate closely to Smith's sculpture, as in *Untitled*, 1963, with two circles separated by a horizontal slab; and the free flowing painterly type in which shapes dart in and out of space, as in *Untitled*, 1962. A clue to the mask used for this last drawing remains in the crushed piece of masking tape in the lower left section.

For Smith, making drawings functioned as thinking, as exploring, as action, as event. And the artist proudly included his drawings in his exhibitions throughout his life. These works are a central aspect of his art; knowing them is essential to a deep understanding of his sculpture. Along with the eighth work in this gift, *Untitled*, 1965, a nude painted in enamel on canvas that reveals another aspect of Smith's calligraphic style, this beautiful and wide-ranging group of drawings joins one other calligraphic sheet and six of Smith's sculptures that are part of the National Gallery's collection.

Ruth E. Fine

NOTES

1. My thanks to Candida Smith and Peter Stevens for information they have provided about these drawings. Typically all seven are *Untitled*; on several, the place or date of execution is appended. In *Untitled (9/3/59)* the signature and date are inscribed within a paint stroke, a format Smith frequently used late in his life. On Smith's drawings specifically see Paul Cummings, *David Smith: The Drawings* [exh. cat. Whitney Museum of American Art] (New York, 1979); Trinkett Clark, *The Drawings of David Smith* [exh. cat. International Exhibitions Foundation] (Washington, 1985); *David Smith: Works on Paper* [exh. cat. Margo Leavin Gallery] (Los Angeles, 1990), with an introduction by Eleanor Green; *David Smith: Drawings of the Fifties* [exh. cat. Anthony D'Offay Gallery] (London, 1988), with an essay, "Living with David Smith," by Jean Freas.

2. Freas in London 1988, 6.

3. Quoted in Cleve Gray, ed., *David Smith by David Smith* (New York, 1968), 72.

4. The dates given for Smith's trip to the Virgin Islands vary; these are those listed by Smith in a biographical note published in Smith 1968, 24.

5. David Smith Papers, Archives of American Art, roll 4, frame 384, quoted in New York 1979, 21.

6. A drawing titled *Chicken Bones*, also 1951, is reproduced in Edward F. Fry and Miranda McClintic, *David Smith: Painter, Sculptor, Draftsman* [exh. cat. Hirshhorn Museum and Sculpture Garden] (Washington, 1983), 101, plate 79.

7. Freas in London 1988, 10, told of giving Smith a book on Zen painting titled *The Spirit of the Brush*.

8. Freas in London 1988, 7.

9. During the 1950s landscape was a major subject in Smith's sculpture and paintings as well. For example, see Rosalind E. Krauss, "The Landscapes of the Fifties," in *Terminal Iron Works: The Sculpture of David Smith* (Cambridge and London, 1979), 76–84; and in Washington 1983, 82–83, plates 53–55.

10. The number "5" inscribed to the left of Smith's signature and the date suggests an ongoing series, not necessarily that this is the fifth drawing on this date.

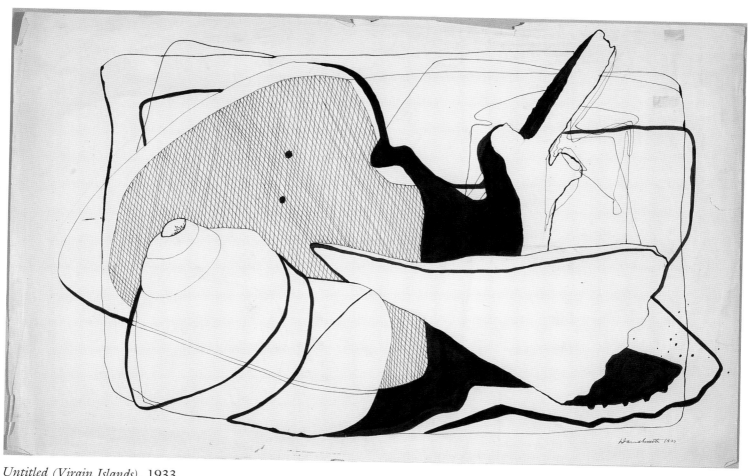

Untitled (Virgin Islands), 1933

Untitled (11–22–58), 1958

Untitled 5 (Sept 13–58), 1958

Untitled (9/3/59), 1959

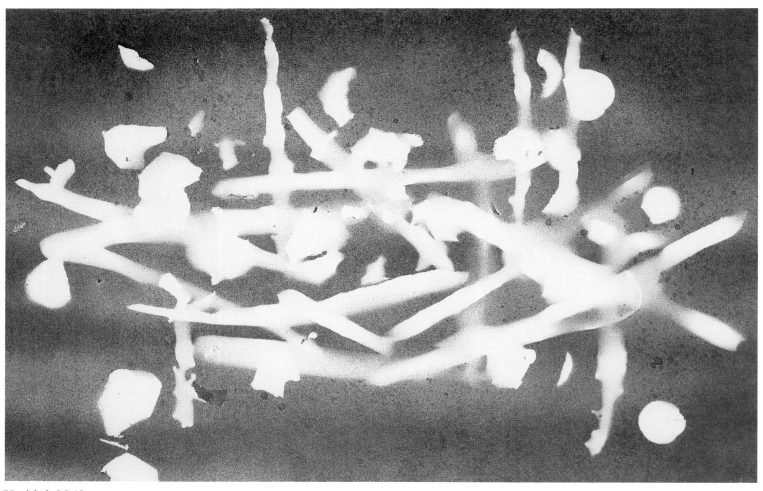

Untitled, 1962

Untitled, 1963

CLYFFORD STILL
1904–1980

1951-N, 1951
Oil on canvas
92⁵⁄₁₆ x 69⅛ (234.61 x 175.58)

Gift (Partial and Promised) of
Robert and Jane Meyerhoff

Although Clyfford Still's best-known work is identified with abstract expressionism and in particular the color-field direction found in Rothko and Newman, its originality bypasses neat categories. Even before making contact with New York art circles from 1945 onward, Still, who had already spent much time in the northwest and then went on to teach in San Francisco, forged a strong individual style from diverse sources. During the next seven years audacious pictorial statements grew rapidly out of those foundations. They are therefore less the total "breakthrough" that critics have imagined than the extraordinary climax of an artistic vision matured over more than a quarter of a century.

Some of these paintings from the later 1940s and early 1950s reduce the ruggedly incisive contours that Still liked to draw with the palette knife to a few dramatic accents set upon unpainted canvas. Others establish a conflict between vertically uprising, eroded, and resistant passages, often heightened by dissonant color combinations. A third tendency was to engulf almost the entire image with a single mass of pigment. *1951-N* belongs more to the latter type yet takes elements from the first two. Its startling appearance—a wall of earthy browns riven by crimson streaks, lemon yellow, and the merest blue sliver at the bottom right edge—comes from an unusual synthesis. On the one hand, everything seems stripped to a bedrock of forms. On the other, this radical abstraction is charged with expressiveness: violent knife work, the sense that action is happening beyond the picture's edge or below its surface, and a denial of ordinary visual space so intense that the viewer is confronted as if before a monolith.

Appropriately, then, Still could comment in the year before *1951-N* that they were "not paintings in the usual sense; they are life and death merging in fearful union."[1] His allusion was evidently to the symbolism underlying the images; ideas whose roots extended back to acute early experiences. As a youth Still homesteaded on the prairies of Alberta where the vast flatness of the landscape made a deep impression. During long periods of drought and recession through the 1920s and after, the situation there became a struggle between the environment and life itself that was translated into the vertical motifs—human, natural, and even mechanical—which rise from the land against expansive stretches of sky or other surroundings in the early works.

By the mid-thirties more cryptic elements began to personify the merger of earth, heavens, and the living presence. It is almost certain that Still, at first a student at Washington State College under an eminent literary scholar, developed them partly from modern studies in Greek mythology that dealt with sinister chthonic figures, dark regions, and blazing flashes from the sky above. When Rothko in 1946 quoted Still's notion that his art was "Of the Earth, the Damned and of the Recreated"[2] it surely echoed such origins. In the meantime he had also absorbed lessons from European avant-garde painters such as Picasso and Miró to reach a spartan manner fully, and aggressively, his own.

Vestiges of past themes remain in *1951-N*: the yellow outburst from on high that answers to the blue literally submerged deep below (scrutiny reveals how most of it was overpainted), a field bristling with forces, and an upright pared down to an alizarin crimson gash whose minute whitish flecks near its break are the final traces of the markings that animated Still's earlier figures. Even more daring is the way these are stated. Not only did the concept of the paint surface itself as a hostile terrain have little parallel at the time, but also the design where shapes are sliced by the edge was groundbreaking and without any debt to cubism. Given no more than a basic date-plus-letter title by Still in order to banish literary associations, the achievements of this period breathe an intense, fearsome spirit. Before them, he wrote, the viewer would "be on his own."[3]

Still concentrated his donations to the public realm in select locations, among them museums in Buffalo and San Francisco. As the first of his works to enter the National Gallery, *1951-N* constitutes a crucial and magnificent addition to its representation of postwar American art.

David Anfam

PROVENANCE
Marlborough Gallery.

NOTES
1. Unpublished statement for an exhibition at the Betty Parsons Gallery, New York.

2. Introduction, *First Exhibition, Paintings, Clyfford Still,* [exh. cat. Art of This Century] (New York, 1946). Still's main source was evidently Jane E. Harrison, *Themis* (Cambridge, 1912). See David Anfam, *Abstract Expressionism* (London, 1990), 68.

3. Letter of 29 December 1949, Archives of American Art.

CLYFFORD STILL
1903–1970

Untitled, 1951
Oil on canvas
108 x 92½ (274.32 x 234.95)

Gift (Partial and Promised) of
Marcia S. Weisman

Rather than progress along a linear path, Clyfford Still periodically mined his own past for inspiration. Established ideas would give birth to breathtaking new compositions. Dating from the same year as *1951-N*, *Untitled* attests to his cycles of growth and reflection.[1] Its blaze of yellow belongs to the period when Still was pushing color to the farthest limits. In 1950 he wrote about creating "explosive forces," and no phrase could better describe the impact that both canvases wield.[2] Yet a sense of design grips those vectors in precarious equilibrium. The excitement is almost tangible.

Echoes and accents offset the massive hold on the viewer's attention exerted by the field. Narrow rills of orange, red, and other strong hues anchor the right side whose asymmetry nonetheless balances the vast radiant gulf. As sharp wedges rear upward from the lower left, almost identical rifts descend from the top. Whites and black establish a dialogue around the entire picture, while the exotic pink at the upper edge resounds against an equally minute blue in the bottom right corner. Belying Still's stereotype as one of the cruder abstract expressionists, these refinements also revolutionize some of his oldest artistic traits.

Colleagues from Still's time as an art instructor remembered an ability to analyze paintings in great detail.[3] Indeed, compositional rhythms he observed in Cézanne in 1935[4] anticipate by a decade or more the tectonics that would hold the subsequent abstractions together beneath their austere surfaces. So do the devices of Still's representational style from the 1920s onward. In a typical case such as the Canadian prairie landscape entitled *Row of Elevators* (National Museum of American Art, Smithsonian Institution, Washington), red and green are poised on either side of the central focus.

He also frequently introduced conventional *repoussoirs* — motifs such as trees or figures that the old masters placed near a picture's edge to frame its interior elements — whose ultimate descendants are the marginal presences seen in *Untitled*. What had begun as traditional practice returns here to amazing effect.

The inimitable palette, involving "hot" colors such as yellows and reds that sometimes overwhelm, at other times themselves are overwhelmed by earth tones and black, may express a similar transformation. Certainly the various yellows that came to the fore in the later 1940s and dominate *Untitled* had once held a special meaning. A fellow art teacher was struck by "great shafts of ocher wheat blades rising upwards from a relentless earth" in his early work[5]; the word "yellow" occurred in three of the titles in his 1943 retrospective[6]; and the famous *Jamais* (Peggy Guggenheim Collection, Venice) contains upright vivid ocher wheat stalks. The latter accompany a dark red sun and an immensely elongated black specter.[7] To cite such a history behind *Untitled* neither trivializes nor denies its sheer rigor, but instead suggests how far Still had traveled in a few years.

Less ferociously wrought than *1951-N*, *Untitled* has perhaps a more exultant tone. In particular, it seems to liberate the verticals that the artist considered indicative of vital energy itself. Moreover, every hue is near maximum saturation. Whereas the Meyerhoff gift presents, on the whole, an unforgettably landlocked mass, the rising movement in the present work runs to infinity as if form and space were a single continuum.[8] Both exemplify Still's art at its most absolute. Together they allow the Gallery to initiate the record of his historic status.

David Anfam

PROVENANCE
The artist.

NOTES

1. Irving Sandler, *The Triumph of American Painting: A History of Abstract Expressionism* (New York, 1970) reproduced the work as *1951 Yellow* (plate XI). This is erroneous since Still stopped using titles (other than simple numerical ones) by 1947: see his 3 March letter of that year to Barnett Newman in the Archives of American Art.

2. Letter of 5 July 1950, Archives of American Art.

3. For example, the late Lois Katzenbach, a teacher at Washington State College, interview with the author, 9 April 1978. Also, Dr. William Bakamis, letter to the author, 21 February 1978.

4. Clyfford E. Still, "Cézanne. A Study in Evaluation" (M.A. thesis in Fine Arts, State College of Washington, Pullman, 1935).

5. Theresa Pollak, *An Art School: Some Reminiscences* (Richmond, Va., c. 1969), 47.

6. At the San Francisco Museum of Art, March.

7. See Angelica Z. Rudenstine, *Peggy Guggenheim Collection, Venice* (New York, 1985), 707–710.

8. See Ti-Grace Sharpless, *Clyfford Still* (Philadelphia, 1963), 9. The concept of space and time as a continuous dimension was well established in American physics by the 1940s, and Still undoubtedly knew the nuclear physicist J. Robert Oppenheimer's writings.

BARNETT NEWMAN
1905–1970

Achilles, 1952
Oil on canvas
96 x 79 (243.84 x 200.66)

Gift of Annalee Newman

Following his second one-man exhibition at Betty Parsons in New York in the spring of 1951, Newman worked on several paintings that, while they did not involve gradual modeling from light to dark, showed brushwork and changes within one hue from more opaque areas to thinner paint handling. This gave the impression of slight changes in value. In *Achilles* it occurs in the broad red area that forms the central field, contrasting with the dark brown sides of the painting that are resolutely opaque.

The most striking feature of *Achilles* is the way that, unlike a narrow zip that races from the top edge to the bottom edge of the canvas, the vivid, broad, central red shape is broken toward the bottom in an irregular jagged manner, cut into by the opaque dark brown at the bottom. Despite the contrast in paint handling, both the red and the brown appear from close up to be on the same plane. The unusual composition has a precedent in a brush and ink drawing of 1949 (fig. 1), where the central swath (the white paper reversed into an image by the black

ink around it) appears to stop with a jagged edge before reaching the lower edge of the paper.[1] Much as brushed ink establishes the bottom of the white central image of the drawing, it seems likely that brown paint established the bottom of the red central area of *Achilles*.

Regarding the title *Achilles*, Thomas Hess has written that Newman referred "to its red and fiery central shape as a 'shield,' thus reiterating his great theme, the act of creation and the artist as a god, through Homer's famous description of that masterpiece of Hellenic realism, the hero's armor wrought by Hephaestus."[2]

Nan Rosenthal

NOTES

1. Brenda Richardson, *Barnett Newman: The Complete Drawings, 1944–1969* [exh. cat. The Baltimore Museum of Art] (Baltimore, 1979), 150-151.

2. Thomas Hess, *Barnett Newman* [exh. cat. The Museum of Modern Art] (New York, 1970), 82.

Fig. 1. Barnett Newman, *Untitled*, 1949. Courtesy Anthony d'Offay Gallery

JOHN MARIN
1870–1953

New Brunswick Sketchbook
(29 drawings), 1951
Graphite, watercolor, and blue ink
13¹⁵/₁₆ x 11¹/₁₆ (35.3 x 28)

Maine Landscapes Sketchbook
(12 drawings), 1952
Watercolor, crayon, graphite, ink
11⅞ x 8⅞ (30.2 x 22.4)

Gift of Norma B. Marin

Drawing is central to John Marin's art. From the 1890s, when Marin was practicing architecture, and throughout his career as a painter, which lasted half a century, he seems habitually to have carried a sketchbook or loose sheets of paper with him, making brief visual notes of his surroundings as he engaged in his daily activities.

In 1986 and 1987 John Marin Jr. donated to the National Gallery of Art an archive collection of his father's work that includes 114 watercolors, thirteen oils, thirteen drawings, twenty etchings, and sixteen sketchbooks that contain more than four hundred drawings and watercolors dating from the 1890s through the 1940s.[1] The two sketchbooks now generously donated by Marin's daughter-in-law probably are the last volumes the artist filled, bringing our rich representation of his drawings to almost the end of his life.

All of the twenty-nine studies in the earlier of the two books are annotated as to place. Most of them document a trip to St. John, New Brunswick, Canada, revisiting and drawing places Marin had first seen as a child of twelve. At the front of the book are several sites in Maine, however, and one in Massachusetts is at the back.[2] The New Brunswick scenes for the most part are linear in approach, using graphite or blue ink—a material distinctive to this sketchbook. Nine of the graphite drawings, including *Near Calais, Maine*,[3] incorporate watercolor, which Marin applied freely with the great versatility for which his art had long been acclaimed. All of the drawings, regardless of medium, are marked by the artist's lively staccato style.

The 1952 sketchbook contains eleven pages plus a twelfth drawing on tracing paper (a drawing surface Marin used often at the end of his life) that was attached to a verso, perhaps by the artist.[4] This book is filled entirely with scenes in Maine where Marin spent a significant part of most years from 1914 through 1953. Annotated like the earlier one, this book features sites not far from his Cape Split home, many of which Marin visited repeatedly during the last years of his life: the Tunk Mountains; Machias; and brilliantly colorful sunsets, perhaps seen from the porch of his cottage overlooking Pleasant Bay.

Most of the scenes were worked in watercolor with graphite, although occasionally ink was employed as well, and they are as highly finished as Marin's individual late watercolors and oils. Patches of paint in counterpoise to the dynamic linear structure evoke rather than depict the various moods of the artist's adopted state. Marin's colors tend to reflect the seasons. The page illustrated here, for example, splendidly illustrates his response to the vivid, burning reds of autumn, a season Marin occasionally also responded to with words:

> —there are the things that grow on the
>   ground—
> flowers trees and such—There are the
>   ledges—not
> forgetting entirely the Ocean and a few
>   wild things—
> birds fishes and animals. . . .
> The day is balmy—the sun is warm—the
>   water sparkles
> The little purple and gold asters in
>   clumps—beautiful
> The (Earth Beautiful) if only those who
>   live on it would
>   —behave in some extent
> As for me—it's back to—the Cities
>   —but I hope for not too long.[5]

Ruth E. Fine

PROVENANCE
Estate of the artist; Mr. and Mrs. John Marin, Jr.

NOTES
1. The drawings in the John Marin Archive gift are briefly described in Ruth E. Fine, "The John Marin Archive at the National Gallery of Art," *Drawing* 9 (September–October 1989), 54–58. Other watercolors and etchings have come to the National Gallery of Art as gifts from Frank and Jeannette Eyerly, Eugene and Agnes E. Meyer, Mrs. Harold Ober, James N. Rosenberg, and the Alfred Stieglitz Collection.

2. On this sketchbook, see Cleve Gray and Dorothy Norman, "John Marin's Sketchbook— Summer 1951," *Art in America* 55 (Sept.–Oct. 1969), 44–53.

3. In color, composition, and the handling of his materials, this sheet is remarkably like the one that follows it, annotated "Near St. Stephen, N.B." The only page in this part of the book said to be a Canadian site, it makes one wonder about the accuracy of the annotations.

4. For illustrations of all pages in this sketchbook except the one on tracing paper see Ruth E. Fine, *John Marin* [exh. cat. National Gallery of Art] (Washington, 1990), 272–280.

5. Letter from Marin to Alfred Stieglitz, 29 September 1943, Cape Split Maine, taken from Dorothy Norman, ed., *The Selected Letters of John Marin* (New York, 1949), 209–210.

New Brunswick Sketchbook

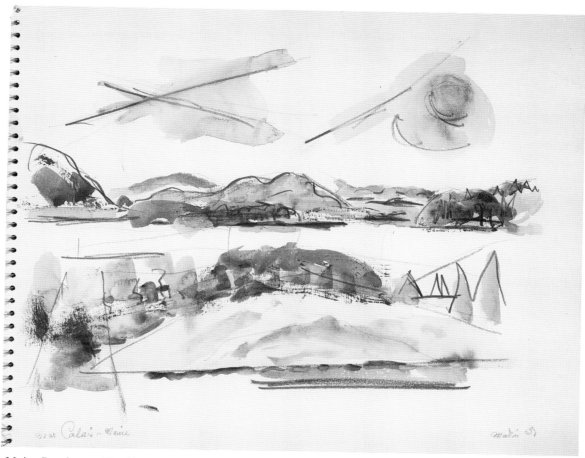

Maine Landscapes Sketchbook

ROBERT FRANK
Born 1924

Black, White, and Things
Bound volume of 34 gelatin silver
photographs, 1952
14⁹⁄₁₆ x 15½ (37 x 40)

Robert Frank Collection,
Gift (Partial and Promised) of
Robert Frank

A few years ago, Robert Frank recalled that as a young man he often "made decisions based on negative feelings." He continued, "I didn't know exactly what I wanted, but I sure knew what I didn't want. I didn't want to be part of the smallness of Switzerland."[1] His revolt against the rigid Swiss middle-class standards of decorum, its circumscribed world view, and its strict moral standards has informed much of his life and art ever since. It not only propelled his immigration to the United States in 1947 and defined his lifestyle once he arrived, but it is also at the very core of his photography. For it is this attitude that challenged and inspired him to reject accepted conventions of photographic style, subject matter, and intention. To this day, it is this rebellion that gives his art its strength and clarity, its frequently unsettling quality, and its compelling sense of honesty.

Thinking back to his early work, Frank also remembered: "I wanted to sell my pictures to *Life* magazine and they never did buy them. So I developed a tremendous contempt for them which helped me. You have to be enraged. I also wanted to follow my own intuition and do it my way, and not make any concessions—not make a *Life* story. . . . It comes back to what I said before, if I rejected life in Switzerland with all its moral values, so the same thing goes here. If I hate all those stories with a beginning, a middle, and an end then obviously I will make an effort to produce something that will stand up to all those stories and not be like them."[2]

For several years in the late 1940s and early 1950s Frank did struggle to have his photographs published in *Life* as well as other magazines. In addition he also made three bound volumes of photographs that begin to address the cumulative and intuitive power of a sequence of photographs: *Peru*, a book of thirty-eight photographs made in 1948 and assembled that same year; an untitled compilation of images of Paris made for his first wife, Mary Lockspeiser; and three cop-

ies of the book *Black, White, and Things*, designed by Werner Zryd, with photographs taken from 1947 to 1952.[3] The first two books were stories in the more traditional sense: *Peru*, although it has no clear progression through time, does convey a sense of Frank's journey through and discovery of that South American country, while Mary Lockspeiser's book is a lyrical poem of photographs of Paris.

Black, White, and Things, however, is a complex, ambitious, and sophisticated work. Instead of exploring just one subject as do *Peru* and the Lockspeiser book, *Black, White, and Things* uses photographs from many of the locales Frank explored in his early years: New York, Peru, Spain, London, and Paris. Not organized thematically, it is divided into units that are grouped conceptually. As Frank wrote on the title page: "sombre people and black events/quiet people and peaceful places/ and things people have come in contact with/ this, I try to show in my photography." The "black" group includes, for example, photographs of London bankers or funerals in Spain. Although it does contain some joyous images, these few lyrical notes are followed by bleaker ones. The "white" section includes photographs of intimate familial details—*My Family, New York*, for example, as well as a Peruvian family and a communion. The final section on "things" is the most emphatic. While it begins with a wistful photograph of a man holding a tulip behind his back, it quickly progresses to a chilling juxtaposition of religion and commerce, between a photograph of a procession with a statue of Christ on a cross, titled *Men of Wood*, and an image of a balloon from the Macy's Thanksgiving Day parade, titled *Men of Air, New York* (fig. 1). These are followed by a haunting photograph of a doll in a plastic bag.[4]

Stylistically and conceptually, *Black, White, and Things* is the precursor for Frank's book *The Americans*, first published in 1958. Like the later work, it uses groupings of photographs and sequences to establish meaning, and, like *The Americans*, it is founded on the power of intuition. No text or captions direct our attention or manipulate our sentiments. Only a brief quote from Antoine de Saint-Exupéry, printed on the title page, sets the tone. It reads: "It is only with the heart that one can see rightly. What is essential is invisible to the eye."

In May 1990 Robert Frank gave the Gallery a major archive, representing his entire career from the 1940s to his most recent work of the late 1980s. Although the Robert Frank Collection contains approximately

2,000 rolls of film, 2,296 contact sheets, 999 work prints, and sixty-one rare vintage photographs, one of its most compelling items is *Black, White, and Things*. It, perhaps more than anything, makes us fully appreciate the ambition and intention of the young photographer.

Sarah Greenough

PROVENANCE
Rosie and Henry Frank, Zurich, 1952; Robert Frank, 1983.

NOTES
1. "History—His Story," by William S. Johnson, in "The Pictures are a Necessity: Robert Frank in Rochester, NY, November 1988," *Occasional Papers No. 2* (Rochester, 1989), 28.

2. Johnson 1989, 37–38.

3. Anne Tucker and Philip Brookman in *Robert Frank: New York to Nova Scotia* [exh. cat. Museum of Fine Arts] (Houston 1986), 9, noted that Frank made four copies of *Black, White, and Things*. However, further research indicates that only three copies were made: in addition to this one, given by Frank to his parents, he gave one to Edward Steichen, which is now in the collection of The Museum of Modern Art, New York, and one unbound copy is in a private collection.

4. The sequencing of photographs in the two intact copies is different, particularly in the more complex section of "things." Steichen's copy, for example, does not juxtapose *Men of Wood* with *Men of Air*, but has them on successive double-page spreads. See Houston 1986, 94.

Fig. 1. *Men of Air, New York*, 1948

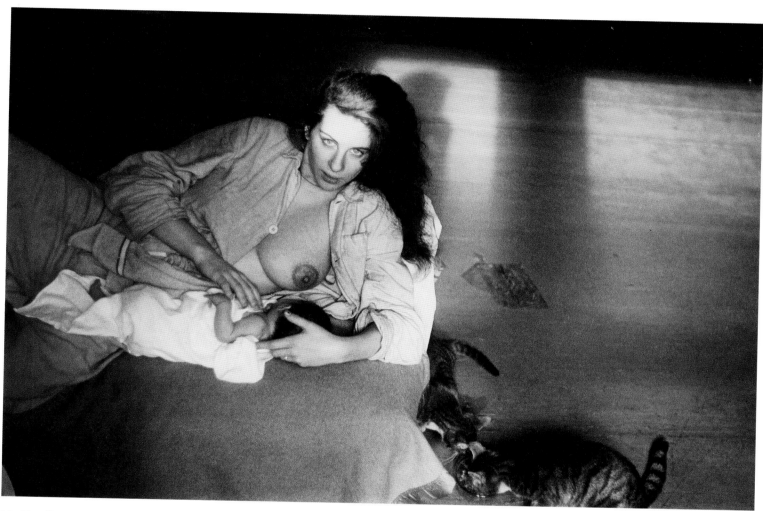

My Family, New York, 1951

ROBERT FRANK
Born 1924

City of London, 1952
Geltin silver photograph
9 x 13¼ (22.9 x 33.7)

Parking Lot, 1952
Gelatin silver photograph
9⅛ x 13³⁄₁₆ (23.2 x 33.5)

Robert Frank Collection,
Gift of The Howard Gilman
Foundation

In 1976 Robert Frank admitted that there is an element of the stranger present in his art. "Well, I think that's quite a good observation," he said, "I guess I am an observer, in a way. It also had to do with the fact that a lot of my work deals with myself, especially my films. It's very hard to get away from myself. It seems, almost, that's all I have. That's sort of a sad feeling. But that feeling of being a stranger — it has to do with years of photographing, where you walk around, you observe, and you walk away, and you begin to be a pretty good detective."[1]

When Frank moved to New York in 1947 he had walked like a stranger through the city, acutely observing anonymous people and perceptively capturing their isolation while moving through the urban environment. In 1951, after living in New York for four years, he returned to Europe for a stay that lasted a little less than two years. While there he made several photographic essays, including ones on a Welsh miner, chairs and flowers in Paris, and bankers in London. A few of these essays, such as the one on Ben James, the Welsh miner, were the result of a close communication between Frank and his subject, but most were silent records, made without any interaction between the photographer and the people he depicted.

Perhaps nowhere did he better perfect his role as the silent, almost invisible observer than in the series of photographs he made in London in December 1952 of English bankers. As in the *City of London*, the elegant but arrogantly self-confident bankers stride past Frank, oblivious to his presence and his intention. Fascinated with their top hats, overcoats, and umbrellas, Frank was also intrigued with their deportment — in how they carried their canes, angled their hats, and moved through the streets. Permeated with fog, the images, like *Parking Lot*, are fused with a soft gray light that blurs all outlines both in the foreground and background, merging near and far, object and air — so much so, in fact, that one senses that Frank too was enveloped and thus unobtrusively melted into the surroundings.

He made several photographs of the bankers, and as a group this work has an important position in the evolution of his art. He later recalled that at this time he was still trying to create the single photographic masterpiece. And yet in looking at several published in the most recent edition of *The Lines of My Hand* one can see that it was in the group as a whole that Frank found the most meaning. As much as anything else it is the differences between the images — the way one banker tucks his umbrella under his arm while another uses it as a cane, the way another walks precisely with legs close together while yet one more lanky figure work. On the one hand this group harks back to Walker Evans' subway series, while at the same time it predicts Frank's own bus series, the last group of photographs he made in the late 1950s before abandoning still photography for film.

City of London and *Parking Lot*, both vintage prints, are two of a total of six photographs of London bankers whose purchase was made possible by a grant from the Howard Gilman Foundation. All six works are reproduced in Frank's most recent edition of *The Lines of My Hand* and thus are the images the artist selected to represent this important group of photographs.

Sarah Greenough

NOTE
1. "Robert Frank," in *Photography within the Humanities*, ed. Eugenia Parry Janis and Wendy MacNeil (Danbury, New Hampshire, 1977), 64.

ROBERT FRANK
Born 1924

Parade—Hoboken, New Jersey,
1955–1956
Gelatin silver photograph
9⅛ x 13³⁄₁₆ (23.2 x 33.5)

Approaching New York Harbor, 1953
Gelatin silver photograph
9¹³⁄₁₆ x 13¹³⁄₁₆ (23.3 x 33.2)

Robert Frank Collection,
Anonymous Gift

"The photographing of America" is a large order—read at all literally, the phrase would be an absurdity. What I have in mind, then, is observation and record of what one naturalized American finds to see in the United States that signifies the kind of civilization born here and spreading elsewhere.

Robert Frank
Guggenheim Fellowship application, 1954[1]

On 17 March 1953 Robert Frank sailed from Southampton, England, back to New York. In many ways, he left behind his earlier work. During his two years in Europe he had created some of his most lyrical images: passionate, tender, evocative, at times romantic, they speak of a young photographer at peace in his surroundings. For someone born in Zurich, the cities of London and Paris as well as the countries of Wales and Spain had proved fertile subjects, their atmosphere safe and familiar. Yet, like the four people on the Mauretania, Frank was on a journey of thoughtful reflection, looking in many different directions for something else.

What he found, of course, was *The Americans,* a series of eighty-three photographs of the United States made in 1955 and 1956 and published in 1958, which are radically different from his previous work: tough, gritty, often abrasive, they tell of a world that is separated by more than an ocean from Frank's previous abode. *The Americans* is one of the most compelling and influential photographic publications ever produced. With the eyes of a European he looked freshly on the American scene and saw a country plagued by alienation and angst, by extreme contrasts of rich and poor, and by discrimination. He photographed both the empty symbols that had come to stand for American culture—and particularly the flags, parades, and politicans—as well as its true objects of veneration—cars, juke boxes, and the open road. As in *Parade—Hoboken, New*

Jersey, the first image in the book, he looked behind all these symbols, both real and imagined, to see something deeper. He was concerned with revealing how symbols had obscured reality, literally blotting out the people, land, and ideas they supposedly represented. And he was concerned with showing how the people themselves were often blind to the world around them, unable or unwilling to see because their eyes were closed or literally shrouded by these false icons.

Although there are many images in this book that have come to be accepted as masterpieces of the art of photography and through our veneration of them become icons in themselves, it is, perhaps, wrong to extract any one photograph from the work as a whole. For part of Frank's purpose in constructing *The Americans* was to get away from the idea of the singular photographic masterpiece and create, as he said, "a more sustained form of visual [expression]. It would have to last longer. There had to be more pictures that would sustain an idea or a vision or something. I couldn't just depend on that one singular photograph any more. You have to develop; you have to go through different rooms."[2] Originally Frank created four separate rooms or sections in *The Americans,* each of which began with an image of the flag: *Parade—Hoboken, New Jersey* is the first photograph in the book; *Fourth of July—Jay, New York* announced the second room; *Bar—Detroit,* a photograph of a flag fluttering surreally between two portraits of Washington and Lincoln, began the third; and *Political Rally—Chicago* opened the last.

Eventually he merged the sections so that it became one seamless whole, but nevertheless flags remain a powerful, recurrent theme. It was a bold subject on which to frame his idea, for the flag carried with it the potential to be nothing more than a cliché—an obvious, sentimental, fatuous object, stripped of its meaning and conviction. Yet by using it as the prelude to each section, by repeatedly drawing our attention to its hollowness, Frank emphatically demonstrated that it was time to look more clearly at the true nature, not just of the emblems of American life and culture, but of the reality of America itself.

Parade—Hoboken, New Jersey and *Approaching New York Harbor* are part of a larger anonymous gift of twelve photographs by Robert Frank from the years 1951 to 1956. Selected by the artist himself to represent this early period in his work, they are a superb addition to the Robert Frank Collection from this donor, whose support has been crucial to the growth of the photography collection at the Gallery.

Sarah Greenough

NOTES

1. Robert Frank, as quoted in *Robert Frank: New York to Nova Scotia* [exh. cat. Museum of Fine Arts] (Houston, 1986), 20.

2. As quoted by William S. Johnson, "History—His Story," in "The Pictures are a Necessity: Robert Frank in Rochester, NY, November 1988," *Occasional Papers No. 2* (Rochester, 1989), 38.

1955 HOBOKEN

Robert Franck

ROBERT FRANK
Born 1924

Drug Store—Detroit, 1955
Gelatin silver photograph
18⅞ x 12⁷⁄₁₆ (47.9 x 32.7)

Gift of
Christopher and Alexandra Middendorf

Paint Rock Post Office, Alabama, 1955
Gelatin silver photograph, early 1970s
4 x 16⅝ (10.2 x 42.2)

Gift of George F. Hemphill and
Lenore A. Winters

It is all too easy to fall into nostalgia and reverie when looking at Robert Frank's photographs, and particularly those published in *The Americans.* For many the discovery of this book, whether it occurred in the late 1950s when it was published or in subsequent years, was a profound revelation. It was not just Frank's subject matter—gas stations, diners, and juke boxes—or the raw, grainy style of his photographs that gave his work of this period its greatest impact. Nor was it his suggestion that these things, rather than the majestic landscape or towering skyscrapers, were the true icons of American civilization. Instead, as in *Drug Store—Detroit,* it was the sense of loneliness, isolation, and angst that pervaded his haunting images and was so at odds with the myth of postwar prosperity that deeply affected his viewers. In an age that was strongly polarized, that mouthed slogans and paraded endless empty symbols, Frank seemed to be someone who saw clearly and spoke both honestly and passionately.

These photographs so eloquently address not just the social and political issues of the late 1950s and 1960s but more fundamentally its *zeitgeist* that it becomes difficult to separate ourselves from the art. So direct

and powerful is their statement that we have a tendency to project into them our own (possibly idealized) vision of the time, and, more specifically, of who we were and what we believed in. Thus, as our sentiment descends into sentimentality, it is hard to extract the myth of *The Americans* from its reality and the myth of ourselves from this art.

But Robert Frank is not so confused. Sensing the perils of succumbing to a style rather than an expression, Frank stopped photographing in the late 1950s and turned to filmmaking. In the early 1970s when he looked back to *The Americans* he saw a different picture. *Paint Rock Post Office, Alabama* is composed of three negatives taken in 1955 while Frank was traveling around the United States making the photographs for *The Americans.* None of the three was published in that work. In the early 1970s when Frank was working on the first edition of his book *The Lines of My Hand* he printed them as a triptych. The image recalls the empty, evocative interiors of many of the photographs of Walker Evans, Frank's close friend. Yet this is not merely a tribute, nor is it any simple resurrection or appropriation of the past. By combining three neg-

atives, an act clearly indicative of his career as a filmmaker, Frank was taking a broader look at his past, allowing us to see the wider panorama of possibilities available to him. And ultimately, perhaps, this is an attempt to diffuse or at least partially allay the iconic grandeur of his earlier work.

Drug Store—Detroit, graciously donated by Christopher and Alexandra Middendorf, *Paint Rock Post Office, Alabama,* given by George F. Hemphill and Lenore Winters, along with a third photograph, *Platte River, Tennessee,* 1961, from the Middendorf Gallery, are significant additions to the National Gallery's growing collection of Robert Frank's photographs. They particularly enhance our representation of Frank's innovative work from the middle of the 1950s to the early 1960s.

Sarah Greenough

PROVENANCE
Drug Store—Detroit: Christie's, New York, 1985; Christopher and Alexandra Middendorf, 1985. *Paint Rock Post Office, Alabama*: Sotheby's, New York, 1987; George F. Hemphill and Lenore A. Winters, 1987.

1955

R. Frank

MARK ROTHKO
1903–1970

White and Orange, 1955
Oil on canvas
59½ x 49¾ (151.13 x 126.37)

Promised Gift of Mrs. Paul Mellon

White and Orange beautifully exemplifies Mark Rothko's mature art. Starting with depictions of single or isolated figures during the 1930s, Rothko gradually replaced them with more fantastic protagonists inspired by surrealism in the subsequent decade until, around 1950, the images were distilled to tiers of floating rectangles. Throughout this long evolution one of his fundamental concerns was the interaction between the living presence and its environment. In works such as *White and Orange* the dialogue becomes abstract, initiating not just tensions between the two main forms and their narrow surrounding space but also the drama of the spectator's encounter with mysterious veils of color. These canvases therefore carry a wealth of associations within their seemingly plain format and represent what the artist had earlier called "the simple expression of the complex thought."[1]

Although often linked to Clyfford Still and Barnett Newman as an exponent of the so-called "color-field" idiom of abstract expressionism, Rothko denied the value of formal effects in themselves, instead insisting upon the expression of "basic human emotions."[2] Yet his technique still shows a remarkable blend of power and subtlety. It owed much to a longstanding penchant for watercolor that climaxed in the atmospheric washes evoking some primal, aqueous world in the mid-1940s works on paper. The translucency and layerings typical of the medium were then developed to the utmost in his far larger "classic" abstractions. In them oil pigment was thinned with solvents so that it would soak into the canvas as a series of superimposed films. The result was fragile but richly tinted surfaces from which light appears to emanate. Frayed or unfocused edges to their interior forms intensify the hypnotic mood, as if the viewer were looking at an evolving vision where nothing remains altogether static but rather dissolves, rematerializes, and shimmers like a mirage. Vestiges of themes from the 1940s such as the processes of natural growth and the

passage of time are distantly recalled here. Indeed, Rothko once spoke of his pictures "expanding and quickening in the eyes of the sensitive observer."[3]

As early as 1952 Rothko experimented with the enormous, almost murallike dimensions sometimes chosen by other abstract expressionists, including Still, Newman, and Jackson Pollock, to engulf the onlooker.[4] Critics have compared their sweep to the melodramatic impact sought by late eighteenth- and nineteenth-century painters of "sublime" landscapes. Nevertheless, *White and Orange* maintains an essentially human scale. Its warm hues, particularly characteristic of the period, also heighten the sensuous immediacy. One source for this is hinted at by the title of a canvas executed in the previous year, namely *Homage to Matisse* (private collection, New York), but another may lie in the glowing harmonies of Pierre Bonnard whose 1948 retrospective at the Museum of Modern Art in New York the artist is likely to have seen. Unique to Rothko, however, are the suggestions of undertows and contradictions present within the main fields. The uppermost white expanse, for instance, shades imperceptibly into a second and slightly denser oblong occupying the middle of the composition. Both are scumbled over a virtually concealed golden ground. This itself extends beneath the evanescent glazes of a somewhat more reddish cast that constitute the lower field and, in turn, melt into the peripheral orange. Ironically, much seems to be hidden by this forthright, lucid facade.[5]

Thus *White and Orange* alludes to the opposing forces that typify Rothko's artistic language and, at its best, are held in an unresolved tension. With the most extensive public collection of his works in the world, the National Gallery is singularly able to place this outstanding gift from Mrs. Paul Mellon in context. Holdings from the 1930s given by the Mark Rothko Foundation like *Street Scene XX* (fig. 1) show the play of animate life against inscrutable planes that would remain as abstract qualities in *White and Orange*, while its high-key tones are foretold by *Untitled* (1948, Rothko estate no. 5094.48). But the Gallery's finest companion to *White and Orange* is surely *Orange and Tan* (1954, gift of Enid A. Haupt), which it matches in design, amplitude, and haunting refinement.

David Anfam

PROVENANCE
Marlborough Gallery.

NOTES
1. Marcus Rothko and Adolph Gottlieb, letter to the *New York Times*, 7 June 1943.

2. Quoted in Selden Rodman, *Conversations with Artists* (New York, 1957), 93.

3. Statement in *The Tiger's Eye* 2 (1947), 44.

4. A 1952 canvas by Rothko (estate no. 5136.52) measures 117 x 174 in.

5. In a 1958 lecture at the Pratt Institute, New York, Rothko included "irony" among the ingredients of his "recipe" for art.

Fig. 1. Mark Rothko, *Street Scene XX*, late 1930s, National Gallery of Art, Washington, Gift of The Mark Rothko Foundation

411

MARK ROTHKO
1903–1970

Red, Black, White on Yellow, 1955
Oil on canvas
105 x 93 (266.7 x 236.22)

Promised Gift of Mrs. Paul Mellon

Any highly distinctive or original style tends to hold its creator in thrall. With his quintessential idiom of the 1950s, Rothko, like other major abstract expressionists, committed himself to extracting the greatest range of expression from a limited vocabulary. He had no fears about this, saying to a friend, "If a thing is worth doing once, it is worth doing over and over again—exploring it, probing it, demanding by this repetition that the public look at it."[1] Nothing better illustrates the fruits of that resolve than the contrast between *Red, Black, White on Yellow* and the other Rothko given on this occasion by Mrs. Mellon, *White and Orange* of the same year. Together they offer a microcosm of the competing directions that helped to keep his output at the time, despite its steadfastness, diverse and alive.

In fact his paintings were meant to be shown closely together to resonate against each other and in 1954 Rothko wrote that "by saturating the room with the feeling of the work, the walls are defeated and the poignancy of each single work [becomes] more visible." Furthermore, hanging them "low rather than high" entailed their being "encountered at close quarters, so that the first experience is to be within the picture."[2] The intentional lack of frames—a situation ideally applicable to all the "classic" works—also stresses their palpable transaction with the viewer. But it was this very point, the interplay between image and onlooker, that Rothko began to ponder with growing concern during the 1950s. By the close of the decade it would contribute to a radical shift in his methods. Both the various mural series (which began with those planned for a room in New York's Seagram Building in 1958) and his exploration of a more somber pictorial world after 1957 articulated a changing notion of how to confront an audience. Already, however, the special character of such compositions as *Red, Black, White on Yellow* appears prophetic.

Besides physically larger and more imposing dimensions than *White and Orange,*

any overt lyricism is eschewed. Among the few inflections are the faint rose tones that grace the white region toward its upper left. Otherwise the handling and conception are different and a relatively uniform sense of touch creates flatter planes, monolithic and quite implacable. Whatever may be lost in atmospheric depth is gained in severity and drama: a reminder that Rothko had soon been upset by those who saw his art as merely beautiful and instead wrote the previous year that it was "the opposite of what is decorative."[3]

A certain starkness indeed informs the relation of the fields to their ambience. Whereas *White and Orange* was built of seductive superimposed veils, the presences here hover upon (rather than within) the ultra-thin tan ground. Adamant yet enigmatic, they perhaps contain the germ of impulses that led to the clear-cut motifs found in his subsequent mural series and related pieces like the Gallery's *Sketch for Mural H* (fig. 1). The effect is architectonic. Equally instructive are the links between *Red, Black, White on Yellow* and another Gallery holding such as an *Untitled* (Rothko estate no. 5028.53) from two years before. Their affinities demonstrate how the harder shapes and an "iconic" look were by no means belated additions to Rothko's repertoire.

The palette of *Red, Black, White on Yellow* is also significant because its strong tonal contrasts, whereby the black band thrusts like a portent between the uppermost light red and the lurid white below, allude to a lengthy involvement with polarities. Rothko described them bluntly in 1957 as ". . . tragedy, ecstasy, doom."[4] At least one canvas already in the National Gallery, a strange counterpoint involving white and black female nude figures from the early 1930s (estate no. 3100.30), suggests that these oppositions had deep imaginative roots. *Red, Black, White on Yellow,* nonetheless, is preeminently an important abstract statement from a period when the artist had concluded that "there are some painters who

want to tell all, but I feel that it is more shrewd to tell little."[5] Within that terseness it summarizes much, poised between the first brilliance that marks Rothko's flowering in the early 1950s and the monumental, darker vision that lay ahead.

David Anfam

PROVENANCE
Marlborough Gallery.

NOTES
1. Ida Kohlmeyer, "About Rothko," *Arts Quarterly* 4, no. 4 (Oct./Nov./Dec. 1982), 59.

2. Correspondence with Katharine Kuh, Archives of the Art Institute, Chicago.

3. Correspondence with Katharine Kuh, Archives of the Art Institute, Chicago.

4. Selden Rodman, *Conversations with Artists* (New York, 1957), 93.

5. Lecture, Pratt Institute, New York, 1958.

Fig. 1. Mark Rothko, *Sketch for Mural H,* 1962. National Gallery of Art, Washington, Gift of The Mark Rothko Foundation

413

MILTON AVERY
1885–1965

Mountain and Meadow, 1960
Oil on canvas
60 x 68 (152.4 x 172.7)

Gift of Sally Michel Avery

In a memorial address delivered upon the death of Milton Avery, Mark Rothko spoke eloquently of his friend: "His is the poetry of sheer loveliness, of sheer beauty. . . . This alone took great courage in a generation which felt that it could be heard only through clamor, force and a show of power. But Avery had that inner power which can be achieved only by those gifted with magical means, by those born to sing."[1] For Rothko and other painters of his generation such as Adolph Gottlieb and William Baziotes, Avery's example contributed significantly to their artistic development. Yet Avery himself never followed the path toward pure abstraction. He consistently looked to the physical world and its inhabitants for his subjects, all the while regarding nature as a pretext for the formal exploration of chromatic and spatial relationships, sometimes attaining such a degree of abstraction that only the title of the work reveals its subject.

The landscapes Avery produced in the last decade of his life are among the finest works of his career and of American art in this century. In 1955 Avery and his family spent the summer in Yaddo, an art colony near Saratoga Springs, New York. While driving near the border of Vermont and Massachu-

setts, they stopped in a meadow for a picnic where Avery sketched the landscape that he eventually painted as *Mountain and Meadow.* It was not atypical of the artist's working methods in that five years elapsed between the initial recording of a motif and its realization in paint. Rather than representing a specific locale, Avery captured the general mood of the place by abstracting its essence in a characteristically tranquil, harmonious view of nature.

By the late 1950s Avery had begun to paint in a larger format, increasing the size of many of his canvases from approximately forty by fifty inches to sixty by seventy. With the enlarged scale came the new breadth in composition and remarkable simplicity of color and form so beautifully exemplified in *Mountain and Meadow.* Avery here reduced the compositional elements to a few gracefully interlocking forms that convey little in the way of illusionistic space but imply a spatial expansiveness and a gently palpable atmosphere. By mixing his colors with white and thinning them with turpentine, he created a dry, subtly worked surface and luminous coloristic effects. His highly refined color sensibility could produce surprising layerings and juxtapositions of hues, such

as the pale pink of the sky that has been painted over thin shades of light blue.

Avery, who was notably reticent about his own art, aptly summarized his aims in 1951. "I like to seize the one sharp instant in nature, to imprison it by means of ordered shapes and space relationships. To this end I eliminate and simplify, leaving apparently nothing but color and pattern. I am not seeking pure abstraction; rather the purity and essence of the idea—expressed in its simplest form."[2] With an absolute economy of means, Avery created in *Mountain and Meadow* a lyrical, radiant vision of nature. This work is the first painting by this key figure of American modernism to enter the collection of the National Gallery.

Marla Prather

NOTES
1. Reprinted in Barbara Haskell, *Milton Avery* [exh. cat. Whitney Museum of Art] (New York, 1982), 181.

2. Quoted in Robert Hobbs, *Milton Avery* (New York, 1990), 166.

414

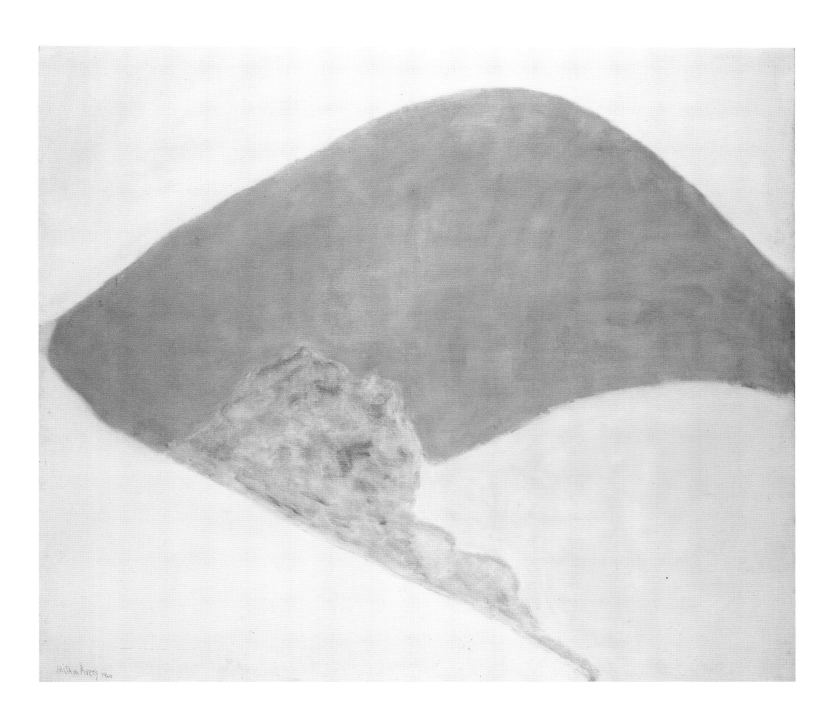

HANS HOFMANN
1880–1966

Staccato in Blue, 1961
Oil on canvas
59¾ x 83⅞ (151.8 x 213)

Gift (Partial and Promised) of
Mr. and Mrs. Gilbert H. Kinney

Born in Weissenburg, Bavaria, and raised in Munich, Hofmann spent the decade from 1904 to 1914 in Paris. There he painted and befriended the inventors of the new movements in European modernist painting, fauvism and cubism, just as these styles were emerging. He was particularly close to Robert Delaunay and shared his interest in attempting to merge the high-key color of fauvism and German expressionism with the compositional grid and shallow space of cubism.

Caught in Germany by the start of World War I, Hofmann deepened his exposure to German expressionist painting, became familiar at first hand with Kandinsky's "improvisation" pictures, and, always concerned to analyze and explain, opened his first art school, in Munich. In 1930 he moved his teaching activities to the United States, at first as a guest at the University of California and soon afterward on the East Coast where he settled. He became an American citizen in 1941. In the course of the 1940s and 1950s Hofmann's art schools, in New York City and in summers on Cape Cod in Provincetown, Massachusetts, became legendary both for the clarity with which he presented and assessed formal problems of European modernism and for Hofmann's encouragement of students to exploit their intuition and spontaneous gesture when painting. Among Hofmann's many students were I. Rice Pereira, Lee Krasner, Helen Frankenthaler, Larry Rivers, and the critic Clement Greenberg, who further disseminated Hofmann's teachings in his own essays about Matisse, cubism, and color-field abstraction.

Although a generation older than American abstract expressionist painters of the New York school, Hofmann developed in the 1940s as one of them, anticipating Pollock in his use of pouring techniques in oils such as *Spring,* 1940. In 1958, in his late seventies, he ceased teaching, began to paint full-time, and during the final eight years of his life accomplished his most inspired work. The most characteristic abstract paintings of Hofmann's great final years are composed of rectangular slabs of intensely saturated and highly impastoed color, aligned parallel to the picture plane in balanced asymmetrical grids somewhat reminiscent of Mondrian's compositions yet unlike them in Hofmann's richly varying, tactile surfaces and use of vibrant, jarring, even dissonant hues. In these works Hofmann seems to have arrived at a highly original solution to an old challenge: merging fauvism and cubism into a new style that calls vivid attention to the canvas surface.[1]

It was characteristic of Hofmann always to set himself new problems. Having achieved vivid abstract paintings with rectangular slabs of thick oil in the years around 1960, in 1961 he made a series of paintings in which roughly rectangular planes are set down on a white ground in balanced, nearly transparent washes of a single color. The diluted paint is applied in broad swaths and the path of the wide brush is evident. The presence of a compositional grid remains, yet each wide rectangular element has become slightly askew from a position parallel to canvas perimeters. The effect is a kind of syncopation, lending a sense of motion to these nearly monochrome canvases much as dissonant color lends vitality to the thickly painted works. *Staccato in Blue,* similar in style to the better-known, ocher-colored *Agrigento* (University Art Museum, Berkeley, California) of the same year, is an outstanding example in this group of nearly monochrome works. It is the first painting by Hofmann to enter the collection of the National Gallery. In terms of the energy of its strokes it relates to abstract paintings in the collection by Franz Kline, and in terms of its thinly washed paint application it relates closely to works in the collection by color-field painters such as Frankenthaler.

Nan Rosenthal

PROVENANCE
Andre Emmerich Gallery, Inc., New York; Sarah Campbell Blaffer Foundation, Houston, Texas; Mr. and Mrs. Gilbert Kinney, purchased from Vivian Horan Fine Art, New York, November 1987.

NOTE
1. Irving Sandler, *The Triumph of American Painting* (New York, 1970), 144.

417

ROY LICHTENSTEIN
Born 1923

Look Mickey, 1961
Oil on canvas
48 x 69 (121.92 x 175.26)

Dorothy and Roy Lichtenstein,
Partial and Promised Gift of the Artist

Look Mickey is a monument of vanguard American postwar painting, representing the artist's first mature adaptation of the subject, style, and source of comic-strip illustration to his art. Here Lichtenstein applies the imagery of popular culture to so-called "high" art and achieves a complete creative and functional transformation. The artist and this bold, challenging work helped define those vital international activities later called Pop art.

Lichtenstein has long been fascinated with the way we perceive the world around us, especially as it is graphically represented or surprisingly juxtaposed in mass communication: newspapers, books, or ephemeral printed material. Working during the early 1950s in a youthful abstract-expressionist idiom (mixed with reverential wit for both European and American master artists and their subjects), he freely portrayed themes of art history and American art.[1] By the late 1950s Lichtenstein quickly sketched several Walt Disney characters as gifts for his children. These Donald Duck, Mickey Mouse, and Bugs Bunny drawings from 1958 led in 1961 to the artist's more formal paintings of the distinctly American comic figures Popeye, Wimpy, Mickey, or Donald.[2]

The artist recalls that *Look Mickey* was a composition found on a bubble-gum wrapper, and was painted "as is, large, just to see what it would look like."[3] But it was more than merely an enlarged image, and his use of the subject was far more complicated.

Blowing it up from a two by three-inch wrapper to a four by six-foot painting radically changed the effects of the bright saturated colors and obliged a number of artistic alterations. Large flat areas of unmodulated yellow, red, blue, and white now dominate our view. Lichtenstein fashioned new painted lines to suggest the smaller drawn lines on the gum wrapper. He painted through a screen in Mickey's face and Donald's eyes to create a printlike halftone. Although at a distance it looks as if it is made mechanically, this painting is very much made by hand, with visible pencil lines, brushmarks, and his trademark script signature *rfl* in the lower left.

The small lettering in the original word balloon is now large and bold, an emphatic part of the new composition. The message, Donald saying "LOOK Mickey, I've hooked a BIG one!!" refers first to the literal image, the only relevant interpretation in the gum wrapper. But it has a second and more provocative meaning to the world of art. Are viewers, galleries, or collectors the big ones "hooked"? Has Lichtenstein "hooked" a big new style or idea?

The artist has preserved this painting in his personal collection for the last three decades, knowing that it confirmed his mature style by its devious and subtle inventions. The National Gallery collection has two important early Pop works by Andy Warhol[4] and one other Lichtenstein painting, his 1974 *Cubist Still Life*.

Jack Cowart

NOTES

1. Ernst A. Busche, *Roy Lichtenstein, Das Frühwerk 1942–1960* (Berlin, 1988), cats. 51, 52, 220, 55, 114.

2. *Popeye,* 1961 (42 x 56 in.); *Wimpy (TWEET),* 1961 (16 x 20 in.).

3. Diane Waldman, *Roy Lichtenstein* (New York, 1971), 8. However, after contacting Topps Chewing Gum, the manufacturers of Bazooka, and the Walt Disney Archives, we have not been able to find a record of this particular gum wrapper. The artist made no preliminary drawings from the wrapper, choosing instead to enlarge the design directly on the primed canvas.

4. *A Boy for Meg,* 1962 (Gift of Mr. and Mrs. Burton Tremaine) and *Let Us Now Praise Famous Men (Rauschenberg Family),* 1963 (Gift of Mr. and Mrs. William Howard Adams).

419

WAYNE THIEBAUD
Born 1920

Cakes, 1963
Oil on canvas
60 x 72 (152.4 x 182.9)

Gift of the Collectors Committee,
the 50th Anniversary Gift Committee,
and The Circle, with Additional
Support from the Abrams Family
in Memory of Harry N. Abrams

By his own admission, Wayne Thiebaud is a traditional artist. Both as a teacher and a painter he has long been intrigued by the concept of realism, and he admires painters in the realist tradition such as Vermeer, Chardin, Eakins, and Morandi. However, when he began to paint still lifes of food in 1953, he did not resort to time-honored still-life subjects such as bread, onions, and apples, but to the contemporary equivalents of these humble foods consumed daily by his own society.

For Thiebaud, the still-life genre, like the figures and landscapes he has also painted, is a means of investigating formal issues. It is paint's ability to re-create observed reality in an endless variety of ways that constitutes Thiebaud's chief artistic preoccupation. He has said of the challenge offered by realism, ". . . it seem[s] alternately the most magical alchemy on the one hand, and on the other the most abstract construct intellectually. . . . This makes it possible for representational painting to be both abstract and real simultaneously."[1]

By 1960–1961 Thiebaud had developed the distinctive imagery of mass-produced American foodstuffs with which he is associated today. When his paintings of pies, hot dogs, and gum-ball machines were exhibited to much critical acclaim in New York in 1962, they were regarded as indictments of America's desolate consumer culture and earned Thiebaud a reputation as a major exponent of west-coast Pop. Yet he has always resisted the Pop designation and maintained that his subjects are born of admiration and nostalgia rather than contempt.

Thiebaud has said that the ritualistic practices surrounding food—its presentation and consumption—initially attracted him to the subject. Cakes, particularly the celebratory kind depicted here, are ceremonial in function. They are elaborately decorated with mounds of frosting to commemorate birthdays, anniversaries, and marriages. In *Cakes,* the display counter arrangement isolates the confections against a neutral background and structures them within a simple compositional grid. Thus, Thiebaud interfaces the essential geometry of the cakes with what he has called their "organic messiness." While these objects may share certain formal characteristics with Pop art—a deadpan, non-hierachical presentation, a conformity of one object to another—these are not brand-name goods or commercially printed designs, but objects carefully observed in space. Though monotonous at first glance, the individual units are infinitely varied by subtle manipulations of color, light, and texture, all made possible through the descriptive powers of oil paint. Most importantly, while Pop artists took care to mitigate the subtleties of touch, Thiebaud took impasto to new heights and, ultimately, new meaning. *Cakes* is one of the most delectable examples of Thiebaud's mastery of the brush and pure delight in the handling of the medium. With skillful precision he reproduces the very substance of buttery, creamy frosting. A trademark of his style, this technique has been described by the artist as "object transference," that is using paint to re-create literally the look and feel of the substance it depicts, whether mustard, meringue, or frosting.

Thiebaud's highly developed chromatic sense is in full evidence here. His practice of underdrawing in several hues eventually produced the rainbowed lines that define the perimeters of his objects. These brilliant colors, which depart from any sense of local description, endow the objects with a remarkable luminosity and prismatic vibration, like blinking colored neon lights traveling around the edges of the cakes. These contours are echoed in the surrounding paint, creating an effect of halation that is both a means of activating the monochromatic ground and expressing a light that seems to radiate from the objects themselves.

Monumental in scale and ambitious in execution, *Cakes* figures among Thiebaud's most important pictures. From it he generated smaller variations on the subject in the 1970s. It is the first painting by the artist to enter the National Gallery's collection.

Marla Prather

PROVENANCE
Sold in 1963 to Harry N. Abrams by the Allan Stone Gallery, New York.

NOTE
1. Quoted in Karen Tsujimoto, *Wayne Thiebaud* [exh. cat. San Francisco Museum of Art] (Seattle and London, 1985), 39.

OSSIP ZADKINE
1890–1966

Le Jouvenceau, c. 1961
Ebony, 42⅛ x 10½ x 6 (107 x 26.67
x 15.24)

Torso, c. 1963
Ebony, 41¾ x 10 x 6½ (106 x 25.4 x
16.51)

Gift (Partial and Promised) of
Mr. and Mrs. Nathan L. Halpern

Although Ossip Zadkine was born and passed his childhood in Russia, he was an artist essentially of the school of Paris rather than the Russian avant-garde. He established himself in Paris in 1909, entering (briefly) the Ecole des Beaux-Arts and the atelier of the academic sculptor Injalbert.[1] Soon he was frequenting the cafés and salons of Montparnasse, and his early sculptures reflect the currents of cubism and primitivism running through advanced Parisian art.

Those currents continued to run through Zadkine's work for the remainder of his long career. He preferred to work in several manners concurrently, choosing his manner according to his subject. Sculptures of similar theme or subject are thus quite close in style, even if thirty years separate their making. Most often referred to as a cubist sculptor, Zadkine frequently applied elements of the cubist formal vocabulary to three-dimensional figurative objects, treating forms in terms of simplified geometric shapes.

Zadkine distinguished himself above all in his feeling for materials, especially wood. It is worth noting that he descended from an English shipbuilder brought to Russia by Peter the Great at the end of the seventeenth century. His mother's family had remained builders of wooden ships in the city of Vitebsk.[2] Zadkine carved sculptures from a variety of woods including, most dramatically, ebony.

Torso and *Le Jouvenceau* (the youth), although carved at the end of Zadkine's career, typify the artist's work in ebony. *Torso*, in fact, is one of a series of sculptures of that title that stretches back to 1918, the first ebony *Torso* dating from 1922. The Halpern *Torso* may be the most refined of that series: it is a matter of smoothly flowing lines and softly undulating shapes that contrast only with the incised crossing of buttocks and thighs. Anatomical and decorative detail have been eliminated in favor of an unusual purity of form.

Le Jouvenceau, too, has a long pedigree in Zadkine's oeuvre. A sculpture of *Demeter* of 1918 (Stedelijk Van Abbemuseum, Eindhoven) carved in elm displays much the same classical pose as *Le Jouvenceau*, standing with legs apart, one arm held behind a tilted head, the other arm hanging down with elbow turned outward, a pose maintained as well by several later sculptures. Like the *Demeter*, Zadkine's figures in this pose are mostly women. *Le Jouvenceau* may be said to possess a hermaphroditic character, its sex defined only by the masculine gender of its title.

In both *Torso* and *Le Jouvenceau* Zadkine highlighted the smooth, polished surface afforded by ebony. Although ebony is among the hardest and most obdurate of woods, Zadkine makes it appear soft and almost pliant, lending these sculptures a distinctly tactile quality. Although they were conceived independently, *Torso* and *Le Jouvenceau* make a revelatory pair. They are the first works by Zadkine to enter the collection of the National Gallery.

Jeremy Strick

PROVENANCE
Le Jouvenceau: from the artist to Halpern collection; *Torso*: from the artist to Sam Salz to the Halpern collection.

NOTES
1. Ionel Jianou, *Zadkine* (Paris, 1964), 64.

2. Jianou 1964, 64.

DAVID SMITH
1906–1965

Untitled, 1964
Enamel on canvas
27½ x 43 (69.86 x 109.22)

Gift of Candida and Rebecca Smith

More than many artists, David Smith responded to the nature and abundance of his materials.[1] He liked to work with large quantities of things, and his series of works are often defined as much by medium as by subject. The painted steel Tanktotems, for example, all incorporate the lids of oil drums, the Voltri series had its origins in the scrap metal of an abandoned factory, and the Agricolas were made up of elements of farm machinery. Much the same principle applied to Smith's graphic oeuvre. The extensive series of calligraphic drawings produced in the late 1950s and early 1960s can be understood partly as Smith's response to the soft, broad brush and to the black egg ink that he mixed himself in large batches.

Smith may remain best known for his last great sculptural series, the Cubis of 1963–1965, which, if covertly figurative, are most evidently defined as assemblages of geometric volumes of polished stainless steel. The Cubis represented a technical departure for Smith, as they were constructed of designed rather than found elements. Interestingly, at the same moment that Smith was engaged in what was his ultimate sculptural departure, he was pursuing a quite different technical departure in another medium: painted nudes.

Throughout his career Smith had drawn the female nude. These drawings were shown as a group for the first time in 1964 at the Marlborough Gallery, paired in an exhibition with Smith's Cubis, and again in spring 1990 at Knoedler & Company and at the Montclair Art Museum. Altogether, they are remarkable for the direct power of their linear forms. The brush and ink reclining nudes of 1953 suggest both figure and landscape, while the vertical figures of 1963 embody much the same disturbing force as de Kooning's Women.

Smith's interest in the female nude culminated in 1964 with a series of paintings in which he applied enamel paint, mostly black, to white canvas. These paintings had their most evident precedent in the late black pourings of Jackson Pollock, but technically Smith's nudes differed from Pollock's paintings in two ways. Smith applied his enamel to linen that he bought commercially prepared with a white ground, as opposed to the unprimed canvases employed by Pollock, and Smith made use of a novel applicator for his paint: an ear syringe.[2] Smith painted on unstretched linen, leaving the cutting and stretching of the linen as his final compositional act.

The remarkable results of Smith's technique are evident in *Untitled*, 1964. Because the black enamel is applied to a prepared canvas, it is only partly absorbed into the fabric. The painted line is soft, but it does not fade at the edges. Especially at those points where paint has pooled, it reflects light. The figure described in *Untitled* is defined by sweeping, apparently gestural lines. As a manipulable painting tool, the syringe must stand somewhere between a paintbrush and the sticks Pollock used to drip and toss paint. Like a brush it was held in Smith's fingers, but at such an angle as to limit the artist's range of digital and manual dexterity. Most of the movement whose traces we see on the surface of *Untitled* had to come from the artist's arm rather than his fingers or wrist. Still, Smith could achieve an impressive variety of marks, even within this one painting: from short blunt strokes to sweeping, elegant arcs. The black paint has pooled slightly at the beginning of each stroke, and tapers at its end. Changes of direction are also marked by pooling.

Of the enamel nudes that Smith painted in 1964, *Untitled* is among the most refined. Whereas others in the series apparently engage in a dialogue with works by De Kooning, Pollock, and Picasso, *Untitled* seems informed above all by the spirit of Matisse. The deceptive ease of the connected lines of *Untitled* link it to Matisse's line drawings, as do the evident anatomical distortions that here appear both lovely and necessary. As in all of the black enamel nudes, Smith's image extends to the edges of the canvas. The elegance of his line detracts not at all from the monumentality of his nude's tri-angular form, which seems compressed into an image of restrained power.

Untitled, the first David Smith painting on canvas to come to the National Gallery, makes a stunning addition to the collection. Part of a gift from Candida and Rebecca Smith that also includes seven works on paper, *Untitled* joins six David Smith sculptures already in the collection. Combined with *Cubi XXVI* and the two untitled spray paintings on paper of 1962 and 1963 also included in this fiftieth-anniversary gift, it completes a compelling overview of the great innovative achievements of David Smith's last years. It will make a fascinating companion to Jackson Pollock's great black pouring, *Number 7, 1951*.

Jeremy Strick

NOTES
1. Edward F. Fry and Miranda McClintic, *David Smith: Painter, Sculptor, Draftsman* [exh. cat. Hirshhorn Museum and Sculpture Garden] (Washington, 1983), 33.

2. Paul Cummings, "The Figure and David Smith," in *David Smith Nudes: Drawings and Paintings from 1927–1964* [exh. cat. Knoedler & Company] (New York, 1990).

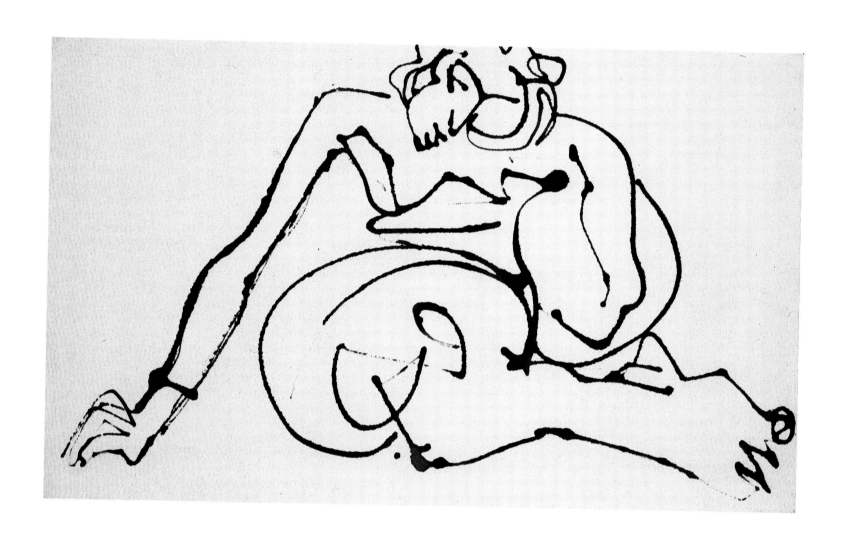

ANDY WARHOL
1928–1987

Green Marilyn, 1964
Silkscreen on synthetic
polymer paint on canvas
20 x 16 (50.8 x 40.6)

Gift of William C. Seitz and
Irma S. Seitz

Andy Warhol's well-known works based on Marilyn Monroe are his youthful Pop-art challenge to Willem de Kooning's earlier *Marilyn Monroe,* 1954, and de Kooning's even more notorious abstract-expressionist Woman paintings.[1] The issue became larger, however, as Warhol expanded beyond a local conflict with the preceding generation of New York artists and moved into a more complicated dialogue with our new media-saturated society. The artist was fascinated by our movie-star system, the persuasive role of media imagery, and questions of originality in art raised by the emerging Pop artists' use of collaboration, derivation, and mechanical, "neutral," or media-like methods.

Warhol had made movie-star drawings and paintings in 1962, notably after Natalie Wood, Liz Taylor, Warren Beatty, Troy Donahue, and Elvis Presley. But his greatest series of the 1962 paintings would focus on Monroe after her death in that year. In 1963 he added other potent icons to his portrait themes: Leonardo de Vinci's *Mona Lisa* and Jacqueline Kennedy after President Kennedy's assassination.

Warhol's subsequent Marilyns would thus subsume almost any- and everything that these prior sources bring to mind: beauty, movie stars, theatricality, publicity, ideal symbols, cult worship, fate, tragedy, and so much more. In 1964 the artist produced his twenty- by sixteen-inch series of pastel-colored Marilyns. *Green Marilyn* is a remarkable painting from this historic suite, works that were immediately acquired by some of the most influential and respected people in contemporary art: Alfred Barr, William Seitz, Jasper Johns.

In many of his early Pop portraits, this small twenty- by sixteen-inch format was a prevalent and critical dimension.[2] The silkscreen portrait's meanings and effects, however, are large and immediate. We are confronted by an image reminding us of snapshots, postcards, passports and identity cards, or photo-booth frames.

Green Marilyn began when Warhol cropped a publicity still of Monroe that had been taken by Gene Kornman for the 1953 film *Niagara.*[3] Rauschenberg and Warhol, among others, began experimenting by late 1962 in the use of silkscreen to apply images in paintings.[4] The black and white photograph was transferred to a photosensitized screen. But the *Green Marilyn* and others were still largely painted by hand. At least nine colors were used after outlining this head on the canvas. Then the green background was brushed on. Following were the darker green of the collar, two skin tones (an underpaint of lavender and a covering of a warmer pigment), the yellow hair, the light and dark blues of the eyes, the green eye shadow, and a soft white over the white primed canvas where the teeth would be. Only now was the black silkscreen printed over the paint. Subsequently came the painting of the red lips and the touch ups: tightening around the neck with green and the lips with lavender. The result is a jewel, a provocative addition to the Gallery's growing collection of postwar art.

The National Gallery has two larger, earlier Warhol paintings (*A Boy for Meg,* 1961/ 1962, and *Let Us Now Praise Famous Men* [*Rauschenberg Family*], 1963), and thirty-eight of his prints. *Green Marilyn* is especially welcome as the collection's only Warhol image on the subject of Marilyn. The painting also has a striking relationship to the Hirshhorn Museum and Sculpture Garden's *Marilyn Monroe's Lips,* 1962, the silkscreen painting composed of 168 floating Monroe mouths in rows on large white and pink panels.

Jack Cowart

NOTES
1. De Kooning's astonishing and controversial Woman paintings began in the early 1940s, reaching their full critical impact by the early and mid-1950s.

2. It is the same proportion for Monroe's head in The Museum of Modern Art's great *Gold Marilyn Monroe,* 1962, and screens of the de Vinci painting images used for *Mona Lisa,* 1963, his own notable double self-portrait of 1964, *Ethel Scull Thirty Six Times,* 1963, *Jackie (The Week That Was),* 1963, and *Sixteen Jackies,* 1964, among others. Warhol's own radical *Campbell's Soup Cans,* 1962, is composed of thirty-two hand-painted canvases each measuring twenty by sixteen inches.

3. *Andy Warhol, A Retrospective* [exh. cat. The Museum of Modern Art] (New York, 1989), 72, fig. 15.

4. See *Robert Rauschenberg: The Silkscreen Paintings 1962–64* [exh. cat. Whitney Museum of American Art] (New York, 1990) and Marco Livingstone, "Do It Yourself: Notes on Warhol's Techniques," New York 1989, 69–72.

427

RICHARD DIEBENKORN
Born 1922

*Still Life: Cigarette Butts
and Glasses,* 1967
Ink, conté crayon, charcoal,
and ball-point pen
13¹⁵⁄₁₆ x 16¾ (35.2 x 42.5)

Gift of
Mr. and Mrs. Richard Diebenkorn

Drawing plays a central role in Richard Diebenkorn's art. In his paintings and prints as well as in his drawings themselves, the sense of his searching for form, of altering, of refining is a salient characteristic. Images such as *Still Life: Cigarette Butts and Glasses,* depicting a table in the artist's studio, provide an alternate form of self-portrait.[1] In the mid to late 1960s particularly, having moved from the lyrical abstraction that dominated his work of the late 1940s and early to mid 1950s, Diebenkorn made many paintings and drawings related to this one, which tell not only about the artist's vision but also about his daily habits.

Depicted here, in addition to the cigarette butts mentioned in the title, are two pipes; and of glasses, also mentioned in the title, there are two kinds, those for drinking and those with which one sees. There is a beverage can as well. Those objects might be found any number of places, but this is clearly an artist's studio, as is evident from the tools for drawing and cutting strewn across the table.[2] The locale is reinforced by the several drawings lying about. Some are more highly finished than others. An example is the upside-down landscape that reminds us of another subject that occupied Diebenkorn's imagination at this time.

The composition of *Still Life: Cigarette Butts and Glasses* at first looks random, as if the artist walked into his studio, sat down, and drew precisely what he happened to see.

And perhaps he did. But the taut relationships between the various elements that are revealed by studying the drawing suggest that as part of his working process Diebenkorn uncovered a hidden structure within the scene, making critical adjustments to the objects' arrangement, aligning edges, creating shapes between forms, augmenting rhythms, suggesting formal echoes. Ovals, triangles, and eccentric rectangles work together to predict the highly structured Ocean Park paintings of the following decades. No form is locked into a specific space; instead, each element seems to shift in recognition of its relationships to other things. A pulsating surface results, amplifying the sense of inner light with which Diebenkorn's art is always imbued.

The careful structuring of pictorial elements in *Still Life: Cigarette Butts and Glasses* is heightened by the sensuousness of the artist's touch. A meandering blue pen line appears throughout the sheet, outlining shapes, setting in touches of tone visible from beneath the dense black washes, suggesting directions in which the eye should move. Presumably this blue line was used for laying in the preliminary composition. After setting it in, Diebenkorn employed a variety of other media to achieve his painterly surfaces. Wet washes forming puddles and veils and dry strokes, often layered to create rich tones and textures, are placed over and under or adjacent to each other,

working together to create a second kind of pulsation, vivacity. The dynamic plane, the structuring of space, and the sensuous handling of materials are characteristic of Diebenkorn's work in all media.

This is the first of Diebenkorn's drawings to enter the Gallery's collection, joining a 1955 oil, *Berkeley, No. 52,* as well as twenty-two lithographs and drypoints dating from 1962 to 1985.

Ruth E. Fine

NOTES

1. See Gerald Nordland, *Richard Diebenkorn* (New York, 1987), 136; John Elderfield, *The Drawings of Richard Diebenkorn* [exh. cat. The Museum of Modern Art] (New York, 1988), 117; *Richard Diebenkorn: Paintings and Drawings, 1943–1976* [exh. cat. Albright-Knox Art Gallery] (Buffalo, 1976), 104, drawing no. 43; on Diebenkorn's prints see *Richard Diebenkorn: Etchings and Drypoints 1949–1980* [exh. cat. The Minneapolis Institute of Arts] (Houston, 1981), with an introduction by Mark Stevens.

2. Tools for eating—knives, forks, spoons—also have been important components of Diebenkorn's still lifes.

CLAES OLDENBURG
Born 1929

Soft Drainpipe—Red (Hot) Version, 1967
Vinyl, styrofoam, canvas, metal
120 x 60 x 45 (304.8 x 152.4 x 114.3)

Robert and Jane Meyerhoff Collection

In 1967 Oldenburg created provocative and witty drawings, models, and sculptures on his new theme of Colossal Monuments. Plans for monuments in Toronto, Stockholm, and London were shown at the Sidney Janis Gallery.[1] According to the artist, they were to be "poetic ideas that express the reality of a place, even if they are never put into effect."[2] The visionary monument intended for Toronto was a giant drainpipe. At the horizontal gutter top of this 850-foot-high structure was to be a heliport and swimming pool. Water would flow down the vertical pipe and exit at the bottom into a great dam generating hydroelectric power. Oldenburg proposed this as Toronto's civic answer to nearby Niagara Falls.[3] Relating to the five-foot painted wooden model of this scheme[4] were a lively series of large drainpipe drawings, a styrofoam model, and two other soft sculptures.

Generally called a Pop artist, Oldenburg maintains a special ability to analyze everyday objects and transform them into serio-comic sculptures whose fine-art meanings are multiple and cleverly contradictory. The "soft sculptures" constructed of loose canvas, kapok, or vinyl are his special invention. He began this style in the early 1960s, and by 1966 and 1967 these objects became metamorphosed, antiheroic monuments representing a major part of his production. Oldenburg attempted in these works to idealize life and, following the aspirations of the new public art of the sixties, to push the viewer into a new relationship with the daily world.

The Tate Gallery, London, owns *Soft Drainpipe—Blue (Cool) Version,* 1967, made of painted canvas, with a pulley and ropes that can retract the soft downspout. It is in many ways the artistic and emotional opposite of the Meyerhoffs' *Red (Hot) Version.* The former hangs like a relief painting on the wall, while the latter is a suspended sculpture on its freestanding metal rack. The red version is made of shiny glistening vinyl, not the matte stained canvas of the blue version. Oldenburg's sketchbooks and finished drawings show the quite surprising evolution of this common object. He first saw an advertisement showing gutter and downpipe sections in a Swedish newspaper. The gutter *T* reminded him of his middle initial; the *T* racks in his studio from which he hung other sculptures; the shape of crucifixes and the form of the sagging body on this cross; human body parts; and elephant trunks. It fits into the artist's evocative and systematic index of powerful found shapes where *L* shapes are equated with ray guns and *T* shapes are so-called "double ray guns." In this creative process the drainpipe accumulated all of these legitimate references. But another Oldenburg, in his wall relief composed of twenty metal *T*-shapes titled *Exercising Drainpipes,* reminds us that the artist views all of these sculptures as kinetic, animate objects, loaded with associations but also all the energy of our daily life.

Oldenburg exercises our skills at seeing the lush world around us and our complicated visual history. In this aggressive and odd-looking *Soft Drainpipe—Red (Hot) Version,* the artist, working with his wife, Pat, who cut and assembled the fabric, has produced one of his signature sculptures. It is the first large-scale Oldenburg to enter the Gallery's collection. We have numerous Oldenburg prints, small object multiples produced by Gemini, G.E.L., and an expanding collection of major paintings and drawings by other Pop artists. This Meyerhoff gift provides the Gallery with a significant and dramatic work from the historic period of Oldenburg's early and large soft sculptures.

Jack Cowart

Fig. 1. Claes Oldenburg, *Proposed Colossal Monument for Toronto-Drainpipe,* 1967. Art Gallery of Ontario, Toronto. Purchased with Assistance from Trier-Fodor Foundation

PROVENANCE
Mr. & Mrs. Roger Davidson, Toronto; Sotheby Parke Bernet, 21 October 1976, lot 217, Leo Castelli Gallery; Robert and Jane Meyerhoff.

NOTES
1. *New Work by Claes Oldenburg,* Sidney Janis Gallery, 26 April–27 May 1967.

2. Grace Glueck, "Sidney Janis Gallery," *Art in America* 55 (May 1967), 116.

3. Claes Oldenburg, "About the Famous Toronto Drainpipe," *ArtsCanada* 25 (August 1968), 40–41.

4. Ludwig Museum, Cologne, Germany.

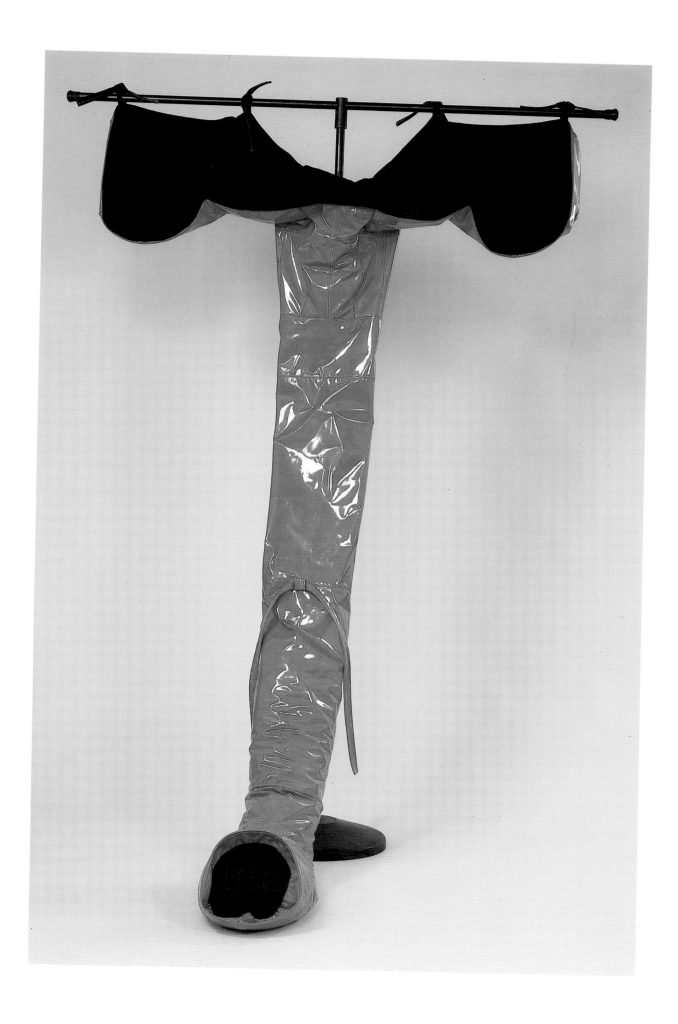

JASPER JOHNS
Born 1930

Color Numeral Series: *Figure 0*,
1968–1969, Lithograph
38 x 31 (96.5 x 78.7)

Color Numeral Series: *Figure 9*,
1968–1969, Lithograph
38 x 31 (96.5 x 78.7)

Gift of Gemini G.E.L.

These two lithographs complete the National Gallery's set of Jasper Johns' Color Numerals series, which are among his most admired prints. Prints have played a central role in Johns' art.[1] Since 1960 he has completed more than 250 editions using all of the major media—lithography, etching, screenprint, woodcut, and monoprint—distinctively exploring each process to locate its particular characteristics in relation to his art. He has worked with many renowned printmaking workshops, starting with Universal Limited Art Editions (U.L.A.E.) and including Atelier Crommelynck, Simca Print Artists, and Gemini G.E.L.

The alphabet, flags, targets, and numbers were among the "things the mind already knows" that have stimulated Johns' imagination throughout his career.[2] He began to use numerals as a subject in his paintings in 1955, and in one of his earliest prints, a 1960 lithograph in black and white titled *0 Through 9*,[3] the ten individual figures were superimposed upon each other. Also in 1960 Johns began four series of prints in which 0, 1, 2, 3, 4, 5, 6, 7, 8, and 9 appear as individual figures each of which is placed on the page below two rows of smaller figures: 0, 1, 2, 3, 4 above 5, 6, 7, 8, 9.[4] All four series were made at U.L.A.E.

Johns' first print project with Gemini G.E.L. was his Black and White Numerals series; the Color Numerals closely followed, and *Figure 0* and *Figure 9* are two of these ten ambitious color lithographs.[5] For the Black Numerals, Johns' drawings on lithograph stones were printed in black and transparent gray, and the same stones were used unaltered for all of the color prints that followed except *Figure 9*, because its original drawing was lost when the stone was used for the color edition.[6] In addition, a third printing element was used for the opaque white layer added for each color image.

Whereas each of the Figures is self-contained, each also plays a specific role within the group. This is evident, for ex-

ample, in the manner by which Johns has structured his bands of color. He started with *Figure 0*, comprising the primary colors, and introduced a secondary hue, violet, in *Figure 1*; and moving through the series he introduced a different color at the top band of each print, shifting down one level the color that had appeared at the top of the previous Figure. In *Figure 9* the secondaries—orange, green, and violet—are featured. Johns' signature functioned within a second scheme; each print was signed in a pencil the color of the top printed band, for example *Figure 0* is signed in red whereas *Figure 9* is signed in orange.

The sense of sequential movement within a specific framework as seen here is an important component of Johns' art. So, too, is the clear structuring of individual parts within a larger whole. Also vividly apparent in these two prints is the artist's extraordinary ability to suggest the full range of tonal and textural possibilities within the medium of lithography. Delicate line work and broad washes, marks that maintain their autonomy and marks that merge to suggest a broader field, play a role in Johns' rich visual language.

The National Gallery's collection includes two drawings by Jasper Johns, *Untitled (from Untitled 1972)* donated by the artist and included in this catalogue, and *Numbers*. Johns' prints are represented at the Gallery by more than a hundred impressions, most of which are part of our Gemini G.E.L. Archive. Others came into our collection as donations from Lessing J. Rosenwald, William W. Spieller, Dr. and Mrs. Maclyn E. Wade, and The Woodward Foundation, Washington, D.C.

Ruth E. Fine

NOTES
1. Catalogues of Johns' prints include Richard S. Field, *Jasper Johns: Prints 1960–1970* [exh. cat. Philadelphia Museum of Art] (Philadelphia, 1970); Richard S. Field, *Jasper Johns: Prints 1970–*

1977 [exh. cat. Center for the Arts, Wesleyan University] (Middletown, Conn., 1978); Judith Goldman, *Jasper Johns: Prints 1977–1981* [exh. cat. Thomas Segal Gallery] (Boston, 1981); Riva Castleman, *Jasper Johns: A Print Retrospective* [exh. cat. The Museum of Modern Art] (New York, 1986); and the Universal Limited Art Editions catalogue raisonné with introduction by Richard S. Field (forthcoming).

2. Quoted in Leo Steinberg, "Jasper Johns: The First Seven Years of His Art," in *Other Criteria: Confrontations with Twentieth Century Art* (New York, 1972), 31.

3. Philadelphia 1970, no. 4. See also Nan Rosenthal and Ruth E. Fine, *The Drawings of Jasper Johns* [exh. cat. National Gallery of Art] (Washington, 1989), cats. 18–23.

4. Philadelphia 1970, nos. 17–46.

5. Philadelphia 1970, nos. 94–113. *Figure 0* is printed in an edition of forty plus eleven artist's proofs and thirty-two other proofs; *Figure 9* is in an edition of forty plus twelve artist's proofs and eighteen other proofs.

6. Philadelphia 1970, no. 113.

GERHARD RICHTER
Born 1932

9 Objekte, 1969
Portfolio of 9 offset lithographs
17⅝ x 17⅝ (44.9 x 44.9)

Gift of Wolfgang Wittrock

How is reality known? This philosophical question guides Gerhard Richter's artistic quest. The "answers" to date constitute a diverse output that is dominated by his activity as a painter but also encompasses film-making, sculpture, photography, and related graphic works such as the print portfolio *9 Objekte.* Like his friend Sigmar Polke (they met while students at the Düsseldorf Kunstakademie), Richter seems acutely aware of his historical place at the end of an entire western art tradition and, moreover, modernism itself. As he remarked: "I see myself as the heir to an enormous, great, rich culture of painting, and of art in general, which we have lost, but which obligates us."[1] From that perspective he is bound to analyze, deconstruct, and reassemble the elements of vision itself, scrutinizing how images are created. His development has been neither chronological nor stylistically monolithic. Instead, disparate explorations of a constant theme exist side by side.

In the same year as *9 Objekte* Richter therefore also made abstract "Star Paintings" related to Jackson Pollock's tangled mazes of pigment alongside "Photo Paintings" depicting idyllic landscapes with painstaking care. All three directions in fact share a single target: the innate human tendency—indeed need—to process raw experience into usable "models," whether for creating art or to render everyday life easier.[2] Photographs, the basis of numerous paintings and the *9 Objekte,* exert a special appeal for Richter because they occupy a zone where perception and cognition merge, bridging the divide between what is visible and how it can be recorded. He explained that the photographic medium was "a crutch to help me understand reality."[3] Within such a context these nine prints quiz the tantalizing nature of representation.

The forms in the series are variations on "impossible" solids: configurations like the notorious "Penrose triangle" whose sides can be visualized yet could never join in three dimensions since they amount to a contradictory whole. At first we are even doubtful whether Richter just took shots of real constructions (insofar as such objects can be physically fabricated and, if seen from a fixed point, fool the eye into believing they are integral), or rather has more likely altered the original photographs. Various degrees of focus confound the dilemma, notably in the backgrounds that are at times ambiguous and echo patterns in the Star Paintings. In 1966 the artist made a totally blurred film. He associates haziness with his own insecurity toward the world, adding, nonetheless, that a picture can never be blurred.[4] That is, it remains always a sharp image of something else and thus a paradox. Banality, however, resides in the general matter-of-factness: gray tones, an apparently almost mechanical technique and the contrast between the wooden conundrums themselves and domestic artifacts such as teacups or a folding chair. Here Richter's initial interest in Pop still lingers. Overall, though, the competing messages neutralize each other to leave a dialectic on the inexplicable and the known, reality and abstraction. Two years before Richter had built assemblages with glass panes and noted, tellingly, how in them we "see everything and grasp nothing."[5] That comment might well summarize the thought-provoking *9 Objekte.*

In their ironic detachment these prints balance the more vigorously crafted graphics by such Germans as Baselitz and Immendorff that are among other fiftieth anniversary gifts and, again, firsts of their kind at the National Gallery. By a happy coincidence Jasper Johns' *Untitled (From Untitled 1972)* also explores, in an altogether different framework, kindred ideas about illusion and the structures of knowledge. Both will be at home with an even earlier picture in the Gallery that delves deep into metaphysics, René Magritte's *The Human Condition.*

David Anfam

PROVENANCE
Edition Heiner Friedrich, G. von Pape, Munich.

NOTES
1. Quoted in Roald Nasgaard, *Gerhard Richter. Paintings* (Chicago, 1988), 21.

2. See for instance Ernst Gombrich's speculative writings on this topic, especially *Meditations on a Hobby Horse* (London, 1971).

3. Heiner Stachelhaus, "Doubts in the Face of Reality: The Paintings of Gerhard Richter," *Studio International* 184 (Sept. 1972), 79.

4. Jürgen Harten, ed., *Gerhard Richter: Paintings 1962–1985* (Cologne, 1986), 23.

5. Harten 1986, 32.

ROY LICHTENSTEIN
Born 1924

Study for *Untitled Head II*, 1970
Aluminum and wood
30 (76.25)

Gift of Gemini G.E.L.

Much of Roy Lichtenstein's art from the mid-1960s forward can be understood as a brilliant, idiosyncratic revision of the history of modern art. Cubism, futurism, German expressionism, surrealism, and abstract expressionism are among the styles that Lichtenstein has made over into his own distinct pictorial language. One of the richest veins that Lichtenstein mined was 1930s *art moderne*, or art deco. Beginning in 1966, Lichtenstein produced an extended series that included paintings, drawings, prints, as well as a number of sculptures, all in a witty approximation of art deco style.

Untitled Head II belongs squarely within that series of art deco explorations but, typical of Lichtenstein's work, it makes reference to a number of objects and artists as well as styles. This unique study for an edition of thirty with three artist's proofs[1] was produced between 1969 and 1970 at Gemini G.E.L. The *Untitled Head II* edition, eventually executed in wood, was part of a group that included *Untitled Head I* as well as a related series of prints and reliefs, *Modern Head #1–5*, and *Modern Head Relief*. This group of prints and sculptures marked something of a departure in Lichtenstein's art deco series, for most of his earlier works in that style (and especially the sculpture) had focused on the decorative and applied arts vocabulary of *art moderne* rather than the human figure. In fact, Lichtenstein has noted that his original inspiration for the Modern Head series came not from art deco but rather from the paintings of Alexej von Jawlensky that he saw at the Pasadena Art Museum.[2]

Of the Gemini group, *Untitled Head I* and *Untitled Head II* are the only freestanding sculptures. Ironically, they read as two-dimensional works, revealing themselves fully only in profile. Lichtenstein's approach to sculpture is deeply informed by the work of Alexander Calder and David Smith, both of whom made objects that function as draw-ings in space rather than volumetric masses.[3] But whereas the two sides of *Untitled Head I* are entirely flat and the sculpture is articulated only in profile, *Untitled Head II* is marked by a series of setbacks and indentations that lend it particular richness and complexity.

Iconographically, *Untitled Head II* refers to the ancient tradition of Janus, the two-headed god of beginnings. Since the Renaissance, Janus figures have symbolized the co-existence of opposite characteristics in a single being. That conception is evident in *Untitled Head II*, where one side of the head is formed of straight lines and regular geometric forms and the opposite side is fluid and irregular. The regular, geometric side is close to one of the two heads in the *Peace through Chemistry* prints and relief that Lichtenstein produced at Gemini at about the same time that he made the Untitled and Modern heads.

This unique piece is an especially important gift of Gemini G.E.L. and the artist. It makes complete the National Gallery's representation of Lichtenstein's collaboration with Gemini of 1969–1970, joining *Untitled Head #1* and *Modern Head Relief* among others. The Gallery's collection of works by Roy Lichtenstein now numbers seventy-five prints, four sculptures in multiple editions and two maquettes for edition, and two paintings, including *Look Mickey*, which has been donated by the artist in honor of the Gallery's fiftieth anniversary.

Jeremy Strick

NOTES
1. John Coplans, *Roy Lichtenstein: Graphics, Reliefs & Sculpture* [exh. cat. Gemini G.E.L.] (Los Angeles, 1970), 40.

2. Los Angeles 1970, 9.

3. Jack Cowart, *Roy Lichtenstein 1970–1980* (New York, 1981), 152.

ALEXANDER CALDER
1898–1976

A Group of Ten Bent-Metal,
Painted Sculptures, 1970–1971, 1976
Cut, bent, and painted sheet metal

Gift of Mrs. Paul Mellon

These small sculptures, all but one of a type known as "Animobiles," date from the later years of the artist's life. They combine his positive, humorous outlook with his life-long interest and delight in animals. As a child Calder collected Noah's Ark sets with his sister Peggy[1] and designed animal figures. In 1925–1926 he made a series of nearly 250 drawings of animals in the Bronx and Central Park zoos, a group of which were published in his 1926 book *Animal Sketching*. It was also during this period that he became enthralled with the circus, making sketches at the Ringling Brothers/Barnum & Bailey Circus in 1925 for the *National Police Gazette*. This experience, which gave him many opportunities to explore the artistic and comic possibilities of animals, led to the creation in Paris between 1926 and 1931 of one of Calder's best-known, most-loved works, *The Circus*, a miniature functioning circus complete with an elephant and a roaring lion. Although Calder's use of animal motifs in his art never waned — they are found in every stage of his career, in every medium, including cast bronze, wood, wire sculpture, paper sculpture, jewelry, drawing, and gouache — it is perhaps symptomatic of a revitalized interest that Calder reinstalled *The Circus* in 1970[2] and that he brought out his zoo drawings in 1972,[3] both during the period in which he was creating the present works, his Animobiles.

This term was coined by Louisa Calder, the artist's wife, combining "animaux" and "mobiles." Only nine of the present works fall into this category; the tenth, *Les Flèches* (arrows), is related in size and technique but was made five years later than any of the others and contains no overt animal references. Each Animobile is made of a flat sheet of metal that is cut, folded, and painted. The flat sheet generally stands perpendicular to the ground, forming the body of the animal, with the cut-out legs bent to allow it to stand. A back-and-forth folding process makes extra volume in the so-called "crinkly" areas, Calder's term for such passages as the

neck of the *Crinkly Taureau* or the body of the *Crinkly Worm*. Finally, a mobile head (in most cases) balances carefully on the pointed neck. These heads are also made of cut and bent sheets of metal, are usually punched or pierced for eyes and nostrils, and can have hanging attachments, as in the horns of *La Vache* or the *Crinkly Taureau*; some Animobiles have recognizable animal bodies, but with "heads" that are purely abstract mobiles.[4] Originally Louisa's term for the group applied to animals with movable heads, but later it came to include others of the period, such as the *Crinkly Worm*.[5] Another important element of most Animobiles is the brightly colored paint, often with two contrasting colors on the animal's two different flanks, so that the two principal views differ radically in character, as in the *Horse*, the *Red and Yellow Bull with Blue Head*, and the *Blue and Red Bull with Yellow Head*. A slightly different construction technique is used in both *Deux Angles Droit* (which, despite its non-figural descriptive title "Two Right Angles," depicts a seal with large, white tusks attached to its round face) and *Les Flèches*. In these two the support for the mobile element is made from a flat piece shaped somewhat like a wide boomerang, one arm folded upright and the other lying flat on the ground as a base.

This technique of cutting, bending, and painting sheet metal calls to mind an earlier, similar technical approach in the work of the ubiquitous Pablo Picasso, such as his *Bust of Sylvette* of 1954 or, more significantly, his *Man with Sheep* of 1961, whose sheep (carried on the man's shoulders in a classical pose) is remarkably comparable in character to the Animobiles, albeit on a smaller scale.[6] Calder himself used folded sheet metal as early as c. 1930–1932 for his *Old Bull* in the Whitney Museum of American Art, but manipulated it in a much more complex fashion than did Picasso or than he himself did in his own Animobiles. Nor did Calder paint the early sculpture.

Beyond their technical aspects in common, the Animobiles share an overriding

sense of whimsy. Among the group of five bovines, the *Crinkly Taureau* is the natural leader because of his large size and his fancy, harlequinlike neck. His long haughty face and his insouciant gaze, coupled with over-size horns, give him an air of foolish, condescending importance. In contrast to him is *La Vache*, whose angled eyes give her an irritated squint that is offset by the humor of her lopsided horns and her black-and-white, wire-attached teats. *Blue and Red Bull with Yellow Head* has one ear larger than the other and horns that curl in opposite directions: one up, the other down. The small *Red Cow with Black Head* has one horn slightly higher that the other and a somewhat worried expression on her small head. *Red and Yellow Bull with Blue Head* also has a small head, with a bluntly angled nose and long, droopy ears. His punched eyes are larger and rounder than those of his herd mates, giving him a surprised demeanor.

The *Horse*, with his long neck and one ear longer than the other, has a blankly expectant gaze. Alert, uneven ears give his small friend the *Camel*, on the other hand, an eager look. He is perhaps the most richly humorous of the bunch, with a looped neck, two tiny humps (echoed in the little "Adam's apple" on his neck), and a protruding red tongue, as if chewing his cud or licking something off his face.

The seal (*Deux Angles Droits*) has a fat body topped by a flat moon-like face. His silly expression is the result of closely spaced eyes at the top, widely spaced nostrils in the middle, and goofy tusks attached at the bottom. Only the *Crinkly Worm* has any hint of menace — diamond-shaped eyes and pointed snout — but this is negated by bright coloring and the crinkly tail.

Les Flèches is more abstract than the Animobiles. Its top pivots on the point of its simple, bent base, allowing continual change in the direction of the "arrows" and drawing attention in and out of its central locus. It thus makes a very basic statement about movement, space, and direction in kinetic sculpture.

The deceptively simple construction of these sculptures reflects Calder's knowledge of engineering gained from four years of study, starting in 1915, at the Stevens Institute of Technology in Hoboken, New Jersey, before entering the Art Students League in 1923.[7] In addition to the careful balance of the kinetic heads (on all but the *Crinkly Worm*), many exhibit a complex, well-thought plan that cleverly uses the metallic sheet. For instance, in the *Camel* the bottom edge of its swag-like neck, were it to be rebent flat, would lie against the forward edge of the right front leg, which itself would match with the edge of the left leg. Similarly, the front and back legs of the *Horse* would fit together if flattened, the hooves of both right legs fitting in the notched-out fetlocks of the left legs and the length of the legs joining together. The legs of the *Blue and Red Bull with Yellow Head*, the *Red and Yellow Bull with Blue Head*, the *Red Cow with Black Head*, and the back legs of the *Crinkly Taureau* are all similarly devised.

The *Crinkly Worm*, however, is the most complex in plan. If it were laid flat it would form a solid ovoid sheet, with only the cut-out eyes missing: the right side of the worm's head would nestle against the inside of the loop of the body, with the rest of the tail wrapping around the tip of the nose and then curling around on itself.

The Animobiles (designated as such) made their exhibition debut in February 1971, at the Galerie Maeght, Paris, followed by a showing at the Galleria dell' Obelisco, Rome; they were shown later that year at Perls Galleries, New York, during October and November.[8] Though not styled as Animobiles, two of the type were shown three years earlier at Dayton's Gallery 12, Minneapolis[9]: a *Cheshire Cat* with long wire whiskers and an *Iguana* with a mobile-like head, both made in 1967. One of the earliest, however, is the *Foxy Dog* of 1958, which might actually be considered as a precursor rather than an actual Animobile, since its head is made of shiny unpainted brass.[10] The production of Animobiles ceased sometime after

1972, one of the latest examples being *The Crested Crow* of that year, a black bird with a colorful crest of colored disks on the ends of black wires.[11] The Animobile series seems perhaps to have metamorphosed into a new type, the Critters, which are humanoid, three-legged creatures in a similar technique (though generally larger in scale and more impish in character), which were shown at Perls Galleries in 1974.

Until now the National Gallery had relatively few works by Calder, even though one of these, the *Mobile* of 1973–1977,[12] functions as a symbol of the Gallery's East Building. This piece shows the full potential of Calder's public works, both in its grand size and its impact. The Gallery's *Obus* of 1972,[13] also donated by Mr. and Mrs. Mellon, is a Stabile. The Gallery also owns three color lithographs by Calder.[14] Both monumental works of sculpture contrast with the Animobiles, which represent Calder at his most lighthearted, playful, and intimate. The Mellon Animobiles were briefly displayed at the National Gallery as part of the ceremonies celebrating the opening of the East Building in May of 1978.

Donald Myers

PROVENANCE
Purchased at Galerie Maeght, Paris: *Crinkly Taureau, La Vache, Red and Yellow Bull with Blue Head, Blue and Red Bull with Yellow Head, Deux Angles Droits,* and *Black Camel with Blue Head and Red Tongue* in March 1978; *Horse, Crinkly Worm, Red Cow with Black Head,* in April 1978, with *Les Flèches.*

NOTES
1. Jean Lipman, *Calder's Universe* [exh. cat. Whitney Museum of American Art] (New York, 1976), 45.

2. At the Whitney Museum of American Art; see New York 1976, 338.

3. New York 1976, 81; some of these were published in 1974 by the Archives of American Art, Smithsonian Institution, in a portfolio entitled *Calder at the Zoo.*

4. As in *The Blunt-Tailed Dog* of 1970, which has a large red disk on a wire balancing five white disks on several wires; illustrated in Jean Lipman, *Calder Creatures Great and Small* (New York, 1985), 15.

5. *Calder Animobiles—Recent Gouaches* [exh. cat. Perls Galleries] (New York, 1971), n.p., second page.

6. The entire height of the *Man with Sheep* is 17¼ inches; see Roland Penrose, *The Sculpture of Picasso* [exh. cat. The Museum of Modern Art] (New York, 1967), 148, 181.

7. Ugo Mulas and H. Harvard Arnason, *Calder* (London, 1971), 9–12.

8. Giovanni Carandente, *Calder* [exh. cat. Palazzo a Vela] (Turin, 1983), 146; New York 1976, 338; see also *Derrière le Miroir* [exh. cat. Galerie Maeght, no. 190] (Paris, Feb. 1971).

9. April 17–May 11, 1968; the exhibition was entitled simple *Calder*, and was done in collaboration with Perls Galleries, New York.

10. Lipman 1985, 73.

11. Lipman 1985, 19.

12. Accession number 1977.76.1; the Gallery also owns the *Model for the East Building Mobile*, 1975.114.1.

13. 1983.1.49, Collection of Mr. and Mrs. Paul Mellon.

14. 1964.8.444, 1976.55.1, and 1987.42.1.

Crinkly Taureau
39½ (100.3), 1970

Horse, 38⅜ (97.5)
1970

Crinkly Worm
18⅛ (46), 1971

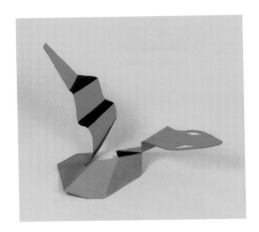

La Vache, 34⅛ (86.7)
1970

*Red and Yellow Bull
with Blue Head*
40⅛ (101.9), 1971

*Blue and Red Bull
with Yellow Head*
39⅛ (99.4), 1971

*Black Camel with
Blue Head and Red Tongue*
21⅛ (53.7), 1971

Deux Angles Droits
20 (50.8), 1971

Red Cow with Black Head
22⅜ (56.8), 1971

Les Flèches
25⅛ (63.8), 1976

SIGMAR POLKE
Born 1941

Kölner Bettler IV, 1972
4 offsets
16⅞ x 23¹⁵⁄₁₆ (42.9 x 60.7)

Figur mit Hand (Es schwindelt mir . . .)
1973
Offset
24¹¹⁄₁₆ x 17⅞ (62.75 x 45.4)

Gift of Wolfgang Wittrock

Born in the Lower Silesia region of East Germany, Sigmar Polke moved to the Federal Republic in 1953 at a time when its "Economic Miracle" was underway. As might be expected of a newcomer, he became fascinated with consumerist society and while studying at the Kunstakademie in Düsseldorf during the earlier 1960s was influenced by both Joseph Beuys' iconoclastic teaching and the eclectic images of the American pop movement. The first broke down distinctions between art and life while the second saw mass culture as packed with layer upon layer of signs, commodities, and visual codes. Subsequently Polke compounded these twin attitudes into a quintessential post-modernist oeuvre that parallels Gerhard Richter's many-sided talents.[1] Yet by comparison Polke's paintings ostensibly recognize no norms whatsoever and incorporate bizarre materials, multiple styles, and even stranger sources.

Although a mere year separates the *Kölner Bettler* (Cologne Beggars) quartet from *Figur mit Hand* (Figure with Hand), they straddle Polke's past and future, apart from being among his most distinctive prints. The movement called "Capitalist Realism" that he launched with Richter and others in 1963 turned a wry gaze on commercial objects. Its implicitly bittersweet view of a society that treated them as fetishes shifted to overt social comment in the *Kölner Bettler* scenes — perhaps darker than anything he did until the references to Nazism that emerged in the paintings of the early 1980s. Rubbish contradicts a slogan proclaiming "Der saubere Weg" (The Clean Street) in prints *I* and *III*, while the violinist-beggar of *IV* is sharply graven unlike his faceless audience. Their shopping bags answer to his one instrument of survival. A prototype exists in Otto Dix's mordant portrayals of First World War veterans and, more recently, the Cologne working-class milieu photographed by Chargesheimer.[2]

Yet documentary as such remains alien to Polke's mentality. After their initial exposure the photographs for *Kölner Bettler* would have been subjected to one or another darkroom technique that was already tried out on pictures taken in Paris the previous year.[3] They include partial solarization and uneven application of the developer to the surfaces. In conjunction with faint traces of violet and brown inks, these devices complicate the prints, bring their spatial design up onto the picture plane, and afford a worn hand-wrought look. Going further still, Polke reached the palimpsest of *Figur mit Hand* the next year. It exhibits all the novel features dramatized in his larger works. Among them is the droll snakeskin-textured commercial paper similar to the fabric chosen for the oil painting *Menschkin* (1972), the later Marcel Picabia's guiding influence, and a montage that superimposes text upon figurative fragments and the obtrusive ground.[4] Since this writing, with its mention of "dizziness," "rosepetals," and "sin" is more a stream-of-consciousness word chain in the surrealist mode than any cogent narrative, it is fair to conclude that we are confronted by Polke's typical stagecraft for evoking the manic, disjunct realm of contemporary experience. Its frank pastiche denies that anything can be out of place to the postmodern mind.

With *Kölner Bettler* the Gallery receives an exemplar inspiring further acquisitions of avant-garde graphics from the 1970s. In turn, *Figur mit Hand* shows that its collection is already choice enough to have an ancestor for Polke's more antic side in Picabia's *Machine, Tournez Vite*.

David Anfam

PROVENANCE
Kölner Bettler: Klaus Staeck, Heidelberg; *Figur mit Hand*: Griffelkunst, Hamburg.

NOTES
1. On postmodernism and consumer society see Frederick Jameson's eponymous essay in Hal Foster, ed., *The Anti-Aesthetic* (Seattle, 1983), 111–125.

2. Pseudonym of Carl-Heinz Hargesheimer (b. 1924). See R. Misselbeck, ed., *Chargesheimer: Photographien 1949–1970* (Cologne, 1983).

3. Stephen Frailey, "Sigmar Polke: Photographic Obstruction," *Print Collector's Newsletter* 16, no. 3 (July–Aug. 1985), 77–80.

4. Compare, for instance, the black silhouettes of Picabia's *Animal Trainer* (1923).

445

VIJA CELMINS
Born 1939

Untitled, 1973
Graphite
29⅞ x 43¾ (75.7 x 111)

Gift (Partial and Promised) of the
Grinstein Family

Untitled is a beautiful drawing that exemplifies a pivotal phase of Vija Celmins' career. Whether in drawings or prints, Celmins' oceans are meditative in their quietness and hypnotic in their constancy. Nothing intrudes upon their peacefulness except for their own rhythmic motion.

Celmins relocated from Connecticut to California in 1962 to continue her graduate studies at UCLA. She had hoped that the move from the environment at Yale to a university in a larger city would provide the stimulation she required to continue her career.[1] Yet a year later Celmins discontinued painting for a period of time, needing to seriously reevaluate her art. When she returned to the canvas, she had deserted her earlier abstract-expressionist approach for a style closer to the Pop art movement in California.

In the late 1960s Celmins began to take photographs of the ocean. She made her first graphite drawing of the Pacific in 1968. This led to intense study of this subject both from nature and from the photographs she took from Venice Pier, which was near her Venice, California, studio, south of Los Angeles.[2] About the same time in her career she also took a break from oil painting. Since then Celmins' primary mode of expression has been drawing.

The early drawings of the ocean surface are large images that fill the page. The ocean is brought so close to the picture plane that the viewer's spatial relationship with the subject is ambiguous. In 1973 she began to explore depth in her drawings, for example in *Untitled*. She reduced the format of her placid views to a narrow horizontal band situated on the lower register of a large sheet of paper. This emphasizes the breadth of the picture and makes it more panoramic. At the same time, the allusion to depth is implied by the boundary placed between the upper edge of the band of water and the vast white ground above the image. This edge can be interpreted as a horizon, something upon which the viewer can focus.

Compressing the image into a narrow band increases the abstract qualities of the situation. One's attention to the drawing shifts to the literal subject. From a distance it may be difficult to identify the scene because the drawing appears three-dimensional. Upon very close inspection one loses sight of the overall place, the surface becoming more engaging. The graphite markings on the page become the focus. Celmins explained, "the art is in the making, not in the object."[3] Her painstaking technique and delicate touch show just how dedicated she is to the process of drawing.

Celmins' drawings of the ocean, distinctive in their density and tonality, seem to have their own individual pulse. They remain her best-known works. This drawing, which represents an important turning point in her career, is the first of Vija Celmins' drawings to enter the collection of the National Gallery. In conjunction with several prints in the collection, the majority of which are part of our Gemini G.E.L. Archive, this drawing will further define the progression of Celmins' imagery.

Carlotta J. Owens

PROVENANCE
Riko Mizuno, sold 1973.

NOTES
1. *Vija Celmins, A Survey Exhibition,* introduction by Susan C. Larsen [exh. cat. Newport Harbor Art Museum] (Los Angeles, 1979), 21.

2. Los Angeles 1979, 27.

3. Kenneth Baker, "Vija Celmins: Drawing Without Withdrawing," *Artforum* 22 (November 1983).

DAVID HOCKNEY
Born 1937

Celia, 1973
Lithograph
42½ x 28¾ (107.9 x 73)

Gift of Gemini G.E.L.

David Hockney has said that "portraits aren't just made up of drawings, they are made up of other insights as well."[1] His investigations into appearances are not only masterful studies in problems of formal drawing, but also moving tributes to the people who share his life. Hockney's lithographs made at Gemini G.E.L. have the same fullness and graphic subtlety that pervade his most sensitive drawings. *Celia* is a lithographic portrayal that is exceptional not only in its economy of means, delicacy, and softness, but also an understanding portrayal of a friend in an unguarded moment.

Some of Hockney's most memorable portraits have been of Celia Birtwell, a London-based textile designer and close friend who became a subject for his prints by 1969. Celia visited Hockney in Los Angeles with some regularity after he moved there from England in the early 1970s, and the artist often celebrated his friend's visits by drawing her. She is seen frontally in this work, her legs shifted slightly one way, her head turned slightly in the other. Gently slumped in the seat, her buoyed shoulders suggest the support of the armrests while the narrow plunging arrow of her neckline emphasizes gravity's pull.

A series of contrasts animates this work. The silvery figure stands out against the warm background, its contours pulsating against the edges of the sheet. This energy is further augmented by the subject's off-center placement. Additionally, the highly finished areas of the face, hands, shoes, and armrests contrast with the notational character of other marks. Details of the hair and eyes are remarkably intense studies that are set like jewels in luminous space. Small, dark areas such as Celia's shoes, the back of her head, and the armrests form an interesting constellation. The ruled lines of the horizon and parts of the chair play against the freehand lines of the figure and have a sense of whimsy when compared with the general treatment. It is interesting to see a prefiguration of

Hockney's later experiments with oriental and cubist spatial representation in the forward-leaning chair in this work. Note too that the artist's use of contrast even stretches to the green crayon signature.

Lithography captures subtle tonalities in *Celia*. Hockney established the figure's structure with litho crayon and then amended it with a wash of tusche. By allowing the tusche to pool and then settle, passages of exquisite luminosity that mimic the gown were created. Even the deckle edges of the textured paper echo the rippled dress. Highlights on Celia's hair and nose are achieved by scraping back to the stone through the litho crayon.

By the late 1960s Hockney's work gravitated toward portraiture and the depiction of space and naturalistic effects. His first collaborations with Gemini occurred in the early 1970s. *Celia* was made in 1973 during a concentrated period of activity at the atelier. Since then, numerous other lithographic portraits have been completed including the Friends series in 1976, featuring a number of celebrated as well as little-known associates. Hockney often does a great deal of self-editing, making "many more lithographic drawings than the number of editions ultimately printed. By proofing all of the images, the artist is able to select those that he finds most successful."[2]

Celia is a notable addition to our collection of fifty-seven prints by Hockney. Some of the other lithographic portraits of Celia in our collection include *Celia, 8365 Melrose Avenue, Hollywood* and *Celia Smoking*, which are two seated portraits from the same period as the present work, a series of calligraphic brushstroke images of her in a variety of attitudes, two expansive reclining portraits, and a series depicting her seated in various kinds of chairs (one of which is both lithograph and screenprint). Most of Hockney's works in the collection have been gifts of Gemini G.E.L. and the artist.

Charles M. Ritchie

NOTES
1. David Hockney as quoted in *David Hockney: Travels with Pen, Pencil and Ink* [exh. cat. The Tate Gallery] (London, 1980), n.p.

2. Ruth E. Fine in *Gemini G.E.L.: Art and Collaboration* [exh. cat. National Gallery of Art] (Washington, 1984), 146.

Gemini imp III   Celia   David Hockney 73

PHILIP GUSTON
1913–1980

Painter's Table, 1973
Oil on canvas
77¼ x 90 (196.22 x 228.6)

Gift (Partial and Promised) of
Mr. and Mrs. Donald Blinken
in Memory of Maurice H. Blinken

By the late 1960s Philip Guston's art had achieved a remarkable but troubling level of freedom. It evolved from his early WPA mural projects, the complex figurative compositions of the 1940s, and his tense and lush abstract expressionist paintings of the 1950s and early 1960s, yet most viewers were not prepared for the famous 1970 exhibition of his new symbolic figuration.[1] But when Willem de Kooning saw the "heresy" of Guston's late work in this breakthrough exhibition, he said, perceptively, "Well, now you are on your own! You've paid off all your debts."[2]

Painter's Table is a work expressing the artist's mature meditations concerning creativity, the dilemma of the solitary artist, the beauty of his materials, and his own desire to involve us in what he felt were the perplexing impossibilities of his artistic search. Painted in 1973 when the artist was sixty, this remarkable canvas contains depictions of simple objects emphatically drawn. Guston said he didn't "arrange" the still life of objects picked up from around the studio and he did enjoy painting the ashtray and cigarette butts, "which began to look like something else."[3]

But the issues of this composition are probably more complex. One can propose that the two flatirons, the shoes, and the rail spikes are examples of mundane reality, though they do have curious extended references to art history. The chain-smoking artist is present in his filled ashtray, his burning cigarette, and his profile eye on a small canvas. We are reminded of his insomnia and his obsessive night working by the light bulb, pull chain, and a haunting window opening out to the dark. His materials are suggested by the pigments on the palette in the center. The various open books on the left may be the Law or Authority. This large and impressive canvas is a more extensive pendant to his 1972 work *Painter's Forms*. It sums up a number of smaller autobiographical paintings and drawings of the period when Guston, without being egotistic, wanted to give the full benefit of his broad introspection and classical training.

Painter's Table is frequently cited in monographs and reviews. The *New York Times* critic John Russell saw this canvas as an "updated version of Chardin's *Attributes of the Arts*."[4] And this it is, with its narrative outline of the sources and studio atmosphere of a deeply thoughtful artist. But the more visceral and mysterious dark manner of the Spanish baroque still lifes of Goya and Meléndez are profoundly connected as well. Noting relationships to early twentieth-century metaphysical and surrealist artists, Dore Ashton saw this as a work made "in order to underscore the strangeness, finally, even of everyday things."[5]

This promised gift from Mr. and Mrs. Blinken is the first Guston painting to enter the Gallery collection. It joins our comprehensive collection of major paintings by Jackson Pollock, Barnett Newman, Mark Rothko, Arshile Gorky, and Franz Kline, among others, all of whom were Guston's close artistic friends in New York. By its subject this work by Guston continues a figurative tradition, but by its expressive surface, handling, and worried content there are compelling relations to various modes of twentieth-century modernist expression, and most particularly those of recent times.

Jack Cowart

PROVENANCE
Acquired from the artists in 1974.

NOTES
1. *Philip Guston, Recent Paintings*, Marlborough Gallery, New York, November, 1970.

2. Musa Mayer, "My Father, Philip Guston," *New York Times Magazine* (7 August 1988), 55.

3. *Philip Guston. Paintings 1969–1980* [exh. cat. Whitechapel Art Gallery] (London, 1982), 55.

4. John Russell, "Art: Guston's Last Tape Mislaid," *New York Times* (23 November 1974), 38.

5. Dore Ashton, *Yes, but . . .* (New York, 1976), 173.

ROBERT RAUSCHENBERG
Born 1925

Hoarfrost Editions: *Ringer State,* 1974
Lithography and newspaper print
transfers and paper and fabric collage
70 x 36 (177.7 x 91.4)

Gift of Gemini G.E.L.

Robert Rauschenberg's art seeks to contain the world by utilizing its objects. This "realism" mirrors our cluttered, complex lives, generating surprising results through unusual juxtapositions of subject and form. The contemporary world is seen in a fresh context presented with extraordinary sensitivity to materials and atmosphere. Not only the content of Rauschenberg's art but also the technology frequently used to help create it are indicative of the modernist aesthetic.

A group of nine printed Hoarfrosts was made for Gemini G.E.L. in 1974. *Ringer State* is a slightly different version of *Ringer*, which is also in the series. The word "state" implies that the print is presented at another stage in its development. Composed of soft cheesecloth and delicate silks and satins, the Hoarfrosts drift and overlap like drapery. Everything is in visual flux due to shifting support and, as Rauschenberg wrote, "imagery in the ambiguity of freezing into focus or melting from view."[1] The restrained palette of *Ringer State* evokes a coating of frost over a field of delicate images. Rauschenberg has remarked about them that "the first ones were very obscure. They were almost like brushstrokes. And in many cases you had to know what the image was in order to see it. The last Hoarfrosts got clearer and clearer, and they got more into construction."[2] Restraint is further emphasized in this work by the loose bilateral symmetry that underpins and balances the whole. Metaphorical associations with clothing and skin give it a tactile, vulnerable feeling.

The artist appropriated images and texts from the print media. While some images may echo certain themes, other inclusions simply open the imagination rather than expand upon an issue. Thus, the image at the upper left of a bull with a nose ring can be seen as a reference to the title; no other explanation for it is apparent. Other articles and images may have subtle interrelationships, whether intended or not, but each has its own integrity. It is not unlike the associations that occur when reading a newspaper, and it is understandable why Rauschenberg "considers himself more journalist than artist—a reporter-commentator on the ironies, foibles, horrors—and the beauty—of the world we inhabit."[3]

Ringer State is a fine example of art served by technology. Inks from newspaper and journal cutouts were transferred to cloth using solvent and the heavy pressure of a lithography press. During edition printing "approximately one hundred copies of the Sunday Los Angeles Times were separated into sections and organized into neat, discrete piles (a pile of one hundred magazine covers, for example, next to a pile of one hundred front sheets from the entertainment section). These piles and the enlarged offset sheets were, in effect, Rauschenberg's palette."[4] As Rauschenberg commented, "The Hoarfrosts were built of such excesses. The sound of making them is very dramatic. The presses are going on and the paper is being crumpled . . . we use gas masks. It's all poisonous too, so we send the dogs out of the room because they don't have gas masks. I mean it's like Cecil B. De Mille to make a Hoarfrost."[5]

The National Gallery has long sought the works of Rauschenberg, and is fortunate to have 241 of his works in the collection. *Ringer State* will help complete our series of Gemini G.E.L. Hoarfrosts.

Charles M. Ritchie

NOTES

1. Quoted in Lawrence Alloway, *Robert Rauschenberg* [exh. cat. National Collection of Fine Arts, Smithsonian Institution] (Washington, 1976), 22.

2. Arthur Perry (interviewer), "A Conversation between Robert Rauschenberg and Arthur Perry," *artmagazine* 10 (Nov.–Dec. 1978), 32.

3. Mary Lynn Kotz, "Robert Rauschenberg's State of the Universe Message," *Artnews* 82 (Feb. 83), 58.

4. Ruth E. Fine, *Gemini G.E.L. Art and Collaboration* [exh. cat. National Gallery of Art] (Washington, 1984), 112.

5. Perry 1978, 32.

453

LEE KRASNER
1908–1984

Imperative, 1976
50 x 50 (127 x 127)
Oil, charcoal, and paper on canvas

Gift of
Mr. and Mrs. Eugene Victor Thaw

Throughout her career Lee Krasner periodically turned to the medium of collage, one she employed on a scale comparable to that of her large oil paintings. Many of the collages figure among the peak achievements of this important figure of first-generation abstract expressionism. When Krasner produced her first collage painting in 1938, she made cutouts from her own paintings to construct an entirely new composition.[1] Utilizing a similar method in 1976, she made *Imperative* to inaugurate a startling new series of collages.[2]

Imperative consists of pieces of paper that have been sliced and slivered into angular shapes and glued to sized, unpainted canvas. These elements are fragments of charcoal and oil drawings Krasner made as a student between 1937 and 1940. In the summer of 1974 the artist came across the drawings in her East Hampton studio while rifling through old portfolios. Produced while Krasner was studying with Hans Hofmann in New York, the drawings were dynamic figure studies in charcoal, graphite, or brown chalk on paper as well as colorful still-life studies in oil and gouache. Krasner later avowed that she had learned the rudiments of cubism at the Hofmann school, and her figure drawings are boldly conceived, highly abstracted compositions demonstrating her vigorous interpretation of Picasso's analytical cubist drawings from 1910.

Fiercely self-critical, Krasner frequently destroyed her own work. In mutilating the drawings from the thirties, she cast, in her own words, "a cold eye" over her early work and reclaimed it for a new context. Each collage in the series carries a title of a grammatical tense or mood. The title of *Imperative,* the first of the group, implies an obligatory act. As Krasner explained, "I experienced the need not just to examine these drawings, but a peremptory desire to change them; a command as it were to make them new."[3]

The elements of *Imperative,* as with the other works in the series, are structured within a grid. The canvas is here bisected horizontally. Each half is divided into rectangular sections, although areas of collage frequently transgress the borders of the grid. Some of the collages preserve entire drawings, leaving the figure intact. *Imperative,* however, embodies a ruthless dissection of several charcoals that defy reconstitution but present tantalizing remnants of figuration within an otherwise abstract composition.

Departing from Krasner's collage paintings of the fifties, in which pieces are torn and left ragged, the cutout shapes that make up *Imperative* are hard-edged and sharp. The forms overlap and interpenetrate one another so that, in their reconstituted form, the drawings of the thirties function ironically like cubist shards. Dark, monochromatic sections of charcoal alternate with occasional chromatic flourishes provided by the oil studies. These brilliant flashes of impastoed color serve as a reminder of Krasner's gestural canvases and, like the reserved areas of bare canvas, constitute dramatically luminous passages.

Krasner said that the rediscovery of her forty-year-old drawings forced her to think of "time and its inexorable passage."[4] Her self-appropriation of that work introduces an autobiographical dimension that is central to her production. Though an ostensibly harsh judgment of her student work, the destructive reordering of the thirties drawings made possible a creative regeneration and synthesis.

As a key example of Krasner's late work, *Imperative* will provide a striking counterpoint to her earlier monumental painting *Cobalt Night,* 1962, in the Gallery's collection.

Marla Prather

PROVENANCE
Purchased by Eugene Thaw from the Pace Gallery exhibition, 1977.

NOTES
1. Barbara Rose, *Lee Krasner* [exh. cat. The Museum of Fine Arts, Houston and the Museum of Modern Art, New York] (New York, 1983), 148.

2. This series of collages was the subject of an exhibition *Lee Krasner: Eleven Ways to Use the Words to See* at the Pace Gallery, New York, in 1977. On Krasner's entire collage production, see *Lee Krasner Collages* [exh. cat. Robert Miller Gallery, New York] (New York, 1986).

3. John Bernard Myers, "Naming Pictures: Conversations Between Lee Krasner and John Bernard Myers," *Artforum* 23, no. 3 (Nov. 1984), 71.

4. Myers 1984, 71.

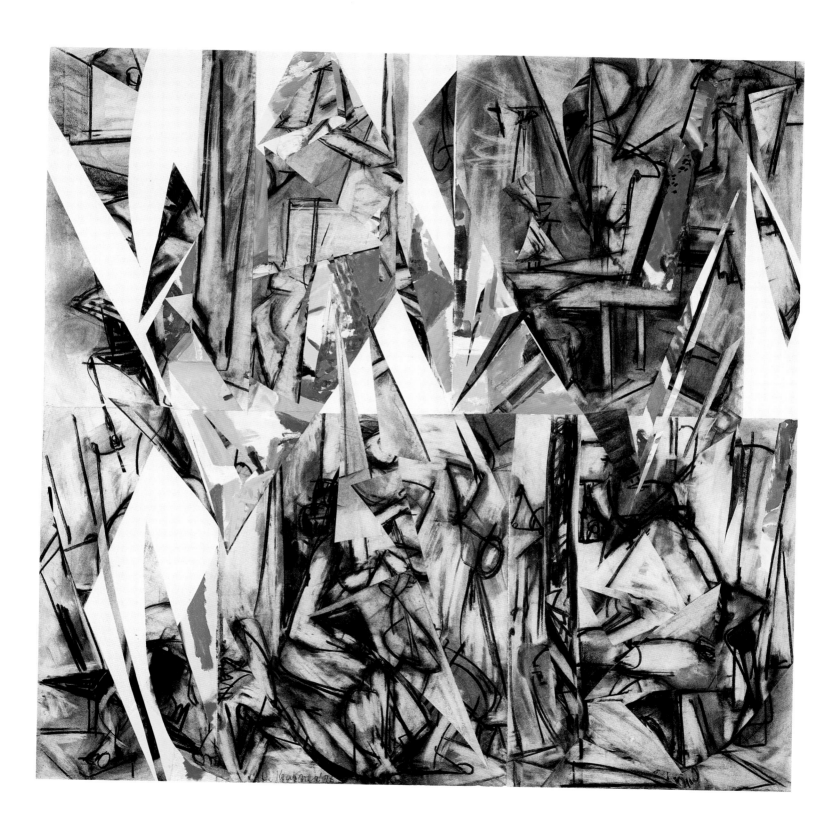

JASPER JOHNS
Born 1930

Untitled (from Untitled 1972)
1975–1976
Pastel and graphite pencil on paper
15³⁄₁₆ x 37³⁄₄ (38.5 x 95.9)

Gift of Jasper Johns

Like most of Jasper Johns' drawings, this pastel followed the painting on which it is based, offering a reworking of imagery previously executed in another medium. It is one of five drawings Johns made between 1973 and 1976 based on his monumental four-panel painting, *Untitled, 1972* (Museum Ludwig, Cologne).[1] That oil, encaustic, and collage painting is a pivotal work, drawing upon motifs employed by the artist since the late 1960s and introducing imagery critical to the work of the following two decades. Its far left panel of green, violet, and orange cross-hatching marks Johns' earliest use of a motif that frequently recurred in works throughout the 1970s and 1980s.[2] The two middle panels reproduce in red, black, and white a flagstone pattern Johns said he glimpsed on a wall in Harlem and that he first incorporated into a painting from 1968 called *Harlem Light*. Attached to the far right panel of *Untitled* are wooden slats which in turn carry flesh-colored body parts that have been cast from life in wax. Multicolored paint has been dripped over the surface of the these objects as well as the canvas.

Three of the drawings based on *Untitled, 1972* are identical in size and were based on the entire composition of the painting. The first of the three is a black ink on plastic drawing from 1975; the last, dating from 1976, is made with metallic powder that has been suspended in acrylic. Unlike those monochromatic works, the present drawing, a richly textured pastel on gray paper, closely reproduces the color and composition of the painting, although subtle vari-

ations can be detected throughout. For example, the cross-hatching in the first panel of the pastel is composed on a scale commensurate with that of the painting but in different configurations, and the color scheme has been enhanced with additions of blue, brown, and yellow.

The flagstone patterns of the pastel carefully replicate those of the painting, yet there is no analogy here for the two different media in the painting: oil and collage in the left and encaustic and collage in the right. In 1969, Johns wrote about the perceptual game at work in the flagstone panels:

Flagstone ptg. 2 panels. one in oil.
*   "   " encaustic.*

An imagined unit the square of the height of these canvases.

The flagstones enclosed by a border (within this imagined square). The left rectangle (oil?) will include area A.B.C.D. The right (encaustic?) will include E.F.G.H. The meeting B.D. and E.G. will not have borders. (Or will they? Aim for maximum difficulty in determining what has happened?) (The possibility of these — or others — in gray.)

Whether to see the 2 parts as one thing or as two things.

Another possibility: to see that something has happened. Is this best shown by "pointing to" or by "hiding" it.[3]

This "imagined square" results when one flagstone panel shifts over the other, aligning the patterns and forming a single square panel.

The silhouetted shapes in the far right panel of the pastel only schematically suggest the three-dimensional boards and casts of the painting. The warm tones and shimmering layers of pastel echo but by no means duplicate the palette of the painting. Each of the boards in the pastel is marked with a discrete band of "matching" color at either end. This device replaces the "L" and "R" (left and right) stenciled on either end of the boards in the painting.

Beginning in 1973, Johns made several prints based on the 1972 painting. These include two four-sheet sets published by Gemini G.E.L. and included in the National Gallery's substantial holdings of Johns' prints. The Gallery's collection contains one other drawing by Johns, *Numbers* from 1966.

Marla Prather

NOTES

1. On these drawings see *The Drawings of Jasper Johns* [exh. cat. National Gallery of Art] (Washington, 1990), nos. 63–66.

2. Johns was driving on the Long Island Expressway and saw a crosshatch design painted on a passing car.

3. Jasper Johns, "Sketchbook Notes," *0 to 9*, no. 6 (July 1969), 1–2.

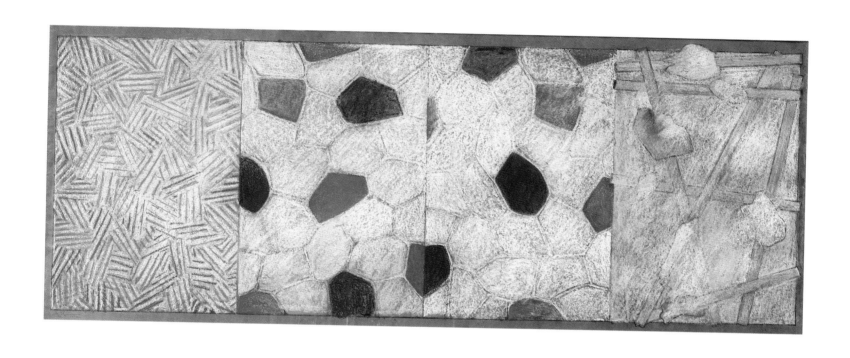

457

JASPER JOHNS
Born 1930

#6 (after 'Untitled 1975'), 1976
5 lithographs from a set of
15 progressive proofs
30⅛ x 29¾ (76.6 x 75.8)

Gift of Gemini G.E.L.

The process of working is a central subject in Jasper Johns' art. Methods, materials, and systems suggest components of its meaning. Printmaking, in particular, provides Johns with a splendid arena for documenting a work's evolution, keeping a record of its development, tracking the steps made along the way. This is because impressions of a print in progress may be made at various points throughout the working process. When such impressions are made in the course of the artist's changing the marks on the matrix they are called state proofs; when the impressions are drawn or painted upon by the artist in further developing an idea, they are called touched proofs or working proofs; and when a systematic record is maintained of each plate or element as it is successively added to build a multiplate image the proofs are called progressive proofs.

For virtually all of his printed editions Johns has come to retain various types of proofs, many of them quite special.[1] For color prints he tends to have his printers make a proof in black of each separate plate in a multiplate image as well as progressive color proofs such as the five seen here for *#6 (after 'Untitled 1975')*. These five from a set of fifteen progressive proofs have been selected to show the image at several immediately discernible, dramatically different stages.[2]

#6 (after 'Untitled 1975') is the last of six variants based on a 1975 painting in encaustic and oil.[3] According to Richard S. Field, *#6* is worked from some of the plates used for earlier works in the series as well as from plates assembled from cut-out portions of other of the earlier plates. Sixteen print runs, many of them very subtle in effect, were used to complete the lithograph, including four of a varnish glaze.

Progressive Proof 1 features gray lines that divide the format into four segments, echoing the four panels of the painting from which it derives: a vertical rectangle at left adjacent to a vertical rectangle one-half its width, this right one composed of three almost square units stacked one above the other. The regularity of these divisions provokes an imaginative leap in which one sees the print's surface divided into nine smaller units, which together suggest the various divisions explored in the series titled "6 Lithographs (after 'Untitled 1975')."

On view with these proofs is an earlier gift of Gemini G.E.L., the final version of the subject (opposite, lower right). In it the glow of the glaze layers along the right third of the image subtly differentiate each of the stacked squares, the lower right segment being the richest in effect. This use of glazes achieves a partly matte and partly gloss surface similar to the one achieved in the *Untitled* painting in encaustic and oil from which this image derives.[4]

The Gallery's collection includes more than a hundred of Johns' prints. However, this is our first group of his special proofs.

Ruth E. Fine

NOTES

1. Johns' proof impressions were the subject of the exhibition *Working Proofs*, organized by Christian Geelhaar for the Kunstmuseum Basel in 1979.

2. The number II/II in the margins indicates it is one of two sets.

3. Richard S. Field, *Jasper Johns: Prints 1970–1977* [exh. cat. Center for the Arts, Wesleyan University] (Middletown, Conn., 1978), cats. 249–254.

4. Johns first explored the crosshatch motif seen in these six lithographs in *Untitled*, 1972, oil, encaustic, and collage (Museum Ludwig, Cologne). See the drawing after the 1972 painting also in this catalogue. See also James Cuno and others, *Foirades/Fizzles: Echo and Allusion in the Art of Jasper Johns* [exh. cat. The Grunwald Center for the Graphic Arts, Wight Art Gallery, University of California] (Los Angeles, 1977); Nan Rosenthal and Ruth E. Fine, *The Drawings of Jasper Johns* [exh. cat. National Gallery of Art] (Washington, 1989), especially cats. 64–84.

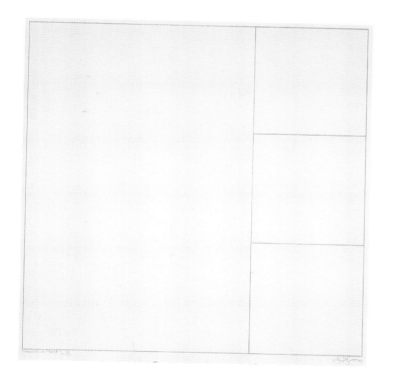

459

DAVID HOCKNEY
Born 1937

The Blue Guitar, 1976–1977
Portfolio of 20 etchings with aquatint
20⅝ x 18 (52.1 x 45.5)

Gift of Mrs. Robert A. Hauslohner

The title plate for *The Blue Guitar* informs us that the series comprises "Etchings by David Hockney who was inspired by Wallace Stevens who was inspired by Pablo Picasso." Hockney also has written that he

read Wallace Steven's (sic) poem [The Man With the Blue Guitar] in the summer of 1976. The etchings themselves were not conceived as literal illustrations of the poem but as an interpretation of its themes in visual terms. Like the poem, they are about transformations within art as well as the relation between reality and the imagination, so these are pictures within pictures and different styles of representation juxtaposed and reflected and dissolved within the same frame.[1]

Picasso's blue-period painting *The Old Guitarist*, 1903 (The Art Institute of Chicago) was the impetus for Stevens' 1936 poem to which Hockney, forty years later, responded. Hockney's etched rendition of *The Old Guitarist*, surrounded by a border of visual notes on other Picassoesque subjects, follows the title plate for the series. Next is a medley of landscapes, interiors, still lifes, and figure compositions remarkable for their visual inventiveness. Together they chart the artist's fertile imagination, suggesting and transforming images from the natural and fantastic worlds, using graphic media with great variety and subtlety. The blue guitar itself, musical staves, architectural details, furniture, draperies, flowers, figures, drawing instruments are all to be found.

Hockney's drawing here tends toward the playful and the schematic, yet portrait heads including one of Wallace Stevens on the plate titled "The Poet" capture keen likenesses. And references to cubism, surrealism, and others of Picasso's modes abound, lest we naively be charmed by Hockney's own delight in capturing essences with his ostensibly simplified approach.

All of the prints have individual titles, some of which refer to Picasso and his subjects. Others employ phrases from Stevens' poem: "Discord merely magnifies," "Tick it, tock it, turn it true." One title, "Etching is the Subject," responds to Stevens' line "Poetry is the subject of the poem." For this plate Hockney juxtaposed a heavily worked portrait head, with strong volumes developed by using a variety of etched marks one upon the other, and another head described by a few highly selective fine lines. Other areas of the plate show Hockney further exploring his medium, his stated subject.

On "Made in April," part of Stevens' poem appears in reverse, starting with the last four lines of verse xvi through the first four lines of verse xviii, the latter of which are quoted here:

*A dream (to call it a dream) in which
I can believe, in face of the object,*

*A dream no longer a dream, a thing
Of things as they are, as the blue guitar.[2]*

Hockney's etchings were printed by Maurice Payne, each of them from two copper plates inked with a selection from five colors: red, yellow, blue, green, and black. The white paper functions actively throughout the series as a foil for these bright hues that create patterns moving in space, set in counterpoise to rhythmic developments across the surface. *The Blue Guitar* was published by Petersburg Press, London and New York, in an edition of two hundred (of which this is number eighteen) plus thirty-five proof copies.

The National Gallery is fortunate to own fifty-seven etchings and lithographs by David Hockney, but this is the first of his illustrated portfolios or books to enter our collection. It makes a splendid addition not only to our representation of Hockney's art, but to our holdings of modern illustrated books and portfolios as well.

Ruth E. Fine

PROVENANCE
Purchased from Associated American Artists, Philadelphia, 1982.

NOTES
1. Quoted on the jacket flap for a small facsimile catalogue of the series published by Petersburg Press in 1977 simultaneously with the original. See *From Manet to Hockney: Modern Artists' Illustrated Books* [exh. cat. Victoria and Albert Museum] (London, 1985), color plate 30 and no. 157, where it states that Henry Geldzahler introduced the artist to the Stevens poem.

2. *The Palm at the End of the Mind: Selected Poems and a Play by Wallace Stevens*, ed. Holly Stevens (New York, 1972), 142; the poem in its entirety is found on 133–150.

461

JIM DINE
Born 1935

Me in Horn-Rimmed Glasses, 1979
Etching and drypoint with pastel
25½ x 19¾ (64.8 x 50.1)

Gift of Richard A. Simms

At the start of his career, Jim Dine's images of bathrobes were considered self-portraits.[1] As his work evolved from a less personalized approach into an intensely introspective art, his self-portraits moved from the symbolic and theoretical to the more immediately referential. Indeed, while Dine still is engaged by the bathrobe theme, it is now viewed as a metaphor for everyman as much as for the artist alone. Among his other important subjects has been his own countenance. Especially in his prints and mixed media drawings, Dine has studied himself repeatedly and with great concentration, as if seeking meaning in both life and art within his own visage.[2]

Speaking broadly about his use of figuration, Dine has signaled his work in printmaking as being particularly important:

Making prints is as important to me now as making drawings or paintings. As a matter of fact, it was the only medium, in which, until just recently, I felt free enough to be figurative when the pressure was still on to make those field paintings with the tools hung on them. Probably because the process was one step removed from me (with the printer in between), I felt that I could start to do that. I'm not sure exactly why I did it, but making prints was the first place my interest in figurative art raised its head.[3]

Me in Horn-Rimmed Glasses is the sixth of a series of nine self-portraits from 1979, eight of which, including this one, were printed at the Burston Graphic Center in Jerusalem by Ami Rosenberg, with the final one proofed by Aldo Crommelynck and printed at Atelier Crommelynck in Paris.[4] The first two of the prints, *Self-Portrait in Gray* and *The Hand Painted Portrait on Thin Fabriano,* include the artist's shoulders and

bare chest. With each succeeding stage of the plate's development the artist reduced its size, so that the focus became increasingly involved with the face itself and its individual features.

This self-portrait series has been worked with etching and drypoint, using both hand tools and the power tools that Dine has come to wield with such authority. Many of the group incorporate direct work with paint, grease crayon, or pastel. Most are printed in very small editions. *Me in Horned-Rimmed Glasses,* for example, is in an edition of eight impressions (plus six proofs, some on different papers), printed with an overall layer of surface tone on Canson Mi Fientes rust-colored paper. The warmth of the sheet is enhanced by the red and orange pastels, which emphasize the volume of the face. White and black pastels also are used, highlighting and drawing attention to the artist's intense gaze.

As has been Dine's method for many of his etchings, for *Me in Horned-Rimmed Glasses* and other works in this series, the plate was run through the press two times, slightly off-register, so each of the lines and marks appears twice, one darker than the other and with a slight space between them, adding a suggestion of movement and agitation to the image.

Commenting to David Shapiro on solipsism, Dine has indicated that "the unleashing of inner thoughts in an exciting way, in an appropriate way, is never a problem. I love exposure."[5] More than any of his other subjects, Dine's self-portraits enforce our awareness of this introspective view. *Me in Horn-Rimmed Glasses* is the first of Dine's self-portraits to enter our collection, thereby adding an important dimension to our representation of his work.

Ruth E. Fine

PROVENANCE
Christie's, New York, 7 November 1984, no. 462.

NOTES
1. Graham W. J. Beal and others, *Jim Dine: Five Themes* [exh. cat. Walker Art Center] (Minneapolis, 1984), 70–93.

2. For a selection of Jim Dine's self-portrait drawings see *Jim Dine Drawings 1973–1987* [exh. cat. The Contemporary Arts Center] (Cincinnati, 1988), nos. 7, 9, 17, 20, 53, 54, 58, 75, 76. For self-portrait prints, see Thomas Krens, ed., *Jim Dine Prints: 1970–1977* (New York, 1977), for example nos. 159–161, 176–192, 194–196; also see Ellen G. D'Oench and Jean E. Feinberg, *Jim Dine: Prints 1977–1985* (New York, 1986) for several others including *Me in Horn-Rimmed Glasses,* no. 47.

3. In "Conversations with Jim Dine" in Krens 1977, 32.

4. D'Oench and Fineberg 1986, nos. 42–50.

5. "Dine on Dine" in David Shapiro, *Jim Dine: Painting What One Is* (New York, 1981), 206.

6/8   1979

A. R. PENCK (RALF WINKLER)
Born 1939

8 Erfahrungen, 1981
Portfolio of 8 woodcuts with title page
30⅛ x 22¹³⁄₁₆ (76.5 x 58)

Gift of Wolfgang Wittrock

The art of A. R. Penck embraces polarities: light and dark, positive and negative, beginning and end, hope and doubt, West and East, and existence and nonexistence. His pragmatic and magical use of signs reflects upon mankind's earliest origins. These signs also act as symbols of hope for its continuation. Although intended as communication, the artist strives to keep his "message unspecific and at times ambiguous. Only the structure . . . has to be logical. The sequence of signs has to be accessible so that the viewer can work somehow with the information."[1] In this way Penck seeks to regain prerational thought for the viewer, allowing him or her to form subjective associations from visual information of primal integrity.

8 Erfahrungen (eight experiences) is a portfolio of woodcuts printed in black on white paper. Signs and images emerge in mesmerizing variety from constantly reversing figure and ground relationships. While activating the entire surface with pattern, Penck maintains a general balance of light and dark from image to image. Each print is a meditation on the self based on personal experiences of the artist and, metaphorically, the eight individual experiences of creating these woodcuts.

Two works from the portfolio are illustrated. Number 6 from *8 Erfahrungen* is a dancing figure in black silhouette, whose arms and legs swing out in expressive diagonals toward the edges of the image. Highly reminiscent of work by the artists of the Brücke movement, this print has strong subject and compositional similarities to a woodcut of a nude dancer by Christian Rohlfs entitled *Tanzender Akt,* 1909–1910.[2] Additionally, it echoes elements from a woodcut by Emil Nolde entitled *Kerzentänzerinnen,* 1917, a depiction of two partially-clad women dancing with lighted candles at their feet.[3] The candles find equivalents in the small, dark, starlike forms that occupy the foreground of Penck's work. Other prints in the portfolio have notable correspon-

dences to earlier work such as the full-faced portrait Number 3 from *8 Erfahrungen* (not illustrated), which is highly reminiscent of the vigorous gouging and angular style of woodcut portraits by Karl Schmidt-Rottluff.[4] It is important to note that while many contemporary German artists are overtly troubled by the Nazi past, there are those such as Penck whose work celebrates great German artistic achievements.

Number 8 from *8 Erfahrungen* is compositionally divided in half, with the left side suggesting the artist standing before his work and the right side the world of symbols he composes. Traversing the image from top to bottom, the silhouetted artist swings open his arms toward the slightly off-vertical demarcator that leans with a gentle dynamism in his direction. The right side of the composition is filled with glyphs, some of which combine to evoke a female form. Penck's characters are created with the most rudimentary elements and some have multiple readings much like a Rorschach inkblot. The artist's stick figures in particular have been described as representing "the holocaust of anonymity in perpetual, pervasive process in the modern administered world."[5] While such doubt is at the heart of the artist's work, it is important to remember the hope implied in his attempts to communicate.

Many aspects of Penck's technical approach to printmaking relate to that of earlier German expressionists. The utilization of blotter paper and other papers with heavy physical presence is similar. This kind of support provides a vital interaction of image and surface. Also like his forbears, Penck has a predilection for woodcut and has noted that "the resistance of the material almost forces the shape on the artist."[6] It is easy to see in the artist's enthusiasm for the elemental act of cutting wood in these works, an aspect that mirrors the gouging of the block by earlier expressionists. Note too that the frequently consistent width of the cutting line generates a harmony that extends through the entire series.

Much of Penck's artistic philosophy developed during his years behind the Iron Curtain where he absorbed writings on politics and philosophy. He also took an interest in natural sciences with a focus on research into primal origins. Penck emigrated to the west in 1980, but his works were known outside East Germany fifteen years before because of special export arrangements. His several pseudonyms were a means of self-defense and a way to facilitate

the export of his paintings from the German Democratic Republic. The name A. R. Penck was borrowed from the geologist Albrecht Penck (1858–1945), whose writings on the Ice Age the artist admires. The present works are signed both A. R. Penck and α γ, another adopted appellation.

The National Gallery welcomes the addition of this portfolio, which is the first of Penck's work to enter the collection and represents one of the artist's most important printmaking achievements.

Charles M. Ritchie

PROVENANCE
Peter Blum Editions, New York.

NOTES
1. Dorothea Dietrich, "A Talk with A. R. Penck," *The Print Collector's Newsletter* 14 (July–Aug. 1983), 95.

2. For illustration see Paul Vogt, *Christian Rohlfs Das graphische Werk* (Recklinghausen, 1960), CR 3.

3. For illustration see Gustav Schiefler, *Emil Nolde Das Graphische Werk Holzschnitte und Lithographien* (Cologne, 1967), CR 127.

4. For illustrations see Gerhard Wietek, *Schmidt-Rottluff Graphik* (Munich, 1971), 152–153.

5. Donald Kuspit, *A. R. Penck* [exh. cat. Magasin 3 Stockholm Konsthall] (Stockholm, 1989), n.p.

6. Dietrich 1983, 94.

17/30   α. Y. (as perdtz)

GEORG BASELITZ
Born 1938

Lesender Mann, 1982
Woodcut with painted additions,
unique proof of first state
33¹³⁄₁₆ x 24¹⁄₁₆ (85.8 x 61.1)

Joshua P. Smith Collection

Georg Baselitz has been of international importance since the 1970s with art that he has referred to as "Stil Malerei" (style painting). This mode of working is often surprising in its impact, with aggressive marking and crude yet facile portrayals of simple, even banal subjects. A simpler direction is shared with earlier German expressionists such as the artists of the Brücke movement, who likewise cultivated an interest in primitive art and the art of the insane, the search for a Germanic voice in art, and a revitalization of printmaking, particularly the woodcut. Nevertheless, Baselitz' art is different, often lacking the brilliant color, the optimistic radicalism, and even the psychological component that were key elements for the earlier group.

As is common in Baselitz' work, in *Lesender Mann* (man reading) the artist has turned the figure upside down, forcing the viewer to consider the formal aspects of the print before the represented subject, and also suggesting the problems of orientation in our complex contemporary society. Baselitz frequently places his subject in compositional center, viewed from front or side, giving the work a balanced, monumental quality despite the churning, expressionist mark making. Indeed the figurative elements in *Lesender Mann* are often overwhelmed by the sparkling contrast between whites left open in the printing process and the blacks of the soft printing ink and the viscous paint. Drips, spatters, fingerprints, as well as strokes of paint used to later adjust and redefine the image are evidence of the charged heat and artifice associated with Baselitz' creative process.

Lesender Mann is a fine example of the artist's work, featuring the inverted profile of a man holding an open book close to his face. While the subject is not necessarily a self-portrait, the artist frequently depicts himself, his wife, his studio, and the landscape nearby his castle in Derneburg where he lives and works in relative isolation. Interestingly, Baselitz' subjects are drawn from memory and imagination rather than directly from the model because he is interested in "invented figurations" rather than "illustrative method."[1] The artist's concern with portraiture, genre, and landscape subjects reflects not only his own interest in representation, but also the return by many artists throughout the world to figuration during the 1980s. In particular, the fragmented human body has been used by Baselitz and other contemporary artists to show "corrosion and dissolution of the human body as a metaphor for the erosion of value and belief in the modern world [and] for a sense of historical loss."[2]

The print is also an outstanding example of both the renaissance of interest in the woodcut medium and the flowering of the unique print that have occurred in the past decade. Printed by the artist and his wife in limited rather than large editions, Baselitz' prints have a personal quality and are frequently enlivened with variation and experiment. It has been noted that his prints of the early 1980s "were often informed by Baselitz' activities as a sculptor, which began in 1980. His attack of the wood or linoleum block (sometimes even with a chain saw) is similar to the aggressive manner in which his wooden sculptures were brought to form."[3] The woodblock surface of *Lesender Mann* was gouged by a power tool, the effect of which can be seen as regularized skips in some of the white areas. The sculptural qualities of creating a woodcut are apparent when looking at this print, especially the brutality of cutting into the block and the tactile aspects of printing it. Even the expressive overpainting emphasizes the print's physicality.

This significant work will begin to fill a major gap in our collection. *Lesender Mann* is not only the first work by Baselitz to be offered for the Gallery's collection of prints and drawings, it is also one of the first by any of the major contemporary European neo-expressionists.

Charles M. Ritchie

NOTES
1. Jill Lloyd, "Georg Baselitz Comes Full Circle: The Art of Transgression and Restraint," *Art International* 5 (Winter 1988), 89. For a discussion of Baselitz' views concerning his art and an overview of his artistic development see this article, 86–96.

2. Lloyd 1988, 90.

3. Joanna E. Fink, *Georg Baselitz: Selected Prints 1963–1985* [exh. cat. The Alpha Gallery] (Boston, 1985), n.p.

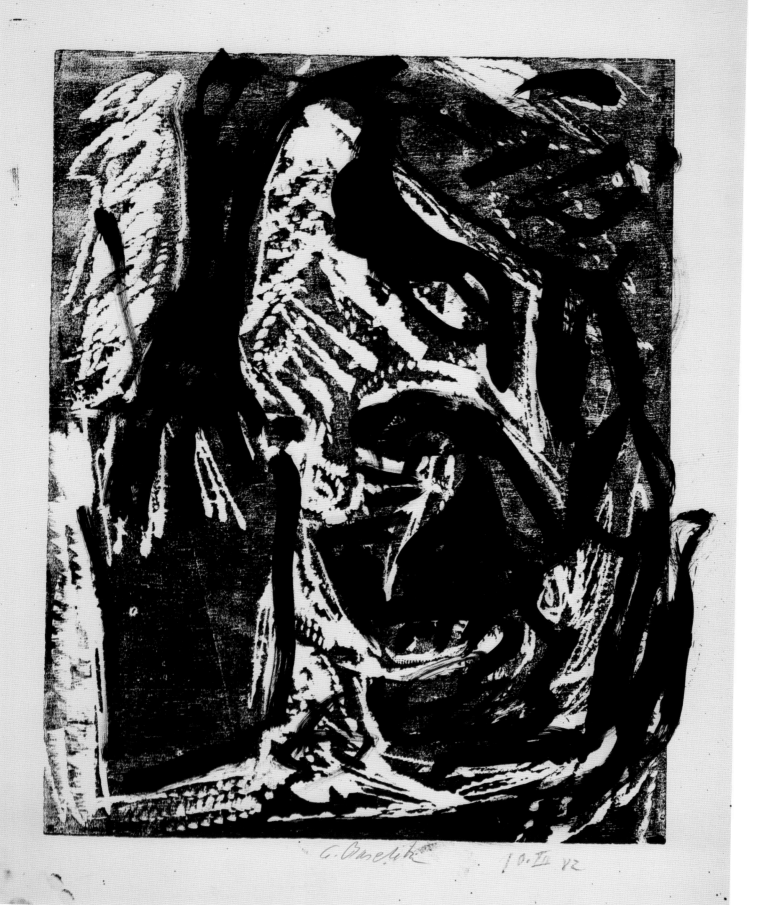

467

FELIX DROESE
Born 1950

Glocke, 1982
Three unique impressions of a woodcut
9⅜ x 15⅜ (23.8 x 39.1)
13⅝ x 16⅛ (34.6 x 41)
10¼ x 17 (26.1 x 43.2)

Gift of Wolfgang Wittrock

Broken planks, wood ravaged and eroded by nature, wrappers from consumer goods, and other discarded entities inspire the artistic impulses of Felix Droese. It has been noted that the artist's "'stigmatized' supporting materials conform exactly with the themes of his works, which are concerned with such social questions as freedom and responsibility, suffering and redemption, and reflect the ethical position of the artist."[1] Droese's art transforms these substances into powerful statements about the forces that control our lives and poses questions about the role of the artist in contemporary society.

The three present works, each entitled *Glocke* (bell), are from a series of impressions made from the same block. Small, nearly triangular in shape, the matrix itself is not unlike the flaring shape of a bell. In the image, a mysterious black figure with featureless head confronts a bell-shaped form, which displaces it toward the left side of the composition. The bell, one of the artist's most important themes, evokes a variety of interpretations: as "warnings of disaster," a call for "freedom," and a caution to a "world ruled by reason."[2]

Each sheet responds to the image in a different way. One version on wrapping paper is traversed laterally by bands of red hearts. Its two pinked edges and numerous folds attest to its previous life as packaging. The hearts are both a cliché from popular culture and an ageless symbol. One wonders if the artist scorns their superficiality or endorses their sentiment, or both? Irony is fundamental in the contrast between the cheery background and enigmatic image. It is interesting to note how the vibrant hearts generate energy, much like waves of sound from a bell.

Another version is printed on an unfolded package of organically grown rye flour. Green labeling shows through from the verso, and torn edges remain along the bottom edge of the folded sheet, on which the image is printed twice. The choice of this support reflects not only the artist's environmental

consciousness, but also evokes his concern that forces directing our food supply are insensitive to the individual.

The third version on deep purple is actually the verso of a book cover. The image is printed twice, and the overprintings interact in an interesting manner. Note too how the subtle orange rectangle on the right half adds a stimulating color contrast. The verso of the image is printed with "East/West Painting Poems by Sheila Isham," a title that reminds us of the artist's global and political concerns. In each print the artist has shifted the context of the printed image, forcing us to consider essential themes such as love and physical and intellectual nourishment.

Droese's expressive, bladelike line often assumes the quality of silhouette. Indeed, a group of scissor-cut images drew acclaim for the artist in the early 1980s, and he has also created larger sculpture that sustains these traits. The artist's sensitivity to the materials he chooses is clearly seen in the *Glocke* prints.

Droese's approach to woodcut technique recalls many aspects of his German predecessors in the Brücke. He prefers to print using only the most primitive methods. Note the inscription "handgedruckt" (printed by hand) on two of the prints, denoting his absorption with the unassisted act of printing the image. This method sustains im-

mediacy and cultivates irregularities that are so important to his process. Printing his works in very small editions, the artist also explores a wide range of printing surfaces: maps, newspaper pages, and other extraordinary supports. Droese studied with Joseph Beuys, whose political and social activism has inspired many contemporary German artists. In the spirit of Beuys, Droese finds the artist's role as a manufacturer of goods for middle-class society problematic. He attempts to subvert the system by adopting the orphans of our culture, transforming them into desirables, and placing them in the hands of the collector. Much like the phoenix rising from the flames, the magical is born of ashes and engages us with its thorny beauty. Metaphorically, these three prints are small bells ringing us awake to the failures of our consumer culture and the threat of political darkness in the late twentieth century.

Charles M. Ritchie

NOTES

1. Annie Bardon, "New Paths in Germany: The Woodcuts of Droese, Kluge & Mansen," *Print Collector's Newsletter* 17 (Nov.–Dec. 1986), 158.

2. For a discussion of the importance of the bell motif in Droese's work, see Bardon 1986, 159.

JIM DINE
Born 1935

*The Apocalypse: The Revelation
of Saint John the Divine*
Arion Press, San Francisco, 1982
Bound volume with 29 woodcuts
14⅞ x 11 (37.8 x 28.3)

Gift of Mrs. Robert A. Hauslohner

The Apocalypse: The Revelation of Saint John the Divine is the earliest of three volumes with images by Jim Dine that have been published by Andrew Hoyem's Arion Press in San Francisco.[1] The story of the Apocalypse has been a source of inspiration for many painters and printmakers, notable examples being Albrecht Dürer and William Blake. Thus it is not surprising that an artist with so strong a sense of art history as Jim Dine would tackle the complexities of the theme. Dine's immediate inspiration, however, was his reading of *Unforgettable Fire: Pictures Drawn by Atomic Bomb Survivors*.[2]

Dine's *Apocalypse* opens with a full-page frontispiece self-portrait entitled "The Artist as Narrator." The balance of the woodcuts, varied in size and shape and individually titled, are spaced throughout the volume's twenty-two chapters. Many images long associated with Dine's art make close connections with the text: tools ("Pruning Shears"); bathrobes ("Robes Were Given Unto Every One"); hearts ("The Voice of the Bridegroom and of the Bride"); trees ("The Two Olive Trees"); gates ("Every Several Gate was of One Pearl").[3] In addition, images that have since been used frequently as part of Dine's vocabulary made an early appearance here, for example hands and skulls. Many of the woodcuts seem specific to this text, however, such as "That Old Serpent, Called the Devil," "I Saw Another Angel," and "Behold a White Horse."

Dine carved his images into oak. His masterful control of the woodcut is evident throughout the volume. Using both hand tools and the power tools that he wields with great authority, the artist has provided us with a virtual dictionary of woodcut marks, from the finest, most delicate of lines through complex and varied textures to broadly worked shapes that are refined with incisive clarity. The role of the grain of uncarved expanses of wood varies from print to print, sometimes serving as a broad textured tonal area, other times providing a quiet activity among many dynamically carved surfaces.

Beginning with the artist's own vivid likeness, each of Dine's compositions is characterized by a striking interplay of dramatic black and white contrasts. Sometimes darkness prevails, sometimes blinding light. In a number of prints volumetric form and qualities of light are emphasized; in others one responds first to the drama of an event or situation; or the qualities of atmosphere, of smoke, of fire become paramount. Some images handsomely demonstrate the economy with which Dine is able to convey a form, whereas in others the accumulative vigor of Dine's extraordinary ability to conflate many ways of working takes precedence. In several instances two images of similar subjects — hands, bathrobes, trees — fill a double-page spread, inviting comparisons between their structure, their emotional impact, their facture.

The volume is printed on French handmade paper from the Richard De Bas Mill, with every page a pleasure to touch. The text, from the 1611 King James Bible, is set in several typefaces — Monotype Garamond Bold, Hadriano, and Stempel Garamond Titling. The pages are bound in oak veneer plywood boards stained with an image of a lightning bolt; the spine is white pigskin.

This is the first book with Jim Dine's prints to enter the Gallery's collection. It is also one of our first volumes printed and published by Arion Press, one of the most admired fine printers in America. Thus it makes a doubly important addition to our representation of modern illustrated books.

Ruth E. Fine

PROVENANCE
Purchased from Associated American Artists, Philadelphia, 1983.

NOTES
1. *The Apocalypse: The Revelation of Saint John the Divine* was printed in an edition of 150 (of which this is number 36) plus 15 copies *hors commerce*. In the current catalogue raisonné of Jim Dine's prints, Ellen G. D'Oench and Jean E. Feinberg, *Jim Dine Prints 1977–1985* (New York, 1986), *The Apocalypse* is listed as no. 141. Dine's other two Arion Press books are *The Temple of Flora* (D'Oench and Fineberg 1986, 177), with twenty-nine prints incorporating drypoint and engraving and poetry by John Ashbury, Hart Crane, Kenneth Rexroth, among others (1984) and, most recently, *Biotherm*, with offset lithographs accompanying the last poem of Frank O'Hara (1990).

2. See D'Oench and Fineberg 1986, 128.

3. On these themes see Graham W. J. Beal and others, *Jim Dine: Five Themes* [exh. cat. Walker Art Center] (Minneapolis and New York, 1984).

THE APOCALYPSE

THE REVELATION

of

SAINT JOHN THE DIVINE

THE LAST BOOK OF THE NEW TESTAMENT

FROM THE KING JAMES VERSION OF THE BIBLE, 1611,

WITH TWENTY-NINE PRINTS FROM WOODBLOCKS CUT BY

JIM DINE

PRINTED AND PUBLISHED IN 1982 BY

THE ARION PRESS

SAN FRANCISCO

EDWARD RUSCHA
Born 1937

I Think I'll . . ., 1983
Oil on canvas
53¾ x 63¾ (136.53 x 161.93)

Gift (Partial and Promised) of
Marcia S. Weisman

Edward Ruscha was born in 1937 in Omaha, Nebraska, and raised in Oklahoma City. After high school he moved to Los Angeles where from 1956 to 1960 he attended Chinouard Art Institute, a school known then as a training ground for Disney illustrators and animators. He majored in painting and also took courses in commercial art. While a student Ruscha worked as a printer's devil, setting type by hand, pulling proofs, and cleaning presses, and also in a mail order gift house that personalized toys by enameling children's names on them in showcard lettering. Ruscha's interest in using words, as visually important elements and wry, quizzical carriers of meaning, dates back to his paintings and collages of the very early 1960s.

Although regarded from almost the beginning as a leader of West Coast Pop art, Ruscha has found that label narrow. While his paintings (as well as his drawings, prints, and humorous, narratively charged printed books of photographs) have involved incorporating elements of quotidian popular culture in the form of images and words, his work has often achieved its impact from the kinds of odd juxtapositions found in the surrealism of an artist such as Magritte. Ruscha's work often apposes the sweeping scale and magnificence of nature in America with manifestations of our conspicuously manufactured products. Both categories are rendered with meticulous craftsmanship, as if to make us consider carefully what it means to live in a culture that may equalize the value of a gasoline station and a subtly modulated sky. Ruscha's craftsmanship may also be thought of in the wake of the American precisionists of the years between the world wars. The flawless finish that characterizes precisionist art, whether the stretched perspectives and sharply angled industrial landscapes of Charles Sheeler or the graphic signs atop Charles Demuth's urban scenes, appear to be distant ancestors of Ruscha's words in the sky and views from the freeway.

The 1983 oil *I Think I'll . . .* is the first painting by Ruscha to enter the Gallery's collection. It joins three drawings and forty-one lithographs and screenprints dating from 1963 to 1982. The painting is one of a group from 1983 in which words with an ambiguous message float on red skies suggesting smog-filled sunsets over Los Angeles. The upper-case lettering resembles the sans serif type style Helvetica, except that straight edges have been set at angles where curves normally would be, as on the *B*s and *S*s. By combining graphic lettering associated with the flat surface of the printed page and an illusionistically rendered sky that describes infinite depth, Ruscha has created a lush, highly witty sight gag about a classic issue of modernist painting: calling attention to the surface of the work, its two-dimensionality, more than to the capacity of painting to engender an illusion of three dimensions behind the surface. This issue has concerned Ruscha often during his career. The step-down drift of the larger letters in the painting ("I THINK MAYBE I'LL . . .") from the upper left to the lower right of the canvas rectangle is reminiscent of the way Ruscha bisected the canvas diagonally, leaving the upper triangle as empty sky, in much earlier compositions involving Standard gasoline stations, the 20th Century Fox trademark, or the Los Angeles County Museum in flames. The fiery color of the sky in *I Think I'll . . .*, combined with the indecisive nature of the message, create an ominous mood that links this work directly to another of the 1983 red-sky paintings, in which the message reads "A CERTAIN FORM OF HELL."

Nan Rosenthal

PROVENANCE
From the artist to the donor.

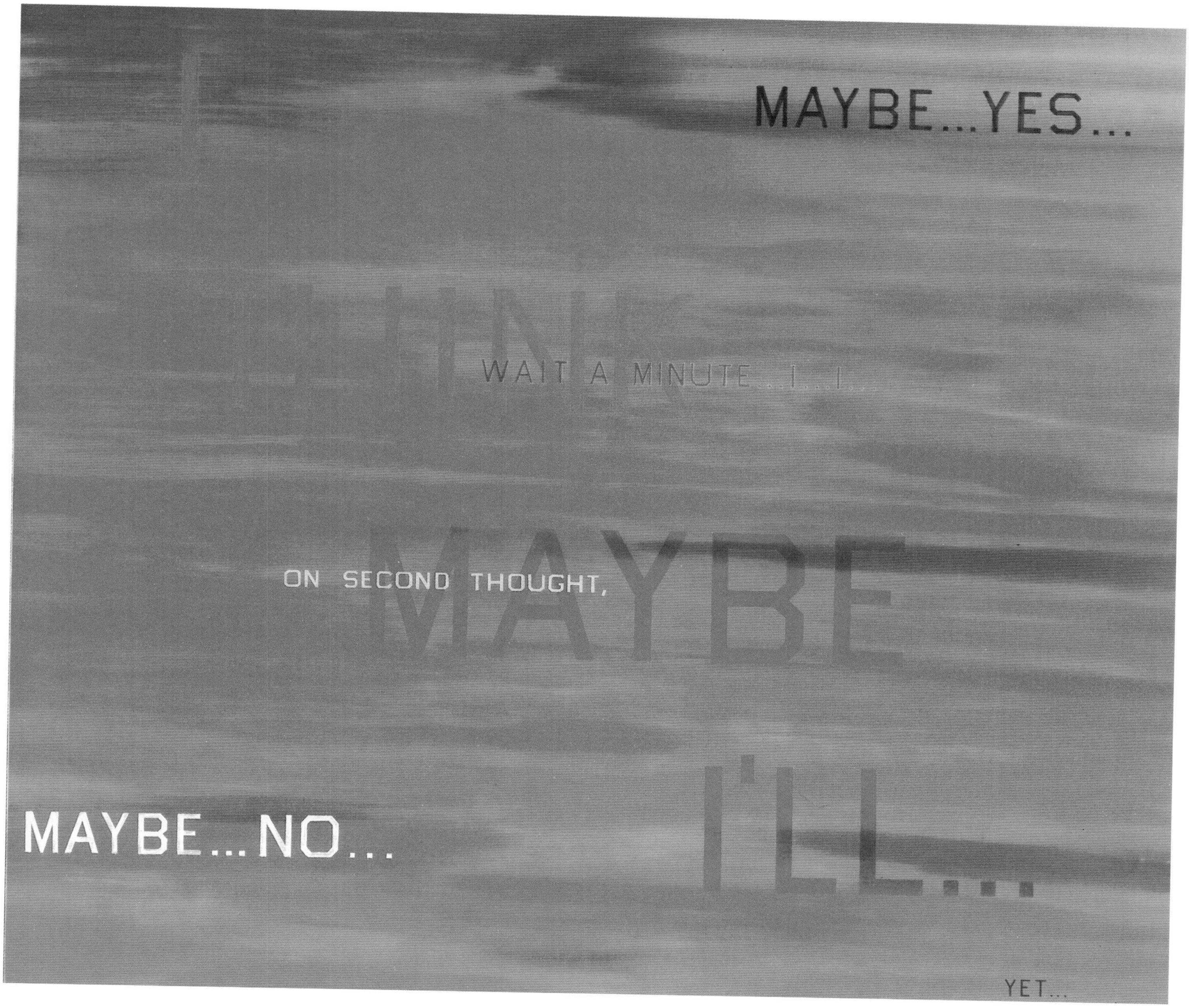

MAYBE...YES...

THINK

WAIT A MINUTE...I...I...

ON SECOND THOUGHT, MAYBE

MAYBE...NO...

I'LL....

YET...

473

HELEN FRANKENTHALER
Born 1928

Untitled, 1983
Acrylic on paper
23⅛ x 31⅜ (58.74 x 80.45)

Gift of Helen Frankenthaler

Untitled is from a group of paintings on paper that Helen Frankenthaler made in Connecticut during a very productive August and September of 1983. Annotated 10 August, *Untitled* is one of at least two works painted that day.[1] While high-key colors are often associated with Frankenthaler's art, she has also explored a more somber palette throughout her career and especially in the 1980s. This aspect of *Untitled* may be associated with several paintings on canvas, among them *Brother Angel*, 1983, and *Halley's Comet*, 1985.[2] Fascinating is the fact that these earth-toned paintings have titles suggestive of heavenly themes.

The seminal importance of Helen Frankenthaler's work has been acclaimed since the early 1950s. Her *Mountains and Sea*, 1953, referred to at the time as a "bridge between Pollock and what was possible,"[3] continues to evoke extraordinary interest and praise. Worked from memories of the Nova Scotia landscape, Frankenthaler said, "I knew the landscapes were in my arms as I did it."[4] John Elderfield has responded to Frankenthaler's words by pointing out that "'in my arms' . . . is not a casual figure of speech: deriving not only from landscape but from the experience of painting landscape, the picture releases stored knowledge and memories of that experience in its physical creation."[5]

This release of stored memories as an aspect of physical creation is an important factor in Frankenthaler's art; and one of her major concerns has been to explore the expressive power of the painterly touch. On canvas and on paper she has expanded and refined her intensely personal exploration of the nature of her medium. In each work she creates a unique visual space, an atmosphere, a mood, the layers and details of which are uncovered in stages as one looks closely.

Frankenthaler often employs beautifully colored handmade papers, and *Untitled* is painted on a tan sheet visible around the upper left corner. It provides a foil for the dominant, pulsating brown that shifts in space. Puddles and pools, splashes and strokes create a shimmering arena for the artist's bold touches of color and of gold. Some areas emerge from the distance, float forward, whereas others feel as if they are spreading across the surface as we watch.

Frankenthaler's lush, fluid brown and golden washes are enhanced by clear delineation of edges within them, by the brilliant red hovering to the right of center, the smoky white that modifies it, and the strongly felt white shapes that jump across the lower edge just above the dryly brushed dark brown stroke. There is a significant shift in "feel" when moving from these washed and brushed markings to Frankenthaler's colorful "clumps," to use Elderfield's word for the artist's touches of thickly applied paint. These dabs of subtle, metallic blues and greens function as accents, as turning points, as momentary anchors for the forms that attach themselves to them.

And then there is the daring use of gold. More visually insistent than the clumps of color, these dabs and strokes evoke heavenly bodies, fireworks, explosions of light, acting with the color touches as counterpoints to the earth tones throughout.[6]

The National Gallery's collection of works by Helen Frankenthaler includes one painting, *Wales*, 1966, two paintings on paper, and sixteen prints; primarily the gifts of The Woodward Foundation, other donors include Lessing J. Rosenwald and Louis J. Hector. This beautiful acrylic on paper, a generous gift from the artist, is an enormously important addition to our representation of her work.

Ruth E. Fine

NOTES
1. Karen Wilkin, *Frankenthaler Works on Paper 1949–1984* [exh. cat. International Exhibitions Foundation] (New York, 1984), in her chronology, 123, cited this as a particularly fertile period. The present work is plate 73 in this catalogue; plate 75, also *Untitled*, is also dated to 10 August. The present work also appears in John Elderfield, *Frankenthaler* (New York, 1989), 336.

2. In Elderfield 1989, these are reproduced respectively on 340 and 360.

3. The frequently quoted statement by Morris Louis after seeing *Mountains and Sea* in 1953 can be found in Elderfield 1989, 65.

4. Elderfield 1989, 66.

5. Elderfield 1989, 66.

6. The artist's assistant, Maureen St. Onge, suggested relationships between this *Untitled* painting on paper and *Grey Fireworks*, an acrylic on canvas of 1982, reproduced in Elderfield 1989, 329.

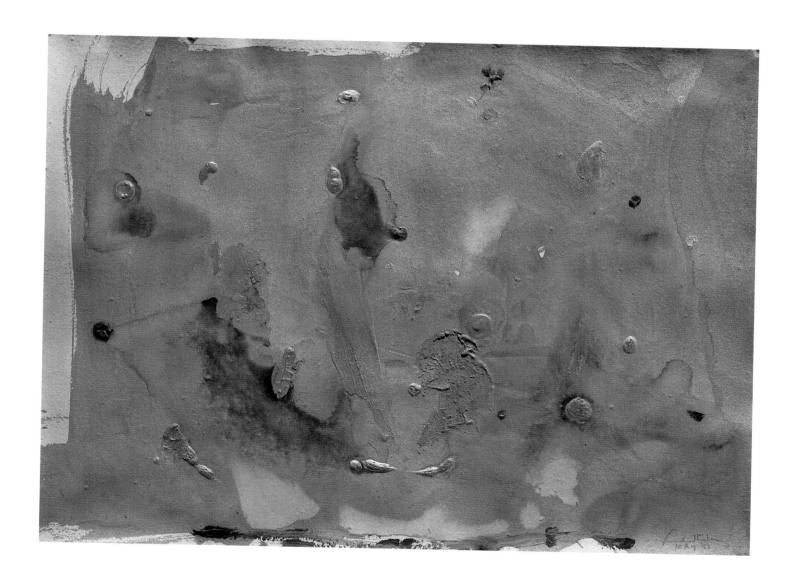

JÖRG IMMENDORFF
Born 1945

Café Deutschland gut: *folgen*, 1983
Linocut with painted additions
70⅞ x 90⁹⁄₁₆ (180 x 230)

Joshua P. Smith Collection

Jörg Immendorff has stated that "art is the only way for me to clarify my political viewpoint."[1] Intending his art as a catalyst for political and social change, the artist presents allegorical subjects as a way of commenting on contemporary issues. This activism is an extension of the artistic approach of Joseph Beuys, an early influence on Immendorff and a leader of an artistic revolution that began in Germany in the 1960s. Expanding upon Beuys' declaration that art is a powerful instrument and life force, Immendorff and others such as Anselm Kiefer and Markus Lüpertz have sounded it as a clarion call for a troubled Germany and an ideologically divided world.

Folgen (consequences) is from a series of ten linocuts entitled "Café Deutschland gut," all printed from the same matrix but with variations in color scheme. The subject is an imaginary bar based on the Rattinger Hof, a Düsseldorf gathering place. Created by Immendorff as a stage on which to dramatize symbolic events, it involves famous characters from history, writers, notables from popular culture, revolutionaries, spies, and other political figures. All are depicted in a style and color reminiscent of comics. It has been noted that Immendorff "is satisfied with the representation of the world as undertaken by the media. He only recasts [its] figures and stage props."[2] Indeed, the cramped perspective and lurid light of these works seems related to the visual and aural clutter of the media. One can almost hear the crashing pop music emanate from this, its visual equivalent.

While identities in these narratives are important, they are sometimes difficult to read.

The artist's imagination embraces the famous and obscure, the obvious and arcane. Immendorff himself can be seen at center, poking his head through a crumpled image of Chairman Mao. Above him is a helmeted German soldier, a specter from the past who looks away from a blue mirrored column. Just to the left is a rather unstable-looking Brandenburg Gate and at the far right is a tumbling horse, part of the Roman Victory that once topped the gate. On the left side of the composition is a broken eagle, a symbol for the West German state. The top of the round table in the foreground has a scrambled red swastika-like insignia, while the broken arms of black swastikas fall from above. A yellow oval glares with an interrogation-room-like light, with figures such as Marx, Stalin, and Lenin in attendance.[3]

Although it is smaller and a reverse image, *folgen* is a transcription of a 1982 painting entitled *Café Deutschland XII / Adlerhalfte*. Immendorff's work is in the tradition of history painting, using grand scale as a way of inviting the viewer to participate in the events depicted. While *folgen* does this, its fractured arrangement is less than accessible. The frenetic energy of color and line create a tension that invokes a feeling of threat and claustrophobia, undermining certain narrative qualities. In addition, the hand-painted red background adds a fiery undercurrent to the chaotic action formed in shadowy brownish black.

The linocut has sometimes been neglected in the fine arts, perhaps because of its image as a crafts process, the industrial nature of the material, and its characteristic requirement for simplification of line. The tech-nique and its populist associations would seem to be an obvious printmaking choice for Immendorff. Linoleum is easy to cut and allows the artist to work quickly on a large, relatively lightweight surface. Further, it does not require a press but can be printed by hand using a spoon to rub the back of paper while in contact with the matrix. This aspect has been particularly useful to Immendorff who has chosen to print smaller sections of this image as distinct new compositions.

A work of monumental power and scope, *folgen* is the first work by Immendorff to enter the National Gallery's collection. It represents a primary theme by this important artist and provides a cornerstone from which our collection of his art can be developed.

Charles M. Ritchie

PROVENANCE
Maximilian Verlag-Sabine Knust, Munich.

NOTES
1. Rainer Crone, "Jörg Immendorff," in Elizabeth Armstrong and Marge Goldwater, *Images and Impressions: Painters Who Print* [exh. cat. Walker Art Center] (Minneapolis, 1984), 34.

2. Ulrich Krempel, *Café Deutschland gut* (Düsseldorf, 1983), n.p.

3. For brief discussions of iconography see Armstrong and Goldwater, also Ellen S. Jacobowitz and Ann Percy, *New Art on Paper* [exh. cat. Philadelphia Museum of Art] (Philadelphia, 1988), 30.

VIJA CELMINS
Born 1939

Concentric Bearings, A, 1983-1985
Drypoint, aquatint, photogravure, and
burnishing
Two plates:
(left) 8⅛ x 5⅜ (20.5 x 13.5)
(right) 9½ x 7 (24.0 x 17.7)

Gift of Gemini G.E.L. and the Artist

Concentric Bearings, A is the first in a series
of four mixed intaglio prints titled *Concentric Bearings* that was printed by Vija Celmins at the Gemini G.E.L. workshop in Los Angeles. The series consists of four images on individual plates of various sizes that have been aligned in different combinations and printed on large sheets of paper. Two of these images, a galaxy field and Marcel Duchamp's *Rotary Glass Plates [Precision Optics]*, appear in *Concentric Bearings, A*. Two more images can be seen in the other prints in the series: a smaller version of a galaxy field and a monoplane in flight.[1]

In 1968 Celmins abandoned her earlier paintings and drawings of large-scale everyday objects and began graphite drawings of the ocean surface seen close-up on a shallow plane. This new investigation occupied her almost exclusively for five years, after which she expanded her subjects to include the desert floor, the lunar surface, and the galaxy. By the early 1970s these themes were carried over to the print medium. Celmins created many variations on these motifs, often executing them in the same format but always looking at them with slightly different sensibilities.

The source for her image of the star cluster in *Concentric Bearings, A* is a photograph taken by a NASA observatory. Celmins has meticulously redrawn the image on the plate and further worked it with aquatint and drypoint. The Duchamp motorized machine is also taken from a photograph that she transferred to the plate by photogravure and then reworked with drypoint, aquatint, and burnishing. Celmins does not intend to imitate the texture and character of the photographs she employs, but rather reinterprets these images into a surface that is true to whatever graphic medium she is using. The results provide sensuous and tangible surfaces that are physically pleasing and never wearisome to the eye, through which the artist hopes the viewer will reexperience a familiar sight,

for example the dark starry heavens. Celmins explains, "You really have to quiet yourself to see how physical they are."[2] It is this physical quality and the art of picture making that she finds challenging.

Celmins' pairing of the constellation with the image of Duchamp's machine makes for an exceptionally beautiful print. Besides being aesthetically pleasing, *Concentric Bearing, A*, along with the entire series, is Celmins' witty commentary on perception. Both images address similar concerns with the optical illusion of space and motion, but ironically one is man-made and the other made by nature.

The National Gallery owns ten prints by Celmins. The earliest is a lithograph of an ocean view that she printed at the Tamarind Lithography Workshop, Inc., in 1970 and was a gift to the Gallery from Dorothy J. and Benjamin B. Smith. In 1986 the Gallery acquired Celmins' largest print of a galaxy view from Mr. and Mrs. Roger P. Sonnabend. Since then the Gallery's Celmins holdings have continued to expand, thanks to the generous gifts in 1988 and 1989 from Gemini G.E.L. and the artist. Because of their continuous support the Gallery's series of *Concentric Bearings* is now complete.

Carlotta J. Owens

NOTES
1. Duchamp made his motorized device in 1920 to demonstrate optical illusion. It consists of five rectangular glass plates of graduated lengths attached to a metal rod. When the rod is turned the black lines painted on the ends of the plates appear as a continuous circle.

2. Kenneth Baker, "Vija Celmins: Drawings without Withdrawings," *Artforum* 22 (Nov. 1983), 64–65; and Carter Ratcliff, "Vija Celmins: An Art of Reclamation," *Print Collector's Newsletter* 14, no. 6 (Jan.–Feb. 1984), 193–196.

 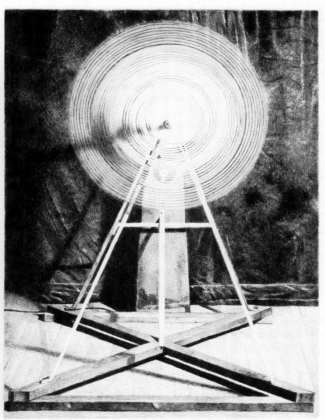

JIM DINE
Born 1935

The Gate, Goodbye Vermont, 1985
Wood, steel, tools, and paint
111½ × 170 × 62½
(283.21 × 431.80 × 158.75)

Gift (Partial and Promised) of
a San Francisco Collector

Jim Dine first attained recognition in the early 1960s as a kind of "Pop-assemblagist," an artist who, instead of depicting or re-making the objects of popular culture, brought the objects themselves into his works. During the later 1960s and through-out the 1970s Dine continued to incorpo-rate various objects into his paintings at the same time that his painterly technique be-came ever more lush and complex. In these years Dine's work increasingly lost its "Pop" edge. His iconography grew more personal, and the objects he incorporated into his works became linked to a private world of memory and association.

Much of Dine's work, it has been noted, revolves around five themes: tools, robes, hearts, trees, and gates.[1] Gates are the most recent of these themes to enter the artist's oeuvre, introduced in 1981. Dine's imme-diate inspiration for the theme came from the nineteenth-century iron gate outside the house and studio of the French master printer Aldo Crommelynck, with whom Dine worked over a period of many years.[2] He first addressed the gate in paintings and drawings, but in 1983 it inspired the cre-ation of a monumental bronze sculpture, *The Crommelynck Gate with Tools*.

To make *The Crommelynck Gate with Tools*, Dine employed the technique of direct cast-ing. Casts of tools were taken in wax, then heated and reshaped before being cast in bronze. The bronze casts were then welded to the frame of the gate. Also affixed to either side of the gate were direct casts of two tree branches. The themes of tools and trees were thus explicitly incorporated into *The Crommelynck Gate with Tools*, as were, implicitly in the curving tendrils of the frame, the themes of hearts and robes.[3]

The ability of the gate to incorporate a number of separate themes is all the more evident in Dine's *The Gate, Goodbye Ver-mont*, 1985. Here Dine returned to the tech-nique of straightforward assemblage. The work is constructed from actual tools, pieces of scrap steel, and tree branches, all welded and bolted into place. There is a reminis-cence of *The Crommelynck Gate with Tools*, especially in the arabesque of tracery at top, but in most other specifics *The Gate, Goodbye Vermont* differs from its predecessor. Most important, the tools in *The Gate, Goodbye Vermont*, rather than appearing as appen-dages to a structure, participate in defining the structure of the work. Moreover, the heart theme, implicitly stated in the earlier sculpture, is made prominent in *The Gate, Goodbye Vermont* by the inclusion of a large, painted metal heart.

The Gate, Goodbye Vermont is at once ag-gressive and intensely personal. The tools, many sharp or pointed, stick out from the sculpture at all angles. At the same time these objects, made to be held and used, seem to proffer themselves to our hands. Working with his son Nicholas and his son's friend John Labine, Dine made *The Gate, Goodbye Vermont* shortly before he moved to Connecticut from the Vermont home where he had lived since 1971.[4] There is an elegiac quality to *The Gate, Goodbye Ver-mont*, a sense of tools being put away for the last time, tools transformed from objects of work into a work of memory and art.

Jim Dine regards *The Gate, Goodbye Ver-mont* as one of his most important works. At the National Gallery it joins a number of the artist's prints, drawings, and sculpture in multiple editions. A monumental work, *The Gate, Goodbye Vermont* will serve as a virtual cornerstone to the Gallery's Dine col-lection, summing up the artist's past and pointing toward his future.

Jeremy Strick

PROVENANCE
From the artist via Pace Gallery to the Fisher collection.

NOTES
1. Graham W. J. Beal, *Jim Dine: Five Themes* [exh. cat. Walker Art Center] (New York, 1984).

2. Beal 1984, 136.

3. Beal 1984, 46.

4. Conversation with the artist, 15 October 1990.

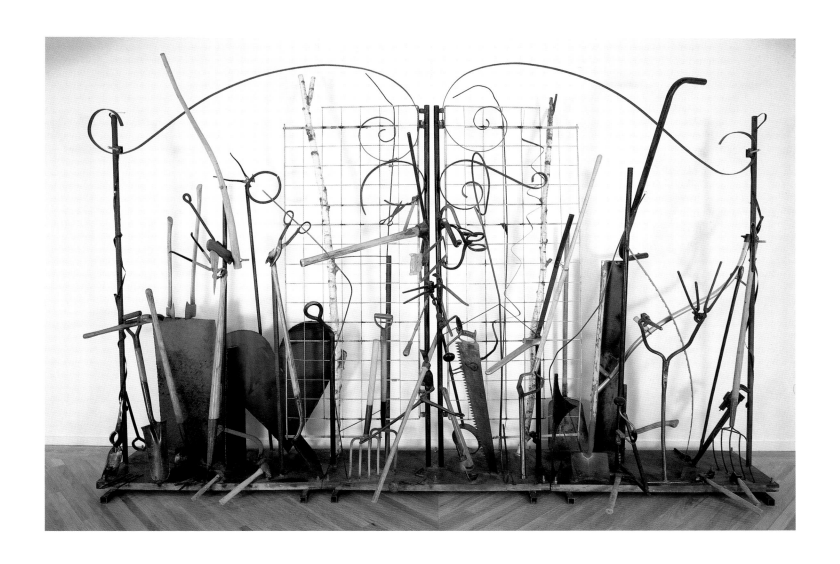

MICHAEL HEIZER
Born 1944

Platform #2, 1982–1985
Drypoint and collage
50 x 65 (127 x 165.1)

Gift of Gemini G.E.L. and the Artist

First known in the late 1960s for his vast earth sculptures in the Mohave Desert, Michael Heizer has also completed major works for public sites including *This Equals That* (1980) for the State Capitol complex in Lansing, Michigan, and his *Effigy Tumuli* (1983–1985) at Buffalo Rock State Park, along the Illinois River south of Chicago; site-specific pieces privately commissioned; and a significant body of paintings, drawings, and prints.[1] Heizer has worked in printmaking intermittently, approaching each project with the same sense of exploration that spurs his massive sculptures.

The artist's first prints were made at Gemini G.E.L. in 1975, and he since has worked in a variety of print media including etching, screenprint, and monoprint. In addition, printed elements play a significant role in his complex drawings, often functioning as a base from which he further develops his images using spray paint, Paintstik, and other media.

Platform #2 is one of three prints in the Platform series, published together in 1985, that feature similar configurations: a rectangular central section divided into four long bands, two of them further divided into smaller rectangular units; and four panels separated from but enclosing the central section. Within these outer panels are divisions bearing a variety of relationships to those in the central section. In some instances the divisions on these four surrounding panels continue the internal sectioning; in others they set up new systems.

Whereas the general configuration of the three Platform prints is quite similar, their surfaces are varied. For *Platform #1* the aluminum plates were etched to achieve distinctive, textural effects. The plates for both *Platform #2* and *Platform #3*, by contrast, feature "natural" or "found" drypoint markings, resulting from the ravages of time and activity, reflecting two operations—scratch-

ing and corrosion. They are similar to the plates used for Heizer's series of six Scrap Metal Drypoints, published by Gemini in 1979.[2] *Platform #2* is especially rich, with pale overall surface articulation set in contrast to darker indentations.

Heizer's art is rooted in a far-ranging curiosity, coordinating archaeology, anthropology, folklore, and myth as well as art and architecture of many cultures: a wedding of his explorations of materials and processes and his respect for cultural history.[3] The idea for the Platform prints, for example, stems from the artist's interest in Meso-American sacrificial platforms, often thirty feet square and standing some four feet high. Steps on all four sides allow access to and egress from the top.[4] Heizer's exploration of his subject suggests the format of an engineering drawing, with the four sides flattened for visibility on a single plane.

The aluminum plates used for the Platform series were somewhat thicker than standard etching plates, and each individual segment of the sections was actually a separate piece of metal, cut and roughly beveled by Heizer at his Nevada studio before being brought to the Los Angeles workshop for printing.[5] To hold these slabs to their desired configuration for printing, the plates were mounted on thin sheets of metal to form the five units.

Monumentality is virtually always an issue in Heizer's work, and the format of this idea was larger than the Gemini presses could accommodate at that time. To achieve the scale of his intentions, each of the five sections used for *Platform #2* was printed as a separate element, and then collaged together onto a single large sheet of paper.

Platform #2 joins twenty-one prints by Michael Heizer in the Gallery's collection, all of them part of our Gemini G.E.L. Archive.

Ruth E. Fine

NOTES

1. For an overview of Heizer's art see Julia Brown, ed., *Michael Heizer: Sculpture in Reverse* [exh. cat. The Museum of Contemporary Art] (Los Angeles, 1984).

2. On the Scrap Metal Drypoints see Ruth E. Fine, *Gemini G.E.L.: Art and Collaboration* [exh. cat. National Gallery of Art] (Washington, 1984), 99–101.

3. Heizer's father, Robert Heizer, was an anthropologist, with whom he traveled to Mexico, Bolivia, Peru, and Egypt. These travels provided the roots for the artist's broad cultural awareness.

4. Telephone conversation with the artist, 13 December 1990.

5. The edition of *Platform #2* is five, plus six proofs including a color variant.

483

RICHARD DIEBENKORN
Born 1922

Trip on the Ground, 1984–1985
Lithograph
37 x 25 (94 x 63.5)

Gift of Gemini G.E.L. and the Artist

Richard Diebenkorn's artistic journey has crossed and recrossed the territories of realism and abstraction in his search for balance and harmony. Full of surprise, growth, tension, doubt, and joyous arrival, his work is a metaphor for life.

Trip on the Ground is the result of an investigation in lithography for the artist at Gemini. Related to the Ocean Park series, which he began in 1967 and which continues to this day, the print is an exquisite tribute to space and light. Inspired by the ambiance of the suburb of Santa Monica where he lives and works, Diebenkorn creates engaging visual equivalents not only for the "pearly moistness of the American West Coast"[1] but also for "the experiences he has known as a painter."[2]

Trip on the Ground is a temporal and spatial journey. Consider the linear expeditions in this work: at times thin and sprightly, at other times coarse and meandering, at still others broken and halting, and at yet others thick and unyielding. All of these variations imply the artist's tactile engagement with his materials and compose a log of "events," as the artist has termed them. Their combination also forms the bones of vectors and planes that structure the viewer's journey into the rectangle. Three strong parallel diagonals lean back toward the right side of the composition, calling to mind spatial recession in oriental art. The path of the leftmost diagonal seems to disappear behind a plane that dominates the center of the image. This plane appears to hide the line from vision while its two counterparts demand that the line be supplied in the imagination. Another avenue moves downward with tumbling chevrons, their points leading to the baseline and also serving as reminders of the corners of image and sheet. Note too the ladder of horizontals that invites one to climb to the edges of the image and into the implied space beyond its boundaries, a space in the viewer's mind.

Consider as well the journey into light and atmosphere. Printed in two colors, a light gray over a deep blue-black, the print has a scrubbed gray patina. Feathery clouds of gray stretch in a veil over the dark background, obscuring yet revealing intricate details of some of the enigmatic hidden spaces. Indeed, the dark background is pulled forward by the similarly colored lines that act as a network across the frontal plane. Pentimenti are seen in several delicate scratches that skim the face of the picture. Like the spatters, dots, and fingerprints that liberate the image from its boundaries, they trace the history of the artist's search. While Diebenkorn is well known for his splendid color sense, this work in grisaille shows the artist's ability to exploit the most restrictive palette. The charged unity of the whole, the vigorous interaction of drawn lines and fluid tones, provide the dynamic energy to propel one through this work.

The artist's figurative art has informed abstract images such as *Trip on the Ground* and the Ocean Park series. During the late fifties and early sixties when abstract painting "was a religion,"[3] "he moved instead, against the current, into representation out of a need to experience the tradition of modern figurations and to explore the permissions and insights of Matisse and Bonnard."[4] Through disciplined study he learned to evoke space and light, balance form, and compose his art in terms of essences. These vocabularies of description have provided material against which the artist measures his painterly experiences. Throughout the artist's career the swings of the pendulum between the two approaches have occurred at critical points affording him fresh possibilities for investigation.

Trip on the Ground is an inviting passage, like a small window or a washed sidewalk, that leads through a delightful landscape of the mind.

Charles M. Ritchie

NOTES
1. John Gruen, *Richard Diebenkorn: The Idea is to Get Everything Right*, ARTnews 85 (Nov. 1986), 86.

2. Dore Ashton, *Richard Diebenkorn: Small Paintings from Ocean Park* (Houston, 1985), n.p.

3. Richard Diebenkorn as quoted in Gruen 1988, 82.

4. Gerald Nordland, *Richard Diebenkorn Paintings and Drawings, 1943–1976* [exh. cat. Albright-Knox Art Gallery] (Buffalo, 1976), 40.

LOTHAR BAUMGARTEN
Born 1944

Untitled, 1985
Offset and screenprint
31½ x 45¼ (80 x 114.94)

Gift of Wolfgang Wittrock

At first sight *Untitled* may baffle most viewers. Odd words seem to confuse a simple picture; alien things interrupt a familiar world. But this stems from Lothar Baumgarten's desire to engage no less than one of western civilization's driving forces: the urge to find and possess realms outside itself. "Though trapped in my Western thought patterns," the artist wrote in 1987, "I have always been interested in the 'other.' "[1] South American natives are Baumgarten's most recurrent "others." During 1978–1980 he lived with a Venezuelan tribe. Their environment and culture populate his art, which, in the tradition begun by Joseph Beuys (Baumgarten followed Richter and Pollock at the Düsseldorf Kunstakademie), knits emblems—text, photographs, material things—into a network with numerous links but no conventional center.

To study the elements in this composition is to be reminded of Baumgarten's admiration for the tableaux of de Chirico and Italian *pittura metafisica* compositions in general, whose narratives lurk just beyond our grasp. Banana leaves make a matted background, reminders of the fruit that gives many people their best and perhaps only contact with South America. Among the leaves are fish skeletons alluding to a companion print entitled *Shaiprabowë*, in which an Indian with hunting arrows sails in a canoe through the water. Names of Venezuelan rivers overprint *Untitled*. It cannot be a coincidence that Baumgarten has deplored the pollution of the continent, including its waterways.[2] Straightforward politics like those that sparked Beuys' actions or the didactic statements alongside the pictures by his fellow German Hans Haacke are not, however, Baumgarten's agenda. His is a subtler path. Hence the background tap-estry in *Untitled* becomes more disconcerting the longer one studies it. The bones sprout as if they were flowers while the viewing angle feels wrong, either too high or close. In fact a critic has noted how the images are consistently cropped, making us aware "of the constraints to our vision."[3] A commonplace of intellectual currency from the late 1970s onward considers the human gaze as an act of possession. Filtering the design through the horizontal canes and, lastly, the screen of words, Baumargaten casts the viewer as transgressor: except for the fact that these tribal names, stamped in colors akin to the natives' own orange-red body paint, stand firm in their alien tongue.

Untitled's hierarchic zones, from botanic (leaves) via zoological (skeletons) to linguistic (names), surely draw upon the French anthropologist Claude Lévi-Strauss who traced such structurings beneath purportedly "savage" cultures.[4] Baumgarten's use of native words contrasts strikingly with the process by which earlier colonists appropriated the continent in naming it after European sites. "Venezuela" for example means "little Venice."[5] In *Untitled*, as in Baumgarten's museum installations and books, the true tribal names such as *Tootoowë* and *Itahi* are literally and metaphorically of the first order (note how the screenprint stencil even raises their hues up slightly from the surface of the paper). Behind lie monochrome memories.

Baumgarten once envisaged artworks that might be "dematerialized, planted into consciousness, they would exist solely in the imagination and might survive untarnished."[6] This daring conceptual slant means that *Untitled* opens a new chapter in the National Gallery's coverage of recent printmaking.

David Anfam

PROVENANCE
Konrad Fischer, Düsseldorf.

NOTES
1. Lothar Baumgarten, "A Project for Artforum," *Artforum* 26, no. 7 (March 1988), 108–111.

2. Craig Owens, "Improper Names," *Art in America* 74 (Oct. 1986), 133.

3. John T. Paoletti, "Lothar Baumgarten: Myths in Prints," *Print Collector's Newsletter* 19, no. 5 (Nov.–Dec. 1988), 178. A wider perspective is also given by Hal Foster, "The 'Primitive' Unconscious of Modern Art," *October* 34 (Fall 1985), 45–69.

4. Lévi-Strauss provided the underyling myth for Baumgarten's 1973–1977 film: see Peggy Gale, "Lothar Baumgarten's *The Origin of the Night*," *Parachute* (June/July/Aug. 1986), 4–9.

5. See Owens 1986.

6. Baumgarten 1988.

JONATHAN BOROFSKY
Born 1938

Berlin Dream with Steel Window Frame at 2,978,899, 1986
Lithograph with Herculene, plexiglas and metal frame, prismacolor, painting
33⅞ x 41¾ (86.0 x 106.1)

Gift of Gemini G.E.L. and the Artist

With seriousness and wit, Jonathan Borofsky's art probes the psychological, political, and social turbulence of our times. The chatter of the inner mind and the restless drama of the outer world are scrutinized equally with a seemingly childlike directness. Much like the dada artists of the the early twentieth century who tried to destroy the boundary between life and art, Borofsky uses the exhibition space as metaphor for the world, challenging the viewer to confront a wide range of often-difficult and sensitive issues. His one-man shows are carnivals of paintings, drawings, and sculpture that are unconventionally displayed and frequently animated with mechanical, video, and recorded sound elements that interact with other exhibition objects and the viewer.

Berlin Dream with Steel Window Frame consists of a dark steel frame with window bars, which encases a depiction of a strange doglike creature carrying away a bird from a furrowed field covered with birds. The creature's ears are alert and it seems to hesitate as if being accosted by an unknown predator. The endless regiment of birds that recedes out of the picture plane lends a feeling of doom that subverts the playful quality of the drawing. Deep and boxlike, the frame is an oppressive container that contrasts with the smooth, frosty image it contains. The overall static quality of the work is relieved by the diagonals of the furrows and the warped sweep of the horizontal window bar.

Borofsky frequently uses his dreams as subjects for his art. Although they are always self-referential, he tends to select those that he feels will have universal meaning. The artist has noted, "I had a dream when I was living and working in West Berlin—near the Berlin Wall. I dreamed a dog forced its way into a garden of birds because the fence was broken. It picked up one of the birds in its mouth. Later, when I was awake, the memory of this dream fragment led me to thoughts about freedom and aggression, fear of 'the enemy' and the need for personal space."[1] It has been noted that in this subject "the extinguished lives of the birds symbolize for Borofsky the lives of the East Germans, who were themselves unable to flee."[2]

Borofsky's work matured in the late sixties and early seventies and some of the predominating conceptual themes from that period are evident in his work: art as a form of theater, as a means of documenting experiences, and as a means of communicating ideas. The number painted at the lower right of the frame of the present work is a thread from one of Borofsky's most important conceptual experiments. In 1969, during a period when he rejected making "things," he began counting from one to infinity on sheets of eight-and-a-half- by eleven-inch paper. For several years he worked continuously, drifting into variations that eventually became the doodles that led the artist back to image-making.[3] His counting has remained an ongoing project, however, and he assigns the next consecutive number to each new piece.

Borofsky often recycles his imagery to find fresh nuances of meaning in new materials. *Berlin Dream with Steel Window Frame at 2,978,899* is a lithograph based on a 1983 charcoal drawing on paper. The subject has been drawn, painted, projected, traced onto exhibition walls, and even reproduced as a lamp. The National Gallery has three variations in its collection. Two are different colored versions in photogravure and the other presents the image as a sheet of stamps on photographic paper. Part print, part sculpture, this gift is a major addition to our holdings of this important theme by the artist. In addition to the three previously mentioned works, there are currently nineteen prints and edition sculptures of various subjects by Borofsky in the collection, all of which were published by Gemini G.E.L. All but two were gifts of Gemini and the artist. The other two were the first to enter the collection and were donated by Mr. and Mrs. Roger P. Sonnabend.

Charles M. Ritchie

NOTES
1. Dean Sobel, *Jonathan Borofsky Drawings* [exh. brochure, Milwaukee Art Museum] (Milwaukee, 1986), n.p.

2. Mark Rosenthal and Richard Marshall, *Jonathan Borofsky* [exh. cat. Philadelphia Museum of Art] (Philadelphia, 1985), 20.

3. Philadelphia 1985, 33.

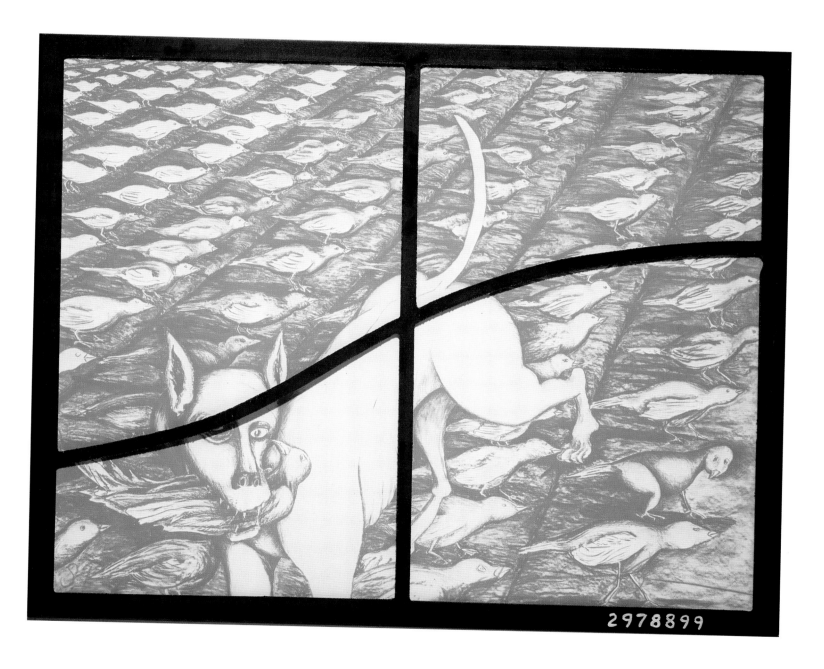

2978899

SUSAN ROTHENBERG
Born 1945

Boneman, 1986
Mezzotint
30 x 20 7/8 (76.2 x 52.9)

Gift of Gemini G.E.L. and the Artist

Susan Rothenberg is one of a number of contemporary artists who have reinvested subject matter with mystery. Her fragmented figures emerge from atmospheric voids as enigmatic symbols inviting interpretation. Developed organically out of webs of expressionist marks, her characters are products of improvisation and intuition rather than preconception. Interestingly, "while grouped with the Neo-Expressionists, Rothenberg's expressionism is not concerned with raw extroverted emotionalism but rather with the more powerful inner emotional psychological state of her subject."[1] This state is conveyed to the viewer in subtle, multilayered ways.

In *Boneman*, a profile figure sits in solitary blackness, drumming a wide, shimmering path of light out of the upper-right portion of the composition. It is as if the musician is conducting a beam of bones and sound into a field beyond the picture plane. The levitation of both figure and bones seems magical. Indeed, the viewer may be reminded of the artist and musician's ancient role as shaman in society. Rothenberg's figures frequently have the directness of primitive art. Similar to pictographic cave drawings, they act as elements of language featuring universal symbols such as bones, heads, hands, and horses as vocabulary. Rhythm and movement propel this work. Repetitive marks are the basis for the figure and its force field and are a natural characteristic of the wood grain's pattern. Momentum is emphasized through a key harmonic element, the wedge shape. This acute angle is echoed throughout the composition; in the cropped corner at the upper right, in the beam of activity projecting from the figure, and in angles formed by the drumming legs and arms. Further, the wooden triangle acts as a dynamic force, an arrowhead that points the beam of energy beyond the boundaries of the image area. Interestingly, it also acts to unify the three distinct sections of the composition, like a small magnet attracting a similarly toned band across a field of darkness. Another unifying factor is the wood grain that traverses and gives structure to the dense black image area.

It has been noted that "Rothenberg's prints are not directly derived from painting images. Her approach in each case is a spontaneous response to the specific materials — for example, the shape of a block of wood — as much as a development of her own visual themes."[2] Thus the choice of medium and its specific qualities are critical to the artist's creative process. The wood veneer paper on which *Boneman* is printed is an inherently rich textural surface and its brown tonality suffuses the print with warmth. Further, mezzotint is a process that creates some of the richest blacks attainable in printmaking. To do this, the entire surface of the plate is pitted beforehand with tiny holes that become reservoirs for ink. The artist then burnishes or smooths areas to create highlights. The medium requires working from dark to light, and is highly suitable for coaxing a phantom figure from inky blackness as Rothenberg has done in this print.

Boneman is an important acquisition for the Gallery because it reflects Rothenberg at her most technically and conceptually experimental and because it is beautiful, representative of her finest work.

Charles M. Ritchie

NOTES

1. Eliza Rathbone, *Susan Rothenberg* [exh. cat. The Phillips Collection] (Washington, 1985), 19.

2. Ruth Fine, "Susan Rothenberg," in Richard S. Field and Ruth E. Fine, *A Graphic Muse: Prints by Contemporary American Women* [exh. cat. Mount Holyoke College Art Museum] (South Hadley and New York, 1987), 139.

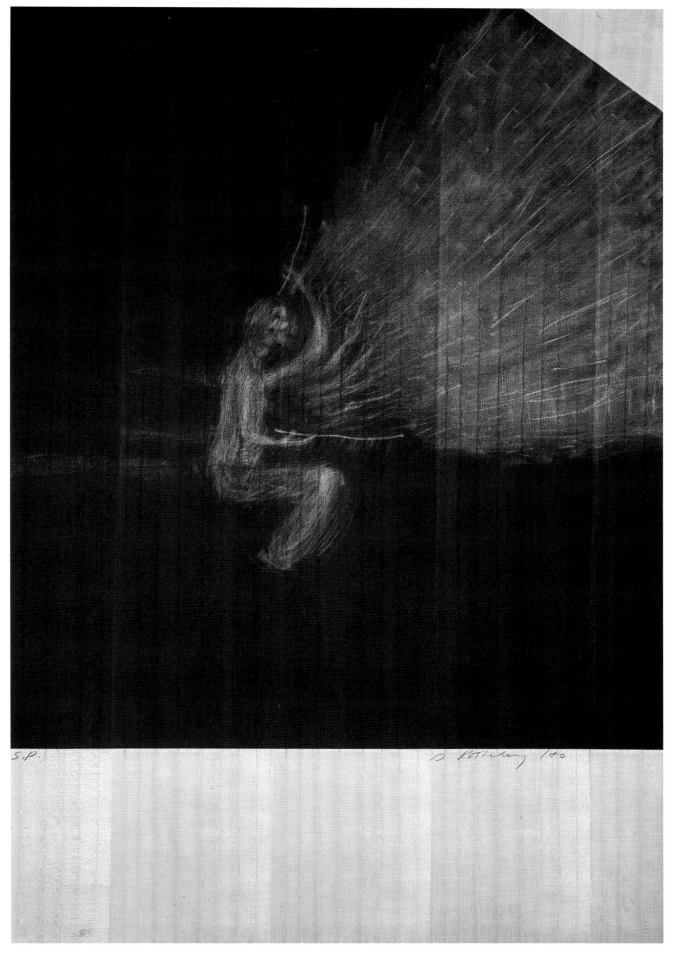

S.P.   S. Rothenberg '86

ROBERT RAUSCHENBERG
Born 1925

Fifth Force, 1986
Bronze, Xerox transfer on silk, thread,
shot
83¼ x 15 x 45 (211.5 x 38.1 x 114.3)

Gift of Graphicstudio, U.S.F.
and the Artist

Fifth Force is quintessential Rauschenberg, merging history and current events, seriousness and wit while combining diverse materials and techniques. The keystone of the piece is a cast bronze plaque that replicates part of a dictionary page featuring an image of the campanile of Pisa as the illustration for the word "tower"; the page is surrounded by a grid pattern. The plaque was cast from a photoengraved plate of a small collage Rauschenberg had created during the 1950s in which he mounted the page at an angle on a piece of graph paper so that the tower would appear straight, thereby "correcting" the tower's famous tilt.[1]

On the white silk hanging below the plaque is a portrait of the Italian astronomer and physicist Galileo (1564–1642), applied to the fabric through the process of Xerox transfer. The portrait appears twice, doubled in a mirror image of itself, recalling the convex and concave lenses that form the telescope, the Dutch invention that Galileo perfected.

Legend has it that Galileo, who was born in Pisa, climbed to the top of the "leaning tower" and dropped cannonballs of differing weights in a public demonstration of his theory of motion. Galileo's theories were once again brought to public notice in 1986, when two physicists reported that preliminary results from their experiments seemed to challenge Galileo's findings, suggesting the existence of a fifth force in the universe, in addition to the four already known. An article that appeared in *Time* magazine about these experiments was the impetus for Rauschenberg's *Fifth Force,* which evokes the centuries-old Galileo story in its combination of images, while its title suggests contemporary scientific investigation.[2] The frozen motion of the "cannonball" on the floor, tenuously reigned in by the delicate waxed thread that connects it to the fabric, seems to exert the force that "corrects" the tower's angle.

The dialogue between disparate materials is at the heart of Rauschenberg's art, as is clearly evident in *Fifth Force.* The hard, rigid, and reflective surface of the cast bronze plaque is counterbalanced by the free-flowing softness of the shimmering white silk, which gently gathers where it joins the bronze and then falls in sensuous soft folds that are projected outward by the apparent "pull" of the cannonball.

The added color on the plaque highlights the straightened tower, which has been given a rich purple tone complimented by an adjacent area of red, while the blues and greens at the bottom of the plaque provide a subtle transition to the similarly colored Xerox transfer. The color is not on the surface of the plaque, but rather fills the recesses in the same way ink is wiped onto an etching plate.

Fifth Force was executed at Graphicstudio in anticipation of an exhibition of Rauschenberg's work in Italy in conjunction with the Rauschenberg Overseas Culture Interchange (ROCI) project.[3] ROCI, announced by Rauschenberg at the United Nations in 1984, was established by the artist as a touring exhibition meant to promote world peace through the exchange of cultural information and the sharing of artistic ideas. ROCI will have traveled to ten international locations before its showing at the National Gallery of Art in the spring of 1991. The Italian venue, however, ultimately was not included on the tour.

Fabric has long had an important place among the varied materials used by Rauschenberg in the making of his art. *Fifth Force* is a welcome recent example, joining many other works in the National Gallery's collection that feature this material. Among them are the Airport series, also produced at Graphicstudio, and the Hoarfrost Editions, published by Gemini G.E.L., both from the mid-1970s.

Mary Lee Corlett

NOTES

1. Information about the collage and the various processes used to produce the piece comes from Donald Saff, former director of Graphicstudio, in conversation with Ruth Fine, June 1990.

2. See "A Fifth Force?" *Time* 127 (20 Jan. 1986), 51–52.

3. The sculpture was planned in an edition of twenty-five, eleven of these having been completed at this writing, along with five proofs.

493

SAM FRANCIS
Born 1923

King Corpse, 1986
Color screenprint
42 x 59 (101.7 x 149.9)

Gift of Gemini G.E.L. and the Artist

Sam Francis has pursued printmaking throughout his career, completing more than six hundred etchings, lithographs, screenprints, and monoprints in both black and white and color.[1] Indeed, his commitment to printmaking is such that since 1970 he has maintained his own print workshop, The Litho Shop, in Santa Monica, California. At the present time, two printers, one in etching and one in lithography, are part of the shop's full-time staff.[2]

Francis has worked intermittently at Gemini G.E.L. since 1971, and *King Corpse,* printed in fifteen runs, is one of a group of four screenprints and one lithograph they published in 1986.[3] The screenprints were printed by Ron McPherson at his La Paloma workshop. *King Corpse* was issued in an edition of sixty-five plus forty proofs, fourteen of which are color trials.

Forms hovering, streaks darting, broad slabs mapping areas across the surface, Francis' visual world is charged with activity. His layering of discrete, vivid areas of hue builds to an exuberant crescendo, the intensity of his colors achieved by using rich pigments that are dissolved in a wetting agent alone. This allows for maximum brilliance of hue, rather than having the color effects diluted by large quantities of binder.[4] Moreover, Francis' meticulous attention to color is reflected in the fact that he has many of his inks made to his personal specifications.[5] Layers of transparent and transluscent hues

one on another enable him to achieve a pulsating density of color and to greatly expand the visual effect of his palette. In *King Corpse* pure reds, yellows, and oranges are juxtaposed with more muted greens, blues, and violets, presenting a field that is simultaneously brilliant and subtle.

Francis "like[s] to work on prints continuously, at a slow pace, where things change in a natural way."[6] His drawings on mylar for each individual color were transferred to the screens as the starting point for *King Corpse*; and the same mylars were used for the lithograph in this group. The lithograph, titled *Beaudelaire,* is printed entirely in variations of yellow, its impact very different from that of the multicolor screenprint. In approaching his work Francis drew each color layer with the certainty of how it would interact with all of the others, a reflection of his years of experience in printmaking. Reflected, too, is a sense of the artist's great joy in the act of working.

Francis' fluid markings—brushed, poured, splattered—establish an explosive rhythmic field of great visual richness. As *King Corpse* immediately makes clear, all of the freshness and spontaneity one associates with Francis' paintings and unique works on paper is retained when he approaches his prints. Forms at once seem to grow out of the depths of the cosmos and hover on the surface of the sheet, suggesting infinite space and flatness constantly shifting in tense equilibrium.

Ruth E. Fine

NOTES

1. A catalogue raisonné is forthcoming from Hudson Hills Press, compiled by Connie Lembark with an introduction by Ruth E. Fine.

2. See Brooke Alexander's interview with one of Francis' master printers, George Page, in *Sam Francis: The Litho Shop 1970–1979* [exh. cat. Brooke Alexander, Inc.] (New York, 1979), n.p. In addition to maintaining the shop Francis also has founded Lapis Press for the publication of texts he finds of interest as well as finely printed artists' books in limited editions.

3. For a summary of Francis' activity at Gemini to 1984, see Ruth E. Fine, "Sounds and Silences: Sam Francis," in *Gemini G.E.L.: Art and Collaboration* [exh. cat. National Gallery of Art] (Washington, 1984), 178–189.

4. My thanks to printer Ron McPherson, long associated with both Gemini G.E.L. and Sam Francis, for discussing these particular inks with me; and to George Page for supplying much information.

5. An ink mixing section manned by Dan Cytran is set up in The Litho Shop.

6. New York 1979.

SANDRO CHIA
Born 1946

Father and Son Song, 1987–1989
Woodcut with assemblage
85¾ x 75⅝ x 4¼
(217.8 x 192.0 x 10.7)

Gift of Graphicstudio, U.S.F.
and the Artist

Sandro Chia is a member of the European vanguard who helped reestablish figuration as an essential medium of expression after the minimalist and conceptual emphasis of the 1970s. Borrowing from the great tradition of western art, particularly the themes and attitudes characteristic of the Renaissance, the vigorous dynamics of futurism, and the beefy figures of realist art of the 1930s and 1940s, Chia both assimilates and transforms his sources into vital, ambitious, and personal statements. Chia is well known for his innovative work in etching and other intaglio print processes. *Father and Son Song* is a splendid example of his ability to leap technical and conceptual boundaries in the woodcut medium as well.

As is characteristic of much of the artist's work, *Father and Son Song* presents an obscure narrative in heroic scale unfolding on fields of exuberant color. The subject, a large male figure accompanied by a smaller one, is common in Chia's mythology. Numerous works pertain to this theme. Indeed the artist often recycles not only themes but particular figures as well. Both the large reclining figure and the small climbing figure can be found in variations in other works by the artist and can be related to subjects in works by Michelangelo and Rodin. Despite clues in the title, the mysterious subject defies identification. Does the artist refer to the experience of raising a son? Is this a self-portrait with an oblique homage to the tradition of western painting? It has been suggested that Chia "offers the experience of puzzling over his work as a stand-in for the process of making sense of the world in which the painting is . . . immersed." [1]

A game of formal relationships also in-vites contemplation. Each wooden shape that hovers about the edge of the composition relates directly to a printed area, much as if the original print matrices had been included in the frame. In matching each "puzzle" piece to each print area, the viewer begins to unravel the subtle internal harmonics beneath apparent cacophony. The title, then, may also be seen as an echo of the parent and offspring relationship that exists in the song of the matrix and its print. Even the two black clouds serve to stabilize and give contrasting texture to the work, the exceptionally rich surface of which is due to the sensitively printed woodgrain whose inherent beauty is further enhanced by its shifting directions.

This is the second work by Chia to enter the National Gallery's collection. The first was *Flowers Fight,* which was also created at Graphicstudio and also explored the heliorelief process developed there. In this process a light-sensitive block of basswood is exposed through an ink drawing on translucent Mylar and is then cut by sandblasting, thus creating a bas-relief.

Chia masterfully discerns possibilities inherent in materials and processes while making his art, and his contributions have helped to make the recent period of printmaking rich in discovery. *Father and Son Song* is a fine example of the new scope of contemporary printmaking, a field that welcomes invention and blurs media distinctions.

Charles M. Ritchie

NOTE
1. Carter Ratcliff, "On Iconography and Some Italians," *Art in America* 70 (Sept. 1982), 154.

JAMES ROSENQUIST
Born 1933

Welcome to the Water Planet, 1987
Aquatint
75⁹⁄₁₆ x 59⁹⁄₁₆ (191.9 x 151.2)

Gift of Graphicstudio, U.S.F.
and the Artist

Rosenquist's *Welcome to the Water Planet* is related to a series of works that includes a 1987 painting of the same name and composition and comprises other paintings and prints. "Water planet" refers to Earth, the only known planet with water, and reflects Rosenquist's environmental concern.

To create this image, the artist imaginatively stepped back to view the planet's fragile inhabitants from space, alluding to the vulnerability of "spaceship Earth" in a monumental but disjointed spectacle. Among stars, fish, and a great water flower in shimmering reflection, a jagged rupture reveals a woman's face with hand over mouth. Other faces are hinted at in the ghostly galactic clouds and in other fragmented areas. Rosenquist began using the interlocking fingerlike device (which he calls "crosshatching") by the early 1980s as a means of pictorial invention. He has observed that "crosshatching filled with imagery leaves space for more forms." [1] These layers of imagery shift constantly and are impossible to absorb at a glance. They elicit our attention and invite our interaction to decode the composition.

Rosenquist's early work recycled images and objects of American consumer culture in fragmentary views and disjointed spaces. As a painter of billboards in New York in the late fifties, he started to explore ways of incorporating into his own canvases oversize images like the ones that he was painting above the city streets. His startling juxtapositions force the viewer to see the everyday images in new ways, both humorous and threatening. Rosenquist's recent work has explored several specific images—women's faces, flowers, stars—combined with his jagged forms. Both ironic and poetical, *Welcome to the Water Planet* is an excellent example of this direction in his work.

This is technically one of the most impressive prints created by Rosenquist at the Graphicstudio workshop. One of the difficulties of producing large works in intaglio is the limitation imposed by the width of the press. In order to work as large as Ro-senquist desired, the piece was printed in halves in two runs from two copper plates on a single sheet of folded paper. The aquatint process seems both liquid and atmospheric, naturally suited to the subjects, and its silvery shadow and light lend an austere feeling to what is an unusually solemn, reflective image for the artist.

Welcome to the Water Planet is an important addition to the Gallery's collection of fifty-nine prints by Rosenquist. The artist has consistently produced numerous prints at Graphicstudio, U.S.F. and Gemini G.E.L., all of which are part of the National Gallery's archive collection from the two ateliers.

Charles M. Ritchie

NOTE
1. Bernice Rose, *New Work on Paper 3* [exh. cat. The Museum of Modern Art] (New York, 1985), n.p.

498

National Gallery of Art Seoul   Welcome to the Water Planet   Laura Anderson 4/7

RICHARD SERRA
Born 1939

Muddy Waters, 1986–1987
Screenprint
74 x 60½ (188 x 153.7)

Gift of Gemini G.E.L. and the Artist

I continually attempt to confront the contradictions of memory and to wipe the slate clean, to rely on my own experience and my own materials even if faced with a situation which is beyond hope of achievement. To invent methods about which I know nothing, to utilize the content of experience so that it becomes known to me, to then challenge the authority of that experience and thereby challenge myself.[1]

Although Richard Serra made this statement when discussing his sculptures, it is the principle that governs virtually all of his art. Monolithic steel sculptures are what Serra is most widely known for, yet over the course of the last decade his prints have emerged as a significant extension of them. Serra has explained, "The prints are mostly studies made after a sculpture has been completed. They are the result of trying to assess and define what surprises me in a sculpture, what I could not understand before a work was built. . . . The shapes originate in a glimpse of a volume, a detail, an edge, a weight."[2]

Muddy Waters is one of seven screenprints Serra made in 1986–1987, most of which relate to his Corten steel sculpture. This is the second group of prints in which Serra has employed his special technique of screenprint using ink and Paintstik, a combination Serra began in 1983. (In other contexts Paintstik has been one of Serra's often-used graphic materials, one he initially started using in some of his drawings in the early 1970s.)

Muddy Waters and the entire series were executed with the assistance of printmaker Ron McPherson at his print workshop La Paloma. McPherson has worked as an outside collaborator on silkscreen projects for Gemini G.E.L. since the mid 1970s.[3] His expertise in the area of silkscreen has been essential to the successful production of this and several others of Serra's projects.

In executing *Muddy Waters*, as in all of Serra's screenprints with Paintstik, the first step is coating the paper with urethane in order to prevent any degradation of it by the oil-based Paintstik. Then the essential shapes are screenprinted in black ink. Using the same screen, the Paintstik is pressed across its surface, forcing the dense black pigment through the woven network of the material, leaving a layer of Paintstik over the entire surface of the form.[4] The textural surface of the print is further developed with an additional layer. Each layer requires several days to dry. The final result is a dramatic surface of irregular vertical striations that communicate Serra's forceful encounter with the medium.

Muddy Waters has an imposing presence that demands our attention much like Serra's sculptures. Large in scale, the black form has a weight and mass that dominates the paper, and its orientation relative to the paper's edge further defines the weight of this image.

Although this work is part of an edition of twenty prints, each one has its own distinctive character because of the hands-on application of the Paintstik. The extraordinary subtlety of the layered Paintstik on *Muddy Waters* merits close inspection; thus, Serra insists that the work not be obstructed by glass. The bare surface of the print beckons the viewer to contemplate its richness and variety.

The National Gallery has thirty-three of Serra's prints, almost all donated by Gemini G.E.L., at whose atelier Serra has produced the major part of his print oeuvre.

Carlotta J. Owens

NOTES

1. Richard Serra, introduction, *Axis* [exh. cat. Kunsthalle Bielenfeld] (Bielenfeld, 1990), 37.

2. Richard Serra, introduction, *Richard Serra at Gemini 1983–1987* (Los Angeles, 1988), n.p.

3. Ruth E. Fine, *Gemini G.E.L.: Art and Collaboration* [exh. cat. National Gallery of Art] (Washington, 1984), 75–76.

4. Melinda Wortz, "Richard Serra: Prints," *Print Collector's Newsletter* 27, no. 1 (March–April 1986).

I.P. R Ane 87

JIM DINE
Born 1935

Youth and the Maiden, 1987–1988
Woodcut, etching, and drypoint with
paint, in three sections
Left and right 78⅜ x 24¼
(199.1 x 61.6); center 78⅜ x
91⅜ (199.1 x 232.1)

Gift of Graphicstudio, U.S.F.
and the Artist

Printmaking has been central to Jim Dine's art. In the course of the past three decades he has completed more than six hundred etchings, lithographs, woodcuts, and screen prints, often, as here, combining several processes to create an image.[1]

Youth and the Maiden is Dine's largest print to date, virtually enveloping the viewer in its mysterious presence.[2] Its triptych format conjures memories of altarpieces. And the complex of images Dine has juxtaposed makes reference to the breadth of his explorations in religion, myth, and art history while developing his own artistic vocabulary.

Dine's use of a vast and varied selection from the art of the past for his inspiration is well documented in his many published interviews and statements.[3] Among the works that played a role in the development of *Youth and the Maiden* were two from the sixteenth century: Andreas Vesalius' anatomical text, *De humani corporis fabrica,* illustrated by skeletal figures that are enhanced, like the figures in *Youth and the Maiden,* by vast areas of sky; and Domenico delle Greche's woodcut after Titian's *The Death of Pharaoh and His Army Submerged in the Red Sea.* Cut from twelve separate blocks that together measured approximately 46 x 88 inches, this was a massive woodcut among prints of the sixteenth century just as Dine's is among prints of the twentieth.

Trees in foliage, skeletons and a flayed figure, a sheathed central woman based on a Hellenistic sculpture: all carry ritualistic overtones. By repeating these elements in his own work Dine has made them as much his as are the robes and hearts long associated with his art.[4] Less pervasive in their shared meanings or associations with Dine's art are the braided doll figures. Yet they recall his 1972 etching, *Braid (First State),* and other works featuring hair from that period. At the same time they suggest German peasant dolls thought to have mystical powers on behalf of fertility as well as curative powers if burned to ashes and swallowed.

Youth and the Maiden was printed from multiple copper plates and woodblocks. The plates were drawn in several of the etching media, including spit-bite and softground along with drypoint. The woodblocks were both hand cut and worked in a heliorelief process recently developed at Graphicstudio. In this method, Dine's drawings on transparent mylar were transferred to specially light-sensitized wood blocks, after which the images were cut into the blocks by sandblasting.

In working these various printmaking processes, Dine's enormous sensitivity as a draftsman is vividly evident. And in his layering of surfaces, repetition of images, atmospheric color, and references to both a cultural and personal history he invites us to share his own responses to the pleasures and pains of modern life.

Youth and the Maiden is one of more than forty-five works by Jim Dine in the National Gallery's collection, including drawings, prints—many of which are working proofs with hand-drawn additions—and sculpture. His work is central to our Graphicstudio Archive, donated by the University of South Florida Foundation or Graphicstudio and the artist. Dine has also made several independent contributions to the archive of especially important works. Other gifts of Dine's work have come from Robert Rauschenberg, Lessing J. Rosenwald, Joshua P. Smith, and the Woodward Foundation.

Ruth E. Fine

NOTES

1. Catalogues raisonné documenting Dine's prints are *Jim Dine: Complete Graphics* (Berlin, 1970); Thomas Krens, ed., *Jim Dine Prints: 1970–1977* (New York, 1977); and Ellen G. D'Oench and Jean E. Feinberg, *Jim Dine Prints: 1977–1985* (New York, 1986), which includes a chronology of the artist's major printmaking activities.

2. For a discussion of this print in context with other prints of the period see Donald Saff, "Youth and the Maiden: A Morphology of Complex Boundaries in the Art of Jim Dine," in *Jim Dine: Youth and the Maiden* [exh. cat. Waddington Graphics] (London, 1989), 30–39. Saff's essay and a conversation with the artist in New York on 26 September 1990 are the sources for information here.

3. For example, see "Conversations" in Constance W. Glenn, *Jim Dine's Drawings* (New York, 1985), 31–51, and "Dine on Drawing" in the same volume, 196–210; see also David Schapiro, *Jim Dine: Painting What One Is* (New York, 1981), 203–211.

4. For Dine's best-known subjects, see Graham W. Beal and others, *Jim Dine: Five Themes* [exh. cat. Walker Art Center] (Minneapolis, 1984); the catalogue includes comments by the artist throughout.

MATTHIAS MANSEN
Born 1958

Studio—Head and Feet, 1987
Woodcut
79⁷⁄₁₆ x 27³⁄₁₆ (218 x 69)

Gift of Wolfgang Wittrock

Time, decay, and loss are constant references in the woodcuts of Matthias Mansen. His themes are explored not only with traditional subjects chosen from everyday life, but in the highly radical creative strategy he employs. By utilizing discarded materials, decaying matrices, and by selecting subjects that often dematerialize within a printed sequence, the artist invests old concepts with a new emotional resonance. Mansen and a number of other contemporary German artists have been responsible for a revivification of the German woodcut, breaking down our notion of what it represents, how it is seen, and expanding the possibilities of what it can be.

While full of graphic activity, a haunting absence pervades *Studio—Head and Feet*.[1] The strongly vertical composition is established around the outlines of a full figure, seen frontally and appearing nearly actual size. Its featureless presence questions the viewer and invokes the imagination. Head, hands, and feet are frequent subjects for the artist, symbols of mental and physical activity. Mansen portrays them in a fragmented state, suggesting a kind of powerlessness. This is emphasized in the horizontal sectioning of the figure and the disconnected nature of the hands, cropped by the left side of the composition. These hands, working with wood tools at a table, are seen almost from above while the bare studio is seen from a slightly lower perspective extending down to a grid that evokes a window. The stiff wooden legs of a table in the foreground are a metaphorical echo of the immobile legs of the figure.

Mansen frequently utilizes a tall format that introduces a temporal element into his work by forcing the eye to travel over an image that cannot be absorbed as a compositional whole. In *Studio—Head and Feet*, two long white verticals (representing seams between boards of the matrix) are spines on which horizontal ribs of the composition are attached. Superimposed lines representing the edges of the tabletop and studio walls construct a grid that finds relief in the

diagonals of the arms and the inverted *V* shapes at the base of the table legs. Broken and irregular cutting lines further emphasize a feeling of impermanence. Recessive earth colors predominate. The coppery-brown central area, the peripheral border of black, and sections of green at the base of the table legs form a tonal scaffolding that supports the brightly colored spots of modulated red, blue, and yellow scattered throughout open passages of the figure, which are applied in monotype fashion on the woodblock.

Mansen is uninterested in making reproductions of an image. Most of his prints are unique variants. Primarily done in series, his works represent stages of arrested metamorphosis. Changes are frequently introduced by recutting the block between printings, varying color arrangements, and by affixing or overprinting new blocks. Sometimes Mansen exhibits a series of prints as a single work in which the variations become the focus of the work. The old boards and disassembled pieces of furniture that he uses as matrices frequently limit the number of printings because the "blocks are partially worked with sculptor's tools, and, after intensive use of the drill, they have so many holes they look like a sieve."[2] It has been noted about Mansen's work that "the impression of day-to-day life is emphasized again and again—even if not intentionally— by the choice of materials."[3] Usually Mansen works in oil paint, often applying it to the printing surface by hand. These colors tend to seep into the nontraditional supports such as wrapping or industrial paper that he uses, adding further to the informal character of his work.

Studio—Head and Feet contains references to past, present, future. The old planks used to print this work speak of their previous existence as objects in the world, not only as wood construction but also as trees. Presently they are seen as vehicles for art, but the future is foretold in the bits of wood clinging to some of the printed surfaces, subtly alluding to decay and the inevitable return of wood to dust.

Mansen produced the present work while he was working in London; it is directly related to an important series of head-and-feet images he created there. The present woodcut is the first work by the artist to enter the National Gallery's collection and an excellent example of the powerful content for which he is known best.

Charles M. Ritchie

NOTES
1. This work has been exhibited as *Mann in Studio* (Man in Studio). The artist stated, on 18 December 1990, his preference for the present title.

2. Annie Bardon, "New Paths in Germany: The Woodcuts of Droese, Kluge & Mansen," *Print Collector's Newsletter* 17 (Nov.–Dec. 1986), 162.

3. Bardon 1986, 161.

ELLSWORTH KELLY
Born 1923

Untitled, 1988
Bronze
119½ x 24¼ x 1 (303.5 x 62.2 x 2.5)

Gift of the Artist

One side straight, the other gently bowed, the pure, dark form of *Untitled* springs directly from the floor. Despite its asymmetry, Ellsworth Kelly's sculpture seems a miracle of balanced poise. The contrasting sides create a dynamic equilibrium between expansion and contraction, upward and outward movement, action and repose. The inherent tension of the sculpture is only enhanced by the mystery of its support. Held in place by an invisible subsurface mechanism, the nearly ten-foot-high sheath of bronze appears to rest directly on the floor, magically balanced on its inch-thick edge.

Untitled, the artist's copy in an edition of one, is the first Ellsworth Kelly sculpture to enter the National Gallery collection. It relates to a series of the artist's sculptures known as the Standing Totem Curves.[1] Begun in 1974, this series comprises tall, dramatically thin, stele-like sculptures. The vertical perimeters of each sculpture in the series delineate a curve based upon the arc of an enormous circle. The Standing Totem Curves have been fabricated in aluminum, weathering steel, stainless steel, wood, and, most recently, bronze. The bronze sculptures, including *Untitled,* appear to be solid pieces of metal. In fact they are hollow, each composed of five separate bronze pieces that are welded together.

Most of the Standing Totem Curves are symmetrical both horizontally and vertically. That is, not only are both sides curved, but the centers of the curves are placed at the center of the sculpture, so that top and bottom of the sculpture are of equal width. *Untitled* is unique in Kelly's oeuvre in that it is asymmetrical in both dimensions.[2] The two sides are unequal (one curved, the other straight), and the center of the single curve is placed low, so that the bottom of the object is considerably wider than the top.

Kelly's art, which often reads as precisely calibrated geometric form, always relates to objects or shapes that the artist has observed, often in nature. Kelly has described the visual effect of *Untitled* as akin to his memory of seeing a shark's fin cutting through water.[3] Because the curves of *Untitled* are unequal, one senses that one sees only a fragment of a larger form, that the sculpture continues beneath the ground. As if one spotted a shark's fin, a presence beneath the surface is felt.

The first public exhibition of *Untitled* occurred in 1989 at the National Gallery of Art in a room devoted to Ellsworth Kelly's work. This also marked the first time that the artist's painting and sculpture had been exhibited together. Both Kelly's paintings and his sculpture explore the subtle interrelationships of shape, space, and color. The close ties between Kelly's sculptural and painterly interests are vividly apparent in the comparison of *Untitled* and an Ellsworth Kelly painting in the National Gallery collection, *White Curve VIII,* 1976 (Gift of Mr. and Mrs. Joseph Helman). Painting and sculpture both explore the contrasts and tensions of curved and straight lines. In *White Curve VIII* opposing blocks of black and white are brought into dynamic interplay. In *Untitled* it is form, color, and their surrounding space that Kelly at once opposes and unites.

Jeremy Strick

NOTES
1. Patterson Sims and Emily Rauh Pulitzer, *Ellsworth Kelly: Sculpture* (New York, 1982), 110.

2. Conversation with the artist, June 1990.

3. Conversation with the artist, June 1990.

507

ELLSWORTH KELLY
Born 1923

Red Curve, 1987–1988
Lithograph
26 x 84 (66 x 213.4)

Gift of Gemini G.E.L. and the Artist

The year 1970 marked the beginning of Ellsworth Kelly's long and productive association with Gemini G.E.L.'s graphic workshop. Over the course of twenty years Kelly has worked at Gemini fairly regularly, producing more than 184 prints and eighteen sculptures in multiple editions. *Red Curve* is one of several related lithographs he printed at Gemini in 1977–1988 based on his fan-shape motif. This motif first engaged Kelly in his paintings in 1972 and appeared later in his weathering steel and painted aluminum wall reliefs of 1974. Kelly introduced this motif into his prints in *Red Curve* and the other lithographs in this group.

During his years in Paris, 1949–1954, Kelly gravitated toward the forms and colors of the artists Constantin Brancusi, George Vantongerloo, Jean Arp, and Sophie Taeuber-Arp.[1] Although his early direction was perhaps guided by their work, Kelly assimilated these influences and forged his own personal style of nonobjective flat hard-edged shapes that he conceived from forms he has observed in nature and his environment.

Kelly's first experiment with printmaking was in 1949 while he was enrolled at the Ecole des Beaux-Arts, but it was fifteen years before he created another print. By that time he was already recognized as a distinguished painter and sculptor. Over the last twenty-seven years, Kelly has produced an impressive body of prints, which represents a major portion of his oeuvre. His paintings, sculptures, and prints often evolve in tandem and are mutually enriched because of their shared vocabulary. With all of his art forms, the creative process usually begins the same way. Kelly explained, "The form is usually the first situation. The form is made and color is applied. Sometimes form and color happen simultaneously."[2]

In *Red Curve* Kelly substituted his flat pristine colors for a more painterly surface. The print is made with two lithographic plates. One holds the brushed surface of the print, which he produced with tusche wash, and the other is the key color plate. He explored similar gestural brushwork in his Saint Martin series of lithographs made at Gemini in 1983–1984.[3] Kelly is conscious of how his shapes and colors interact with his expressive surfaces. He intuitively weaves these elements together in order to achieve a harmonious whole. In the other lithographs related to *Red Curve*, the surface, color, and size of the fan shape varies; in turn, the viewer's perception and response to each print differs. Studied together, the prints offer a challenging visual experience.

With this recent gift, the Gallery now owns 134 of Ellsworth Kelly's prints. Among the holdings are a few of his early prints from 1964, examples of some of the first lithographs Kelly collaborated on at Gemini in 1970, and several transfer lithographs from his 1974 and 1978 botanical series. Other highlights are his elegant Colored Paper Images, a series of twenty-three colored and pressed paper pulp pieces he produced at Tyler Graphics Ltd. in 1976–1977 and the Concorde series, 1981–1982, which combines etching and aquatint. Both series demonstrate major stages in Kelly's early interest in the textural surface of his prints and provide an instructional comparison to *Red Curve*, which continues his investigation of surface character. Apart from his prints, the Gallery's collection includes one graphite drawing, a painting from 1976, and four sculptures. *Red Curve* and a large portion of the prints in the collection have come to the Gallery as gifts from Gemini G.E.L. and the artist. Other important donors who have

added Kelly's prints to the Gallery's holdings include Mr. and Mrs. Roger P. Sonnabend, Mr. and Mrs. Burton Tremaine, Dr. and Mrs. Maclyn E. Wade, and the Woodward Foundation, Washington, D.C.

Carlotta J. Owens

NOTES

1. Ellsworth Kelly, "Notes from 1969," *Ellsworth Kelly: Paintings and Sculptures 1966–1977* [exh. cat. Stedelijk Museum] (Amsterdam, 1979), 32.

2. Ruth E. Fine, *Gemini G.E.L.: Art and Collaboration* [exh. cat. National Gallery of Art] (Washington, 1984), 127–128.

3. Richard H. Axsom with the assistance of Phylis Floyd, *The Prints of Ellsworth Kelly: A Catalogue Raisonné 1949–1985* (New York, 1987), 161–167.

ROY LICHTENSTEIN
Born 1923

Green Face, 1987–1989
Lithograph, woodcut, and screenprint
with encaustic and waxtype
58⅞ x 41 (149.5 x 104.1)

Gift of Graphicstudio, U.S.F.
and the Artist

Roy Lichtenstein's *Green Face* is one of a series of "portraits" developed and produced at Graphicstudio between February 1987 and March 1989. Each print in the group represents an arrangement of several kinds of Lichtenstein's distinctive brushstroke characters. *Green Face* shows the artist at his wittiest. It is a compendium of many of his characteristic printmaking techniques.

Framed by a metallic oval of silver strokes, a wild array of brilliantly colored forms coalesces loosely into a bust as if seen in a distorted mirror. The viewer is spurred to query which details represent which features and whether the viewer is reflected or the artist himself depicted. Donald Saff, collaborator on this project, has observed that Lichtenstein "views not only the world and his relation to it, but he also views himself looking at himself engaged in the life of the world." [1] Indeed the artist has frequently used mirrors as subjects for paintings as well as prints; his work "is further loaded by the implied allusion to the histories of art and literature which are stocked with mirrors and mirroring." [2]

During the 1950s Lichtenstein was exploring the idea of using the expressionist brushstroke to create comic figures. In doing so he parodied the art of the predominant abstract expressionists whose marks, drips, and spills on canvas were presented as records of intense feeling. While sensing the humor and irony of using the expressionist gesture to re-create cartoon and other "low art" motifs, Lichtenstein, like the other Pop artists, introduced new subjects into painting, borrowing from a variety of popular media sources. Lichtenstein's prints feature stripes, Ben Day dots, and other elements derived from commercial printing processes. By 1980, however, he had begun to reintroduce freehand drawing and his brushstroke into his work. *Green Face* in-corporates this and other more mechanically conceived "brushstrokes" from his vocabulary.

A great beauty of the "brushstroke" elements is the wide range of printmaking media used to create them: hard-edged bands in woodcut with lightly grained tone, dots of pure direct color created in screenprint, lithography strokes with a broad tonal range, and waxtype with its inviting, translucent surface that has beautiful relief qualities. Waxtype is a new screenprint process developed at Graphicstudio in which wax is pressed through the screen to print the image. After printing, the wax may be left with the screen's texture as part of its surface, or it may be made smooth by using heat in a traditional encaustic manner, and it also may then be burnished to a high sheen.

This is a welcome addition to our collection of seventy-five prints by this artist. In addition to the works by Lichtenstein that have been given to us as a part of the Graphicstudio and Gemini archives, others of his prints have been donated to the National Gallery of Art by Lessing J. Rosenwald, J. Carter Brown, Charles Parkhurst, Mr. and Mrs. Burton Tremaine, the Woodward Foundation, Washington, D.C., Dr. and Mrs. Maclyn E. Wade, David Gensburg, Benjamin B. Smith, and Mr. and Mrs. Roger P. Sonnabend.

Charles M. Ritchie

NOTES
1. Donald Saff, *Roy Lichtenstein: New Prints and Sculptures from Graphicstudio* [exh. cat. Wetterling Gallery] (Gothenburg, Sweden, 1989), unpaginated.

2. Jack Cowart, *Roy Lichtenstein 1970–1980* [exh. cat. The St. Louis Art Museum] (St. Louis, 1981), 16.

MALCOLM MORLEY
Born 1931

Rite of Passage, 1988–1989
Spit-bite and aquatint
46½ x 32½ (118.1 x 82.5)

Gift of Gemini G.E.L. and the Artist

The British-born Malcolm Morley graduated from the Royal College of Art, London, in 1957. He was influenced by abstract expressionism, especially the work of Willem de Kooning. The following year he settled in New York where he met Barnett Newman, who became an important stimulus for Morley during his early career. Morley strove for a personal means of expression, his super-realist paintings of the mid-1960s being what first brought him recognition in the art world. He avoids ties to any particular style, which accounts for the innovation and assorted modes of expression seen in his oeuvre.

Although Morley's discipline is primarily painting, throughout his career he has sporadically produced prints. His watercolors have often been the bases for paintings and prints. These sequences provide an insightful look at Morley's creative process.

Rite of Passage is derived from several watercolors of the same subject. The metamorphosis of this image can be traced from the very first watercolor he made to the watercolor *Rite of Passage with Complementaries and Tertiaries, Tondo,* which was the direct inspiration for the round format of this print. There is a certain consistency between the print and the watercolor after which it is modeled. The print adheres closely to its predecessor's composition and colors and approximates its fluid quality. Yet Morley did not attempt to force the print medium to imitate the characteristics of the watercolor. Rather, he explored the physical qualities of the spit-bite and aquatint with a painterly sensibility. His goal is "to make whatever happens, the content, the image, in terms of the medium itself and not in terms of making the medium look like another medium, thus beating it to death. I would rather let the medium itself be free."[1]

The elegant colors in *Rite of Passage* seem to penetrate the paper as they flow across the page, giving the image rhythm and motion. The circular format amplifies the spatial depth and the viewer's high perspective. Likewise, it heightens the closeness of the two sails and figures to the foreground and their dominance over the composition. As a compliment, the tondo is surrounded by a field of transparent and opaque gray washes interspersed with pools and streams of various colors. These nuances enhance the richly orchestrated colors within the tondo.

Morley is one of the more recent artists to work at Gemini G.E.L.; prior to *Rite of Passage,* he had completed twelve prints in their workshop. The National Gallery has two other prints by Morley, both in the Gemini G.E.L. Archive. These prints, two versions of *Eve Born of Adam* (1987), are bold figurative studies with broad lines and more gestural handwriting. *Rite of Passage* is a sensually handsome work and offers an interesting comparison to the two earlier prints.

Carlotta J. Owens

NOTE
1. *Malcolm Morley,* interview with Malcolm Morley by Arnold Glimcher [exh. cat. Pace Gallery] (New York, 1988).

S.P. Malcolm Morley

513

NANCY GRAVES
Born 1940

Canoptic Legerdemain, 1990
Brushed stainless steel, aluminum mesh,
cast resin, cast paper, aluminum
panels, cast epoxy, color lithograph
85 x 95 x 37 (215.9 x 241.3 x 93.9)

Gift of Graphicstudio, U.S.F.
and the Artist

Color, line, and form interlock in *Canoptic Legerdemain,* Nancy Graves' first edition sculpture.[1] The openness of the sculpture, enhanced by the transparency of the overlapping elements, belies its tightly interwoven and interactive structure; its shifting planes extend outward at various angles, twisting and turning in and around each other in complex, dynamic fashion.

Every element in *Canoptic Legerdemain* leads a double life, serving an iconographical as well as a compositional function. The imagery reflects the artist's ongoing study of art history, culture, and archaeology, bringing together Byzantine, Egyptian, and Christian sources while interweaving male and female historical and mythological roles. For example, the "hand of God," seen in the lithograph incorporated in the piece and again as a relief element, is obviously taken from Michelangelo's Creation of Adam on the ceiling of the Sistine Chapel, while a related Sistine fresco served as the basis for the face of Eve printed in red on the lithograph, from which the hand of God extends. The snake has cross-cultural associations, including the creature's role in the temptation in the Garden of Eden.

On the left side of the composition, Graves rendered the sixth-century Byzantine empress Theodora in an intricate and open design that suggests the tesserae of the mosaic in San Vitale (Ravenna) on which Graves' image is based. Interwoven with the likeness are references to the Egyptian calendar — blue stars and circular forms superimposed with a sunburst-like image. Other references to ancient Egyptian culture include the fishing scene, cut from stainless steel with a laser that had been digitally programmed from the artist's drawing, itself a composite of images from Theban tombs. The ducks featured on the left side of the lithographic element are also from a Theban source, and the canopic (burial) jars referred to in the work's title can be found beneath the ducks.

In 1983 Graves had introduced classical Greek forms as well as references to ancient Greek culture into her work. Here these are seen in the resin bust of Aphrodite, from a cast in the artist's collection taken from the Elgin marbles. On the lithograph's right side are Greek mourning women whose arms are raised in the ancient gesture of grief, while on the left is a portion of a Greek robe, which the artist chose in part "for its graphic configuration and the way it would contrast with the laser-cut."[2]

Throughout her career, Graves has consistently pursued technical alternatives for their expressive potential, and *Canoptic Legerdemain* is clearly a tour de force in this regard. A remarkable interplay of color, texture, and pattern is achieved using a number of innovative processes, including the laser-cut steel and the cast resin already mentioned. The river element is also molded resin, cast from plasticene-covered styrofoam that the artist manipulated with her fingers, and other tools, rope, and wire. The Theodora panel is epoxy mixed with sand and marble dust, from a clay original to which palm leaves dipped in wax, wax stars, and styrofoam balls had been added. The grittiness of the surface of the panel was enhanced by sandblasting before painting.

Both the skeletal structure and the skin of the snake are actually "found" materials; the diamond-shaped aluminum mesh of its skin was manufactured for use over screen doors, while its internal armature is a section of prefabricated aluminum grating.

In *Canoptic Legerdemain* Graves' recent explorations in both painting and sculpture are merged, making it an exciting addition to the Gallery's collection. It joins one other Graves sculpture, the wonderfully whimsical *Spinner* (bronze with polychromed and baked enamel, 1985), which was acquired by the Gallery in 1986 as a gift of the Lila Acheson Wallace Fund.

Mary Lee Corlett

NOTES
1. An edition of seven was produced, plus seven proofs.

2. Nancy Graves in a telephone conversation with Mary Lee Corlett, 25 October 1990.

ROBERT FRANK
Born 1924

Untitled, 1952–1990
Gelatin silver photographs, video prints,
board, wire, nails, colored paper, paint,
and acetate
40⅛ x 29⁷⁄₁₆ (101.9 x 75.6)

Mute/Blind, 1989–1990
Type C color photographs, video
prints, acetate, foil, nails, and board
41⅛ x 31⅞ (104.5 x 81)

Robert Frank Collection,
Gift of Isabel and Fernando Garzoni,
Switzerland

One senses, at times, that Robert Frank's past weighs heavily on him, that it has been both a burden and a source of inspiration. His early work, and particularly *The Americans*, catapulted him into the forefront of American art, but it also served to define and thus potentially confine him ever since. However, while Frank may not wish to disown his previous work, he clearly recognizes that it is inadequate to express his present feelings.

In his video *Home Improvements*, 1985, he dealt with his past by having a friend drill holes through a large stack of prints from *The Americans* as well as other early work. Even within this highly personal examination of his relationship with his wife and son as well as his art, it was a brutal, abrupt, and unexplained action. In *Untitled* he significantly expanded upon this act by wrapping the stack of photographs with wire, driving nails through it, and mounting it onto a piece of wood. Before he did this, however, he selected as the top photograph not his more romantic study of flowers in Paris or his highly charged image of a flag, *Parade—Hoboken, New Jersey*, that are so clearly destroyed in *Home Improvements*, but rather a photograph of a bull in Valencia, Spain. With a sword stuck in its back, the bull is a wounded relic of the past, struggling to live in the present. Covered with dirt and aggressively raw, *Untitled*, like the bull itself, is a clear statement of Frank's abhorrence of the preciousness and sanctity ascribed to most works of art.

Although the various components of *Untitled* and its companion piece *Mute/Blind* were made over many years—from the early 1950s to the late 1980s—they were assembled for a group show in January 1990 at Frank's dealer, Pace/MacGill, to inaugurate

new galleries on 57th Street in New York. It may have amused viewers, and possibly even the photographer himself, to see *Untitled*, with its conscious, violent desecration of a large number of marketable prints, within this context. However, Frank was not mocking the art world. Instead, as he has done so often in his career, he seized the occasion of this group exhibition, which included work by senior photographers as well as the most current younger practitioners, to unequivocally separate himself and his art from the crowd. In addition, it should be recognized that while *Untitled* does speak to the gross commercialization of art and photography in the 1980s, it and *Mute/Blind* are more fundamentally about change and continuity, both within Frank's life and within the medium of photography.

Untitled consists not only of the stack of photographs nailed to a board, but also several thermal transfer prints of video stills from *Home Improvements*. As well as showing his wife, June Leaf, in the hospital and his "happy" neighbor in Canada, one of the stills in the center of the composite is of Frank himself, filming directly into a reflecting window at his house in Canada. Recognizing the continuity in his work as well as his struggle to simply keep going, Frank in the film tells the viewer, "I'm always doing the same images. I'm always looking outside trying to look inside. Trying to tell something that's true. But maybe nothing is really true. Except what's out there and what's out there is always different." The highly fugitive video stills, even now only pale shadows of their original intensity, will change and fade with time, as has Frank's relationship with his earlier stack of photographs.

Mute/Blind, composed of stills shot for

Frank's 1989 film *Hunter*, is also about what is out there and the struggle to see and know. Inspired by Kafka's parable, "The Hunter Gracchus," the film, as Frank wrote in the press release, is about "a man whose destiny is—not to find a destination. A man who fears that he will never find what his imagination compels him to look for." It is also the journey of a traveler seeking to know the German people, attempting to reconcile his past feelings with their present reality, "looking for Evil and Hate. But they are all nice people—the Germans—and if they hear you explain you're Jewish they are especially nice."[1] Yet, while *Mute/Blind* is derived from the film, it is an independent work. The stills in *Mute/Blind*, many of which are outtakes that were never included in *Hunter*, are primarily of a blind dog and a statue of a deer. Blindness and muteness, particularly as they affect close friends and family, are recurrent themes in Frank's work. In *Mute/Blind* the dog and the statue are both deeply appealing and at the same time very disturbing figures. Profoundly real, the dog is not a prop or a foil for a joke. It is not a dog by William Wegman (whose photographs were also shown in the group exhibition at Pace/MacGill), posed as if it were a human being, but a genuine animal with piercing, haunting eyes. The statue of the deer, which is in a park in Zurich notorious for the consumption of drugs, is not only mute, but it too has been blinded, literally defaced by park inhabitants so that it is unable to see. In a gesture that seems to allude painfully to Frank's feelings for Zurich, his birthplace, he has further altered the deer's eye, adding color so that it appears almost to bleed and weep.

The power of *Untitled* and *Mute/Blind* resides not only in their compelling imagery,

but also in their innovative exploration of new technological inventions. Signaling his acceptance of the transformation of the medium of photography, Frank constructed a piece that is largely dependent on electronic imagery. Only the stack of photographic prints, which is dirty and defiled, has been made using traditional photographic methods: even the color prints in *Mute/Blind* were taken from a video screen. Yet no relationship within this mixture is stable. Although at the present time the video prints in *Mute/Blind* have an extremely strong physical and psychological intensity, like those in *Untitled* they are fugitive and will fade. Just as the deer was assaulted by vandals and forced to find a new definition in a new context, so too will both *Untitled* and *Mute/Blind* continue to change with time and be forced to find other meanings. They are, as Frank wrote on the edge of *Untitled*, "Monuments of Glory and Regret."

This rich, complex piece has been generously given to the Gallery by Isabel and Fernando Garzoni, old friends of Frank's from Switzerland. Their donation of this elegiac but triumphant work, which is at one and the same time redolent of the past but expressive of the most pressing issues of the artist's present, is a fitting tribute to the endurance of their friendship.

Sarah Greenough

PROVENANCE
Isabel and Fernando Garzoni, 1990.

NOTE
1. Press release for *Hunter*, adapted by Paul Hofman, August, 1989.

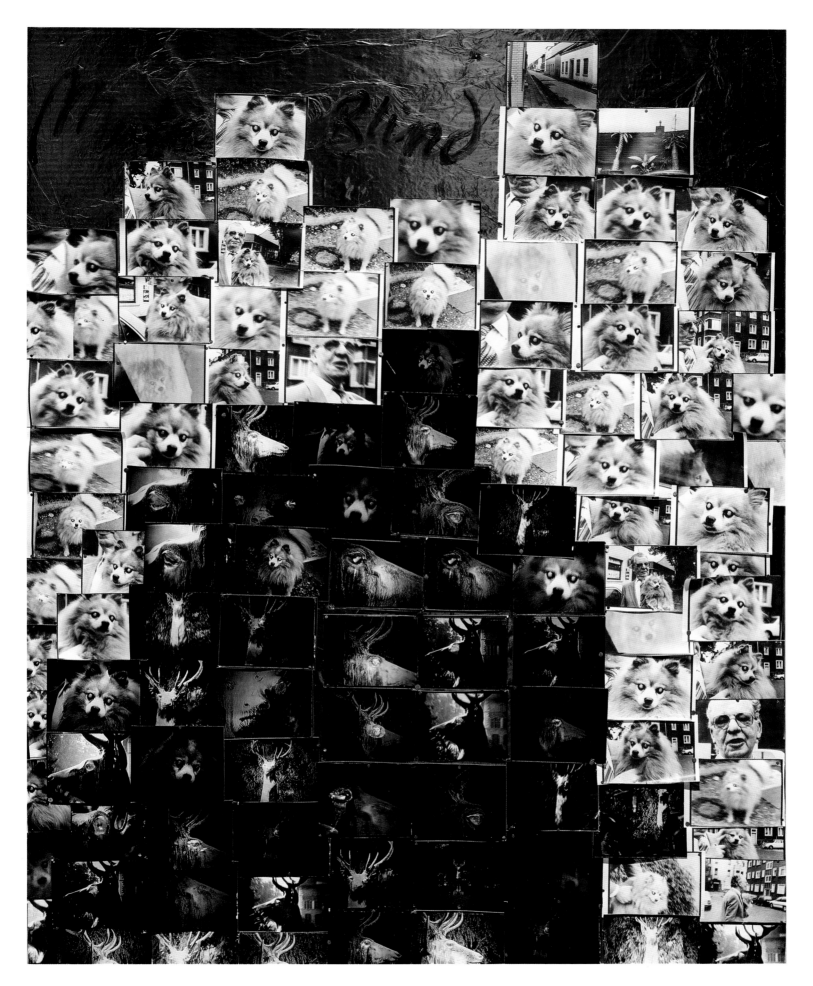

519

CLAES OLDENBURG
Born 1929

Profiterole, 1989–1991
Painted cast bronze
5¾ x 8 x 8⅝ (14.6 x 20.32 x 21.91)

Gift of Gemini G.E.L. and the Artist

Although by no means Claes Oldenburg's only subject, food is among his most frequent. His comestibles tend to the sweet and the popular: pies, cakes, and ice cream; hamburgers, hot dogs, and baked potatoes. Always they are presented in a manner that is at once appreciative and ironic, excessive and transgressive.

Food had long been a traditional subject of still-life painting, but to make sculpture of individual foodstuffs as Oldenburg first did in 1961 was a novelty. More challenging to the idealizing tradition of still life was Oldenburg's early representations of food as messy, seeping, and sagging. He made objects of humorous revulsion as well as desire. In recent years, however, Oldenburg's representations of food have become increasingly pristine. Part of their humorous and aesthetic charge comes not from messiness, but from an impossible perfection.

Such is certainly the case with *Profiterole*. That most excessive of deserts — ice cream, pastry, and chocolate sauce — is re-created in painted bronze to appear as immaculate as in a food-magazine photograph. The puff pastry is perfectly shaped, the ice cream has the correct degree of softness, and the thick chocolate sauce flows slowly down and outward to form neat crosses.

One of Oldenburg's favored devices involves dramatic shifts in scale, enlarging everyday objects out of all proportion to their normal appearance and function. *Profiterole*, however, is made to life scale. It is in every respect a perfectly realized simulation. Its special punch derives from a curious contradiction: the very perfection of its realization renders more striking the fact that it is utterly unconvincing. Despite the brilliance of illusion, one is instantly aware that the *Profiterole* is not real. That has partly to do with Oldenburg's ephemeral subject. Seen in any setting other than a dining table, the *Profiterole* simply could not be. By its extreme realism, then, *Profiterole* paradoxically widens the gap between art and life.

If many of Oldenburg's large sculptures can be termed mock heroic monuments, *Profiterole* belongs to a category that might be called mock precious. It is the size of an *objet d'art*, and its subject, as desserts go, is more rarefied than popular. Equating the *objet d'art* with a precious dessert, Oldenburg wittily draws attention to the correspondence and contradictions of aesthetic and gustatory desire.

Oldenburg's *Profiterole* was made by Gemini G.E.L. in an edition of 113, 75 of which were made as a benefit for the Hereditary Disease Foundation, along with a color lithograph of the same subject. It makes an interesting counterpoint to Oldenburg's *Soft Drainpipe — Red (Hot) Version*, 1967, donated to the Gallery in honor of the fiftieth anniversary by Robert and Jane Meyerhoff. *Soft Drainpipe — Red (Hot) Version* uses pliable materials to represent hard metal, whereas *Profiterole* uses bronze to represent soft ice cream.

Jeremy Strick

INDEX BY ARTIST

INDEX BY DONOR

gather

gather

CASUAL COOKING FROM WINE COUNTRY GARDENS

JANET FLETCHER

PHOTOGRAPHY BY MEG SMITH

Jennifer Barry Design Books

For information, write to
Jennifer Barry Design Books, LLC
229 Tamalpais Road, Fairfax, CA 94930, USA

First Edition

ISBN: 978-0-578-75194-8

Library of Congress Control Number: 2020916129

Produced and designed by Jennifer Barry Design, Fairfax, CA
Text by Janet Fletcher
Photography by Meg Smith
Food Styling by Abby Stolfo
Prop Styling by Thea Chalmers
Copy Editing by Sharon Silva

www.jenniferbarrydesign.com
www.janetfletcher.com
www.megsmith.com

Printed in China

Preceding pages: *Young fava beans at
Wheeler Farms; Wheeler Farms co-owner
Daphne Araujo in the winery's culinary garden*

Above and right: *Ha'ogen melon, a prized
Israeli variety, at Cakebread Cellars; thriving
stand of corn soaks up the Napa Valley sun at
Regusci Winery*

contents

Left: *Pickled carrots in the kitchen at
Alexander Valley Vineyards; Dolores Cakebread
with Cakebread Cellars chef Brian Streeter*

introduction   *An Invitation to Gather*

Northern California is wine country, among the most acclaimed viticultural regions on earth. Not coincidentally, this paradise for Pinot Noir and Chardonnay is also a sublime place to garden. The same mild Mediterranean climate that wine grapes love is what many herbs, fruits, and vegetables appreciate, too. Fertile soil, abundant sun, and moderate temperatures allow edible gardens to thrive year-round in the area's scenic wine valleys. To the surprise of many wine country visitors, some of the most delightful of these culinary gardens reside at wineries. *Gather: Casual Cooking from Wine Country Gardens* takes you on a tour of these picturesque plots and into the kitchens of those fortunate cooks who reap the harvest.

What beautiful food comes out of these gardens! And vintners want you to taste it. Most of them make wine, after all, because they relish sharing it with others. They believe that many of life's most pleasurable moments happen around the table, with friends and well-prepared food. Like gardeners, they embrace the rhythms of nature: the calm of winter, the optimism of spring, the adrenaline rush of harvest. They love creating a product that encourages hospitality and contributes to a healthy lifestyle. For many vintners, an abundant garden is essential to the life they want to lead and the zest for living they want to convey.

Gather: Casual Cooking from Wine Country Gardens showcases thirteen Northern California wineries with inspiring edible gardens. These enterprises differ in many ways, but they share the belief that

Above: *(clockwise from left) Laura Regusci in the Regusci garden; Trefethen Vineyards tomatoes and dried chile powders; Cakebread Cellars melon; Trefethen chef Chris Kennedy; apples at Wente Vineyards*

fresh, seasonal, garden-to-table meals are the most satisfying and flattering companions for their wines.

These charming gardens serve many ends. They provide some of the produce used in meals served to visitors, as at Cakebread Cellars, where Dolores Cakebread's marvelous garden has delighted and fed guests for almost fifty years. Wente Vineyards' large organic garden has long supported its restaurant and robust visitor events, while the mountain garden maintained by Clif Family Winery keeps its popular Bruschetteria food truck supplied daily.

At other wineries, the garden inspires handmade gifts for guests, such as chef Sarah Heller's edible flower cookies at Wheeler Farms, or the southern-style pickled okra that chef Angel Perez puts up every summer at Regusci Winery, a nod to vintner Laura Regusci's Kentucky roots. At Beringer Vineyards, winery hosts use the sensory garden as a teaching tool for guests, a way to make wine aromas more discernible by connecting them to more familiar scents in nature.

A culinary garden makes a scenic backdrop for many winery events and receptions. At The Prisoner Wine Company, private events often begin in the garden, giving guests a chance to congregate casually outdoors with a glass of wine and explore the unusual culinary

Wine country culinary gardens make a scenic backdrop for many winery events and receptions.

herbs that fill the deep raised beds. A garden tour is one of the opportunities that Robert Mondavi Winery offers guests, who get to cook with what they harvest and enjoy a family-style lunch in the garden.

Some wineries, such as Trefethen Family Vineyards, view the garden primarily as a staff perk, a creative way of investing in employee health and wellness by encouraging staffers to take home what the winery chef doesn't use. The garden at Alexander Valley Vineyards feeds many families. The winery operates a farm stand at the nearby farmers' market, so locals can enjoy fresh eggs from the winery's pastured hens and the tomatoes and peppers that winery co-owner Hank Wetzel delights in growing.

Skipstone owner Fahri Diner grew up in rural Cyprus surrounded by fruit trees and free-range hens, and he and his wife, Constance, want their young children to have a similar experience. At B Cellars and HALL Wines, the garden reflects a deep-rooted commitment to sustainability and a belief that diversity creates a healthier ecosystem.

In this book, so stunningly photographed by Meg Smith, you will visit thirteen magical gardens—some of them open to the public, some not. I hope you will gather ideas for your own culinary garden, tips on what to plant, and techniques for keeping the garden healthy and productive. You will, I hope, gather inspiration for your own cooking and make time to re-create some of these mouthwatering meals. Above all, I hope this book will compel you to gather friends and family around the table, open a bottle of California wine, and celebrate the unending generosity of the earth.

Right: *Napa Valley chef Sarah Scott prepares garden tomato sauce; a vineyard view for an alfresco meal*

Above and right: *Kikinda gourds dangle from a trellis at Cakebread Cellars; Katie Wetzel Murphy prepares garden citrus for marmalade.*

Alexander Valley Vineyards: *Farmers' Market Favorite*

Healdsburg

For the Wetzel family, Cyrus Alexander is ever present, a hovering spirit who perpetually reminds them of their property's storied past. Family members live, garden, and make wine on the historic Alexander estate, the long-ago home of the pioneering settler who gave Alexander Valley its name. This landmark property's roots plunge deep, like those of its massive olive and oak trees.

"We think Alexander parked himself here because the soil is great," says Katie Wetzel Murphy, whose father purchased the heritage acreage in 1962 from Alexander's heirs. The site is a half mile from the Russian River but not in the floodplain, an ideal spot for fruit trees and other food crops, which Alexander planted. A teetotaler, he left it to later generations to plant the first wine grapes in what became one of California's most esteemed wine appellations.

Ironically, Alexander was scouting ranchland, not vineyard, when he traveled north from San Diego in the late 1830s. He found a suitable tract near the future town of Healdsburg, and for four years he managed the vast Rancho Sotoyome for his patron. His reward was a fertile parcel of his own where he started a family and, in 1842, built an adobe home. The old adobe still stands, gently restored and used for winery events, adjacent to the Victorian-style home where Katie's brother Hank and his wife, Linda, live now.

Today, Hank, Katie, and their families oversee Alexander Valley Vineyards, the enterprise their parents started after purchasing the Sonoma County estate sight unseen. Gradually, Maggie Wetzel, their mother, transformed the neglected landscape with rose gardens, dahlias, and espaliered pears. She planted citrus trees around the swimming pool and asparagus beds that still produce, but she was really more of an ornamental gardener, says Hank.

The five acres of edible gardens that make Alexander Valley Vineyards such a draw for visitors today are largely Hank's doing. He has worked in the family vineyards since childhood, but it's the vegetable patch that kindles his sense of awe. "Planting a seed and having it produce something edible feels like a miracle," says Hank, who is something of a celebrity at the Healdsburg Farmers' Market.

Hank has operated a popular stand at this lively local market since 2014, when he decided to test it as a sales venue for the estate's extra virgin olive oil. To make his stall more alluring, he began growing tomatoes and peppers, melons and zucchini, lettuces and lima beans. "I love the phenomenon of farm to table," says the vintner. "I have a regular clientele who would never think of missing the market."

Left and above: *Five acres behind the Wetzel family home yield produce for the Healdsburg Farmers' Market; Hank Wetzel at the market with his sought-after eggs*

With garden manager Javier Patino, Hank oversees the planting and pampering of at least ten different types of cherry tomatoes (Chocolate Cherry is a favorite), sauce tomatoes, and slicers, such as Mortgage Lifter, Brandywine, and Pineapple. In one of several separate garden plots, lemon cucumbers weave their way over decorative wrought-iron trellises, while wire arches cloaked in pole beans create verdant tunnels. Picture-perfect rosettes of Salanova lettuce are farmers' market favorites, but it's the farm's eggs that have the real cult following, especially among local chefs.

"When the chickens have that first flush of green grass to eat, the eggs are fantastic," says Katie. Coyotes are a constant menace, but the eggs have too much of a fan club to let the coyotes prevail. Hank buys baby chicks online, and the post office calls him when the chirping

box arrives; he adopts roosters from city folks who want only hens. The birds' mobile coop can be towed from one vineyard block to another so the chickens can do pest control. During the day, they wander freely, feasting on insects and worms and fertilizing as they go; at night, they retreat to the safety of the coop and a dinner of garden scraps.

A separate plot near the winery caves is allocated to employees. Javier oversees this productive patch of tomatillos, chiles, tomatoes, corn, watermelon, and squash. Staffers can take whatever they want, a treasured perk for those who lack the time or space to garden at home.

Despite the energy and resources directed at the garden, it is no profit center. "I have a goal to make money from the garden before I die," sighs Hank, but no one really believes that the bottom line drives him. The winery's business is wine. For the Wetzel clan, the garden is

Above: *(clockwise from top) stately olive tree; garden manager Patino; espaliered Bartlett pears; Katie prepping marmalade; fresh-dug carrots and Salanova lettuce, a top farmers' market seller*

The garden tells a story about the Wetzel family's passion for their land and for the Eden that is Sonoma County. "To not have a garden in a place like this would be a crime," says Katie.

a lifestyle choice and a way to honor their parents, who had the foresight to purchase such a fertile parcel. It is also a vehicle for telling stories: about their passion for the land; about the Eden that is Sonoma County; about the pleasures of a life that revolves around home-grown food and good wine.

Or mostly wine. A few tasks require stronger stuff. "We drink bourbon and shell limas on the porch," admits Hank. "That's a favorite habit of mine."

Hank cooks, but Katie cooks better, he says. Among the four siblings, she is the one who accompanied her mother to La Varenne, the Parisian cooking school, and inherited the French copper cookware. She makes the tangerine marmalade that overnight visitors find in the

guesthouse, and she is the family's preserver in chief, responsible for transforming extra produce into pickled green beans, bread-and-butter pickles, spicy ketchup, tomatillo salsa, fruit chutney, preserved lemons, and dried cherry tomatoes for pizza, bruschetta, and spaghetti sauce.

When the Healdsburg Farmers' Market reopens each May, the Alexander Valley Vineyards garden is ready for it with soft spring lettuces, asparagus, radishes, turnips, beets, and, of course, plenty of fresh eggs. Throughout the summer, the evenings are warm enough to eat on the front porch, and the garden brims with tender young vegetables, the only excuse this close family needs to gather for a dinner alfresco.

Above and right: *(clockwise from left) Hank's Victorian home; trellised pear-shaped tomatoes for salad; Alexander Valley Vineyards' farmers' market stand; bean trellis with gopher-deterring euphorbia*

A chilled bottle of Gewürztraminer makes the rounds with Katie's creamy pimiento cheese (made with garden pimientos in season) and a sliced baguette from the local bakery. As the sun sets, a big platter of crudités, boiled eggs, and olives appears with a salsa verde–avocado dip, a favorite family recipe that Katie perfected after encountering it in Mexico. The summer garden yields plenty of dip-worthy vegetables, with radishes, slender scallions, baby carrots, sugar snap peas, green beans, cauliflower, and beets among them. To follow, Katie roasts a quartered chicken the way Maggie often did: with a basting of butter, French mustard, garden tarragon, and honey to brown and crisp the skin. Linda takes charge of the salad, a jumble of lettuces, mild spring onions, early tomatoes, and lemon cucumbers, tossed with the vinaigrette that she perfected and that everyone in the family makes now. A pear and blackberry crisp made with ranch pears and topped with Katie's homemade granola provides the finale.

Surveying this lush landscape, nature seems endlessly generous and benign. But the Wetzels have seen nature's fury, too. In the autumn of 2019, a windstorm-whipped fire tore through this dry valley, causing major damage at neighboring properties. Alexander Valley Vineyards lost some of Maggie's citrus trees, Hank's greenhouse, and other outbuildings, but fortunately the family home and the grandest old trees survived. Hank can still forage for breakfast under the sprawling fig, peach, and apple trees with nothing but a pocket-knife. One of the apple trees, an old Russian variety called Red Astrachan, may have been planted in Cyrus Alexander's day.

As fierce preservationists, the Wetzels recognize that they have a treasure to protect and nurture. Fortunately, Hank's sons, Harry and Robert, are involved in the winery, preparing to perpetuate what their grandparents started. Hank's ambitious garden will evolve—gardens always do—but it should still be ripening tomatoes a generation from now. "We have water, sun, and soil," says Katie. "To not have a garden in a place like this would be a crime."

menu

Katie's Pimiento Cheese
Alexander Valley Vineyards Dry Rosé of Sangiovese or Gewürztraminer

Crudités with Avocado Salsa Verde
Alexander Valley Vineyards Dry Rosé of Sangiovese

Summer Garden Salad with Linda's Dressing
Alexander Valley Vineyards Chardonnay

Maggie's Ranch Chicken
Alexander Valley Vineyards Merlot

Pear, Blackberry, and Granola Crisp
Alexander Valley Vineyards Gewürztraminer

Katie's Pimiento Cheese

Makes about 3½ cups

1 small pimiento pepper or red bell pepper, about 4 ounces

½ cup mayonnaise

1 tablespoon fresh lemon juice

1½ teaspoons dry mustard, such as Colman's

½ teaspoon Worcestershire sauce

1 pound sharp Cheddar cheese, coarsely grated

Optional additions: minced scallion, chopped fresh
flat-leaf parsley, chopped roasted pecans, chopped
green olives, ground cayenne, Tabasco sauce

Wine: Alexander Valley Vineyards Dry Rosé of Sangiovese
or Gewürztraminer

---

katie's tip:

Pack pimiento cheese in a decorative
jar for a hostess gift. It's a great
appetizer for Thanksgiving or a large
dinner party because you can make
it well ahead. "It lasts for days if it
doesn't get eaten," says Katie.

Katie discovered pimiento cheese on a business trip to Charleston, South Carolina, and fell in love with this classic Southern specialty. She uses sweet pimientos from the garden when they ripen in late summer and fall and grills them over charcoal if she has time. No wonder many of her friends say, "For my birthday, I'd like pimiento cheese." Serve with a sliced baguette.

Roast the pepper until blackened all over by your preferred method: over a charcoal fire, over a gas flame, or under a broiler. Let cool, then peel and remove the stem, seeds, and ribs. Cut the pepper into small dice.

In a bowl, using an electric mixer, combine the pepper, mayonnaise, lemon juice, mustard, and Worcestershire sauce and beat on medium speed until blended. Add the cheese and beat again until blended. Stir in the optional ingredients to your taste.

Crudités with Avocado Salsa Verde

Makes 1⅓ cups salsa

1½ pounds tomatillos, husked and coarsely chopped (about 4 cups)

1 Anaheim or poblano chile, seeded and coarsely chopped

1 jalapeño chile, seeded and coarsely chopped

3 cloves garlic, peeled

½ small white onion, sliced

Sea salt

½ large avocado, peeled

1 small handful arugula

⅓ cup coarsely chopped fresh cilantro leaves and stems

¼ cup extra virgin olive oil

2 tablespoons fresh lime juice

Assorted vegetables, hard-cooked eggs, and olives, for serving (see headnote)

Wine: Alexander Valley Vineyards Dry Rosé of Sangiovese

Preheat the oven to 350°F. Put the tomatillos, Anaheim chile, jalapeño chile, garlic, and onion in a 9-by-13-inch baking dish and stir to mix. Bake, stirring halfway through, for 1 hour. Let cool slightly, then put all the ingredients into a blender, add ½ teaspoon salt, and blend until smooth. Set aside 1 cup of this salsa and refrigerate the remainder for another use.

Return the reserved 1 cup salsa to the blender and add the avocado, arugula, cilantro, oil, 2 tablespoons lime juice, and ¾ teaspoon salt. Blend until smooth, adding a splash of water if the sauce needs thinning. Taste for salt and lime juice. Serve the salsa with the assorted vegetables, hard-cooked eggs, and olives.

This dip, which Katie discovered in Baja, may well become your go-to sauce for crudités, steamed vegetables, or fish. In spring, Katie serves it with steamed artichokes or a platter of fresh radishes, spring onions, lightly steamed baby carrots, sugar snap peas, baby turnips, and roasted beets. In summer, think tomatoes, bell peppers, blanched green beans, and steamed zucchini. Hard-cooked farm eggs and olives round out the platter.

Summer Garden Salad with Linda's Dressing

Makes 1 cup dressing

Linda's Dressing:

⅓ cup extra virgin olive oil

⅓ cup grapeseed oil

⅓ cup red wine vinegar

1 teaspoon sea salt

1 teaspoon dry mustard, such as Colman's

1 heaping teaspoon sugar

½ teaspoon freshly ground black pepper

Optional additions: chopped shallot, minced fresh herbs, Worcestershire sauce

Salad ingredients from the garden such as lettuces, cherry tomatoes, sweet peppers, lemon cucumbers

Wine: Alexander Valley Vineyards Chardonnay

Everybody in the Wetzel family makes this salad dressing, but they all switch it up a bit. This recipe is Linda's version. (Katie adds a dash of Worcestershire sauce.) It can be kept on the kitchen counter because it doesn't contain anything perishable. The one constant, of course, is Alexander Valley Vineyards extra virgin olive oil. The dressing complements whatever lettuces and vegetables the garden provides, so feel free to improvise.

Prepare the dressing: Combine all the ingredients in a tightly capped glass jar and shake well.

Combine the salad ingredients of your choice in a large bowl. Add just enough dressing to coat the salad lightly and toss. Taste for salt and pepper. Serve immediately.

Left and right: *Lemon cucumbers climb an ornamental garden trellis; harvest of Little Gem lettuces from the Alexander Valley Vineyards garden*

Maggie's Ranch Chicken

Serves 4

One whole fresh chicken, 4 to 4½ pounds, backbone removed, quartered

Sea salt and freshly ground black pepper

⅓ cup honey

4 tablespoons salted butter

1 tablespoon Dijon mustard

4 six-inch sprigs fresh tarragon

Wine: Alexander Valley Vineyards Merlot

Ranch chicken has nothing to do with ranch dressing, says Katie. "It's what we called this dish as kids," she recalls. "It seems that my mother only made it when we came to 'The Ranch,' which is what we called the vineyards before we had a winery." Baked with honey, mustard, and tarragon, the quartered chicken emerges with a crisp brown skin, and the sweet aroma draws everyone to the kitchen. "Kids like it and adults like it," says Katie, "and most of the food we make has to be that way."

Preheat an oven to 350°F. Season the chicken all over with salt and pepper.

In a small saucepan, combine the honey, butter, and mustard and stir over low heat until the butter melts.

Put the chicken quarters in a 9- by 13-inch baking dish and pour the honey mixture over them. Place a tarragon sprig on each quarter. Bake for 30 minutes, then remove the dish from the oven, spoon the juices over the chicken, and return to the oven for 30 minutes more. The chicken will be fully cooked, with beautifully browned skin. Let rest at least 15 minutes before serving to allow the juices to settle.

Right: Hank's sons, Robert (left) and Harry Wetzel, enjoy the family's wine in front of the entrance to the winery cave.

Above and right: *Katie checks on the laying hens in the mobile chicken coop; pasture-fed chickens produce eggs with thick, creamy yolks.*

katie's tip:

Katie makes her own granola for family breakfasts. If you want to include dried fruits, such as raisins, add after baking so the fruit doesn't burn. If you want to substitute store-bought granola, choose one with no dried fruit.

Pear, Blackberry, and Granola Crisp

Serves 6 to 8

4 firm but ripe pears, peeled, halved, cored, and sliced

2 cups blackberries

¼ cup Demerara or turbinado sugar

3 cups Katie's Granola (recipe follows)

4 tablespoons unsalted butter, melted

Wine: Alexander Valley Vineyards Gewürztraminer

Preheat the oven to 375°F. In a large bowl, toss the pear slices and blackberries with sugar. Transfer to an 11-by-9-by-3-inch baking dish and spread in an even layer. Top with the granola, patting it into place. Pour the butter evenly over the granola.

Bake the crisp until fruit has softened and the topping has browned and crisped, about 25 minutes. Serve warm (not hot) or at room temperature with whipped cream or ice cream if desired.

This crisp showcases the ranch's abundant late-summer pear crop. The property has many Bartlett pear trees, reminiscent of a time before wine grapes became the primary crop in the Alexander Valley. Unlike most fruits, Bartlett pears are harvested while still green and hard. They will soften and turn yellow in a few days on the kitchen counter.

Katie's Granola **Makes about 7 cups**

⅓ cup pure maple syrup

⅓ cup packed light brown sugar or Demerara sugar

1 tablespoon plus 1 teaspoon pure vanilla extract

½ teaspoon sea salt

1 teaspoon ground cinnamon

½ cup vegetable oil

5 cups old-fashioned rolled oats

2 cups raw walnuts, broken into chunks

Position an oven rack in the upper-middle position. Preheat the oven to 325°F. Line a 12-by-17-inch baking sheet with parchment paper.

In a large bowl, whisk together the maple syrup, sugar, vanilla, salt, and cinnamon. Whisk in the oil. Fold in the oats and walnuts until thoroughly coated.

Transfer the mixture to the prepared pan and spread into an even layer. Using a stiff metal spatula, compress the mixture until very compact. Bake the granola, rotating the pan back to front halfway through, until lightly browned, 40 to 45 minutes. Place the pan on a rack and let the granola cool to room temperature. Break into pieces or crumble. Store in an airtight container at room temperature.

B Cellars: *New Ways to Engage*

Napa

When Jim Borsack and Duffy Keys envisioned the winery they intended to build, they knew B Cellars would need to deliver a unique visitor experience. Napa Valley already had plenty of wineries with welcoming tasting rooms and friendly staff. How does a new venture break out of that pack? How do you connect with guests in a way that they won't soon forget?

"For the most part, the Napa Valley wine-tasting experience seemed pedestrian to me," says Duffy, a longtime luxury-hotel executive. "We wanted to change the way visitors engage with a winery; we wanted to go beyond the expected."

Mission accomplished. Opened in 2014, B Cellars quickly became a top destination for wine country travelers, a winery that other wineries recommend to their guests. Five years in, more than a third of B Cellars guests are repeat visitors, people who clearly feel a rapport with the place and the people.

Who wouldn't want to return to this stylish and inviting venue, with its strollable edible gardens and shady terraces? The outdoor armchairs look so comfy, it's a wonder guests don't curl up and stay all day. The tasting room, christened the Hospitality House, is equally hard to leave, with multiple seating areas and a stunning open kitchen with a wood-burning hearth. First-timers may wonder if they took the wrong driveway and mistakenly landed at a chic boutique hotel.

Left and above: *Galvanized-steel troughs make handsome planters for the winery herb garden; chef Derick Kuntz (left) can snip chives, sage, or tarragon as needed for the creative "B bites" served to visitors.*

"We wanted to create an environment where all your senses were engaged the moment you came in the door," says Duffy. "That's why we put the kitchen and the living room together in our Hospitality House."

The seduction starts as soon as guests gather in the arrival courtyard. Within moments, they have wine in hand, perhaps the plush B Cellars Dutton Ranch Chardonnay. After a sip or two, and a welcome from their guide, an elegant one-bite appetizer arrives, maybe featherlight pumpkin gnocchi in a porcelain spoon.

Chef Derick Kuntz oversees the kitchen, henhouse, apiary, and culinary garden; he's the mastermind behind these petite and pretty "B bites"—more than sixty different ones every year to showcase B Cellars wines. "The garden is part and parcel of the kitchen," says general manager Curtis Strohl. "The experience wouldn't be the same without it. Guests are seeing vegetables and flowers on their plate that thirty minutes ago they saw in the garden."

With glass in hand, visitors take a guided stroll that leads them past the culinary herb garden, a series of deep aluminum troughs filled with rosemary, mint, nasturtiums, chives, and sage. Around the corner, the edible garden is an orderly grid of rectangular beds separated by gravel walkways. In late summer, tall spires of feathery red amaranth tower above rows of peppers, both sweet and hot (the chiles are for the daily staff meals); heirloom tomatoes; yard-long beans; cucumbers; and sunchokes. A dormant asparagus bed promises a tasty crop the following spring, when the garden will also be flush with Kalette (a kale–Brussels sprout cross), kohlrabi, Chioggia beets, baby zucchini, arugula, Nantes carrots, spring garlic, young basil, and salad greens.

"I like growing things that others don't typically try," says the chef, pointing to the finger limes whose tart, caviar-like "pearls" he uses for garnishes, the huckleberries he adds to sauces and house-made sausage, a caper bush, and a leafy horseradish plant. His treasured Espelette peppers, a rare variety from France's Basque region, ripen to red in early fall. After drying them, Derick will grind them for a fragrant, gently spicy, pumpkin-colored seasoning he uses all year. Pineapple guava, an attractive shrub with deep-pink blossoms and gray-green leaves, provides fuzzy egg-shaped fruits, while cherry, apple, peach, pear, Asian pear, Meyer lemon, and blood orange trees are just getting settled into this young landscape.

"What I love most about the garden is that people will come lean against the fence while I'm working," says Michael Christophel, a professional gardener who helps with the plant sourcing and maintenance. "I get to meet people from all over the world, and they get to

Above: *(clockwise from left) The winery garden is at the base of a hillside blanketed with ancient walnut trees that the owners spared from vineyard development; onion patch; plaque commemorating the vineyard planting date; a carrot bouquet; Tuscan kale; a home for the winery's hens*

"It's rewarding to see our vineyards in harmony with barn owls, hawks, falcons, and wild turkeys," says Duffy. "There's diversity here, and that's what we like."

taste something right out of the garden." Michael plants lemon verbena, cherry tomatoes, and strawberries in the corners, so even guests who don't venture into the garden can snatch a taste as they pass.

A scheduled visit to B Cellars typically includes a barrel tasting—a privilege reserved for VIPs at most wineries—before guests return to the Hospitality House for a sit-down wine sampling. The winery produces small lots of many types—single-varietal and single-vineyard bottlings as well as complex blends—so Derick has a relentless creative challenge. Every wine has its own precise accompaniment, a fully realized mini dish designed to enhance it. "We set our wines up for success," says Curtis, and the property's fruits, vegetables, and herbs provide a big assist, subtly echoing wine aromas and textures.

In late spring, the release of the winery's lively rosé coincides with the start of California salmon season. To highlight the pink wine's freshness and brisk acidity, Derick pairs it with salmon tartare, adding finely diced garden strawberries and cucumbers to lighten and brighten the rich, fatty fish. It's a surprising, even shocking, combination, but it works, complemented by the wine's youthful fruitiness.

Above and right: *(clockwise from left) Renowned for its ambitious hospitality program, the winery entices visitors with creative food offerings, such as handmade beet tortellini with elk* sugo *and kale chips; B Cellars Rosé; outdoor tastings have a vineyard view.*

Summer is the garden's peak moment, of course, when the estate's stone fruits and tomatoes grow ripe and sweet. For B Cellars Blend 23—a marriage of Sauvignon Blanc, Chardonnay, and Viognier—Derick composes a salad of tomatoes, watermelon radishes, burrata, and peaches in vivid summer hues. The tomatoes and spicy radishes connect with the Sauvignon Blanc, the creamy burrata speaks to the Chardonnay, and the peach echoes the aromatics in the Viognier.

By late autumn, the cool-weather-loving root vegetables in the garden are sizing up. Derick showcases the season's first parsnips with seared scallops, preparing the underappreciated vegetable two ways: a silky puree for the dish's foundation and fried ribbons for crunch on top.

In winter, to match the winery's Blend 24 and to nudge guests out of their comfort zone, the chef often looks to farm-raised game, such as ostrich and elk. "You should get a little nervous about one of the bites, I think," says Derick. Certainly, any guests uneasy about the chef's elk *sugo* will quickly be won over. The meaty braise, like the Super Tuscan–style Blend 24, is concentrated and rich, with a mirepoix of garden vegetables adding sweetness. The winery's heirloom chickens contribute the eggs for the tortellini dough (and for the staff's Saturday buffet breakfast), but Derick fills and shapes every dumpling by hand.

"One club member told me, 'My husband never eats vegetables except when he's here,'" says Curtis.

Jim's retailing background schooled him in creating experiences that make an impression—that aren't quite what guests expected when they got out of the car. "We have a shared vision of excellence," says Duffy about his business partner. "We take pride in our wine, in the warmth of our employees, in the beauty of our surroundings. And it's rewarding to see our guests appreciate them, too."

From the beginning, Jim and Duffy imagined an integrated estate, with gardens, orchards, grapevines, and honeybees in symbiosis with the native landscape. "There's diversity here," says Duffy, "and that's what we like."

menu

Strawberry Salmon Tartare
B Cellars Rosé

Heirloom Tomato and Peach Salad with Burrata
B Cellars Blend 23

Seared Sea Scallops with Parsnips Two Ways
B Cellars Chardonnay

Elk Sugo with Herb Cheese Tortellini
and Kale Chips
B Cellars Blend 24

Dijon-Crusted Lamb Chops with Pistachio Puree,
Chard, and Huckleberry Gastrique
B Cellars Cabernet Sauvignon

Strawberry Salmon Tartare

Serves 6

Pickled Peppers:

3 baby bell sweet peppers, preferably a mix of colors

1 jalapeño chile, halved lengthwise

¼ cup white wine vinegar

¼ cup sugar

¼ cup water

5 to 6 ounces skinless salmon fillet, pin bones removed, in small, neat dice

3 large strawberries, hulled, in small, neat dice

1½ teaspoons extra virgin olive oil

Finely grated zest of 1 lemon

Sea salt

1 small lemon cucumber or 2-inch chunk English cucumber, peeled if desired, halved lengthwise, and very thinly sliced crosswise (12 half-moons)

12 fresh chive batons, each 1 to 2 inches long, for garnish

Wine: B Cellars Rosé

"When I taste our rosé, the two flavors that come to mind are salmon and strawberries," says Derick. "The wine is tart, so the fat of the salmon helps. And the rosé can stand up to a lot of spice." The combination of ingredients is unusual, but the recipe is among the most requested at B Cellars. If you can't find Baby Bell sweet peppers, choose a long, narrow sweet pepper, such as Corno di Toro or Anaheim, so the rings are small.

Make the pickled peppers: Cut off the tip of each pepper, then slice thinly crosswise with a vegetable slicer. Put the pepper slices and jalapeño in a heatproof bowl. In a small saucepan, combine the vinegar, sugar, and water and bring to a simmer over medium heat, stirring to dissolve the sugar. Pour the hot mixture over the peppers. Let cool, then cover and chill for at least 1 day. The pickled peppers can be made up to 2 weeks ahead.

In a bowl, combine the salmon, strawberries, oil, and lemon zest, season with salt, and toss gently. Taste for salt.

Divide the salmon mixture evenly among twelve Chinese porcelain soupspoons. (Derick uses two small spoons to shape the salmon mixture into neat quenelles, but that's optional.) Top each portion with a cucumber half-moon and a sweet pepper ring. Garnish each with a chive baton. Serve immediately.

chef's tips:

Immersing shaved watermelon radishes in ice water helps them stay crisp.

For long keeping, wrap fresh herbs in a moist paper towel and refrigerate in a lidded container.

Heirloom Tomato and Peach Salad with Burrata

Serves 6

Pickled Red Onion:

½ cup sugar

½ cup white wine vinegar

½ cup water

½ red onion, ends removed, thinly sliced from stem to
    root end

2 large or 3 small yellow peaches, halved, pitted, and cut
    into wedges

3 tomatoes, preferably a mix of colors, cut into wedges

1 tablespoon extra virgin olive oil, plus more for the cheese

Sea salt and freshly ground black pepper

1 small watermelon radish, thickly peeled, then halved
    and thinly shaved

½ pound burrata cheese, drained, at room temperature

1 lemon cucumber or Persian cucumber, peeled if desired,
    then thinly shaved

Carr's Ciderhouse Cider Syrup, for drizzling

1 bunch watercress, upland cress, or peppercress,
    thick stems removed

Wine: B Cellars Blend 23

*This gorgeous summer salad is always a riot of color but never exactly
the same, says Derick. Depending on what's coming out of the garden,
he may change up the tomatoes, or the type of cucumber, or the way he
arranges the components. Sometimes he uses microgreens in place of
the cress or adds Spanish black radishes from the garden. "I have fifty
pictures of these salads and no two are identical," says the chef.*

Make the pickled red onion: In a small saucepan, combine the sugar,
vinegar, and water and bring to a simmer over medium-high heat,
swirling the pan to dissolve the sugar. When the sugar has dissolved,
remove from the heat and let cool completely. Put the onion slices into
a bowl and pour the cooled liquid over them. Cover and refrigerate for
at least 24 hours.

Put the peach and tomato wedges on a platter. Drizzle with the
oil and season with salt and pepper. Let stand for 30 to 45 minutes to
absorb the seasonings.

Put the shaved radish into a bowl with ice water to cover and let
stand for about 30 minutes to crisp.

Divide the burrata into 6 equal slices and put 1 slice on the
center of each of six salad plates. Season each slice with salt and pepper
and a few drops of olive oil. Surround with the peach and tomato
wedges and the cucumber. Drain the radishes, pat dry, and add them
to the plates, scattering them attractively. Place slivers of pickled onion
here and there. Drizzle each portion with about ½ teaspoon cider
syrup. (A squeeze bottle is helpful.) Garnish each serving with tufts of
cress. Serve immediately.

Seared Sea Scallops with Parsnips Two Ways

Serves 6

6 small Chioggia beets, greens removed

½ cup sugar

½ cup white wine vinegar

½ cup water

2 parsnips, about ¾ pound total, peeled

Sea salt

Canola oil, for deep-frying

Vinaigrette:

1 small navel orange

1 lemon

1 lime

¼ cup apple cider vinegar

1 teaspoon sea salt

1 tablespoon honey

1 vanilla bean

1 cup extra virgin olive oil

1 cup canola oil

½ cup raw hazelnuts

2 small navel oranges

12 sea scallops, feet removed

1 tablespoon B Cellars Blend 7 (see Note)

2 tablespoons extra virgin olive oil

3 small heads frisée, pale inner hearts only

Wine: B Cellars Chardonnay

This complex dish demonstrates how Derick approaches the challenge of creating "bites" that heighten the wine experience. Buttery scallops and hazelnuts are classic with Chardonnay, but B Cellars' Chardonnay shows more bright citrus fruit and acidity than many. Weaving citrus into the dish helps highlight those qualities. The fruit, beets, and parsnips all come from the property, and this dish always makes new fans for the humble parsnip.

Put the beets into a saucepan with lightly salted water to cover and bring to a simmer over medium heat. Adjust the heat to maintain a simmer and cook uncovered until the beets can be pierced easily, about 30 minutes. Drain. When cool enough to handle, peel the beets and put them into a small, heatproof bowl.

In a small saucepan, combine the sugar, vinegar, and water and bring to a simmer over medium-high heat, swirling the pan to dissolve the sugar. When the sugar has dissolved, remove from the heat and pour over the beets. Let cool to room temperature, then cover and refrigerate for 24 hours.

With a vegetable peeler, shave the parsnips lengthwise into ribbons. Stop when you have used about half of each parsnip and set the ribbons aside. Cut the remaining half of each parsnip into ¾-inch pieces and put them into a saucepan with lightly salted water to cover. Bring to a simmer over medium heat, then adjust the heat to maintain a simmer and cook until the parsnips are tender when pierced, about 15 minutes. Drain, reserving the cooking liquid. In a blender, puree the parsnips with enough of the reserved cooking liquid to make a silky puree. Season with salt.

Pour canola oil to a depth of 3 inches into a heavy saucepan and heat to 340°F. Add the parsnip ribbons and fry, agitating them constantly, until golden, about 2 minutes. With a wire-mesh skimmer, lift them out and drain on paper towels. Season with salt.

Make the vinaigrette: With a rasp grater, remove the zest from the orange, lemon, and lime. Cut all the citrus in half, then squeeze the juice and strain. Combine the juices and zests in the blender with

the vinegar and add the salt and honey. Halve the vanilla bean lengthwise and, with the tip of a small knife, scrape the seeds into the blender. Blend briefly. With the blender running, add the oils slowly. Taste for salt.

Preheat the oven to 350°F. Toast the hazelnuts on a baking sheet until fragrant and lightly colored, about 10 minutes. Let cool, then chop coarsely.

Cut a thin slice off both ends of 1 orange so it will stand upright. Stand the orange on a cutting surface and, using a sharp knife, remove all the peel and white pith by slicing from top to bottom all the way around the orange, following the contour of the fruit. Cut along the membranes to release the individual segments and place them in a bowl. Repeat with the second orange.

Season the scallops on both sides with the Blend 7. Heat two large skillets over medium-high heat. Add 1 tablespoon of the olive oil to each skillet. When the oil is hot, add the scallops and sear until lightly browned on the bottom, about 1 minute. Turn and cook the other flat side until nicely colored, about 1 minute, then reduce the heat and continue cooking until the scallops are just barely cooked at the center, about 2 minutes longer.

Spoon about 1½ tablespoons of the parsnip puree onto each of six salad plates and spread it thinly. Scatter the hazelnuts around the rim of each plate. Toss the frisée with just enough of the vinaigrette to coat it lightly. Arrange a tuft of frisée on the parsnip puree on each plate, then nestle 2 scallops alongside the frisée. Quarter the beets and scatter them and the orange segments attractively around each salad. Place the fried parsnips on top and serve immediately.

Note: *B Cellars Blend 7 is a proprietary spice mix that includes dried thyme, orange peel, onion, lemon verbena, Espelette pepper, sugar, and salt. It is available for purchase in the winery's tasting room. Alternatively, use salt and pepper only or create your own blend using some or all of the listed spices to your taste.*

Elk Sugo with Herb Cheese Tortellini and Kale Chips

Serves 6

Derick buys elk from a Montana farm, but you can order it from a good butcher. The meat is dark, deeply flavorful, and lean. Substitute beef top or bottom round or lamb shoulder, if you prefer. For sugo (Italian for "meat sauce"), the elk is always braised slowly with diced garden vegetables, and the flavor improves overnight. If making tortellini seems daunting, substitute store-bought pappardelle.

Elk Sugo:

2 pounds boneless elk sirloin, in ¾-inch dice

2 tablespoons B Cellars Blend 8 (see Note)

¼ cup extra virgin olive oil

1 large yellow onion, in ½-inch dice

1 large carrot, in ½-inch dice

3 large celery ribs, in ½-inch dice

1 medium fennel bulb, in ½-inch dice

10 cloves garlic, chopped

1 cup dry red wine

4 cups diced Roma tomatoes (no need to peel)

1 bay leaf

½ teaspoon chile flakes, or to taste

1 cup chicken broth or water

Sea salt and freshly ground black pepper

Tortellini Dough:

2 large whole eggs plus 4 large egg yolks

1 tablespoon extra virgin olive oil

1 tablespoon water

2 cups Italian "00" flour

¾ teaspoon sea salt

Tortellini Filling:

½ pound whole-milk ricotta cheese (about 1 cup)

¼ cup grated Parmigiano-Reggiano cheese

2 tablespoons chopped fresh flat-leaf parsley

1 tablespoon chopped fresh sage

¼ teaspoon freshly ground black pepper

Sea salt

Fine semolina, for dusting

1 whole egg beaten with 1 teaspoon water, for egg wash

Kale Chips:

Canola oil, for deep-frying

¼ pound Tuscan kale (½ bunch), ribs removed

Sea salt

Extra virgin olive oil, for drizzling

_____

Wine: B Cellars Blend 24

_____

Make the elk *sugo*: Season the elk all over with the Blend 8. Let stand at room temperature for 1 hour.

In a large, heavy pot, heat the olive oil over high heat. Add the elk and sear without stirring for about 2 minutes. Stir briefly and continue searing the meat on all sides, stirring as little as possible to avoid drawing out the meat juices. It will take 5 to 10 minutes to sear the elk properly. Reduce the heat as needed to prevent burning.

Add the onion, carrot, celery, and fennel and cook over medium heat, stirring, for about 5 minutes to soften the vegetables. Add the garlic and cook, stirring, until fragrant, about 2 minutes. Add the wine and simmer until reduced by half. Add the tomatoes, bay leaf, chile flakes, and broth, then season with salt and pepper. Bring to a simmer, adjust the heat to maintain a gentle simmer, and cook uncovered until the meat is tender, about 1 hour. Remove the bay leaf. Taste for seasoning. You can prepare the *sugo* up to 1 day ahead and refrigerate.

Make the tortellini dough: In a bowl, whisk together the eggs, egg yolks, olive oil, and water.

In another bowl, whisk together the flour and salt. Transfer the flour to a work surface and make a well in the center large enough to contain the eggs. Make sure the flour "walls" are high enough to keep the eggs from escaping. Pour the egg mixture into the well. With a fork, begin drawing in the flour from the sides and whisking it with the eggs. Take care not to let the runny eggs breach the flour walls. When the dough becomes too stiff to mix with the fork, continue with your hands, kneading until you have incorporated all the flour and the dough is smooth and elastic. Divide the dough into 4 equal portions, shape each portion into a ball, flatten slightly, and wrap in plastic wrap. Let rest for 1 hour at room temperature.

Make the tortellini filling: In a bowl, combine the cheeses, parsley, sage, and pepper and mix with a wooden spoon until blended. Season to taste with salt.

To shape the tortellini, line a baking sheet with parchment paper and dust the parchment with semolina. Set up a pasta machine. Work with 1 dough portion at a time and keep the others covered with plastic wrap or a dish towel to prevent drying.

With a rolling pin, flatten the dough into a rectangle thin enough to pass through the pasta machine set at the widest setting. Pass the dough through the rollers twice at the widest setting, then continue passing it through the rollers, tightening the rollers by one setting each time, until the dough is as thin as you can manage. (Derick flattens the dough through setting #7 on his machine.)

Lay the flattened dough sheet on a work surface and cut into rounds with a 3¾-inch cutter. Put 1 rounded tablespoon of the filling on the center of each round. Brush the edge of a round lightly with egg wash, then fold the round into a half-moon, pressing the edges to seal. With the straight edge facing you, grasp the two ends, bring them together, and pinch to secure, brushing with a little egg wash if needed to help them seal. Place the tortellino on the prepared pan and repeat with the remaining filling-topped rounds and then the remaining dough and filling. You should have 18 to 20 tortellini. Let them dry uncovered at room temperature for about 30 minutes before cooking them.

While the tortellini rest, make the kale chips: Pour canola oil to a depth of 3 inches in a deep saucepan and heat to 340°F. Cut the kale crosswise into 2-inch-wide pieces. Dry thoroughly. Working in small batches, add the kale to the hot oil (be careful, as the oil can pop) and fry, agitating constantly, until the kale crisps, about 2 minutes. With a wire-mesh skimmer, lift out the chips and drain on paper towels. Sprinkle with salt while warm.

At serving time, reheat the elk *sugo* if necessary. Bring a large pot of salted water to a boil over high heat. Add the tortellini and cook at a gentle simmer, until they float and the pasta is fully cooked, about 2 minutes. (Lift one out and taste a bit of the pasta to be sure.) With the skimmer, lift them out into a bowl and drizzle lightly with olive oil.

Divide the *sugo* among six pasta bowls. Arrange 3 tortellini around the *sugo* in each bowl. Perch kale chips on top of the *sugo* to garnish. Serve immediately.

Note: *B Cellars Blend 8 is a proprietary spice mix that includes salt, ginger, onion, garlic, black pepper, rosemary, oregano, and chile. It is available for purchase in the winery's tasting room. Alternatively, use salt and pepper only or create your own blend using some or all of the listed spices to your taste.*

Dijon-Crusted Lamb Chops with Pistachio Puree, Chard, and Huckleberry Gastrique

Serves 6

Huckleberries are one of Derick's favorite crops from the B Cellars estate. They ripen in late summer but freeze well. He often uses them in dishes to complement the winery's Cabernet Sauvignon, which typically has a huckleberry scent. The tiny marble potatoes, chard, and garlic for this recipe also come straight from the winery garden. Garlic oil and garlic confit are part of Derick's toolbox at the winery and at home. He spreads the confit on crackers ("it's like candy") and uses the aromatic oil on vegetables.

Garlic Confit:

¼ cup peeled whole garlic cloves

1 cup extra virgin olive oil (or part canola oil, if desired)

Pistachio Puree:

½ cup raw pistachios

½ cup whole milk

½ cup water

¼ cup coarsely chopped fresh flat-leaf parsley

1 tablespoon coarsely chopped fresh tarragon

1 teaspoon Banyuls or sherry vinegar

¼ teaspoon sea salt

Huckleberry Gastrique:

½ cup huckleberries, thawed if frozen

2 cups dry red wine

3 tablespoons sugar

2 tablespoons Banyuls or sherry vinegar

½ teaspoon sea salt

2 tablespoons Dijon mustard

2 tablespoons B Cellars Blend 9 (see Note)

2 tablespoons extra virgin olive oil

12 lamb rib chops, about 1 inch thick

1 pound marble potatoes, about 1 inch in diameter

2 tablespoons extra virgin olive oil

Chard:

2 small bunches chard, ribs removed

1 large shallot, ends removed, then halved lengthwise and thinly julienned lengthwise

1 cup dry red wine

2 tablespoons extra virgin olive oil

Sea salt and freshly ground black pepper

1 cup panko (Japanese-style bread crumbs)

½ cup canola oil

Wine: B Cellars Cabernet Sauvignon

(continued)

Dijon-Crusted Lamb Chops with Pistachio Puree and Huckleberry Gastrique *(continued)*

Make the garlic confit: In a small saucepan, combine the garlic cloves and olive oil and bring to a simmer over medium-high heat. Reduce the heat to maintain a gentle simmer and cook uncovered until the cloves are tender and just starting to color, 10 to 15 minutes. Drain the garlic, reserving both the cloves and the garlic oil. The oil will keep refrigerated for weeks. The garlic will keep refrigerated for up to 1 week.

Make the pistachio puree: In a small saucepan, combine the pistachios, milk, and water and bring to a simmer over medium-high heat. Reduce the heat to maintain a gentle simmer and cook uncovered until the nuts are tender, about 15 minutes. Let the mixture cool to room temperature.

In a blender, combine the pistachios and any liquid in the pot, the parsley, tarragon, vinegar, and salt and blend until smooth. Taste for salt.

Make the huckleberry gastrique: In a small saucepan, combine the huckleberries, wine, sugar, vinegar, and salt and bring to a simmer over medium heat. Simmer until reduced to a scant 1 cup. Let cool slightly.

In a small bowl, stir together the mustard, Blend 9, and olive oil to make a paste. Slather the paste on both sides of each lamb chop. Set the chops on a platter and let rest at room temperature for 45 minutes.

Preheat the oven to 375°F or 350°F with a convection fan. Put the potatoes on a baking sheet and toss with the olive oil. Bake until tender when pierced, about 15 minutes. Let cool on the pan, then smack the potatoes with your palm or the back of a plate until they split. Season to taste with salt. Drizzle with 1 tablespoon of the garlic oil and toss gently to coat. Scatter the cooked garlic cloves all around the potatoes. Leave the oven on.

Meanwhile, prepare the chard: Stack the chard leaves in batches and cut crosswise into thirds or quarters. You should have about 2 quarts loosely packed. In a small skillet, combine the shallot and wine and bring to a simmer over medium heat. Simmer until the wine has evaporated completely, about 15 minutes.

At serving time: Return the potatoes to the oven until they are lightly crisped, about 10 minutes.

To finish the chard, heat a large skillet over high heat. Add the olive oil, then add the red wine–cooked shallots and stir for about 30 seconds. Add the chard, season with salt and pepper, and cook, tossing with tongs, until the chard has wilted and softened but is not fully tender, about 2 minutes. Keep warm.

Coat the lamb chops on both sides with the panko. Heat two large skillets over medium-high heat until very hot. Add ¼ cup of the canola oil to each skillet. When the oil is hot, add the lamb chops, dividing them evenly between the skillets, and sear on one side until the panko is browned, about 2 minutes. Turn and transfer the skillet to the oven. For medium-rare, cook the chops until they are somewhat firm to the touch but still have some give, about 5 minutes.

To serve, put about 1½ tablespoons pistachio puree on each of six dinner plates and spread it thinly. Divide the chard and potatoes among the plates. Arrange 2 lamb chops artfully on each plate. Drizzle the huckleberry gastrique around the edge of each plate. Serve immediately.

Note: *B Cellars Blend 9 is a proprietary spice mix that includes coriander, cinnamon, cumin, pepper, rosemary, salt, garlic, thyme, and chile. It is available for purchase in the winery's tasting room. Alternatively, use salt and pepper only or create your own blend using some or all of the listed spices to your taste.*

uncommon edibles:

B Cellars chef Derick Kuntz likes to grow produce he can't easily buy. Here are a few top performers in the B Cellars garden.

Espelette pepper: This French red pepper is usually dried and ground for a spice; it resembles hot paprika but is less earthy.

Finger lime: The green-skinned fruit looks like a tiny cucumber. Inside are hundreds of pale, sweet-tart caviar-like beads that pop in the mouth.

Hibiscus: Known as *jamaica* in Spanish, this plant (*Hibiscus sabdariffa*) produces beautiful red blossoms. The petals can be dried and then steeped for a tart tea, served hot or cold.

Huckleberry: Similar to blueberries, huckleberries are crunchier, seedier, and more intense in flavor.

Kalette: A cross between kale and Brussels sprouts, this new hybrid produces leafy green and violet florets.

Pineapple guava: Also known as *feijoa*, this lovely shrub yields egg-shaped fruits with juicy, sweet-tart flesh and a pineapple-like flavor.

Right: *Huckleberries thrive in the B Cellars winery garden.*

Beringer Vineyards: *A Sensory Teaching Garden*

St. Helena

One of the most visited wineries in Napa Valley, Beringer Vineyards enchants guests with its historic nineteenth-century architecture and expansive, shady grounds. The winery was the first in the valley to offer public tours, laying the foundation for the polished hospitality offerings at Napa Valley wineries today. Yet many who make a beeline for the Beringer tasting room, drawn by the renown of its wines (its Cabernet Sauvignon and Private Reserve Chardonnay are California standard bearers), miss the experience of discovering its handsome landscape and gardens.

People with time for a more leisurely visit can enjoy an hour-long Taste of Beringer tour, which includes a guided stroll through the winery's sensory garden. Located behind the Rhine House, the seventeen-room mansion that is the centerpiece of the property and former home of cofounder Frederick Beringer, the sensory garden is a verdant teaching venue for people who want to deepen their perception of wine. Beringer's wine educators consider it a scratch-and-sniff playground, a compendium of smells and textures that helps them make wine components more vivid for guests.

Left and above: *(clockwise from bottom left) Fresh tarragon; winery entrance; garden haul; Beringer's sensory garden plantings replicate some of the aromas found in wine; the property's 19th-century Rhine House is a Napa Valley historic landmark.*

Devoted primarily to scented and edible plants that echo the aromas and sensations of wine, the garden allows Beringer's wine educators to make sensory connections for visitors that are harder to convey in the tasting room. Tannins in particular can be challenging to explain. A winemaker might describe tannin as bitter or astringent, or contributing a rough, sandpaper texture. Yet Merlot has soft, velvety tannins, similar to the velour-like feel of a sage leaf, a correlation that Beringer's hosts can highlight in the garden.

Strawberries thrive in small, sunny patches in the sensory garden, along with blueberries, kumquats, pomelos, blood oranges, Valencia and navel oranges, Asian pears, and pomegranates. Depending on what's blossoming or bearing fruit, hosts can open an appropriate wine and help guests understand what wine experts mean when they describe a red wine as smelling of red fruits, black fruits, or blue fruits.

Many of Beringer's white wines have vibrant citrus notes. In the garden, guides can parse that scent more finely, pointing out the subtle differences between lemon verbena, lemon pith, lemon blossom, or Meyer lemon with its sweetness. Beringer's ambition for the sensory garden was to help guests connect more easily with the aromas in wine given that the senses of taste and smell are so closely linked.

The sensory garden's plantings of rosemary, mint, lavender, and fennel provide other opportunities for Beringer wine educators to help guests plumb the depths of aromas in their wineglass. Cabernet Sauvignon, especially from mountain-grown fruit, often exhibits the anise scent of fresh fennel. For many visitors, a whiff of fresh rosemary warmed by the summer sun elicits memories of grilled meat, an association that clears a path to Cabernet Sauvignon or Cabernet Franc. Chocolate mint speaks to the richer red wines in the Beringer portfolio, such as the Merlot, which has deep mocha notes.

These exercises in aromatic discernment help guests become more comfortable with describing fine wine and, perhaps, more confident about wine and food pairing. Beringer patrons fortunate enough to dine at the winery's Hudson House—a special-event venue—can experience these principles put into practice by the culinary team.

The gracious Hudson House, the historic home of Jacob Beringer, Frederick's younger brother and winery cofounder, dates from about 1850. Originally, it stood where the Rhine House is today. But Frederick coveted that site for his own home, so he had the Hudson House moved two hundred feet north in 1883. For a decade, beginning in 1990, the Hudson House hosted the School for American Chefs, a rigorous two-week training session for professional chefs overseen by the eminent French cooking teacher Madeleine Kamman. Today, the

updated Hudson House hosts many VIP guests for lunch and dinner, with the culinary team drawing ingredients and inspiration from a small culinary garden at the rear of the house.

This almost-secret nook consists of several curved beds arranged in a circular pattern around a central fountain. Tuteurs and wire trellises for pole beans and tomatoes give the design some verticality, while large terra-cotta pots filled with rosemary topiary, bushy mint, and silvery curry leaf add texture. Clusters of marigolds provide pest protection, lavender chive blossoms dance in the breeze, and lush, burgundy-hued opal basil tempts visitors to snitch a fragrant sprig. Paths of decomposed granite separate the planting beds, the coarse material crunching underfoot as cooks harvest zucchini, cucumbers, eggplants, and sweet peppers and snip culinary herbs.

Above: *(clockwise from left) Culinary program manager Gina Baldridge harvests vegetables; magnificent walnut tree; classical garden statue; harvesting navel oranges from the winery citrus grove; ripening tomatoes; snipping fragrant lemon verbena*

Beringer's wine educators view the sensory garden as a scratch-and-sniff playground, a compendium of smells and textures that help them make wine components more vivid for guests.

The adjacent outdoor kitchen sees action in good weather, but the primary kitchen, inside the Hudson House, produces most of the wine-driven, garden-based cooking that defines Beringer's entertaining. In spring, when the first few fava beans land in the kitchen, a meal at the Hudson House might begin with a glass of steely Sauvignon Blanc and crostini topped with white beans and fava bean pesto—a clever way to celebrate favas when the garden has delivered only a handful. The winery's navel oranges peak in sweetness in spring, prompting the kitchen to prepare a gazpacho of golden beets, olive oil, and orange juice. Edible spring flowers make a delicate garnish.

An elaborate salad of roasted carrots, sugar snap peas, baby greens, and garden herbs features two creamy dressings, a composition

Above and right: *(clockwise from lower left) Garden blueberries work well in dishes paired with Beringer Vineyards Merlot; Hudson House; Hudson House interior; Beringer's wines echo the aromas and flavors found in its gardens; garden stairway*

that welcomes the lushness of the Private Reserve Chardonnay. With pomegranate-glazed lamb chops, a slam-dunk choice for Beringer's concentrated Cabernet Sauvignon, the kitchen pairs couscous sweetened with finely diced garden vegetables.

Dessert can be a challenging course at wineries that don't produce sweet wines, but Beringer has no such problem. Its much-admired Nightingale, a Sauternes-inspired dessert wine from Sémillon and Sauvignon Blanc, brings meals to a memorable close all by itself, but the culinary team has developed a German honey-spice cake to match it and honor the winery's German heritage. Served with oranges from the estate and orange-scented mascarpone, the dessert heightens the honey and tangerine notes in this luscious wine.

"Scent is associated with our deepest memories," says Ryan Chernick, Beringer's premium experiences manager. "In the garden, and in our wines, we help people reconnect with scent and the long-ago experiences we still carry with us."

pairing help from the garden:

Many of the flavors in garden produce can create a bridge between a dish and a wine or amplify the character of a wine, creating a pairing that soars. Beringer's Wine Education Team has a few favorite affinities.

Sauvignon Blanc: Consider adding peaches, apricots, or citrus, especially pomelo, to the dish. Chervil is a compatible herb, and this variety is the go-to wine for asparagus.

Chardonnay: If the wine has been through malolactic fermentation, it will have a rounder, creamier mouthfeel, compatible with buttery apples and pears. Barrel-fermented or barrel-aged Chardonnay will have toasty notes; look to grilled onions or shallots for a flavor bridge. Lemon, lemon basil, citrus blossoms, and tarragon are other complementary scents with this variety.

Pinot Noir: Raspberries, strawberries, and pomegranates speak to the red fruit in Pinot Noir. Consider a pairing with roast duck and raspberries, or roast lamb with a pomegranate glaze. Thyme and lavender are also compatible with this variety.

Merlot: Blueberries can find an aromatic echo in Merlot. Add blueberries to a pan sauce for roast chicken or to a garden greens salad with shredded rotisserie chicken.

Cabernet Sauvignon: Rosemary, fennel, and chocolate mint hint at aromas found in this variety. Top a rib-eye steak with rosemary butter.

Zinfandel: Beringer's fig trees also create pairing opportunities for the winery's culinary team, as several of the winery's red wines exhibit hints of fig. Consider serving Zinfandel with a main course of grilled pork and figs.

menu

Crostini with White Bean Puree and
Fava Bean Pesto

Beringer Vineyards Sauvignon Blanc

Spring Lettuces with Sugar Snap Peas and
Roasted Carrots

**Beringer Vineyards Private Reserve
Chardonnay**

Golden Beet Gazpacho

Beringer Vineyards Luminus Chardonnay

Lamb Rib Chops with Garden-Vegetable Couscous

**Beringer Vineyards Cabernet Sauvignon
Reserve Knights Valley**

German Honey Cake with Orange Mascarpone

Beringer Vineyards Nightingale

Crostini with White Bean Puree and Fava Bean Pesto **Serves 4**

This recipe yields more bean puree and fava bean pesto than you need, but you'll be glad for that. Serve the white bean puree with roast leg of lamb or salmon or as a sandwich spread. Use the pesto on pasta or pizza.

White Bean Puree:

1 cup dried cannellini or other white beans, soaked overnight in water to cover

2 cups chicken broth

2 garlic cloves, peeled

¼ yellow onion

2 fresh thyme sprigs

2 fresh flat-leaf parsley sprigs

2 bay leaves

1 teaspoon black peppercorns

1 cup pure olive oil (not extra virgin)

Sea salt

Fava Bean Pesto:

½ cup fully cooked peeled fava beans

¼ cup freshly grated Parmigiano-Reggiano cheese

20 large fresh basil leaves

1 tablespoon fresh oregano leaves

2 tablespoons pine nuts

¼ cup pure olive oil (not extra virgin)

Sea salt

8 baguette slices, each cut on the diagonal ¼ inch thick

Extra virgin olive oil, for brushing

Fleur de sel

Fresh fava bean blossoms or rosemary blossoms, for garnish

Wine: Beringer Vineyards Sauvignon Blanc

Make the white bean puree: Drain the soaked beans. Put them into a small saucepan with the broth, garlic, and onion. Tie the herbs and peppercorns in a cheesecloth bag and add to the pan. Bring to a simmer over medium-low heat, adjust the heat to maintain a gentle simmer, and cook, uncovered, until the beans are just tender and have absorbed most of the liquid, 30 minutes or more, depending on their age.

Remove the cheesecloth bag. Transfer the contents of the pan to a food processor and puree until smooth. With the motor running, add the oil slowly through the feed tube, then continue to puree until the mixture is completely smooth, about 5 minutes. Press the puree through a fine-mesh sieve to remove any bean skins. The puree will be fairly thin. Season well with sea salt. You should have about 3 cups. Set aside ¼ cup for the crostini. Pour the remainder into an airtight container, press plastic wrap against the surface of the puree to prevent browning, cover tightly, and refrigerate for up to several days.

Make the fava bean pesto: Put the beans, cheese, basil, oregano, and pine nuts into a food processor and process until nearly smooth. With the motor running, add the oil slowly through the feed tube and process until smooth. Season with sea salt. You will have about ½ cup. Set aside 2 tablespoons plus 2 teaspoons for the crostini. Put the remainder into an airtight container, press plastic wrap against the surface of the puree to prevent browning, cover tightly, and refrigerate for up to 1 day.

Preheat the oven to 350°F. Brush the baguette slices on both sides with oil and season lightly with salt. Arrange in a single layer on a baking sheet and toast until golden brown, 10 to 15 minutes. Let cool.

Top each toast with about 1½ teaspoons bean puree, spreading it to cover most of the toast. Top the bean puree with about 1 teaspoon fava bean pesto. Sprinkle a little fleur de sel on each toast, then garnish with blossoms.

Spring Lettuces with Sugar Snap Peas and Roasted Carrots **Serves 4**

Pickled Onions:

2 yellow onions, halved and sliced

2 cups water

1 cup raspberry vinegar

Quince Raspberry Dressing:

1 cup raspberries

¼ cup quince paste

2 tablespoons raspberry or apple cider vinegar

1½ teaspoons whole-grain Dijon mustard

½ cup canola or grapeseed oil

Yogurt Tahini Sauce:

½ cup full-fat plain Greek yogurt

¼ cup tahini

Grated zest of ½ lemon

8 slender, young carrots, preferably a mix of colors, peeled

Canola oil, for coating

1 tablespoon za'atar

Sea salt

12 sugar snap peas, trimmed

1 small handful microgreens

12 fresh tarragon or chervil leaves

¼ pound mixed baby salad greens

12 raspberries

4 teaspoons minced fresh herbs (mint, basil, and flat-leaf parsley)

Pansies or other edible flowers, for garnish

Wine: Beringer Vineyards Private Reserve Chardonnay

In spring, the Beringer garden yields big harvests of leafy greens, tender herbs, sugar snap peas, and sweet baby carrots. The winery's culinary team unites them in this pretty salad with two different dressings. Note that you need to pickle the onions at least 1 day ahead.

Make the pickled onions: Put the onions into a heatproof bowl. In a saucepan, combine the water and vinegar and bring to a boil over high heat. Pour the hot liquid over the onions. Let cool, then cover and refrigerate overnight before using. The onions will keep for weeks.

Make the quince raspberry dressing: In a food processor, combine the raspberries, quince paste, vinegar, and mustard and blend until smooth. With the motor running, add the oil through the feed tube. Blend until smooth.

Make the yogurt tahini sauce: In a small bowl, whisk together all the ingredients until smooth.

Preheat the oven to 350°F. Put the carrots into a small baking dish and toss with just enough oil to coat them. Add the za'atar, season with salt, and turn to coat with the seasonings. Cover and bake until tender, about 10 minutes. Let cool.

Bring a small pot of salted water to a boil over high heat and prepare a bowl of ice water. Add the sugar snap peas to the boiling water and blanch for about 30 seconds, then drain and immediately transfer to the ice water. When cool, drain, pat dry, and halve crosswise.

To serve, put about 2 tablespoons yogurt tahini sauce on half of each of four salad plates. Spread the sauce into a thin layer with the back of a spoon but keep it confined to half of the plate. Top the sauce on each plate with 2 carrots, a tuft of microgreens, and 3 tarragon or chervil leaves.

Lift about one-fourth of the pickled onions out of the pickling liquid and place them in a bowl. Add the salad greens and just enough of the quince raspberry dressing to coat them lightly. Toss gently, then season with salt. Divide among the four plates, placing the greens on the uncovered half of the plate. Top with the sugar snap peas and raspberries. Put 1 teaspoon minced herbs on top of each salad. Garnish each plate with pansies.

Golden Beet Gazpacho

Serves 6

3 extra-large golden beets, greens and any roots removed

1 cup extra virgin olive oil, plus more for coating beets and garnish

½ yellow onion, in 2 pieces

2 bay leaves

4 cloves garlic, peeled

Stems from 1 bunch fresh flat-leaf parsley

½ bunch fresh thyme

1 tablespoon black peppercorns

Sea salt

1½ cups water

2 navel oranges

Fleur de sel

Fresh micro cilantro or finely sliced cilantro, for garnish

Pansies, violas, or other edible flowers, for garnish

Wine: Beringer Vineyards Luminus Chardonnay

---

chef's tip:

Save the nutrient-packed beet greens and boil or steam them, then cool and squeeze dry. Reheat with olive oil and minced garlic and serve with feta.

Citrus trees of several types grace the grounds at Beringer Vineyards. When the navel oranges and golden beets overlap in spring, Beringer's culinary team uses them both in this silky, sunflower-colored soup. You can serve the soup chilled or at room temperature.

Preheat the oven to 350°F. Coat the beets lightly with oil, then put them into a baking dish with the onion, bay leaves, garlic, parsley, thyme, peppercorns, 1 teaspoon sea salt, and ½ cup of the water. Cover tightly and bake until the beets are tender when pierced, 45 minutes or more, depending on size. Peel the beets while warm and cut into quarters. Strain the juices in the baking dish and reserve.

Cut a slice off both ends of each orange. Stand each orange on a cutting surface and remove all the peel and white pith by slicing from top to bottom all the way around the orange, following the contour of the fruit. Quarter each peeled orange.

Put the beets, oranges, and strained juices into a blender and blend well. With the blender running, add the oil and the remaining 1 cup water through the opening in the blender lid and blend until smooth. Strain through a fine-mesh sieve, then season with sea salt.

Divide the soup among six bowls. Top each serving with a pinch of fleur de sel and a drizzle of oil. Garnish with cilantro and flowers.

Lamb Rib Chops with Garden-Vegetable Couscous

Serves 4

Lamb Chops:

1 tablespoon plus 1 teaspoon extra virgin olive oil

1 tablespoon plus 1 teaspoon canola oil

1 tablespoon plus 1 teaspoon pomegranate molasses

1 yellow onion, halved and sliced

4 cloves garlic, thinly sliced

Leaves from 3 fresh thyme sprigs

Leaves from 3 fresh flat-leaf parsley sprigs

1 teaspoon sea salt

½ teaspoon sumac

½ teaspoon ras el hanout

½ teaspoon za'atar

8 lamb rib chops, preferably not frenched

Couscous:

2½ tablespoons extra virgin olive oil

1 yellow onion, chopped

1 red onion, chopped

½ teaspoons ras el hanout

1 tablespoon Garlic Confit (recipe follows), mashed to a paste

½ cup golden raisins

1 cup pearl couscous

1⅓ cups chicken broth, heated

1 small carrot, peeled, in ¼-inch dice

1 parsnip, peeled, in ¼-inch dice

1 small zucchini, in ¼-inch dice

1 small crookneck yellow squash, in ¼-inch dice

In late spring, Beringer's culinary team harvests tender baby vegetables from the winery garden for this refined version of couscous. The recipe uses pearl couscous (sometimes called Israeli couscous), which is larger than the familiar North African pasta, and the kitchen team cooks it separately from the lamb. Pomegranate molasses in the marinade gives the lamb chops a subtle sweetness and a beautiful sheen.

1 medium Yukon Gold potato, peeled, in ¼-inch dice

1 teaspoon pomegranate molasses

1 tablespoon finely minced mixed fresh herbs (mint, basil, and flat-leaf parsley)

Sea salt

¼ cup sliced almonds, toasted

Wine: Beringer Vineyards Cabernet Sauvignon Reserve Knights Valley

---

Marinate the lamb: In a large bowl, mix together the oils, pomegranate molasses, onion, garlic, thyme, parsley, salt, sumac, ras el hanout, and za'atar. Add the lamb and toss to coat evenly with the seasonings. Cover and refrigerate for at least 2 hours or up to 24 hours, turning occasionally to redistribute the seasonings. Bring to room temperature before cooking.

Prepare the couscous: Heat 1 tablespoon of the oil in a saucepan over medium heat. Add half each of the yellow onion and red onion and all the ras el hanout and sauté until the onions soften, about 5 minutes. Add the garlic and raisins and sauté, stirring, for about 1 minute. Add the couscous and cook, stirring, for about 2 minutes to toast it. Pour in the broth, bring to a simmer, cover, reduce the heat to low, and cook until the liquid is absorbed, about 15 minutes. Set aside to rest.

Bring a small pot of salted water to a boil over high heat and prepare a bowl of ice water. Add the carrot to the boiling water and cook for 30 seconds, then drain and immediately transfer to the ice water. When cool, drain again.

Warm the remaining 1½ tablespoons oil in a skillet over medium heat. Add the remaining yellow and red onion and sauté until softened, about 5 minutes. Add the parsnip, zucchini, yellow squash, and potato and sauté until the vegetables are tender and almost caramelized, about 10 minutes. Stir in the carrots and cook until they are hot, about 1 minute. Keep warm.

Preheat the oven to 325°F. Heat a heavy ovenproof skillet large enough to hold all the chops and warm it over medium-high heat. (Use two skillets if necessary.) When hot, add the chops and sear on both sides, about 1 minute per side, adjusting the heat to prevent smoking or burning. Transfer the skillet to the oven and roast until the lamb is done to your taste, about 5 minutes for medium.

Transfer the couscous to a bowl and fluff with a fork. Add the sautéed vegetables, pomegranate molasses, and mixed herbs and fluff with a fork. Season with salt.

Divide the couscous among four plates. Scatter the almonds over the couscous then top each portion with 2 chops.

Garlic Confit
Makes about ½ cup

12 large garlic cloves, peeled
½ cup vegetable oil

In a small saucepan, combine the garlic cloves with vegetable oil to cover. Cook over low heat until the cloves are soft but not colored, about 20 minutes. (Use a flame tamer if necessary to keep the cloves from browning.) Let cool, then refrigerate in a covered container for up to 1 week.

German Honey Cake with Orange Mascarpone

Serves 12

Nonstick cooking spray, for the pan

2 cups all-purpose flour

2 teaspoons baking powder

2 teaspoons sea salt

1 teaspoon ground cloves

1 teaspoon ground allspice

1 teaspoon ground ginger

2 oranges

4 large eggs

1 cup honey, plus more for drizzling

½ teaspoon orange blossom water

Orange Mascarpone:

½ cup heavy cream

½ cup powdered sugar

¼ teaspoon orange blossom water

1 cup mascarpone

Wine: Beringer Vineyards Nightingale

To honor Jacob Beringer, the winery's German cofounder, the winery's culinary team developed this cake from an old German recipe. Richly spiced, it contains no fat, so it is almost more like bread than cake. Sweet oranges from the winery's garden moisten the cake, and orange blossom water scents the creamy topping. Beringer's much-admired dessert wine makes the perfect accompaniment.

Preheat the oven to 325°F. Spray an 8-inch round cake pan generously with cooking spray. Line the bottom of the pan with parchment and spray the parchment.

Sift together the flour, baking powder, salt, cloves, allspice, and ginger into a bowl.

Grate the zest of 1 of the oranges directly into the bowl of a stand mixer. Place the bowl on the mixer and fit the mixer with the whisk attachment. Add the eggs and beat on medium speed until well blended. Add the honey and orange blossom water and beat until light. Switch to the paddle attachment and, on low speed, add the flour mixture and mix just until blended. Do not overmix.

Transfer the batter to the prepared pan and spread it evenly. Bake until a cake tester inserted into the center comes out clean, about 45 minutes. Let cool in the pan on a rack for 10 minutes, then invert onto another rack. Lift off the pan, turn the cake right side up, and let cool completely.

Cut a slice off both ends of the zest-free orange so it will stand upright. Stand the orange on a cutting surface and, using a sharp knife, remove all the remaining peel and the white pith by slicing from top to bottom all the way around the orange, following the contour of the fruit. With the knife, cut along both sides of each orange segment to free the segment from its membrane. Put the segments into a small bowl. Repeat with the second orange.

Make the orange mascarpone: In a bowl, whisk together the cream and sugar until soft peaks form. Whisk in the orange blossom water, then whisk in the mascarpone until blended.

To serve, cut the cake into 12 wedges. Transfer to dessert plates and top each slice with a generous dollop of orange mascarpone, 2 orange segments, and a generous drizzle of honey.

Cakebread Cellars: *Farm-to-Table Pioneers*

Rutherford

In 1972, Jack and Dolores Cakebread impulsively bought twenty-two acres of cow pasture in the heart of Napa Valley. They were excited about having a place in the country, a weekend respite from their Oakland home and auto-repair business. They figured they would develop a vineyard and sell the grapes, but one of the first things Dolores did was plant a vegetable garden. An enormous one.

Predictably the two-and-a-half-acre plot produced far more than the Cakebreads and their three boys could manage. Every available family member was recruited to help harvest the Rutherford garden and haul produce back to Oakland in lug boxes. Faced with a deluge of tomatoes and beans, Dolores carved out a pantry under the stairs of their Oakland home. She put her elderly father to work washing and peeling vegetables, and soon the pantry was stocked with enough jars to carry the family through the winter.

"Then we learned that in Napa Valley you can grow a winter garden," recalled Dolores. "So we didn't need any of the canned food."

When the fertile land just kept churning out produce, Dolores converted the property's small pump house into an honor-system farm stand. Soon enough, locals and Napa Valley tourists—there weren't many of either in those days—were veering off the highway to stock up on fresh fruits and vegetables. The property's caretaker teased Dolores that if she and Jack didn't make it in the wine business, he would move the farm stand to the highway and she could make apple pies.

Decades later, Cakebread Cellars is a Napa Valley landmark, its redwood-clad compound—expanded several times—a favorite stop for wine tourists. The vegetable garden has moved a few times to accommodate vineyard development and now measures a sensible three-quarters of an acre, but it remains a key element of the visitor experience and of the family's legendary hospitality.

"The garden is part of our DNA and one of the great perks of working here," says Cakebread Cellars culinary director Brian Streeter, who started in the winery kitchen in 1989, straight out of cooking school, and has never left. A restaurant chef may be tied to the same menu for weeks or months, notes Streeter. His own menu making for Cakebread visitors starts fresh every day, responding to what gardener Marcy Snow has to offer.

Left and above: *Winery chef Brian Streeter returns from the garden with heaped bins of sweet peppers and tomatoes; a tasting plate at the ready for a Cakebread Cellars guest*

For many years, the garden was Dolores's domain. A certified Master Gardener, she decided what to plant every year and doggedly promoted the garden as part of the winery's identity. Today, under Marcy's management, it is colorful, prolific, and welcoming, with neat fir-bark paths and signage to educate unaccompanied guests. "We have small beds and lots of variety so our guests can smell and taste things," says Brian.

Whenever Brian conducts a cooking class or prepares a meal for winery guests, they tour the garden first. "It hits home when people sit down for lunch and find vegetables on the plate they just saw," says the chef. Many have never seen the lacy foliage of an asparagus bed or the garnet-red hibiscus flowers that Mexicans dry, then steep for a sweet-tart tea.

Brian now works closely with Marcy to select the seeds for each season's plantings. Marcy loves the visual showstoppers, such as climbing purple hyacinth beans, towering sunflowers, and the gourds that dangle like baseball bats from an arbor. Brian, of course, wants the basics that define the California kitchen: heirloom tomatoes, purple basil, lemon cucumbers, Tuscan kale. But he also peruses seed catalogs for novelties to jazz up his plates, such as yellow romano beans, toadskin melons, Italian flint corn for polenta, and Mexican gherkins. The collaboration produces a year-round harvest that evolves a bit every year to keep both gardener and chef energized.

Feeling the physical demands of the job, Marcy tried to retire in 2018 but failed. "After six months away, I was so sad," she admits. The

Above: *(clockwise from left) The garden in autumn; dangling kikinda gourds and purple amaranth; red hibiscus for tea; sign designates a Certified Bee Friendly garden; Marcy Snow with purple asparagus; hyacinth beans*

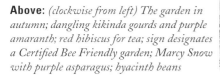

"The garden is part of our DNA and one of the great perks of working here," says culinary director Brian Streeter. "Our menu making for visitors starts fresh every day."

winery welcomed her back part-time, with an assistant to do the heavy lifting, and the indefatigable gardener is once again staking corn, outsmarting voles, and nurturing the lush borders of zinnias, marigolds, and borage that keep bees and beneficial insects on the job. "I'm so happy to be here, you wouldn't believe it," says Marcy. She regularly makes bouquets for employees to brighten their day; when her beds yield more than the kitchen can use, staffers take home the bounty.

With the garden only a short walk from the kitchen, Brian's cooking can be hyper-seasonal, reflecting not just the month but the moment. If Marcy has pulled some perfect baby turnips or radishes, they will find their way onto the plate.

A vegetable garden enables, but it also challenges, demanding flexibility. A supermarket shopper can choose carrots that are all the same size, but at Cakebread, the day's harvest may include a few baby carrots and some bigger ones, a handful of early fava beans and asparagus spears, the first spring garlic, a bunch of tarragon, and a few pounds of peas. Brian's answer to this delivery is likely to be a vivid vegetable medley, merging all these ingredients into a succulent side dish for spring salmon or lamb.

Many vintners ask chefs to steer clear of asparagus and artichokes, two vegetables notorious for challenging wine, but "we're not that kind," said Dolores, who passed away in late 2020. "We can drink wine with almost anything." Roasting artichokes or combining them with other vegetables mitigates their wine-altering impact, says Brian, and

Above: *(clockwise from lower left) Dolores Cakebread harvests sunflowers and purple basil for a colorful arrangement; Brian and Dolores discuss menu ideas; butternut squash are ready for harvest.*

Cakebread's steely Sauvignon Blanc can manage asparagus. When you appreciate vegetables and wine as much as the Cakebreads do, any pairing "don'ts" are easy to sweep aside.

For more than two decades, Brian has volunteered monthly in an elementary school classroom, introducing Napa fourth graders to the pleasures of garden-based cooking. They make tortillas with fresh salsa and learn the cultural origins of different foods. Once a year, the kids come to the winery for a garden tour and lunch. "You'll never see kids as excited about carrots as when they pick them," says Brian.

For a menu designed to showcase the Cakebread garden in full autumn glory, Brian turned to carrots for his opening salvo. Heirloom varieties in multiple colors are sliced and briefly sautéed, then piled on crostini spread with local goat cheese, a delightful match for the winery's Sauvignon Blanc. Cranberry beans—one of the chef's favorite crops—anchor a classic minestrone topped with Tuscan kale pesto, a cool-weather alternative when the basil starts to fade. The orchard at Cakebread's River Ranch vineyard provides buttery pears for a chicory salad with cubes of sweet delicata squash, a composition of contrasting flavors and textures that blossoms with a lush Chardonnay. Thanks to Napa Valley's mild fall weather, Brian can prepare the main course outdoors, first grilling salmon fillets on a cedar plank, then glossing them with a roasted-tomato butter. Red wine with fish? Absolutely. A French prune tree in the orchard contributes fruit for the meal's finale. Brian dries the fresh prunes, plumps them in brandy, and then folds them into homemade coffee ice cream. Sublime.

Cakebread Cellars' eventual success did save Dolores from the pie business, but she still dreamed of relaunching the farm stand. Stocked with fruits and vegetables from the orchard and garden, it would reinforce what the Cakebreads have always advocated: simple cooking, shared meals, good wine. From the beginning, the family's wine country adventure was never just about the wine. "We had to grow vegetables," said Dolores. "You wouldn't buy vegetables when you had this wonderful land to grow them on."

menu

Crostini with Garden Carrots,
Goat Cheese, and Dukkah
Cakebread Cellars Sauvignon Blanc

Autumn Squash, Pear, and Arugula Salad
Cakebread Cellars Chardonnay Reserve

Winter Vegetable and Bean Soup with
Tuscan Kale Pesto
Cakebread Cellars Chardonnay

Cedar Plank Salmon with Roasted-Tomato Butter
**Cakebread Cellars Two Creeks Pinor Noir,
Anderson Valley**

Profiteroles with Coffee Ice Cream,
Armagnac-Soaked Prunes,
and Chocolate-Caramel Sauce

Crostini with Garden Carrots, Goat Cheese, and Dukkah

Serves 6

Rainbow carrots from the Cakebread garden—purple, red, orange, and yellow—display their stunning colors atop these crostini. Dukkah, an Egyptian nut-and-spice blend, is the captivating seasoning that keeps you coming back for just one more toast. You will have leftover dukkah, but that's no problem. Store it in an airtight container and enjoy it later in the classic way, dipping bread first in extra virgin olive oil and then in dukkah. On another occasion, substitute sliced roasted beets or butternut squash for the sautéed carrots.

12 baguette slices, each cut ¼ inch thick on the diagonal

Extra virgin olive oil

Dukkah:

¼ cup chopped raw pecans or raw whole pistachios

1 tablespoon sesame seeds

1 tablespoon coriander seeds

1½ teaspoon cumin seeds

½ teaspoon sea salt

Freshly ground black pepper

¼ pound small carrots, preferably a mix of colors, scrubbed but not peeled

1 tablespoon extra virgin olive oil

¾ cup fresh rindless goat cheese, at room temperature

1 tablespoon thinly sliced fresh chives

Honey, warmed enough to drizzle

Wine: Cakebread Cellars Sauvignon Blanc

Preheat the oven to 375°F. Brush the baguette slices lightly on both sides with oil. Arrange in a single layer on a baking sheet and toast until golden brown, about 15 minutes. Set aside to cool. Leave the oven on.

Prepare the *dukkah*: Put the pecans or pistachios into a pie pan and toast in the oven until fragrant and lightly colored, 5 to 10 minutes. If using pistachios, chop roughly. Toast the sesame seeds in a dry skillet over high heat, stirring constantly, until lightly colored and fragrant, 1 to 2 minutes. Let cool. Add the coriander and cumin seeds to the skillet and toast, stirring, until fragrant and starting to darken. With a mortar and pestle, coarsely grind the coriander and cumin seeds. Transfer to a small bowl and stir in the pecans or pistachios, sesame seeds, salt, and a few grinds of pepper.

Slice the carrots into ⅛-inch-thick rounds. Heat a large skillet over high heat. Add the oil and carrots, season with salt and pepper, and sauté, stirring, until the carrots are tender and starting to brown, about 5 minutes. Transfer to a plate and let cool to room temperature.

In a bowl, mash together the goat cheese and chives with the back of a spoon until smooth and spreadable.

To assemble the crostini, spread 1 tablespoon of the goat cheese on each toast and arrange on a platter. Top each toast with a few rounds of carrots, using a mix of colors on each, and a generous pinch of *dukkah*. Drizzle the toasts with honey, using a total of about 2 teaspoons. Serve immediately.

Autumn Squash, Pear, and Arugula Salad

Serves 6

Some people think wine doesn't go with salad, but that has never been the thinking at Cakebread Cellars. The family loves salads of every kind, in every season, and Brian finds ways to make his salads wine friendly. In autumn, juicy pears and sweet roasted squashes balance the bitterness of chicories, with toasted pumpkin seeds and Vella Dry Jack for nutty richness. Brian goes easy on the vinegar to make the salad more compatible with wine.

5 tablespoons extra virgin olive oil

2 cups peeled and diced butternut squash (½-inch dice)

Sea salt and freshly ground black pepper

½ delicata squash, about ½ pound, seeded, ends removed, and sliced crosswise about ¼ inch thick

1 tablespoon pure maple syrup

¼ cup raw green pumpkin seeds (pepitas)

Vinaigrette:

1 small shallot, minced

1 teaspoon Dijon mustard

1½ tablespoons sherry vinegar or golden balsamic vinegar

½ cup extra virgin olive oil

2 handfuls arugula (about 2 ounces total)

2 Belgian endives, chopped

½ head radicchio, chopped

1 Bartlett pear, halved and cored (no need to peel)

Vella Dry Jack cheese, for shaving

Wine: Cakebread Cellars Chardonnay Reserve

Heat a large nonstick skillet over medium heat and add 2 tablespoons of the oil. When hot, add the butternut squash and season with salt and pepper. Sauté, stirring occasionally, until the squash is lightly browned and tender, about 7 minutes. Transfer to a plate.

Return the skillet to medium heat and add 2 tablespoons of the oil. When hot, add the delicata squash and season with salt and pepper. Cook, stirring occasionally, until lightly browned and almost tender, about 5 minutes. Add the maple syrup and cook for about 1 minute longer to glaze the squash slices. Transfer to the plate with the butternut squash.

In a small skillet, heat the remaining 1 tablespoon oil over medium-high heat. Add the pumpkin seeds and sauté, stirring almost constantly, until they darken, about 2 minutes. Season with salt and scoop out onto paper towels to drain.

Prepare the vinaigrette: In a small bowl, stir together the shallot, mustard, and vinegar. Whisk in the oil, then season with salt and pepper.

In a large salad bowl, combine the arugula, endives, and radicchio. Slice the pear lengthwise and add to the bowl along with the sautéed squashes. Add enough vinaigrette to coat the salad lightly (you may not need all of it) and toss gently. Taste for salt and pepper.

Divide the salad among six salad plates. Top with the pumpkin seeds, dividing them evenly. With a vegetable peeler, shave a few ribbons of Dry Jack over each salad. Serve immediately.

Winter Vegetable and Bean Soup with Tuscan Kale Pesto

Makes 3½ quarts; serves 8 generously

Beans:

½ pound dried cranberry (borlotti) beans (1 rounded cup)

½ yellow onion

1 carrot, in large chunks

1 celery rib, cut into large chunks

1 fresh sage sprig

Sea salt

Tuscan Kale Pesto:

¼ cup pine nuts

1 bunch Tuscan kale (about ½ pound), ribs removed

1 large clove garlic, chopped

3 tablespoons grated Parmigiano-Reggiano cheese

½ cup plus 2 tablespoons extra virgin olive oil

3 tablespoons extra virgin olive oil

1 yellow onion, minced

2 carrots, neatly diced

2 celery ribs, neatly diced

2 cloves garlic, minced

¼ pound prosciutto, neatly diced

½ cup chopped fresh flat-leaf parsley

One 28-ounce can Italian tomatoes, crushed by hand, with juice

4 cups chicken broth, plus more if needed

2 small zucchini, preferably 1 green and 1 yellow, diced

1½ cups small dried pasta, such as tubettini or small elbows

Grated Parmigiano-Reggiano cheese, for garnishing

Wine: Cakebread Cellars Chardonnay

Almost any type of dried bean, from cannellini to lima to chickpea, will work in this hearty minestrone. Marcy grows several types in the Cakebread Cellars garden: cranberry beans, the heirloom Good Mother Stallard, and French Tarbais beans that Brian uses in an annual cassoulet cooking class at the winery. Tuscan kale is a winter staple in the garden, and it makes a great cold-weather stand-in for basil in pesto.

Prepare the beans: Soak the beans overnight in water to cover. The next day, drain, transfer to a deep saucepan, and add water to cover by 1 inch. Add the onion, carrot, celery, and sage and bring to a simmer over medium heat, skimming off any foam. Cook uncovered at a simmer until the beans are tender, about 1 hour, adding water as needed to keep the beans covered. Remove from the heat, season with salt, and let cool in the liquid. With tongs, remove the onion, carrot, celery, and sage.

Prepare the pesto: Preheat the oven to 350°F. Put the pine nuts into a pan and toast until lightly colored and fragrant, about 5 minutes. Let cool. Bring a large pot of salted water to a boil over high heat. Add the kale and cook until just wilted, about 1 minute. Drain and cool under cold running water. Squeeze dry and chop coarsely. Put the kale into a food processor with the garlic, cheese, and pine nuts and pulse until blended. With the motor running, add the oil through the feed tube, pureeing until smooth. Transfer to a bowl and season with salt.

Heat the oil in a large soup pot over medium heat. Add the onion, carrots, celery, garlic, prosciutto, and parsley and sauté until the vegetables have softened, about 10 minutes. Add the tomatoes with their juice and simmer briskly for 5 to 10 minutes. Add the broth, the beans and their cooking liquid, and the zucchini and simmer gently until the zucchini are almost tender, about 10 minutes.

Bring a pot of salted water to a boil over high heat. Add the pasta and cook until just al dente, according to package directions. Drain and add to the soup. Thin the soup with broth or water if necessary. Taste for salt. Ladle the soup into bowls. Spoon a dollop of kale pesto on top of each serving and garnish with Parmigiano-Reggiano. Serve immediately.

Cedar Plank Salmon with Roasted-Tomato Butter

Serves 6

Roasted-Tomato Butter:

½ pound San Marzano or Roma tomatoes, halved lengthwise

Sea salt and freshly ground black pepper

1 tablespoon extra virgin olive oil

1 teaspoon coarsely chopped fresh thyme leaves

2 cloves garlic, unpeeled

1 cup unsalted butter, at room temperature

2 tablespoons coarsely chopped fresh basil

1 teaspoon fresh lemon juice

Pinch of ground Espelette or cayenne pepper

2 pounds skin-on salmon fillets, pin bones removed

Extra virgin olive oil

Wine: Cakebread Cellars Two Creeks Pinot Noir, Anderson Valley

---

For this recipe, you will need an untreated 1 by 6 cedar plank, available at most lumber stores. The smoke it generates when placed on the grill will infuse the salmon, a much easier approach than grappling with a complicated smoker. The recipe makes more butter than you need, but you can freeze what you don't use. It's nice to have on hand for use on steamed clams, grilled lobster, or swordfish. Accompany the salmon with fresh-dug potatoes, greens beans, or corn on the cob.

Soak a 1 by 6 cedar plank (see headnote) in cold water to cover for at least 2 hours.

Prepare the roasted-tomato butter: Preheat the oven to 400°F. Turn on the convection fan, if available. Line a baking sheet with aluminum foil and place the tomatoes, cut side up, on the pan. Season the tomatoes with salt and pepper, then drizzle with the oil and sprinkle with the thyme. Put the garlic cloves on the baking sheet as well. Bake the tomatoes until they are tender and starting to color and shrink, about 45 minutes.

Let the tomatoes cool, then remove the skins and put the flesh into a food processor with any juices from the pan. Squeeze the garlic flesh out of it skins into the food processor, then add the butter and pulse until smooth and creamy. Add the basil, lemon juice, and Espelette pepper and pulse to blend. Taste for salt. Scoop into a bowl and set aside.

Prepare a hot fire in a charcoal grill or preheat a gas grill to high. Brush the fish lightly all over with oil and season with salt and pepper. Place the fillets, skin side down, on the plank and set the plank on the grill directly over the fire. Watch carefully and have the grill lid ready with vents open. The smoldering plank will generate a lot of smoke. When the edges of the plank start to flame, cover the grill and cook the salmon until you can easily slide a metal offset spatula between the skin and the flesh, 8 to 10 minutes, depending on the thickness of the fillets.

With the spatula, transfer the fillets to dinner plates, leaving the skin behind. Top each portion with 1 tablespoon of the tomato butter. Serve immediately.

Profiteroles with Coffee Ice Cream, Armagnac-Soaked Prunes, and Chocolate-Caramel Sauce **Serves 6**

An adult version of an ice-cream sandwich, this luscious finale showcases the winery's succulent French prunes. Brian dries them, then steeps them in Armagnac (French brandy) before folding them into coffee ice cream. The prune recipe is adapted from A New Way to Cook by Sally Schneider and must be made at least 1 week before you plan to serve the profiteroles. If you're pressed for time, substitute store-bought ice cream.

Ice Cream:

2 cups whole milk

2 cups heavy cream

1 tablespoon instant coffee (not instant espresso)

¾ cup granulated sugar

6 large egg yolks

1 cup diced Armagnac-Soaked Prunes (recipe follows)

Profiteroles:

1 cup water

½ cup unsalted butter, diced

¼ teaspoon sea salt

1 cup all-purpose flour

4 large eggs

Chocolate-Caramel Sauce:

¾ cup granulated sugar

Pinch of cream of tartar

¼ cup water

½ cup heavy cream

½ cup crème fraîche

3 ounces bittersweet chocolate, chopped

Powdered sugar, for dusting

Prepare the ice cream: In a saucepan, combine the milk, cream, and instant coffee and bring to a simmer over medium heat, whisking to dissolve the coffee. Remove from the heat.

In a large heatproof bowl, whisk together the granulated sugar and egg yolks until pale yellow. Slowly add half of the hot milk mixture while whisking constantly. Add the remaining milk mixture and whisk to blend. Return the mixture to the saucepan over low heat and cook, stirring with a wooden spoon, until the mixture visibly thickens and reaches 178°F on an instant-read thermometer; do not let it boil or it will curdle. The mixture has cooked sufficiently when a finger drawn across the back of the spoon leaves a trail that does not fill immediately.

Strain the custard through a fine-mesh sieve into a heatproof bowl. Nest the bowl in an ice bath, stir the custard occasionally until cold, then refrigerate until well chilled. Freeze in an ice-cream maker according to the manufacturer's directions. Stir in the prunes by hand, transfer to a lidded container, and place in the freezer to harden.

Prepare the profiteroles: Preheat the oven to 400°F. Line a baking sheet with parchment paper or a silicone mat. Combine the water, butter, and salt in a saucepan and bring to a simmer over medium heat. When the butter melts, remove the pan from the heat, add the flour all at once, and stir it in vigorously with a wooden spoon. Return the saucepan to medium heat and cook, stirring constantly, until the batter pulls away from the sides of the pan, about 1 minute.

Transfer the batter to a stand mixer fitted with the paddle attachment. Turn on the mixer to medium speed and add the eggs one at a time, waiting for each egg to be incorporated before adding another. When all the eggs are well blended, transfer the batter to a pastry bag fitted with a large straight ½-inch tip. Pipe 1-inch mounds of dough about 1 inch apart on the prepared pan. You should have enough batter to make 24 mounds. With a moistened finger, flatten the peak of each mound.

Bake the profiteroles until golden brown and firm, 25 to 35 minutes. Turn the oven off and let the profiteroles dry in the oven for about 15 minutes before removing.

Prepare the chocolate-caramel sauce: Put the granulated sugar, cream of tartar, and water into a small, heavy saucepan and bring to a boil over medium heat. Cook without stirring until the sugar begins to caramelize and turn golden brown, about 5 minutes, swirling the pan so the sugar colors evenly. (Be very careful to avoid burning yourself with spattering caramel; for extra safety, don a hand mitt.) Remove the pan from the heat and carefully whisk in the cream; it will hiss and boil vigorously. Whisk in the crème fraîche and then the chocolate, whisking until the chocolate melts. Keep the sauce warm over low heat.

To serve, cut each profiterole in half horizontally with a serrated knife. Place 3 bottom halves on each of eight dessert plates. Put a small scoop of ice cream in each half. Top with the upper halves of the profiteroles. Spoon the warm chocolate-caramel sauce over the profiteroles, dust with powdered sugar, and serve immediately.

Armagnac-Soaked Prunes
Makes about 3 cups

1½ cups water

2 tablespoons sugar

1 vanilla bean

¾ pound large dried pitted prunes

½ cup Armagnac, or more to taste

Combine the water and sugar in a small saucepan. Halve the vanilla bean lengthwise and, with the tip of a small knife, scrape the seeds into the saucepan. Add the pod as well. Bring to a simmer over medium-high heat, stirring until the sugar dissolves. Remove from the heat.

Put the prunes into a clean heatproof glass jar or crock. Pour the hot syrup, including the vanilla bean, over the prunes, let cool, and then stir in the Armagnac. Cover and refrigerate for at least 1 week before using. The prunes will keep in the refrigerator indefinitely.

marcy's garden tips:

Take advantage of verticality. Use towering sunflowers and bean trellises to shade lettuces from summer heat. But be mindful that tall plants can also block sun from plants that need it.

Control invasive vegetables like sunchokes by planting in pots or halved wine barrels.

Keep detailed maps of garden beds so you can plan crop rotations. Plants in the Solanaceae family (eggplants, tomatoes, peppers, potatoes) should not be grown in the same location two years in a row or soil diseases may get established.

Plant a blanket of Blue Spice basil around the base of tomatoes to deter nighttime predators, such as raccoons.

Plant marigolds lavishly. Their roots repel root-knot nematodes, soil-dwelling pests that can damage beets, chard, and spinach.

Marcy often starts a second planting of squash, melons, or basil after most gardeners think the window for success has passed. If good weather holds, she gets a crop. If not, she has lost nothing but seeds.

Above and right: *Towering sunflowers create vertical interest and shade more delicate plantings from the summer sun; gardener Marcy Snow inspects Floriani Red Flint corn, an heirloom variety prized for polenta.*

Clif Family Winery: *Farm to Truck to Table*

St. Helena

Napa Valley has fine restaurants galore, but some of the freshest, most engaging fare in this famous wine region comes from a food truck. Parked most days outside Clif Family Winery's tasting room, the kelly-green vehicle draws a lunchtime crowd for bruschette with inventive toppings and pristine salads that taste like the lettuces were still growing that morning.

Clif Family Bruschetteria—the truck's official name—is a business on a mission. Encouraging healthy communities, organic farming, outdoor activity, shared food and wine—these are the notions that inspire Kit Crawford and Gary Erickson, the truck's married owners who are also proprietors of the Clif Family Winery and creators of the energy-bar pioneer Clif Bar.

"When we decided to get into winemaking, we didn't want to plant only vineyards," says Kit. "We wanted to create biodiversity."

In the late 1990s, the couple purchased a remote parcel overlooking Pope Valley, on the east side of Napa Valley. Surrounded by a forest of oak and fir, the secluded Howell Mountain location provided just what they sought: trails for cycling and horseback riding and enough sunny acreage for a small vineyard, ambitious vegetable garden, and chicken coop. Kit and her brother planted olive and fruit trees, and over time the vegetable plot evolved into a five-acre farm, a productive paradise of peppers, tomatoes, melons, citrus, herbs, and asparagus.

Left and above: *Avid cyclists and Clif Family owners Gary Erickson and Kit Crawford bike to Bruschetteria, their food truck adjacent to the winery tasting room and a local favorite for lunch.*

By the time the couple opened the St. Helena tasting room to showcase their wines, the farm's output had surpassed the needs of its weekly produce-box subscribers. The Clif Family Bruschetteria, as a companion to the tasting room, would allow them to share their organic-farming philosophy and the bounty of their property, whose residents had grown to include 180 free-range chickens. Inspired by the bruschette they had enjoyed on cycling vacations in northern Italy, the couple hired chef John McConnell and let him loose to devise a flexible menu that would showcase the fruits, vegetables, herbs, and eggs from their farm.

Bruschette, as it turns out, make the perfect neutral stage for presenting whatever farm manager Tessa Henry has in abundance. Using *pain au levain* from a nearby bakery, John can devise tantalizing toast from virtually anything Tessa grows, from Brussels sprouts, kale, and spinach to persimmons and peaches.

Every week, Tessa sends John a harvest list, and they meet at the farm biweekly. "That helps me determine what's high priority," says John. "Instead of writing the menu first, the farm dictates the menu."

This type of cooking in the moment produces flashes of genius, like the truck's Mater Melon Salad, an inspired composition of ripe tomatoes, muskmelon, and watermelon that helped utilize a bumper melon crop. (Clif Family's vibrant extra virgin olive oil, pressed from the farm's Greek and Italian olive varieties, is often the unsung hero on these composed salad plates.) John's no-waste mentality means that whatever Tessa sends his way will find a home. "You have to see opportunity in everything that's coming through the door," says the chef, but that's a talent that can frustrate diners who don't always

appreciate that the bruschetta they enjoyed the week before is not repeatable. Nature has moved on.

A farm visitor senses immediately that Kit and Gary's Howell Mountain endeavor is a hybrid: not quite a production farm managed for yield but far more than a hobby garden. Managing the so-called Lower Garden, a large basin surrounded by digger pines and Douglas fir, "feels more like farming," says Tessa. This broad, flat parcel yields close to a ton of tomatoes each summer, many destined for the organic tomato sauce that wine-club members sometimes receive in their shipments. Chile peppers in brilliant hues—some the color of egg yolks, others the size of a cherry—soak up the midday sun, auditioning for their role in single-variety hot sauces for the Clif Family brand. Tessa also grows Floriani Red Flint corn here, an heirloom Italian

Above: *(clockwise from far left) Chef John McConnell; farm box; orchard peaches; lower garden; sauce from estate tomatoes; red flint corn for polenta; cherry peppers; greenhouse-started seedlings*

"We want to educate and inspire others," says Kit. "Sustainably farmed grapes, fruits, and vegetables are so important to the health of our community and our planet."

variety that John dries and grinds by hand for polenta.

The upper area is more relaxed, with raised beds and smaller plots. It could be the fruit and vegetable garden of a large and very hungry family, with a hoop house for seed starting and a tidy storage shed where red onions, garlic, and peppers hang to dry. Fruit trees surround the hoop house but only one or two of each type: Arkansas Black apples, Asian pears, pomegranates, peaches, persimmons, plums, figs, and citrus. A nearby property, which became part of the Clif Family Farm later, hosts a more intensive orchard and supplies the blueberries, blackberries, citrus, and stone fruits for the Clif Family's small-batch marmalades, jams, and preserves.

Whatever the season, both properties will be blanketed in blooms. The IPM (integrated pest management) techniques that Tessa employs rely on California native plants and colorful blossoms to lure beneficial insects, and many of these plants do double duty as plate garnishes. Zinnias, marigolds, amaranth, borage, pineapple sage, pincushion flowers, snapdragons, white salvia, and verbena thrive in thick stands, and Tessa lets parsley, cilantro, and fennel mature until they flower and set seed. John occasionally sends his cooks to the farm to work for a day—"It connects the dots for them," he says—and they

Above and right: *(clockwise from left)*
Yellow ground cherries; farm manager Tessa Henry delivers a farm box to the chef; red onions dry in the potting shed; sunflowers brighten the lower garden in late summer

come back to the restaurant's prep kitchen with trays of painstakingly gathered marigold petals or dill pollen.

Working with John has helped Tessa realize how many parts of a plant may be edible. He harvests fennel pollen—a tedious task—to season the truck's popular *porchetta* and uses the leaves from citrus prunings to flavor his pork brine. The delicate blossoms of chives, parsley, and nepitella add beauty and freshness to the Clif Family Bruschetteria plates. In spring, the chef serves young, tender fava beans, pod and all, like green beans. Sometimes, Tessa will tell John she's thinking of turning over a tired bed, and he'll say, "But there's still something usable out there."

Hospitality at Clif Family often centers around John's juicy *porchetta*, a simplified version of the rosemary- and garlic-scented pork roast of Tuscany. Polenta is its usual sidekick, made with the farm's freshly ground dried corn. "It tastes miraculously different from what you can buy," says John. "There are so many nuances in whole-grain polenta."

To launch a late-spring *porchetta* dinner, John looks to the farm's last, lingering brassicas—cauliflower, kale, broccoli—and roasts them to top a bruschetta with the season's first peas. The hardy winter chicories are also about to bow out, so they're celebrated in a colorful salad with spring radishes. Fresh-dug potatoes get an unusual two-part treatment that makes them extra crisp. Accompanied by olives, boiled farm eggs, and a dressing thick with spring herbs, they're about as enticing as potatoes can get. For a sweet finale, John concocts a dreamy parfait, alternating layers of Meyer lemon curd, poppy seed shortbread, and sugared farm blueberries steeped in Clif Family red wine.

Today, Kit and Gary own ninety acres of Napa Valley vineyards, all certified organic, and have helped other grape growers transition to organic production. Leading by example is, fundamentally, what their Clif Family project is about. "We want to educate and inspire others," says Kit. "Sustainably farmed grapes, fruits, and vegetables are so important to the health of our community and our planet."

menu

Bruschetta with Brassicas, Peas, and Burrata
**Clif Family Oak Knoll Sauvignon Blanc
or Rosé of Grenache**

Mixed Chicory Caesar
with "Cacio e Pepe" Croutons
Clif Family Chardonnay or Grenache

Fingerling Potato "Tostones" with Olive
Salsa Verde and Farm Eggs
Clif Family Rosé of Grenache or Viognier

Clif Family Porchetta with Creamy Polenta
Clif Family Grenache or Chardonnay

Meyer Lemon Curd Parfait with
Poppy Seed Crust and
Red Wine–Macerated Blueberries
Clif Family Arriva Petite Sirah Dessert Wine

uncommon edibles:

Shake up your edible garden with these unusual plants, all star performers on the Clif Family farm.

Ground cherries: Also known as Cape gooseberries, ground cherries look like miniature gold tomatillos and taste like a cross between a tomato and mango. John halves them and scatters them on tomato bruschetta.

Nepitella: *(Calamintha nepeta)* Sometimes called Tuscan mint or calamint, nepitella has oregano-like leaves and an aroma that mingles mint, oregano, and licorice. John especially likes it with watermelon.

Greek dwarf basil: This delicate herb grows in small, compact mounds and has tiny leaves. "You can use the leaves whole, so they don't oxidize like cut basil," says John, who uses this variety in Clif Family tomato sauce.

Cabernet red onions: The name is a plus, but more important, the variety is useful at multiple stages: as a mild spring onion, a mature summer onion, and a dry storage crop.

Flavor King and Dapple Dandy pluots: These two varieties thrive in Kit and Gary's orchard and are among the sweetest examples of this plum-apricot cross.

Above and right: *Cabernet red onions hanging in the garden shed; upper garden at the Clif Family farm*

Bruschetta with Brassicas, Peas, and Burrata **Makes 6 toasts**

John likes to use the leaves and tender pared stems of broccoli and cauliflower, parts that less resourceful cooks discard. "I love the taste and the contrast," says the chef. "Instead of just roasted florets, you have the crisp, golden-brown leaf tips as well." For this springtime bruschetta, he spreads creamy burrata on hot, crunchy toast, then tops it with roasted brassicas (such as broccoli, Romanesco broccoli, and cauliflower) and sweet English peas, all from the Clif Family farm.

Vinaigrette:

½ cup extra virgin olive oil

¼ cup plus 1½ teaspoons fresh lemon juice

⅛ teaspoon freshly cracked black pepper

4 tablespoons Thai or Vietnamese fish sauce, or to taste

1½ quarts small florets, tender leaves, and coarsely chopped stems of mixed brassicas, such as cauliflower, broccoli, and broccoli Romanesco

2 tablespoons extra virgin olive oil, plus more for brushing the toasts

Kosher or sea salt

¾ to 1 cup shelled English peas

6 slices day-old pain au levain or other sourdough loaf, about 4 inches by 2 inches and ½ inch thick

1 large clove garlic, halved

½ pound burrata cheese

Torn fresh mint leaves, for garnish

Wine: Clif Family Oak Knoll Sauvignon Blanc or Rosé of Grenache

---

Make the vinaigrette: In a small bowl, whisk together the oil, lemon juice, and pepper. Whisk in the fish sauce 1 tablespoon at a time until the flavor is strong enough for your taste. Depending on the brand of fish sauce, you may need less than 4 tablespoons.

Preheat the oven to 375°F with a convection fan or 400°F without a fan. Line a baking sheet with parchment paper. In a bowl, toss the brassicas with the oil and with salt to taste. Arrange the brassicas on the prepared pan and bake until lightly browned in spots, about 10 minutes.

Have ready a bowl of salted ice water. Bring a small pot of unsalted water to a boil over high heat. Add the peas and blanch for about 1 minute, then drain and plunge immediately into the ice water to stop the cooking. Drain again and pat dry.

Toast the bread on both sides by your preferred method—on a stove-top grill pan, in a toaster oven, under a broiler, or on a grill—brushing each side with oil partway through toasting. The bread should be crusty on the outside but still soft inside. While hot, rub one side of each slice with the garlic.

Slice the burrata into 6 roughly equal pieces. Put a piece of burrata on the garlic-rubbed side of each slice of hot toast and smash the cheese with the back of a spoon so it covers most of the toast.

Put the roasted brassicas into a bowl and toss them with just enough of the vinaigrette to coat lightly. Top each toast with the roasted brassicas and the peas, dividing them evenly. Scatter mint on top and drizzle with a little more vinaigrette. Serve immediately.

Mixed Chicory Caesar with "Cacio e Pepe" Croutons **Serves 6**

Creamy Anchovy Dressing:

½ cup mayonnaise

1½ teaspoons fresh lemon juice

1½ teaspoons Thai or Vietnamese fish sauce

½ teaspoon Dijon mustard

⅛ teaspoon freshly ground black pepper

"Cacio e Pepe" Croutons:

½ sourdough baguette, torn into rough ½-inch pieces

1 tablespoon extra virgin olive oil

¼ teaspoon freshly cracked black pepper

¼ cup freshly grated Parmigiano-Reggiano cheese

3 quarts torn mixed chicories and other bitter greens, such as radicchio, escarole, frisée, dandelion, puntarella, and arugula

1 cup thinly sliced mixed radishes, including small daikon and watermelon radishes if available

Chunk of Parmigiano-Reggiano cheese, for shaving

Wine: Clif Family Chardonnay or Grenache

Inspired by the Roman pasta dish spaghetti cacio e pepe, *John got the idea to toss hot toasted croutons with grated cheese and black pepper. The cheese melts on contact. Instead of slicing the baguette for the croutons, he tears it into rough chunks. It's more rustic and creates more crevices to trap the seasonings. The croutons are best warm, so if you've made them ahead, reheat them before adding them to the salad. Leftover dressing is great with steamed artichokes, cauliflower, or other steamed vegetables.*

Make the creamy anchovy dressing: In a small bowl, whisk together all the dressing ingredients. Taste and adjust the seasoning.

Make the "cacio e pepe" croutons: Preheat the oven to 375°F or 350°F with a convection fan. Line a baking sheet with parchment paper. In a bowl, toss the baguette pieces with the oil and pepper, then arrange them in a single layer on the prepared pan. Bake until lightly browned in spots, about 8 minutes. Immediately transfer them to a bowl and, while they are hot, toss them with the cheese.

Toss the chicories and radishes with enough of the dressing to coat lightly. Arrange attractively on a serving platter, then scatter the warm croutons on top. Using a vegetable peeler, shave a little Parmigiano-Reggiano over the top. Serve immediately.

chef's tips:

After washing the chicories, soak them in ice water for 30 minutes, changing the water once. The ice water helps crisp them. Spin dry and, if not using them immediately, layer them with paper towels and refrigerate in a plastic bag.

wine for all seasons:

Working daily with the fruits and vegetables from the farm has shaped John's ideas about pairing fresh produce with Clif Family winemaker Laura Barrett's wine.

Spring: "Peas and fava beans from the farm are tender, sweet, and delicate. I can't help but associate that flavor with freshness and white wines with heightened acidity, like our Sauvignon Blanc. Laura's style is exuberant and expressive."

Summer: "A really crisp, cold glass of Clif Family Rosé of Grenache goes hand in hand with what's coming from the garden— herbs, zucchini, eggplants, tomatoes—and the Provençal-type dishes we're making."

Autumn: "We're getting winter squashes, potatoes, beets, and Brussels sprouts from the garden, and we're doing more braising. Our Grenache is lovely with those earthier flavors."

Winter: "I'm roasting root vegetables and cooking the garden chicories in duck fat. Those bold flavors marry with a full-bodied red wine, like Gary's Improv Zinfandel."

Fingerling Potato "Tostones" with Olive Salsa Verde and Farm Eggs **Serves 6**

Faced with a deluge of spring herbs, fingerling potatoes, and fresh eggs from Clif Family's farm, John devised this dish to showcase them. It weaves together many influences—the tostones (fried plantain chips) of Puerto Rico, the chimichurri of Argentina, Italy's salsa verde, the South American pairing of olives and eggs. The result seems like a dish that was always meant to be: crusty potatoes under a zippy dressing, with the creamy complement of perfectly boiled eggs.

12 fingerling potatoes, about 1½ pounds total

Olive Salsa Verde:

1 cup loosely packed fresh flat-leaf parsley leaves, plus more whole leaves for garnish

½ cup loosely packed fresh dill leaves

⅓ cup loosely packed fresh tarragon leaves

5 or 6 large green olives, such as Picholine or Castelvetrano, pitted

4 whole cornichons

1 tablespoon brine-packed capers, rinsed

1½ teaspoons Thai or Vietnamese fish sauce

1½ teaspoons sherry vinegar

½ teaspoon kosher or sea salt

½ cup extra virgin olive oil

3 large eggs, at room temperature

¼ cup extra virgin olive oil

½ teaspoon kosher or sea salt

Wine: Clif Family Rosé of Grenache or Viognier

Preheat the oven to 400°F or 375°F with a convection fan.

Put the potatoes into a saucepan with salted water to cover by 1 inch. Bring to a boil over high heat, then lower the heat to maintain a simmer. Cook until you can pierce the potatoes with a skewer or small knife, about 20 minutes. Drain well, then put the potatoes back into the warm saucepan and cover with a lid. Set aside for about 10 minutes to cool slightly.

Make the olive salsa verde: In a food processor, combine the parsley, dill, tarragon, olives, cornichons, capers, fish sauce, vinegar, and salt and pulse until well chopped. Add the oil and puree until smooth, stopping to scrape down the work bowl once or twice. You should have a generous 1 cup.

Have ready a bowl of ice water. Put the eggs into a small saucepan and add water to cover by an inch or so. Remove the eggs. Bring the water to a boil over high heat, then lower the heat to avoid jostling the eggs when you add them. With a spoon, carefully lower the eggs, one at a time, into the simmering water, then adjust the heat to maintain a gentle simmer. Cook for exactly 8½ minutes. With a slotted spoon, transfer the eggs into the ice water. When cool, drain and peel, then cut each egg lengthwise into 8 wedges.

Put a potato between two sheets of parchment paper and flatten the potato with the bottom of a skillet. The potato should be crushed flat but still mostly in one piece. Repeat with the remaining potatoes.

Put the flattened potatoes in a shallow bowl with any scraps. Drizzle with the oil and sprinkle with the salt. Toss gently, then spread the potatoes out on a baking sheet, minimizing any overlap. Bake until crusty, about 12 minutes.

With an offset spatula, transfer the potatoes to a serving platter. Drizzle with 4 to 5 tablespoons of the salsa verde and surround with the egg wedges. Scatter parsley leaves on top. Serve hot.

Clif Family Porchetta with Creamy Polenta Serves 12

Spice Rub:

½ cup whole fresh rosemary leaves

¼ cup whole peeled garlic cloves (about 12)

¼ cup ground fennel seed

½ teaspoon sea salt

¼ cup extra virgin olive oil

One 4-pound piece skinless pork belly

2½ pounds boneless center-cut pork loin, chain attached, silverskin removed

2½ tablespoons sea salt

Polenta:

3 cups polenta

½ cup heavy cream

4 tablespoons unsalted butter

1 cup coarsely grated Fontina Val d'Aosta cheese

⅓ cup freshly grated pecorino romano cheese

Sea salt

Wine: Clif Family Grenache or Chardonnay

Make the spice rub: Put the rosemary, garlic, fennel, salt, and oil into a food processor or blender and process until smooth. You should have about ½ cup.

Customers of Clif Family's popular Bruschetteria food truck would riot if the porchetta *ever left the menu. Modeled on the famous Tuscan preparation of pork loin wrapped in pork belly, chef John's* porchetta *makes a dramatic party dish, a juicy, garlicky, crusty roast scented with rosemary and fennel. If the total weight of your* porchetta *is heavier or lighter than the assembled 6½-pound* porchetta *in this recipe, adjust the quantity of spice rub accordingly. You need about 1½ tablespoons rub per pound of meat.*

Pork belly is typically sold with the skin attached. Ask the butcher to remove the skin for you, leaving all the fat on the belly. You can also choose to have the butcher butterfly the belly for you, or you can follow the method described here. The short sides of the rectangular pork belly should be the same length as the pork loin so the belly will encase the loin completely.

To butterfly the pork belly, put it skinned side down on a work surface with a longer side nearest you. With a sharp boning knife, make a vertical cut down the center of the belly, slicing only halfway through. Starting from that center cut, slice horizontally through the belly from the center to the left end without cutting all the way through. Make a similar horizontal cut from the center to the right end without cutting all the way through. You will have two flaps that you can open like a book and lay flat. The belly is now twice as long and half as thick as it was before.

Season the pork belly and the loin all over with the salt. Then spread the spice rub over the belly and loin, using all of it and slathering it evenly over all the surfaces.

Wrap the pork loin in the butterflied pork belly, jelly-roll style. Tie tightly with butcher's twine in five to seven equidistant places, starting from the center and working out toward the ends. Line a roasting pan or a baking sheet with aluminum foil and place a flat rack on it. Set the tied roast, seam side down, on the rack and refrigerate uncovered for 24 hours.

Two hours before cooking, remove the *porchetta* from the refrigerator. Preheat the oven to 500°F or 450°F with a convection fan.

Roast the pork, rotating the pan back to front after 10 minutes, until the exterior begins to brown, about 20 minutes. Reduce the oven temperature to 325°F or 300°F with a convection fan. Continue cooking, rotating the pan occasionally, until an instant-read thermometer inserted into the center of the roast registers 130°F to 135°F, about 2 hours. Transfer the pork, still on the rack, to a baking sheet that can collect any drippings. The internal temperature will rise about 10°F as the meat rests. Let rest for at least 1 hour before carving.

While the *porchetta* rests, make the polenta: In a large pot, bring 4 quarts lightly salted water to a boil over high heat. Add the polenta gradually, whisking constantly. When the polenta begins to thicken, lower the heat to maintain a gentle bubble. Cook, whisking often and occasionally scraping down the sides of the pan with a heat-resistant rubber spatula, until the polenta is creamy and no longer gritty, about 45 minutes. Whisk in the cream and butter, then remove from the heat and whisk in the cheeses. Taste for salt.

Transfer the *porchetta* to a cutting board. Remove the twine and slice about ½ inch thick. Divide the slices among twelve dinner plates. Pour any collected juices from the board and pan over the sliced pork. Spoon the polenta alongside. Serve immediately.

Meyer Lemon Curd Parfait with Poppy Seed Crust and Red Wine–Macerated Blueberries

Serves 6 to 8

Poppy Seed Crust:

1¼ cups unbleached all-purpose flour, plus more for the work surface

2 tablespoons granulated sugar

1 tablespoon poppy seeds

⅛ teaspoon kosher or sea salt

½ cup cold unsalted butter, in small pieces

1 large egg yolk

2 to 3 tablespoons cold heavy cream

Meyer Lemon Curd:

¾ cup Clif Family Meyer Lemon Marmalade or other marmalade

½ cup granulated sugar

6 tablespoons fresh lemon juice

3 large eggs, at room temperature

3 large egg yolks, at room temperature

¼ teaspoon kosher or sea salt

½ cup plus 2 tablespoons unsalted butter, at room temperature, in small pieces

Marmalade made with Meyer lemons from the Clif Family farm is a favorite souvenir for visitors to the winery's tasting room. (It's also available online.) John often uses the marmalade in a lemon curd filling for tarts. In a genius moment, he got the idea to deconstruct the tart, breaking up the shortbread-like crust into shards and layering the pieces with the lemon curd and macerated berries. Serve the parfait shortly after assembly, but you can prepare all the components a day ahead.

Macerated Berries:

2 pints blueberries or blackberries

¼ cup powdered sugar

2 tablespoons red wine

1 teaspoon fresh lemon juice

6 to 8 fresh mint sprigs, for garnish

Wine: Clif Family Arriva Petite Sirah Dessert Wine

Make the poppy seed crust: In a food processor, combine the flour, sugar, poppy seeds, and salt and pulse to blend. Add the butter and pulse just until the mixture resembles coarse meal. Whisk together the egg yolk and 2 tablespoons of the cream, then drizzle them evenly over the dry mixture. Pulse just until the dough begins to come together, adding another 1 tablespoon cream if the dough seems dry. Handling the dough as lightly as possible, shape it into a flattened disk, wrap in plastic wrap, and refrigerate for at least 1 hour or up to 1 day.

Preheat the oven to 350°F. Remove the dough from the refrigerator about 15 minutes before rolling to soften it slightly. On a lightly floured work surface, roll the dough out ¼ inch thick. The shape doesn't matter as long as it will fit on your pan. Transfer the rolled dough to a baking sheet. Pierce the dough in several places with a fork.

Bake until golden brown, 20 to 30 minutes. Let cool on a wire rack to room temperature. Gently break the crust into pieces small enough to fit in your serving glasses. Store in an airtight container at room temperature until you are ready to assemble the parfaits.

Make the Meyer lemon curd: Put a bowl into the refrigerator to chill. Put all the ingredients into a blender and puree until completely smooth. Pour the mixture into the top of a double boiler and set over (but not touching) simmering water. Cook, whisking almost constantly and scraping down the sides of the bowl or pan occasionally, until the mixture visibly thickens and registers 178°F to 180°F on an instant-read thermometer. Do not allow the curd to boil or it will curdle. Immediately remove from the heat and whisk the curd for a minute or so to cool it. Transfer it to the chilled bowl and cover with plastic wrap, pressing it directly onto the surface of the curd to prevent a skin from

forming. Let cool to room temperature, then refrigerate until chilled. You can make the curd a day ahead and refrigerate it.

Make the macerated berries: In a bowl, gently stir together all the ingredients until the sugar dissolves. Let macerate at room temperature for about 30 minutes to draw some juices out of the berries.

Assemble the parfaits: Set aside a few blueberries to garnish each serving. Put a scoop of lemon curd in each of six to eight clear glass cups or parfait glasses, using about one-third of the curd. Top the curd with poppy seed crust pieces, using about half of the pieces. Spoon macerated berries and juices on top, using about half of the berry mixture. Repeat the layering of lemon curd, crust, and berries. Top with the remaining lemon curd and garnish with the reserved berries and a mint sprig. Serve immediately so the crust stays crisp.

HALL Wines: *Solutions in Nature*

St. Helena

Kathryn and Craig Hall are such enthusiastic consumers of fresh, seasonal produce that they have not one garden, but two. A vegetable plot, herb garden, and fruit trees at their hilltop Napa Valley home supply their table when this busy couple is in residence. But the larger garden, at HALL Wines, is even more ambitious: twenty-six long, sunny beds overseen by an energetic manager whose devotion to organic and sustainable methods is as deep as the Halls'.

"Being organic and sustainable is who we are in our vineyards, so it makes sense to carry that through to the garden," says Kathryn, a former attorney and US ambassador to Austria who founded the winery with her husband in 2003. "It's heartening to see how much our team loves the garden and how proud they are of it. Shelley has taken it to another level."

Shelley Kusch, a longtime Napa Valley professional gardener, keeps both gardens prolific and producing food and flowers year-round. "This is a 365-day garden," says Kusch of the winery's edible landscape. "It needs to always look beautiful."

The winery often hosts visiting chefs for charitable events, and Kusch gives them free rein to forage in the garden. Employees also take home a lot of the harvest, and many of the flowers go into lush bouquets for the tasting room and for events. And, of course, winery visitors are encouraged to stroll the garden, wineglass in hand, and enjoy the dahlias and zinnias, sniff the roses, and admire the sculptures—some of them, like the cast-bronze apple tree, commissioned by the Halls for the garden site.

Left and above: *HALL Wines in St. Helena includes both a contemporary tasting room and gallery and the restored 1885 Bergfeld Winery, now known as the Founder's Cellar; Kathryn and Craig Hall at home*

"I farm using Amish methods," says Shelley. "The Amish garden for inner peace and for productivity—a big yield from a little space. It involves a lot of companion planting."

With a degree in botany and decades of experience in organic gardening, Shelley has learned to look to nature for solutions. In the HALL garden, many plants provide pest or disease protection to their neighbors. "Chives and tomatoes are best friends," says Shelley; plant them together and the tomatoes will be stronger. Radishes growing around cucumbers deter cucumber beetles. Society garlic repels gophers. For additional gopher protection and disease resistance, Shelley plants garlic around all the fruit trees—a collection that includes Blenheim and Moorpark apricots, Babcock white peach, Harko nectarine, Gala apple, Warren pear, and Lapin cherry. The garlic also helps the fruit grow bigger and sweeter, says this avid naturalist.

But Shelley reserves her highest praise for borage, a leafy herb with attractive blue flowers. "It's God's gift to the plant world," says the gardener. "It attracts all the good bugs and repels the bad ones." Bees love it, strawberries love it, and chefs appreciate it, too. The leaves have a cucumber-like flavor and make a tasty addition to soups, and the dainty blossoms embellish salads.

"All of my gardens have edible flowers," says Shelley, who manages some restaurant and private gardens as well. "You need them to attract pollinators. The winery staff uses the flowers on cheese plates, and whatever doesn't get used for culinary purposes makes the garden more lovely for visitors." Pansies, alyssum, and sweet Williams in spring give way to marigolds, calendula, and sunflowers, a fall palette that harmonizes with the autumn colors in the winery's adjacent Bergfeld Vineyard. Bulbs are the only nonedibles that Shelley permits in the garden, with irises and calla lilies, ranunculus and daffodils all doing double duty as gopher deterrents.

Shelley starts almost all of her edibles from seed to be sure the seedlings are disease-free. Although she grows heaps of tomatoes, peppers, kale, and green beans, she has a soft spot for the novelties and curiosities that few others grow. Espelette pepper, a mildly spicy red pepper from France's Basque region, is a favorite, as is luffa. The slender, pendulous gourd is a powerful bee attractant and edible when young, with a flavor like summer squash. As it matures, the fleshy interior turns fibrous and can be harvested for sponges. "Everybody thinks luffa comes from the ocean," says Shelley.

Above: *(clockwise from far left) Vintage tractor; alpine strawberries; sculpture by Anya Gallaccio; chef Ken Frank picks beans; yellow romano beans; summer green beans; Kathryn's harvest; gardener Shelley Kusch*

"Being organic and sustainable is who we are in our vineyards, so it makes sense to carry that through to our garden."

After winter's relative calm, the arrival of spring paints the winery garden in vivid shades of green. Tarragon, chives, and anise hyssop reawaken; green garlic's strappy leaves poke through the earth; and plump artichokes beckon from their silvery fronds. Fava beans quickly spurt to five feet, and the air is heady with the honeyed scent of sweet alyssum.

Summer brings tomatoes in profusion, peppers, potatoes, sweet corn, eggplants, melons, and yellow wax beans. By autumn, when gardeners in other climates might be putting their tools to rest, Shelley is harvesting cranberry beans and sunchokes and making sure the Halls' rock-walled vegetable bed is churning out alpine strawberries, kale, chard, basil, and winter squashes for their home kitchen.

The idea that a fine bottle of red wine needs red meat alongside is not how the Halls approach food and wine pairing. Kathryn is not a meat eater and Craig is a longtime vegan, yet they still find room for red wine every night. "That's never been a problem," laughs Kathryn. "We have at least one glass of red wine with every meal." They certainly have choices: the couple's wine ventures also include WALT, a Pinot Noir and Chardonnay brand, and BACA, which focuses on Zinfandel.

Above and right: *(clockwise from left) Shelley harvests baby shallots; garden bed at the Hall home; companion planting of flowers and edibles; edible flowers for garnish are a fixture in the HALL Wines garden.*

Between their businesses and their philanthropy, the Halls maintain packed schedules, but making time for a relaxed evening meal is a priority. Ken Frank, proprietor of the Michelin-starred La Toque in Napa, is among the chefs they most admire in the Napa Valley, and they occasionally engage him to cook for winery events. Ken is also a celebrity judge in the winery's annual Cabernet Cookoff, a fundraiser that pits teams of prominent chefs against one another to benefit local nonprofits.

Challenged to create a menu using autumn produce from the winery garden, Ken immediately saw the possibilities in the young root vegetables and shelling beans. He prepares a multicourse vegetarian menu nightly at his restaurant, so he is accustomed to putting produce in the spotlight. Ken's recipe for roasted sunchoke soup transforms the humble-looking tubers into a velvety puree fit for guests but easy enough for family meals, too. With carrots and parsnips, he created a light slaw dressed with lemongrass oil—a stand-alone salad that could also accompany grilled shrimp, grilled tofu, or rotisserie chicken. The chef's stunning beet and citrus salad relies on a clever technique—charring citrus—to introduce a subtle burnt-sugar note.

Shelley's harvest of cranberry beans inspired Ken's Pinot Noir–friendly main course, a pan-seared pork chop with garlicky wild mushrooms and a shelling bean ragout. Alpine strawberries, still producing in early fall, prompted Ken to turn to a classic dessert that everyone loves but few people make. Not surprisingly, this French-trained chef produces crêpes that would please a Michelin inspector, with nutty brown butter scenting the warm strawberry filling. Fruit truly does seem to grow better and sweeter at HALL, a testament both to the site and the nature-knows-best gardening practices.

"The garden emphasizes the connection between food and wine, so it seems natural to us to have it," says Kathryn. "In Napa Valley, we take for granted that we can grow fresh produce year-round, but for people from elsewhere, the abundance makes an impression. Touring the garden is part of the enjoyment of visiting HALL."

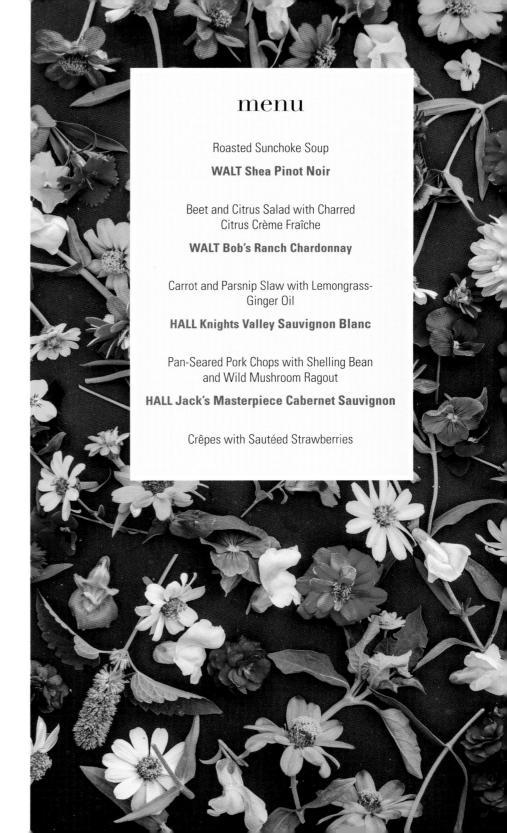

menu

Roasted Sunchoke Soup

WALT Shea Pinot Noir

Beet and Citrus Salad with Charred
Citrus Crème Fraîche

WALT Bob's Ranch Chardonnay

Carrot and Parsnip Slaw with Lemongrass-
Ginger Oil

HALL Knights Valley Sauvignon Blanc

Pan-Seared Pork Chops with Shelling Bean
and Wild Mushroom Ragout

HALL Jack's Masterpiece Cabernet Sauvignon

Crêpes with Sautéed Strawberries

Roasted Sunchoke Soup

Makes about 6½ cups; serves 8

1½ pounds sunchokes, scrubbed but not peeled

2 large shallots, peeled

2 tablespoons extra virgin olive oil

2 large cloves garlic, peeled

1 leek, white and pale green part only

4 cups water

¾ cup dry white wine

¾ cup heavy cream

2 teaspoons sea salt

Porcini Crème Fraîche:

3 tablespoons crème fraîche

¼ teaspoon porcini powder (see Note)

Wine: WALT Shea Pinot Noir

Oven roasting caramelizes the abundant natural sugar in sunchokes and helps develop their nuttiness. They make a surprisingly velvety soup blended with roasted shallots and garlic, with cream supplying richness and white wine brightening the flavor. The porcini powder that Ken uses in the garnish is "like magic," says the chef. "Anything you put it in tastes better." Add it to risotto, to broth, or to pasta in tomato or cream sauce.

Preheat the oven to 400°F. In a bowl, toss the whole sunchokes and shallots in 1 tablespoon of the oil. Arrange the vegetables in a single layer on a baking sheet and roast until they begin to caramelize, about 1 hour, shaking the pan occasionally and turning the sunchokes and shallots if necessary to promote even browning. Add the garlic cloves and roast for an additional 10 minutes. The sunchokes, shallots, and garlic should be completely tender and lightly caramelized in spots.

Halve the leek lengthwise and rinse thoroughly between the leaves; leeks can hide a lot of dirt. Slice crosswise into ½-inch-thick pieces. Heat the remaining 1 tablespoon oil in a large saucepan over medium heat. Add the leek and sauté, stirring, until softened, about 5 minutes. Add the roasted sunchokes, shallots, and garlic, then pour in the water, wine, and cream and add the salt. Bring to a simmer, adjust the heat to maintain a simmer, and cook uncovered for 30 minutes to marry the flavors. Set aside to cool for about 15 minutes, then blend in a blender until completely smooth. Rinse the saucepan and pour in the pureed soup.

Prepare the porcini crème fraîche: In a small bowl, whisk together crème fraîche and porcini powder until smooth.

Reheat the soup gently to serve. Divide among bowls and garnish each serving with a drizzle of the crème fraîche. Serve immediately.

Note: *To make porcini powder, place dried porcini in a spice or coffee grinder and grind to a powder. Store in an airtight container. In spring, garnish the soup with crème fraîche, sliced chives, and chive blossoms.*

Beet and Citrus Salad with Charred Citrus Crème Fraîche

Serves 4

¼ cup raw pistachios

12 small beets, preferably a mix of colors (about 1 pound trimmed)

1 tablespoon extra virgin olive oil, plus more for the greens

Dressing:

5 kumquats, halved lengthwise

¼ cup crème fraîche

Pinch of sea salt

¼ teaspoon honey

½ teaspoon grated orange or tangerine zest

1 blood orange, navel orange, or Cara Cara orange

2 tangerines

2 kumquats, thinly sliced crosswise

4 small tufts baby arugula, mâche, or frisée

Wine: WALT Bob's Ranch Chardonnay

This beautiful composed salad has appeared on the tasting menu at La Toque, Ken's elegant Napa Valley restaurant, but it's easily reproduced at home. Charring the citrus heightens its flavor, enhancing its contribution to the salad dressing. You can replace the kumquats with a halved tangerine, navel orange, or blood orange; grapefruit is too bitter.

Preheat the oven to 400°F. Toast the pistachios on a baking sheet until fragrant and lightly colored, 8 to 10 minutes. Let cool, then chop coarsely.

In a bowl, toss the beets with the oil. Arrange in a single layer on a baking sheet and bake until tender when pierced, 45 to 50 minutes. When the beets are just cool enough to handle, peel them. (They are easier to peel while warm.) Cut into quarters.

Prepare the dressing: Preheat a griddle to high or preheat a cast-iron skillet over high heat. Place the kumquats, cut side down, on the griddle or in the skillet and cook until blackened on the cut side, about 5 minutes. When cool enough to handle, squeeze the pulp, juice, and seeds from the kumquats into a bowl, then add the spent rinds to the bowl. Add the crème fraîche and salt and use the back of a spoon to smash the kumquats even more so their flavor infuses the crème fraîche. Pass the mixture through a sieve into a bowl, pressing on the kumquat solids with a rubber spatula. Whisk in the honey and orange zest and taste for salt.

Cut a slice off both ends of the orange. Stand the orange upright on a cutting board and, using a sharp knife, remove all the peel and white pith by slicing from top to bottom all the way around the orange, following the contour of the fruit. Cut along the membranes to release the individual segments and place them in a bowl. Remove any seeds. Repeat with the tangerines; add them to the same bowl.

To serve, arrange the beets on a platter or individual plates. Scatter the citrus segments and sliced kumquats among the beets. Drizzle with the dressing. In a small bowl, gently toss the arugula with a pinch of salt and just enough oil to gloss it lightly. Top the salad with tufts of the arugula. Scatter the pistachios all around. Serve immediately.

Carrot and Parsnip Slaw with Lemongrass-Ginger Oil

Serves 4

Dressing:

1 tablespoon unseasoned rice vinegar

¼ teaspoon tamarind pulp (optional)

Pinch of sea salt

¼ cup Lemongrass-Ginger Oil (recipe follows)

2 large carrots

2 large parsnips

Chopped cilantro leaves or whole microgreens, for garnish

Wine: HALL Knights Valley Sauvignon Blanc

Prepare the dressing: In a small bowl, whisk together the vinegar, tamarind pulp (if using), and salt. Whisk in the lemongrass oil.

Peel the carrots and parsnips and cut them crosswise into 3-inch chunks. With a mandoline or other vegetable slicer, carefully slice the chunks lengthwise into thin slabs about ⅛ inch thick. Stack a few slabs at a time and slice lengthwise as thinly as possible to make a fine julienne. If you don't have a vegetable slicer, grate the chunks lengthwise on the large holes of a box grater to produce long strands. You should have 2 cups each of julienned or grated carrots and parsnips.

Combine the carrots and parsnips in a bowl and add the dressing. Toss with your hands to coat evenly. Taste for salt and vinegar. Let rest for 15 to 30 minutes to soften the slaw slightly.

Divide the slaw among four salad plates. Top each serving with a tuft of cilantro. Serve immediately.

The underappreciated parsnip has many cheerleaders at HALL. Shelley enjoys growing them, the Halls love to eat them, and Ken knows how to prepare them in ways that even skeptics want to try. This lively slaw is scented with lemongrass oil prepared with lemongrass from the winery garden. Make the slaw your own by adding toasted peanuts, chiles, or Asian basil, or add a splash of fish sauce to the dressing.

Lemongrass-Ginger Oil

Makes 1 cup

1 small stalk lemongrass

1 cup canola oil

3 thin slices fresh ginger (no need to peel)

Cut the lemongrass crosswise into thirds. With a mallet, pound the lemongrass pieces to shatter the fibers. Put the lemongrass pieces, oil, and ginger into a small saucepan, place over medium-low heat, and warm until the oil reaches 145°F on an instant-read thermometer. Set aside for 24 to 48 hours, then strain. Store the oil in an airtight container at room temperature if using within a few days or refrigerate for longer keeping.

Pan-Seared Pork Chops with Shelling Bean and Wild Mushroom Ragout **Serves 4**

Fresh cranberry beans from the HALL garden make a creamy bed for thick, succulent pork chops. Sometimes, when he has a night off from the restaurant, Ken will cook cranberry beans, adding chopped tomatoes and cavatelli *for an easy* pasta e fagioli. *As for cooking pork chops, he has two rules: always brine them and let them rest after cooking. If you follow that advice and don't overcook them, the chops will be tender and juicy.*

Brine:

2 cups water

¼ cup plus 1 tablespoon sea salt

1 tablespoon plus 1 teaspoon sugar

4 bone-in pork loin chops, 10 to 12 ounces each

Beans:

2 slices thick-cut bacon

¼ yellow onion, cut into ¼-inch dice

½ large celery rib, cut into ¼-inch dice

½ carrot, peeled and cut into ¼-inch dice

2 cups fresh cranberry beans, fava beans, or other fresh
    shelling beans (from about 1½ pounds unshelled)

1 fresh thyme sprig

Sea salt

½ pound mixed wild mushrooms or cultivated maitake or
    oyster mushrooms, cleaned

Freshly ground black pepper

Canola oil

¼ cup extra virgin olive oil

2 cloves garlic, minced

¼ cup minced mixed fresh herbs, such as flat-leaf parsley, chives,
    tarragon, and chervil

Wine: HALL Jack's Masterpiece Cabernet Sauvignon

(continued)

Pan-Seared Pork Chops with Shelling Bean and Wild Mushroom Ragout *(continued)*

Prepare the brine: In a container just large enough to hold the pork chops, combine the water, salt, and sugar and stir to dissolve the salt and sugar. Add the pork chops. They should be submerged. Let stand at room temperature for at least 30 minutes or up to 1 hour, turning them over once halfway through. Remove from the brine and pat dry with paper towels.

Prepare the beans: Halve the bacon slices lengthwise, then cut crosswise into ¼-inch pieces. Place in a saucepan and cook over medium heat until the bacon renders some of its fat and begins to sizzle and color, about 5 minutes. Add the onion, celery, and carrot and cook, stirring, for about 2 minutes. Add the beans, thyme, and enough water just to cover the beans and bring to a simmer. Cover the beans with a round of parchment paper cut just to fit inside the pot and simmer gently until the beans are tender, 20 minutes or more, adding water if needed to keep the original level. Remove from the heat, season to taste with salt, and remove the thyme. Let the beans cool in the liquid if time allows.

Trim the mushrooms of any blemishes or dried ends. Tear them into bite-size pieces if they are tender or slice them with a knife if they are firm.

Heat two 10-inch skillets over medium-high heat. Season the pork chops well on both sides with pepper. (They won't need additional salt.) Add enough canola oil to each skillet to film it generously, about 1½ tablespoons per skillet. Don't skimp on the oil or the pork chops won't sear properly. When the skillets are hot, put 2 chops into each one and sear on the underside until well browned, about 2 minutes. Adjust the heat if needed to prevent scorching. With tongs, turn the chops and continue cooking until the second side is richly browned and the chops are almost done, about 3 minutes; when probed in the center, they should feel neither flabby nor firm. They will continue to cook as they rest. Transfer the chops to a rack to rest while you cook the mushrooms.

Reheat the beans if necessary and keep warm.

Heat a large skillet over medium-high heat. Add the olive oil. When it is almost smoking, add the mushrooms and season with salt and pepper. Cook briskly until they are almost tender, about 4 minutes, then add the garlic and sauté until it is fragrant, about 1 minute. Add half of the mixed herbs, toss well, and remove from the heat.

Make a bed of beans on each of four dinner plates. (You may not use them all.) Top with a pork chop, then spoon the mushrooms on top of the chops, dividing them evenly. Garnish with the remaining herbs and serve immediately.

Left: *The Halls, assisted by Rocky, their Cavalier King Charles Spaniel, harvest Tuscan kale and chard from their stone-walled beds at home on a warm Napa Valley evening.*

Crêpes with Sautéed Strawberries

Serves 6

¾ cup sliced almonds

½ cup heavy cream

2 tablespoons crème fraîche

1 teaspoon powdered sugar

Crêpes:

2 large eggs, at room temperature

⅔ cup unbleached all-purpose flour

¼ teaspoon sea salt

4 tablespoons unsalted butter, melted, plus more for the pan

¾ cup whole milk

Strawberries:

1 pound strawberries, hulled and quartered

4 tablespoons unsalted butter

¼ cup plus 2 tablespoons granulated sugar

Preheat the oven to 350°F. Toast the almonds on a baking sheet until fragrant and light brown, about 10 minutes. Let cool.

In a bowl, whisk together the cream, crème fraîche, and powdered sugar to soft peaks. Cover and refrigerate until needed.

Tender crêpes topped with berries are a timeless dessert that never goes out of fashion. Ken's brilliant idea is to cook the HALL garden's fragrant strawberries in brown butter and sugar, adding a caramel note to the sauce that is totally luscious. Serve with whipped cream or ice cream. Peaches or blueberries can replace the strawberries on another occasion.

Prepare the crêpes: In a bowl, whisk together the eggs, flour, and salt until smooth. Whisk in the warm melted butter, followed by the milk. The mixture should be smooth and thin. Let the batter rest for 15 minutes so any bubbles can dissipate.

Lay a large sheet of parchment paper near the stove top. Heat a well-seasoned crêpe pan or 8-inch nonstick skillet over medium-low heat. When hot, brush with melted butter. Add 1 ounce (2 tablespoons) batter, swirling to coat the pan evenly. (If the batter does not flow readily, thin the batter with a splash of milk.) Cook until the crêpe is golden brown in spots on the bottom and lightly colored around the edge, 30 to 45 seconds, then flip and cook the second side until lightly colored and no longer damp, 30 to 45 seconds. Transfer the crêpe to the parchment and continue with the remaining batter, brushing the pan lightly with butter before cooking each crêpe and adding the finished crêpes to the parchment, overlapping them slightly so you have an edge to grab. You should have enough batter for 12 crêpes.

Prepare the strawberries: Heat a 10-inch skillet over medium-high heat. When hot, add the butter and swirl the pan constantly as the butter melts and sizzles. When the butter turns a deep caramel color, add the strawberries and sugar and cook briskly, stirring, until the berries soften and the mixture becomes almost jam-like, 3 to 4 minutes.

Fold each crêpe into quarters and put 2 crêpes on each of six dessert plates. Spoon the warm strawberries and sauce over the crêpes. Top each serving with almonds and a dollop of whipped cream. Serve immediately.

The Prisoner Wine Company: *A Courtyard Garden*

St. Helena

Many wineries with edible gardens situate the beds out of sight because, truth be told, vegetable plantings can have their unsightly moments. But at The Prisoner Wine Company, the edible garden gets the limelight. Arriving guests can't help but notice the ten handsome, deep corten steel beds in a courtyard adjacent to the winery entrance, their coppery finish glinting in the setting sun. Many after-hours events here begin in the garden, an aromatic alfresco reception room where guests can meander, wineglass in hand, among the rosemary, eggplant, and thyme.

As its many fans know, little about The Prisoner Wine Company is conventional. From its inception, the winery has colored outside the lines, building its reputation on blended wines from purchased grapes at a time when critics reserved their highest marks for single-variety, estate-grown bottlings. Founder David Phinney, who has since sold the company, unknowingly unleashed a movement when he debuted The Prisoner in 2000. Winemaker Chrissy Wittmann enjoys the creative freedom of blending multiple grape varieties from many sources, and wine lovers embrace these bold yet balanced wines.

"Dave is a visionary," says The Prisoner Wine Company's brand manager Euming Lee. "The way he thinks is different from the norm, and we try to embody that spirit in all we do today."

Designed and built in 2018, after new owners purchased The Prisoner Wine Company, the courtyard garden and the petite fruit orchard alongside can't begin to supply all the produce that this winery's busy kitchen needs. But chef Brett Young appreciates every last basil sprig, and the hospitality team uses the garden as a sensory experience for visitors. Touring the garden with a winery host, guests are introduced to scents they might not know, such as lemon verbena, winter savory, and anise hyssop.

"The garden is an extension of the aromatics found in our wines," says Alex Brisoux, one of the winery's managers. "Visiting the garden makes it easier to correlate those aromas."

Even the winemaker finds that the garden has expanded her sensory vocabulary. "It's sometimes hard to pull those descriptors out," says Chrissy, who takes regular strolls around the beds. "The garden helps me describe wine better, and it has been an inspiration for starting a garden at home."

For Brett, the garden provides an endless palette of toppings for the pizzas he prepares for guests. In spring, he scatters delicate thyme and chive blossoms on top of a leek and bacon pizza. In the cooler months, there's almost always wispy rustic arugula, an heirloom variety that he can strew on top of pizzas when they emerge from the oven, and in early summer, baby zucchini and sliced zucchini blossoms make an alluring topping.

Left and above: *Winery chef Brett Young has access to an enviable variety of culinary herbs just steps from his kitchen; situated on Napa Valley's main highway, The Prisoner Wine Company sees many visitors.*

Herbs thrive in these sunny, west-facing beds constructed of food-safe weathering steel and built almost waist-high so they're easy to plant and harvest. Commonplace types, like parsley and mint, play only minor roles in the collection. Instead, the choices seem designed for adventure as unexpected as the winery's uncommon wine blends. Persian basil, Lettuce Leaf basil, and Green Goddess basil jostle for space with Mexican tarragon, German parsley, and caraway thyme. Brett transforms the fragrant lemon verbena leaves into a tangy fermented kombucha—"like a tart lemon tea," says the chef, a pickling and fermenting enthusiast. The kombucha adds citrus-like acidity to his vinaigrettes. "We can't grow enough lemon verbena."

For the colorful plates of pickles that Brett likes to serve tasting-room visitors, the garden always includes a few vegetables that welcome a quick brining, like oblong Badger Flame and Touchstone Gold beets, French Breakfast radishes, Trieste fennel, sweet Tokyo turnips, and the burgundy-skinned, yellow-fleshed Purple Elite carrots. In Napa Valley's mild climate, the beds remain productive year-round, providing winter cabbage and kohlrabi for sauerkraut to utilize Brett's fermentation skills.

Once each season, Brett sits down with edible-garden expert Stefani Bittner of the Bay Area–based Homestead Design Collective to plan the future harvest. What will he want to cook in three months? What herbs and vegetables will help him and his staff create eye-opening matches for the winery's bottlings? Most winery chefs stick with proven pairing tactics so their food doesn't challenge the wines. At The Prisoner Wine Company, it's all about bending the norms. "We expect the chef and our wine educators to put together uncommon pairings,"

Above: *(clockwise from left) The setting sun bathes the garden in golden afternoon light; harvesting lemon verbena; a garden peach; beans clamber up trellises; inspiration for tasting menus starts in the garden.*

"The garden is an extension of the aromatics found in our wines. Visiting the garden makes it easier to correlate those aromas."

says Alex. "It leads to some interesting debates."

The Prisoner Wine Company garden is a chef's garden first and foremost, but it's also a show garden that has to look groomed all the time. Thoughtful design makes that possible. The dramatic beds and trellises give the garden a pleasing visual structure even when the plantings are in transition. Heights are layered, with tall, vining beans or peas in the center of the beds and cascading or low-growing plants, such as creeping thyme, tarragon, and salad greens, at the edges. Repeating materials also helps, so beds, ornamental tuteurs, and tomato trellises are all made of the same weathering steel. Herbs are planted in large groupings to create a cohesive look, and an allée of ornamental Wild Magic basil hints at a garden entrance.

Like any organic garden, the plantings rely on beneficial insects to keep pests in check. Herbs are allowed to bloom to attract desirable bugs and pollinators, and the beds are thickly planted with edible flowers, from violas and lavender in spring to sunflowers, calendulas, and marigolds in summer and fall. Companion planting also helps combat pests and diseases. Signet marigolds, known to deter root-knot nematodes, surround the tomatoes like a fortress. What's more, they are edible. Brett uses the flowers for garnish and the young foliage for microgreens.

Above and right: *(clockwise from left): The winery's handsome open kitchen enhances the guest experience; the winery entrance is steps away from its neat courtyard garden; pizza with leeks and bacon; outdoor mural*

For most of the private events at The Prisoner Wine Company, Brett likes to serve family-style from large bowls and platters. A casual dinner might not follow the flow of a conventional multicourse menu but instead consist of several garden-influenced dishes—a few of them meatless—served more or less at once.

Conjuring a warm spring evening in The Yard, the winery's interior courtyard with its pizza oven, Brett might start the meal with a platter of garden vegetables—some raw, some blanched—and an updated reading of 1970s onion dip with goat cheese and caramelized spring onions. Tender Little Gem lettuces follow, dressed in a fruity vinaigrette that finds echoes in the winery's complex, creamy white wine blend, Blindfold. Brett's pizza mastery elevates a pie topped with bacon, fromage blanc, and caramelized young leeks. A vegetarian fried rice—incorporating whatever the garden provides that day—seduces with its green-garlic fragrance and the season's first peas. And Brett's buttery potato gnocchi prove that, in capable hands, even asparagus—considered a problem vegetable by some wine lovers—can be wine friendly.

With this lush, well-maintained garden just steps from his kitchen, Brett can harvest what he needs *à la minute*. Herbs go from garden to table in minutes—a seize-the-moment approach to cooking that echoes how the winery's staff speaks about the wines. "I often tell people these are wines for the impatient," says Alex. "They are meant to drink sooner rather than later. If you see a bottle of The Prisoner at the store, take it home and drink it."

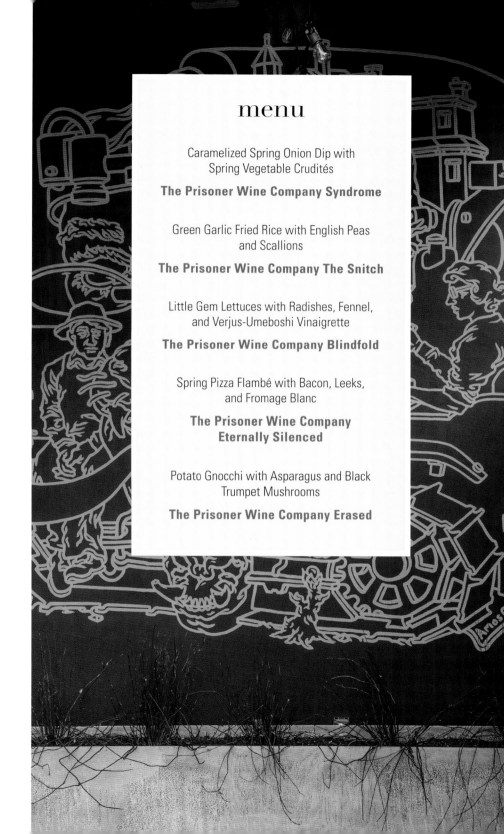

menu

Caramelized Spring Onion Dip with
Spring Vegetable Crudités

The Prisoner Wine Company Syndrome

Green Garlic Fried Rice with English Peas
and Scallions

The Prisoner Wine Company The Snitch

Little Gem Lettuces with Radishes, Fennel,
and Verjus-Umeboshi Vinaigrette

The Prisoner Wine Company Blindfold

Spring Pizza Flambé with Bacon, Leeks,
and Fromage Blanc

**The Prisoner Wine Company
Eternally Silenced**

Potato Gnocchi with Asparagus and Black
Trumpet Mushrooms

The Prisoner Wine Company Erased

Caramelized Spring Onion Dip with Spring Vegetable Crudités **Makes about 2½ cups**

Every guest who visits The Prisoner for a wine tasting enjoys some small bites along with the wine. Brett has developed a repertoire of dips for this purpose, all of them easy to make in quantity. This caramelized onion dip is understandably a favorite, whether served with potato chips or a cornucopia of garden vegetables. In spring, many of the dippers— like radishes, baby rainbow carrots, and baby fennel—can be served raw, but Brett likes to briefly blanch asparagus, baby zucchini and sugar snap peas, to heighten their color. The dip keeps for 4 days in the fridge.

2 tablespoons canola oil

3 cups chopped spring onions, white and pale green part only

Sea salt and freshly ground black pepper

1 cup fresh rindless goat cheese (about 4 ounces), at room temperature

⅔ cup crème fraîche

¼ cup plus 2 tablespoons buttermilk

2 tablespoons onion powder

1 tablespoon garlic powder

Thinly sliced fresh chives, for garnish

Spring vegetable crudités (see introduction)

Wine: The Prisoner Wine Company Syndrome

Heat the oil in a saucepan over medium-high heat. Add the onions and a pinch of salt, lower the heat to medium, and cook, stirring often and reducing the heat as needed to prevent burning, until the onion is meltingly soft, dark, and sweet, about 35 minutes. Add a splash of water whenever the onions threaten to stick or scorch. Transfer the onions to a bowl or baking sheet and let cool completely.

In a bowl, whisk together the goat cheese, crème fraîche, buttermilk, onion powder, garlic powder, 1 teaspoon salt, and black pepper to taste. Whisk in water as needed to thin to dip consistency. Stir in the caramelized onions. Transfer to a serving bowl and garnish with chives. Surround with crudités and serve.

Green Garlic Fried Rice with English Peas and Scallions **Serves 6**

2 tablespoons canola oil

2 teaspoons minced garlic

1 teaspoon peeled and minced fresh ginger

1½ cups jasmine rice

1 teaspoon sea salt

2⅔ cups water

¾ cup shelled English peas

1 tablespoon Chinese or Japanese sesame oil

1½ cups very thinly sliced green garlic, white and pale green parts only, sliced on a sharp diagonal, plus more for garnish

½ cup very thinly sliced scallions, white and pale green parts only, sliced on a sharp diagonal, plus more for garnish

2 tablespoons soy sauce

½ preserved lemon, pulp discarded and rind finely julienned

2 large eggs, beaten

Wine: The Prisoner Wine Company The Snitch

Preheat the oven to 375°F or 350°F with a convection fan.

Heat the canola oil in an ovenproof saucepan over medium heat. Add the garlic and ginger and stir until fragrant, about 30 seconds. Add the rice and salt and cook, stirring, for 1 minute to coat the rice with oil and toast it slightly. Stir in the water and bring to a simmer. Cover the pan, transfer it to the oven, and bake for 20 minutes. Remove from the oven and let rest in the pan for 5 minutes, then spread the

Brett makes fried rice often for The Prisoner's family-style guest meals, and he likes to keep it meatless for the winery's many vegetarian visitors. The dish is an accommodating showcase for garden vegetables and herbs. In late spring, the last of the green garlic—mild, immature garlic harvested before the bulb forms—and the first tender English peas overlap, inspiring a particularly fragrant and colorful variation. Note that you need to cook the rice several hours ahead, and preferably a day ahead, so it has time to chill.

rice on a baking sheet to cool quickly. Refrigerate uncovered for at least 4 hours or up to overnight.

Bring a small pot of salted water to a boil over high heat and prepare a bowl of ice water. Add the peas to the boiling water and blanch until they no longer taste raw, about 2 minutes, then drain and transfer to the ice water. When cool, drain again and pat dry.

Break up the chilled rice with your hands so there are no clumps. Heat a 12- to 14-inch nonstick skillet over high heat. Add the sesame oil. When it is almost smoking, add the rice and spread it flat with a wooden spoon. Let it cook without stirring for about 2 minutes to allow it to color slightly, then stir. Add the peas and green garlic and stir to combine. Add the scallions and cook, stirring, until they soften slightly, about 30 seconds. Add the soy sauce and preserved lemon and toss well.

Remove the skillet from the heat and scoot the rice to one side of the pan, leaving half the pan bare. Add the beaten eggs to the bare area, then return the skillet to high heat and scramble the eggs with a wooden spoon until barely set, about 1 minute. Toss the eggs and rice together and taste for salt. Transfer to a serving dish and garnish with a few shreds of raw green garlic and scallion. Serve immediately.

Little Gem Lettuces with Radishes, Fennel, and Verjus-Umeboshi Vinaigrette

Serves 4 to 6

Verjus-Umeboshi Vinaigrette:

1¼ cups red verjus

6 tablespoons canola oil

2 tablespoons pure olive oil (not extra virgin)

2 tablespoons umeboshi paste

2 tablespoons fresh lemon juice

¾ teaspoon xanthan gum (see Chef's Tip)

Sea salt

½ fennel bulb, stalks removed

4 radishes, preferably a mix of colors, leaves removed

5 Little Gem lettuces

Sea salt and freshly ground black pepper

Edible flowers, for garnish

Wine: The Prisoner Wine Company Blindfold

Make the vinaigrette: In a blender, combine the verjus, both oils, umeboshi paste, lemon juice, and xanthan gum and blend until smooth. Transfer to a bowl and whisk in salt to taste.

Have ready two bowls of ice water. With a mandoline or other vegetable slicer, slice the fennel and the radishes paper-thin. Put each into its own bowl of ice water. Refrigerate for 1 hour to crisp, then drain and pat dry.

This pretty salad might be on the table when guests visit The Prisoner in spring for a family-style lunch. It adapts to what's in the garden, but the unusual vinaigrette remains unchanged. Like a lot of Brett's food, the vinaigrette merges wine country flavors, such as verjus, the sweet-tart juice from underripe wine grapes, with international ingredients, such as umeboshi paste, an intense fermented seasoning derived from dried Japanese plums. It's difficult to make the dressing in a small volume, so you will have some left over for dressing other salads or saucing grilled fish. It has a fruity, strawberry-like taste.

Quarter 2 of the Little Gem lettuces through the core. With a pastry brush, lightly brush the quartered lettuces all over with the vinaigrette. Sprinkle with salt and pepper, then arrange the quarters around the edge of a shallow salad bowl.

Chop the remaining 3 lettuces into bite-size pieces and put them into a bowl. Add the fennel and half of the radishes, then drizzle with enough of the vinaigrette to coat the salad lightly and toss well. Season to taste with salt and pepper. Transfer to the salad bowl, heaping it in the middle. Garnish with the remaining radish slices and with edible flowers. Serve immediately.

chef's tip:

Xanthan gum, a powder available at some supermarkets, creates an emulsified vinaigrette that does not separate. It has no flavor. Brett uses it in almost all his salad dressings.

Spring Pizza Flambé with Bacon, Leeks, and Fromage Blanc

Makes two 11-inch pizzas

Pizza Dough:

2½ cups pizza flour or all-purpose flour

¾ cup plus 2 tablespoons cold water

¼ teaspoon instant dry yeast

1 tablespoon warm water

3 tablespoons sourdough starter

1 teaspoon olive oil, plus more for the bowls

2 teaspoons sea salt

Topping:

1 tablespoon canola oil

2 cups leeks, white and pale green part, in ½-inch-thick slices

¼ pound thick-sliced bacon, diced

½ cup fromage blanc

1 tablespoon crème fraîche

Grated zest of 1 lemon

¼ teaspoon sea salt

2 teaspoons fresh herb flowers, such as thyme and chervil blossoms, or 2 teaspoons minced fresh thyme

All-purpose flour, for dusting

Wine: The Prisoner Wine Company Eternally Silenced

Make the pizza dough: In a large bowl, combine the flour and cold water and stir with a wooden spoon until the mixture forms a shaggy mass. Knead lightly until it comes together, cover, and let rest for 30 minutes.

In a small bowl, dissolve the yeast in the warm water. Add to the dough along with the sourdough starter and olive oil. Knead for 1 minute, then add the salt and continue kneading until the dough is

The Prisoner Wine Company's outdoor pizza oven gets a workout in good weather, when the winery hosts many groups for alfresco events. The garden always provides something enticing for the topping—in spring, tender leeks to caramelize and bake with clumps of fresh cheese and tiny herb blossoms to scatter on after baking for a burst of fragrance.

smooth and elastic, about 10 minutes. The dough will seem very wet and sticky at first, but the flour will eventually absorb the liquid and the dough will become more manageable. Transfer the dough to an oiled bowl. Cover and refrigerate for at least 12 hours or up to overnight.

Divide the dough in half and shape each half into a ball. Place the balls in an oiled bowl or tub, cover, and refrigerate for at least 24 hours or up to 5 days. On baking day, take the balls out of the refrigerator. Set them on a floured surface, cover with a clean kitchen towel, and let rise at room temperature until doubled.

Make the topping: Heat the canola oil in a skillet over medium-high heat. Add the leeks and cook, stirring almost constantly, until they caramelize and darken, about 5 minutes, adding splashes of water if they threaten to stick or burn. Set aside to cool.

Put the bacon into a cast-iron skillet and set over medium heat. Cook, stirring often, until the bacon crisps, about 10 minutes. Transfer to paper towels to drain and cool.

In a bowl, whisk together the fromage blanc, crème fraîche, lemon zest, and salt.

At least 30 minutes before baking, put a baking stone in the oven and preheat the oven to 550°F or the highest setting.

On a floured surface, flatten 1 dough ball with your hands into a 12-inch round. Transfer it to a well-floured pizza peel. Scatter half of the leeks over the dough, leaving a ½-inch rim. Using half of the fromage blanc mixture, place 8 or 10 dollops of the mixture on the dough. Top with half of the bacon and half of the herb blossoms. Transfer the pizza to the baking stone and bake, rotating it 180 degrees halfway through baking, until well browned on the bottom and the rim, about 8 minutes. Cut into wedges and serve immediately. Repeat with the remaining dough ball.

Potato Gnocchi with Asparagus and Black Trumpet Mushrooms **Serves 6**

Brett learned to make gnocchi from a master, and he has since perfected his own technique. His gnocchi are beautiful and light, and he attributes the good outcome to two key practices: he insists on quickly transforming the cooked potatoes into dough, and he uses a bench scraper to mix the ingredients and keep gluten from forming. In spring, he likes to pair the gnocchi with asparagus, pureeing some of the cooked stalks for a buttery sauce and tossing in the tender tips at the end.

⅓ cup dried black trumpet mushrooms, cleaned

2 russet potatoes, 8 to 10 ounces each

¼ cup plus 2 tablespoons Italian "00" flour (page 196), plus more for dusting

Sea salt and freshly ground black pepper

1 large egg, beaten

2 tablespoons extra virgin olive oil, plus more for garnish

12 large asparagus spears (about 1 pound), ends trimmed and stalks peeled

5 tablespoons unsalted butter

1 cup water

1 cup grated pecorino romano cheese, plus more for garnish

½ lemon

Wine: The Prisoner Wine Company Erased

Soak the mushrooms in hot water to cover until soft, about 30 minutes, then drain and set aside.

Preheat the oven to 400°F or 375°F with a convection fan. Pierce the potatoes all over with a fork. Place on a baking sheet and bake until tender, about 1 hour. Let them rest for 5 minutes, then cut the potatoes in half lengthwise and scoop the flesh into a food mill fitted with the medium blade. Pass the flesh through the food mill onto a work surface. Measure out 1½ cups lightly packed milled potatoes (9 ounces) and discard the remainder or reserve for another use.

In a small bowl, whisk together the flour and ½ teaspoon salt. Sprinkle ¼ cup plus 1 tablespoon of the flour mixture over the potato and then drizzle with the egg. Working with a metal bench scraper, use a chopping and folding motion to incorporate the ingredients gently. When the flour is largely incorporated, knead lightly and briefly by hand until you have a smooth dough, adding the remaining 1 tablespoon flour mixture if needed.

Cut the dough in half. On a floured work surface, roll each half by hand into a rope about 1 inch thick and 14 inches long. Cut each rope crosswise into 1-inch pieces. Use a dinner fork to form the gnocchi in this manner: Put a piece of dough on the fork and pinch it until it is the same width as the fork. With the side of your thumb, make a shallow crosswise indentation in the middle of the dough. Still using the side of your thumb, roll the dough off the tines of the fork lengthwise so the dough curls like a loose jelly roll. The exterior should have shallow ridges from the tines of the fork.

Bring a large pot of salted water to a boil over high heat and add the oil. Prepare a large bowl of ice water. Working in small batches, boil the gnocchi until they float to the surface; wait for another 20 seconds, then transfer them to the ice water with a wire skimmer. When all the gnocchi are cooked, drain them and place them in a single layer on a clean kitchen towel.

Bring a pot of salted water to a boil and prepare a bowl of ice water. Cut off the top 3 inches of each asparagus spear. Set aside 3 of these tips. Cook the remaining tips until crisp-tender, about 2 minutes, then transfer to the ice water with the wire skimmer. Cook the stalks until tender, about 3 minutes, then transfer to the ice water. Drain both and pat dry. Cut the cooked tips in half lengthwise. With a vegetable peeler, shave the raw tips lengthwise.

Put the cooked stalks into a blender, add enough water (about ½ cup) to make a puree with a sauce consistency, and blend until smooth. Transfer to a saucepan, add 1 tablespoon of the butter, and warm over low heat until the butter melts. Season with salt and pepper and keep warm.

Melt the remaining 4 tablespoons butter in a large skillet over medium-high heat. Add the water and bring to a simmer. Add the gnocchi and the halved asparagus tips and season with salt and pepper. Simmer briskly until the liquid has reduced but is not fully absorbed, about 2 minutes. Add the mushrooms and toss until they are hot. Add the cheese and toss until it melts, adding a splash of water if the mixture looks dry.

Divide the asparagus puree among four shallow bowls, spreading it thinly with the back of a spoon. Top with the gnocchi, dividing them evenly. Garnish each portion with shaved raw asparagus, a few drops of lemon juice, a drizzle of olive oil, and a sprinkle of pecorino. Serve immediately.

must-have herbs:

The garden beds at The Prisoner Wine Company offer an enormous palette of culinary herbs for freshening chef Brett Young's creations. Here are five herbs he can't live without.

Lemon thyme: for flavoring marinades and scattering over a hot pizza

Mexican tarragon: less aggressive in its anise scent than French tarragon; for brightening salads and vinaigrettes

Thai basil: for folding into Asian noodle dishes and stir-fries just before serving

Lemon verbena: for fermenting to make kombucha and for perfuming vinaigrettes

Mexican oregano: for contributing authentic flavor to Mexican-inspired dishes

Above and right: *Unusual varieties of culinary herbs flourish in The Prisoner Wine Company's garden beds; a chef's bouquet of Mexican tarragon, lemon verbena, and rosemary*

Regusci Winery: *Italian-American Abbondanza*

Napa

Visitors come to Regusci Winery for its celebrated wines, but few leave without a stop at the Garden Wagon to fill their totes with estate-grown fruits and vegetables. "Wine-club members never go home empty-handed," says proprietor Laura Regusci, who makes sure the honor-system farm stand is especially bountiful before winery events.

Neighbor kids bike up the Reguscis' long walnut tree–lined drive to fill their baskets with strawberries and cherry tomatoes. Their parents, many of them internationally known vintners, shop for dinner and fresh flowers at the rustic fruit-and-vegetable wagon. For vintners Laura and Jim Regusci, the expansive garden and produce stand make a personal statement: we are farmers first, on this ranch for more than a century, with Italian roots and an Italian love of *abbondanza*.

Jim's immigrant grandfather purchased the original 286-acre parcel in Napa Valley's prestigious Stags Leap District. Today, Jim's busy farming company, Regusci Vineyard Management, services his own vineyards and those of dozens of other grape growers. In addition,

Left and above: *Laura Regusci harvests okra with the help of canine friends; Regusci farm stand, a riot of color, operates on the honor system.*

the family raises chickens, turkeys, pigs, goats, sheep, and cattle for its own table and for special events; bottles olive oil; and harvests a cornucopia of orchard fruits and nuts, from apples and plums to persimmons, pomegranates, and walnuts. The family menagerie is missing only a dairy cow, ironic in that the Regusci Dairy, a business Jim's grandfather started in the 1930s, supplied Napa Valley with milk and cream for almost forty years. "Our family has always produced its own food," says Jim, "but now it's chic."

In 2010, when Jim decided that a Cabernet Sauvignon block on the home ranch needed replanting, he asked Laura about its viability as a garden. Laura quickly saw the potential in that idea, believing that an edible garden would create lasting memories for winery guests and distinguish the experience of visiting Regusci. Validation came quickly on social media. "I look at people's images, and they've taken pictures of the vegetable stand," acknowledges Jim.

Raised in Kentucky, Laura fell in love with farming as a way of life while living with farm families in northern Europe during high school. She earned a master's degree in agriculture education, then launched a twenty-year academic career, teaching organic farming and gardening at the junior-college and high-school level and installing edible gardens wherever she went. To bolster youth interest in the local food, wine, and hospitality industries, she helped create California's first high-school viticulture and winemaking curriculum at St. Helena High School, which Jim's children attended.

It wasn't long before Laura and Jim discovered their mutual passions, and soon Laura was sketching garden designs for the former vineyard block. Over time, Laura has softened the beds' angularity with tall, arched trellises for beans and tomatoes and with swaths of

colorful cosmos and sunflowers. Gardening in a grid is functional, says Laura, making irrigation and planting plans easier.

"This garden is about more than just eating fresh or eating local," says Laura. "For us, growing is a passion." Laura's gardening talents are also evident at the ranch home she shares with Jim, an Eden of olive and avocado trees, strawberry beds, lemon verbena for scenting pitchers of water, and a cutting garden lush with zinnias and sunflowers.

The vegetable garden's annual output could satisfy a dozen Italian grandmothers, with 280 basil plants yielding so heavily that Laura supplies a local juice shop and many of her favorite restaurants in the valley. Pesto and basil oil made in the ranch kitchen find their way into gift baskets for VIP wine-club members, with plenty of basil left to share with employees.

Nine large square beds of perennials and fruit trees—raspberries, pomegranates, figs, strawberries, fennel, asparagus, artichokes, and culinary herbs—form the core of the landscape, so the garden's heart remains largely green year-round. The larger twenty-by-forty-foot beds on the perimeter change with the seasons. In summer, they're home to twenty varieties of tomatoes planted in rows by color; shishito, Padrón, and banana peppers and thick stands of broom corn; Rosa Bianca and Nadia eggplants for estate chef Angel Perez's famous eggplant parmigiana; green beans; cucumbers; mini watermelons; and multiple types of summer squash. Perez is Oaxacan, so this wine country garden always includes an abundance of fiery chiles for salsas and pickles, as well as many of the ingredients that make up his mother's laborious mole.

Above: *(clockwise from left) Napa Valley vista; garden coordinator Jim Bachor (left) harvests with chef Angel Perez; Shooting Stars eggplant; colorful blooms lure beneficial insects; ripening chiles; farm stand bounty*

"In nature, more diversity creates a resilient garden," says Laura, who views the whole Regusci estate as an ecosystem where "everything feeds everything else."

Cherry tomato and gourd vines clamber over arches made of hog-wire fencing, creating shady, mysterious tunnels that beckon children.

Autumn weather ripens the butternut squash that Angel uses for one of the family's favorite soups. A vast pumpkin patch bordered with white cosmos has its moment in the spotlight, and the estate's walnut trees deliver their annual treasure.

In winter, the pace is slower compared to summer's marathon. Half the garden will be carpeted with mustard, a cover crop that improves the soil, while the other half will furnish garlic, cabbage, fava beans, leeks, kale, Brussels sprouts, collards, beets, and carrots for the family kitchen and for employees. "The cabbages here are ridiculous," says Jim. "Let's just say they may not go through a basketball hoop."

And always, year-round, bees and beneficial insects will find welcoming thickets of blooms: sunflowers, lavender, lemon verbena, zinnias, salvias, scabiosa, and roses, garden residents valued for the habitat they provide and the charming bouquets they inspire.

To create a more integrated and sustainable system, Laura has gradually introduced heritage livestock to the ranch. Now the pasture supports beef cattle, sheep, turkeys, and goats; chickens and ducks provide eggs for the winery kitchen; and squealing litters of piglets grow to maturity on garden scraps. It's an ancient and synergistic approach, with landscape nurturing livestock and vice versa.

Left and above: *Laura enjoys feeding the ranch turkeys; Jim and Laura relax at sunset with a glass of Regusci Winery Block 3 Cabernet Sauvignon.*

"In nature, more diversity creates a resilient garden," says Laura, who views the estate as an ecosystem where "everything feeds everything else." The animals provide manure that nourishes the soil. The garden provides produce—misshapen or overripe—that nourishes the animals. Strategically planted insectaries keep an army of good bugs on patrol so pests rarely get the upper hand.

"That's the way we garden, by understanding the biological aspects," says Jim Bachor, the garden coordinator and a former student of Laura's.

Above and right: *(clockwise from left) Angel heads for the kitchen with jumbo heirloom tomatoes; farm stand artichokes and avocados; historic Regusci stone winery; sun-ripened cherry tomatoes*

The bonanza of vegetables and fruits from this garden would be daunting without a resourceful cook to manage it. Angel, whose wife, father, sister, and brothers also work at Regusci, has a long résumé with Napa Valley restaurants and an experimental bent that serves him well when the garden delivers a deluge. He makes crackers incorporating oven-dried tomatoes and grissini flavored with pureed artichokes. He puts up numberless jars of fig jam, marinara sauce, pickled jalapeños, spicy *giardiniera*, and—Laura's favorite—pickled okra. He makes spiced walnuts for cakes and cheese boards, pistachio pesto for visitor gifts, and avocado-tomatillo salsa and chips for business meetings.

Angel's talents and the garden bounty merge most impressively at Thanksgiving, when Jim and Laura host a crowd. Italian-American, Mexican, and southern foodways mix and mingle in a feast that always showcases a turkey raised on the ranch and begins with a massive charcuterie board. Pickled okra makes an appearance, as does Angel's butternut squash soup with balsamic reduction, a cornbread dressing with Italian seasonings, Brussels sprouts with apples (estate grown, of course), and a persimmon-walnut pudding that nods to a nut crop that once rivaled grapes in Napa Valley.

If Jim had any doubts about Laura's ability to realize her garden vision, they are long gone. As he has learned in the years since they married, she has an almost supernatural green thumb. Jim likes to tell about the time the couple visited the former World Trade Center site in New York City and Laura spotted a few acorns under the only surviving oak tree. Those forlorn acorns are now thriving young oaks at Regusci Winery.

Jim's vineyard-management business is a dusty world of pickup trucks, tractors, and tool sheds. Now, at its center, is an orderly oasis of greenery and calm. "Laura has softened the ranch with her garden," says Jim, and that's surely a good return on investment.

menu

Antipasto Platter with Southern-Style Pickled Okra
Regusci Winery Rosé

Roasted Butternut Squash Soup with Pomegranate and Pumpkin Seeds
Regusci Winery Merlot

Brussels Sprouts with Bacon, Apples, and Pistachios

Italian Cornbread Dressing
Regusci Winery Zinfandel

Steamed Persimmon and Walnut Pudding
2001 Regusci Winery Cabernet Sauvignon

Antipasto Platter with Southern-Style Pickled Okra

Makes 6 pints

3 pounds small okra

6 cups distilled white vinegar

4 cups water

½ cup kosher or sea salt

¼ cup sugar

For Each Pint Jar:

¼ teaspoon yellow mustard seeds

¼ teaspoon dill seeds

6 black peppercorns

6 cumin seeds

2 cloves garlic, peeled

1 fresh oregano sprig

1 bay leaf

Pinch of ground coriander

Pinch of red chile flakes

Wine: Regusci Winery Rosé

Have ready six sterilized pint canning jars and two-part lids. Trim the okra stems if needed to fit the whole pods upright in the jars. Otherwise, leave the stems intact.

Laura developed a passion for pickling in her grandmother's Kentucky kitchen. The family pastime began as a way to preserve vegetables for winter and share homegrown gifts with neighbors. Today, Laura carries on the tradition, growing okra and other seasonable vegetables in the Regusci estate garden for pickling. Each Thanksgiving, pickled okra adds a southern spirit to the family's antipasto board alongside salumi, figs, grissini, and marinated artichokes.

In a saucepan, combine the vinegar, water, salt, and sugar and bring to a simmer over medium-high heat, stirring to dissolve the sugar. Keep hot.

Into each of the six jars, put the mustard seeds, dill seeds, peppercorns, cumin seeds, garlic, oregano, bay leaf, coriander, and chile flakes. Fill the jars with the okra, packing it in upright—alternating the stems up and down if needed—as tightly as possible. Fill the jars with the hot liquid, leaving ¼-inch headspace, and top each jar with a flat lid and screw band. Process the jars in a boiling water bath for 15 minutes, then cool on racks without disturbing.

Refrigerate any jars that failed to seal and use within 2 weeks. Store sealed jars in a cool, dark place for up to 1 year. Wait for at least 1 week before opening a jar to allow the flavor to mellow.

Roasted Butternut Squash Soup with Pomegranate and Pumpkin Seeds

Makes 10 cups; serves 10 to 12

1 butternut squash, about 4 pounds

7 tablespoons unsalted butter

1 tablespoon brown sugar

Sea salt and freshly ground black pepper

1 teaspoon extra virgin olive oil

1 large white onion, chopped

2 celery ribs, sliced

1 large carrot, peeled and sliced

2 cloves garlic, minced

½ large shallot, sliced

1 teaspoon peeled and minced fresh ginger

Kosher or sea salt and freshly ground white pepper

1 bay leaf

1 fresh thyme sprig

6 cups water

½ teaspoon ground cumin, toasted in a dry pan

Freshly grated nutmeg

10 to 12 small winter squashes, about 1 pound each, stems attached

For Garnish:

Bottled balsamic vinegar reduction or glaze

Pomegranate arils (seeds)

Roasted and salted pumpkin seeds (pepitas)

Thinly sliced fresh chives

Angel's festive soup is a fixture at the Regusci family's Thanksgiving table and holiday parties. Served in hollowed-out miniature squashes, this creamy soup is topped with pomegranate arils, pepitas, and a drizzle of balsamic vinegar reduction. During the winery's annual wreath-making event, wine club members enjoy this signature soup from mugs. A handsome tureen is another serving option if you can't find mini squashes.

Wine: Regusci Winery Merlot

Preheat the oven to 350°F. Line a baking sheet with parchment paper. With a cleaver or heavy chef's knife, cut off the stem end of the butternut squash, then cut the squash crosswise where the bulbous base meets the straight neck. Cut both pieces in half lengthwise. Remove the seeds and stringy membranes from the cavities. Put the squash halves, skin side down and generously spaced, on the prepared pan. Using 4 tablespoons of the butter, dot the surface and cavities of the squash. Sprinkle with the sugar and season with sea salt and black pepper. Bake until the squash is tender when pierced and lightly caramelized, 50 to 55 minutes. Let cool, then scrape the flesh from the skins.

In a large pot, melt the remaining 3 tablespoons butter with the oil over medium heat. Add the onion, celery, carrot, garlic, shallot, and ginger and season with kosher salt and white pepper. Sauté until the vegetables soften, 7 to 8 minutes; do not allow them to brown. Add the bay leaf, thyme sprig, and 4 cups of the water. Bring to a boil over medium-high heat, adjust the heat to maintain a gentle simmer, and simmer uncovered for 45 minutes.

Remove the bay leaf and thyme sprig, then add the squash flesh, breaking it up with a wooden spoon. Stir in the remaining 2 cups water, the cumin, and a few scrapes of nutmeg and bring the soup back to a boil, stirring often. Let cool, then puree in batches in a blender until completely smooth and pour into a clean saucepan.

(continued)

Gently reheat the soup, stirring often and adding a little more water if it is too thick for your taste. Season to taste with kosher salt and white pepper.

To make the squash bowls, use a heavy chef's knife or cleaver. Working very carefully, slice off the tops just below the stem. The easiest and safest way to do this is to score the squash first, slicing all the way around but not all the way through. Once you have scored the squash, you can more easily slice all the way through and remove the top. With a soupspoon, scoop out the seeds and membranes. You can prepare the bowls several hours ahead.

Just before serving, place the squash bowls on a parchment-lined baking sheet and bake at 350°F until very warm, about 5 minutes.

Set the warm squash bowls on individual plates. Ladle hot soup into the cavities, stopping short of the rim; you should have enough room for about ¾ cup. Drizzle with balsamic vinegar reduction (using a squeeze bottle if you have one). Scatter a few pomegranate arils, pumpkin seeds, and chives on top of each serving and cover each squash bowl with its top. Serve immediately.

Brussels Sprouts with Bacon, Apples, and Pistachios **Serves 6**

If there's one Thanksgiving dish the Regusci family can't be without, it's this Brussels sprout preparation. Made with young, mild sprouts from the estate garden, this side dish will turn even Brussels sprout skeptics into believers. You can blanch the sprouts 1 day ahead. Pat dry and refrigerate in a plastic bag.

1½ pounds Brussels sprouts, trimmed and halved lengthwise

1 tablespoon canola oil

½ pound thick-sliced bacon, in large dice

½ large white onion, sliced

Sea salt and freshly ground black pepper

½ teaspoon minced fresh thyme

¼ cup apple cider vinegar whisked with 2 teaspoons sugar

1 apple, halved, cored, and sliced about ¼ inch thick

½ cup chopped roasted and salted pistachios

Bring a large pot of salted water to a boil over high heat. Add the Brussels sprouts and blanch for 1½ minutes. Drain into a sieve or colander. Let dry completely, patting dry with paper towels if necessary. They must be completely dry to sear properly.

Heat the oil in a large skillet over medium-high heat. Add the bacon and sauté until it renders most of its fat but is not yet crisp, about 5 minutes; lower the heat if necessary to keep the bacon from burning. With a slotted spoon, transfer the bacon to a bowl. Add the onion to the skillet and sauté just until it softens slightly but does not color, about 1 minute. With a slotted spoon, transfer the onion to the bowl with the bacon. Pour off and reserve the bacon fat and wipe the skillet clean.

Return 2 tablespoons bacon fat to the skillet and set over high heat. When the fat is hot, add the Brussels sprouts and let them sear without stirring for about 3 minutes so they brown well on one side. Season with salt and pepper, then stir briefly to redistribute them and let them again sear without stirring for about 3 minutes. Lower the heat if necessary to keep them from burning and add another 1 tablespoon bacon fat if the pan seems dry.

Remove from the heat and stir in the thyme. Immediately add the cider-sugar mixture, bacon and onion, apple slices, and pistachios and toss to mix. Taste for seasoning, then serve.

Above: *A Regusci family Thanksgiving includes Roasted Butternut Squash Soup, Italian Cornbread Dressing, and Brussels Sprouts with Bacon, Apples, and Pistachios to accompany ranch-raised turkey.*

Italian Cornbread Dressing

Serves 8

Jalapeño and Fresh Corn Cornbread:

1 jalapeño chile

1 cup fresh corn kernels (from about 1 ear corn)

1 cup unbleached all-purpose flour

1 cup yellow cornmeal

1 cup sugar

¼ cup cake flour

2 tablespoons baking powder

1½ teaspoons kosher or sea salt

4 large eggs

1 cup whole milk

½ cup buttermilk

¾ cup unsalted butter, melted and cooled

⅓ cup canola oil

6 tablespoons unsalted butter

1 teaspoon extra virgin olive oil

6 carrots, chopped

1½ white onions, chopped

4 large celery ribs, thinly sliced

3 cloves garlic, minced

1 shallot, thinly sliced

Sea salt and freshly ground black pepper

¼ cup dry white wine

3 tablespoons chopped fresh flat-leaf parsley

½ teaspoon finely minced fresh thyme

3 fresh sage leaves, finely minced

½ teaspoon red chile flakes

1 cup chicken broth

1 cup chopped toasted pecans (optional)

Wine: Regusci Winery Zinfandel

The perfect Thanksgiving accompaniment to ranch-raised ham and turkey, the family's cornbread dressing is a recipe that will be shared with generations to come. Angel's wife, Adriana, bakes the cornbread, then Angel and Laura prepare the dressing with sautéed vegetables and herbs.

Prepare the cornbread: Preheat the oven to 350°F. Line a 12-by-17-inch baking sheet with parchment paper.

Toast the whole jalapeño in a dry small skillet over medium heat, turning it with tongs until it is blistered all over. Immediately wrap the chile in plastic wrap and let steam until cool. Unwrap and discard the skin, stem, and seeds, then finely chop.

Toast the corn in the same dry skillet over medium heat, stirring constantly, until the corn loses its raw taste, about 2 minutes. Let cool.

In a large bowl, whisk together the all-purpose flour, cornmeal, sugar, cake flour, baking powder, and salt. In a medium bowl, whisk together the eggs, milk, buttermilk, butter, and canola oil. Add the liquid ingredients to the dry ingredients and whisk to blend. Stir in the jalapeño and the corn.

Transfer the batter to the prepared pan and bake the cornbread, rotating the pan back to front halfway through, until lightly browned and firm to the touch, 20 to 30 minutes. Transfer the pan to a rack.

Set aside half of the cornbread to enjoy warm and let the other half cool completely. Transfer the cooled half to a cutting board and cut into ½-inch cubes. Leave to dry out at room temperature overnight.

Preheat the oven to 350°F. Put the cornbread cubes on a baking sheet and bake until lightly browned, about 15 minutes. Let cool. Leave the oven on.

In a 12-inch skillet, melt the butter with the olive oil over medium-high heat. Add the carrots, onions, celery, garlic, and shallot, season with salt and pepper, and sauté until lightly colored, about 5 minutes. Add the wine and cook, stirring, until it evaporates, about 1 minute. Add the parsley, thyme, sage, and chile flakes and cook, stirring, for about 1 minute. Add the broth, bring to a simmer, and remove from the heat. Stir in the toasted cornbread and the pecans, if using. Spread the dressing in an 11-by-9-by-2½-inch baking dish. Cover with aluminum foil and bake for 15 minutes. Serve immediately.

Steamed Persimmon and Walnut Pudding

Serves 12

Sharing recipes is an honored tradition among Napa Valley agricultural families. This family recipe comes from Regusci garden coordinator and friend Jim Bachor. Walnuts are plentiful on the Regusci Ranch and recall the days before grapes became the valley's mainstay. The pudding calls for Hachiya persimmons, the heart-shaped variety that is harvested firm. Leave them on the kitchen counter until they are squishy, then remove the cap, cut in half, and inspect for seeds before pureeing, skin and all.

⅓ cup unsalted butter, melted, plus more for the mold

1 cup sugar

1 cup all-purpose flour

2 teaspoons baking soda

1 teaspoon ground cinnamon

½ teaspoon sea salt

½ cup raisins

½ cup coarsely chopped toasted walnuts

1 teaspoon pure vanilla extract

½ cup whole milk

1 large egg

1 cup Hachiya persimmon pulp (about 2 ripe persimmons)

Powdered sugar, for dusting (optional)

Whipped cream, for serving (optional)

Wine: 2001 Regusci Winery Cabernet Sauvignon

Place a steamer rack in the bottom of a large pot and add enough water to come to within 1 inch of the top of a 1½-quart pudding mold. Bring the water to a boil over high heat. With melted butter, brush the interior and the underside of the lid of the pudding mold and set aside.

In a large bowl, whisk together the sugar, flour, baking soda, cinnamon, and salt until blended. Stir in the raisins and walnuts. In a medium bowl, whisk together the butter, vanilla, milk, egg, and persimmon. Fold the wet ingredients into the dry ingredients just until blended.

Transfer the batter to the prepared mold and clamp on the lid. Place on the rack in the boiling water, cover the pot, and reduce the heat to maintain a gentle simmer. You should see some steam escaping from the pot throughout the cooking. Cook for 1¼ hours.

Carefully transfer the pudding mold to a rack. Let cool for 30 minutes, then remove the lid and unmold the pudding onto a serving dish. Serve warm or at room temperature. If desired, dust with powdered sugar just before serving and accompany with whipped cream.

chef's tip:

Hachiya persimmon puree freezes well. Freeze in 1-cup containers and use another time to make this moist steamed pudding or fruit smoothies year-round.

Left and above: *Laura gathers dried fava beans to plant for next year's crop; a bed of sunflowers and blooming fennel frames a view of the vineyards and distant Mayacamas Mountains.*

top habitat plants for healthy gardens:

The Regusci garden puts out the welcome mat for bees and beneficial insects. Some of Laura's favorite plants for luring good bugs and butterflies include the following:

Cosmos	Milkweed
Dill	Red Valerian
Echinacea	Salvia
Fennel	Yarrow

Robert Mondavi Winery: *Garden Carved from a Vineyard*

Oakville

Robert and Margrit Mondavi were legendary hosts whose warm approach to wine country hospitality persists at Robert Mondavi Winery years after the couple's passing. Margrit, especially, was a fresh-air and fresh-food enthusiast who believed that a vegetable garden was as essential to the winery as the prime vineyards alongside it. From its beginning in 1966, the Robert Mondavi Winery, with its mission-style architecture, exemplified the relaxed California way of life. Entertaining visitors with a garden-to-table meal only underscored the message, then as now.

Today, winery executive chef Jeff Mosher manages the edible garden with his culinary team. They plant it and tend it, harvest its bounty and cook what it yields. Christened the "Piccolo" To Kalon Garden, after the adjacent To Kalon Vineyard, source of the winery's finest Cabernet Sauvignon, the garden is a small (*piccolo* in Italian) parcel carved out of a world-renowned vineyard. Given the market value of the wine grapes that this terrain could produce, the garden speaks volumes about the winery's priorities.

"The garden communicates the winery's commitment and connection to the land," says Nova Cadamatre, senior director of winemaking. "It's about following the seasonal cycle, like we do in the vineyard. Jeff's menus are always driven by what is growing right now."

With its low redwood-framed beds and shredded bark paths, the edible garden is as understated as the winery, a compound acclaimed for its tasteful design and lack of ostentation. The garden, a neat, flat grid

Left and above: *Winery chef Jeff Mosher harvests spring vegetables at the foot of the Mayacamas Mountains; from the To Kalon Vineyard, a view of the winery's mission architecture*

of raised beds surrounded by fig, olive, and citrus trees, supplies only a small portion of the produce this busy winery—one of Napa Valley's most visited—needs. But it serves as a scenic backdrop for some of the visitor experiences and an educational venue as well.

From late spring until fall, the garden stars in some of the winery's small-group offerings. Guests who opt for these experiences will tour the garden with a winery chef, gather herbs and produce, and then decamp to the winery's nearby kitchen for a hands-on cooking lesson. They'll prepare a dish or two with the produce they picked, then tour the winery while the culinary staff completes and serves the meal.

With the culinary garden only steps from the kitchen, Jeff and his crew can pop out to snip fresh chives the moment they're needed or gather violas, dianthus, nasturtiums, or calendulas to add vivid color to their plates. "It's hard for us to plant enough onions, but we can plant enough flowers," says the chef.

In spring's gentle light, the culinary garden has a newborn softness and freshness. Trellises and stakes are in place for the vining squashes, tomatoes, and towering sunflowers that will cover them in the weeks to come, but the garden's inhabitants in May are mostly low growing: tufts of chives, fragile lettuces, the tender tops of French breakfast radishes, wisps of arugula. The To Kalon vines, bare all winter, are steadily pushing out their leafy canes against the stately backdrop of the Mayacamas Mountains.

For Jeff and his team, the garden also expands the potential for food and wine pairing and heightening guests' experience of Robert Mondavi wines.

"It's a nice collaboration," says Nova. "I'll take a new wine to him and his team and we'll taste it together. We'll talk about the different flavors in the wine and toss ideas back and forth. Jeff's team does an amazing job of teasing out subtle differences that even my winemaking team doesn't perceive because we're not as familiar with the flavors of fruits and vegetables."

The conventional "red wine with red meat" approach to wine pairing doesn't begin to describe the pairing strategies that emerge when a chef has a culinary garden at arm's reach.

"One of the things Jeff's team has opened my eyes to is how well fennel goes with our Fumé Blanc," says Nova. The wine that Robert Mondavi christened—Fumé Blanc was his poetic rebranding of Sauvignon Blanc—has some of the same fresh, faint licorice or anise scent that fennel contributes to a dish. "Pairing that wine with shaved fennel or candied fennel is always mind-blowing," says Nova.

Above: *(clockwise from left) The winery garden abuts the famous To Kalon Vineyard; Jeff samples spring peas; garden signage; iconic winery entrance; French Breakfast radishes; nasturtium pesto prep*

"The garden communicates the winery's commitment and connection to the land. Jeff's menus are always driven by what is growing right now."

While a grilled steak is a slam-dunk pairing for Robert Mondavi's classic Cabernet Sauvignon, a wine that has long been a standard bearer for California wine around the world, the accompanying vegetables can make the match even more profound. "Jeff does this great braised kale that goes so well with Cabernet Sauvignon," says Nova. "Kale has a strong flavor and crunch, but our Cabernet is strong and structured, so it marries well with that type of vegetable."

With the winery's Chardonnay, the kitchen turns to creamy vegetables that welcome butter, such as potatoes, sweet potatoes, and butternut squash. Even parts of the plant that cooks rarely use, such as nasturtium leaves, become elements of the kitchen's palette, employed to help highlight aspects of a wine. For a composed salad of spring

vegetables and ricotta, Jeff adds nasturtium leaves to the accompanying pesto, believing that their peppery, herbal character produces a more intriguing match for the Fumé Blanc Reserve. Nasturtiums thrive in these garden beds, so the peppery pesto makes other appearances, often with grilled bread, burrata, and spring vegetables.

To see such creative, high-level cooking coming from this kitchen is no surprise. Robert and Margrit Mondavi were tireless supporters of the arts, bringing world-renowned chefs, musicians, painters, and performers to the winery to enrich the valley's cultural life. For many years, the Robert Mondavi Winery's Great Chefs

Above and right: *(clockwise from lower left) Ripening blueberries; harvesting radishes; beehives and fruit trees add diversity to the winery garden; sunset and moon over To Kalon Vineyard*

cooking school lured culinary luminaries to Napa Valley, establishing this wine valley as a destination for food enthusiasts, too.

In April and May, the winery garden yields delicate greens, sweet baby carrots, pristine English peas, and a profusion of edible flowers and wispy herbs. The gorgeous dishes that Jeff and crew create from this bounty practically beg for a painter to capture them; Margrit Mondavi, an avid watercolorist, would have relished the chance.

An appetizer tostada topped with avocado, cured yellowtail, and sweet-tart beads of finger lime complements the winery's unoaked Chardonnay, a bright, citrus-forward interpretation of this variety. Fluffy house-made ricotta and a bouquet of spring vegetables pair up for the next course, a ravishing salad, but the showstopper is sous-chef Lisa Moore's edible flower *croccante*, cracker art produced by pressing garden blossoms and leaves into the dough. A pasta course follows, to showcase the garden's first spring peas, fava beans, and sweet onions. Lisa is the crew's pasta specialist, transforming ten egg yolks and a cup of flour into a heap of golden fettuccine.

For the main course, a seared rib-eye steak, Jeff forages in the garden for tender herbs for a salsa verde. Fresh-snipped parsley, chives, and marjoram bring this classic Italian sauce to life, and the accompanying grilled vegetables, still growing that morning, give the composition a California stamp. Like many meals at the Robert Mondavi Winery, this one concludes with Moscato d'Oro, the winery's signature dessert wine from Muscat grapes. Blueberry bushes in the winery garden produce just enough fruit to share occasionally with VIP guests; sous-chef Lissette Garay stretches a few cups of the precious berries into a dessert for a dozen by transforming them into a gelée to top a silky cheesecake.

Napa Valley wineries offer visitors countless ways to explore their properties and products, but a vineyard lunch at the Robert Mondavi Winery is surely among the most pleasant. Dining outside by the edible garden, enjoying the scent of Meyer lemon blossoms and Jeff's exquisite garden-based food, would be a highlight of anyone's valley experience.

menu

Hamachi Crudo Tostada with Finger Limes
and Avocado

**Robert Mondavi Winery Napa Valley
Unoaked Chardonnay**

Spring Vegetable Salad with Ricotta,
Nasturtium Pesto, and Edible Flower Croccante

**Robert Mondavi Winery Napa Valley
Fumé Blanc Reserve**

Parsley Fettuccine with Fava Beans, Peas,
Spring Onions, and Parmesan Cream

**Robert Mondavi Winery Napa Valley
Carneros Pinot Noir Reserve**

Grilled Rib Eye with Grilled Spring Vegetables
and Salsa Verde

**Robert Mondavi Winery Napa Valley
Cabernet Sauvignon Reserve**

Cheesecake with Blueberry Gelée

**Robert Mondavi Winery Napa Valley
Moscato d'Oro**

Above and right: *Just-picked edible spring flowers and nasturtium leaves are pressed into a cracker dough with a pasta machine; the baked sheet makes a crisp cracker or croccante.*

Hamachi Crudo Tostada with Finger Limes and Avocado **Serves 4**

The winery's lone finger-lime tree (Citrus australasica) *produces an abundant crop of these tiny, tangy fruits. The caviar-like beads inside are crunchy, sweet-tart, and juicy, a refreshing garnish for this lovely tostada. You can make all the components a few hours ahead—even the cured and sliced fish—and then assemble the tostada just before serving.*

Hamachi Crudo:

½ cup kosher salt

½ cup light brown sugar

¼ pound skinless hamachi (yellowtail) fillet

Vegetable oil, for deep-frying

4 corn tortillas

Sea salt

1 large or 2 small ice cubes

1 avocado, halved, pitted, and peeled

½ medium jalapeño chile, seeded

1½ teaspoons extra virgin olive oil

Juice of 1 lime

Garnishes:

4 finger limes, or a few drops of fresh lime juice for each tostada

Fresh edible flowers, baby miner's lettuce, bronze fennel fronds, or chives

---

Wine: Robert Mondavi Winery Napa Valley Unoaked Chardonnay

Prepare the hamachi crudo: In a bowl, combine the kosher salt and sugar and mix with your hands until no lumps remain. Bury the fish in the mixture and let stand at room temperature for 15 to 30 minutes.

Pour vegetable oil to a depth of 2 inches into a heavy saucepan and heat to 350°F. With a 3-inch round cookie cutter, cut out a round from each tortilla. Pierce each round in a few places with the tip of a

knife to keep it from curling in the hot oil. Fry the rounds, agitating them almost constantly to keep them submerged in the oil and flipping them halfway through, until lightly colored, about 1½ minutes. Lift them out of the hot oil with tongs or a wire-mesh skimmer and transfer to paper towels to drain. Sprinkle with sea salt while hot.

Put the ice cube into a blender and add the avocado, jalapeño, olive oil, lime juice, and a pinch of sea salt. Blend until smooth. Taste for salt.

Remove the fish from the salt mixture. Rinse well and pat dry on paper towels. Slice against the grain on the diagonal into 12 thin slices.

Top each tostada with about 1 tablespoon of the avocado puree, spreading it evenly with the back of a spoon. (Save leftover avocado puree for another use.) Arrange 3 slices of fish on top of each tostada. Slice the tip off of each finger lime and squeeze the caviar-like seeds directly onto the fish, using 1 lime per tostada. Garnish with flowers and serve immediately.

Spring Vegetable Salad with Ricotta, Nasturtium Pesto, and Edible Flower Croccante **Serves 4**

Whatever is most tender and tempting in the winery's spring garden can find a place in this salad: radishes, baby carrots, fennel, spring onions. Young nasturtium leaves paired with basil produce a lightly spicy pesto that brings even more of the garden to the plate. Jeff makes his own ricotta, but a good store-bought ricotta, such as Calabro, works as well.

Pickled Red Onions:

2 red onions (about 1 pound)

2 cups red wine vinegar

2 cups water

½ cup sugar

1 tablespoon plus 1 teaspoon kosher salt

1 tablespoon black peppercorns

6 fresh thyme sprigs

2 bay leaves

2 whole star anise

2 whole cloves

Edible Flower Croccante:

1¼ cups all-purpose flour, plus more for dusting

¼ cup cornstarch

½ teaspoon sea salt

¼ teaspoon baking powder

2 tablespoons extra virgin olive oil, plus more for brushing

½ cup water, plus more if needed

Nonstick cooking spray, for the parchment

Fresh edible flowers, nasturtium leaves, and fava leaves

Flaky sea salt, such as Maldon

Nasturtium Pesto:

1 tablespoon pine nuts

2 cups lightly packed fresh nasturtium leaves

2 cups lightly packed fresh basil leaves

½ cup grapeseed oil

¾ teaspoon finely minced garlic

1 tablespoon plus 1 teaspoon freshly grated
    Parmigiano-Reggiano cheese

Pinch of sea salt

1 teaspoon fresh lemon juice

½ large fennel bulb, stalks removed

10 small radishes, leaves removed

1 medium carrot

2 cups sugar snap peas (about ¼ pound)

2 tablespoons plus 2 teaspoons extra virgin olive oil

2 tablespoons plus 2 teaspoons fresh lemon juice

Sea salt

¾ cup whole-milk ricotta cheese

Flaky sea salt, such as Maldon

Small fresh basil and nasturtium leaves, for garnish

Wine: Robert Mondavi Winery Napa Valley Fumé Blanc Reserve

Prepare the pickled red onions: Cut off both ends of each onion, halve through the root end, and then peel. Thinly slice each half from stem to root. Put the onion slices into a nonreactive container.

In a saucepan, combine the vinegar, water, sugar, kosher salt, peppercorns, thyme, bay leaves, star anise, and cloves. Bring to a simmer over medium heat, stirring to dissolve the sugar. Remove from the heat and let steep for 30 minutes, then pour over the onions.

(continued)

chef's tip:

Refrigerate extra pesto in an airtight container, pressing a sheet of plastic wrap directly onto the surface, and use within a day. Or freeze in ice cube trays, then transfer the cubes to a plastic bag and store in the freezer for up to 3 months.

Spring Vegetable Salad *(continued)*

Let cool, then cover and refrigerate for at least 1 day before using. They will keep for up to 2 weeks.

Make the edible flower croccante: In a food processor, combine the flour, cornstarch, salt, and baking powder and pulse to blend. Add the oil and pulse several times until evenly blended. Pour in the ½ cup water and pulse just until the mixture comes together into a dough, adding a little more water if too dry. Gather into a ball, wrap in plastic wrap, and refrigerate until chilled.

Preheat the oven to 425°F or 400°F with a convection fan. Line a heavy baking sheet with parchment paper and spray the parchment with cooking spray.

Set up a pasta machine. On a lightly floured work surface, flatten the dough with a rolling pin into a rectangle thin enough to pass through the pasta machine set on the widest setting. Pass the dough through the rollers twice at the widest setting, then continue passing it through the rollers, tightening the rollers by one setting each time, until you have a 20-inch-long sheet. Lay the sheet on a work surface and lightly brush half the sheet (widthwise not lengthwise) with water. Arrange edible flowers and leaves on the moistened half, placing them close together—even overlapping—until they cover the surface. Fold the other half over to enclose the flowers, pressing with your hands to seal. Lightly flour both sides, then feed the dough sheet through the pasta machine, tightening the rollers by one setting each time, until the sheet is almost as thin as fresh pasta and you can see the flowers easily.

Cut the sheet into lengths that fit the prepared baking sheet. Transfer to the baking sheet (you may need to bake in batches), brush lightly with oil, sprinkle with flaky sea salt, and prick all over with a fork. Bake until lightly browned and crisp, about 8 minutes. Let cool, then break into rough pieces by hand.

Make the nasturtium pesto: Preheat the oven to 350°F. Toast the pine nuts in a pie pan until lightly colored and fragrant, 4 to 5 minutes. Let cool. Bring a large pot of salted water to a boil over high heat and prepare a bowl of ice water. Add the nasturtium leaves, push them under the water, and cook until just tender, about 45 seconds. Lift them out with a wire skimmer and transfer immediately to the ice water. When the water returns to a boil, add the basil, push the leaves under the water, and cook for about 30 seconds, then lift them out with the wire skimmer and transfer immediately to the ice water. When cooled, drain them and squeeze to remove as much water as possible.

Pour the grapeseed oil into a blender and add the greens, breaking them up a bit as they go into the jar. Add the pine nuts, garlic, cheese, and sea salt and blend until very smooth. Transfer to a bowl and taste for salt. You should have about ¾ cup pesto. Set aside ¼ cup pesto (and the 1 teaspoon lemon juice) for the salad and reserve the remainder for another use (see Chef's Tip).

Have ready a bowl of ice water. Halve the fennel bulb through the root. With a mandoline or other vegetable slicer, slice the fennel thinly from top to bottom (not crosswise). Put the fennel slices into the ice water to help them crisp and curl. Slice the radishes thinly with the mandoline or vegetable slicer. Add the radishes to the ice water to keep them crisp. Peel the carrot and, using a vegetable peeler, shave it lengthwise into thin ribbons.

Bring a small pot of salted water to a boil over high heat and prepare a bowl of ice water. Add the sugar snap peas to the boiling water and blanch for about 1 minute, then drain and immediately transfer to the ice water. When cool, drain and pat dry.

To assemble the salad, drain the fennel and radishes and pat dry. Put them into a bowl with the carrot and sugar snap peas. With a fork or slotted spoon, retrieve about one-fourth of the pickled red onions from the pickling liquid and add them to the bowl. (Reserve the remaining pickled onions for another use.) Add the olive oil, lemon juice, and sea salt to taste and toss gently.

Stir the lemon juice into the pesto to brighten the flavor. On each of four salad plates, put 1 tablespoon pesto and spread thinly with the back of a spoon. Put 3 tablespoons of the ricotta in the center of the plate. Mound the dressed vegetables on top of the ricotta, dividing them evenly. Sprinkle with flaky sea salt and garnish with basil and nasturtium leaves. Place 3 or 4 croccante shards around each salad and serve.

Parsley Fettuccine with Fava Beans, Peas, Spring Onions, and Parmesan Cream **Serves 6**

The garden's early fava beans and English peas are so moist and tender they hardly need cooking. Jeff tosses them with handmade fettuccine and a delicate cream sauce with just enough cheesy flavor to make the case for Pinot Noir.

Fettuccine:

1 cup Italian "00" flour (page 196), plus more for dusting

1 tablespoon finely minced fresh flat-leaf parsley

1 teaspoon sea salt

10 large egg yolks

1 teaspoon extra virgin olive oil

2 tablespoons water

Fine semolina, for dusting

Cream Sauce:

4 tablespoons unsalted butter

4 cloves garlic, thinly sliced

2 shallots, thinly sliced

3 cups heavy cream

Two 2-ounce pieces Parmigiano-Reggiano cheese rind

Sea salt and freshly ground white pepper

Grated zest of 1 lemon

1 cup shelled English peas

1 cup shelled and peeled fava beans

2 small spring onions, thinly sliced

Fresh edible flowers, for garnish

Wine: Robert Mondavi Winery Napa Valley Carneros
Pinot Noir Reserve

Make the fettuccine: In a bowl, whisk together the flour, parsley, and salt. Make a well in the center. Put the egg yolks, oil, and water into the well. Mix with a fork, incorporating the flour gradually, then turn the dough out onto a work surface and knead until smooth and elastic, dusting lightly with flour as needed. Wrap in plastic wrap and refrigerate to rest for 30 minutes.

Stretch the dough with a pasta machine into a long, thin sheet. Cut into 10-inch lengths, then use the fettuccine attachment to cut noodles or cut by hand about ⅓ inch wide. Put the noodles on a baking sheet lightly dusted with semolina and let dry at room temperature for about 1 hour.

Make the cream sauce: Melt the butter in a saucepan over medium heat. Add the garlic and shallots and sauté until softened, about 3 minutes. Add the cream, cheese rinds, and a pinch each of salt and pepper and simmer gently until slightly thickened, about 20 minutes. Strain and transfer to a wide skillet large enough to hold the pasta. Add the lemon zest and taste for salt. Keep warm.

Bring a large pot of salted water to a boil over high heat and prepare a bowl of ice water. Add the peas and blanch for 1 minute, then transfer with a wire skimmer to the ice water. Drain when cool.

Add the pasta to the boiling water and cook until al dente. While the pasta cooks, add the peas, fava beans, and spring onions to the cream sauce and bring just to a simmer. With tongs, transfer the pasta to the skillet and toss to coat. Divide among six bowls, garnish with flowers, and serve.

Grilled Rib Eye with Grilled Spring Vegetables and Salsa Verde **Serves 4**

Salsa Verde:

½ cup plus 2 tablespoons extra virgin olive oil

¼ cup chopped fresh flat-leaf parsley

2 tablespoons minced fresh chives

1½ tablespoons minced fresh marjoram

1½ teaspoons minced garlic

1½ teaspoons brine-packed capers, well rinsed and coarsely chopped

¼ teaspoon red chile flakes

Grated zest of 1 lemon

Pinch of sea salt

Two ¾-pound boneless rib-eye steaks, at room temperature

Sea salt and freshly ground black pepper

4 small spring onions, ends trimmed

8 baby turnips, peeled and halved

8 baby carrots, peeled

12 broccoli di cicco (sprouting broccoli) florets

¼ pound king trumpet mushrooms, cleaned and halved lengthwise

Extra virgin olive oil

½ lemon

Wine: Robert Mondavi Winery Napa Valley Cabernet Sauvignon Reserve

To flatter the winery's signature wine, Cabernet Sauvignon, Jeff often grills thick steaks. A salsa verde with garden herbs makes a brighter, more contemporary accompaniment than a reduction sauce, and the vegetable garnish can change with the seasons. In spring, a bouquet of grilled baby turnips, carrots, spring onions, and sprouting broccoli gives the garden a chance to shine.

Make the salsa verde: In a medium bowl, combine all the ingredients and mix well.

Prepare a hot charcoal fire or preheat a gas grill to high. Season the steaks well on both sides with salt and pepper. Grill until well seared on one side, about 5 minutes, then turn and grill until done to your taste, about 4 minutes longer for medium-rare. Set aside to rest while you grill the vegetables.

Coat all the vegetables and mushrooms lightly with oil. Season with salt and pepper. Grill, turning as needed, until just tender. The spring onions will cook the fastest, in about 2 minutes. The turnips and carrots will take the longest, about 5 minutes.

Put the salsa verde into a small saucepan and warm gently over low heat. Do not allow it to boil. Remove from the heat and add a squeeze of lemon juice to brighten the flavor.

Slice the steaks on the diagonal to desired thickness. Divide the steak and the vegetables and mushrooms among four plates. Drizzle the salsa verde over all and serve.

Cheesecake with Blueberry Gelée

Serves 12

Crust:

½ cup unsalted butter, at room temperature, in small cubes

¼ cup granulated sugar

Pinch of sea salt

1 large egg yolk

¾ cup all-purpose flour, measured then sifted

Filling:

1 pound cream cheese, at room temperature

1 cup granulated sugar

4 large eggs

1 teaspoon pure vanilla extract

Pinch of sea salt

Topping:

¾ pound blueberries

⅓ cup loosely packed light brown sugar

Pinch of sea salt

8 sheets leaf gelatin

Garnish:

2 cups blueberries, some halved

24 strawberries, hulled and quartered

Granulated sugar

Fresh edible flowers

Wine: Robert Mondavi Winery Napa Valley Moscato d'Oro

The winery garden yields just enough blueberries to use them judiciously in desserts—as a wine-dark gelée on top of a cheesecake, for example. With this strategy, a dozen people can enjoy a taste of this sweet-tart fruit without wiping out the week's harvest. The winery's fragrant Moscato d'Oro, with its honeysuckle aroma, was a favorite of Margrit Mondavi.

Make the crust: In a stand mixer fitted with the paddle attachment, cream the butter on medium speed until smooth. Gradually add the granulated sugar, stopping to scrape down the sides of the bowl once or twice. Add the salt, then the egg yolk and beat until blended. On low speed, add the flour and beat just until blended. Gather the dough, flatten it into the shape of a hamburger patty, wrap in plastic wrap, and refrigerate for at least 30 minutes or up to 1 day.

Preheat the oven to 350°F. Unwrap the dough and place it between two sheets of parchment paper. With a rolling pin, flatten it into a 9-inch round of even thickness. With scissors, trim the excess parchment. Lift off the top sheet of parchment. If it threatens to stick, return the dough to the refrigerator until chilled, then try again. Invert the dough onto the bottom of a 9-inch springform pan with the sides removed and lift off the parchment. Reattach the sides of the springform pan.

Bake the crust, rotating the pan 180 degrees halfway through baking, until very lightly colored, 8 to 12 minutes. Let cool on a wire rack for 30 minutes.

Make the filling: In a stand mixer fitted with the whisk attachment, whip the cream cheese on medium speed until creamy. Scrape down the sides of the bowl and the whisk. Gradually add the granulated sugar and beat until light and smooth. Add the eggs one at a time, beating well after each addition. Add the vanilla and salt, mixing well.

Pour the filling into the springform pan. Grasping the sides of the pan, tap the pan vigorously two or three times on a work surface to deflate any bubbles. Bake the cake, rotating the pan 180 degrees halfway through baking, until a cake tester inserted into the center comes out clean, about 45 minutes. Let cool on the rack.

Make the topping: In a small saucepan, combine the blueberries, brown sugar, and salt. Cook over medium-low heat, stirring until the sugar dissolves and mashing the blueberries lightly with a wooden spoon to release some of their juices, for 5 to 10 minutes. Transfer to a blender and blend until smooth. For extra smoothness, press the mixture through a fine-mesh sieve into a bowl.

Put the gelatin sheets into a bowl of ice water to cover and let soften until pliable, about 3 minutes. Lift them out and squeeze dry. Put them into a small saucepan over low heat just until they melt, then stir them into the warm blueberry puree. Let the puree cool until it begins to set, about 30 minutes.

Pour the blueberry mixture on top of the cooled cheesecake, spreading it almost to the edge but leaving a narrow rim. You may not need all the blueberry mixture. With an offset spatula, level the topping. Refrigerate the cheesecake until chilled.

To serve, slice the cheesecake into 12 wedges, wiping the knife after every cut. Transfer to individual plates and scatter the blueberries around each slice. Toss the strawberries with sugar to taste. If desired, arrange the sugared berries on a baking sheet and use a kitchen torch to melt and caramelize the sugar. Otherwise, simply scatter the sugared berries around each slice. Garnish with edible flowers.

Skipstone: *A Mediterranean Tribute*

Geyserville

Maybe you can't go home again, but Fahri Diner has come close with Skipstone. The hilly, hidden two-hundred-acre property near Healdsburg so closely resembles his native Cyprus that the first sight of it brought him to tears. After a year of searching for a wine country getaway, he had found the one he had to own. A former cattle ranch, the bowl-shaped parcel had grapevine-covered hillsides and a hilltop home with an unparalleled view of the Alexander Valley. The son and grandson of Cypriot olive growers, Fahri had grown up in the Eastern Mediterranean, playing among olive, citrus, and almond trees, and he wanted a similar rural experience for his children.

In 2000, he purchased the parcel and began to transform it. He replanted the vineyards with top-tier wine in mind and established more olive and fruit trees. "Olive oil is in my DNA," says Fahri, a technology entrepreneur and venture capitalist. The Alexander Valley has long been a prime region for apples and plums, but Fahri added to the collection, planting peaches, pears, quinces, figs, pomegranates, persimmons, loquats, and almonds in homage to the island landscape of his childhood.

"Almonds are everywhere in Cyprus," says the vintner. "You can eat them from March to September. In early spring, you can bite into them like a fruit." A spongy green hull surrounds the moist, skinless almond kernel initially. At that early stage, says Fahri, you can pound the soft almonds with water, then strain the mixture to produce sweet fresh almond milk. Over the summer months, the kernel develops its papery brown skin and pockmarked shell, and the hull hardens until it splits open to release the delectable nut.

The Skipstone vegetable garden is a handsome collection of raised beds built from stones gathered on the property, then edged in red brick and surrounded by soft bark paths. Frilly lettuces make a burgundy and emerald-green carpet in some of the beds. In others, cucumbers clamber up a bamboo trellis constructed on a slant so the dangling fruits will be easy to spot. Tomatoes consume much of the real estate in summer, with other produce essential to the Cypriot table—sweet peppers, eggplants, zucchini, potatoes, basil, red onions, and garlic—in supporting roles. Patches of tomatillos, jalapeños, and red hibiscus (dried and used for beverages in the Mexican kitchen) reflect Fahri's insistence that the "family" this family garden serves includes every member of the mostly Hispanic staff. Employees eat from the garden more often than he does.

Left and above: *(clockwise from bottom left) Trellised cucumbers; spring's green (unripe) almonds are moist and tasty; flourishing lettuces; Skipstone's outdoor tasting pavilion; winery owners Fahri and Constance Diner*

Fahri and his own family—his wife, Constance, and four children—live on the property only part time, but those days are treasured ones. The two younger children love to gather strawberries from the raised beds and fresh eggs from the chicken coop, a pristine two-level residence for several pampered free-range hens. The youngsters are "always out there," says their father, "and that's important to me. I think it's part of their whole education, playing in the dirt and picking olives. I want them to learn respect for the soil."

Fahri and Constance, a former luxury-brands marketer, travel widely and sample the local specialties with enthusiasm, but the Mediterranean way of eating appeals to them most—a diet driven by what's in the garden, prepared with minimal manipulation.

"My philosophy of cooking is salt, pepper, and olive oil," jokes Fahri. "I'm very simple. I run in the morning, and when I come back for breakfast, I have cucumbers, tomatoes, and fried eggs."

His tastes may be humble but Fahri loves to cook, and his outdoor kitchen—designed with large gatherings in mind—has the capabilities any serious chef would want: a wood-burning oven, built-in grill, huge cast-iron skillets, and vast granite countertops. Just steps from the garden, the cooking pavilion is the stage in this peaceful natural amphitheater, embraced by hills cloaked in grapevines and oaks.

Several times during the year, Fahri and Constance host alfresco dinners for fans of their wines. As Fahri had hoped, the site has proven to be a world-class vineyard, and Skipstone wines—a Viognier and three red bottlings from Bordeaux varieties, all crafted by acclaimed

Above: *(clockwise from far left) Vineyard at the base of the hills; Fahri and Constance inspect the fall garden; newly planted stone beds; sheep control vineyard weeds; hillside vines; drying garlic; salad greens*

Skipstone's garden evokes the sweetest moments from Fahri's Cyprus childhood, and he and Constance hope to create similar memories for their own children.

winemaker Philippe Melka—are prized by collectors. The annual harvest party in September gives enthusiasts a chance to savor these superb wines in the setting that birthed them, with food prepared by Laura and Sayat Ozyilmaz, young San Francisco chefs who help Fahri bring his Mediterranean heritage to the table. Lamb raised on the property is typically the centerpiece (Skipstone relies on sheep for organic weed control), and the chefs have the run of the garden.

Sayat is Turkish and Laura is Mexican, a culinary marriage that, unlikely as it might seem, results in some delightfully original food. Collaborating with the Diners on an autumn menu to showcase Skipstone wines, the chefs devised a first course that plays cleverly with color. The painterly composition pairs Fuyu persimmons from

Skipstone trees with sashimi-style salmon, lightly salt cured and garnished with coral-colored pearls of salmon roe. Small dollops of *zhug*, an Egyptian herb paste, are the genius touch that shakes everything up. The plating is lovely, the combination inspired. What's more, it goes with Rose de Constance, a brut Champagne that Fahri commissioned to honor his wife.

Skipstone's Viognier is bright and fresh, with lively aromas of citrus blossom and stone fruit, a refreshing complement to a dish rich in olive oil. To match this graceful white, the menu looks next to

Above and right: *(clockwise from left)*
Signature Skipstone wines and estate olive oil; green almonds are a delicacy in Cyprus, Fahri's native country; Alexander Valley sunset view; estate vineyards in the setting sun

zeytinyağli, a classic Turkish cooking method for slowly poaching vegetables—in this case, flat romano beans simmered gently in Skipstone extra virgin olive oil with tomato and garlic. The beans become silky and heightened in flavor, and they improve in the fridge overnight. Skipstone's wood-burning oven is fired up for the accompanying *pide*, or flatbread, spread with mellow Turkish red pepper paste and olives.

Skipstone's powerful red wines welcome bigger flavors from the garden: smoky eggplant, concentrated tomato, roasted garlic, well-browned potatoes. For Faultline Vineyard, the winery's blend of Cabernet Franc and Merlot, a modern *imam bayildi* reimagines the beloved Turkish home-style recipe of braised eggplant, tomato, and onions. In this deconstructed version, the dish is a sophisticated eggplant carpaccio on a bed of saffron-scented tomato sauce.

To showcase Oliver's Blend, Skipstone's Cabernet Sauvignon–dominated bottling, thick lamb shoulder chops are seasoned with an herb-and-spice mixture as complex as the wine. Seared on the outdoor grill and served with crusty creamer potatoes, the lamb demonstrates how compelling a sizzling, simply cooked chop can be with a profound red wine.

The almond trees at Skipstone don't produce enough crop to sell but plenty for snacking and the occasional dessert. Fahri's fondness for the nuts determined the meal's finale, an almond and semolina cake perfumed with grated citrus zest. After baking, the warm cake is brushed repeatedly with citrus syrup, a reference to the syrup-drenched semolina cakes of Turkey and Greece. Fruit from the garden almost always accompanies it: poached quinces or pears in autumn; citrus in winter; loquats in late spring; *fraises des bois* or sugared peaches in summer.

For Fahri, Skipstone calls to mind the sweetest scenes and sounds from his childhood: walks with his grandfather, fields of sunflowers, grazing sheep, squawking chickens. Hoping to create a similar highlight reel for his own children, he and Constance have fashioned a wine country escape that others can enjoy as well.

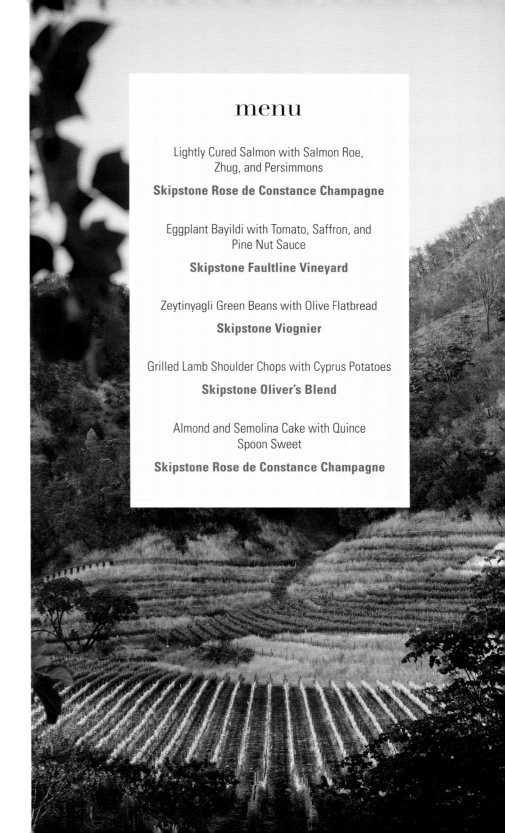

menu

Lightly Cured Salmon with Salmon Roe, Zhug, and Persimmons

Skipstone Rose de Constance Champagne

Eggplant Bayildi with Tomato, Saffron, and Pine Nut Sauce

Skipstone Faultline Vineyard

Zeytinyagli Green Beans with Olive Flatbread

Skipstone Viognier

Grilled Lamb Shoulder Chops with Cyprus Potatoes

Skipstone Oliver's Blend

Almond and Semolina Cake with Quince Spoon Sweet

Skipstone Rose de Constance Champagne

Lightly Cured Salmon with Salmon Roe, Zhug, and Persimmons **Serves 6**

¾ pound sushi-grade fresh skinless salmon fillet,
    pin bones removed

½ teaspoon sea salt

2 tablespoons Zhug (recipe follows)

2 tablespoons extra virgin olive oil

1 tablespoon fresh lemon juice

1 large or 2 small Fuyu persimmons

6 tablespoons salmon roe (about 3 ounces)

Wine: Skipstone Rose de Constance Champagne

Season the salmon all over with the salt. Put the salmon on a parchment-lined plate, cover with plastic wrap, and refrigerate for 1 hour to firm the flesh.

In a small bowl, mix together the *zhug*, oil, and lemon juice to make a paste.

Remove the persimmon cap. Cut the persimmon in half through the stem. Lay cut side down and slice paper-thin by hand or with a mandoline. You will need a total of 30 half-moon slices.

Slice the salmon in half down the center, then slice crosswise about ⅛ inch thick. You will need a total of 30 slices.

On six serving plates, alternate slices of salmon and persimmon, using 5 slices of each for each serving. Dot each serving with 1 teaspoon of the *zhug* paste, then spoon 1 tablespoon salmon roe over each serving.

The Fuyu persimmon trees at Skipstone inspired this dish, which plays on the visual similarity between the fruit and the fish. Nectarines, peaches, or even pears can replace the persimmons when they are out of season.

Classic zhug, the Egyptian hot sauce, relies primarily on cilantro and parsley, but Laura and Sayat often incorporate other herbs from the Skipstone garden, such as tarragon, chives, and chervil. Zhug will last for up to 1 month, refrigerated, if you add the lemon juice just before using; with the lemon juice, it will last up to 5 days.

Zhug **Makes about 1 cup**

½ cup extra virgin olive oil

¼ cup chopped fresh cilantro

¼ cup chopped fresh flat-leaf parsley

2 teaspoons sea salt

1 teaspoon Garlic Confit (recipe below)

½ teaspoon ground cardamom

¼ teaspoon ground cloves

¼ teaspoon ground cumin

¼ teaspoon ground fenugreek

¼ teaspoon Aleppo pepper

Fresh Meyer lemon juice

In a bowl, whisk together all the ingredients, adding the lemon juice to taste.

Garlic Confit: In a small saucepan, combine 12 peeled large garlic cloves and vegetable oil to cover (about ½ cup). Cook over low heat until the cloves are soft but not colored, about 20 minutes. (Use a flame tamer if necessary to keep the cloves from browning.) Let cool, then scoop out the garlic cloves, reserving the flavorful oil for another use. Puree the garlic in a small food processor or spice grinder or pound to a paste in a mortar. Makes about 2 tablespoons.

Eggplant Bayildi with Tomato, Saffron, and Pine Nut Sauce

Serves 6

1 large globe eggplant, 1¼ to 1½ pounds

Sea salt

¼ cup plus 3 tablespoons extra virgin olive oil, plus more
  for drizzling

1 large yellow onion, diced

5 large cloves garlic, thinly sliced

2 tablespoons mild Turkish red pepper paste

Pinch of saffron threads

1 cup diced Roma tomatoes (no need to peel)

⅓ cup untoasted pine nuts, plus toasted pine nuts for garnish

½ cup water

Mixed fresh whole herb leaves, such as dill, cilantro,
  flat-leaf parsley, thyme, and mint, for serving

18 cherry tomatoes, quartered

Wine: Skipstone Faultline Vineyard

This dish is an updated interpretation of imam bayildi—"the priest fainted"—the classic Turkish stuffed-eggplant recipe. Supposedly, he fainted with pleasure. Who knows what might have happened had he encountered this magnificent version? Laura and Sayat deconstruct the original dish, arranging smoky eggplant "carpaccio" on a bed of tomato and pine nut sauce. A whole-leaf herb salad on top adds a burst of freshness.

Over a gas flame or charcoal fire, roast the eggplant, turning it often, until it is blackened all over and completely soft, 10 to 20 minutes. The stem area is the last part to soften, so be sure to check there. Transfer the eggplant to a bowl and cover the bowl tightly with plastic wrap; let the eggplant steam until cool, then peel carefully, removing all traces of burnt skin. Break up any large pieces with your hands, season with salt, and then drain the eggplant flesh in a sieve for 30 minutes.

While the eggplant drains, heat 3 tablespoons of the oil in a saucepan over medium heat. Add the onion and garlic and sauté until soft and sweet, about 10 minutes. Add the pepper paste and saffron and sauté, stirring, for about 2 minutes, then add the Roma tomatoes and cook, stirring often, until the tomatoes have broken down and the mixture is thick, about 10 minutes. Add the pine nuts, 1½ teaspoons salt, and ¼ cup of the water, reduce the heat to low, and cook, stirring occasionally, until the mixture is very thick, about 15 minutes.

Transfer the contents of the saucepan to a blender, add the remaining ¼ cup water, and blend well. With the blender running, add the remaining ¼ cup olive oil, blending until smooth.

Return the sauce to the saucepan and cook over low heat, stirring often, until it darkens, about 15 minutes, adding a splash of water to thin if needed. Taste for salt. Keep warm.

Put ¼ cup of the roasted eggplant between two sheets of plastic wrap and flatten gently with the bottom of a 1-cup measuring cup into a 6-inch circle of even thickness. Repeat to make 5 more rounds.

Put about 3 tablespoons of the warm tomato sauce on each of six salad plates. Spread the sauce thinly with the back of a soupspoon. Working with 1 eggplant round at a time, remove the top sheet of plastic wrap and invert the eggplant round onto one of the prepared salad plates. Carefully peel off the second sheet of plastic. Repeat with the remaining eggplant rounds.

Put a tuft of mixed herbs on each eggplant round. Scatter the cherry tomatoes and toasted pine nuts on top, dividing them both evenly. Sprinkle with a little sea salt and drizzle with oil. Serve immediately.

Zeytinyagli Green Beans with Olive Flatbread **Serves 6**

1 pound green beans, preferably romano type, ends trimmed

⅓ pound cherry tomatoes

1 large yellow onion, very coarsely chopped

3 cloves garlic, peeled

2 cups extra virgin olive oil

Juice of 1 lemon

2½ tablespoons sea salt

2 cups water

Vegetable oil, for deep-frying

¼ cup plus 2 tablespoons brine-packed capers, rinsed and patted thoroughly dry

Fresh thyme or lemon thyme sprigs, for garnish

Olive Flatbread (recipe follows)

Wine: Skipstone Viognier

In a heavy pot, combine the green beans, tomatoes, onion, garlic, olive oil, lemon juice, salt, and water. The liquid will not cover the beans. Cover the beans with a round of parchment paper cut just to fit inside the pot.

Zeytinyağli is the Turkish name for vegetables cooked slowly in olive oil until tender. Many vegetables are prepared this way—green beans, carrots, artichokes, potatoes, celery root, red peppers—and they last for several days in the fridge. Typically, they are served at room temperature as part of an assortment of appetizers, or meze. For this contemporary presentation, the soft green beans are topped with crunchy fried capers and served with an olive-topped flatbread to soak up the juices.

Bring the liquid to a bare simmer over medium heat and adjust the heat to maintain a bare simmer. Cook until the beans are almost tender, about 25 minutes. Remove from the heat and let the beans cool in the liquid to room temperature. They will continue to cook as they cool and should be tender after cooling.

In a small, heavy saucepan, pour vegetable oil to a depth of 2 inches and heat to 375°F. Add the capers and fry until crisp, about 2 minutes. Transfer them with a wire-mesh skimmer to paper towels to drain.

With a slotted spoon, transfer the green beans and tomatoes to a platter or individual plates. Garnish with the fried capers and a few sprigs of thyme. Drizzle with some of the olive oil from the pot. Serve immediately with the flatbread.

chef's tip:

Don't be put off by the amount of olive oil required. The oil picks up flavor from the green beans and seasonings, and you can use it for salad dressings or on fish or steamed vegetables.

Olive Flatbread

Makes 3 flatbreads; serves 6

Dough:

¾ cup plus 2 tablespoons warm water (105°F to 115°F)

1½ teaspoons active dry yeast

1 cup plus 1 tablespoon unbleached all-purpose flour, plus more for dusting

1 cup plus 1 tablespoon bread flour

2 teaspoons sugar

1½ teaspoons sea salt

1½ tablespoons extra virgin olive oil

Topping:

1 cup coarsely chopped green olives, such as Castelvetrano, Lucques, or Picholine

6 tablespoons mild Turkish red pepper paste

3 tablespoons extra virgin olive oil

The chopped-olive topping on this flatbread is a tribute to Fahri and his upbringing as the son of an olive grower. Add chopped walnuts to the topping, if you like.

Prepare the dough: Combine the water and yeast in the bowl of a stand mixer and whisk to dissolve the yeast. In a bowl, whisk together both flours and the sugar to blend. Add to the yeast mixture, fit the mixer with the dough hook, and mix on low speed until a shaggy mass forms, about 1 minute. Let stand for 20 to 30 minutes.

Add the salt and mix on low speed for 2 minutes. Increase the speed to medium and mix for 5 minutes. Turn off the mixer, add the oil, and then mix on low speed until blended. If the mixer does not readily incorporate the oil, remove the bowl from the mixer, knead the dough by hand until the oil is incorporated, and then return the bowl to the mixer. Increase the speed to medium and mix for 2 minutes.

Remove the dough hook, cover the bowl, and let the dough rise at room temperature for 1 hour. Transfer the dough to a work surface and fold in thirds, then place in a lightly oiled bowl or tub, cover, and refrigerate for at least 8 hours or up to 24 hours. Remove the dough from the refrigerator 1 hour before shaping it. Divide the dough into 3 equal balls. Put the balls on a lightly floured work surface and cover lightly with a clean kitchen towel. Let rest for 20 minutes.

Put a pizza stone in the oven and preheat the oven to 500°F for at least 30 minutes. If the oven has a convection fan, turn it on.

Prepare the topping: In a bowl, mix together the olives, pepper paste, and oil.

On a large sheet of parchment paper lightly dusted with flour, roll 1 ball of dough into an oval roughly 12 inches long and 7 inches wide. Cover with one-third of the topping, spreading it evenly to the edges. Trim any excess parchment with scissors.

Slide a rimless baking sheet or pizza peel under the parchment, then slide the flatbread, still on the parchment, onto the preheated pizza stone. Bake until golden brown, 7 to 8 minutes. Transfer to a cutting board and cut into 6 equal pieces. Repeat with remaining 2 dough balls. Serve hot or warm.

Grilled Lamb Shoulder Chops with Cyprus Potatoes **Serves 4**

Lamb Marinade:

¼ cup extra virgin olive oil

1½ teaspoons honey

Grated zest of 1 small orange

1½ teaspoons sea salt

½ teaspoon dry mustard

½ teaspoon minced fresh rosemary

½ teaspoon dried lavender flowers

½ teaspoon dried oregano

½ teaspoon Sichuan peppercorns

¼ teaspoon cumin seeds

¼ teaspoon caraway seeds

4 lamb shoulder blade chops, about ½ pound each

Cyprus Potatoes:

1½ pounds Yukon Gold potatoes, 1½ inches in diameter

3 ounces cherry tomatoes (about 15)

2 large cloves garlic, peeled

1 Meyer lemon, sliced

1½ cups extra virgin olive oil

1½ tablespoons sea salt

4 cups water

1 tablespoon Garlic Confit (page 174)

Grated zest of 1 Meyer lemon

¼ cup thinly sliced fresh chives

Wine: Skipstone Oliver's Blend

The rosemary and lavender that grow so profusely at Skipstone are go-to seasonings for the ranch's lamb. The crusty potatoes that accompany the chops are first poached in olive oil, then crisped in a hot oven just before serving. Lemon zest and garlic confit take them over the top. Small waxy creamer potatoes are ideal. Save the flavorful poaching oil and use it in vinaigrettes or on steamed vegetables or fish.

Prepare the marinade: In a small bowl, combine the oil, honey, and orange zest. In a spice grinder or in a mortar, combine the salt, mustard, rosemary, lavender, oregano, Sichuan peppercorns, cumin seeds, and caraway seeds and grind finely. Whisk into the oil mixture. Coat the lamb with the marinade, then put the lamb into a heavy-duty resealable plastic bag and refrigerate for 24 hours. Bring to room temperature before grilling.

Prepare the potatoes: In a saucepan, combine the potatoes, tomatoes, garlic, sliced lemon, oil, salt, and water and bring to a simmer over medium heat. Adjust the heat to maintain a bare simmer and cook until the potatoes are just tender when pierced, 20 to 40 minutes, depending on size. Let cool in the liquid.

Prepare a hot charcoal fire or preheat a gas grill to high. Also preheat the oven to 475°F or 450°F with a convection fan. Line a baking sheet with parchment paper.

Grill the chops to desired doneness, about 5 minutes per side for medium, depending on thickness. (Shoulder chops are best when cooked to at least medium.) Set aside to rest for 5 minutes.

While the chops are on the grill, lift the potatoes out of the cooking liquid with a slotted spoon (leaving the tomatoes behind) and transfer to a bowl. Add the garlic confit and salt to taste and toss well to coat the potatoes evenly with the garlic. Arrange the potatoes on the prepared baking sheet and bake until crisp and sizzling, about 10 minutes. Transfer to a serving bowl, add the lemon zest and chives, and toss well. If desired, add 1 to 2 tablespoons oil from the cooking liquid—just enough to make the potatoes glisten—and toss again.

Divide the chops among four dinner plates and spoon some of the hot potatoes alongside. Serve immediately.

Almond and Semolina Cake with Quince Spoon Sweet

Serves 12

2¼ cups almond flour

1¼ cups fine semolina

2 teaspoons baking powder

Pinch of sea salt

4 large eggs, at room temperature

1 cup plus 2 tablespoons sugar

1 teaspoon pure vanilla extract

1 tablespoon fresh lemon juice

1 tablespoon fresh orange juice

Grated zest of 1 lemon

Grated zest of 1 orange

1 cup extra virgin olive oil

1 cup whole milk

Syrup:

⅓ cup fresh orange juice

⅓ cup sugar

⅓ cup water

2 tablespoons honey

Quince Spoon Sweet:

2 cups sugar

2 cups water

3 pineapple quinces, peeled, each cut into 8 wedges, and cored (reserve peels and core)

Fresh lemon juice

Wine: Skipstone Rose de Constance Champagne

Made with extra virgin olive oil, this moist cake speaks to Fahri's childhood among the olive groves his father and grandfather tended. It welcomes a fruit accompaniment, such as berries or poached quince. These hard, knobby fruits are beloved in Cyprus, and Fahri made sure to plant some at Skipstone. When simmered for several hours in light syrup, they turn a gorgeous ruby color and resemble the preserve-like "spoon sweets" enjoyed in Greece.

Preheat the oven to 350°F. Butter the bottom and sides of a 10-by-3-inch round cake pan. Line the bottom with a round of parchment paper, then flour the pan sides, shaking out any excess.

In a bowl, whisk together the almond flour, semolina, baking powder, and salt. In a stand mixer fitted with the whisk attachment, whip together the eggs, sugar, and vanilla on medium speed until very light, about 5 minutes. Add the lemon and orange juices and zests and whip until blended.

Reduce the speed to medium-low, add the oil, and beat until blended. Then gradually add the dry ingredients, beating just until blended. Scrape down the sides of the bowl, reduce the mixer speed to low, add the milk, and beat just until blended. The batter will be thin. Pour the batter into the prepared pan. Bake the cake until the top is golden brown and a cake tester inserted into the middle comes out clean, about 55 minutes. Let rest in the pan on a rack for 20 minutes. Run a paring knife around the perimeter of the pan to loosen the cake. Invert the cake onto the rack, remove the pan, peel off the parchment, and then invert again onto another rack to finish cooling.

Prepare the syrup: In a small saucepan, combine the orange juice, sugar, water, and honey and bring to a simmer over medium-low heat, stirring to dissolve the sugar. Let cool. Brush the top of the cooled cake generously with the syrup. Wait for 5 minutes, then brush again. Repeat until you have used all the syrup.

Prepare the spoon sweet: In a heavy saucepan large enough to hold the quince, bring the sugar and water to a boil over high heat, stirring to dissolve the sugar. Add the quince wedges, peels, and cores and return to a simmer. Cook uncovered until the fruit turns a deep burgundy, which may take as long as 3 hours. Transfer the quince wedges to a heatproof bowl. Using a fine-mesh sieve, strain the syrup over the wedges and discard the peels and cores. Add lemon juice to taste to the syrup. Let cool, then chill.

Cut the cake into 12 equal portions. Accompany each portion with 2 quince wedges and some of the quince syrup.

Above and right: *Estate-grown olives ripening; olive trees line the road to the top of the hill, where the sweeping view encompasses much of the Alexander Valley.*

Trefethen Family Vineyards: *A Joyful Jumble*

Napa

Some wine country gardens look as if they are tidied around the clock, with nary a wilted leaf or pebble out of place. The Trefethen family takes a different approach in managing the flat, sunny plot that employees refer to as La Huerta—Spanish for a garden or small farm. This joyful jumble of clambering kiwi vines, sprawling squash plants, and towering tomatoes is more about nourishing people than impressing them. In a garden largely grown for employees, yield trumps tidiness.

"It's a bit of a wild garden," admits Hailey Trefethen, the third-generation vintner who oversees nearly an acre of beds behind the winery in Napa's Oak Knoll District. "We don't mind some weeds."

Even so, a lot more than weeds comes out of this fertile former vineyard: hundreds of pounds of chiles, eggplants, tomatoes, tomatillos, and green beans along with more esoteric heirloom produce, such as Jimmy Nardello sweet red peppers, Indigo Apple tomatoes, and Mexican sour gherkins. Although winery chef Chris Kennedy uses some of the harvest for guests, the vast majority goes straight to the staff.

Left and above: *Late-summer garden at Trefethen Vineyards yields heirlooms tomatoes, nasturtiums, eggplant, Jimmy Nardello sweet peppers, chard, and herbs; Janet Trefethen (left) and daughter Hailey*

Hailey grew up on garden produce—her mother, Janet, is an avid gardener and renowned home cook—and her grandmother Katie planted many of the fruit trees that still thrive at Trefethen. "Our family ate out of our garden most of the time," recalls Hailey. "So why didn't we do the same for employees? Why didn't we have a garden at the winery so people could go home with produce grown where they work?"

The family has always tried to promote wine as part of a healthy lifestyle; enabling employees to make better food choices seemed a good fit with that message. With that goal in mind, winery executive Jon Ruel initiated the garden program in 2008, and the garden now produces year-round, its harvest supplemented by the fig, persimmon, quince, kumquat, apple, and stone-fruit trees on the premises.

The produce is picked into bins and delivered to different departments on rotation; employees take what they want. "We switch it up so not all the zucchini are going to the tasting room," says Hailey, who also posts pictures, descriptions, and usage ideas for less-familiar produce. Chris often contributes an easy recipe, especially for an item, like the skinny Jimmy Nardello peppers or the mild shishito peppers, that staffers might otherwise pass up.

Many winery owners might look at this garden and see only an expense that's hard to defend, but the Trefethens think otherwise. "The employees value it," says Janet, "and we get paid back in their satisfaction."

Chiles, both hot and hotter, are the most in-demand crop, says Hailey; no matter how many seedlings she plants, it's never enough. Around Labor Day, an annual salsa-making competition encourages employees to flaunt their own creativity. All tomatoes, chiles, and tomatillos used in the salsas must come from La Huerta, and the

winning entry is determined by popular vote of the staff. "We are trying to increase everybody's connection to the garden," says the vintner.

The prolific edible landscape at Trefethen was one of the lures for Chris when he accepted the job. What chef would not feel stimulated and challenged by the bounty this property yields? In Hailey and head gardener Paul Hoffman, he has found partners willing to experiment with planting African cucumbers, yellow wax beans, okra, and rhubarb. And Hailey can be sure that whatever Paul harvests, Chris will make it his mission to use every edible part.

"I like using what most people would get rid of," says the chef. In his toss-nothing kitchen, tender carrot tops aren't jettisoned for compost; they're chopped and used for *chimichurri* with peppery extra virgin olive oil pressed from Trefethen's own fruit. Nasturtium blossoms

aren't merely strewn over salads. They're braised with the leaves and sautéed shallots, then blended, reemerging as a peppery, emerald-green sauce for fillet of beef. Convinced that toasted sunflower seeds make a great bridge to the winery's Chardonnay, Chris extracts the seeds from the mature sunflower heads by hand.

"The garden has honed my palate," says Chris, a longtime chef and restaurateur. Far more than most chefs, he pays close attention to how fruits and vegetables interact with wine (see sidebar, page 199). In regular wine-tasting sessions with Janet, he notes the scents and textures that might find an echo or complement in the garden: Riesling with citrus and cilantro, Merlot with fire-roasted red peppers, Chardonnay with melon and tarragon. From those tasting trials, he develops a wish list of wine-friendly fruits and vegetables to plant.

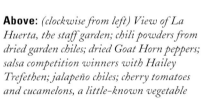

Above: *(clockwise from left) View of La Huerta, the staff garden; chili powders from dried garden chiles; dried Goat Horn peppers; salsa competition winners with Hailey Trefethen; jalapeño chiles; cherry tomatoes and cucamelons, a little-known vegetable*

"Our family ate out of our garden most of the time. Why didn't we have a garden at the winery so people could go home with produce grown where they work?"

"The thousand pounds of chiles we grow do not fit in that realm," jokes Hailey. But the chiles might find their way into the monthly "blue-plate lunches" that Trefethen hosts for small groups of employees, so staffers can connect across departments and get some fresh ideas for their own home meals.

Good cooking and home entertaining have been part of the Trefethen brand since at least 1973, when Janet and her mother-in-law, Katie, helped to start the Napa Valley Cooking Class at the winery. The valley had few good restaurants then, and vintners had visiting customers to entertain. Initially, the vintners' wives taught favorite recipes to one another, but the school's ambitions quickly grew, and over the next twenty-five years, many celebrity chefs held classes in the

Trefethen winery kitchen. "I grew up on a stool there," says Hailey.

The valley has countless fine restaurants now, but many wine country visitors still seek to have a more personal wine-and-food experience at a winery. Weather permitting, Trefethen's guests get a quick tour of La Huerta, and they reap its benefits in the small seasonal bites that Chris prepares for the winery's Taste the Estate sessions.

"Chris continues to expand what we can pair with our wines," says Hailey. "He thinks up so many ways to process what we grow."

A serious student of food preservation—salting, drying, fermenting, pickling—Chris keeps testing the limits of where fruits and vegetables can go. In the fall, he makes *hoshigaki*, Japanese-style dried persimmons, but he has applied the same techniques to kiwis and apples. He hangs colorful *ristras* of Goat Horn peppers to dry in the potting shed and then grinds them for a sweet spice to use all year. He dries tomatoes, blueberries, apples, kale, and oregano. He pickles cucumbers and eggplants, cans hundreds of quarts of tomatoes, and makes wine vinegar and sweet-tart verjus from the juice of underripe grapes. Many cooks make salt-preserved lemons, but Chris makes salt-preserved kumquats scented with star anise for use in salads and vinaigrettes.

This informal garden is at its most riotous in late summer, when peppers, beans, squashes, and melons jostle for space. But every season here has its allure. For a late-spring menu, Chris makes the most of the garden's tender sweet carrots, beets, spring onions, and English peas and the leafy delicacy of spring cilantro and thyme. The meal opens, as it often does at Trefethen, with the winery's beloved Dry Riesling and concludes with its elegant Cabernet Sauvignon, a demonstration in five courses of the delicious possibilities when linking garden to glass.

Left and right: *Winery chef Chris Kennedy processing dried Goat Horn peppers; chard is one of the many crops that provide a treasured benefit to Trefethen employees.*

menu

Dungeness Crab Roll with Pickled Ginger, Cilantro, and Yuzu Crème

Trefethen Dry Riesling

Oven-Roasted Baby Carrots with Cumin Yogurt, Carrot Top Chimichurri, and Spiced Pumpkin Seeds

Trefethen Chardonnay

Handmade Pappardelle with Wild Mushroom Ragout and Peas

Trefethen Merlot

Spring Lamb Chops Scottadito with Charred Tomato and Black Olive Tapenade

Trefethen Dragon's Tooth

Black Pepper–Crusted Beef Ribeye with Balsamic Spring Onions and Smashed Beets

Trefethen Cabernet Sauvignon

Dungeness Crab Roll with Pickled Ginger, Cilantro, and Yuzu Crème   **Makes 8 rolls; serves 4**

This West Coast spin on a lobster roll is a popular passed appetizer at Trefethen events. The winery's Dry Riesling, with its refreshing minerality, loves Dungeness crab, but Chris has found that cilantro and green apple create even more flavor bridges.

2 brioche hot dog buns

2 teaspoons unsalted butter, melted

¼ cup plain whole-milk Greek yogurt

1½ teaspoons crème fraîche

1½ tablespoons bottled yuzu juice or fresh lime juice

2 teaspoons coarsely chopped fresh cilantro, plus 8 whole leaves for garnish

½ teaspoon finely minced pickled ginger

½ apple, preferably a tart, crisp variety such as Granny Smith, peeled, cored, and diced small

½ pound fresh Dungeness crabmeat, preferably in large pieces, picked over for shells

Sea salt and freshly ground black pepper

Wine: Trefethen Dry Riesling

Preheat the oven to 375°F. Slice each bun crosswise into 4 equal chunks. Make a similar cut down the middle of each chunk (vertically, not horizontally) but do not cut all the way through. Brush these slots with the melted butter. Place on a baking sheet and bake until lightly toasted on the edges but not crisp, about 3 minutes. Set aside while you assemble the filling.

In a bowl, whisk together the yogurt, crème fraîche, yuzu juice, cilantro, and pickled ginger. Stir in the apple. Gently fold in the crab, trying not to break up the pieces. Season to taste with salt and pepper.

Refrigerate for 10 to 15 minutes to allow the flavors to marry. Don't let the mixture sit too long or it will start to throw liquid.

Set aside 8 pretty pieces of crabmeat, then use the remaining crab mixture to fill the buns, dividing it evenly. Top each bun with a reserved piece of crabmeat, then garnish with a whole cilantro leaf. Serve immediately.

chef's tip:

If you can't find baby carrots, you can trim larger ones down, selecting those with the most tender, freshest greens. If your carrots don't have greens attached, replace with chopped fresh flat-leaf parsley, cilantro, or both.

Oven-Roasted Baby Carrots with Cumin Yogurt, Carrot Top Chimichurri, and Spiced Pumpkin Seeds **Serves 4**

Chris is a big advocate of using every edible part of a fruit or vegetable, including the tender leafy tops of young carrots. These frilly greens make a surprising substitute for chopped parsley in chimichurri, *the Argentine sauce often drizzled on grilled beef. In this dish, the* chimichurri *enlivens roasted baby carrots. Use any leftover sauce on a steak the following day.*

24 baby carrots with greens attached, about 1 pound after removing greens

Extra virgin olive oil, for drizzling

Sea salt and freshly ground black pepper

¼ teaspoon cumin seeds or ground cumin

¼ cup plain whole-milk Greek yogurt

Carrot-Top Chimichurri:

¼ cup white wine vinegar or verjus

1 small shallot, finely minced

⅓ cup finely chopped carrot greens

¼ cup olive oil (not extra virgin)

Spiced Pumpkin Seeds:

⅓ cup raw green pumpkin seeds (pepitas)

1 teaspoon extra virgin olive oil

Pinch of Spanish smoked paprika (pimentón de la Vera)

Wine: Trefethen Chardonnay

Position a rack in the upper third of the oven and preheat oven to 425°F.

Remove the carrot greens. Trim the greens, discarding the stems and keeping only the frilly leaves. Wash and dry the leaves well, then chop finely. Set aside ⅓ cup chopped leaves for the chimichurri.

Scrub the carrots under running water, then "polish" them with a rough dish towel to remove any clinging bits of soil, paying special attention to the area where the greens were attached. Place them on a heavy baking sheet, drizzle with just enough extra virgin olive oil to coat them lightly, and season with salt and pepper. Roast the carrots, shaking and rotating the pan halfway through to ensure even cooking, until the carrots are lightly caramelized and tender when pierced, about 20 minutes. Remove from the oven. Leave the oven on.

If using cumin seeds, toast in a dry small skillet over medium heat until darkened and fragrant. Let cool, then, with a mortar and pestle, pound until finely ground. Put the yogurt into a small bowl and whisk in the cumin, a pinch of salt, and a few grinds of pepper.

Prepare the chimichurri: In a small bowl, combine the vinegar and shallot. Add a pinch of salt and a few grinds of pepper and let stand for at least 10 minutes to soften the shallots. Add the carrot greens and olive oil, season with salt and pepper, and whisk well.

Prepare the spiced pumpkin seeds: Spread the pumpkin seeds in a pie pan and toast in the oven until lightly colored, about 5 minutes. Transfer them to a bowl and, while they are hot, add the olive oil and toss to coat well. Add the paprika, salt to taste, and a grind or two of pepper and toss again. Let cool.

At serving time, spoon the yogurt onto the bottom of a serving platter and spread thinly with the back of a soupspoon. Arrange the warm carrots on top in an artful mound, then put small dollops of chimichurri on the carrots, using as much as you like. Scatter the pumpkin seeds all over and serve immediately.

Handmade Pappardelle with Wild Mushroom Ragout and Peas

Serves 6

Pasta Dough:

3 large whole eggs plus 5 large egg yolks

1 tablespoon extra virgin olive oil, plus 2 tablespoons for the pasta water and more for drizzling

1½ teaspoons sea salt

2 cups Italian "00" flour or all-purpose flour, plus more for dusting

Ragout:

2 cups shelled English peas

1 tablespoon extra virgin olive oil

1 clove garlic, minced

1 large shallot, diced

Sea salt and freshly ground black pepper

1 pound wild mushrooms, cleaned and cut or torn into large pieces

1 tablespoon unsalted butter

½ cup Trefethen Chardonnay or other white wine

1 tablespoon chopped fresh flat-leaf parsley

1 teaspoon chopped fresh thyme

Chunk of Parmigiano-Reggiano cheese, for grating

Wine: Trefethen Merlot

Sweet, tender English peas are a fleeting treat in the Trefethen garden, so Chris makes sure they get star billing during that brief window. Spring morels would be his first choice for the mushroom ragout, but chanterelles or even cultivated oyster mushrooms will work.

Prepare the pasta dough: In a bowl, whisk together the eggs, egg yolks, oil, and salt. Place the flour on a large work surface and make a well in the center large enough to contain the eggs. Make sure the flour "walls" are high enough to keep the eggs from escaping. Pour the egg mixture into the well. With a fork, begin drawing in the flour from the sides and whisking it with the eggs. Take care not to let the runny eggs breach the flour walls. The mixture should come together into a slightly tacky dough. Dust with additional flour as needed and knead by hand until the dough is firm and no longer tacky.

Knead the dough by hand until it is smooth and elastic, 7 to 10 minutes. It should bounce back when poked with a finger. Divide the dough into 4 equal portions. Shape each portion into a ball, flatten slightly, and wrap in plastic wrap. Let rest at room temperature for about 1 hour.

(continued)

chef's tip:

Look for Italian "00" flour in well-stocked supermarkets and specialty stores. It is more finely ground than all-purpose flour. Fresh pasta made with "00" flour is easier to roll by hand and has a more pleasing texture.

Handmade Pappardelle with Wild Mushroom Ragout and Peas

(continued)

Work with 1 dough portion at a time, keeping the others covered. With a pasta machine or by hand with a rolling pin, roll the dough into a sheet thin enough to see your fingers through it. Dust with flour as needed to keep it from sticking to the machine or work surface.

Starting at a narrow end, loosely roll the sheet like a jelly roll, leaving a 1-inch tail. With a sharp chef's knife, cut the roll crosswise into ¾-inch-wide ribbons. Grab the noodles by the exposed ends and lift them so they unfurl. Place them on a baking sheet, dust lightly with flour, and toss gently to separate. Repeat with the remaining 3 dough portions. Let the noodles dry while you prepare the ragout.

Prepare the ragout: Bring a small pot of water to a boil over high heat. Prepare a bowl of ice water. Boil the peas until barely tender, then drain and immediately immerse in the ice water. When cool, drain again and set aside.

Put the oil and garlic into a pot large enough to hold the pasta and place over low heat. Cook slowly, stirring occasionally, until the garlic begins to color, about 5 minutes; watch carefully to prevent burning. Add the shallot and a pinch of salt and cook over low heat, stirring occasionally, until the shallot is translucent, about 5 minutes. Raise the heat to medium-low, add the mushrooms, and season well with salt and pepper. Cook, stirring, until the mushrooms release their liquid, about 5 minutes. Add the butter, raise the heat to medium-high, and cook until the liquid has mostly evaporated and the mushrooms have begun to caramelize. Reduce the heat to medium-low, add the wine, and simmer until all the liquid has evaporated. Keep warm.

Bring a large pot of well-salted water to a boil over high heat. Add the 2 tablespoons oil to keep the noodles from sticking. Add the pasta and cook to desired doneness, about 2 minutes, depending on dryness. Add 1 cup of the pasta water to the mushrooms, then drain the pasta and return it to the warm pot, off the heat. Drizzle with a little oil and toss gently to keep the noodles from sticking.

Add the parsley and thyme to the mushrooms and simmer until the liquid is reduced by half. Add the peas and turn off the heat. Add the pasta, toss gently but well, and taste for seasoning. Divide among six bowls and garnish each portion with a generous amount of grated Parmigiano-Reggiano and pepper. Serve immediately.

what grapes want:

Although many cooks focus their wine pairing on the "center of the plate"—such as seafood, chicken, or beef— Chris finds that many fruits and vegetables can echo or complement the textures and aromas in a wine. Over frequent tastings with Janet, Chris has refined his ideas about the garden produce that flatters each of Trefethen's key wines.

Dry Riesling: green apples, Asian pears, Bosc pears, cucumbers, braised cabbage, quinces, kiwis, cilantro, citrus, chiles

Chardonnay: tarragon, melons, golden apples, fennel, butternut squashes, radishes, sunflower seeds, persimmons, brassicas, corn, carrots, delicata squashes, zucchini, romaine, white figs, oranges

Merlot: mushrooms, stewed tomatos, grilled peppers, nasturtiums, Swiss chard, sage, roasted squashes, figs, charred corn, polenta, green garlic

Dragon's Tooth (Bordeaux-style blend): mushrooms, toasted garlic, charred sweet peppers, Goat Horn peppers, parsley, nasturtiums, mustard greens, eggplants

Cabernet Sauvignon: thyme, carrots, mushrooms, potatoes, arugula, caramelized onions, toasted garlic, beets, chives, eggplants

Spring Lamb Chops Scottadito with Charred Tomato and Black Olive Tapenade *Serves 4*

4 lamb shoulder chops, each about 6 ounces and ½ inch thick

Sea salt and freshly ground black pepper

¼ cup extra virgin olive oil, plus more for drizzling

1 teaspoon minced fresh rosemary

3 teaspoons minced garlic

4 San Marzano or Roma tomatoes, halved lengthwise

½ teaspoon anchovy paste

⅓ cup pitted and neatly diced black olives, such as Niçoise or Kalamata

⅓ cup neatly diced caper berries

½ cup coarsely chopped fresh flat-leaf parsley

1 teaspoon fresh lemon juice

Wine: Trefethen Dragon's Tooth

The garden's beautiful old caper bush yields a lot of edible berries that Chris preserves for use all year. Its tiny buds are the familiar capers found bottled in brine. Left on the bush, they open into a gorgeous flower, which then sets an edible berry. Chris uses the berries in a zesty warm tapenade for lamb chops. Scottadito, an Italian word, implies the pan-seared chops are so hot they will burn your fingers if you pick them up.

Line a baking sheet with parchment paper. To keep the chops from curling as they cook, make a few small notches in the rim of fat on each chop. Season the chops on both sides with salt and pepper. In a small bowl, combine the oil, rosemary, 2 teaspoons of the garlic, and a pinch of salt. Put the chops on the prepared pan and spoon the seasoned oil evenly over them, coating both sides. Refrigerate uncovered for at least 2 hours or up to 24 hours. Bring to room temperature before cooking.

Heat a cast-iron or nonstick skillet over medium-high heat until very hot. Season the cut side of the tomatoes with salt, then place them, cut side down, in the hot skillet. Do not move them. Let them cook without moving or turning until they are soft to the touch and charred on the cut side, 7 to 8 minutes. Turn the heat off and let them rest in the pan while you cook the lamb.

Heat a large cast-iron or nonstick skillet over medium-high heat until very hot. Add the lamb chops in a single layer. Cook until they are well browned on the bottom, about 2 minutes, then turn and cook on the other side until they are well browned and fairly firm to the touch, 2 to 3 minutes longer. (Shoulder chops are best when cooked to at least medium.) Transfer the chops to a serving platter and reduce the heat to low. Discard any burnt garlic.

When the skillet has cooled a bit, add the remaining 1 teaspoon minced garlic and the anchovy paste and stir for about 30 seconds. Add the olives and caper berries and stir until aromatic, about 30 seconds. Add the parsley and cook, stirring, just until it wilts slightly, about 30 seconds. Stir in the lemon juice and remove from the heat.

Top each chop with 2 tomato halves and the olive mixture, dividing it evenly. Drizzle with a little oil, then serve immediately.

Black Pepper–Crusted Beef Ribeye with Balsamic Spring Onions and Smashed Beets **Serves 4**

Chris works many robust flavors into this dish—a peppery spice rub on the steaks, a balsamic marinade on the onions, and a tart poaching liquid for the beets—but Trefethen's elegant Cabernet Sauvignon can handle them. He harvests young onions from the garden when they resemble thick leeks, with a bulbous base that has just begun to swell. To use golden beets, substitute Chardonnay and white wine vinegar in the poaching liquid.

Beef:

2 beef ribeye steaks, about 1 pound each, trimmed of excess fat (leave some fat)

2 tablespoons sea salt

2 tablespoons chopped fresh thyme

2 tablespoons freshly ground black pepper

1 tablespoon olive oil

Spring Onions:

2 whole spring onions, roots removed, trimmed to 12 inches, and quartered lengthwise

1½ teaspoons sea salt

¼ cup extra virgin olive oil

¼ cup aged balsamic vinegar

1 teaspoon freshly ground black pepper

Beets:

4 cups water

½ cup Trefethen Cabernet Sauvignon

½ cup red wine vinegar

1 tablespoon sea salt

1 teaspoon freshly ground black pepper

12 small red beets, greens and roots removed

Olive oil, for searing the steaks

Vegetable oil, for frying the beets

Wine: Trefethen Cabernet Sauvignon

Prepare the beef: Season the steaks on both sides with the salt. Let rest at room temperature for 10 minutes to draw out moisture. Lightly pat the steaks dry but do not rinse or remove the salt.

In a small bowl, mix together the thyme, pepper, and olive oil to make a loose paste. Coat the steaks on both sides with the paste and put them into a lidded container. Cover and refrigerate for at least 4 hours or up to 24 hours, occasionally turning the steaks and massaging them lightly to encourage the seasonings to penetrate.

Prepare the spring onions: Season the onions with the salt and let rest at room temperature for 10 minutes to draw out moisture. Pat dry but do not rinse or remove the salt. In a small bowl, whisk together the olive oil, vinegar, and pepper. Put the onions and marinade into a lidded container and toss to coat. Cover and refrigerate for at least 4 hours or up to 24 hours, occasionally turning the onions and massaging them lightly to encourage the seasonings to penetrate.

Prepare the beets: In a pot, combine the water, wine, vinegar, salt, and pepper. Add the beets and bring to a simmer over high heat. Reduce the heat to maintain a gentle simmer and cook until the beets are just tender when pierced, about 30 minutes. They will be cooked more later so be careful not to overcook at this stage. With tongs, transfer the beets to a rack to cool. Try to keep the skins intact. Let cool to room temperature. With your palm, smack the beets to crack them and flatten them slightly.

(continued)

Black Pepper–Crusted Beef Ribeye with Balsamic Spring Onions and Smashed Beets *(continued)*

Remove the steaks from the container but do not pat them dry. They should still have bits of thyme and pepper on them. Bring them to room temperature. Heat a large cast-iron skillet over medium-high heat. Add enough olive oil to cover the bottom. When the oil is hot, add the steaks and let sear without moving them for 5 to 8 minutes to allow a crust to form. With tongs, turn the steaks and cook on the second side until done to your taste, another 5 to 8 minutes for medium-rare. Transfer the steaks to a cutting board to rest.

Pour off any fat in the skillet but do not wipe it clean. Return the skillet to medium heat. Remove the spring onions from their marinade, reserving the marinade. Add the onions to the warm skillet, cut side down, and cook, rotating as needed to keep them from burning, until they are richly caramelized and almost tender. Remove from the heat but leave the onions in the skillet.

Set another large cast-iron skillet over medium-high heat and pour in enough vegetable oil to come halfway up the sides of the beets. When the oil is hot, carefully add the beets to the pan. Cook until crisp on the bottom, 3 to 5 minutes, then turn and crisp the other side, 3 to 5 minutes longer. Drain on paper towels. Season with salt and pepper.

Divide the onions and beets evenly among four dinner plates. Slice the steaks to desired thickness and divide among the plates. Drizzle with the reserved spring onion marinade and serve immediately.

Wente Vineyards: *Deep Roots in One Place*

Livermore

Gardens are forever evolving, their colors changing as plants come and go. They fall quiet in winter but perk up after a spring rain. They even look different at dawn and at dusk. And when a longtime caretaker moves on, a garden will shift shape, subtly or dramatically, again.

These images of the Wente Vineyards garden capture an especially sweet time in its life, the final season for its longtime manager, Diane Dovholuk, who retired at the end of 2019 after thirty-three years. How the garden will evolve is a story that hasn't been written yet, but Diane's long collaboration with the winery's culinary team has enhanced the experience of visiting this landmark Livermore Valley estate.

Fourth-generation vintner Carolyn Wente hired Diane in 1986 but not for the garden. Diane had been Carolyn's favorite server at a local steak house, and when Wente opened its own restaurant, Carolyn encouraged Diane to join the dining-room staff. She soon became its top salesperson and a keen observer of the restaurant kitchen.

Left and above: *Two generations of Wente women (CEO Carolyn and Aly Wente) share a patio meal near the winery's Cresta Blanca Room, a popular event center; garden manager Diane Dovholuk gathers sweet peppers in the autumn garden.*

"Carolyn, did you know you're spending $40,000 a year on herbs?" she asked one day. Diane was certain she could start an organic garden and deliver fresh herbs for much less than that, including her salary.

Carolyn and her brothers, Phil and Eric, agreed to transition a small vineyard parcel that was proving too shady for wine grapes. But Diane's herb garden thrived there, and her edible empire eventually grew to almost an acre. Predictably, fresh herbs were just the proverbial camel's nose under the tent. By the time she retired, Diane was harvesting two thousand pounds of tomatoes a year, plus eggplants, peppers, cucumbers, and specialties such as ground cherries, Italian Corona beans, and purple tomatillos. Along the way, a greenhouse went up so Diane, relentlessly frugal, could start plants from seed.

"The garden has paid for itself the entire time," says Carolyn, an avid home gardener herself whose family has deep roots in Livermore Valley agriculture. Her paternal grandfather, Ernest, who managed Wente's vineyards in his day, also cultivated citrus, avocado, fig, and persimmon trees at his Livermore home and started a cattle ranch to help the family survive Prohibition. "My grandparents lived from the land," recalls Carolyn, "and I remember working with them all the time in their garden." Returning an edible garden to the Wente estate would help visitors appreciate the profound connection to place that has long defined this pioneering wine family.

From the beginning, the garden's harvest has always remained on the property, supplying the restaurant, the golf-course grill, and, to a lesser extent, the winery's many catered events. Coordinating supply with kitchen demand is no easy task; nature throws curveballs and, despite the pampered soil and enviable climate, not every crop on the

chefs' wish list is feasible. "In spring, I give them seed catalogs and they pick out what they want," says Diane. "Then I tell them what we can grow."

Fortunately for Wente's culinary team, Diane has rarely met a food plant she didn't want to grow. A stroll along the bark paths of this colorful, prolific garden turns up many novelties: baby butternut squash, long-necked Trombetta squash, holy basil, trendy Salanova lettuces with their tightly packed emerald and burgundy leaves, elderberries for syrup, hibiscus for tea, and red flint corn for polenta. Small fruit trees provide peaches, nectarines, apriums, and pluots for the pastry kitchen, as well as crisp Fuji apples and prized heirloom varieties, such as Cox's Orange Pippin and Hudson's Golden Gem.

The Wente garden is a compelling billboard for the sustainable growing methods that the family has long embraced in its vineyards. "We replenish our soil all the time," says Diane. All food waste from Wente events and the restaurant—ten thousand pounds a year—is composted and returned to the garden. Winter cover crops also nourish the soil, and the bark paths build humus, too, as the materials gradually decompose.

By planting densely, Diane has made the beds less welcoming for weeds. "You see how tight the basil and peppers are," she points out. "That's closer than what it says on the seed packets. Plus, I never walk by a weed. I pick it up."

Drifts of colorful blooms do more than beautify this sunny

Above: *(clockwise from far left) Cox's Orange Pippin; Wente Riesling with dessert; winery chef Jeff Farlow surveys the garden bounty; tomatillos; winery visitors on a garden tour; shucking red flint corn; chiles galore*

"My grandparents lived from the land," says Carolyn. "I remember working with them all the time in their garden."

parcel, a level plot embraced by hills. Asters, zinnias, hollyhocks, pansies, Maximillian sunflowers, and society garlic take their turn on the stage, luring pollinators and providing blossoms the chefs can use to garnish plates. Calendulas, dianthus, and bachelor's buttons are combined and delivered to the kitchen to scatter on salads. Aware that visitors routinely pocket seeds from unusual plants they admire—a trait shared by plant lovers the world over—guests are now treated to seed packets for garden standouts.

"Every herb we could need is out there," says Wente executive catering chef Jeff Farlow. Plus, he has access to every edible part of a plant—the pea tendrils, leafy pea greens, and the sweet peas

themselves—at the ideal moment. In early spring, Wente guests might find a warm pea greens salad on the menu and, weeks later, sautéed peas with lavender.

"Before I worked with Diane, I wasn't nearly as comfortable with improv cooking," says Jeff. The garden has made him a more flexible and more creative cook, willing to make a temporary home on the menu for a small harvest of squash blossoms or to turn a surfeit of *ají amarillo* chiles into a fermented hot sauce.

Above and right: *(clockwise from left)*
Aly and Carolyn Wente enjoy cooking together; Aly in her aunt Carolyn's garden; Carolyn harvests navel oranges from her trees on the winery estate; Carolyn's citrus grove

Carolyn maintains her own extensive edible garden, including a large collection of citrus, at her home on the winery estate. An accomplished cook, she hosts many philanthropic events on the winery's behalf and has a kitchen spacious enough to accommodate a catering crew when the occasion requires it. For her own dinner parties, she may re-create a dish from the winery's restaurant, but then round out the menu with courses drawn from her own repertoire.

Phil's daughter, Aly Wente, is part of the fifth generation running the winery and a self-confessed foodie who clearly inherited the interest, both from her aunt Carolyn and her mother, Julie, a skilled cook. Carolyn and Aly occasionally collaborate in the kitchen.

To showcase the early-autumn harvest from the winery garden, Carolyn and Aly settled on a menu with butternut squash hummus as the starter. A best seller at the winery's Tasting Lounge, the silky hummus makes a versatile dip—for homemade fried pita crisps, radishes, cucumber spears, roasted beets, or fennel wedges—and a casual companion for the evening's first glass of wine. For the next course, late-ripening tomatoes of many varieties are roasted with onions and blended for soup, a last hurrah before the vines decline. Risotto follows, prepared by Aly, who stirs in a handful of garden arugula at the last minute. Wente's famed Chardonnay accompanies the grilled halibut and its vegetable entourage.

As pioneer vintners in the Livermore Valley, the Wentes have been the region's most prominent and tireless advocates. Long before tasting rooms were widespread, the family was welcoming guests to the property. Carolyn's generation introduced the culinary experiences, and the fifth generation intends to build on them. "For decades, we've believed that wine and food belong together," says Aly. "That's how we live, and we try to share that lifestyle with visitors."

menu

Butternut Squash Hummus with
Pepita Aillade and Pita Chips
Wente Vineyards Brut Sparkling Wine

Roasted Tomato Bisque
Wente Vineyards Sauvignon Blanc

Risotto with Pancetta and Arugula
**Wente Vineyards Riva Ranch Vineyard
Pinot Noir or Sandstone Merlot**

Grilled Halibut with Cauliflower-Leek Puree,
Roasted Zucchini, and Pistachio Pesto
Wente Vineyards Eric's Chardonnay

Blood Orange Crème Brûlée
Wente Vineyards Riesling

Butternut Squash Hummus with Pepita Aillade and Pita Chips **Serves 8**

Hummus:

2 pounds peeled butternut squash, in 1-inch cubes

2 cups drained home-cooked or canned chickpeas

½ cup tahini

3 tablespoons Champagne vinegar

2 tablespoons extra virgin olive oil

1 tablespoon honey

½ teaspoon ground nutmeg

¼ teaspoon ground turmeric

Juice of 1 to 2 lemons

Sea salt

Pepita Aillade:

⅓ cup roasted and salted pumpkin seeds, roughly chopped

1 small clove garlic, minced

¼ cup extra virgin olive oil

Red chile flakes

Canola oil, for deep-frying

4 pita rounds, cut into triangles

Wine: Wente Vineyards Brut Sparkling Wine

Make the hummus: Preheat the oven to 425°F. Line a baking sheet with parchment paper. Spread the squash cubes on the prepared pan. Bake until tender and lightly browned in spots, 25 to 30 minutes.

Wente Vineyards chef Jeff Farlow dreamed up this hummus variation to use the deluge of autumn squashes from the garden. Beware: the fried pita chips are as addictive as the hummus. Jeff tops the hummus with a pumpkin seed aillade, a French word for a rustic, garlicky sauce. With garden vegetables for dipping—radishes, cucumbers, tomatoes, peppers— and some meaty olives, this appetizer could become a light meal.

In a food processor, combine the squash, chickpeas, tahini, vinegar, olive oil, honey, nutmeg, turmeric, the juice of 1 lemon, and a large pinch of salt. Process until smooth. Taste and adjust with more lemon juice or salt if necessary.

Make the pepita aillade: In a small bowl, stir together the pumpkin seeds, garlic, olive oil, and chile flakes to taste.

Pour canola oil to a depth of 3 inches into a heavy saucepan and heat to 360°F. Working in batches, add the pita triangles and fry, turning once with tongs, until golden brown on both sides, about 1 minute. As they are done, use the tongs to transfer them to a rack. Sprinkle with salt and let cool.

To serve, spread the hummus on a platter. With the back of a spoon, make a well in the center and spoon the aillade into the well. Serve with the pita chips for scooping.

Roasted Tomato Bisque

Makes 6 cups, to serve 4 to 6

3 pounds tomatoes of any color, including some
   cherry tomatoes for garnish

6 cloves garlic, peeled

2 large yellow onions, halved and sliced

½ cup extra virgin olive oil

Sea salt and freshly ground black pepper

1½ cups chicken broth

½ cup dry white wine

1 teaspoon minced fresh thyme

1 teaspoon minced fresh rosemary

4 tablespoons unsalted butter

Crème fraîche or thinned sour cream, for garnish (optional)

Thinly sliced fresh basil leaves, for garnish (optional)

Wine: Wente Vineyards Sauvignon Blanc

Preheat the oven to 450°F. Line two baking sheets with parchment paper. Core the large tomatoes and cut into quarters. Leave the cherry tomatoes whole. In a large bowl, combine the tomatoes, garlic, onions, oil, and salt and pepper to taste. Toss gently, then spread the vegetables on the two prepared pans. Roast until the tomatoes have softened and begun to caramelize and the onions are lightly colored, 25 to 30 minutes. Set the roasted cherry tomatoes aside.

Scrape the remaining vegetables and any juices into a soup pot and add the broth, wine, thyme, rosemary, and butter. Bring to a simmer, adjust the heat to maintain a simmer, and cook uncovered

The annual tomato harvest from the Wente garden is almost over-whelming—hundreds of pounds of lemon-yellow, sunset-orange, pink, carmine, and purple fruits. What to do with this river of ripeness? Carolyn freezes some and dries some, and many pounds become soup. This bisque is a family favorite. Roasting concentrates the tomato flavor, and garden herbs round out the scent.

until the volume has reduced by about one-third and the tomatoes are completely soft. Remove from the heat and let cool for a few minutes.

Working in batches, puree the mixture in a blender until smooth. Strain through a fine-mesh sieve to remove the tomato skins and seeds, pressing hard on the solids with a rubber spatula. Adjust the seasoning with salt and pepper.

Return the soup to the pot and reheat gently. Ladle into bowls and garnish with the reserved cherry tomatoes and with a drizzle of crème fraîche and a scattering of basil, if desired.

Risotto with Pancetta and Arugula **Serves 4**

1 tablespoon extra virgin olive oil

¼ pound pancetta, diced

1 small yellow onion, minced

1 clove garlic, minced

1 cup Carnaroli or Arborio rice

4 to 5 cups chicken broth, simmering

2 cups baby arugula

⅓ cup freshly grated Parmigiano-Reggiano cheese, plus more for topping

Fresh lemon juice

Sea salt and freshly ground black pepper

Wine: Wente Vineyards Riva Ranch Vineyard Pinot Noir or Sandstone Merlot

---

Warm the oil and pancetta in a heavy saucepan over medium heat. Cook, stirring, until the pancetta has rendered most of its fat and is almost crisp. With a slotted spoon, transfer the pancetta to paper towels. Add the onion and garlic and sauté until the onion has softened, about 5 minutes. Add the rice and cook, stirring, until the grains are coated with oil and have just started to color, about 2 minutes.

Begin adding the hot broth ½ cup at a time. Adjust the heat to maintain a gentle simmer and cook, stirring frequently and adding more broth only when the previous addition has been absorbed. It should take 20 to 25 minutes for the rice to absorb most of the broth and become al dente. Taste often and stop cooking when the rice is just tender enough for your taste. It will soften a bit more as it rests.

Aly learned to make risotto from her aunt Carolyn and has gradually mastered the technique, a useful one for gardeners because almost any vegetable can find a home in risotto. For this autumn version, she stirs in a handful of arugula when the rice is almost done. The greens wilt during the few minutes the rice needs to rest.

Stir in the pancetta, arugula, cheese, and the lemon juice to taste. Season with salt and pepper. Stir in another ¼ cup of the broth, cover, and let rest for about 3 minutes.

Divide the risotto among four bowls, sprinkle a little more cheese on top, and serve immediately.

wine-pairing tips from two pros:

Vintners are often more casual about wine pairing than their customers might imagine. "For me, it's more about the wine I want to drink that evening," admits Carolyn Wente. "Then I think about what's in the garden and open the fridge." The pairing dos and don'ts that make many people self-conscious are often relaxed in her household. "There were so many rules when I was growing up," recalls Carolyn. "'You can't have asparagus with wine; you can't have artichokes with wine.' Well, I think you can."

Her niece, Aly, concurs. "I like to drink what I'm in the mood for and eat what I'm in the mood for," says the fifth-generation vintner. If you want to serve a steamed artichoke with white wine, marinate it in olive oil and vinegar, then finish it on the grill, suggests Aly. "I'm a believer that salt and acid can fix anything."

Grilled Halibut with Cauliflower-Leek Puree, Roasted Zucchini, and Pistachio Pesto **Serves 4**

Carolyn often gets inspiration from the Wente Vineyards restaurant for her own home entertaining. This recipe is one example: a restaurant-caliber dish that any home cook can do. The cauliflower-leek puree is simple. Young garden zucchini roast in the oven while the halibut is on the grill. An impressive dinner-party dish, it gets a big assist from the garden and from a bottle of Wente Vineyards Chardonnay.

Pistachio Pesto:

1 cup loosely packed fresh basil leaves

½ cup loosely packed fresh flat-leaf parsley leaves

½ cup unsalted roasted pistachios

1 tablespoon chopped garlic

1 teaspoon sea salt

½ cup extra virgin olive oil

Freshly ground black pepper

1 cup chicken broth

1 large leek, white and pale green parts only, thinly sliced

1 medium cauliflower, cored and separated into florets

Sea salt and freshly ground black pepper

½ lemon

2 small green zucchini

2 small yellow zucchini

2 tablespoons extra virgin olive oil, plus more for the fish

1 tablespoon sherry vinegar

4 cloves garlic, minced

4 skin-on halibut fillets, 5 to 6 ounces each

Wine: Wente Vineyards Eric's Chardonnay

Make the pistachio pesto: In a food processor, combine the basil, parsley, pistachios, garlic, and salt and pulse to blend. With the motor running, add the oil in a thin, steady stream, blending until smooth.

Stop and scrape down the sides of the work bowl once or twice. Transfer the pesto to a bowl and stir in pepper to taste.

In a saucepan, heat the broth over medium-high heat. Add the leek and simmer until softened, about 5 minutes. Add the cauliflower florets, season with salt, cover, and adjust the heat to maintain a simmer. Cook until the cauliflower is tender, about 10 minutes. Drain into a sieve set over a bowl, reserving the liquid. Transfer the leeks and cauliflower to the food processor and puree until very smooth, thinning as needed with the reserved cooking liquid. Return the puree to the pan and season with salt, pepper, and a squeeze of lemon juice. Cover and keep warm.

Preheat the oven to 400°F. Prepare a medium charcoal fire or preheat a gas grill to medium. Preheat the grill rack to prevent the fish from sticking.

Line a baking sheet with parchment paper. Slice all the zucchini lengthwise about ⅜ inch thick. In a bowl, toss the zucchini slices with the oil, vinegar, and garlic and season with salt and pepper. Arrange them on the prepared pan and roast until tender and golden, 15 to 20 minutes. Keep warm.

Coat the halibut on both sides with oil and season with salt and pepper. Place the halibut, skin side down, on the preheated grill rack. Cook for about 5 minutes, then turn and cook on the flesh side until the fish barely flakes, about 3 minutes longer. The fish will continue to cook as it cools.

To serve, spoon some of the cauliflower-leek puree on each plate. Arrange the zucchini slices alongside and top them with the fish. Spoon the pesto over all and serve immediately.

Blood Orange Crème Brûlée

Serves 6

4 blood oranges

2 tablespoons Wente Vineyards Riesling

6 tablespoons granulated sugar

2 cups heavy cream

1 vanilla bean

6 large egg yolks

Pinch of sea salt

6 tablespoons superfine sugar

Wine: Wente Vineyards Riesling

With a rasp grater, grate enough blood orange zest to yield 1 tablespoon. Working with 1 orange at a time, cut a thin slice off both ends so it will stand upright. Stand the orange on a cutting surface and, using a sharp knife, remove all the peel and white pith by slicing from top to bottom all the way around the orange, following the contour of the fruit. Cut along the membranes to release the individual segments and place them in a small bowl. Repeat with 2 more of the oranges. Remove any seeds.

Add the Riesling and 1 tablespoon of the granulated sugar to the segments and toss gently.

Carolyn has a potted blood orange tree just outside her kitchen door—convenient for breakfast juice—and another in her hillside orchard. No wonder she dreamed up this gorgeous crème brûlée, with Riesling-steeped oranges on the bottom of the ramekin and a ruby-red orange slice on top.

Pour the cream into a small saucepan and add the orange zest. Halve the vanilla bean lengthwise and, with the tip of a small knife, scrape the seeds into the saucepan. Add the pod as well. Bring just to a simmer over medium heat. Cover, remove from the heat, and let steep for 5 minutes, then remove the pod.

In a bowl, whisk together the egg yolks, the remaining 5 tablespoons granulated sugar, and the salt. Add the warm cream ½ cup at a time, whisking constantly.

Drain the orange segments and divide them evenly among six 6-ounce heatproof ramekins. Pour the custard mixture into the ramekins, dividing it evenly. Place the ramekins in a baking dish just large enough to hold them. Add boiling water to come halfway up the sides of the ramekins. Cover the baking dish tightly with aluminum foil and bake until the custards are just set, about 30 minutes. They will be slightly puffy on top and still a bit jiggly. With a jar lifter or pot holders, carefully lift the ramekins out of the hot water and set on a wire rack to cool. When cool, cover and refrigerate until chilled, at least 4 hours or up to overnight.

Preheat the oven to 350°F. Remove the peel and pith of the remaining blood orange as described for the first 3 oranges. Then, instead of removing the segments, slice the orange crosswise into 6 thin slices. With the tip of a knife, remove the white pith at the center of each slice. Remove any seeds.

Place an orange slice on each chilled custard. Top each custard with 1 tablespoon of the superfine sugar in an even layer. With a kitchen torch, heat the sugar until it melts and caramelizes; do not allow it to burn. Let cool briefly, then serve.

Wheeler Farms: *Restoring Diversity*

St. Helena

Most people place their vegetable gardens out of visitors' sight, knowing that tomato vines and melon patches can look ragged by season's end. Keeping an edible garden camera ready year-round takes persistence and the ability to see beauty in autumn's decline and winter's comparative bareness.

"We put in front what most people put in back," acknowledges Daphne Araujo about the landscape plan she settled on for Wheeler Farms, the estate she purchased with husband, Bart, and partners in 2014. From their experience at Araujo Estate, the Calistoga winery they formerly owned, the couple knew that an edible garden, front and center, should be a key feature of their new venture.

"Gardens are such a magnet," says Daphne, a former landscape architect. At Araujo, tasting-room visitors would hear the chickens and then want to see the chickens. "It dawned on us that the people who were coming to wine country wanted the whole 'country' experience," says the vintner. "We want to give them that experience at Wheeler Farms."

Left and above: *Wheeler Farms proprietor Daphne Araujo is a former landscape architect and avid gardener; Daphne and husband, Bart, enjoy a glass of the winery's Sauvignon Blanc in the garden at sunset.*

Working with San Francisco landscape architect Ron Lutsko, the Araujos have restored the agricultural diversity that defined the property when J. H. Wheeler owned it in the late 1800s. Inheriting part of a large Spanish land grant, Wheeler cultivated wine grapes as well as fruit, nut, and citrus trees on more than one hundred acres. The family's holdings dwindled over the decades, and the parcel the Araujos and their partners purchased is only a sliver of the original farm. But by reviving the Wheeler name, the Araujos are signaling their commitment to preserving the land's farming past. Adding a state-of-the-art winery and planting Cabernet Sauvignon and Sauvignon Blanc grapes, the couple has created a nearly self-sufficient estate.

"We took out vineyard to make room for the orchard," says Daphne, "and that was not a hard decision. We wanted fruits and vegetables coming into the kitchen that you could cook with and decorate with."

That orchard now supplies the kitchen with more than twenty different heirloom fruits, from prized (and endangered) Royal Blenheim apricots to Elephant Heart plums, Northern Spy apples, and sought-after Suncrest peaches. Growing winter cover crops in the orchard has helped restore the soil's tilth, and in keeping with the Araujos' commitment to organic and biodynamic practices, weeds are managed by hand. California poppies and other wildflowers carpet the orchard with color in spring and provide habitat for beneficial insects. A thriving beehive generates honey for the kitchen, but its occupants are valued more for their contribution as pollinators.

Lutsko, known as a brilliant plantsman as well as for his genius with hardscape, designed steel planter boxes of varying heights to give the garden a strong visual structure. Filled with ornamental plants and edibles and surrounded by decomposed granite paths, the burnished copper-colored beds occupy a sunny walled courtyard with views of the Mayacamas Mountains. "Even if the beds are empty, the garden looks good," says Daphne. "When things grow, the joy is in the growth, and when the trellises come down, you can see the garden's bones again."

But these handsome, deep raised beds are rarely empty. Soft mounds of white alyssum bloom almost nonstop, wafting a gentle, honeyed scent that bees love. Ladybugs, butterflies, and other desirable visitors know they will always find blooming plants here, from cheery violas and pansies in late winter to sweet peas, nasturtiums, bachelor's buttons, sunflowers, salvias, and cosmos as the seasons progress. "A lot of what goes on in that garden is about attracting beneficial insects," says Daphne.

But fundamentally, the garden is about farm-to-table eating and celebrating the synergy between good cooking and fine wine. Wheeler Farms' Cabernet Sauvignons draw serious collectors to its Hospitality House for tasting, and the Araujos initially viewed the property as something of a demonstration farm, a model of sustainable Napa Valley living. But their ambitions grew with the arrival of Sarah Heller, a talented and energetic young chef and experienced gardener.

"She is a perfectionist on the French Laundry level," says Daphne, who soon delegated garden management to Sarah. "Every now and then I'll make a suggestion, but she knows what to do."

Above: *(clockwise from left) Winery chef Sarah Heller oversees both garden and kitchen; broccoli Romanesco; well-loved hen; gathering eggs; spring peas; fresh eggs headed for the winery kitchen*

"Gardens are such a magnet," says Daphne. "The people coming to wine country want the whole 'country' experience, and we want to give them that."

Following a monthly planting calendar, Sarah has greatly expanded the garden's variety, preferring smaller harvests but more diversity. A greenhouse on the premises allows her to start seeds for specialty produce rarely available in nurseries, such as purple jalapeños; Mr. Stripey, Blondkopfchen, and Hawaiian Pineapple tomatoes; Gadzukes zucchini; Graffiti and Fairy Tale eggplants; six varieties of cucumber; and eight types of basil.

In spring, the beds are flush with tender herbs like chervil, chives, and lime thyme; mild spring onions, spring garlic, and garlic flowers; baby kale; five types of radishes; and blossoming fava beans and peas, whose delicate blossoms Sarah plucks to garnish plates. By summer, the onslaught of tomatoes, peppers, eggplants, beans, and basil means

long days for Sarah in the farm's light-filled contemporary kitchen making tomato sauce, fermenting hot peppers, and pickling cucumbers.

Now, Wheeler Farms visitors have a more elevated tasting experience, engineered by a chef who understands the harmonies between garden produce and wine. "I try to make the food complement the wine instead of mimic the flavors," says Sarah. "If the wine tastes of tropical fruit, I won't make a dish with tropical fruit, but I'll use complementary ingredients like shrimp and green vegetables."

Above and right: *(clockwise from left) Sarah preserves much of the garden harvest for visitor gifts; the chef discusses the dinner menu with the Araujos; Daphne in the garden; Wheeler Farms' handsome kitchen; Sarah's edible flower cookies*

The winery's powerful Cabernet Sauvignons love rich red meats, but the garden supplies pairing options, too. "You can cook a carrot to go with Cabernet if you grill it and use complex spices," says the chef. The Cabernet-friendly dishes she makes for vegetarian guests often include roasted or grilled eggplant, caramelized onions, roasted peppers, and sturdy herbs like rosemary, oregano, and lavender.

"So much of the food that goes with red wine is brown and white," says the chef, "but I like to make pretty food." The garden, with its riot of color, solves that dilemma, offering golden beets, flowering mint, Thumbelina carrots, purple bean blossoms, and other edibles in gemstone hues for her plates.

Even the chicken eggs are colorful here. The Wheeler Farms flock resides in the Taj Mahal of coops, a pristine residence for heirloom-variety laying hens that looks as if a housekeeper tidies up daily. Many Wheeler Farms visitors go home with a half dozen of these exceptional eggs, or a jar of Wheeler Farms apricot preserves, or a cellophane bag of sugar cookies stamped with pressed flowers.

For a dinner showcasing the late-spring garden and built around Wheeler Farms wines, Sarah first surveys what the raised beds have to offer: English peas, fresh-dug potatoes, fava beans, fragrant mint, spring onions and garlic, tender broccoli shoots, and, from the orchard, the first apricots. From that inventory, a menu takes shape: chilled spring vegetable soup with a lemony shrimp garnish to show off the Sauvignon Blanc; a poached egg on potato puree with fava bean pesto and fried shallots, a dish robust enough for a vineyard-designated Cabernet Sauvignon; and for the main course, well-marbled short ribs with broccoli di cicco and farro—a Cabernet Sauvignon slam dunk. Apricots in lemon verbena syrup and a dainty quenelle of olive oil–sea salt ice cream reflect Sarah's tendency to end meals on a light note. A parting gift of flower cookies sends guests home with a souvenir of a wine estate with a distinctive vision and purpose.

menu

Chilled Spring Garden Soup with Bay Shrimp
Wheeler Farms Sauvignon Blanc

Poached Farm Egg with Potato Crème, Fava Bean Pesto, and Crispy Shallots
Wheeler Farms Beckstoffer Georges III Cabernet Sauvignon

Slow-Roasted Beef Short Ribs with Broccoli di Cicco and Farro
Wheeler Farms Beckstoffer Missouri Hopper Cabernet Sauvignon

Lemon Verbena Apricots with Olive Oil–Sea Salt Ice Cream

Edible Flower Cookies

Chilled Spring Garden Soup with Bay Shrimp **Serves 4**

¾ pound English peas, chopped into ½-inch pieces (including the pods)

2 spring onions

1 small bunch spinach (about 6 ounces), stemmed

½ bunch fresh flat-leaf parsley, stems included

4 fresh mint sprigs

2 tablespoons extra virgin olive oil

2-inch piece green garlic, coarsely chopped

Kosher or sea salt and freshly ground white pepper

2 cups low-fat milk

½ teaspoon grated Meyer lemon zest

Fresh Meyer lemon juice, as needed

Shrimp Salad:

¼ pound bay shrimp (about ¾ cup), halved crosswise

2 tablespoons plain Greek yogurt

1 teaspoon fresh Meyer lemon juice

¼ teaspoon grated Meyer lemon zest

1 teaspoon thinly sliced fresh chives

Sea salt and freshly ground white pepper

Fresh chive blossoms or mustard blossoms, for garnish (optional)

Wine: Wheeler Farms Sauvignon Blanc

In spring, the Wheeler Farms garden is flush with delicate leafy greens and tender fresh herbs. Sarah likes to blend them together in an emerald-green cold soup brightened with Meyer lemon. Low-fat milk keeps the texture airy; even so, the soup has depth and plenty of body. Sugar snap peas, asparagus, leeks, or dill could also play a role if you have them. A spoonful of lemony shrimp salad on top dresses up the soup and supplies a bridge to the winery's seafood-friendly Sauvignon Blanc.

Bring a pot of salted water to a boil over high heat and prepare a large bowl of ice water. Add the peas to the boiling water and boil until the pods are just tender, about 2 minutes. With a wire skimmer, transfer the peas to the ice water to chill quickly.

Cut the leafy green tops from the spring onions. Chop the green tops and the white stalks coarsely but keep them separate. Add the green tops to the boiling water along with the spinach, parsley, and mint. Boil just until the onion tops are tender, about 1½ minutes, then drain and transfer to the ice water. When cool, drain well.

Heat the olive oil in a saucepan over medium-low heat. Add the green garlic and white spring onion stalks, season with salt and pepper, and sauté until translucent, about 5 minutes. Add the milk and lemon zest, bring to a simmer, then reduce the heat to low and cook gently for about 10 minutes to infuse with flavor. Remove from the heat.

In a blender, combine the boiled herbs and vegetables and the milk mixture and puree until smooth. Blend only as long as necessary to avoid overheating the mixture, which can dull the color. Strain the mixture through a fine-mesh sieve, pressing on the solids. Cover and chill.

Make the shrimp salad: In a small bowl, combine the shrimp, yogurt, lemon juice and zest, and chives and mix gently. Season to taste with salt and pepper.

Taste the soup for salt and add a squeeze of lemon juice to brighten the flavor if needed. Divide the soup among four bowls. Spoon the shrimp salad on top of each portion, dividing it evenly. If desired, garnish with chive blossoms. Serve immediately.

Poached Farm Egg with Potato Crème, Fava Bean Pesto, and Crispy Shallots **Serves 4**

Potato Crème:

1 large russet potato, about 10 ounces, peeled,
    in ¾-inch cubes

Kosher or sea salt

¾ cup low-fat milk

2 tablespoons unsalted butter

¼ teaspoon freshly grated nutmeg

Freshly ground black pepper

Fava Bean Pesto:

2½ pounds fava beans

⅓ cup freshly grated Pecorino Romano cheese

1 tablespoon extra virgin olive oil

1 tablespoon fresh Meyer lemon juice

½ teaspoon grated Meyer lemon zest

Fried Shallots:

Canola oil, for deep-frying

1 large shallot, peeled

Unbleached all-purpose flour, for dusting

Sea salt

Eggs:

6 cups water

1 tablespoon kosher salt

1 tablespoon white wine vinegar

4 large farm eggs

Extra virgin olive oil

Sliced fresh chives, for garnish

Wheeler Farms' heirloom chickens supply golden-yolked eggs that deserve center stage. In spring, Sarah poaches them and presents them on a bed of potato foam (a simple potato puree works, too) with tender spring fava beans transformed into pesto. On another occasion, spoon the fava pesto on ricotta-topped crostini.

Wine: Wheeler Farms Beckstoffer Georges III Cabernet Sauvignon

---

Make the potato crème: In a saucepan, combine the potato, 1 tablespoon salt, and cold water to cover and bring to a simmer over medium heat. Cook at a gentle simmer until the potato is tender, about 20 minutes. Drain, reserving about ½ cup of the potato water. While the potato cooks, in a small saucepan, combine the milk, butter, nutmeg, several grinds of black pepper, and ½ teaspoon salt. Warm over low heat until the butter melts; keep warm.

In a blender, combine the boiled potato and the warm milk mixture and blend just until smooth, adding enough reserved potato water—about ⅓ cup—to make a creamy, pourable puree. Do not overblend or the potato may turn gummy. Taste for salt. Transfer the puree to a whipped-cream dispenser or to a small saucepan.

Make the pesto: Shell the fava beans. You should have about 2 cups beans. Bring a small saucepan of water to a boil over high heat and prepare a bowl of ice water. Add the beans to the boiling water and blanch for about 30 seconds (a little longer if they are large), then drain and transfer to the ice water. When cool, drain again. Peel the beans; the skins should slip off easily. You should have a scant 1 cup peeled beans. Put the beans into a food processor and add the pecorino, olive oil, and lemon juice and zest. Pulse a few times to make a coarse but blended mixture. It should not be smooth.

Make the fried shallots: In a small saucepan, pour canola oil to a depth of 2 inches and heat to 325°F. While the oil heats, slice the shallot thinly on a vegetable slicer. Toss the shallot slices in flour, shaking off

the excess. Add the slices to the hot oil and fry, agitating constantly, until deep golden brown, about 2 minutes. With a wire skimmer, transfer the slices to paper towels to cool; sprinkle with salt.

Cook the eggs: In a wide saucepan, combine the water, salt, and vinegar and bring to a simmer over medium heat. Adjust the heat to maintain a bare simmer. Break each egg into a small ramekin or cup. Stir the simmering water to create a vortex, then slide the eggs in one at a time. Adjust the heat to make sure the water does not boil; it should barely bubble. Poach until the egg whites are set, 3 to 4 minutes. Meanwhile, put about 2 teaspoons olive oil into a shallow bowl. With a slotted spoon, lift the eggs out of the water and into the bowl. The oil will keep them from sticking.

If the potato puree is in a whipped-cream dispenser, activate the charger. If the puree is in a saucepan, reheat it gently. Divide the puree among four plates. Top with the fava pesto, dividing it evenly. Put a poached egg on top of the pesto, then scatter the fried shallots and chives over the top. Serve immediately.

Slow-Roasted Beef Short Ribs with Broccoli di Cicco and Farro

Serves 4

1½ pounds boneless beef short ribs, preferably USDA Prime, trimmed of silverskin

Sea salt and freshly ground black pepper

Farro:

¼ cup extra virgin olive oil

1 cup farro

2 fresh thyme sprigs

⅓ cup finely diced red onion

1 large clove garlic, peeled

1 tablespoon unsalted butter

3 cups chicken broth or water

1 teaspoon balsamic vinegar

Kosher or sea salt

Broccoli:

3 tablespoons extra virgin olive oil

1 large clove garlic, very thinly sliced

4 cups loosely packed broccoli di cicco (sprouting broccoli) or broccolini florets

Wheeler Farms ground chile ají amarillo or other mildly spicy ground chile

Kosher or sea salt

¼ cup veal demi-glace (optional)

1 teaspoon finely minced mixed fresh herbs, such as oregano, thyme, and savory (optional)

Wine: Wheeler Farms Beckstoffer Missouri Hopper Cabernet Sauvignon

---

No recipe for beef could be easier than this slow-roasting method. The ribs aren't even browned first, but after four hours in a slow oven, they are the color of mahogany. To balance their richness, Sarah serves them with nutty farro and broccoli di cicco, an Italian variety that produces tender side shoots rather than a single head. This prized crop thrives in the Wheeler Farms raised beds in late spring and again in fall.

Preheat the oven to 200°F. Pat the short ribs dry, then season all over with salt and pepper. Arrange the short ribs, not touching, in a single layer in an ovenproof skillet or on a baking sheet. Roast uncovered for 4 hours without opening the oven door. They will release some fat and turn a deep, dark brown. Let rest for at least 30 minutes before slicing. (Note: You can cool the ribs and refrigerate them, covered, overnight. Shortly before serving, slice the meat ¼ inch thick, stack the slices against one another in a baking dish, and reheat in a preheated 350°F oven until hot, 3 to 5 minutes.)

Make the farro: Heat the oil in a saucepan over medium heat. Add the farro and cook, stirring constantly, until it smells like toasted wheat, about 3 minutes. Add the thyme, onion, garlic, and butter and cook, stirring, for about 2 minutes. Then add the broth and bring to a simmer. Adjust the heat to maintain a gentle simmer and cook uncovered until the farro is tender and the liquid has been absorbed, about 40 minutes. Remove the thyme sprigs, stir in the vinegar, and season to taste with salt. Keep warm.

Make the broccoli: Heat a large skillet over medium-low heat. Add the olive oil and garlic, and when the garlic begins to color, add the broccoli, chile, and salt to taste. Cook, tossing often with tongs, until the broccoli is tender but not soft, about 5 minutes.

If using the demi-glace, warm it in a small saucepan over low heat. Stir in the mixed herbs.

Slice the short ribs about ¼ inch thick. Divide the broccoli and the farro evenly among four dinner plates. Top with the sliced short ribs. Brush the meat with demi-glace, if using. Serve immediately.

Lemon Verbena Apricots with Olive Oil–Sea Salt Ice Cream

Serves 4

Ice Cream:

3 cups half-and-half

1 cup sugar

1 teaspoon vanilla bean paste, or seeds from 1 vanilla bean, halved lengthwise

½ teaspoon sea salt

5 large egg yolks

3 tablespoons extra virgin olive oil

Lemon Verbena Apricots:

½ cup sugar

2 tablespoons fresh Meyer lemon juice

1 tablespoon vanilla bean paste, or seeds from 1 vanilla bean, halved lengthwise

½ cup water

20 fresh lemon verbena leaves, chopped medium-fine, or 2 tablespoons chopped dried lemon verbena leaves

2 large or 4 medium apricots, halved, pitted, and sliced

Flaky sea salt, such as Maldon, for garnish

Make the ice cream: In a saucepan, combine the half-and-half, sugar, vanilla paste, and salt. Bring to a simmer over medium heat, whisking to dissolve the sugar. Remove from the heat. Put the egg yolks into a blender and, with the motor running, gradually add the hot half-and-half mixture, blending well. Return the mixture to the saucepan and cook over medium heat, stirring constantly, until the mixture visibly thickens and coats a wooden spoon. Do not let it boil or it may curdle. Transfer the custard to a clean bowl, let cool, and then chill.

Apricots aren't the easiest fruit to grow in Napa Valley, but Wheeler Farms has a tree that yields enough for two to three weeks of desserts and out-of-hand eating. Sarah likes to toss the sliced fruit in a light lemon-verbena syrup and pair it with olive oil ice cream. You can replace the apricots with pitted cherries, blackberries, nectarines, strawberries, or figs.

Churn the custard in an ice-cream maker according to manufacturer's directions, adding the oil when the ice cream is almost frozen. Transfer to a container and freeze for at least 1 hour to firm.

Make the apricots: In a small saucepan, combine the sugar, lemon juice, vanilla, and water and bring to a simmer over medium heat, stirring to dissolve the sugar. Remove from the heat. If using dried lemon verbena, add to the syrup while it is hot. If using fresh lemon verbena, let the syrup cool, then add the leaves. Let steep for at least 10 minutes, but overnight is better.

Put the apricots into a small bowl and add about 2 tablespoons of the syrup, enough to coat them lightly. Toss gently. Divide the apricots evenly among four dessert plates. Spoon a little more syrup over the apricots. Place a scoop of ice cream alongside. Top the ice cream with a few salt flakes. Serve immediately.

Edible Flower Cookies

Makes forty-eight 2½-inch round cookies

Visitors to Wheeler Farms often go home with a gift bag of these exquisite cookies, each one decorated with a pressed edible flower from the garden. The buttery cookies make a memorable accompaniment to ice cream, sorbet, poached fruit, or a pot of hot tea.

48 fresh edible flowers of any type

1¼ pounds plus 2 tablespoons unsalted butter, in small cubes, at room temperature

2 cups powdered sugar, sifted

1 large egg

1 teaspoon sea salt

1 teaspoon vanilla bean paste

½ teaspoon violet extract

8 cups sifted all-purpose flour

Egg Wash:

½ cup granulated sugar

½ cup water

1 large egg white

½ teaspoon citric acid or 1 tablespoon lemon juice

Place the flowers in a single layer between two sheets of parchment paper and put heavy weights, such as books, on top to flatten them. Press overnight.

In a stand mixer fitted with the paddle attachment, cream together the butter and powdered sugar on medium speed until light. Add the egg and mix until fully incorporated. Add the salt, vanilla, and violet extract and mix well. On low speed, add the flour and mix until just combined. Cover and chill the dough for at least 2 hours or overnight.

Preheat the oven to 325°F. Line four heavy baking sheets with parchment paper.

Make the egg wash: To make a simple syrup, combine the sugar and water in a small saucepan and bring to a simmer over medium heat,

stirring to dissolve the sugar. Remove from the heat, let cool, and then chill well. In a small bowl, whisk together ¼ cup of the simple syrup, the egg white, and citric acid until well blended. Reserve the remaining simply syrup for another use.

Roll out the dough ½ inch thick. Brush the entire dough sheet with the egg wash. Using a 2½-inch round cutter (or a cutter of another desired size), cut out as many cookies as possible. Transfer them to the prepared baking sheets, spacing them 1 inch apart. Carefully place a flower in the center of each cookie and brush again with the egg wash.

Place the baking sheets in the freezer for 10 minutes, then bake the cookies, in shifts if necessary, until they just start to brown around the edges, about 12 minutes. Transfer the cookies to a wire rack to cool.

daphne's garden tips:

Keeping a vegetable garden attractive all year takes attention to detail. Daphne's advice:

Create an aesthetically pleasing structure—"good bones"—so even if the beds are empty, the garden looks inviting.

"Tidy is important," say Daphne. "It takes discipline to constantly deadhead and thin and remove wilted leaves, but you have to get them out of there." A neat garden is more sanitary, too, which keeps disease at bay.

Plan to have something in bloom always. Orange cosmos, poppies, and alyssum are among Daphne's favorites. "If not much else is happening, the eye goes to color," says the vintner.

Plant a cover crop to conceal bare ground and improve the soil.

Left and right: *Sarah snips pansies and other edible flowers for her captivating butter cookies; Daphne's ambitious objective is to have these handsome garden beds productive, tidy, and beautiful year round.*

visitor guide

All of these wineries welcome visitors, although most require a prior appointment. Check the website for guest policies and hospitality programs. Many of the wineries offer experiences that include a tour of the garden.

Alexander Valley Vineyards
8644 Highway 128
Healdsburg
707-433-7209
www.avvwine.com

Clif Family Winery
709 Main Street
St. Helena
707-968-0625
www.cliffamily.com

B Cellars
703 Oakville Cross Road
Napa
707-709-8787
www.bcellars.com

HALL Wines
401 St. Helena Highway South
St. Helena
707-967-2626
www.hallwines.com

Robert Mondavi Winery
7801 St. Helena Highway
Oakville
888-766-6328
www.robertmondaviwinery.com

Wente Vineyards
5565 Tesla Road
Livermore
925-456-2305
www.wentevineyards.com

Beringer Vineyards
2000 Main Street
St. Helena
707-257-5771
www.beringer.com

The Prisoner Wine Company
1178 Galleron Road
St. Helena
877-283-5934
www.theprisonerwinecompany.com

Skipstone
2505 Geysers Road
Geyserville
707-433-9124
www.skipstonewines.com

Wheeler Farms
588 Zinfandel Lane
St. Helena
707-200-8500
www.wheelerfarmswine.com

Cakebread Cellars
8300 St. Helena Highway
Rutherford
800-588-0298
www.cakebread.com

Regusci Winery
5584 Silverado Trail
Napa
707-254-0403
www.regusciwinery.com

Trefethen Family Vineyards
1160 Oak Knoll Avenue
Napa
707-255-7700
www.trefethen.com

Above and right: *A scarecrow encourages a happy harvest at Regusci Winery; spring garden radishes at Robert Mondavi Winery*

acknowledgments

This book was a dream project that brought together my three principal interests: cooking, wine, and gardening. My greatest pleasure in writing it was meeting so many others who share these passions and who were generous in sharing what they knew. I am indebted to Cate Conniff for the magazine assignment on winery gardens that planted the seed for this book, and I am deeply grateful to all the vintners, winery chefs, winery gardeners, and their teams who took time to work with me and educate me. The beauty you create in your gardens and kitchens will inspire my own gardening and cooking for years to come.

I have been privileged to collaborate on this book with a team of top-tier professionals. Photographer Meg Smith and her assistant, Antonio Fernando, produced images more beautiful than I dared to imagine. Thank you to food stylist Abby Stolfo; her assistant, Natalie Drobny; and prop stylist Thea Chalmers for interpreting the recipes with such care and style. Copy editor Sharon Silva has an attention to detail and concern for clarity that always make my manuscripts better.

Designer Jennifer Barry made these gardens come to life with her creative vision and good taste. Jenny has been my partner on this book from the beginning, as producer and general wrangler on a project with many moving parts. The trains run on time when Jenny is in charge and *Gather* would never have happened without her.

—*Janet Fletcher*

index